The College Writer

A Guide to Thinking, Writing, and Researching

Randall VanderMey
Westmont College

Verne Meyer
Dordt College

John Van Rys
Dordt College

Dave Kemper

Pat Sebranek

HOUGHTON MIFFLIN COMPANY
BOSTON   NEW YORK

Senior Sponsoring Editor: Suzanne Phelps Weir
Senior Development Editor: Sarah Helyar Smith
Senior Project Editor: Aileen Mason
Senior Production/Design Coordinator: Sarah Ambrose
Cover Coordinator: Diana Coe
Senior Manufacturing Coordinator: Priscilla Bailey
Senior Marketing Manager: Cindy Graff Cohen

Cover Design: Colleen Belmont
Illustrations: Chris Krenzke
CD: Lester Smith, Janae Sebranek, Chris Erickson, Kathy Kahnle, Claire Ziffer
Editorial: Pat Kornelis, Kim Rylaarsdam, Mike Vanden Bosch, Sonneke Kok, Kathy Henning, Stuart Hoffman, Mariellen Hanrahan, Mary Ann Hoff, Lois Krenzke
Production: Sherry Gordon, Jean Varley, Ellen Leitheusser, Colleen Belmont, Sandy Wagner

(Credits appear on page 685, which constitutes an extension of the copyright page.)

Printed in the U.S.A.

Library of Congress Control Number: 2001133342

ISBN (paper): 0-618-40541-0
ISBN (cloth): 0-618-40542-9

2 3 4 5 6 7 8 9 –DOC– 07 06 05 04

Preface

The College Writer is a rhetoric, reader, research guide, and handbook that offers streamlined, nuts-and-bolts writing instruction. It is so thorough, helpful, and graphically designed that students in first-year composition courses at both community colleges and four-year schools will claim it as their own.

Features and Benefits

1. Content

The College Writer is divided into four parts:

Part I, the **rhetoric,** shows students how to think and read critically and how to apply these skills to the full writing process—from understanding the assignment, the purpose, and the audience through selecting a topic, planning, drafting, revising, editing, proofreading, and submitting the paper. A full chapter is dedicated to following one student writer as she develops and completes an essay assignment.

Part II, the **reader,** contains practical guidelines and activities for **strategies and models**. Students will learn about the academic forms of writing (narration and description, analysis, and persuasion) as well as three kinds of reports. Special forms of writing show students both academic and real-world applications, including writing about literature and the arts, taking essay exams, writing across the curriculum, writing for the workplace, writing for the Web, and preparing oral presentations.

Part III, the **research guide,** provides practical information on managing the research writing process, avoiding plagiarism, and using the library and the Internet. MLA and APA documentation guides support sample student research papers.

Part IV, the **handbook,** covers the grammar, punctuation, syntax, usage, mechanics, and sentence structure that college writers need to know. *The College Writer* also offers a full chapter on ESL issues.

2. Streamlined Coverage for the First-Year Writing Course

The College Writer provides the most helpful information available in a thoughtfully streamlined format. Fluff is out; almost every spread is self-contained. Information is carefully offered using prioritized lists, bulleted points, diagrams, questions, suggestions, and brief discussions. *The College Writer* presents materials in a clear, straightforward, yet engaging manner. The clarity of the organization and presentation keeps students centered on their task and on the objectives of each section. The numerous annotated models (42 student essays and 19 professional essays), explanations, and demonstrations promote active learning, freeing the instructor to conduct class more effectively through small-group instruction, peer tutoring, and in-class or online composing. *The College Writer* will become a favorite in many college writing centers, too.

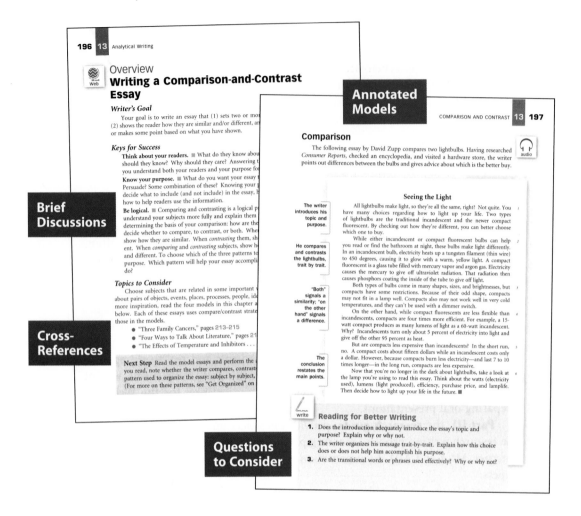

196 13 Analytical Writing

Overview
Writing a Comparison-and-Contrast Essay

Writer's Goal
Your goal is to write an essay that (1) sets two or mor[e]
(2) shows the reader how they are similar and/or different, an[d]
or makes some point based on what you have shown.

Keys for Success
Think about your readers. ▪ What do they know abou[t]
should they know? Why should they care? Answering t[he]
you understand both your readers and your purpose fo[r]
Know your purpose. ▪ What do you want your essay [to]
Persuade? Some combination of these? Knowing your p[urpose]
decide what to include (and not include) in the essay, h[ow]
how to help readers use the information.
Be logical. ▪ Comparing and contrasting is a logical p[rocess]
understand your subjects more fully and explain them
determining the basis of your comparison: how are the[y]
decide whether to compare, to contrast, or both. Whe[n]
show how they are similar. When *contrasting* them, sh[ow]
ent. When *comparing* and *contrasting* subjects, show h[ow]
and different. To choose which of the three patterns to
purpose. Which pattern will help your essay accompli[sh]
do?

Topics to Consider
Choose subjects that are related in some important [way]
about pairs of objects, events, places, processes, people, id[eas]
more inspiration, read the four models in this chapter a[nd]
below. Each of these essays uses compare/contrast strate[gies]
those in the models.

- "Three Family Cancers," pages 213–215
- "Four Ways to Talk About Literature," pages 21[]
- "The Effects of Temperature and Inhibitors . . . [

Next Step Read the model essays and perform the a[ctivities]
you read, note whether the writer compares, contrasts
pattern used to organize the essay: subject by subject,
(For more on these patterns, see "Get Organized" on

Brief Discussions

Cross-References

Annotated Models

COMPARISON AND CONTRAST **13 197**

Comparison
The following essay by David Zupp compares two lightbulbs. Having researched *Consumer Reports*, checked an encyclopedia, and visited a hardware store, the writer points out differences between the bulbs and gives advice about which is the better buy.

audio

Seeing the Light

The writer introduces his topic and purpose.

All lightbulbs make light, so they're all the same, right? Not quite. You have many choices regarding how to light up your life. Two types of lightbulbs are the traditional incandescent and the newer compact fluorescent. By checking out how they're different, you can better choose which one to buy.

He compares and contrasts the lightbulbs, trait by trait.

While either incandescent or compact fluorescent bulbs can help you read or find the bathroom at night, these bulbs make light differently. In an incandescent bulb, electricity heats up a tungsten filament (thin wire) to 450 degrees, causing it to glow with a warm, yellow light. A compact fluorescent is a glass tube filled with mercury vapor and argon gas. Electricity causes the mercury to give off ultraviolet radiation. That radiation then causes phosphors coating the inside of the tube to give off light.

"Both" signals a similarity; "on the other hand" signals a difference.

Both types of bulbs come in many shapes, sizes, and brightnesses, but compacts have some restrictions. Because of their odd shape, compacts may not fit in a lamp well. Compacts also may not work well in very cold temperatures, and they can't be used with a dimmer switch.

On the other hand, while compact fluorescents are less flexible than incandescents, compacts are four times more efficient. For example, a 15-watt compact produces as many lumens of light as a 60-watt incandescent. Why? Incandescents turn only about 5 percent of electricity into light and give off the other 95 percent as heat.

The conclusion restates the main points.

But are compacts less expensive than incandescents? In the short run, no. A compact costs about fifteen dollars while an incandescent costs only a dollar. However, because compacts burn less electricity—and last 7 to 10 times longer—in the long run, compacts are less expensive.

Now that you're no longer in the dark about lightbulbs, take a look at the lamp you're using to read this essay. Think about the watts (electricity used), lumens (light produced), efficiency, purchase price, and lamplife. Then decide how to light up your life in the future. ▪

write

Reading for Better Writing

1. Does the introduction adequately introduce the essay's topic and purpose? Explain why or why not.
2. The writer organizes his message trait-by-trait. Explain how this choice does or does not help him accomplish his purpose.
3. Are the transitional words or phrases used effectively? Why or why not?

Questions to Consider

---

3. Dynamic, Four-Color Design

Today's students are quick at reading visual cues, and many are truly visual learners. *The College Writer* is designed to engage all readers and enhance their learning and writing abilities. The judicious use of four-color coding, drawings, and graphic organizers will appeal to a student body that favors pragmatism and practicality, including the Web-savvy student, the returning student, and the busy student with a family and/or a demanding job.

4. Quick-Reference Features

The College Writer is designed for ease of use: get in, find the information, get out. Step-indexing provides tabbed quick-reference codes so students will know exactly where to find important information in the book. Chapters and sections are clearly laid out and encourage students to move back and forth within the text. The text contains plenty of cross-references, mini-indexes, clear headings and

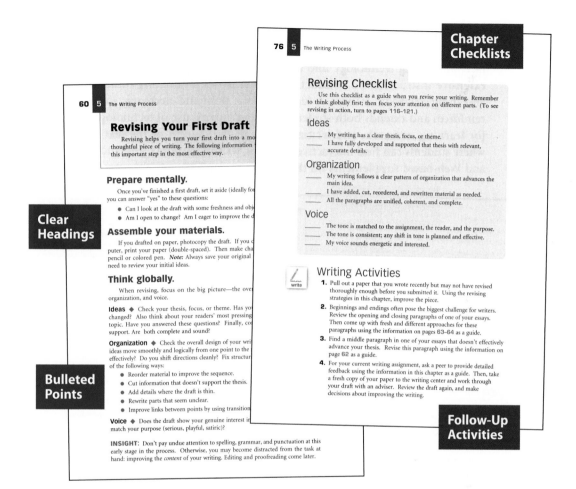

Clear Headings

Bulleted Points

Chapter Checklists

Follow-Up Activities

subheadings, boxes, tabs, and simple labeling. It simplifies content with numerous checklists and summary boxes to which students can refer anytime. The crisp presentation and organization greatly enhance the book's usefulness as a reference.

5. Friendly, Coaching Tone: Students First

First-year students want to get help, find what they're looking for, do well, be respected as learners, and enjoy their work. *The College Writer* grew out of actual classroom experience, and it shows. Whether fresh out of high school or returning as adults, students will take immediately to the book because it addresses their needs and interests. The collegial tone and follow-up activities respect students as thoughtful, self-motivated learners. *The College Writer* will become students' companion, the first book they turn to for help with writing in all their courses—and the one they choose to keep for work after college.

6. Complete Coverage on Using Technology for Research and Writing

The College Writer helps meet one of the greatest challenges that instructors face: integrating technology into the composition course. Student are provided extensive instruction on conducting Web searches, evaluating online sources, and citing electronic sources. A full package of print and electronic supplements reinforces and extends both students' and instructors' use of technology as tools for learning, research, and writing. Icons in the margin of the text highlight where students can find interactive exercises, writing prompts, and audio, visual, and Web-based supplements on the accompanying CD and Web site.

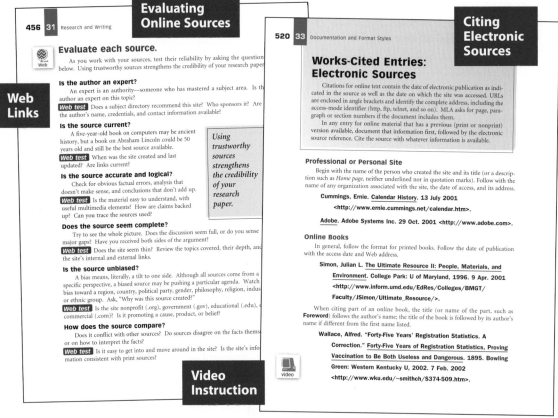

Evaluating Online Sources

456 **31**   Research and Writing

Web Links

Evaluate each source.

As you work with your sources, test their reliability by asking the question below. Using trustworthy sources strengthens the credibility of your research paper

Is the author an expert?

An expert is an authority—someone who has mastered a subject area. Is th author an expert on this topic?

Web test Does a subject directory recommend this site? Who sponsors it? Are the author's name, credentials, and contact information available?

Is the source current?

A five-year-old book on computers may be ancient history, but a book on Abraham Lincoln could be 50 years old and still be the best source available.

Web test When was the site created and last updated? Are links current?

Is the source accurate and logical?

Check for obvious factual errors, analysis that doesn't make sense, and conclusions that don't add up.

Web test Is the material easy to understand, with useful multimedia elements? How are claims backed up? Can you trace the sources used?

Using trustworthy sources strengthens the credibility of your research paper.

Does the source seem complete?

Try to see the whole picture. Does the discussion seem full, or do you sense major gaps? Have you received both sides of the argument?

Web test Does the site seem thin? Review the topics covered, their depth, and the site's internal and external links.

Is the source unbiased?

A bias means, literally, a tilt to one side. Although all sources come from a specific perspective, a biased source may be pushing a particular agenda. Watch bias toward a region, country, political party, gender, philosophy, religion, indus or ethnic group. Ask, "Why was this source created?"

Web test Is the site nonprofit (.org), government (.gov), educational (.edu), commercial (.com)? Is it promoting a cause, product, or belief?

How does the source compare?

Does it conflict with other sources? Do sources disagree on the facts thems or on how to interpret the facts?

Web test Is it easy to get into and move around in the site? Is the site's info mation consistent with print sources?

Video Instruction

Citing Electronic Sources

520 **33**   Documentation and Format Styles

Works-Cited Entries: Electronic Sources

Citations for online text contain the date of electronic publication as indicated in the source as well as the date on which the site was accessed. URLs are enclosed in angle brackets and identify the complete address, including the access-mode identifier (http, ftp, telnet, and so on). MLA asks for page, paragraph or section numbers if the document includes them.

In any entry for online material that has a previous (print or nonprint) version available, document that information first, followed by the electronic source reference. Cite the source with whatever information is available.

Professional or Personal Site

Begin with the name of the person who created the site and its title (or a description such as *Home page*, neither underlined nor in quotation marks). Follow with the name of any organization associated with the site, the date of access, and its address.

Cummings, Ernie. Calendar History. 13 July 2001

<http://www.ernie.cummings.net/calendar.htm>.

Adobe. Adobe Systems Inc. 29 Oct. 2001 <http://www.adobe.com>.

Online Books

In general, follow the format for printed books. Follow the date of publication with the access date and Web address.

Simon, Julian L. The Ultimate Resource II: People, Materials, and

Environment. College Park: U of Maryland, 1996. 9 Apr. 2001

<http://www.inform.umd.edu/EdRes/Colleges/BMGT/

Faculty/JSimon/Ultimate_Resource/>.

When citing part of an online book, the title (or name of the part, such as **Foreword**) follows the author's name; the title of the book is followed by its author's name if different from the first name listed.

Wallace, Alfred. "Forty-Five Years' Registration Statistics. A

Correction." Forty-Five Years of Registration Statistics, Proving

Vaccination to Be Both Useless and Dangerous. 1895. Bowling

Green: Western Kentucky U, 2002. 7 Feb. 2002

<http://www.wku.edu/~smithch/S374-509.htm>.

video

7. Exceptional ESL Coverage

ESL issues, such as idiomatic expressions and troublesome noun and verb forms, are thoroughly covered in a chapter dedicated to nonnative speakers of English. *The College Writer* also incorporates abbreviated versions of the instruction directly into the handbook in the form of ESL tips. ESL writers have the option of reading the full treatment of a certain topic in the separate chapter or getting just the facts from a quick look at the related chapter in the handbook. The concise, clear instruction, colorful presentation, and abundant examples make this text especially practical for ESL students.

Supplements for the Student

CD-ROM for *The College Writer* is an electronically enhanced version of the textbook, bringing multimedia instruction into the classroom. The CD makes using the book more efficient through electronically searchable text and internal hypertext links. It also provides audio and video illustration, interactive exercises, word-processing links and writing prompts, and external links to the Web.

***The College Writer* Web site** for students, at <**www.thecollegewriter.com**>, provides support directly related to the book. The fully integrated Web site contains expanded writing assignments and exercises, a resource center for adult returning students, real-world Web links, writing assignments, annotated readings, journal support, reading comprehension exercises, video and music activities, a game, an interactive calendar, a guide to publishing your work, and links to other helpful sites.

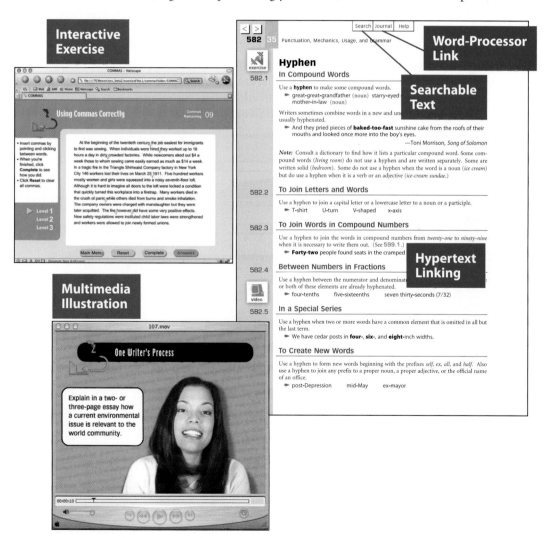

The Student Resource Center at the Houghton Mifflin Web site for students, <**http://college.hmco.com/english**>, provides additional support for coursework.

- **Internet Research Guide** contains Learning Modules on the purpose of research; e-mail, listservs, newsgroups, and chat rooms; surfing and browsing; evaluating information on the Web; building an argument with Web research; and plagiarism and documentation.

- **eLibrary** is full of self-quizzes that give students the opportunity to increase their grammar and writing skills in 30 areas. As they sharpen their skills and strengthen their knowledge with more than 700 exercises, they can work at their own pace wherever they want—home, computer lab, or classroom.

- **SMARTHINKING™** provides online tutoring in English (as well as in seven other disciplines). Students have three different kinds of support. *Live Help* provides access to 20 hours per week of real-time, one-on-one instruction from Sunday to Thursday, 9 p.m.–1 a.m. Eastern time. *Questions Anytime* allows students to submit questions 24 hours a day, 7 days a week, for response by an e-structor within 24 hours. *Independent Study Resources* connects students around the clock to additional educational services, ranging from interactive Web sites to frequently asked questions.

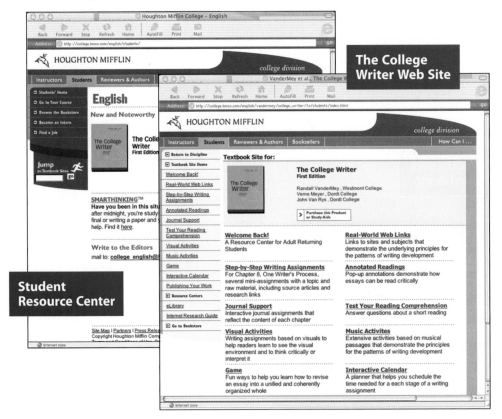

Supplements for the Instructor

Instructor's Resource Manual contains an overview of the course, sample syllabi, chapter summaries, a discussion of each professional and student essay, support for the writing assignments, masters of key lists and visuals, and more.

Teaching Writing with Computers: An Introduction, by Pamela Takayoshi and Brian Huot, addresses writing technologies for composition pedagogies, learning to teach with technology, teaching beyond physical boundaries, teaching and learning new media, and assigning and assessing student writing.

The Writing Teacher's Companion: Planning, Teaching, and Evaluating in the Composition Classroom, by Rai Peterson, helps instructors with organization of the course, assessment, classroom management, and selection of textbooks.

Instructor's Resource Center, located at the Houghton Mifflin Web site,<**http://college.hmco.com/english**>, provides numerous and varied sources of assistance:

- **Instructor's Resource Manual Online** is a downloadable version of the print IRM, enhanced with an overview of Web site offerings, instructions on how to use the site most effectively, and Web links for instructors.

- **SMARTHINKING™** provides personalized, text-specific tutoring to students when they need it—online during their typical study hours—leaving instructors more time for other demands on campus. The three levels of unparalleled service and innovative use of Web-based educational technology provide increased support for instructors and help improve student performance.

- **Guide to the Current Conflict,** a cross-curricular resource center, enables instructors to help students learn more about Afghanistan's cultural and political history, the world of Islam, the al Qaeda network, and more. The wealth of resources can be used as discussion starters, for homework assignments, or for further research. Some topics also include model lesson plans and tips for teaching.

- **After the Test**. Taking a final exam signifies the end of class work for students, but for instructors, the work is just beginning when exams are turned in. See the tips on grading tests and dealing with students after they have received their grades.

- **Adjuncts.com** is dedicated to helping adjunct faculty make the most of their teaching careers.

- **eduSpace**, by Houghton Mifflin, offers diagnostic tests linked to exercises that instructors prescribe for students based on their individual needs.

Web/CT e-Pack provides a flexible, Internet-based education platform containing text-specific resources to enrich students' online learning experience.

Blackboard Course Cartridge provides flexible, efficient, and creative ways for instructors to present materials and manage distance-learning courses. Instructors can use an electronic grade book, receive papers from students enrolled in the course via the Internet, and track student use of the communication and collaborative functions.

Acknowledgments

The authors wish to express their gratitude to the following persons who have contributed their valuable time, energy, and ideas in the development of *The College Writer* and its supplements:

Mary Adams, *Peru State College;* Jim Addison, *Western Carolina University;* Susan Aguila, *Palm Beach Community College;* Edmund August, *McKendree College;* Patricia Blaine, *Paducah Community College;* Deborah Bradford, *Bridgewater State College;* Susan Callender, *Sinclair Community College;* Sandy Cavanah, *Hopkinsville Community College;* James William Chichetto, *Stonehill College;* Sandra Clark, *Anderson University;* Keith Coplin, *Colby Community College;* David Daniel, *Newbury College;* Rachelle L. Darabi, *Indiana University, Purdue University Fort Wayne;* Judy C. Davidson, *University of Texas, Pan American;* Helen Deese, *University of California, Riverside;* Carol Jean Dudley, *Eastern Illinois University;* Chris Ellery, *Angelo State University;* Kelly A. Foth, *University of Dubuque;* Julie Foust, *Utah State University;* Gregory R. Glau, *Arizona State University;* Patricia Glynn, *Middlesex Community College;* Karla Hayashi, *University of Hawaii, Hilo;* Stan Hitron, *Middlesex Community College;* Karen Holleran, *Kaplan College;* Maurice Hunt, *Baylor University;* Barbara Jacobskind, *University of Massachusetts, Dartmouth;* Nina B. Keery, *Massachusetts Bay Community College;* Margo LaGattuta, *University of Michigan, Flint;* Richard Larschan, *University of Massachusetts, Dartmouth;* Dusty Maddox, *DeVry University;* Bonnie J. Marshall, *Grand Valley State University;* Kate Mohler, *Mesa Community College;* Ed Moritz, *Indiana University, Purdue University Fort Wayne;* Deborah Naquin, *Northern Virginia Community College;* Julie Nichols, *Okaloosa-Walton Community College;* Laura Robbins, *Portland Community College;* Matthew Roudané, *Georgia State University;* Robert E. Rubin, *Wright State University;* Nancy Ruff, *Southern Illinois University, Edwardsville;* Christine M. Ryan, *Middlesex Community College;* Larry W. Severeid, *College of Eastern Utah;* Diane Thompson, *Northern Virginia Community College;* Monica Parrish Trent, *Montgomery College;* Shonda Wilson, *Suffolk County Community College;* Frances J. Winter, *Massachusetts Bay Community College;* Kelly Wonder, *University of Wisconsin, Eau Claire;* Deanna L. Yameen, *Quincy College.*
Also Mark Gallaher, Kelly McGuire, Julie Nash, and Dee Seligman.

Randall VanderMey
Verne Meyer
John Van Rys
Dave Kemper
Pat Sebranek

Contents

The College Essay

II. A Reader: Strategies and Models

Narrative and Descriptive Writing

I. A Rhetoric: College Student's Guide to Writing

Reading, Thinking, and Writing

CONTENTS

1　Critical Thinking and Reading

Chapter 1
Critical Thinking and Reading

audio

Sometimes writing is a way of showing what you know or what you have learned. However, successful writing for college courses—and for the world outside of college—will often demonstrate more. That is, it will show your ability to think about what you've learned. Such thinking includes the following:

- Analyzing complex processes and concepts
- Synthesizing ideas
- Weighing the value of things
- Designing new patterns and creating new forms

All of these examples involve critical thinking, a crucial ability for students and professionals alike. Improving your critical thinking skills will make you a better writer and reader. Improving your writing and reading skills will, in turn, make you a better thinker. In this chapter, you'll find several strategies for critical thinking and reading that will help you improve your writing.

What's Ahead
- Thinking Critically, Writing Well
- Using Logical Reasoning Guidelines
- Thinking by Analysis, Synthesis, Evaluation, and Application
- Thinking and Reading Critically
- Reading Actively
- Checklist and Writing Activities

Overview
Thinking Critically, Writing Well

Critical thinking starts with good thinking habits. The suggestions below will help you move beyond superficial responses to develop deeper insights. Like everything worthwhile, improving your thinking skills takes time and practice. But it's worth it. Sound critical thinking will pay off in sound, thoughtful writing.

1. **Be curious.** Ask "why?" Cultivate your ability to wonder; question what you see, hear, and read—both inside and outside class.

2. **Be patient.** Don't expect every puzzle or problem to solve itself instantly. Divide your thinking into manageable steps. Find rewards in the process of thinking.

3. **Focus.** Move away from distractions. Remind yourself of what is important about your subject. Learn to enhance your powers of concentration.

4. **Make connections.** Look at how details tie together. Apply what you already know to new situations. Use comparisons, analogies, and metaphors to clarify difficult ideas.

5. **Value other points of view.** Look at issues from another person's perspective, and think about how to balance other perspectives with your own.

6. **Tolerate ambiguity.** Play devil's advocate, debating two opposing views if both seem to have merit.

7. **Avoid jumping to conclusions.** Focus on issues, not personalities. Admit your blind spots and examine your prejudices. Evaluate, don't judge.

8. **Test the evidence.** Be properly skeptical about all claims. Look for corroboration (verification) in other sources.

9. **Be creative.** Don't settle for obvious answers. Look at things in a fresh way: redesign, reinvent, reenact, and rewrite.

10. **Write things down.** Writing helps you clarify and stretch ideas. It can help you sort out your thinking and discover things you didn't know you knew. In addition, it can show you weaknesses in your thinking, what you need to learn.

11. **Get involved.** Read books, journals, and newspapers. Watch documentaries. Join a club or discussion group. Volunteer for activities that expose you to new perspectives.

12. **Be open to new ideas.** Approach thinking as an adventure, looking for discoveries along the way.

For more help with thinking skills such as making and supporting claims, recognizing logical fallacies, and dealing with opposition, see "Strategies for Argumentation and Persuasion," pages 253–268.

Using Logical Reasoning

Reasoning usually leads in one of two major directions: from specific information toward general conclusions (*induction*) or from general principles toward specific applications (*deduction*).

Organize inductively or deductively.

Organizing your thinking inductively or deductively can add strength and clarity to your ideas. Inductive reasoning begins with specific details or observations (as shown at the base of the diagram below), then moves "up" to broader ideas and eventually to a generalization. In contrast, deduction starts at the top and works down, beginning with a generalization, then using it to explain particular instances.

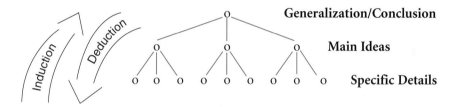

Induction and Deduction in Action

When you are writing, induction and deduction are helpful ways to organize the material in sentences, paragraphs, and essays. Study the two paragraphs below from the essay "If We Are What We Wear, What Are We?" (pages **285–286**). The first paragraph works deductively, the second paragraph inductively.

Deduction: generalization to specific details

1   The American excuse for owning multiples is that clothing styles change so rapidly. At the end of the '80s, trends in high fashion changed every two and a half months (During 95). Even for those of us who don't keep up with high fashion, styles change often enough that our clothing itself lasts much longer than the current trend. Perhaps this is one of the reasons the average American spent $997 on clothing in 1996 (U.S. Department of Commerce).

Induction: specific details to a generalization

2   While Americans are spending a thousand dollars on clothing a year, people in Ethiopia make an average of only $96 a year, those in Bangladesh $280, and the average Filipino worker makes $1,052 (United Nations Statistics Division). I, on the other hand, made over $5,000 last year, and that job was only part-time. When an American college student can earn more money at her part-time job than three billion people each make for a living, it's time to question our culture and ask, as Alan During did, "How much is enough?"

Guidelines
Thinking and Writing

Note: At college and on the job, your writing may require specific modes of thinking. These guidelines explain how to tackle many of these thinking tasks, starting with the most elementary. (See pages 9–12.)

When you are asked to _____ , be ready to _____ .

Know
		call to mind what you have learned
define	memorize	■ Recall information
identify	name	■ List details
list	recall	■ Define key terms
match	recognize	■ Identify main points

Understand
		show what you have learned
comprehend	grasp	■ Connect related examples
connect	restate	■ Summarize important details
explain	summarize	■ Explain how something works
interpret		■ Interpret what something means

Analyze
		break down information
characterize	contrast	■ Divide a whole into its parts
classify	examine	■ Group things into categories
compare	divide	■ Analyze causes and effects
		■ Examine similarities and differences

Synthesize
		shape information into a new form
assemble	imagine	■ Bring together a body of evidence
combine	invent	■ Blend the old with the new
construct	link	■ Predict or hypothesize
formulate		■ Construct a new way of looking at something

Evaluate
		determine the worth of information
assess	monitor	■ Point out a subject's strengths and weaknesses
check	rank	■ Evaluate its clarity, accuracy, logic, value, and so on
critique	rate	■ Convince others of its value/worth
judge	measure	

Apply
		use what you have learned
anticipate	propose	■ Propose a better way of doing something
choose	select	■ Generate a plan of action
generate		■ Offer solutions to a problem

Thinking by Analysis

The word *analyze* literally means "to loosen or undo." When you analyze something, you break it down into parts and examine each part separately. You classify information, compare objects, trace a process, or explain causes.

Analyzing

As you analyze, think about the questions listed below. Note that each type of thinking answers certain kinds of questions. Remember, too, that thinking tasks often require two or more kinds of analysis supporting one another.

- *Categories:* How are things grouped, divided, or classified?
- *Structures:* What are the parts or elements? How are they related?
- *Comparisons:* How are things similar? How are they different?
- *Causes/effects:* Why did this happen? What were the results?
- *Processes:* How does it work or happen? What are the stages?

Example: Read through the passage below from "A Fear Born of Sorrow" (pages 200–201), in which the writer compares and contrasts the September 11, 2001, attack on the World Trade Center with the Oklahoma City bombing in 1995, and analyzes the causes and effects of both events.

The writer develops contrasts signaled by "However." While doing so, she also analyzes causes and explains effects.

> The Oklahoma bombing was grievous and alarming, but localized. The bomber was soon arrested, his motives deduced, and justice served. While lives were changed and a nation was shaken, the world community remained composed. However, the September 11 attack unsettled us more, in part because the World Trade Center stood for so much more than the Oklahoma Federal Building did. The Twin Towers symbolized American domination of world finances: they were a major center for the Internet, a hub for international business, and an emblem of American life. The fall of the towers struck violently at the nation's psyche, and the manner in which they were destroyed—with America's own airplanes filled with passengers— has raised questions about America's security and future. Threatened to their core, Americans have demanded retaliation—but against whom? The terrorists' identity is not clear, and evidence seems elusive. In a sense, an unknown offender has injured Americans, and they beat the air in the dark. In such a case, terrorism is aptly named, for America's outcry expresses more than sorrow—it also expresses fear.

Thinking by Synthesis

As the opposite of analysis (which breaks things into parts), synthesis combines different elements so that they form a new whole. In your writing, when you pull together things that are normally separate, you are synthesizing. Common ways of synthesizing are predicting, inventing, redesigning, and imagining.

Synthesizing

Working with synthesis involves stretching your imagination. Start by looking closely at what you have. Then think of ways to combine that information with other material, to reshape it into another form, or to see it a different way. In other words, think "sideways" rather than straight ahead. Ask the following kinds of questions of your topic:

- *Combining:*   How can things be linked, associated, or blended?
- *Predicting:*   Under these conditions, what might happen?
- *Inventing:*   What new thing can be made?
- *Proposing:*   What fresh changes can you suggest?
- *Redesigning:* How can it be done better?
- *Imagining:*   How can the topic be looked at differently?

Example: Read through the passage below from "Hair Today, Gone Tomorrow" (pages **230–231**), in which Verne Meyer describes the process of how hair grows. Meyer asks readers to imagine the scalp as a pitcher's mound.

The writer uses his imagination to look at the topic differently.

Imagine a pitcher's mound covered with two layers of soil: first a layer of clay and on top of that a layer of rich, black dirt. Then imagine that 100,000 little holes have been poked through the black dirt and into the clay, and at the bottom of each hole lies one grass seed.   *1*

Slowly each seed produces a stem that grows up through the clay, out of the dirt, and up toward the sky above. Now and then every stem stops for awhile, rests, and then starts growing again. All the time about 90 percent of the stems are growing and the others are resting. Because the mound gets shaggy, sometimes a gardener comes along and cuts the grass.   *2*

Your skull is like that pitcher's mound, and your scalp (common skin) is like the two layers of soil. The top layer of the scalp is the epidermis, and the bottom layer is the dermis. About 100,000 tiny holes (called follicles) extend through the epidermis into the dermis. . . .   *3*

Thinking by Evaluation

Evaluation measures things—movies, novels, food, and arguments, for example. When you express your judgment about an issue or discuss the weak and strong points of a topic, you are evaluating.

Evaluating

To evaluate a topic, start by learning as much about it as possible. Then consider exactly how you will judge it—what criteria or standards will you apply to measure its value? Next, carefully weigh all aspects of the topic that relate to your standards. Finally, support your judgment with concrete details, examples, illustrations, and comparisons. Essentially, evaluate your topic by asking questions like these:

- *Parts:* What aspects or elements of the topic will you evaluate?
- *Criteria:* What standards will you use?
  On what will you base your judgment?
- *Assessment:* How does it measure up by those standards?
- *Comparison:* How does it compare and contrast with similar things?
- *Recommendations:* What do you advise?

Example: Read through the paragraphs below from Jennifer Berkompas's film review "Wonder of Wonders: *The Lord of the Rings*" (pages **380–381**). Note how she supports her judgments about the film's value by discussing different parts and comparing the film with the novel on which it is based.

Comparing the novel and the film, the writer assesses the film's strengths and recommends the film using her evaluation criteria.

Tolkien fans, be warned: the movie doesn't try to follow the book scene by scene or character by character. If you are fond of Tom Bombadil or elf lord Glorfindel, you won't find them. But the movie does stay close in spirit to the books. The director read the books often to prepare for filming, reading key scenes several times as he shot them. The martial power of Numenoreans, the rustic naivete of the Shire, the peace and beauty of Rivendell and Lothlorien, the presence of evil, the persistence of good and camaraderie, the pain, the power—it's all there.

Having read the books and seen the movie four times, I recommend that you look at the movie with an open mind. Admire the halls of Moria, the bridge of Khazad-dûm, the river of Rivendell, the towering kings, the Argonath—all incredible scenes. Enjoy what Jackson imagines a hobbit or a Numenorean or a wizard to look like.

If you haven't read the books, you can still enjoy the movie for its scenery, gripping plot, good acting, good role models, fight scenes, compelling characters, and chivalric romance and honor rarely seen today in film or life. Peter Jackson and crew capture Tolkien well.

Thinking by Application

Thinking by application involves exploring the practical. It involves using what you know to demonstrate, show, or relate things. For example, using what you have learned about the ecology of forest fires to examine a particular fire and its aftermath—that's application in action.

Applying

Applying involves moving from what you know to what may be possible. First, thoroughly understand the main themes and patterns in the information at hand. Second, explore how to use this information in the given situation. Third, select those facts and details that clarify and support the application. When you are applying, you are asking these kinds of questions:

- *Choices:*　What are the options? Where could we go from here?
- *Uses:*　What practical benefits could come from it?
- *Solutions:*　What steps could resolve the problem?
- *Outcomes:*　What results should appear?

Example: Review the paragraphs from the essay "Practical Wildlife Management" (pages 315–316). In this passage, the writer offers a solution to the problem of deer overpopulation in suburbs. After dismissing other options, he argues for a particular choice and offers an example to support his solution.

> The writer states his solution, explains it in more detail, and offers an example. He concludes by presenting potential benefits.

> The best and most effective solution to controlling deer populations is to stay as close to nature's ways as possible. Game management by hunting meets this criterion. Since we have eliminated the natural predators, we must provide others—hunters. The strongest animals have the best chance of escaping hunters, so natural selection is implemented.   *1*
>
> Hunting with guns in the suburbs is impractical and dangerous. However, bow hunting is a viable alternative. In Fox Chapel Borough, Pennsylvania, a town of 5,600 residents, 45 deer were being killed each year by autos, and deer were destroying greenery. The town implemented a deer management program that matched an experienced bow hunter with a private landowner. Rules were implemented to provide safety for humans and humane treatment of the deer. During the 1993 season, there were no shooting accidents, no wounded deer escaped, and 128 deer were harvested with a bow. In the 1994 hunt, 185 deer were taken by bow. Since the deer herd numbers around 4,300, Fox Chapel Borough still has some deer to cull, but they are on their way to an effective deer management program.   *2*
>
> Of all the methods tried or considered to rid urban and suburban areas of unwanted deer, this last one holds the most promise. . . .   *3*

Thinking and Reading Critically

Applying the habits of critical thinking to your reading can help improve both your reading and your writing. Critical reading puts you mentally on the edge of your seat. It trains your ear. It shows you how other writers create effects with words. You read critically by

- Reading with your brain engaged
- Reading actively, with a purpose and a plan
- Reading to digest, not simply to swallow
- Reading to prepare for whatever you may write

Read critically.

To become a more critical reader, develop the following habits, and use the strategy outlined on pages 14–15.

1. **Be purposeful.** When you read, know your goal. Ask yourself how this text fits into the course, or what this reading adds to your research or writing project.

2. **Be prepared.** Instead of coming at the text cold, get ready for it. Set aside enough time for the task and gather the necessary materials (pens, notebooks, high-lighters, dictionary).

3. **Be active.** Preview the chapter, Web site, or journal article to get the "big picture" of the writing's purpose and structure. Preview titles, headings, and graphics to gain a sense of the whole. Dig for the main ideas, and take clear notes on important information and ideas.

4. **Be curious and engaged.** Ask yourself questions about what you are reading. Make the writer's interests your own, and bring your interests to the discussion. Turn the reading process into a conversation with the text.

5. **Be open and fair.** Give the writer the benefit of the doubt. Read the entire piece, respecting what the writer says even as you evaluate it.

6. **Be a little distant.** Keep a critical distance from everything you read. Hold an argument at arm's length so that you can examine it fairly. Developing a healthy critical distance allows you to measure the value of what you are reading. (Critical distance from your own work is also vital when you revise your own writing.)

7. **Be thorough.** If the reading has been difficult, reread challenging parts and try to connect them to what you do understand. Review your questions and see whether you can find answers to them. Summarize what you've read.

INSIGHT: Readings sometimes take unexpected turns. A reading with a serious purpose may include passages marked by humor, while a comical reading may have an undercurrent of seriousness. Stay open to the unexpected.

Use a reading strategy.

Have you ever read an assignment, closed the textbook, and then thought, "I can't remember a thing I just read!" An effective reading strategy can change that. It will make you a participant—not just a bystander—as you read. One useful strategy for critical reading of textbooks, journal articles, and Web sites is called **SQ3R: Survey, Question, Read, Recite, and Review.** Try this method with your reading assignments and research assignments.

Before you read . . .

Survey ◆ The first step in the SQ3R study method is to survey the material. When you survey a reading assignment, you try to get a general idea of what the reading is about. Surveying gives you a chance to familiarize yourself with main ideas that can become reference points during the actual reading.

Begin by reviewing any questions or study guides you have received. Then read the introductory and concluding paragraphs and look briefly at each page in between. Pay special attention to the headings, chapter titles, illustrations, and boldfaced type. Also, check out the graphics—charts, maps, diagrams, illustrations—for visual reinforcement of key points.

Think about how you will use this material in the future and how you will be tested on it. You may want to create a brief outline of the assignment, jotting down section titles and paragraph headings as the major and minor points. As you move into a more thorough reading, you can fill in your outline with the necessary details.

Discussion Survey serves two important purposes: (1) it gives you the big picture and (2) it gets you into the assignment. Sometimes getting started is the hardest part. So go ahead, preview everything you read. You'll notice the difference almost immediately.

Question ◆ As you perform your survey, you should begin to ask questions about the material—questions that you hope to answer as you read. One quick way of doing this is to turn the headings and subheadings into questions. Asking questions will make you an active reader, keeping you involved and thinking about what is coming up next. Also, check out any questions found at the end of the chapters.

Discussion Another way to generate questions is to imagine a specific test question covering each of the major points in your reading. In fact, once you get to know your instructor, this strategy becomes a very natural way to approach a reading assignment. You may also create questions by entering into a kind of dialogue with the writer. Ask him or her anything. Question everything. Ask who, what, when, where, how, and why.

As you read . . .

Read ◆ Read the assignment carefully, looking for the main ideas and answers to these three questions: "What does this mean? How does it connect to the previous material? What will probably come next?" Keep track of your answers and other key ideas by annotating the text, taking notes, summarizing, mapping, or outlining. Read the difficult parts slowly. (Reread them if necessary.) Look up unfamiliar words or ideas, and use your senses to imagine the events, people, places, or things you are reading about. (See page **18** for more about taking notes.)

Discussion If you feel as though you're stretching beyond your limit of understanding, don't panic. Challenging reading assignments are designed to make you a better thinker. Simply raise any still-unanswered questions in the next class discussion. You'll soon see that other people have similar questions.

Recite ◆ One of the most valuable parts of the SQ3R method is the reciting step. When you have finished reading a page, section, or chapter, try to recite the key points aloud. Answering the *Who? What? When? Where? Why?* and *How?* questions is a quick way of testing yourself on how well you understand what you have read. You can also recite by writing a summary or listing the key points. Reread the material as necessary. (See page **19**.)

Discussion Reciting not only tests your understanding of what you've just read, it also helps you remember the material. In addition, reciting helps you connect the reading content to your personal needs, now and in the future.

After you read . . .

Review ◆ The final step is to review. As soon as you finish, double-check the questions you posed in the "question" stage of SQ3R. Can you answer them? Glance over any notes you made as well. But don't stop there if the reading is especially important. You will remember it much better by spacing out your reviews—spend a few minutes reviewing on each of the next few days.

Discussion If you can't review your reading immediately, make a concerted effort to do so within a day. Research shows that reviewing within 24 hours goes a long way in moving information from your short-term to your long-term memory. Consider reviewing with a classmate, perhaps by meeting a few minutes before each class. When you do take time to review reading material, consider the following helpful memory techniques:

- **Visualize it.**
- **Draw diagrams, illustrations, or clusters.**
- **Put the material in your own words.**
- **Teach it to someone.**
- **Use acronyms or rhymes.**

Reading Actively

Critical reading is interactive reading. As you read, enter into a dialogue with the writer, guessing where the writer will go next and letting the text provide answers and motivate still more questions. To read critically—and actively—use the tips below and try the techniques that follow.

- Read in stretches of thirty to forty-five minutes, followed by short breaks.
- Slow down and respond to the text, asking questions and writing down your reactions.
- Predict or anticipate what will come next.
- Read difficult parts out loud, or take turns reading aloud with a partner.

X-ray the text.

Texts usually have several parts: introductions, bodies, and conclusions. Some texts, such as textbooks, may contain overviews, reviews, summaries, discussions, and questions. Other texts include boxes and sidebars for special features. Use these elements to help you understand the text, but then get to the heart of the piece. As you read, X-ray the content, focusing on the main ideas. Don't become distracted by less important material.

Annotate the text.

Writing in the margins to record your responses activates your thinking and provides a valuable record of your ideas. Annotate using these techniques:

- **Ask questions.** Sometimes a simple "?" in the margin will do. At other times it's best to write out the question in full. What doubt, concern, or confusion do you encounter as you read?
- **Make connections.** Draw arrows to link ideas, or make notes like "see page 36" to link related passages.
- **Add personal asides.** Record what you think and feel while reading.
- **Define terms.** Define any difficult vocabulary words that you want to understand and remember.
- **Create a marginal index.** Write key words in the margin to identify themes, names, main parts, and so on.

INSIGHT: Underlining or highlighting key words or phrases can also be helpful, but don't overdo it. If you're not careful, highlighting or underlining might translate into "I'll learn this later."

Annotating in Action

Below you'll find the first page of an essay on cloning, showing a student's notes and highlighting. Study these annotations to see how the reader engages the text and comments on key ideas. (The full essay appears on pages 323–327.)

What's the connection?

The Media and the Ethics of Cloning

*Who is
he? Check*

If the contemporary debate on cloning has a patron saint, surely it is Andy Warhol. Not only did Warhol assert that everyone would have 15 minutes of fame—witness the lawyers, philosophers, theologians, and bioethicists who found their expertise in hot demand on the nightly moral-ity plays of network television following Ian Wilmut's cloning of the sheep Dolly—but he also placed "clones," multiple copies of the same phenome-non, at the heart of popular culture. Instead of multiple images of Marilyn Monroe and Campbell's soup cans, we now have cloned sheep. Regrettably, it is Warhol's capacity for hyperbole rather than his intelligence and ironic vision that permeates the current debate on cloning.

1

*See
textbook
p. 375*

*Good
definition
of cloning*

*Means
extreme
exaggeration*

It would be unfair to judge hastily written op-ed pieces, popular talk shows, and late-night radio programs by the same standards that one would apply to a sustained piece of philosophical or legal analysis. But the popu-lar media could do more to foster thoughtful public debate on the legal, moral, political, medical, and scientific dimensions of the cloning of humans and nonhuman animals.

2

*Media
needs to
consider
cloning
thought-
fully.*

As did many of my colleagues at the Hastings Center, I participated in several interviews with the media following Ian Wilmut's announcement in *Nature* that he had succeeded in cloning Dolly from a mammary cell of an adult sheep. After clearly stating to one Los Angeles radio broadcaster before our interview that I was not a theologian and did not represent a religious organization, I was rather breathlessly asked during the taping what God's view on cloning is and whether cloning is "against creation." Predictably, the broadcaster didn't want to discuss how religious ethicists are contribut-ing to the nascent public discourse about the ethics of cloning. Instead, he wanted me to provide a dramatic response that would get the radio station's phones ringing with calls from atheists, agnostics, and religious believers of all stripes.

3

*Radio
interviewer
wants
controversy,
not truth.*

*Look it
up?*

*Key point:
the media
should
emphasize
moral
issues of
animal
(not just
human)
cloning.*

In addition to inundating the public with hyperbolic sound bites and their print equivalents, the media have overwhelmingly emphasized the issues involved in cloning humans, paying almost no attention to the moral implications of cloning nonhuman animals. While the ethics of cloning humans clearly need to be debated, the cloning of nonhuman ani-mals has already taken place and deserves to be treated as a meaningful moral concern.

4

Take good notes.

During reading, effective note taking allows you to track information, insights, and reflections. After reading, it helps you gather your annotations into patterns, insights, and responses. Good note taking often forms the foundation of strong writing.

Note: For a thorough treatment of note taking as it relates to research projects, go to pages **457–462**. You'll find note taking methods described and modeled in detail.

The Double-Entry Notebook: A convenient method of note taking that makes sense for close, critical reading is the double-entry notebook. In a notebook, divide each page into columns. (The width may vary.) In one column, take notes from your reading. In the other column, record lecture notes related to the reading and/or your own responses to the reading. A sample entry appears below.

Reading Notes	Personal Response Notes
"The Media and the Ethics of Cloning"	
- Clones are "multiple copies of the same phenomenon"	*Turner seems dead right about the treatment of this issue in the media. The media just don't go very deep especially on science issues, which most people find tough to understand anyway.*
- The current debate about cloning is dominated by pretty thin journalism and sensationalist talk shows	
- Thoughtful public discussion of the issue is needed	*Like most other people, I've focused on the idea of human cloning, afraid of what it could lead to, but am also curious about it. But cloning animals just for the benefit of people, is that right?*
- Aspects of the cloning issue: legal, moral, political, medical, scientific	
- The discussion in the media has focused mostly on the idea of human cloning, but the issue of animal cloning hasn't been addressed very well yet	*Would I approve of human cloning if it benefited me? If it helped someone I love or saved my life? Would I want to be cloned myself???*

INSIGHT: You can set up a double-entry notebook on your computer by using the columns or table function. (Ask a computer expert if you need help.) Such a method allows you to add lecture notes to your reading notes if you use a laptop in class.

Summarize the text.

Writing a summary disciplines you by forcing you to pull out the essentials from a reading—the main points, the thread of the argument. When you summarize a text, you also stretch your ability to comprehend, analyze, and synthesize information—all important thinking skills. To summarize well, follow these steps:

1. Skim first, read closely second. Skim to get a sense of the whole, including the main idea and strategies for its support. Then read carefully, annotating and taking notes as you go. Ask yourself, "What does this text boil down to?"

2. Review your notes and annotations. Take what you've pulled out of the text and consolidate it into a set of main points.

3. Put those points into your own words. If possible, draft your summary without looking at your notes or the original text. Then check it against the original for accuracy and consistency. Follow these guidelines:

- Include only essentials—the main point or thesis, supporting points, key facts.
- Exclude most examples and details.
- Arrange your points in the order of the original, but cut any repetition.

Sample Summary: Following is a summary of "The Media and the Ethics of Cloning" essay that appears on pages 323–327. Compare the original with the summary. Notice how the writer of the summary includes only main points, arranges them in the same order as the original, and phrases them in terms she understands.

Summary: The Media and the Ethics of Cloning

Because of the recent sheep cloning, this topic has become big in the popular media. However, the media are doing a poor job covering cloning. Talk shows and news programs swamp the airwaves with one-sided bits of information. They've focused solely on human cloning and have ignored animal cloning, especially the ethics of cloning animals to create "pharmaceutical factories." Moreover, the media have stressed "genetic essentialism," the idea that people are simply products of their genes, an idea that ignores the complexity of growth. And finally, the media make it sound as though the advance of cloning cannot be stopped. The solution to this mass media dilemma has three parts: First, scientists and ethicists need further training so that they can understand one another's work better. Second, ethicists need to be better communicators in the media, looking especially for science journals publishing articles that can be understood by the nonscientist. Third, a public debate needs to be sponsored by institutions so that the discussion has some grassroots participation.

INSIGHT: Sometimes you may want to write an evaluative summary, adding your judgment of the text's effectiveness to the basic summary.

Map the text.

You may understand a text better by mapping it out graphically, so as to create a visual representation of its component parts. To do so, start with the main topic circled in the center of a page. Then branch out with subtopics, condensing each into a word or phrase. Add graphics, arrows, drawings—anything that helps you visualize the text. *Note:* If the text follows a traditional method of organization, try one of the graphic organizers on pages **46–47**.

Sample Map for "The Media and the Ethics of Cloning"

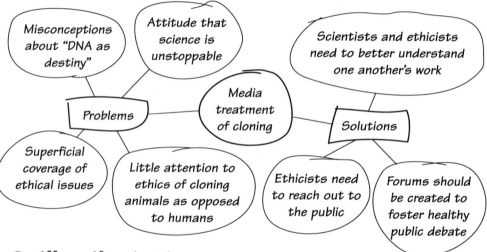

Outline the text.

A traditional way of summarizing a text is constructing an outline. In an outline, you trace the text's thesis, supporting points, and key evidence. *Note:* Outlines can take several forms. See pages **44–45** for details.

Sample Outline for "The Media and the Ethics of Cloning"

1. Introduction: The current debate about cloning is filled with exaggeration.
2. The mass media have confused the debate:
   - Bombarding the public with sound bites
   - Focusing on human cloning and ignoring animal cloning
   - Wrongly stressing that people are products of their genes
   - Promoting a scientific determinism, the idea that scientific "progress" can't be stopped
3. Thesis: The discussion can be improved in three ways:
   - Scientists and ethicists must learn to understand one another's work.
   - Ethicists need to improve how they communicate to the mass media.
   - Public debate about scientific topics must be expanded to forums and outreach programs.
4. Conclusion: We need more intelligent discussions so that the public is not misled by the mass media.

Evaluate the text.

A crucial element of active reading is evaluating—determining the credibility, perspective, and logic of the text. Consider these strategies for testing what you read.

1. **Judge the reading's credibility.** Where was it published? How reliable is the author? How current is the information? How accurate and complete does it seem to be? In addition, consider the tone of the writing, the author's attitude, and any apparent biases.

   Discussion Leigh Turner, the author of "The Media and the Ethics of Cloning" on pages 323–327, tells us that he is a member of the Hastings Center, a nonprofit research institute. How does this information build or break his credibility? Within the article, how does he build credibility?

2. **Put the reading in a larger context.** How do the text's ideas match what you know from other sources? What details of background, history, and social context help you understand this text's perspective? What allusions (references to people, events, and so on) does the writer use? Why?

   Discussion The topic of cloning belongs to the broader subjects of genetic research and ethics. In addition, the topic relates to debates over the nature of human identity. As for allusions, the author refers to the artist Andy Warhol and the cloning of the sheep Dolly. What else is part of this context?

3. **Reflect on how the reading challenges you.** Which of your beliefs and values does the reading call into question? What discomfort does it create? Work through that discomfort.

   Discussion The article may make us feel uncomfortable about several issues: our lack of concern for animals, our inability to see past the media's treatment of cloning, the application of cloning to several areas of life (including replication of ourselves). What other challenges does the article raise?

4. **Evaluate the reasoning and support.**
   - Is the reasoning clear and logical?
   - Are the examples and other supporting details appropriate and enlightening?
   - Are inferences (what the text implies) consistent with the tone and message? (Look especially for hidden logic and irony that undercut what is said explicitly.)

   Discussion In his essay, Turner uses examples and illustrations extensively. He analyzes the problem by breaking it down, and he systematically presents a three-part solution. Is the logic sound?

Note: For additional help evaluating texts and Web sites, see page 456. For information on how to detect logical fallacies often used by writers, go to pages 261–264.

Critical Thinking and Reading Checklist

Use these questions as you work to help improve your critical thinking and reading skills.

____ Which of the habits for critical thinking (page **6**) come most naturally to me? Which require more effort on my part? How might I develop these habits?

____ Can I recognize inductive and deductive reasoning? Can I apply them in my own writing?

____ Can I distinguish among the various thinking and writing modes required in college?

____ Do I recognize what it means to read actively—to engage a text, remain open to its ideas, and yet maintain a critical distance?

____ How can I effectively use the activities of annotating and note taking to increase my understanding and responsiveness to what I read?

____ Do I understand the characteristics of a thoughtful summary? How can I use summarizing to enhance my understanding?

write

Writing Activities

1. What thinking skills are required in your field of study? Reflect on those possibilities in your writing journal, talk with other students in the program, review a textbook for a course in the discipline, or interview one of your instructors.

2. In your experience, what is the relationship between reading and writing? Have you excelled at or struggled with either? How can writing help reading and reading help writing? In a one- to two-page reflective essay, explore these questions and others you can think of about reading and writing.

3. Choose a model essay from the section in this text on persuasive writing (pages **253–330**). As you read it, practice the activities of annotating, note taking, and summarizing. In your journal, explore how these activities influenced your thinking about the essay, your understanding of it, and your responses to it.

4. Choose a subject you know something about. Practice thinking about that subject both inductively and deductively. Then write two paragraphs, one developed through inductive reasoning and one produced through deductive reasoning.

The Writing Process

CONTENTS

The Writing Process

College instructors assign essays for a variety of reasons. One reason is that they want to encourage you to think and figure things out for yourself. This emphasis on clear and logical thought distinguishes college writing from the writing you may have done earlier in your schooling. Fortunately for you, writing occurs through a process, a process that can be learned, practiced, and improved. Once you understand the writing process—from forming a clear sense of the assignment to submitting the final draft—you will be able to produce essays and papers that reflect your best thinking.

This section on the writing process shows you, step by step, how to develop a piece of writing. This process relies on the following premise: An effective essay almost always results from careful planning, writing, and rewriting. The specific steps in the writing process are **getting started, planning, drafting, revising, editing and proofreading,** and **submitting.**

Before you begin, it's important that you understand the following points about the writing process:

- **Writing never follows a straight path.** Don't expect to move neatly through the steps in the writing process. By its very nature, writing includes detours, wrong turns, and repeat visits.

- **Each writer works differently.** Some writers need to talk about their writing early on, while others would rather keep their ideas to themselves. As you continue working with the writing process, your writing personality will develop naturally.

- **Each assignment presents challenges.** For one assignment, you may do a lot of planning and research; for another assignment, you may do little planning before you're ready to write a first draft.

This section discusses the steps in the writing process. Once you understand the strategies and skills associated with each step, you will be ready to develop effective essays and papers.

Web

The Writing Process:
From Assignment to Final Draft

The following flowchart shows the steps in the writing process. Refer to it whenever you need a basic guide during the development of a piece of writing.

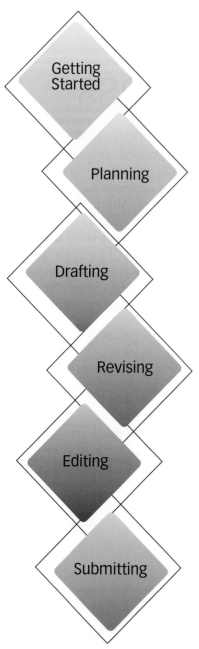

Getting Started

Understanding the assignment
Selecting a topic
Collecting information

Planning

Forming a thesis
Using methods of development
Developing a plan or an outline

Drafting

Opening your draft
Developing the middle
Ending your draft

Revising

Improving ideas, organization, and voice
Revising collaboratively

Editing and Proofreading

Editing for style
Proofreading for correctness

Submitting

Preparing a paper for submission
Checking for page design and documentation

INSIGHT: Notice that the steps in the writing process overlap in the flowchart. When you write, you will sometimes move back and forth between steps.

Chapter 2
Getting Started

video

Before a building contractor begins a new project—let's say an addition to a house—he or she must do some fact finding. For example, a contractor needs to know the purpose of the addition, the customers' budget for the project, and the date when they would like it completed. With this type of information in mind, a contractor can explore possible designs.

You should approach your college writing in much the same way: with some initial fact finding. For example, you need to understand the purpose and intended audience for the piece of writing. You also need to know about what requirements apply concerning the length of the paper and how it will be assessed. Once you understand what is expected, then you are ready to explore possible topics.

Getting started requires you to do three things: (1) gain an understanding of the assignment (the initial fact finding), (2) select a suitable topic, and (3) collect information about it. This section includes guidelines and strategies that will help you "get started" and will make it much easier to plan essays.

What's Ahead

- Understanding the Assignment
- Selecting a Topic
- Collecting Information
- Getting Started Checklist and Writing Activities

Understanding the Assignment

Each college instructor has a way of personalizing a writing assignment, but most assignments will spell out (1) the objective, (2) the task, (3) the formal requirements, and (4) suggested approaches and topics. Your first step, therefore, is to read the assignment carefully, noting the options and restrictions that are part of it. The suggestions below will help you do that. (Also see pages **96–97** for one writer's approach.)

Read the assignment.

Certain words in the assignment explain what main action you must perform. Here are some words that signal what you are to do:

Look for Key Words

Analyze: Break a topic down into subparts, showing how those parts relate.

Argue: Defend a claim with logical arguments.

Classify: Divide a large group into well-defined subgroups.

Compare/contrast: Point out similarities and/or differences.

Define: Give a clear, thoughtful definition or meaning of something.

Describe: Show in detail what something is like.

Evaluate: Weigh the truth, quality, or usefulness of something.

Explain: Give reasons, list steps, or discuss the causes of something.

Interpret: Tell in your own words what something means.

Reflect: Share your well-considered thoughts about a subject.

Summarize: Restate someone else's ideas very briefly in your own words.

Synthesize: Connect facts or ideas to create something new.

Look for Options and Restrictions

The assignment often gives you some choice in topic or approach but may restrict your options to suit the instructor's purpose. Note the options and restrictions in the following short sample assignment:

Reflect on the way a natural disaster or major historical event has altered your understanding of the past, the present, or the future.

Restrictions: (1) you must *reflect on a change in your understanding,* (2) the disaster must be *natural,* (3) the historical event must be *major*

Options: (1) you may choose *any natural disaster or historical event,* (2) you may focus on the *past, present, or future,* (3) you may examine *any kind of alteration*

Relate the assignment . . .

to the goals of the course.

1. How much value does the instructor give it? (The value is often expressed as a percentage.)

2. What benefit does your instructor want you to receive?
   - Strengthen your comprehension?
   - Improve your research skills?
   - Deepen your ability to explain, prove, or persuade?
   - Expand your style?
   - Increase your creativity?

3. How will this assignment contribute to your overall performance in the course? What course goals (often listed in the syllabus) does it address?

to other assignments.

4. Does it build on previous assignments?

5. Does it prepare you for the next assignment?

to your own interests.

6. Does it connect with a topic that already interests you?

7. Does it connect with work in your other courses?

8. Does it connect with the work you may do in your chosen field?

9. Does it connect with life outside of school?

Reflect on the assignment.

1. **First impulses**: How did you feel when you initially read the assignment?

2. **Approaches**: What's the usual approach for an assignment like this? What's a better way of tackling it?

3. **Quality of performance**: What would it take to produce an excellent piece of writing?

4. **Benefits**: To your education? To you personally? To the class? To society?

5. **Key traits**: Reflect further on four key features of any writing assignment.

   Purpose: What is the overall purpose of the assignment—to inform, to explain, to analyze, to entertain? What is the desired outcome?

   Audience: Should you address your instructor? Your classmates? A general reader? How much does the reader already know about the topic? What type of language should you use?

   Form: What are the specific requirements concerning length, format, and due date?

   Assessment: How will the assignment be evaluated? How can you be sure that you are completing the assignment correctly?

Selecting a Topic

For some assignments, finding a suitable topic requires little thinking on your part. If, for example, an instructor asks you to summarize an article in a professional journal, you know what you will write about—the article in question. But suppose the instructor asks you to analyze a feature of popular culture in terms of its impact on society. You won't be sure of a specific writing topic until you explore the possibilities. Keep the following points in mind when you conduct a topic search. Your topic must . . .

- meet the requirements of the assignment,
- be limited in scope,
- seem reasonable (that is, be within your means to research), and
- sincerely interest you.

Limit the subject area.

Many of your writing assignments may relate to general subject areas that you are currently studying. Your task then is to select a specific topic related to the general area of study—a topic limited enough that you can treat it with some depth in the length allowed for the assignment. The following examples show the difference between general subjects and limited topics:

General Subject Area: Popular culture
 Limited Topic: **The Simpsons TV show**

General Subject Area: Energy sources
 Limited Topic: **Using wind power**

Conduct your search.

Finding a writing idea that meets the requirements of the assignment should not be difficult, if you know how and where to look. Follow these steps:

1. Check your class notes and handouts for ideas related to the assignment.

2. Search the Internet. Type in a keyword or phrase (the general subject stated in the assignment) and see what you can find. Or follow a subject tree to narrow a subject. (See page **498**.)

3. Consult indexes, guides, and other library references. *The Readers' Guide to Periodical Literature,* for example, lists current articles published on specific topics and explains where to find them. (See pages **485–493**.)

4. Discuss the assignment with your instructor or an information specialist.

5. Use one or more of the prewriting strategies described on the following pages to generate possible writing ideas.

Explore for possible topics.

You can generate possible writing ideas by using the following strategies. These same strategies can be used when you've chosen a topic and want to develop it further.

Journal Writing

Write in a journal on a regular basis. Explore your personal feelings, develop your innermost thoughts, and record the happenings of each day. Periodically go back and underline ideas that you would like to explore in writing assignments. In the following example of journal writing, the writer came up with an idea for a writing assignment about the societal impacts of popular culture.

> I read a really disturbing news story this morning. I've been thinking about it all day. In California a little girl was killed when she was struck by a car driven by a man distracted by a billboard ad for lingerie featuring a scantily clothed woman. Not only is it a horrifying thing to happen, but it also seems to me all too symbolic of the way that sexually charged images in the media are putting children, and especially girls, in danger. That reminds me of another news story I read this week about pre-teen girls wanting to wear the kinds of revealing outfits that they see in music videos, TV shows, and magazines aimed at teenagers. <u>Too many of today's media images give young people the impression that sexuality should begin at an early age.</u> This is definitely a dangerous message.

Freewriting

Write nonstop for ten minutes or longer to discover possible writing ideas. Use a key concept related to the assignment as a starting point. You'll soon discover potential writing ideas that might otherwise have never entered your mind. Note in the following example that the writer doesn't stop writing even when he can't think of anything to say. *Note also that he doesn't stop to correct typos and other mistakes.*

> Popular culture. What does that include? Television obviously but thats a pretty boring subject. What else? Movies, pop music, video games. Is there a connection between playing violent video games and acting out violent behavior? Most video players I know would say no but sometimes news reports suggest a connection. Is this something I'd want to write about? Not really. What then? Maybe I could think about this a different way and focus on the positive effects of playing video games. They release tension for one thing and they can really be challenging. Other benefits? They help to kill time, that's for sure, but maybe that's not such a good thing. I would definitely read more if it weren't for video games, tv, etc. Maybe I could write about how all the electronic entertainment that surrounds us today is creating ageneration of nonreaders. Or maybe I could focus on whether people aren't gettting much physical exercise because of the time they spend with electronic media. Maybe both. At least I have some possibilities to work with.

Freewriting

QUICK GUIDE

Freewriting is the writing you do without having a specific outcome in mind. You simply write down whatever pops into your head as you explore your topic. Freewriting can serve as a starting point for your writing, or it can be combined with any of the other prewriting strategies to help you select, explore, focus, or organize your writing. If you get stuck at any point during the composing process, you can return to freewriting as a way of generating new ideas.

REMINDERS

- **Freewriting helps you get your thoughts down on paper.** (Thoughts are constantly passing through your mind.)
- **Freewriting helps you develop and organize these thoughts.**
- **Freewriting helps you make sense out of things that you may be studying or researching.**
- **Freewriting may seem awkward at times, but just stick with it.**

THE PROCESS

- **Write nonstop and record whatever comes into your mind.** Follow your thoughts instead of trying to direct them.
- **If you have a particular topic or assignment to complete, use it as a starting point.** Otherwise, begin with anything that comes to mind.
- **Don't stop to judge, edit, or correct your writing;** that will come later.
- **Keep writing even when you think you have exhausted all of your ideas.** Switch to another angle or voice, but keep writing.
- **Watch for a promising writing idea to emerge.** Learn to recognize the beginnings of a good idea, and then expand that idea by recording as many specific details as possible.

THE RESULT

- **Review your writing and underline the ideas you like.** These ideas will often serve as the basis for future writings.
- **Determine exactly what you plan (or are required) to write about.** (You may then decide to do a second freewriting exercise.)
- **Listen to and read the freewriting of others;** learn from your peers.

Listing

Freely list ideas as they come to mind, beginning with a key concept related to the assignment. (Brainstorming—listing ideas in conjunction with members of a group— is often an effective way to extend your lists.)

Following is an example of a student's list of ideas for possible topics on the subject of news reporting:

Aspect of popular culture: News reporting

> **Sensationalism**
> **Sound bites rather than in-depth analysis**
> **Focus on the negative**
> **Shock radio**
> **Shouting matches pretending to be debates**
> **Press leaks that damage national security, etc.**
> **Lack of observation of people's privacy**
> **Bias**
> **Contradictory health news confusing to readers**
> **Little focus on "unappealing" issues like poverty**
> **Celebration of "celebrity"**

Clustering

To begin the clustering process, write a key word or phrase related to the assignment in the center of your paper. Circle it, and then cluster ideas around it. Circle each idea as you record it, and draw a line connecting it to the closest related idea. Keep going until you run out of ideas and connections.

Following is a sample student clustering on the subject of sports:

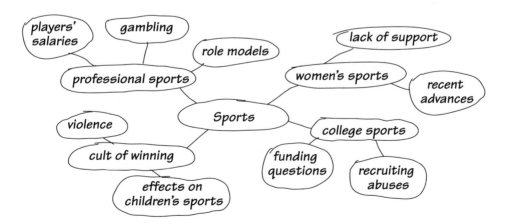

Note: After four or five minutes of listing or clustering, scan your work for an idea to explore in a freewriting. A writing idea should begin to emerge during this freewriting session. (See pages **31–32**.)

Creating a Dialogue

Create a written dialogue between yourself and an intended reader of your piece. The topic of this conversation should relate to your writing assignment. Continue the conversation as long as you can, or until a possible writing idea begins to unfold.

Following is an example of the beginning of a dialogue:

> *Me:* I'm supposed to write a paper about some aspect of popular culture and its influence on society.
>
> *Reader:* Do you have any ideas?
>
> *Me:* Not really. I'd like to avoid trite subjects like advertising.
>
> *Reader:* What else is there?
>
> *Me:* I don't know. I guess I'd really like to write something about barriers in society.
>
> *Reader:* What kinds of barriers?
>
> *Me:* You know. How people don't really communicate very well across ethnic and racial lines.
>
> *Reader:* How could you relate that to popular culture?
>
> *Me:* Stereotypes in the media.
>
> *Reader:* How else?
>
> *Me:* Well, maybe I should start with the idea that racial barriers are an aspect of popular culture in the media and in life and then develop some ideas about how those barriers influence society. . . .

Using the "Essentials of Life Checklist"

Below you will find a checklist of the major categories into which most essential things in our lives are divided. The checklist provides an endless variety of subject possibilities. Consider the fifth category, education. It could lead to the following writing ideas:

- Online education
- Funding higher education (student loans)
- A new approach in education
- An influential educator

Essentials of Life Checklist

clothing	communication	exercise	health/medicine
housing	purpose/goals	community	entertainment
food	measurement	arts/music	literature/books
exercise	machines	faith/religion	recreation/hobby
education	intelligence	trade/money	personality/identity
family	agriculture	heat/fuel	natural resources
friends	environment	rules/laws	tools/utensils
love	science	freedom/rights	plants/vegetation
senses	energy	land/property	work/occupation

Collecting Information

Writer and instructor Donald Murray says that "writers write with information. If there is no information, there will be no effective writing." How true! Before you can develop a thoughtful piece of writing, you must gain a thorough understanding of your topic; to do so, you must carry out the necessary reading, reflecting, and researching. Writing becomes a very satisfying experience once you can speak with authority about your topic. Use the following guidelines when you start collecting information. (Also see the Research Guide in this book.)

- Determine what you already know about your topic. (Use the strategies listed below.)
- Consider listing questions that you would like to answer during your research. (See page **36**.)
- Identify and explore possible sources of information. (See page **37**.)
- Carry out your research following a logical plan. (See page **37**.)

Find out what you already know.

Use one or more of the following strategies to determine what you already know about a writing topic.

Focused Freewriting ◆ At this point, you can focus your freewriting by (1) exploring your limited topic from different angles or (2) approaching your freewriting as if it were a quick draft of the actual paper. A quick version will tell you how much you know about your topic and what you need to find out.

Clustering ◆ Try clustering with your topic serving as the nucleus word. Your clustering should focus on what you already know. (See page **33**.)

Five W's of Writing ◆ Answer the *Five W's—Who? What? When? Where?* and *Why?*—to identify basic information about your subject. Add *How?* to the list for even better coverage.

Directed Writing ◆ Write whatever comes to mind about your topic, using one of the modes listed below. (Repeat the process as often as you need to, selecting a different mode each time.)

    Describe it: What do you see, hear, feel, smell, and taste?

    Compare it: What is it similar to? What is it different from?

    Associate it: What connections between this topic and others come to mind?

    Analyze it: What parts does it have? How do they work together?

    Argue it: What do you like about the topic? Not like about it? What are its strengths and its weaknesses?

    Apply it: What can you do with it? How can you use it?

Ask questions.

To guide your collecting and researching, you may find it helpful to list questions about your topic that you would like to answer. Alternatively, you can refer to the questions below. These questions address problems, policies, and concepts. Most topics will fall under one of these categories. Use those questions that seem helpful as a guide to your research.

	Description	Function	History	Value
P R O B L E M S	What is the problem? What type of problem is it? What are its parts? What are the signs of the problem?	Who or what is affected by it? What new problems might it cause in the future?	What is the current status of the problem? What or who caused it? What or who contributed to it?	What is its significance? Why? Why is it more (or less) important than other problems? What does it symbolize or illustrate?
P O L I C I E S	What is the policy? How broad is it? What are its parts? What are its most important features?	What is the policy designed to do? What is needed to make it work? What are or will be its effects?	What brought this policy about? What are the alternatives to it?	Is the policy workable? What are its advantages and disadvantages? Is it practical? Is it a good policy? Why or why not?
C O N C E P T S	What is the concept? What are its parts? What is its main feature? Who or what is it related to?	Who has been influenced by this concept? Why is it important? How does it work?	When did it originate? How has it changed over the years? How might it change in the future?	What practical value does it have? Why is it superior (or inferior) to similar concepts? What is its social worth?

Identify possible sources.

Finding meaningful sources is one of the most important steps you will take as you prepare to write. Listed below are tips that will help you identify good sources:

1. **Give yourself enough time.** Finding good sources of information may be time-consuming. Books and periodicals may be checked out, your computer service may be down, and so on.

2. **Be aware of the limits of your resources.** Print material may be out-of-date. Online information may be more current, but it may not always be reliable. (See pages **456** and **480** for ways to help you evaluate information.)

3. **Use your existing resources to find additional sources of information.** Pay attention to books, articles, and individuals mentioned in reliable initial sources of information.

4. **Ask for help.** The specialists in your school library can help you find information that is reliable and relevant. These people are trained to find information; don't hesitate to ask for their help. (See pages **485–493**.)

5. **Bookmark useful Web sites.** Include reference works and academic resources related to your major.

Explore different sources of information.

Of course, books and Web sites are not the only possible sources of information. Primary sources such as interviews, observations, and surveys may lead you to a more thorough, meaningful understanding of a topic. (See pages **480–484**.)

Primary Sources	Secondary Sources
Interviews	Articles
Observations	Reference book entries
Participation	Books
Surveys	Web sites

Carry out your research.

As you conduct your research, try to use a variety of reliable sources. It's also a good idea to choose an efficient note-taking method before you start. You will want to take good notes on the information you find and record all the publishing information necessary for citing your sources. (See pages **457–462**.)

Reserve a special part of a notebook to question, evaluate, and reflect upon your research as it develops. The record of your thoughts and actions created during this process will often mean as much as or more to you than the actual information you uncover. It helps you make sense of new ideas, refocus your thinking, and evaluate your progress.

Getting Started Checklist

Use this checklist as a guide to help you plan your writing.

The Assignment *I know . . .*

_____ The main action (key words), restrictions, and options.

_____ The connection to personal and course goals.

_____ The purpose of the writing—to inform, explain, analyze, or persuade.

_____ The audience—who they are, what they know, and what they need.

_____ The form required—essay, narrative, summary, or research paper.

_____ The requirements for length, format, and documentation.

_____ The assessment method that will be used.

The Topic *I have . . .*

_____ Explored possible topics through journal writing, freewriting, listing, clustering, or dialogue.

_____ Chosen a limited topic that fits the assignment and spurs my interest.

_____ Recorded what I already know and what I need to learn.

_____ Developed a workable research plan.

_____ Collected information about the topic.

Writing Activities

1. Andy Rooney once said, "I don't pick subjects so much as they pick me." What do you think he meant? In your experience as a writer, is Rooney's idea valid? Reflect on the topics that have "picked" you— that you have enjoyed exploring or that have challenged you.

2. Review the wording of a recent writing assignment. What are the key words, restrictions, and options? What does the description tell you about the purpose, audience, form, and assessment of the writing? What more would you want to learn from the instructor? What strategies from this chapter would you use to get started?

3. Below is a list of general subject areas. Select one that interests you and do the following: Using the strategies on pages **30–34**, brainstorm possible topics. Then select one of these topics. Finally, using the strategies on pages **35–37**, explore what you know about that topic and what you need to learn.

- **Exercise**
- **Environment**
- **Health/medicine**
- **Housing**
- **Arts/music**
- **Work/occupation**

Chapter 3
Planning

Planning of almost any type requires careful thinking. When you plan an essay, you have two basic thinking objectives: (1) establish a thesis or focus for your writing and (2) organize the supporting information. The amount of organization time required depends on the type of writing. For narratives, very little organizing may be required. For most academic essays, however, you will need to identify the method of development—comparison, cause/effect, classification—that best supports your thesis and then organize your details accordingly. (See pages **42–43**.) At this point, your goal is to establish the general structure of your writing.

Writer and instructor Ken Macrorie offers this important insight about planning: "Good writing is formed partly through plan and partly through accident." In other words, too much early planning can get in the way. Writing, at its best, is a process of discovery. You never know what new insights or ideas will spring to mind until you put pen to paper or fingers to keyboard.

What's Ahead

- Taking Inventory of Your Thoughts
- Forming a Thesis Statement
- Using Methods of Development
- Developing a Plan or an Outline
     Types of Graphic Organizers
- Planning Checklist and Writing Activities

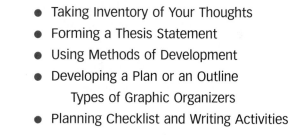

Taking Inventory of Your Thoughts

Suppose you've done some searching, and you've succeeded in discovering some interesting information and perspectives about your subject. Now may be a good time to see how well your findings match up with your topic. After considering the following questions, you should be able to decide whether to move ahead with your planning or to reconsider your topic.

Re-examine your topic.

Writing Task:
- What are the specific requirements of this assignment?
- Do I have enough time to do a good job with this topic?
- Am I writing to inform, to explain, to analyze, or to persuade?

Subject:
- How much do I already know about this topic?
- Do I need to know more? Is additional information available?
- Have I tried any of the collecting strategies? (See pages **35–37**.)

Audience:
- How much does my audience already know about this subject?
- How can I get my audience interested in my idea?

Self:
- How committed am I to my writing idea?
- What can I learn or gain by continuing to write on this topic?

Form and Language:
- What form should my writing take?
- What would be an interesting way to lead into my paper?

Continue the process.

Research ◆ If you need to know more about your topic, continue collecting your own thoughts and/or investigating other sources of information. Remember that it is important to investigate secondary *and* primary sources of information. (See pages **480–484**.)

Review ◆ If you are ready to move ahead, carefully review your initial notes. As you read through this material, circle or underline ideas that seem important enough to include in your writing. Then look for ways in which these ideas connect or relate. The activities on the following pages will help you focus your thoughts for writing.

Web

Forming a Thesis Statement

After you have completed enough research and collecting, you may begin to develop a more focused interest in your topic. If all goes well, this narrowed focus will give rise to a thesis for your writing. A thesis statement identifies your central idea. It usually highlights a special condition or feature of the topic, expresses a specific feeling, or takes a stand.

State your thesis in a sentence that effectively expresses what you want to explore or explain in your essay. Sometimes a thesis statement develops early and easily; at other times, the true focus of your writing emerges only after you've written your first draft.

Find a focus.

A general subject area is typically built into your writing assignments. Your task, then, is to find a limited writing topic and examine it from a particular angle or perspective. (You will use this focus to form your thesis statement.)

FOCUSING A TOPIC

GENERAL SUBJECT	→	LIMITED TOPIC	→	SPECIFIC FOCUS
(Alternative energy sources)		(Wind power)		(Wind power as a viable energy source in the Plains states)

State your thesis.

You can use the following formula to write a thesis statement for your essay. A thesis statement sets the tone and direction for your writing. Keep in mind that at this point you're writing a *working thesis statement*—a statement in progress, so to speak. You may change it as your thinking on the topic evolves.

    A manageable or limited topic (wind power)
+ **a specific focus** (provides a viable energy source in the Plains states)
= **an effective thesis statement**

THESIS STATEMENT: **Wind power provides a viable energy source in the Plains states.**

Thesis Checklist

1. Does the thesis statement reflect a limited topic?
2. Does it clearly state the specific idea you plan to develop?
3. Is the thesis supported by the information you have gathered?
4. Does the thesis suggest a pattern of organization for your essay?

Using Methods of Development

An organizing pattern for your essay may be built into your assignment. For example, you may be asked to develop an argument or to write a process paper. When a pattern is not apparent, one may still evolve naturally during the research and information-collecting steps. If this doesn't happen, take a careful look at your thesis statement. An effective thesis will often suggest an organizing pattern. Notice how the thesis statements below provide direction and shape for the writing to follow. (Also see page **104**.)

Let your thesis guide you.

Thesis (Focus) for a Personal Narrative

What began as a simple prank ended up having serious consequences for all of us who were involved.

Discussion This statement identifies the focus of a personal narrative. It suggests that the essay will recount a personal experience and will most likely be arranged chronologically, beginning with the planning and execution of the prank and then going on to relate the consequences that followed. Writers of personal narratives do not always state a thesis directly, but they will generally have in mind an implied theme or main idea that governs the way they develop their writing.

Thesis for a Descriptive Essay

Although it was no more than an overgrown lot, as children we imagined the property next to my boyhood home to be a forest full of danger and adventure.

Discussion This statement indicates that the writer will describe a special place from childhood. This description might be organized spatially, moving from the edges of the wooded lot to its interior. A description may also be organized thematically, in this case by describing the specific features of the lot through the adventures the children imagined having there.

Thesis for a Cause and Effect Essay

While accepting some stress is inescapable, for our own health and for the well-being of others, we have to do more. We have to understand what stress is—both its causes and its effects.

Discussion This thesis indicates that the writer is developing a cause and effect essay. Essays following this pattern usually begin with one or more causes followed by an explanation of the effects, or they begin with a primary effect followed by an explanation of the causes. To develop the thesis above, the writer will follow the first route, exploring the causes of stress before examining its effects. (The full text of this essay appears on pages **187–189**.)

Thesis for an Essay of Comparison

Bigger in Native Son *and Alan in* Equus *are both entering adulthood and have come to realize that they are controlled by work, religion, and the media.*

Discussion   The writer of this thesis is comparing two literary characters point by point. Comparisons are patterned in two ways: either you discuss one of the subjects completely and then the other (whole versus whole), or you discuss both subjects at the same time (point by point). (See pages **198–199** for this essay.)

Thesis for an Essay of Classification

There are four main perspectives, or approaches, that you can use to converse about literature.

Discussion   The writer is writing an essay of classification. Essays following this pattern identify the main parts or categories of a topic and then examine each one. In this thesis, the writer identifies four ways to discuss literature, and he examines each one in turn. (See pages **216–217** for this essay.)

Thesis for a Process Essay

When a cell begins to function abnormally, it can initiate a process that results in cancer.

Discussion   As indicated in this thesis, the writer of this essay will explain how cancer cells multiply and affect the body. Process essays, such as this one, are organized chronologically. Each step is examined in turn to help readers understand the complete process. (See pages **223–225** for this essay.)

Thesis for an Essay of Definition

My memories, like the things I enjoy, can be described in only one way: eclectic, *a word I find endlessly fascinating.*

Discussion   This essay provides an interesting personal definition of the word *eclectic.* This particular essay of definition is generally organized around explanation and analysis. The writer explains what the word means and analyzes her personal interpretation of the term. (See pages **239–240** for this essay.)

Thesis for an Essay Proposing a Solution

The best solution to controlling deer populations is to stay as close to nature's ways as possible. Game management by hunting meets this criterion.

Discussion   The writer of this thesis is developing a problem/solution essay. Essays following this pattern usually begin with a discussion of the problem and its causes and then examine possible solutions. In this essay, the writer presents a problem's history, causes, and effects. He then identifies and dismisses some solutions before arguing for one solution in particular. (See pages **315–316** for this essay.)

Developing a Plan or an Outline

After writing a working thesis and reviewing the methods of development (pages 42–43), you should be ready to organize the information that you have collected. A simple listing of main points may work for you, or you may need to outline the information or use a graphic organizer.

- **Basic list:** a brief listing of main points
- **Topic outline:** a more formal arrangement, including main points and essential details (See below.)
- **Sentence outline:** a formal arrangement, including main points and essential details written as complete sentences (See page 45.)
- **Graphic organizer:** an arrangement of main points and essential details in an appropriate chart or diagram (See pages 46–47.)

Choose an organization method.

Topic Outline

If you have a good deal of information to sort out and arrange, you may want to use a topic or sentence outline for your planning. In a topic outline, you state each main point and essential detail as a word or phrase. Before you start constructing your outline, write your working thesis statement at the top of your paper to help keep you focused on the subject. Do not attempt to outline your opening and closing paragraphs unless you are specifically asked to do so.

Sample Topic Outline

Thesis: There are four main perspectives, or approaches, that you can use to converse about literature.

I. Text-centered approaches
  A. Also called formalist criticism
  B. Emphasis on structure of text and rules of genre
  C. Importance placed on key literary elements
II. Audience-centered approaches
  A. Also called rhetorical or reader-response criticism
  B. Emphasis on interaction between reader and text
III. Author-centered approaches
  A. Emphasis on writer's life
  B. Importance placed on historical perspective
  C. Connections made between texts
IV. Ideological approaches
  A. Psychological analysis of text
  B. Myth or archetype criticism
  C. Moral criticism
  D. Sociological analysis

Sentence Outline

The sample outline below uses complete sentences to explain the main points and essential details that will be covered in the main part of the essay.

Sample Sentence Outline

Thesis: There are four main perspectives, or approaches, that you can use to converse about literature.
  I. Text-centered approach focuses on the literary piece itself.
    A. This approach is often called formalist criticism.
    B. This method of criticism examines text structure and the rules of the genre.
    C. A formalist critic determines how key literary elements reinforce meaning.
  II. Audience-centered approach focuses on the "transaction" between text and reader.
    A. This approach is often called rhetorical or reader-response criticism.
    B. A rhetorical critic sees the text as an activity that is different for each reader.
  III. Author-centered approach focuses on the origin of a text.
    A. An author-centered critic examines the writer's life.
    B. This method of criticism may include a historical look at a text.
    C. Connections may be made between the text and related works.
  IV. The ideological approach applies ideas outside of literature.
    A. Some critics apply psychological theories to a literary work.
    B. Myth or archetype criticism applies anthropology and classical studies to a text.
    C. Moral criticism explores the moral dilemmas in literature.
    D. Sociological approaches include Marxist, feminist, and minority criticism.

Graphic Organizers

If you are a visual person, you might prefer a graphic organizer when it comes to arranging your ideas for an essay or report. Graphic organizers can help you map out ideas and illustrate relationships between ideas. Here is a graphic organizer—a line diagram—that was used to organize the ideas for the essay.

Sample Graphic Organizer

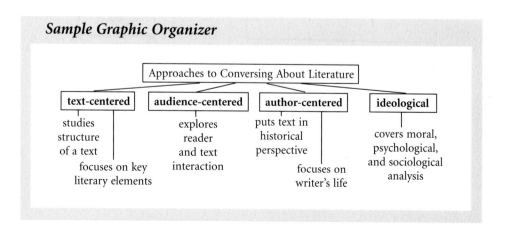

Types of Graphic Organizers

The following organizers are related to some of the methods of development discussed on pages **42–43**. Each will help you collect and organize your information. Adapt the organizers as necessary to fit your particular needs or personal style.

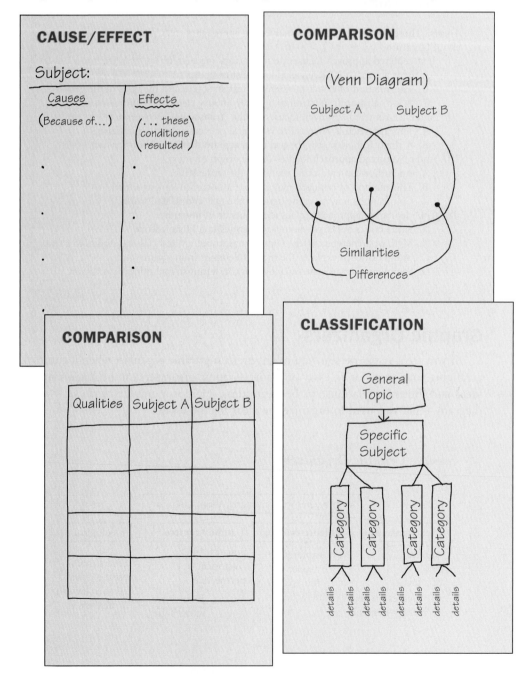

PROCESS ANALYSIS

Subject: _____
(Chronological Order)

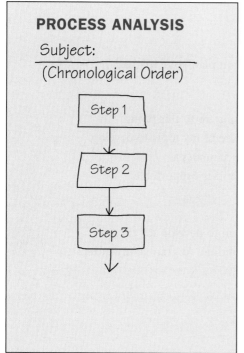

PROBLEM/SOLUTION

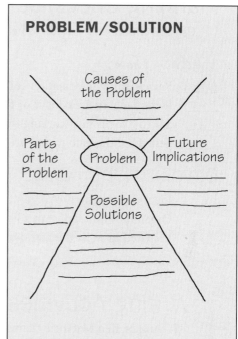

DEFINITION

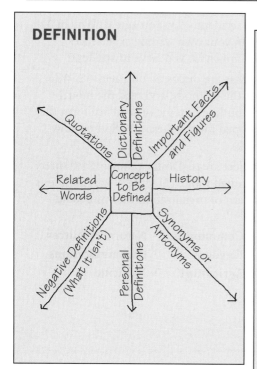

EVALUATION

Subject: _____

Points to Evaluate	Supporting Details
1.	
2.	
3.	
4.	
5.	

Planning Checklist

Use this checklist as a guide to help you plan your writing.

Thesis *I have . . .*

_____ Reviewed my information collecting up to this point.

_____ Identified a specific focus or feature of my topic to develop.

_____ Stated a focus in a working thesis statement.

_____ Tested the thesis to make sure that it is supportable.

Development *I have . . .*

_____ Identified a pattern of organization to develop my thesis.

_____ Organized my support in a list, outline, or graphic organizer.

_____ Prepared to write the first draft.

Writing Activities

1. Author Ken Macrorie claims that "Good writing is formed partly through plan and partly through accident." Do you agree? Why or why not? Relate Macrorie's idea to your own writing experiences. How carefully do you plan? How much do you leave to accident?

2. A number of organizational patterns are discussed on pages **42–43**. Review those pages, select one of the methods, and read the model essay given as an example. Then outline in topic or sentence form the support that the writer has developed for the thesis. Reflect on how that method of development works.

3. Listed below are nine general subject areas. Do the following for three of these subjects: (1) Identify a limited topic, (2) write a working thesis statement, and (3) identify a pattern of organization that you could use to develop the thesis.

- **Exercise**
- **Family**
- **Entertainment**
- **Community**
- **Freedom**
- **Agriculture**
- **Natural resources**
- **Communications**
- **Medicine**

Chapter 4
Drafting

video

The early twentieth-century French novelist Anatole France is reported to have said that one of his first drafts could have been written by any schoolboy, his next draft by a bright upper-level student, his third draft by a superior graduate, his fourth draft by a seasoned professional, and his final draft "only by Anatole France." Even if that report is exaggerated, the point is well taken: the first draft is not the one that will distinguish you as a writer. It's a way of getting material together, starting out, connecting your ideas. A first draft gives you something to work with—verbal wet clay—that will later, through revising and editing, result in a polished piece of writing.

This section provides information and advice about drafting a college-level essay. Our special focus is on the sorts of "moves" that may occur at each major stage of the draft. If you know in advance what moves to make, you'll be in a better position to develop a thoughtful and complete draft.

What's Ahead

- Writing the First Draft
  Basic Essay Structure:
  Major Moves
- Opening Your Draft
- Developing the Middle
- Ending Your Draft
- Drafting Checklist and Writing
  Activities

Writing the First Draft

The American novelist Kurt Vonnegut once laughingly divided writers into two categories: swoopers and bashers. Swoopers write seventeen drafts at high speed before they're done; bashers won't move to sentence number two until they have polished sentence number one. Most writers fall somewhere between the two. When you draft your next paper, you'll strike a better balance between carelessness and care if you consider the following essentials.

Consider the essentials.

Purpose ◆ A draft is meant to pull together the best of your planning and set the actual writing in motion. Ideally, you will put into words all of the crucial points that you want to make about your thesis.

Approach ◆ Keep the following points in mind during drafting:

- Begin when you have found a central focus or promising starting point.
- Use your outline or writing plan as a general guide.
- Write freely without being too concerned about neatness and correctness.
- Include as much detail as possible.
- Complete your first draft in one or two sittings.

Note: Some writers pay special attention to their opening paragraph before they launch into the rest of the first draft; other writers focus on the introduction last.

Ideas ◆ When it comes to ideas, two things are essential: (1) keep your purpose and main point always in sight and (2) allow important new ideas to emerge naturally as you write. Concentrate on developing your ideas, not on producing a final copy. Continue until you reach a logical stopping point. Remember: A first draft is your first look at a writing idea as it develops.

Organization ◆ Try to use your writing plan or any charts, lists, or diagrams you've produced, but don't feel absolutely bound by them. If the type of writing you've been assigned has a prescribed structure, use it. Otherwise, refer to the chart on page **51** to stimulate your thinking so that in the end, the organization of your writing results from your basic writing moves.

Voice ◆ Use the most natural voice you can so that the writing will flow smoothly. If your voice is too formal during drafting, you'll be tempted to stop and edit your words.

INSIGHT: If you have trouble getting started, think of your writing as one-half of a conversation with a reader you invent. Talk to your silent partner. Think about what you've already said and let that help you decide what you should say next.

Basic Essay Structure: Major Moves

The following chart lists the main writing moves that occur during the development of a piece of writing. Use it as a general guide for all of your drafting. Remember to keep your purpose and audience in mind throughout the drafting process.

Opening

Engage your reader.
Stimulate and direct the reader's attention.

Establish your direction.
Identify the topic and put it in perspective.

Get to the point.
Narrow your focus and state your thesis.

Middle

Advance your thesis.
Provide background information and cover your main points.

Test your ideas.
Raise questions and consider alternatives.

Support your main points.
Add substance and build interest.

Build a coherent structure.
Start new paragraphs and arrange the support.

Use different levels of detail.
Clarify and complete each main point.

Ending

Reassert the main point.
Remind the reader of the purpose and rephrase the thesis.

Urge the reader.
Gain the reader's acceptance and look ahead.

Opening Your Draft

The opening paragraph is one of the most important elements in any composition. It should accomplish at least three essential things: (1) engage the reader; (2) establish your direction, tone, and level of language; and (3) introduce your line of thought.

Advice: The conventional way of approaching the first paragraph is to view it as a kind of "funnel" that draws a reader in and narrows to a main point. Often, the final sentence explicitly states your thesis.

Cautions: 1. Don't feel bound by the conventional pattern, which may sound stale if not handled well.

2. Don't let the importance of the first paragraph paralyze you. Relax and write.

The information on the next two pages will help you develop your opening. Also refer to the sample essays in the handbook for ideas.

Engage your reader.

Your reader will be preoccupied with other thoughts until you seize, stimulate, and direct his or her attention. Here are some effective ways to "hook" the reader:

- Mention little-known facts about the topic.
- Pose a challenging question.
- Offer a thought-provoking quotation.
- Tell a brief, illuminating story.
- Offer a little "sip" of what is to follow.

Openings to Avoid

Avoid obvious or worn-out expressions:
"I would like to tell you about . . . "
"Everybody knows that . . . "

Avoid say-nothing sentences:
"A and B are alike in some ways and different in others."
"Crime is an undesirable element in today's society."

Web

INSIGHT: Your opening affects the direction and line of thinking of your entire piece of writing. If you don't like the first or second attempt, keep trying. You'll know when you hit the right version because it will help you visualize the rest of your draft.

Establish your direction.

The direction of your line of thought should become clear in the opening part of your writing. Here are some moves you might make to set the right course:

Identify the topic (issue). ■ Show a problem, a need, or an opportunity.

Deepen the issue. ■ Put the topic into perspective by connecting it to some larger issue; stir the reader's sense of its importance.

Acknowledge other views. ■ Tell what others say or think about the topic.

Get to the point.

You may choose to state your main point up front, or you may wait to introduce your thesis until later. Sometimes your thesis may simply be implied. In any case, the opening should at least establish a "curve" toward the central issue or thesis of your paper. Here are three ways to get to the point:

Narrow your focus. ■ Point to what interests you about the topic.

Raise a question. ■ You can answer the question in the rest of the essay.

State your thesis. ■ If appropriate, craft a sentence that boils your meaning down. You can use the thesis sentence as a "map" for the organization of the rest of the essay. (See pages **41**, **102–103**, and **447–448**.)

Sample Opening

Here is a sample essay opener by a student who has used his first paragraph to describe his subject—the cartoon Simpson family. He uses the second paragraph to raise a question that leads him to a statement of his thesis (underlined).

> The Simpsons, stars of the TV show by the same name, are a typical American family, or at least a parody of one. Homer, Marge, Bart, Lisa, and Maggie Simpson live in Springfield, U.S.A. Homer, the father, is a boorish, obese oaf who works in a nuclear power plant. Marge is an over-protective, nagging mother with an outrageous blue hairdo. Ten-year-old Bart is an obnoxious, "spiky-haired demon." Lisa is eight and a prodigy on the tenor saxophone and in class. The infant Maggie never speaks but only sucks on her pacifier.
>
> What is the attraction of this yellow-skinned family who star on a show in which all of the characters have pronounced overbites and only four fingers on each hand? I contend that we see a little bit of ourselves in everything they do. <u>The world of Springfield is a parody of our own world, and Americans can't get enough of it.</u>

Web

Developing the Middle

The middle of an essay is where you do the "heavy lifting." In this part, you develop the main points that support your thesis statement.

Advice: As you write, you will likely make choices that were unforeseen when you began. Use "scratch outlines" (temporary jottings) along the way to show where your new ideas may take you.

Cautions: 1. Writing that lacks effective detail gives only a vague image of the writer's intent.

2. Writing that wanders loses its hold on the essay's overall purpose.

For both of these reasons, always keep your thesis in mind when you develop the main part of your writing. Refer to the guidelines on the next two pages for help. Also refer to the sample essays in this book for ideas.

Advance your thesis.

If you have stated a thesis in the opening, you can advance it several ways in the middle paragraphs:

Cover your main points. ■ Develop each main point in a paragraph or series of paragraphs.

Fill in the background. ■ Provide some of the history of your topic to help put it into context.

Define terms. ■ Clarify any terms that your reader is not likely to know.

Make distinctions. ■ Explain your exact meaning so that it is impossible to misunderstand.

Sort out the issues. ■ Present issues and ideas in a logical order.

Test your ideas.

When you write a first draft, you're testing your initial thinking about your topic. You're determining whether your thesis is valid and whether you have enough compelling information to support it. Here are some ways to test your line of thinking as you write:

Raise questions. ■ Try to anticipate your reader's questions.

Consider alternatives. ■ Look at your ideas from different angles; weigh different options; reevaluate your thesis.

Answer objections. ■ Directly or indirectly deal with possible problems that a skeptical reader would point out.

Support your main points.

Specific details add substance, depth, and interest to your writing while support-ing your main points. Here are some ways to work with details:

Explain: Provide important facts, details, and examples.

Narrate: Share a brief story or re-create an experience to illustrate an idea.

Describe: Tell in detail how someone appears or how something works.

Define: Identify or clarify the meaning of a specific term or idea.

Analyze: Examine the parts of something to better understand the whole.

Compare: Provide examples to show how two things are alike or different.

Argue: Use logic and evidence to prove that something is true.

Reflect: Express your thoughts or feelings about something.

INSIGHT: In some cases, supporting a main point with examples, facts, and details may not be enough. You may also need to add expert analysis or personal commentary.

Build a coherent structure.

The middle paragraphs form the heart of the essay. Each paragraph should include main points and details that advance your essay logically and coherently.

Define terms. ■ Start a new paragraph whenever a shift or change in the essay takes place. A shift occurs when you introduce a new main point, redirect a point of emphasis, or indicate a change in time or place.

Define terms. ■ It's important that the middle paragraphs are arranged in the best possible way so that they build on preceding paragraphs and flow smoothly from one to the next. To achieve this flow, the first sentence in each new paragraph should somehow be linked to the preceding paragraph. Transitional words are often used for this purpose. (See page **70**.)

Use different levels of detail.

A well-written supporting paragraph often contains three levels of detail, as seen in these sentences from Linda Chavez's essay, "Demystifying Multiculturalism":

Level 1: A topic sentence names the central idea of the paragraph.

Multiculturalists insist on treating race and ethnicity as if they were synonymous with culture.

Level 2: Clarifying sentences support the main point.

They presume that skin color and national origin, which are immutable traits, determine values, mores, language, and other cultural attributes, which, of course, are learned.

Level 3: A clinching sentence completes the point.

Culture becomes a fixed entity, transmitted, as it were, in the genes, rather than through experience.

Web

Ending Your Draft

Closing paragraphs can be important for tying up loose ends, clarifying key points, or signing off with the reader. In a sense, the entire essay is a preparation for an effective ending; the ending helps the reader look back over the essay with new understanding and appreciation. Many endings leave the reader with fresh food for thought.

Advice: Because the ending can be so important, draft a variety of possible endings. Choose the one that flows best from a sense of the whole.

Cautions: **1.** If your thesis is weak or unclear, you will have a difficult time writing a satisfactory ending. To strengthen the ending, strengthen the thesis.

2. You may have heard this formula for writing an essay: "Say what you're going to say, say it, then say what you've just said." Remember, though, if you need to "say what you've just said," say it in new words.

The information on the next two pages will help you develop your ending. Also refer to the sample essays elsewhere in this book for ideas.

Reassert the main point.

If an essay is complicated, the reader may need reclarification at the end. Show that you are fulfilling the promises you made in the beginning.

Remind the reader. ▪ Recall what you first set out to do; check off the key points you've covered; or answer any questions left unanswered.

Rephrase the thesis. ▪ Restate your thesis in light of the most important support you've given. Deepen and expand your original thesis.

Urge the reader.

Your reader may still be reluctant to accept your ideas or argument. The ending is your last chance to gain the reader's acceptance. Here are some possible strategies:

Show the implications:. ▪ Follow further possibilities raised by your train of thought; be reasonable and convincing.

Look ahead. ▪ Suggest other possible connections.

List the benefits. ▪ Show the reader the benefits of accepting or applying the things you've said.

INSIGHT: Sometimes your writing will come to an effective stopping point after you make the last main point. Whenever that is the case, don't tack on a closing paragraph. Leave well enough alone.

Sample Endings

Here are final paragraphs from two of the model essays in this book. Read them and listen to the tone in which they part with the reader. Watch how they consider what has previously been written. And notice how they leave the reader with food for thought.

> **Seven years later I still like to surprise Chinese people with my knowledge of the language when I happen to meet them. I think it is important to show that cultural gaps can be crossed, and without much difficulty as long as there is an open mind. I go back to China when money is available—I visit Beijing and the cow farm, reliving old memories and making new ones. Perhaps one remembers most what one loves.** (See pages **143–145** for the entire narrative.)

> **So what is the best "medication" for people with dementia? While no treatment can stop the illness, understanding the disease and its symptoms is the key to helping people cope. Doctors who understand the science of dementia can prescribe medicine. However, all of us who understand the heartbreaking symptoms and effects of the disease can provide another, possibly more effective treatment. We can respond to the victim of dementia with patience, kindness, and love.** (See pages **241–243** for the complete essay.)

If Endings Could Talk

Here's the last paragraph of an essay about the famous eccentric billionaire Howard Hughes. What does it seem to be saying?

> **Though he died over fifteen years ago, the legend of Howard Hughes lives on. He represented the American Dream turned on itself, a victim of the multibillion-dollar empire that he almost single-handedly created. We will always be fascinated by celebrities, heroes, the wealthy, and the sick. Howard was all of these. And more.**

This ending sums up the story of Howard Hughes by saying, in effect, "Weird, isn't it?" It tells us that our interest in certain celebrities is natural—they'll always get under our skin. Other endings say similar things. If you would take a quick tour through a collection of fine essays, listening to the endings "talk," here are some of the things you would hear the last paragraphs say . . .

- Oh well, . . .
- It all comes down to this: . . .
- Best of all, . . . (or Worst of all, . . .)
- And one more thing . . .
- Here we go round again . . .
- In fact, the opposite is true . . .
- As I think about it now, . . .
- As so-and-so has said, . . .
- And why not?
- I'll say it here for the last time . . .
- And would you believe it, . . .
- But it comes out okay . . .
- It's a strange world, isn't it?
- And here's the difference . . .

Drafting Checklist

Use this checklist as a guide when you develop a first draft for an essay. (To see drafting in action, turn to pages **108–115**.)

Ideas

_____ The opening engages the reader and identifies the thesis or main point of the essay.

_____ The middle advances the thesis.

_____ The ending reasserts the thesis.

Organization

_____ All of the introductory material establishes the direction for the writing.

_____ The main points are arranged logically in separate paragraphs.

_____ The ending thoughtfully leads up to a final point that engages the reader.

Voice

_____ The opening is engaging.

_____ The middle reveals the writer's interest in the topic.

_____ The essay ends in a voice that sincerely connects with the reader.

write

Writing Activities

1. Study the chart on page **51** in this chapter. Based on other material you have read or written, add another writing move for each of the three main parts of the essay: the beginning, middle, and end. Name the move, explain it, and tell in what types of writing it might appear.

2. Read the final paragraphs of any three essays included in this book. Write a brief analysis of each ending based on the information presented on pages **56–57**.

3. Suppose you were asked to write an article about a birthday, a wedding, or a funeral. Choose one. Sketch out a plan for your article, including the main writing moves you would use. More specifically, explain what type of information you would include at each stage of your writing.

Chapter 5
Revising

video

Revising takes courage. Once you have your first draft on paper, the piece may feel finished. The temptation then is to be satisfied with a quick "spell check" before turning in the paper. A word to the wise: Avoid this temptation.

Good writing almost always requires revising, and in some cases, substantial rework. During this step in the writing process, you make changes in the content of your first draft until it says exactly what you mean. To get started, assess the overall quality of the ideas, organization, and voice in your writing. Then be prepared to tinker with your writing until it effectively carries your message. It's also a good idea to share your draft with your instructor, a peer, or a tutor. All writers benefit from sincere, constructive advice during the revision process. This chapter will introduce you to valuable revising guidelines and strategies to use in all of your writing.

What's Ahead

- Revising Your First Draft
- Addressing Whole-Paper Issues
- Revising Your Ideas, Organization, and Voice
- Addressing Paragraph Issues
- Checking for Unity, Coherence, and Completeness
- Revising Collaboratively
- Using the Writing Center
- Revising Checklist and Writing Activities

Revising Your First Draft

Revising helps you turn your first draft into a more complete and thoughtful piece of writing. The following information will help you use this important step in the most effective way.

Prepare mentally.

Once you've finished a first draft, set it aside (ideally for a few days) until you can answer "yes" to these questions:

- Can I look at the draft with some freshness and objectivity?
- Am I open to change? Am I eager to improve the draft?

Assemble your materials.

If you drafted on paper, photocopy the draft. If you drafted on a computer, print your paper (double-spaced). Then make changes with a good pencil or colored pen. *Note:* Always save your original draft in case you need to review your initial ideas.

Think globally.

When revising, focus on the big picture—the overall strength of the ideas, organization, and voice.

Ideas ◆ Check your thesis, focus, or theme. Has your thinking on your topic changed? Also think about your readers' most pressing questions concerning this topic. Have you answered these questions? Finally, consider your reasoning and support. Are both complete and sound?

Organization ◆ Check the overall design of your writing, making sure that your ideas move smoothly and logically from one point to the next. Does your essay build effectively? Do you shift directions cleanly? Fix structural problems in one or more of the following ways:

- Reorder material to improve the sequence.
- Cut information that doesn't support the thesis.
- Add details where the draft is thin.
- Rewrite parts that seem unclear.
- Improve links between points by using transitions.

Voice ◆ Does the draft show your genuine interest in the subject? Does the tone match your purpose (serious, playful, satiric)?

INSIGHT: Don't pay undue attention to spelling, grammar, and punctuation at this early stage in the process. Otherwise, you may become distracted from the task at hand: improving the *content* of your writing. Editing and proofreading come later.

Addressing Whole-Paper Issues

When revising, first look at the big picture. Take it all in. Determine whether the content is interesting, informative, and worth sharing. Note any gaps or soft spots in your line of thinking. Ask yourself how you can improve what you have done so far. The information that follows will help you address whole-paper issues like these.

Revisit your purpose and audience.

Remember why you are writing—your purpose. Are you sharing information, recalling an experience, explaining a process, or arguing a point? Does your writing achieve that purpose? Also consider your readers. How much do they know about the subject? What else do they need to know?

Consider your overall approach.

Sometimes it's better to start fresh if your writing contains stretches of uninspired ideas. Consider a fresh start if your first draft shows one of these problems:

The topic is worn-out. ■ An essay titled "Lead Poisoning" may not sound very interesting. Unless you can approach it with a new twist ("Get the Lead Out!"), consider cutting your losses and finding a fresh topic.

The approach is stale. ■ If you've been writing primarily to get a good grade, finish the assignment, or sound cool, start again. Try writing to learn something, to prompt real thinking in readers, or to touch a chord.

Your voice is predictable or fake. ■ Avoid the bland "A good time was had by all" or the phony academic "When one studies this significant problem in considerable depth . . . ." Be real. Be honest.

The draft sounds boring. ■ Maybe it's boring because you pay an equal amount of attention to everything and hence stress nothing. Try condensing less important material and expanding what's important.

The essay is formulaic. ■ That is, it follows the "five-paragraph" format. This handy organizing frame may prevent you from doing justice to your topic and thinking. If your draft is dragged down by rigid adherence to a formula, try a more original approach.

INSIGHT: Think of revising as an opportunity to energize your writing. If you need to refuel your thinking, consider going back to the getting-started and planning activities described in Chapters 2 and 3.

Revising Your Ideas

As you review your draft for content, make sure that all of the ideas are fully developed and clearly stated. You can strengthen the content by taking action on the following types of issues. (Also refer to pages **253–268** to check the soundness or logic of your ideas.)

Check for complete thinking.

How complete is your thinking on your topic? Have you answered readers' basic questions? Have you sufficiently supported the thesis? The original passage below is too general; the revision is clearly more complete.

Original Passage (Too general)

As soon as you receive a minor cut, the body's healing process begins to work. Blood from tiny vessels fills the wound and begins to clot. In less than 24 hours, a scab forms.

Revised Version (More specific)

As soon as you receive a minor cut, the body's healing process begins to work. In a simple wound, the first and second layers of skin are severed along with tiny blood vessels called capillaries. As these vessels bleed into the wound, minute structures called platelets help stop the bleeding by sticking to the edges of the cut and to one another, forming a plug. The platelets then release chemicals that react with certain proteins in the blood to form a clot. The blood clot, with its fiber network, begins to join the edges of the wound together. As the clot dries out, a scab forms, usually in less than 24 hours.

Check the thesis.

Make sure that your writing centers on one main issue or thesis. The original opening passage below doesn't include a thesis; the revision clearly identifies a thesis statement.

Original Passage (Lacks a thesis)

Teen magazines are popular with young girls. These magazines contain a lot of how-to articles about self-image, fashion, and boy/girl relationships. Girls read them to get advice on how to act and how to look. There are many magazines from which to choose, and girls who don't really know what they want are the most eager readers.

Revised Version (Identifies a specific thesis statement)

Adolescent girls often see teen magazines as handbooks on how to be teenagers. These magazines influence the way they act and the way they look. For girls who are unsure of themselves, these magazines can exert an enormous amount of influence. Unfortunately, the advice these magazines give about self-image, fashion, and boys may do more harm than good.

Revising for Organization

Good writing has structure. It leads readers logically and clearly from one point to the next. When revising for organization, consider four areas: the overall plan, the opening, the flow of ideas, and the closing.

Check the overall plan.

Look closely at the sequence of ideas or events that you share. Does that sequence advance your thesis? Do the points build effectively? Are there gaps in the support or points that stray from your original purpose? If you find such problems, consider the following actions:

- Move material from one section to another. Reorder for emphasis.
- Fill in the gaps with new material. Go back to your planning notes.
- Delete material that wanders away from your purpose.

INSIGHT: What is the best method of organization for your essay? The writing you are doing will often determine the choice. As you know, a personal narrative is often organized by time. Typically, however, you combine and customize methods to develop a writing idea. For example, within a comparison essay, you may do some describing or classifying. See pages **42–43** and **104** for more on the common methods of development.

Check the opening ideas.

Reread your opening paragraph(s). Is the opening organized effectively? Does it engage readers, establish a direction for your writing, and express your thesis or focus? The original opening shown below doesn't build to a compelling thesis statement. In contrast, the revised version engages the reader and leads up to the thesis statement.

Original Opening (Lacks interest and direction)

The lack of student motivation is a common subject in the news. Educators want to know how to get students to learn. Today's higher standards mean that students will be expected to learn even more. Another problem in urban areas is that large numbers of students are dropping out. How to interest students is a challenge.

Revised Version (Effectively leads readers into the essay)

How can we motivate students to learn? How can we get them to meet today's rising standards of excellence? How can we, in fact, keep students in school long enough to learn? The answer to these problems is quite simple. Give them money. Pay students to study and learn and stay in school.

Check the flow of ideas.

Look closely at the beginnings and endings of each paragraph. Have you connected your thoughts clearly? (See page **70** for a list of transition words.) The original opening words of the paragraph sequence below offer no links for readers. The revised versions use strong transitions indicating spatial organization (order by location).

Original First Words in the Four Middle Paragraphs

There was a huge, steep hill . . .

Buffalo Creek ran . . .

A dense "jungle" covering . . .

Within walking distance from my house . . .

Revised Version (Words and phrases connect ideas)

Behind the house, there was a huge, steep hill . . .

Across the road from the house, Buffalo Creek ran . . .

On the far side of the creek bank was a dense "jungle" covering . . .

Up the road, within walking distance from my house . . .

Check the closing ideas.

Reread your closing paragraph(s). Do you offer an effective summary, reassert your main point in a fresh way, and provide readers with food for thought as they leave your writing? Or is your ending abrupt, repetitive, or directionless? The original ending below is uninspiring; it adds little to the main part of the writing. The revision summarizes the main points in the essay and then urges the reader to think again about the overall point of writing.

Original Closing (Sketchy and flat)

Native Son deals with a young man's struggle against racism. It shows the effects of prejudice. Everyone should read this book.

Revised Version (Effectively ends the writing)

Native Son **deals with a young man's struggle in a racist society, but it deals with so much more. It shows how prejudice affects people, how it closes in on them, and what some people will do to find a way out. Anyone who wants to better understand racism in the Unites States should read this book.**

INSIGHT: You may have trouble saying something at the end that keeps readers thinking about your topic. If that is the case, write reflectively about your topic in a journal or notebook. As you write, try to answer questions like these: What have I learned about the topic during my writing? Why is it important? What should it mean to my readers? At some point, a worthy final thought may come to mind.

Web

Revising for Voice

Let your personal writing voice come through in your essays and papers. Writing that has a voice sounds genuine, holds the reader's attention, and reflects the purpose or intent of the assignment. When revising for voice, consider the following two areas.

Check your level of commitment.

Writing that has a voice speaks in an honest and interesting way. It sounds as if the writer is truly stimulated by his or her topic. The original passage that follows lacks a personal voice; it reveals nothing about the writer and his connection with the topic. The revision, on the other hand, shows the writer's genuine interest in cemeteries.

Original Passage (Lacks voice)

Cemeteries can teach us a lot about history. They make history seem more real. There is an old grave of a Revolutionary War veteran in the Union Grove Cemetery. . . .

Revised Version (Personal, sincere voice)

I've always had a special feeling for cemeteries. It's hard to explain any further than that, except to say history never seems quite as real as it does when I walk between rows of old gravestones. One day I discovered the grave of a Revolutionary War veteran. . . .

Check the intensity of your writing.

The academic writing you do in college needs to exhibit control, but your personal essays should express your true concerns with energy and, if necessary, with passion. In the original passage below, the writer's true concern fails to come through because the writing is neutral.

Original Version (Lacks feeling and energy)

Motz blames Barbie dolls for all the problems that women face today. Instead, one should look to romance novels, fashion magazines, and parental training for causes of these societal problems.

Revised Version (Expresses real feelings)

In other words, Motz uses Barbie as a scapegoat for problems that have complex causes. For example, a girl's interest in romance is no more Barbie's fault than the fault of books like *On the Shores of Silver Lake*. Fashion magazines targeted at adolescents are the cause of far more anorexia than is Barbie. And mothers who encourage daughters to find security in men teach female dependency, but Barbie doesn't.

INSIGHT: To develop your personal writing voice, begin each writing assignment by freely recording your thoughts and feelings about the topic.

Addressing Paragraph Issues

While drafting, you may have constructed paragraphs that are loosely held together, poorly developed, or unclear. When you revise, take a close look at your paragraphs for focus, unity, and coherence.

Remember the basics.

Where should paragraph revision start? Remember what a paragraph is—a concise unit of thinking and writing:

- It is typically organized around a controlling idea stated in a topic sentence.
- It consists of supporting sentences that develop the controlling idea.
- It usually concludes with a sentence that summarizes the main point and prepares readers for the next paragraph or main point.
- It serves a specific function in a piece of writing—opening, supporting, developing, illustrating, countering, describing, or closing.

Sample Paragraph

Topic sentence ----- Tumor cells can hurt the body in a number of ways. First, a tumor can grow so big that it takes up space needed by other organs. Second, some cells may detach from the original tumor and spread throughout the body, creating new tumors elsewhere. This happens with lymphatic cancer—a cancer that's hard to control because it spreads so quickly. A third way that **Supporting sentences** tumor cells can hurt the body is by doing work not called for in their DNA. For example, a gland cell's DNA code may tell the cell to produce a necessary hormone in the endocrine system. However, if cancer damages or distorts that code, sick cells may produce more of the hormone than the **Closing sentence** --- body can use—or even tolerate (Braun 4). Cancer cells seem to have minds of their own, and this is why cancer is such a serious disease.

Keep the purpose in mind.

Use these questions to evaluate the purpose and function of each paragraph:

- What specific function does the paragraph fulfill? How does it add to your line of reasoning or the development of your thesis?
- Would the paragraph work better if it broke earlier or was combined with another paragraph?
- Does the paragraph flow smoothly from the paragraph that comes before it, and does it effectively lead into the paragraph that follows?

Checking for Unity

A unified paragraph is one in which all the details help to develop a single main topic or achieve a single main effect. Test for paragraph unity by following these guidelines.

Examine the topic sentence.

Very often the topic of a paragraph is stated in a single sentence called a "topic sentence." Check whether your paragraph needs a topic sentence. If it has one, check whether it is clear, specific, and well focused. Here is a formula for writing good topic sentences:

Formula: A topic sentence = a limited topic + a specific feeling or thought about it.

Example: **The fear that Americans feel** (limited topic) **comes partly from the uncertainty related to this attack** (a specific thought)**.**

Consider the placement of the topic sentence.

Normally, the topic sentence is the first sentence in the paragraph. However, it can appear elsewhere in a paragraph.

- **Middle Placement:** Place a topic sentence in the middle when you want to build up to and lead away from the key idea.

    During the making of *Apocalypse Now,* Eleanor Coppola created a documentary about the filming called *Hearts of Darkness: A Filmmaker's Apocalypse.* In the first film, the insane Colonel Kurtz has disappeared into the Cambodian jungle. As Captain Willard searches for Kurtz, the screen fills with horror. **However, as *Hearts of Darkness* relates, the horror portrayed in the fictional movie was being lived out by the production company.** For example, in the documentary, actor Larry Fishburne shockingly says, "War is fun. . . . Vietnam must have been so much fun." Then toward the end of the filming, actor Martin Sheen suffered a heart attack. When an assistant informed investors, the director exploded, "He's not dead unless I say he's dead."

- **End Placement:** Place a topic sentence at the end when you want to build to a climax, as in a passage of narration or persuasion.

    When sportsmen stop to reflect on why they find fishing so enjoyable, most realize that what they love is the feel of a fish on the end of the line, not necessarily the weight of the fillets in their coolers. Fishing has undergone a slow evolution over the last century. While fishing used to be a way of putting food on the table, most of today's fishermen do so only for the relaxation that it provides. The barbed hook was invented to increase the quantity of fish a man could land in order to better feed his family. **This need no longer exists, so barbed hooks are no longer necessary.**

Review the supporting sentences for unity.

All of the sentences in the body of a paragraph should support the topic sentence. The closing sentence, for instance, will often summarize the paragraph's main point or emphasize a key detail. If any sentences shift the focus away from the topic, revise the paragraph in one of the following ways:

- Delete the material from the paragraph.
- Rewrite the material so that it clearly supports the topic sentence.
- Create a separate paragraph out of the material.
- Revise the topic sentence so that it relates more closely to the support.

Stay on the topic.

Examine the following paragraph about fishing hooks. The original topic sentence focuses on the point that some anglers prefer smooth hooks. However, the writer leaves this initial idea unfinished and turns to the issue of the cost of new hooks. In the revised version, unity is restored: the first paragraph completes the point about anglers who prefer smooth hooks; the second paragraph addresses the issue of replacement costs.

Original (Lacks unity)

According to some anglers who do use smooth hooks, their lures perform better than barbed lures as long as they maintain a constant tension on the line. Smooth hooks can bite deeper than barbed hooks, actually providing a stronger hold on the fish. Some people have argued that replacing all of the barbed hooks in their tackle would be a costly operation.

Revised Version (Unified)

According to some anglers who do use smooth hooks, their lures perform better than barbed lures as long as they maintain a constant tension on the line. Smooth hooks can bite deeper than barbed hooks, actually providing a stronger hold on the fish. These anglers testify that switching from barbed hooks has not noticeably reduced the number of fish that they are able to land. In their experience, and in my own, enjoyment of the sport is actually heightened by adding another challenge to playing the fish (maintaining line tension).

Some people have argued that replacing all of the barbed hooks in their tackle would be a costly operation. While this is certainly a concern, barbed hooks do not necessarily require replacement. With a simple set of pliers, the barbs on most conventional hooks can be bent down, providing a cost-free method of modifying one's existing tackle. . . .

Paragraphs that contain unrelated ideas lack unity and are hard to follow. As you review each paragraph for unity, ask yourself these questions: Is the topic of the paragraph clear? Does each sentence relate to the topic? Are the sentences organized in the best possible order?

Checking for Coherence

When a paragraph is coherent, the parts hang together. A coherent paragraph flows smoothly because each sentence is connected to others by patterns in the language. To strengthen the coherence in your paragraphs, check for the issues discussed below when you revise.

Look for effective use of repetition.

To achieve coherence in your paragraphs, consider using repetition—repeating words or synonyms where necessary to remind readers of what you have already said. You can also use parallelism—repeating phrase or sentence structures to show the relationship between ideas. At the same time, you will add a unifying rhythm to your writing.

Ineffective: **The floor was littered with discarded soda cans, newspapers that were crumpled, and wrinkled clothes.**

Effective: **The floor was littered with discarded soda cans, crumpled newspapers, and wrinkled clothes.** (Three similar phrases are repeated.)

Ineffective: **Reading the book was enjoyable; to write the critique was difficult.**

Effective: **Reading the book was enjoyable; writing the critique was difficult.** (Two similar sentences are repeated.)

Review your transitions.

Linking words and phrases like "next," "on the other hand," and "in addition" connect ideas by showing the relationship between them. There are transitions that show location and time, compare and contrast things, emphasize a point, conclude or summarize, and add or clarify information. (See page **70** for a list of linking words and phrases.) Note the use of transitions in the following examples:

The paradox of Scotland is that violence had long been the norm in this now-peaceful land. In fact, the country was born, bred, and came of age in war. (The transition is used to emphasize a point.)

The production of cement is a complicated process. First, the mixture of lime, silica, alumina, and gypsum is ground into very fine particles. (The transition is used to show time or order.)

INSIGHT: Another way to achieve coherence in your paragraphs is to use pronouns effectively. A pronoun forms a link to the noun it replaces and ties that noun (idea) to the ideas that follow. As always, don't overuse pronouns or rely too heavily on them for establishing coherence in your paragraphs.

Transitions and Linking Words

The words and phrases below can help you tie together words, phrases, sentences, and paragraphs.

- **Words used to SHOW LOCATION:**

above	behind	down	on top of
across	below	in back of	onto
against	beneath	in front of	outside
along	beside	inside	over
among	between	into	throughout
around	beyond	near	to the right
away from	by	off	under

- **Words used to SHOW TIME:**

about	during	next	till
after	finally	next week	today
afterward	first	second	tomorrow
as soon as	immediately	soon	until
at	later	then	when
before	meanwhile	third	yesterday

- **Words used to COMPARE THINGS (show similarities):**

also	in the same way	likewise
as	like	similarly

- **Words used to CONTRAST THINGS (show differences):**

although	even though	on the other hand	still
but	however	otherwise	yet

- **Words used to EMPHASIZE A POINT:**

again	for this reason	particularly	to repeat
even	in fact	to emphasize	truly

- **Words used to CONCLUDE or SUMMARIZE:**

all in all	finally	in summary	therefore
as a result	in conclusion	last	to sum up

- **Words used to ADD INFORMATION:**

additionally	and	equally important	in addition
again	another	finally	likewise
along with	as well	for example	next
also	besides	for instance	second

- **Words used to CLARIFY:**

for instance	in other words	put another way	that is

Checking for Completeness

The sentences in a paragraph should support and discuss the main point. If your paragraph does not seem complete, you will need to add information.

Review the supporting sentences.

If some of your paragraphs are incomplete, they may lack details. Numerous kinds of details exist, including the following:

facts	anecdotes	analyses	paraphrases
statistics	quotations	explanations	comparisons
examples	definitions	summaries	analogies

Add details based on the type of writing you are engaged in.

Describing ◆ Add details that help readers see, smell, taste, touch, or hear it.

Narrating ◆ Add details that help readers understand the events and actions.

Explaining ◆ Add details that help readers understand what it means, how it works, or what it does.

Persuading ◆ Add details that strengthen the logic of your argument.

Include specific details.

The original paragraph below fails to answer fully the question posed by the topic sentence. In the revised paragraph, the writer uses an anecdote to answer the question.

Original (Lacks completeness)

So what is stress? Actually, the physiological characteristics of stress are some of the body's potentially good self-defense mechanisms. People experience stress when they are in danger. In fact, stress can be healthy.

Revised Version (Full development)

So what is stress? Actually, the physiological characteristics of stress are some of the body's potentially good self-defense mechanisms. Take, for example, a man who is crossing a busy intersection when he spots an oncoming car. Immediately his brain releases a flood of adrenaline into his bloodstream. As a result, his muscles contract, his eyes dilate, his heart pounds faster, his breathing quickens, and his blood clots more readily. Each one of these responses helps the man leap out of the car's path. His muscles contract to give him exceptional strength. His eyes dilate so that he can see more clearly. His heart pumps more blood and his lungs exchange more air— both to increase his metabolism. If the man were injured, his blood would clot faster, insuring a smaller amount of blood loss. In this situation and many more like it, stress symptoms are good (Curtis 25–26).

INSIGHT: If a paragraph is getting long, divide it at a natural stopping point. The topic sentence can then function as the thesis for that part of your essay or paper.

72 **5** The Writing Process

Web

Revising Collaboratively

Every writer can benefit from feedback from an interested audience, especially one that offers constructive and honest advice during a writing project. Members of an existing writing group already know how valuable it is for writers to share their work. Others might want to start a writing group to experience the benefits. Your group might collaborate online or in person. In either case, the information on the next two pages will help you get started. (Also see page **119**.)

Know your role.

Both writers and reviewers should know their roles and fulfill their responsibilities during revising sessions. Essentially, the writer should briefly introduce the draft and solicit honest responses. Reviewers should make constructive comments in response to the writing.

Provide appropriate feedback.

Feedback can take many forms, including the three approaches described here.

Basic Description ◆ In this simple response, the reviewer listens or reads attentively and then simply describes what he or she hears or sees happening in the piece. The reviewer offers no criticism of the writing.

Ineffective: "That was interesting. The piece was informative."

Effective: "First, the essay introduced the challenge of your birth defect and how you have had to cope with it. Then in the next part you . . ."

Summary Evaluation ◆ Here, the reviewer reads or listens to the piece and then provides a specific evaluation of the draft.

Ineffective: "Gee, I really liked it!" or "It was boring."

Effective: "Your story at the beginning really pulled me in, and the middle explained the issue strongly, but the ending felt a bit flat."

Thorough Critique ◆ The reviewer assesses the ideas, organization, and voice in the writing. Feedback should be detailed and constructive. Such a critique may also be completed with the aid of a review sheet or checklist. As a reviewer, be prepared to share specific responses, suggestions, and questions. But also be sure to focus your comments on the writing, not the writer.

Ineffective: "You really need to fix that opening! What were you thinking?"

Effective: "Let's look closely at the opening. Could you rewrite the first sentence so that it grabs the reader's attention? Also, I'm somewhat confused about the thesis statement. Could you rephrase it so that it states your position more clearly?"

Respond according to a plan.

Using a specific plan or scheme, like the one described below, will help you give clear, helpful, and complete feedback.

OAQS Method ◆ Use this simple four-step scheme—observe, appreciate, question, and suggest—to respond to your peers' writing.

1. **Observe** means to notice what another person's essay is designed to do, and to say something about its design or purpose. For example, you might say, "Even though you are writing about your boyfriend, it appears that you are trying to get a message across to your parents."

2. **Appreciate** means to praise something in the writing that impresses or pleases you. You can find something to appreciate in any piece of writing. For example, you might say, "You make a very convincing point" or "With your description, I can actually see his broken tooth."

3. **Question** means to ask whatever you want to know after you've read the essay. You might ask for background information, a definition, an interpretation, or an explanation. For example, you might say, "Can you tell us what happened when you got to the emergency room?"

4. **Suggest** means to give helpful advice about possible changes. For example, you might say, "With a little more physical detail—especially more sounds and smells—your third paragraph could be the highlight of the whole essay. What do you think?"

Asking the Writer Questions

Listener-responders should ask the following types of questions while reviewing a piece of writing:

To help writers reflect on their purpose and audience . . .
Why are you writing this?
Who will read this, and what do they need to know?

To help writers focus their thoughts . . .
What message are you trying to get across?
Do you have more than one main point?
What are the most important examples?

To help writers think about their information . . .
What do you know about the subject?
Does this part say enough?
Does your writing cover all of the basics (*Who? What? Where? When? Why?* and *How?*)?

To help writers with their opening and closing . . .
What are you trying to say in the opening?
How else could you start your writing?
How do you want your readers to feel at the end?

Using the Writing Center

In a college writing center or lab, you can develop and strengthen your work in progress by consulting with trained advisers. The questions and answers that follow will help you understand how writing centers work.

Is the writing center just for "remedial" writers?

No. All students are welcome in most writing centers. One mark of a healthy writing environment on campus is widespread use of the writing center by students in all programs and at all levels of ability. Some of the most successful students are the quickest to seek an adviser.

When should I take my paper to the writing center?

You don't even need to provide a complete draft. You can brainstorm with an adviser about writing ideas, or try out your thesis and talk about ways to develop it. The mistake many students make is waiting until it's too late. They come in breathless, ten minutes before closing time on the night before the paper is due, and say, "Can you fix this?" When you need advice about a draft, give yourself at least several days lead time before the assignment's due date.

Is it fair to ask the adviser to fix the paper?

No. A writing center is not a free editing and proofreading service. A well-trained adviser will decline to correct all spelling errors, typos, and other mistakes. That's your job. However, she or he will probably try to point out any systematic type of error and teach you the principles involved in correcting it. The adviser may also show you how to find answers for yourself in standard reference works.

What if the adviser tells me the paper is fine, and I don't think it is?

Advisers aren't perfect, and most papers aren't either. Don't settle for that answer. Ask the adviser to spell out the strengths of the paper. Then think together about different approaches that you could use. Ask how you can get from good to excellent, or from excellent to dynamite!

What's the difference between a peer adviser and an instructor?

A peer adviser is a collaborator and doesn't "grade" papers for a living. He or she may sit in the same classes you do, complete the same assignments, and see the world from your perspective. A peer adviser probably won't lecture you and may have a better overview of writing across the campus than most instructors have time to obtain.

How do most students view the writing center?

At first, many students feel embarrassed or uncertain about going to the center. They think that getting help is a kind of punishment or confession of failure. But afterward, many students are relieved and grateful. Some even come away inspired. And many return again and again.

Web

Be prepared.

When you visit your campus writing center, you can expect the adviser to do certain things. Other things only you can do. For quick reference, refer to the chart of differences below.

ADVISER'S JOB	YOUR JOB
Make you feel at home	Be respectful
Discuss your needs	Be ready to work
Help choose a topic	Decide on a topic
Discuss your purpose and audience	Know your purpose and audience
Help you generate ideas	Embrace the best ideas
Help you develop your logic	Consider other points of view; stretch your own perspective
Help you understand how to research your material	Do the research
Read your draft	Share your writing
Identify problems in organization, logic, expression, and format	Recognize and fix problems
Teach ways to correct weaknesses	Learn important principles
Help with grammar, usage, diction, vocabulary, and mechanics	Correct all errors

tips FOR GETTING THE MOST OUT OF THE WRITING CENTER

- Visit the center at least several days before your paper is due.
- Bring your assignment sheet with you to each advising session.
- Read your work aloud, slowly.
- Expect to rethink your writing from scratch.
- Do not defend your wording—if it needs defense, it needs revision.
- Ask questions. (No question is "too dumb.")
- Request clarification of anything you don't understand.
- Ask for examples or illustrations of important points.
- Write down all practical suggestions.
- Ask the adviser to summarize his or her remarks.
- Rewrite as soon as possible after, or even during, the advising session.
- Return to the writing center for a response to your revisions.

Revising Checklist

Use this checklist as a guide when you revise your writing. Remember to think globally first; then focus your attention on different parts. (To see revising in action, turn to pages **116–121**.)

Ideas

_____ My writing has a clear thesis, focus, or theme.

_____ I have fully developed and supported that thesis with relevant, accurate details.

Organization

_____ My writing follows a clear pattern of organization that advances the main idea.

_____ I have added, cut, reordered, and rewritten material as needed.

_____ All the paragraphs are unified, coherent, and complete.

Voice

_____ The tone is matched to the assignment, the reader, and the purpose.

_____ The tone is consistent; any shift in tone is planned and effective.

_____ My voice sounds energetic and interested.

write

Writing Activities

1. Pull out a paper that you wrote recently but may not have revised thoroughly enough before you submitted it. Using the revising strategies in this chapter, improve the piece.

2. Beginnings and endings often pose the biggest challenge for writers. Review the opening and closing paragraphs of one of your essays. Then come up with fresh and different approaches for these paragraphs using the information on pages **63–64** as a guide.

3. Find a middle paragraph in one of your essays that doesn't effectively advance your thesis. Revise this paragraph using the information on page **62** as a guide.

4. For your current writing assignment, ask a peer to provide detailed feedback using the information in this chapter as a guide. Then, take a fresh copy of your paper to the writing center and work through your draft with an adviser. Review the draft again, and make decisions about improving the writing.

Chapter 6
Editing and Proofreading

video

There comes a point in any writing project (like a fast-approaching due date) when you must prepare your writing for submission. At that time you must edit and proofread your revised writing so that it speaks clearly and accurately. When you edit, look first for words, phrases, and sentences that sound awkward, uninteresting, or unclear. When you proofread, check your writing for spelling, mechanics, usage, and grammar errors.

Before you begin, make sure that you have the proper tools on hand: handbook, dictionary, thesaurus, computer spell checker, and so on. Also, ask one of your writing peers to help you edit your work. Then prepare your final draft, following the guidelines established by your instructor, and proofread it for errors.

The guidelines and strategies given in this chapter will help you edit your writing for style and clarity and proofread it for correctness.

What's Ahead

- Editing Your Revised Draft
- Checking for Sentence Style
- Combining Sentences
- Expanding Sentences
- Editing for Word Choice
- Proofreading Your Writing
- Editing and Proofreading Checklist and Writing Activities

Editing Your Revised Draft

When you have thoroughly revised your writing, you need to edit it, so as to make it clear and concise enough to present to your readers. Use the editing guidelines below to check your revised draft.

Review the overall style of your writing.

1. Read your revised writing aloud. Better yet, have a writing peer read it aloud to you. When your writing doesn't read smoothly and naturally, highlight the awkward area.

2. Check it against three key stylistic reminders.

Be purposeful. ■ Does your writing sound as if you wrote it with a clear goal in mind?

Be clear. ■ Are the ideas expressed concisely and directly?

Be sincere. ■ Does the writing sound authentic and honest?

3. Examine your sentences. Check them for clarity, conciseness, and variety. Replace sentences that are wordy or rambling; combine or expand sentences that are short and choppy. Also, vary the beginnings of your sentences and avoid sentence patterns that are too predicable. (See pages **79–81**.)

Consider word choice.

4. Avoid redundancy. Be alert for words or phrases that are used together but mean the same thing, or close to the same thing.

repeat again   **red in color**   **refer back**

5. Watch for repetition. When used appropriately, repetition can add rhythm and coherence to your writing. When used ineffectively, however, it can be a real distraction.

The man looked as if he were in his late seventies. **The man** was dressed in an old suit. I soon realized that **the man** was homeless. . . .

6. Look for general nouns, verbs, and modifiers. Specific words are much more effective than general ones. (See page **82**.)

The girl moved on the beach. (General)
Rosie slid quietly to the end of the park bench. (Specific)

7. Avoid highly technical terms. Check for jargon or technical terms that are not well known or adequately explained. (See page **83**.)

As the **capillaries** bleed, **platelets** work with **fibrinogens** to form a clot.

8. Use fair language. Replace words or phrases that are biased or demeaning. (See pages **84–86**.)

Checking for Sentence Style

Writer E. B. White advised young writers to "approach sentence style by way of simplicity, plainness, orderliness, and sincerity." That's good advice from a writer steeped in style. It's also important to know what to look for when editing your sentences. The following information will help you edit your sentences for style, correctness, and variety.

Avoid these sentence problems.

Always check for and correct the following types of sentence problems. Turn to the pages listed below for guidelines and examples when attempting to fix problems in your sentences.

Short, Choppy Sentences ◆ Combine any short, choppy sentences, following the examples and guidelines in the handbook. (See page **80**.)

Flat, Predictable Sentences ◆ Rewrite any sentences that sound predictable and uninteresting by expanding them with modifying words, phrases, and clauses. (See page **81**.)

Incorrect Sentences ◆ Look carefully for fragments, run-ons, and comma splices and correct them accordingly. (See pages **657–658**.)

Unclear Sentences ◆ Edit sentences that contain unclear wording, misplaced modifiers, dangling modifiers, or incomplete comparisons. (See pages **659–660**.)

Unacceptable Sentences ◆ Change any sentences that include nonstandard language, double negatives, or unparallel construction. (See page **661**.)

Unnatural Sentences ◆ Rewrite any sentences that contain jargon, flowery language, or clichés. (See page **83**.)

Review your writing for sentence variety.

Use the following strategy to review your writing for variety in terms of sentence beginnings, sentence lengths, and verb use.

- In one column on a piece of paper, list the opening words in each of your sentences. Then decide if you need to vary some of your sentence beginnings.
- In another column, identify the number of words in each sentence. Then decide if you need to change the length of some of your sentences.
- In a third column, list the verbs in each sentence. Then decide if you need to replace any overused "be" verbs (*is, are, was, were*) with more vivid ones (*snap, stare, stir*).

Combining Sentences

Effective sentences often contain several basic ideas that work together to show relationships and make connections. Here are five basic ideas followed by seven examples of how they can be combined into effective sentences.

1. **The longest and largest construction project in history was the Great Wall of China.**
2. **The project took 1,700 years to complete.**
3. **The Great Wall of China is 1,400 miles long.**
4. **It is between 18 and 30 feet high.**
5. **It is up to 32 feet wide.**

Edit short, simplistic sentences.

Combine your short, simplistic sentences into longer, more mature sentences. Sentence combining is generally carried out in the following ways:

- Use a **series** to combine three or more similar ideas.
  The Great Wall of China is 1,400 miles long, between 18 and 30 feet high, and up to 32 feet wide.

- Use a **relative pronoun** (*who, whose, that, which*) to introduce subordinate (less important) ideas.
  The Great Wall of China, which is 1,400 miles long and between 18 and 30 feet high, took 1,700 years to complete.

- Use an **introductory phrase** or **clause**.
  Having taken 1,700 years to complete, the Great Wall of China was the longest construction project in history.

- Use a **semicolon** (and a conjunctive adverb if appropriate).
  The Great Wall took 1,700 years to complete; it is 1,400 miles long and up to 30 feet high and 32 feet wide.

- Repeat a **key word** or phrase to emphasize an idea.
  The Great Wall of China was the longest construction project in history, a project that took 1,700 years to complete.

- Use **correlative conjunctions** (*either, or; not only, but also*) to compare or contrast two ideas in a sentence.
  The Great Wall of China is not only up to 30 feet high and 32 feet wide, but also 1,400 miles long.

- Use an **appositive** (a word or phrase that renames) to emphasize an idea.
  The Great Wall of China—the largest construction project in history—is 1,400 miles long, 32 feet wide, and up to 30 feet high.

Expanding Sentences

Expand sentences when you edit so as to connect related ideas and make room for new information. Length is of no value in itself: the best sentence is still the shortest one that says all it has to say. An expanded sentence, however, is capable of saying more—and saying it more expressively.

Use cumulative sentences.

Modern writers often use an expressive sentence form called the cumulative sentence. A cumulative sentence is made of a general "base clause" that is expanded by adding modifying words, phrases, or clauses. In such a sentence, the details are added before and after the main clause, creating an image-rich thought. Here's an example of a cumulative sentence with the base clause or main idea in boldface:

> In preparation for her Spanish exam, **Julie was studying** at the kitchen table, completely focused, memorizing a list of vocabulary words.

Discussion   Notice how each new modifier adds to the richness of the final sentence. Also notice that each of these modifying phrases is set off by a comma. Here's another sample sentence:

> With his hands on his face, **Tony was laughing,** half-heartedly, looking puzzled and embarrassed.

Discussion   Such a cumulative sentence provides a way to write description that is rich in detail, without rambling. Notice how each modifier changes the flow or rhythm of the sentence.

Expand with details.

Here are seven basic ways to expand a main idea:

1. with **adjectives and adverbs**: *half-heartedly, once again*
2. with **prepositional phrases**: *with his hands on his face*
3. with **absolute phrases**: *his head tilted to one side*
4. with **participial (-*ing* or -*ed*) phrases**: *looking puzzled*
5. with **infinitive phrases**: *to hide his embarrassment*
6. with **subordinate clauses**: *while his friend talks*
7. with **relative clauses**: *who isn't laughing at all*

INSIGHT: To edit sentences for more expressive style, it is best to (1) know your grammar and punctuation (especially commas), (2) practice tightening, combining, and expanding sentence using the guidelines in this chapter, and (3) read carefully, looking for models of well-constructed sentences.

Editing for Word Choice

As you edit your writing, check your choice of words carefully. Are your nouns specific and your verbs vivid? Is your writing free of jargon and clichés? Are your words unbiased? The information on the next five pages will help you edit for word choice.

Substitute specific words.
Choose Specific Nouns

Make it a habit to use specific nouns for subjects. General nouns (*woman, school*) give the reader a vague, uninteresting picture. More specific nouns (*actress, university*) give the reader a better picture. Finally, very specific nouns (*Meryl Streep, Notre Dame*) are the type that can make your writing clear and colorful.

General to Specific Nouns

Person	Place	Thing	Idea
woman	school	book	theory
actor	university	novel	scientific theory
Meryl Streep	Notre Dame	*Pride and Prejudice*	relativity

Use Vivid Verbs

Like nouns, verbs can be too general to create a vivid word picture. For example, the verb *looked* does not say the same thing as *stared, glared, glanced,* or *peeked.*

- Whenever possible, use a verb that is strong enough to stand alone without the help of an adverb.

   Verb and adverb: John fell down in the student lounge.
   Vivid verb: **John collapsed in the student lounge.**

- Avoid overusing the "be" verbs (*is, are, was, were*) and helping verbs. Often a main verb can be made from another word in the same sentence.

   A be verb: Cole is someone who follows international news.
   A stronger verb: **Cole follows international news.**

- Use active rather than passive verbs. (Use passive verbs only if you want to downplay who is performing the action in a sentence. See page **630**.)

   Passive verb: Another provocative essay was submitted by Kim.
   Active verb: **Kim submitted another provocative essay.**

- Use verbs that show rather than tell.

   A verb that tells: Dr. Lewis is very thorough.
   A verb that shows: **Dr. Lewis prepares detailed, interactive lectures.**

Replace jargon and clichés.

You should replace language that is overly technical or difficult to understand. Likewise, you should find alternatives for language that is used so often it has lost its meanings or its impact.

Use Understandable Language

Jargon is language used in a certain profession or by a particular group of people. It may be acceptable to use if your audience is that group of people, but to most ears jargon will sound technical and unnatural.

Jargon: **The bottom line is that our output is not within our game plan.**
Clear: **Production is not on schedule.**

Jargon: **I'm having conceptual difficulty with these academic queries.**
Clear: **I don't understand these review questions.**

Jargon: **Pursuant to our conversation, I have forwarded you a remittance attached herewith.**
Clear: **As we discussed, I am mailing you the check.**

Keep Your Writing Fresh and Original

Clichés are overused words or phrases. They give the reader no fresh view of a concept, no concrete picture. Because clichés spring quickly to mind (for both the writer and the reader), they are easy to write and often slip by.

an axe to grind	**piece of cake**
as good as dead	**planting the seed**
beat around the bush	**rearing its ugly head**
between a rock and a hard place	**stick your neck out**
burning bridges	**throwing your weight around**
easy as pie	**up a creek**

Keep Your Purpose and Voice in Mind

There are other aspects of your writing that may also be tired and overworked. Be alert to the two types of clichés described below.

Clichés of Purpose

● Sentimental papers gushing about an ideal friend or family member, or droning on about a moving experience
● Overused topics with recycled information and predictable examples

Clichés of Voice

● Writing that assumes a false sense of authority: "I have determined that there are three basic types of newspapers. My preference is for the third."
● Writing that speaks with little or no sense of authority: "I flipped when I saw *The Lord of the Rings.*"

Change biased words.

When depicting individuals or groups according to their differences, you must use language that implies equal value and equal respect for all people.

Consider Ethnicity

Acceptable General Terms	*Acceptable Specific Terms*
American Indians, Native Americans	**Cherokee people, Inuit people,** and so forth
Asian Americans (not *Orientals*)	**Chinese Americans, Japanese Americans,** and so forth
Hispanic Americans, Hispanics	**Mexican Americans, Cuban Americans,** and so forth

African Americans, blacks
"African American" has come into wide acceptance, though the term "black" is preferred by some individuals.

Anglo Americans (English ancestry), **European Americans**
Use these terms to avoid the notion that "American," used alone, means "white."

Additional References

Not Recommended	*Preferred*
Eurasian, mulatto	**person of mixed ancestry**
nonwhite	**people of color**
Caucasian	**white**
Americans (to mean U.S. citizens)	**U.S. citizen**

Consider Age

Age Group	*Acceptable Terms*
Up to age 13 or 14	**boys, girls**
Between 13 and 19	**youth, young people, young men, young women**
Late teens and 20's	**young adults, young women, young men**
30's to age 60	**adults, men, women**
60 and older	**older adults, older people** (not *elderly*)
65 and older	**seniors** (*senior citizens* also acceptable)

Consider Disabilities or Impairments

In the recent past, some writers were choosing alternatives to the term *disabled,* including *physically challenged, exceptional,* or *special.* However, it is not generally held that these new terms are precise enough to serve those who live with disabilities. Of course, degrading labels like *crippled, invalid,* and *maimed,* as well as overly negative terminology, must be avoided.

Not Recommended	*Preferred*
handicapped	**disabled**
birth defect	**congenital disability**
stutter, stammer, lisp	**speech impairment**
an AIDS victim	**person with AIDS**
suffering from cancer	**person who has cancer**

Putting People First

People with various disabilities and conditions have sometimes been referred to as though they *were* their condition (*quadriplegics, depressives, epileptics*) instead of people who simply happen to have a particular disability. As much as possible, remember to refer to the person first, the disability second.

Not Recommended	*Preferred*
the disabled	**people with disabilities**
the retarded	**people with a developmental disability**
dyslexics	**students with dyslexia**
neurotics	**patients with neuroses**
subjects, cases	**participants, patients**
quadriplegics	**people who are quadriplegic**
a wheelchair user	**people who use wheelchairs**

Additional Terms

Make sure you understand the following terms that address specific impairments:

hearing impairment	=	partial hearing loss, hard of hearing (not *deaf,* which is total loss of hearing)
visual impairment	=	partially sighted (not *blind,* which is total loss of vision)
communicative disorder	=	speech, hearing, and learning disabilities affecting communication

Consider Gender

● Use parallel language for both sexes:

> The **men** and the **women** rebuilt the school together.
> **Hank** and **Marie**
> **Mr. Robert Gumble, Mrs. Joy Gumble**

Note: The courtesy titles *Mr., Ms., Mrs.,* and *Miss* ought to be used according to the person's preference.

● Use nonsexist alternatives to words with masculine connotations:

> **humanity** (not *mankind*)   **synthetic** (not *man-made*)
> **artisan** (not *craftsman*)

● Do not use masculine-only or feminine-only pronouns (*he, she, his, her*) when you want to refer to a human being in general:

> A politician can kiss privacy good-bye when **he** runs for office.
> (not recommended)

Instead, use *he or she,* change the sentence to plural, or eliminate the pronoun reference:

> A politician can kiss privacy good-bye when **he or she** runs for office.
> Politicians can kiss privacy good-bye when **they** run for office.
> A politician can kiss privacy good-bye when running for office.

● Do not use gender-specific references in the salutation of a business letter when you don't know the person's name:

> **Dear Sir:**   **Dear Gentlemen:** (neither is recommended)

Instead, address a position:

> **Dear Personnel Officer:**
> **Dear Members of the Economic Committee:**

Occupational Issues

Not Recommended	*Preferred*
chairman	chair, presiding officer, moderator
salesman	sales representative, salesperson
mailman	mail carrier, postal worker, letter carrier
insurance man	insurance agent
fireman	firefighter
businessman	executive, manager, businessperson
congressman	member of Congress, representative, senator
steward, stewardess	flight attendant
policeman, policewoman	police officer

Web

Proofreading Your Writing

The following guidelines will help you check your revised writing for spelling, mechanics, usage, grammar, and form. Also refer to the Handbook in this book for additional help. (See pages **573–684**.)

Review punctuation and mechanics.

1. **Check for proper use of commas**: before coordinating conjunctions in compound sentences, after introductory clauses and long introductory phrases, between items in a series, and so on. (See pages **575–579**.)
2. **Look for apostrophes**: in contractions, plurals, and possessive nouns. (See pages **591–592**.)
3. **Examine quotation marks**: in quoted information, titles, or dialogue. (See pages **586–587**.)
4. **Watch for proper use of capital letters**: for first words in written conversation, and for proper names of people, places, and things. (See pages **593–596**.)

Look for usage and grammar errors.

5. **Look for misuse of any commonly mixed pairs of words**: *there/their/they're; accept/except.* (See pages **611–622**.)
6. **Check for verb use.** Subjects and verbs should agree in number: singular subjects go with singular verbs; plural subjects go with plural verbs. Verb tenses should be consistent throughout. (See pages **651–654**.)
7. **Review for pronoun/antecedent agreement problems.** A pronoun and its antecedent must agree in number. (See page **655**.)

Check for spelling errors.

8. **Use a spell checker.** Your spell checker will catch most errors.
9. **Check each spelling you are unsure of.** Especially check those proper names and other special words your spell checker won't pick up.
10. **Consult your Handbook.** Use the list of commonly misspelled words in the Handbook (pages **605–609**) as well as an up-to-date dictionary.

Check the writing for form and presentation.

11. **Note the title.** A title should be appropriate and lead into the writing.
12. **Examine any quoted or cited material.** Are all sources of information properly presented and documented? (See pages **505–536** and **537–568**).
13. **Look over the finished copy of your writing.** Does it meet the requirements for a final manuscript? (See pages **89–92**.)

Editing and Proofreading Checklist

Use this checklist as a guide when you edit and proofread your writing. Edit your writing only after you have revised it. To see editing and proofreading in action, turn to pages **122–125**.

Sentence Structure

_____ Sentences are clear, complete, and correct.
_____ They flow smoothly and have varied lengths and beginnings.

Word Choice

_____ The writing is free of general words, jargon, and clichés.
_____ The language is unbiased and fair.

Correctness

_____ Spelling, punctuation, and mechanics are correct.
_____ Verb tenses are correct.
_____ Subjects agree with their verbs; pronouns agree with their antecedents.
_____ Research documentation is punctuated correctly.

Writing Activities

1. Choose a writing assignment that you have completed recently. Edit the sentences in this writing for style and correctness using pages **78–81** as a guide. Then use pages **82–86** in this chapter to edit the piece of writing for vague words, jargon, clichés, and biased language.

2. Choose one or two editing or proofreading topics that are discussed in this chapter and that you find challenging. Then select another piece of your writing and check it for those problems.

3. Combine some of the following ideas into longer, more mature sentences. Write at least four sentences using page **80** as a guide.

■ **Dogs can be difficult to train.**
■ **The necessary supplies include a leash and treats.**
■ **Patience is also a necessity.**
■ **Dogs like to please their owners.**
■ **Training is not a chore for dogs.**
■ **A well-trained dog is a pleasure to its owner and to others.**

Chapter 7
Submitting

video

Submitting a final paper is the driving force behind writing. It explains why you may have spent so much time planning, drafting, and revising an essay or a paper in the first place—to share a finished piece of writing that effectively expresses your thoughts and feelings. Often, the most immediate and important form of submitting is sharing a finished piece of writing with your instructor and writing peers. It can also be the most helpful. As writer Tom Liner states, "You learn ways to improve your writing by seeing its effect on others."

You can also submit a piece of writing to a school publication or simply place it in your writing portfolio. In addition, you might consider submitting something outside of your school. This chapter will help you prepare your writing for virtually any audience or publication.

What's Ahead

- Formatting Your Writing
- Sharing the Final Copy
- Effective Writing Checklist

Formatting Your Writing

The test of a good page design is that it makes your writing clear and easy to follow. Keep the following information in mind when you produce a final copy of your writing.

Strive for clarity in page design.

Format and Documentation

Keep the design clear and uncluttered. ■ Aim for a sharp, polished look in all your assigned writing.

Use the designated documentation form. ■ Follow all the requirements outlined in the MLA (pages **505–536**) or APA (pages **537–568**) style guide.

Typography

Use an easy-to-read serif font for the main text. ■ *Serif* type, like this, has "tails" at the tops and bottoms of the letters. For most types of writing, use a 10- or 12-point type size.

Consider using a sans serif font for the title and headings. ■ Sans serif type, like this, does not have "tails." Use larger, perhaps 18-point, type for your title and 14-point type for any headings. You can also use boldface for headings if they seem to get lost on the page.

INSIGHT: Because most people find a sans serif font easier to read on screen, consider a sans serif font for the body and a serif font for the titles and headings in any writing that you publish online.

Spacing

Follow all requirements for indents and margins. ■ This usually means indenting the first line of each paragraph five spaces, maintaining a one-inch margin around each page, and double-spacing throughout the paper.

Avoid widows and orphans. ■ Avoid leaving headings, hyphenated words, or single lines of new paragraphs alone at the bottom of a page. Also avoid single words at the bottom of a page or carried over to the top of a new page.

Graphic Devices

Create bulleted or numbered lists to highlight important points. ■ However, be selective; your writing should not include too many lists.

Includes charts or other graphics. ■ Graphics should not be so small that they get lost on the page, nor so large that they overpower the page.

Sharing Your Final Copy

Once you have formatted and proofread your final draft, you should be ready to share your writing. For school assignments, you will often simply turn in your paper to your instructor for evaluation. However, as you work through the final step in the process, keep the following points in mind.

Know your options for submitting your work.

Audiences

Nothing makes writing more real than authentic feedback. Consider the following options:

- Share your writing with peers or family members.
- Submit your work to a local publication or an online journal.
- Post your writing on an appropriate Web site, including your personal Web site.
- Turn in your writing to your instructor.

Methods

You have two basic methods of submitting your work.

- **Paper Submission:** Print an error-free copy on quality paper using a quality printer.
- **Electronic Submission:** If allowed, send your writing as an e-mail attachment.

Writing Portfolio

A portfolio is a collection of writing that shows your skill as a writer, perhaps a collection of your best writing for a semester. To compile your portfolio, keep track of all your writing and stay on top of your work. A portfolio might include these components:

- A table of contents listing the pieces included in your portfolio.
- An opening essay or letter detailing the story behind your portfolio (how you compiled it, how you feel about it, what it means to you, and more).
- A specified number of finished pieces representing your best writing in the class. (Your instructor may require you to include all of your planning, drafting, and revising work for one or more of these pieces.)
- A best "other" piece related to your work in another content area.
- A cover sheet attached to each piece of writing, discussing the reason for its selection, the amount of work that went into it, and so on.
- Evaluation sheets or checklists charting the basic skills you have mastered as well as the skills you still need to fine-tune.

Effective Writing Checklist

Whatever form your writing takes—essay, report, narrative, or research paper—it should demonstrate the following traits. Check your finished work using these traits or standards as a guide.

Stimulating Ideas

The writing . . .

_____ Presents interesting and important information.

_____ Maintains a clear focus or purpose—centered on a thesis, theme, concern, or question.

_____ Develops the focus with sufficient detail.

_____ Holds the reader's attention (and answers his or her questions).

Logical Organization

_____ Includes a clear beginning, middle, and ending.

_____ Contains specific details, arranged in the best order.

_____ Uses transitions to link sentences and paragraphs.

Engaging Voice

_____ Speaks in a sincere, natural way that fits the writing situation.

_____ Shows that the writer really cares about the subject.

Appropriate Word Choice

_____ Contains specific, clear words.

_____ Uses an appropriate level of language.

Overall Fluency

_____ Flows smoothly from sentence to sentence.

_____ Displays varied sentence beginnings and lengths.

_____ Follows a style that fits the situation.

Correct, Accurate Copy

_____ Adheres to the rules of grammar, spelling, and punctuation.

_____ Follows established documentation guidelines.

_____ Exhibits a polished, professional design.

The College Essay

CONTENTS

8 One Writer's Process

Chapter 8
One Writer's Process

audio

An essay is an attempt to understand a topic more deeply and clearly. That's one of the reasons the essay as a basic form of writing is essential in many college courses. It's a tool for both discovering and communicating.

How do you move from an assignment to a finished, polished essay? The best advice is take matters one step at a time, from thoroughly understanding the assignment to submitting the final draft. Don't try to churn out the essay the night before it's due.

This chapter shows up-close how one student followed the writing process outlined in Chapters 2 through 7.

What's Ahead

- Getting Started
- Planning
- Drafting
- Revising
- Editing and Proofreading
- Submitting
- Essay Checklist

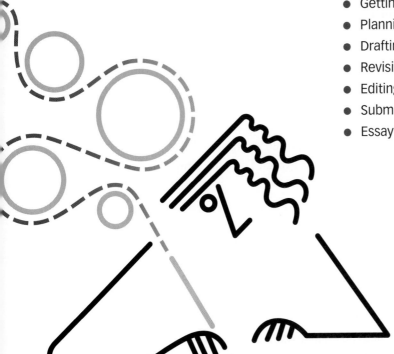

audio

Getting Started
Understanding the Assignment

Writing a good essay begins with understanding the writing assignment. Whether you are writing an informal essay for your communications class or a formal report for your psychology class, it is important to have a clear sense of your purpose, your audience, the form, and the method of assessment for your piece of writing. (Also see pages **28–29**.)

Carefully examine the assignment.

Answering the following questions will help you better understand the writing assignment and find the best way to begin the writing process.

Purpose

- How is this assignment related to other assignments and to the course goals? (See page **29**.)
- Why am I writing this piece—to inform, to persuade, to explain, or to entertain?
- Are there key words in the assignment (such as *describe, explain,* and *compare*) that tell me what I need to do? (See page **28**.)

Audience

- Does the assignment tell me who my readers should be? Should I address my instructor? My classmates? The general reader?
- What does my audience already know about my topic? What do they need to know? Are they interested? Educated? Do they know the technical terms in this subject area?
- What are my readers' attitudes? Skeptical? Accepting? Curious? Enthusiastic?
- What level of diction do my readers expect: Formal? Semiformal? Informal?

Form

- What are the specific requirements of the assignment concerning length, due date, and format?
- Will this be a formal or an informal piece of writing?
- Do I need to include the references I used? If so, which style do I follow (MLA, APA)? See the Research Guide, pages **441–568**, for more on each style.

Assessment

- How will this assignment be evaluated?
- How can I be sure that I am completing the assignment correctly?

video

One Writer's Process

In the pages ahead, you'll follow along with a student, Angela Franco, as she composes an assigned essay. Angela was given the writing assignment below in her environmental studies class. Note how she thought through the purpose, audience, form, and method of assessment.

Angela's Examination of the Assignment

Explain in a two- or three-page essay how a current environmental issue is relevant to the world community. Document any sources you use.

Purpose
- *My purpose is to <u>explain</u> how a current environmental issue is relevant to all people. To me, that means I must show how this issue affects my audience—both positively and negatively.*
- *I'll also need to give enough details and information to be sure my audience understands the issue.*

Audience
- *My audience will be people like me—my neighbors, my classmates, my community.*
- *I'll need to keep in mind what they already know and what they need to know to understand the issue.*

Form
- *I need to explain in <u>essay form</u>—that sounds formal to me.*
- *I'll need to include a thesis statement and references to my sources.*
- *I'll have to get more details about the length, due date, and format.*

Assessment
- *I'll use the guidelines and checklists in the Handbook to evaluate and revise my writing.*
- *I'll get feedback from others, including my instructor, and revise accordingly.*

write

Journal Reflections
- *What other audiences could you imagine for this assignment? How would the writing change with a different audience?*
- *How would a different form—a friendly letter, a short story, an editorial—affect this assignment?*

Exploring Possible Topics

Understanding the assignment doesn't guarantee that the writing process will be easy. However, finding just the right topic and angle of approach will certainly make the process go more smoothly. Begin your search for a topic by using one or more prewriting strategies discussed on pages **30–34.**

Try clustering.

Clustering is a prewriting strategy that allows you to brainstorm quickly and see how your ideas relate to one another. Begin with a key word or phrase related to your writing topic or assignment. Circle it, and then cluster ideas and details around it, circling each idea as you write it and drawing a line connecting it to the closest related idea. (See page **33.**)

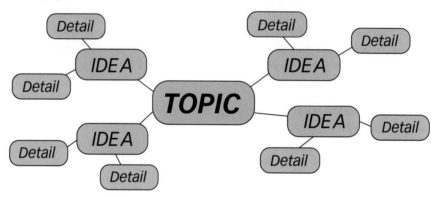

INSIGHT: After a few minutes of clustering, scan your cluster for an idea to explore in a freewriting exercise.

Do a freewriting session.

Freewriting is another effective way to discover possible writing ideas or angles. Simply write nonstop, for five to ten minutes, about whatever topic you're interested in. You'll soon be exploring ideas that might otherwise have never entered your mind. (See pages **31–32.**)

- **Write nonstop and record whatever comes into your mind.**
- **Use your assignment or topic as a starting point.**
- **Don't stop to judge, edit, or correct your writing.**
- **Keep writing, even when you think you have exhausted all of your ideas.**
- **Watch for a potential topic to emerge.**
- **Write about this topic, focusing on specific details.**

One Writer's Process

Angela explored her writing assignment by clustering and freewriting. When she thought about environmental issues, the first thing that came to mind was water pollution. She drew from her own memories and experiences, as well as from classroom discussions and readings, to generate a list of ideas. Note how she clustered the ideas and details into groups.

Angela's Clustering

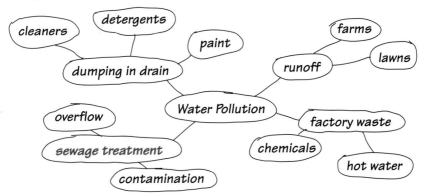

Angela's Freewriting

Angela decided to freewrite about the water pollution caused recently by improper sewage treatment in a small Canadian town. That led her to a narrowed focus in her writing assignment.

> I remember reading an article last summer about problems in a small Canadian town. People actually died. The water they drank was contaminated. This is becoming a problem in developed countries like ours. I thought for a long time this was only a problem in third-world countries. So, who is responsible for sewage treatment? Who guarantees the safety of our drinking water? How is water most often contaminated? Are there solutions for every kind of contamination: mercury, PCBs, sewage, etc.?

Narrowed Writing Assignment: Explain in a two- or three-page essay how the recent water pollution problem in a small Canadian town is relevant to the world community.

Collecting Information

Once you've chosen a narrowed topic, it's time to collect as much information about it as you can. The more you know about your subject, the easier it will be to write about it. (See pages **35–37**.)

Answer the Five *W*'s and *H*.

To gather facts about your narrowed topic, try thinking like a journalist. Pose the questions *Who? What? Where? When? Why?* and *How?* to help you move beyond the obvious aspects of your topic. (Also see page **36**.)

Questions:

- **Who?** Who is involved in or connected to this topic or incident?
- **What?** What is the key problem or issue?
- **Where?** Where did this incident take place?
- **When?** When did this event happen?
- **Why?** Why is this topic important?
- **How?** How did this happen?

Do additional research.

If you can't answer all six questions posed above, you'll have to do some research. It may be as simple as asking a classmate or logging onto the Internet. If your topic is very current or somewhat obscure, however, you may have to dig deeper. (See page **37**.)

Be careful to use only reliable sources, especially if you are researching on the Internet. Also be sure to keep track of your sources if you need to include documentation in your paper. Record the following information for citing your sources:

Author
Title of the book, article and magazine, or entry
Publisher or Web site
Date the material was published (and date accessed for Web sites)
Page numbers

Reserve a special part of a notebook to question, evaluate, and reflect upon your research as it develops. A record of your thoughts and actions during this process will often mean as much as or more to you than the actual information that you uncover. It helps you make sense of new ideas, refocus your thinking, and evaluate your progress.

video

One Writer's Process

Angela first tried answering the journalistic questions about her narrowed topic. She found that these questions further narrowed and focused her topic.

Narrowed Writing Assignment: Explain in a two- or three-page essay how the recent water pollution problem in a small Canadian town is relevant to the world community.

Angela's Answers

Topic: Water pollution in a small Canadian town

Who? - *farm operators, wastewater officials*

What? - *E. coli poisoning*

- *spreads bacteria*

- *causes disease*

- *clean, fresh water is depleted*

Where? - *Walkerton, Ontario*

When? - *May 2000*

Why? - *improper regulation; human error*

How? - *groundwater from irrigation, untreated sewage, and runoff*

Angela's Research

Angela then did some research to check her information and collect more details for her paper. She recorded all the essential data on each source and then listed the specific details related to her topic. Here's one source:

Nikiforuk, Andrew. "When Water Kills." Maclean's. 12 June 2000: 18–21.

- *factory farms hold as many as 25,000 cattle*
- *manure contains things like heavy metals (from mineral-rich feed), nutrients, and pathogens (E. coli)*
- *8,000 hogs can produce as much waste as 240,000 people*
- *six rural Ontario counties had high E. coli 0157 levels in 1990 and 1995*

Planning
Forming a Thesis Statement

The process of writing a working thesis statement leads in funnel fashion from a **general subject** to a **limited topic** to a **specific focus** on that topic. When you write a working thesis statement, you convert your focus into a single sentence expressing the central point you intend to develop in the rest of your essay. Later in the process of drafting or revising, you may further sharpen your thesis statement. The process of forming a thesis statement is described below and on page **41**.

Improve your focus and thesis.

Because your thesis will anchor your essay, take enough time to fine-tune your focus and thesis before you try to develop the rest of your essay.

Your focus should be . . .

(1) clear, (2) specific, and (3) manageable.

Sample focus: **Cause of violence among adult spectators at children's sporting events**

Unacceptable focus:

     Not clear: Sports, violence, and adult spectators
     Not specific: The role of spectators in sports
     Not manageable: The secret thoughts of violent spectators

Your thesis should be . . .

(1) true and (2) clearly organized.

Sample thesis: **Competition among parents contributes to acts of violence by spectators at children's sporting events.**

Unacceptable thesis:

     An exaggeration: Parents who fight at children's sporting events are embarrassments to the human race.
     A figure of speech: Adult spectators who fight at children's sports contests are like flies in the ointment.
     A slang expression: Parents who fight at children's sporting events are wackos.
     A double statement: Children's sports are wonderful and spectators who attack each other should be banned from the games.

The order of words in a thesis statement implies the order of development of the rest of the essay. For example, the sample thesis statement above implies a discussion of cause and effect. First, we would expect to see evidence that **there is competition among parents** and that **it leads to violence**.

One Writer's Process

video

Early in the process, Angela narrowed her focus to water pollution and a recent tragedy in Walkerton, Ontario. Below, we see how she narrowed her focus even further and developed a working thesis.

Angela's Focus

Angela thought about the assignment again to confirm that she was on the right track. Then she decided to focus on how the Walkerton incident happened, what harm it caused, and why it's important to know about it.

FOCUSING A TOPIC

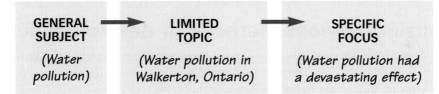

GENERAL SUBJECT	LIMITED TOPIC	SPECIFIC FOCUS
(Water pollution)	*(Water pollution in Walkerton, Ontario)*	*(Water pollution had a devastating effect)*

Angela's Working Thesis

Angela used the following formula to create a working thesis statement:

   A limited topic (water pollution incident in Walkerton, Ontario)
+ **a specific focus** (had a devastating effect)
= **an effective thesis statement**

WORKING THESIS STATEMENT: *The water pollution incident in Walkerton, Ontario, had a devastating effect.*

Thesis Checklist

Angela tested her thesis by asking herself the following questions:
- Does my thesis reflect a limited topic? *Yes, it does.*
- Does it state clearly the specific idea I plan to develop? *Yes.*
- Is the thesis supported by the information I have gathered? *Yes.*
- Does the thesis suggest a pattern of development for my essay? *Yes, cause and effect or problem and solution.*

Using Methods of Development

Once you have a thesis in hand, it is a good idea to consider the overall method of development or pattern of organization for your writing before you begin drafting. See pages 42–43 for more on methods of development.

Review the topic.

1. **Review your assignment.** A pattern of organization may be built into your assignment (process, cause/effect, problem/solution).
2. **Study your thesis statement.** Your thesis may suggest a logical method of development as well.
3. **Review your details.** Look through (or list) the details you plan to use in your writing to see whether they suggest a method of development.

Consider various methods of development.

Almost all academic essays use one or more of the basic methods of development. Knowing how these methods work will help you plan and organize your essays. (The page numbers refer to sample essays in this book.)

Methods	Organizing Principles	Models
Process (How something works)	Chronological order	230–231
Narrative (How something happened)	Chronological order	138–139
Description (How something or someone appears)	Spatial order—location order of interest	168–177
Comparison/contrast (How two things are alike/different)	Whole vs. whole comparison or point-by-point comparison	197–205
Cause/effect (How one thing affects something else)	Identify cause/explore effects or identify effect/explore causes	185–186
Problem/solution (How a problem can be solved)	Study the problem/present solution(s)	315–316
Classification (How something can be categorized)	Name categories/examine each one/divide into categories	213–215
Argumentation (How a position can be made and then supported)	Assert and support/counter the opposition/reassert position	272–273
Definition (How something is identified)	Define a term/distinguish It from similar terms	237–238
Explain and **analyze** (How something is explained or examined)	Move back and forth between explanation and analysis	226–227

One Writer's Process

video

With a thesis selected, Angela thought about the method of development that would best suit her writing.

Angela's Review

1. Review your assignment.

ASSIGNMENT: Explain in a two- or three-page essay how a current environmental issue is relevant to the world community.

My assignment clearly states that I need to explain my topic, so I have a general idea of how my paper will be organized.

2. Study your thesis statement.

THESIS STATEMENT: The water pollution incident in Walkerton, Ontario, had a devastating effect.

After reading my thesis statement, it's obvious that I'm going to be writing about a problem and its causes.

Angela's Method of Development

3. Choose an overall method.

Looking at the list of methods, I see that I can use cause/effect or problem/solution. After making two quick lists of my main points using both approaches, I decide to use a problem/ solution approach. I will still talk about causes and effects in my essay—they just won't be front and center.

With problem/solution, I need to first present the problem clearly so that readers can fully understand it and see why it's important. Then I need to explore solutions to the problem— maybe what they did in Walkerton and what we all need to do to make water safe.

INSIGHT: Many essays you write will be organized according to one dominant method or approach. However, within that general structure, other methods will often come into play. For example, while developing a comparison essay, you may do some describing or classifying.

Developing a Plan or an Outline

Once you've written a working thesis statement and chosen a method of development, you're ready to organize the information (main points, supporting details) that you expect to cover in your essay. A brief list of ideas may be enough to get you going. Then again, you may want to use a more formal outline or graphic organizer. (See pages **44–47** for more details.)

Study the thesis.

Look closely at the phrasing of your thesis statement, concentrating on key words. To support your thesis, what topics, issues, or points must you cover?

Review your prewriting notes, your clusters, and your freewriting. Study all the material you've gathered to this point. Make a list of the key points you want to cover in your essay or the questions you want to answer.

Consider your method of development. Use it to help you arrange your details into a list or outline.

Choose an outline or graphic organizer.

Choose an outline or graphic organizer based on your instructor's requirements, the complexity of the essay, or your own preference.

Basic list: A brief outline, listing only key words or phrases

Topic outline: A basic outline, which includes a detailed list of topics and subtopics

Sentence outline: A detailed outline of key points, supporting evidence, and specific examples written as complete sentences

Arrange details.

List your main points and supporting details. Then arrange these points in an order that best develops and supports your thesis. Ask yourself what logically comes first, second, third, and so on.

Thesis Statement
I. Key point
   A. Supporting detail
   B. Supporting detail
II. Key point
   A. Supporting detail
   B. Supporting detail
III. Key point
   A. Supporting detail
   B. Supporting detail

One Writer's Process

With her working thesis settled and an overall method of development selected, Angela chose to write a sentence outline to guide her first draft.

video

Angela's Study of Her Thesis

THESIS STATEMENT: *The water pollution incident in Walkerton, Ontario, had a devastating effect.*

- *What happened in Walkerton?*
- *Why was it a tragedy?*
- *Who or what caused the pollution?*
- *What were its effects?*
- *Why do we need to pay attention?*

Angela's Outline

SENTENCE OUTLINE:

    I. Walkerton, Ontario, experienced a serious pollution problem.
        A. The water was contaminated from manure runoff.
        B. Nothing was done to protect citizens.
        C. The problem went unnoticed for days.
    II. Several officials shared responsibility.
        A. Water treatment officials failed to diagnose the problem.
        B. The government advisory came too late.
    III. The problem required a series of solutions.
        A. Bottled water was distributed.
        B. Bleach was made available to homeowners.
        C. The town's entire system was flushed.
    IV. This event is important to everyone.
        A. It raises awareness.
        B. People may now take responsibility for their water.

INSIGHT: You don't need to have a fully developed outline to start drafting. You could start with a list or basic outline, then pause after drafting part of your essay to do some detailed outlining for sections or paragraphs. As you develop your outline, you may discover that you need to do more research or prewriting to fully support certain points.

audio

Drafting
Opening the Draft

Think of your essay opening as a bridge that connects the readers' world with the world of your essay. When readers cross this bridge, they move from their own world of concerns and experience into the subject you are exploring in your essay. (See page **51** for more on "major moves" to use when writing openings.)

Engage the reader.

The audience needs a "hook"—some reason to keep reading. Some methods you can use to seize the reader's attention are listed below:
- Share thought-provoking details about your topic.
- Pose a challenging question (or two or three).
- Begin with an interesting quotation.
- Provide a dramatic statement or statistic.

Identify the topic.

Introduce your topic (directly or indirectly) and provide whatever background your reader may need. Ask yourself some questions:
- What terms need to be defined?
- What historical background needs to be provided?
- What basic details do readers need to understand the topic?

Narrow the focus and the thesis.

The thesis often appears near the end of an opening paragraph. However, it can appear elsewhere—and it can be expressed in more than one sentence. Review your thesis before deciding where it should go:
- Does it provide a sharp focus?
- Does it present a definite viewpoint?
- Will it provide a transition to the body of your essay?

fyi

Some writers pay special attention to the exact wording of their opening before they draft the rest of the text. Other writers compose the middle paragraphs before the introduction. Use whatever technique works best for you. (See pages **52–53**.)

One Writer's Process

Angela wanted her readers to want to read her essay, so she talked with several classmates to determine what they did and didn't know about water pollution. She used what she learned from these conversations to connect her readers to her topic.

Angela's Opening: First Attempt

What could be better than a big glass of water on a hot day? What if the water looked clean and pure but wasn't? What if it could make you sick, or even kill you? What if your city's water system was contaminated with E. coli bacteria due to sewage, industry, or waste pollution? That's just what happened in one small Canadian town. The town's well was contaminated, but no one knew it until it was too late. This water pollution incident in Walkerton, Ontario, had a devastating effect.

After reading over her first attempt, Angela decided that she had raised too many questions. She also felt that she hadn't created any concrete images for them and that her thesis statement was too broad. In her next attempt, she tried to draw readers into her essay with some concrete images and a more specific thesis statement.

Angela's Second Attempt

Attention-getting details engage the reader.

> *It's a hot day. Several people just finished mowing their lawns. A group of bicyclists—more than 3,000—have been passing through your picturesque town all afternoon. Dozens of Little Leaguers are batting, running, and sweating.*

The topic is established.

> *What do all these people have in common? They all drink lots of tap water especially on hot summer days. They also take for granted that the water is clean and safe. But in reality, the water they drink could be contaminated and pose*

The thesis is revised slightly.

> *a serious health risk. That's just what happened in Walkerton, Ontario, where a water pollution incident caused serious problems.*

Developing the Middle

When you write the middle paragraphs in your essay, you are beginning to make your point and fulfill your purpose. To do so successfully, you need to state your points in a clear, well-organized manner and support each with appropriate details. (See pages **54–55**.)

Present the main points.

Using your outline or plan as a guide, list the main points you plan to cover in your essay. State each main point in a clear, complete sentence. You can use each of these sentences as a topic sentence for one of your paragraphs (at least for now). The topic sentences will help keep you on track as you develop the body of your essay.

Review the organization.

Review the method(s) of development you selected for your essay. For example, if you are using a problem/solution method, you may want the first paragraphs after the introduction to identify the problem and the next ones to discuss possible solutions. Review the order of your main points in your plan and reorganize them as necessary.

Use specific details.

When writing any paragraph, ask, "What types of details will best support and develop my key idea?" Choose specific details based on your writing situation. Also use different levels of detail. (See page **55**.)

facts	examples	definitions	reasons
statistics	quotations	explanations	comparisons

- If you're **describing** something,
  ask what details would help readers see, smell, taste, touch, or hear what is being described.

- If you're **explaining** something or giving instructions,
  ask what details would help readers understand what this term or concept means, or what details would help them follow this procedure.

- If you're **persuading**,
  ask what details would help readers understand why this argument is reasonable, logical, and true.

- If you're **narrating** something,
  ask what details would help readers understand the progression and significance of the story from beginning to end.

video

One Writer's Process

Angela's next step was to decide which point to develop first and which details she could use to support her point.

Angela's Middle Paragraphs: First Attempt

Walkerton's water supply got contaminated one day in May. The people in this small town learned firsthand what contaminated water meant. The contaminated water should never have reached the people. The rains were heavy and washed cattle manure into the town well. Seven days later people began calling public health officials to tell them they were ill. What was making these people ill was the E. coli bacteria. You may have heard of this bacteria. This tragedy all started on May 12. It wasn't until May 21 that a boil-water alert went out. It was a disaster.

Angela felt her first attempt needed to be organized better, so in her second attempt, she rearranged the same basic facts in chronological order.

Angela's Second Attempt

A direct question opens the paragraph.

Specific details are used to describe the problem.

What happened in Walkerton, Ontario? Heavy rains fell on May 12. It wasn't until May 21 that the townspeople were advised to boil their drinking water. The rains washed cattle manure into the town well. The manure contained E. coli, a bacteria. E. coli is harmless to cattle. It can make people sick. Seven days after the heavy rains, people began calling public health officials. The warning came too late. Two people had already died.

In the same way, Angela then went on to organize and develop the other paragraphs in her essay.

Ending the Draft

An effective closing is an ending—and a beginning. It ends your essay, but begins the readers' further thinking process. Your readers will leave your essay thinking about what you've said—or at least they should. You can close by reviewing, summarizing, asking questions, making comparisons, or looking to the future. (See pages **56–57**.)

Review the main points.

- Review the main focus of your essay.
- Summarize the main points.
- Emphasize the special importance of one of your main points.
- Tie up any loose ends.

Provide a question or comparison.

- Use a thought-provoking question to give your readers something to think about.
- Develop a final comparison or metaphor to provide a lasting image for your readers.
- Come full circle by tying your closing paragraph back to your opening paragraph.

Urge the reader.

- Draw a final conclusion for your reader.
- Look to the future and suggest where this issue fits into the lives of the readers.
- Connect your thesis to your assignment, to the reader's experience, or to society as a whole.

Closing Checklist

___ Does your closing review or summarize the specific focus of your essay?

___ Does your closing help your readers see the importance of your essay to them personally? To the wider society? Now and in the future?

___ Does your essay end with a strong final line?

One Writer's Process

Angela wanted her closing paragraph to add to her readers' understanding of the essay and leave them with something to think about. She opened her paragraph with a question that she answered in the middle of the paragraph.

Angela's Ending: First Attempt

Could there be any good from a tragedy like Walkerton's? Perhaps the good thing is that a tragedy like Walkerton's could raise the general public's awareness of problems with public water. Maybe more people will realize that there can be a breakdown in how water is controlled and that no water is perfectly safe. They might also realize that community officials can make errors. Because of Walkerton's tragedy, ordinary people are starting to be responsible for the water they drink.

Angela's Second Attempt

Angela reviewed her first attempt, found some unnecessary details, and deleted them in her second attempt. She also rearranged some of the sentences to bring her paragraph to a more forceful conclusion.

Questions begin the paragraph.

> *Could any good come from Walkerton's tragedy? Does it have a silver lining? It is possible that more people are aware that water may be contaminated? Today people are beginning to take responsibility for the purity of the water they and their families drink.*

The writer looks to the future.

> *In the end, more and more people will know about the dangers of contaminated water—without learning it the hard way.*

Closing Checklist

Angela tested her closing by asking herself the following questions:

___ Does your closing review the specific focus of your essay? ***Yes.***

___ Does your closing help your readers see the importance of your essay to them personally? To the wider society? Now and in the future? ***Yes, anyone reading my essay would now be aware of the dangers of contaminated drinking water.***

___ Does your essay end with a strong final line? ***I think so.***

Angela's First Draft

After composing her opening, middle, and closing paragraphs, Angela puts together her first draft. She then adds a working title.

The writer adds a title.

Water Woes

She uses a series of images to get the reader's attention.

It's a hot day. Several people just finished mowing their lawns. A group of bicyclists—more than 3,000—have been passing through your picturesque town all afternoon. Dozens of Little Leaguers are batting, running, and sweating. What do all these people have in common? They all drink lots of tap water especially on hot summer days. They also take for granted that the water is clean and safe. But in reality, the water they drink could be contaminated and pose a serious health risk. That's just

The thesis statement introduces the subject.

what happened in Walkerton, Ontario, where a water pollution incident caused serious problems.

What happened in Walkerton, Ontario? Heavy rains fell on May 12. It wasn't until May 21 that the townspeople were advised to boil their drinking water. The rains washed cattle manure into the town well. The

The writer describes the cause of the problem.

manure contained E. coli, a bacteria. E. coli is harmless to cattle. It can make people sick. Seven days after the heavy rains, people began calling public health officials. The warning came too late. Two people had already died.

Once Walkerton's problem was identified, the solutions were known. The government acted quickly to help the community and to clean the water supply. One Canadian newspaper reported that a $100,000 emergency fund was set up to help families with expenses. Bottled water for drinking and containers of bleach for sanitizing and cleaning were donated by local businesses.

The writer discusses other causes of the problem.

So what messed up Walkerton? Basically, people screwed up! According to one news story, a flaw in the water treatment system allowed the infested water to enter the well. The manure washed into the well, but the chlorine should have killed the deadly bacteria. In Walkerton, the PUC group fell asleep at the wheel. *4*

The writer covers the solutions that were used to resolve the problem.

At last, the Provincial Clean Water Agency restored the main water and sewage systems by flushing out all of the town's pipes and wells. The ban on drinking Walkerton's water was finally lifted seven months after the water became contaminated. *5*

The concluding paragraph stresses the importance of public awareness.

Could any good come from Walkerton's tragedy? Does it have a silver lining? It is possible that more people are aware that water may be contaminated. Today people are beginning to take responsibility for the purity of the water they and their families drink. In the end, more and more people will know about the dangers of contaminated water—without learning it the hard way. *6*

audio

Revising
Improving Ideas, Organization, and Voice

Think broadly when you revise. At this point, keep your sights on the big issues of whether the ideas, organization, and voice of the paper work, not on grammar and spelling. (Also see pages **59–76**.)

Use an efficient method of revising.

1. **Pace yourself.** If possible, set your draft aside for a day or more before reviewing it. With some distance, you'll see your writing with fresh eyes.

2. **Print a hard copy.** When you have the printed text in front of you, you can see the whole essay, read it aloud, and mark it up.

3. **Think globally first.** Step back and reassess your thoughts about the subject. Read your entire draft and consider these questions:

   ● Does your thesis still fit your essay, or has a different idea emerged? If necessary, reshape the thesis and rethink the supporting paragraphs.

   ● Does your writing have gaps? Fill them with appropriate ideas and details, doing further brainstorming and research as needed.

   ● Is the organization effective and logical? Are your paragraphs in the best possible order?

   ● Is your writing voice engaging and knowledgeable? Does it fit your topic and your audience? Rewrite passages that are either too formal or not formal enough.

4. **Carefully examine each part.** Once you've looked at your essay for overall sense and organization, you need to study each key part closely.

   ● Does the opening draw readers into your essay and clearly state your thesis?

   ● Do you expand each main point in a separate paragraph?

   ● Have you supported each main point in the body with enough details and examples?

   ● Are the parts of your essay tied together effectively? Do you need to add transitional words or phrases? (See page **70**.)

   ● Does the closing summarize your writing and help readers appreciate the significance of your essay?

5. **Map out a revision plan.** As you look closely at your draft, write notes in the margins about what changes you need to make. Then make these changes, using the notes as a guide but looking for more ways to improve your writing.

video

Angela's First Revision

After finishing her first draft, Angela set it aside. When she was ready to revise it, she looked carefully at global issues—content, organization, and voice. She wrote notes to herself to help keep her thoughts together.

Angela's comments

Water Woes

I need to give my opening more energy.

an unusually   Saturday afternoon⊙
It's a hot ~~day,~~ Several people just finished mowing   *1*
pedal up the street.⊙
their lawns. A group of bicyclists, ~~more than 3,000~~ have
~~been passing through your picturesque town all afternoon.~~
Dozens of Little Leaguers are batting, running, and
sweating. What do all these people have in common? They
all drink lots of tap water especially on hot summer days.
They also take for granted that the water is clean and
safe. But in reality, the water they drink could be

Does my thesis still fit the paper?—yes.

contaminated and pose a serious health risk. That's just
what happened in Walkerton, Ontario, where a water
pollution incident caused serious problems.

What happened in Walkerton, Ontario? Heavy rains   *2*
fell on May 12.[It wasn't until May 21 that the

Using time sequence, put this paragraph in better order.

townspeople were advised to boil their drinking water.]
The rains washed cattle manure into the town well. The
manure contained E. coli, a bacteria. E. coli is harmless to
cattle. It can make people sick. Seven days after the
heavy rains, people began calling public health officials.
The warning came too late. Two people had already died.

Move this paragraph—it interrupts the discussion of causes.

Once Walkerton's problem was identified, the solutions   *3*
were known. The government acted quickly to help the
community and to clean the water supply. One Canadian
newspaper reported that a $100,000 emergency fund was
set up to help families with expenses. Bottled water for
drinking and containers of bleach for sanitizing and
cleaning were donated by local businesses.

My voice here is too informal.

went wrong in
So what ~~messed up~~ Walkerton? ~~Basically, people~~ *Human error was a critical factor.*
First,
~~screwed up!~~ According to one news story, a flaw in the
water treatment system allowed the infested water to
Even after *T*
enter the well. The manure washed into the well ~~but~~ the
chlorine should have killed the deadly bacteria. In

Explain "fell asleep."

Walkerton, the ~~PUC group fell asleep at the wheel.~~

Move paragraph three here and combine.

In addition,
~~At last~~ the Provincial Clean Water Agency restored
the main water and sewage systems by flushing out all of
the town's pipes and wells. The ban on drinking
Walkerton's water was finally lifted seven months after
the water became contaminated.

Could any good come from Walkerton's tragedy? ~~Does~~

Cut the clichés.

~~it have a silver lining?~~ It is possible that more people are
aware that water may be contaminated. Today people are
beginning to take responsibility for the purity of the water
they and their families drink. In the end, more and more
people will know about the dangers of contaminated
water—without learning it the hard way.

*Public Utilities Commission was responsible for overseeing
the testing and treating of the town's water, but they
failed to monitor it properly. Apparently, shortcuts were
taken when tracking the water's chlorine level, and as a
result, some of the water samples were mislabeled. There
was also a significant delay between the time that the
contamination was identified and the time it was reported.*

4

5

6

Revising Collaboratively

Your fellow writers can tell you what does and doesn't work for them in your writing. This feedback is valuable throughout the writing process, but it can prove especially helpful early in the revising process. At this point, you need to find out if your writing makes sense, if it holds the readers' interest, and so on. The guidelines that follow will help whether you are working with a group or one other person. **Note the comments of the reviewer in the margins of Angela's second revision on pages 120-121.** (Also see pages 72-73.)

The Author/Writer

Come prepared with a substantial piece of writing. ▨ Prepare a copy for each person you want to react to your writing.

Introduce your writing. ▨ But don't say too much; let your writing do the talking.

Read the piece out loud. ▨ Speak confidently and clearly.

Listen to the comments carefully and take brief notes. ▨ Don't be defensive about your writing, as taking such an attitude will stop some people from commenting honestly about your work. Answer all of their questions.

Share your concerns with your fellow writers. ▨ Wait until they've had a chance to give you their responses.

The Reader/Listener

Listen carefully as the writer reads. ▨ Take notes, but make them brief so you don't miss the reading.

Imagine yourself to be the writer's intended audience. ▨ If the piece was meant for an admissions office, a civic organization, or a newspaper, react to the text accordingly.

Keep your comments positive, constructive, and concrete. ▨ Instead of "Great job," make more helpful responses: "Including details about the small town helped make your essay more believable—and more powerful."

Focus your comments on specific things you observe. ▨ An observation such as "I noticed many 'There are' statements in the body of your essay" is much more helpful than "Add some style to your writing."

Ask questions of the author. ▨ "What do you mean when you say . . . ?" "Where did you get your facts about . . . ?"

Listen to other comments and add to them. ▨ Listening to everyone's reactions and suggestions can help you and your peers become better writers.

Angela's Second Revision

Next, Angela asked a peer to review her work. Her comments are in the margin. Angela used them to make additional changes.

video

Reviewer's comments

Angela's changes

Water Woes

Use the same verb tense in all examples. --- It's an unusually hot Saturday afternoon. ~~Several~~ *Someone* ~~people just finished~~ *is* mowing ~~their~~ *the* lawn~~s~~. A group of bicyclists ~~pedal~~ *are pedaling* up the street. Dozens of Little Leaguers are batting, running, and sweating. What do all these people have in common? They all drink lots of tap water

Do you need a more interesting thesis statement? --- especially on hot summer days. They also take for granted that the water they drink is clean and safe. But in reality, the water could be contaminated and pose a serious health risk. *Last year for example, the citizens of* ~~That's just what happened in~~ *Walkerton, Ontario, had no idea their water was seriously* ~~Walkerton, Ontario, where a water pollution incident~~ *contaminated—until it was too late.* ~~caused serious problems.~~

The events in Walkerton began when heavy rains fell *, 2000.*

Add the year. --- on May 12. The rains washed cattle manure into the town well. The manure contained E. coli, a bacteria. E. coli is

Add specific details. --- harmless to cattle. It can make people sick. Seven days after the heavy rains, people began calling public health *to complain of nausea and diarrhea.* officials. It wasn't until May 21 that the townspeople were

Add your sources. --- advised to boil their drinking water. The warning came too *, and more than 2,000 were ill (Wickens).* late. Two people had already died. *Several factors contributed to the tragedy in Walkerton,* ~~So what went wrong in Walkerton? Human error was~~ *including human error.* *The Edmonton Journal*

Combine these two sentences? --- ~~a critical factor.~~ First, according to ~~one news story;~~ a flaw in the water treatment system allowed the infested water *(Blackwell)* to enter the well. Even after the manure washed into the

Fix this fragment. --- well. The chlorine should have killed the deadly bacteria. In Walkerton, the Public Utilities Commission was responsible for overseeing the testing and treating of the town's water, but they failed to monitor it properly.

Apparently, shortcuts were taken when tracking the water's chlorine level, and as a result, some of the water samples were mislabeled. There was also a significant delay between the time that the contamination was identified and the time it was reported.

Once Walkerton's problem was identified, ~~the solutions were known.~~ The government acted quickly to help the community ~~and to clean the water supply.~~ One ~~Canadian newspaper~~ *The Edmonton Journal* reported a $100,000 emergency fund was set up to help families with expenses. *Local businesses donated* Bottled water for drinking and containers of bleach for basic sanitizing and cleaning ~~were donated by local businesses.~~ In addition, the Provincial Clean Water Agency restored the main water and sewage systems by flushing out all of the town's pipes and wells. The ban on drinking Walkerton's water was finally lifted seven months after the water became contaminated.]

Again, list your sources.

Rework this paragraph and add more details.

4

5

~~Could any good come from Walkerton's tragedy? It is possible that more people are aware that water may be contaminated. Today people are beginning to take responsibility for the purity of the water they and their families drink. In the end, more and more people will know about the dangers of contaminated water—without learning it the hard way.~~

If any good could come of a tragedy like that in Walkerton, it would be an increased awareness. More people now realize that no water is 100 percent safe and are beginning to take responsibility for the purity of the water they drink. They are installing filtration systems, using bottled water, and boiling tap water. Because of incidents like the one in Walkerton, more people now know about the dangers of contaminated water—without learning it the hard way.

audio

Editing and Proofreading
Editing the Revised Draft

All of the writing, reviewing, reworking, and refining you do will reflect your personal writing style. But you must also look closely at your revised writing to make sure that your ideas are clear and correct. The following list of reminders will help you check your writing for style and word choice.

Check the overall style.

1. Read your revised writing aloud to test it for style. Better yet, have someone read it to you. Your writing should read smoothly and naturally from start to finish.

2. Check for these stylistic reminders:

Be purposeful. ■ Does your writing sound like you know and care about your subject?

Be clear. ■ Are the ideas expressed concisely and directly?

Be creative. ■ Do you present your ideas in a fresh and interesting way?

Examine the sentences.

3. Carefully check your sentences for correctness. Does each sentence express a complete thought? Have you used the most appropriate subordinate conjunction (*although, because,* and so forth) or relative pronoun (*that, who,* and so forth) in your complex sentences?

4. Watch for sentences that sound the same. Rely on your writer's sixth sense to sort out the good from the bad. Listen especially carefully for unwanted repetition of words and ideas.

5. Examine your sentences for variety:

Vary the length. ■ Are your sentences too long and rambling? Have you included too many short, choppy sentences?

Vary the beginnings. ■ Do too many sentences begin with the same pronoun or article (*There, It, The, I,* and so forth)?

Consider the word choice.

6. Replace any potentially awkward or confusing words or phrases. Replace overused words and phrases (clichés) with words and expressions that are specific, vivid, and colorful.

7. Check your writing for the appropriate level of diction. In most cases, academic writing should meet the standards of formal diction.

Angela's Edited Copy

When Angela began editing, she read each sentence aloud to check for clarity and smoothness. **The first page of Angela's edited copy is shown below.**

The writer revises the title.

in Walkerton
Water Woes∧

It's an unusually hot Saturday afternoon. Someone is   *1*
in the next block
moving the lawn. A group of bicyclists are pedaling up the

She makes her opening sentences more parallel (more alike).

street. Dozens of Little Leaguers are batting, running, and
in the park
sweating. What do all these people have in common? They
all drink lots of tap water especially on hot summer days.
They also take for granted that the water they drink
is clean and safe. But in reality, the water could be
contaminated and pose a serious health risk. Last year
for example, the citizens of Walkerton, Ontario, had no
idea their water was seriously contaminated—until it was
too late.

on May 12, 2000,
The events in Walkerton began ∧when heavy rains ~~fell~~   *2*
~~on May 12, 2000.~~ ~~The rains~~ washed cattle manure into

She rewrites and combines several choppy sentences.

the   commonly called
the town well. The manure contained ~~E. coli, a~~ bacteria, E.
While E. coli
coli is harmless to cattle, It can make people sick. Seven
days after the heavy rains, people began calling public
health officials to complain of nausea and diarrhea. It
wasn't until May 21 that the townspeople were advised to
boil their drinking water. The warning came too late. Two
people had already died, and more than 2,000 were ill
(Wickens).

Several factors contributed to the tragedy in Walkerton,   *3*
including human error. First, according to The Edmonton
Journal, a flaw in the water treatment system allowed the
Walkertons
infested water to enter ~~the~~ well (Blackwell). Even after

She adds words for clarity.

the manure washed into the well, the chlorine should have
killed the deadly bacteria. In Walkerton, the Public . . .

Proofreading for Correctness

The following guidelines will help you check your writing for spelling, punctuation, mechanics, usage, and grammar. Also refer to the Handbook for additional help. (See pages 573–662.)

Check mechanics and punctuation.

1. **Review your writing for spelling errors.** (Remember: Your spell checker won't catch them all.)

2. **Check each sentence for proper use of commas**: before coordinating conjunctions (*and, but, or,* and so forth) in compound sentences, after introductory clauses and long introductory phrases, between items in a series, and so on. (See pages 575–579.)

3. **Look for apostrophes in possessives and contractions.** (See pages 591–592.)

4. **Examine quoted information or dialogue for proper use of quotation marks.** (See pages 586–587.)

5. **Review the text for proper use of capital letters**: for first words in sentences and in written conversation; for proper names of people, places, and things. (See pages 593–596.)

Look for usage and grammar errors.

6. **Look for misuse of any commonly mixed pairs of words** such as *accept/except, their/there/they're.* (See pages 611–622.)

7. **Check for subject-verb agreement problems.** Subjects and verbs should agree in number: singular subjects go with singular verbs; plural subjects go with plural verbs. (See pages 651–654.)

8. **Review for pronoun-antecedent agreement problems.** A pronoun and its antecedent must agree in number. (See page 655.)

9. **Use your personal writing checklist.** If you don't already have a personal checklist, begin one by jotting down the errors you find in your writing. Soon you'll have a record of potential errors you'll want to double-check in all of your work.

10. **Check the title.** Did you choose a title that effectively labels your essay and leads into the writing? Is it appropriate for the writing task?

Angela's Proofread Copy

Angela reviewed her edited copy for capitalization and punctuation, agreement issues, and spelling. **The first page of Angela's proofread essay is shown below.**

video

Water Woes in Walkerton

Correct error that spell checker did not pick up.

It's an unusually hot Saturday afternoon. Someone is *1*
mowing ~~moving~~ the lawn in the next block. A group of bicyclists are pedaling up the street. Dozens of Little Leaguers are batting, running, and sweating in the park. What do all these people have in common? They all drink lots of tap

Add a comma for emphasis.

water‸especially on hot summer days. They also take for granted that the water they drink is clean and safe. But‸ in reality, the water could be contaminated and pose a

Add a comma after introductory phrase.

serious health risk. Last year‸for example, the citizens of Walkerton, Ontario, had no idea their water was seriously contaminated—until it was too late.

The events in Walkerton began on May 12, 2000, *2* when heavy rains washed cattle manure into the town well. The manure contained the bacteria commonly called

Underline (or use italics for) a scientific name

<u>E. coli</u>. While <u>E. coli</u> is harmless to cattle‸it can make people sick. Seven days after the heavy rains, people began calling public health officials to complain of nausea and diarrhea. It wasn't until May 21 that the townspeople were advised to boil their drinking water. The warning came too late. Two people had already died, and more than 2,000 were ill (Wickens).

Also underline (or use italics for) the names of newspapers.

Several factors contributed to the tragedy in Walkerton, *3* including human error. First, according to <u>The Edmonton Journal</u>, a flaw in the water treatment system allowed the

Use an apostrophe to show possession.

infested water to enter Walkerton's well (Blackwell). Even after the manure washed into the well, the chlorine should have killed the deadly bacteria. In Walkerton, the . . .

audio

Submitting
Checking the Page Design, Documentation, and Appearance

Before printing a final copy of your essay, check the issues below and make adjustments as necessary.

Consider the form.

- Have you correctly followed MLA, APA, or other format guidelines as required by your instructor?
- Is the spacing correct? Are your margins wide enough, and are lines double-spaced?
- Are the page header and page numbers correct?
- If you used headings, did you keep them short and to the point?
- Is your title centered on the first page?
- If required, have you added a title page and formal outline?

Keep up appearances.

- Have you selected an appropriate typeface and font size (usually 10- or 12-point)?
- Does the text align at the left margin? Have you left the right margin uneven (ragged right)?
- Have you avoided placing headings and the first line of new paragraphs at the very bottom of a page?
- Have you used charts or other graphics if appropriate?
- Have you used a quality printer and printed on quality paper?

Check the documentation.

- Have you avoided unintended plagiarism by rewording and citing your original sources? (See "Avoiding Plagiarism," pages **471–473**.)
- Have you documented your sources correctly within the text? (See "Document your sources," pages **469–470**. For MLA documentation, see pages **505–536**. For APA documentation, see pages **537–568**.)
- Do you have a complete, correct works-cited or references page if one is required? (For MLA Works-Cited format, see pages **508–524** and **534**. For APA Reference-List format, see pages **544–554** and **565-566**.)

video

Angela's Finished Essay . . . with Citations

After proofreading and formatting her essay, Angela added a heading and page numbers. She also added more documentation and a works-cited page at the end.

Franco 1

Complete details are supplied in the heading.

Angela Franco

Professor Rylaarsdam

English 101

12 October 2002

The title is revised.

Water Woes in Walkerton

It's an unusually hot Saturday afternoon. Someone is mowing the lawn in the next block. A group of bicyclists are pedaling up the street. Dozens of Little Leaguers are batting, running, and sweating in the park. What do all these people have in common? They all drink lots of tap water, especially on hot summer days. They also take for granted that the water they drink is clean and safe. But, in reality, the water could be contaminated and pose a serious health risk. Last year, for example, the citizens of Walkerton, Ontario, had no idea their water was seriously contaminated—until it was too late.

An appropriate type font and size are used.

The events in Walkerton began on May 12, 2000, when heavy rains washed cattle manure into the town well. The manure contained the bacteria commonly called E. coli. While E. coli is harmless to cattle, it can make people sick. Seven days after the heavy rains, people began calling public health officials to complain of nausea and diarrhea. It wasn't until May 21 that the townspeople were advised to boil their drinking water. The warning came too late. Two people had already died, and more than 2,000 were ill (Wickens).

Credit is given for a journal and newspaper used as sources.

Several factors contributed to the tragedy in Walkerton, including human error. First, according to The Edmonton Journal, a flaw in the water treatment system allowed the

1

2

3

Franco 2

infested water to enter Walkerton's well (Blackwell). Even after the manure washed into the well, the chlorine should have killed the deadly bacteria. In Walkerton, the Public Utilities Commission was responsible for overseeing the testing and treating of the town's water, but they failed to monitor it properly (Walkerton's). Apparently, shortcuts were taken when tracking the water's chlorine level, and as a result, some of the water samples were mislabeled. There was also a significant delay between the time that the contamination was identified and the time it was reported.

Once Walkerton's problem was identified, the government acted quickly to help the community. The Edmonton Journal reported that a $100,000 emergency fund was set up to help families with expenses. Local businesses donated bottled water for drinking and containers of bleach for basic sanitizing and cleaning. In addition, the Provincial Clean Water Agency restored the main water and sewage systems by flushing out all of the town's pipes and wells. Seven months after the water became contaminated, the ban on drinking Walkerton's water was finally lifted.

If any good could come of a tragedy like that in Walkerton, it would be an increased awareness. More people now realize that no water is 100 percent safe and are beginning to take responsibility for the purity of the water they drink. They are installing filtration systems, using bottled water, and boiling tap water. Because of incidents like the one in Walkerton, more people now know about the dangers of contaminated water—without learning it the hard way.

Writer's name and page number are used on each page.

The writer continues to give credit throughout her essay.

The final essay is printed on quality paper with a quality printer.

Franco 3

Works Cited

Sources used
are listed
correctly, in
alphabetical
order.

Blackwell, Thomas. "Walkerton Doctor Defends Response."
The Edmonton Journal. 9 January 2001
<http://edmontonjournal.com>.

"Walkerton's Water-Safety Tests Falsified Regularly, Utility
Official Admits." The Edmonton Journal. 7 December
2000 <http://edmontonjournal.com>.

Wickens, Barbara. "Tragedy in Walkerton." Maclean's. 5
June 2000: 34-36.

ASSESSMENT: Angela Franco's essay works well for a variety of reasons.

1. It consistently focuses on a single, manageable topic—the events in Walkerton and what they mean for the larger community.

2. The development is logical, moving from a statement of the problem, to a discussion of its causes, to a description of solutions.

3. The paper is engaging. It offers some drama and delivers a clear insight into the topic.

4. The research is appropriate. While news articles aren't strong academic resources, they fit this assignment.

Journal Reflections Based on this assessment and on your own reading of this essay, consider these questions:

- *How did this essay connect with you as a reader? What did it give you or teach you?*
- *What can you take from this essay that you can apply to your own essay writing?*
- *If you had written the essay, what would you have done differently? Why?*

Essay Checklist

Stimulating Ideas

The essay . . .

_____ Focuses on a specific, narrowly defined topic.

_____ Contains a clear, insightful thesis statement about the topic.

_____ Develops and supports the thesis with facts, examples, quotations, and other evidence.

Logical Organization

_____ Includes an interesting opening paragraph that pulls the reader into the topic, narrows the focus, and states the thesis.

_____ Uses organizational patterns appropriate to the type of essay (compare/contrast, problem/solution, cause/effect).

_____ Uses transitions to link ideas in sentences and paragraphs.

_____ Includes an effective closing paragraph.

Engaging Voice

_____ Speaks clearly and knowledgeably.

_____ Shows that the writer is truly interested in the subject.

_____ Is tailored for the intended audience.

Appropriate Word Choice

_____ Defines and explains unfamiliar terms.

_____ Contains specific nouns and strong action verbs.

_____ Maintains the appropriate level of formality.

Overall Fluency

_____ Flows smoothly from one idea to the next.

_____ Displays varied sentence length and structure.

Correct, Accurate Copy

_____ Follows the standard rules for writing (from grammar to usage).

_____ Follows the format required by the instructor.

II. A Reader:
Strategies
and Models

Narrative and Descriptive Writing

CONTENTS

Chapter 9
Personal Narrative

A personal narrative is a story—a story that mirrors you and your experiences. In it, you may tell about a time when you were afraid, lost something (or someone), found joy, learned a tough lesson, or discovered some secret. Whatever the topic, your story should help readers see, hear, touch, and taste those details that make your experience come alive.

As you prepare to choose your story and share it with others, get ready to relive the story yourself—to reexperience all that you felt, thought, or sensed during the original event. But also get ready to learn something new about the event, about others, and even about yourself. That's what writing a personal narrative can do.

What's Ahead

Overview
Writing a Personal Narrative

Writer's Goal

Your goal is to write a personal narrative about something significant that has happened to you. Write in a way that allows your readers to vividly relive the experience and learn something about you, and themselves.

Keys for Success

Be passionate. ■ Choose an experience from your life, anchored in your memory, that still makes you feel happy, angry, humble, afraid, or some other strong emotion.

Include characters. ■ Make the people in your narrative come to life. Let your story unfold through their actions and words. Above all, show how you—and these other people—react to the experience.

Create memorable descriptions. ■ Choose details that create pictures in your readers' minds. First, use your senses to trigger the readers' senses. What did you see? What did you hear? Next, choose strong nouns and active verbs. Finally, show—don't tell.

Topics to Consider

Memorable experiences can be categorized in a number of ways. Understanding these categories may help you identify possible subjects for your narratives. *Remember:* Your personal narratives should show something significant about yourself and about human nature in general.

- **Initiation:** Think of a time when you had to prove yourself, test your abilities, or "grow up." Share this "test" with your reader.
- **Loss:** Explore a time when you lost someone or something that was important to you.
- **Run-In:** Consider an unavoidable confrontation with another person. How did you react to the situation? What did you learn about yourself?
- **Arrival:** Recall when you were the new kid on the block or in school. How did the experience change your life? Or remember a time when someone new arrived in your life. How did this person affect you?
- **Occasion:** Focus on a revealing get-together, celebration, holiday, party, or vacation experience. What did you learn from the experience?

Next Step Read the model essays and perform the activities that follow. As you read, think of "defining experiences" in your life. How did each shape you? Would your readers find something of value for themselves in your experiences? Would they sense the importance of your experience?

Personal Narrative

A common personal narrative is the anecdote—a short, direct story that adds spark to your writing while introducing a topic or illustrating an idea. Below are two anecdotes taken from essays in this book.

Anecdote introducing a topic:

The story gets our attention and shows some causes and effects of stress.

1 It was 8:00 a.m., her husband Lance had left for work without filling the tank on the Mazda, and her daughter Gina had gotten on the school bus without her show-and-tell bunny. "Great!" thought Jan, "now I have to get gas at Demler's, stop by Gina's school, and drop Alex off at day care— all before my 9:30 class!" Quickly she grabbed the diaper bag, picked up the baby, and headed for the door. At 9:35, with her heart pounding and hands sweating, she scrambled into the classroom, found an open seat, and was hurriedly pulling out her psych notes when the prof asked, "So . . . precisely what does Jung mean by 'collective unconscious'—Jan?"

The transition links the anecdote and the thesis.

2 "Uh . . . what was the question?" she responded.

3 Does the scene sound familiar—too much work, too little time, and too much stress?

From "Life-Threatening Stress," page **187**

Anecdote illustrating a point:

The transition tells why the anecdote is used.

1 Steve is a good example. When he entered the nursing home just six months ago, he was experiencing the early stages of dementia. Today, however, his illness is much more advanced. The stress of moving into this new environment and leaving his wife at home alone affected Steve deeply. When he first arrived, Steve often cried and begged to be taken home. "I'll give you $20—please just take me home," he'd plead.

The quote and description show how a dementia patient feels.

2 Painfully, I would explain, "Steve, this is your home." After some time, the situation got so bad that he would not sleep or eat. He was depressed, and he cried often, thinking that no one cared about him. Eventually, Steve was given stronger drugs to help with the depression. For a few months, the medication seemed to work—he laughed at jokes and occasionally told one himself. But then Steve's dementia returned. Soon he was asking his same sad questions: "Where am I?" and "Do you know what I'm doing here?"

The transition shifts the focus.

3 So what is the best "medication" for people with dementia?

From "Understanding Dementia," page **241**

write

Reading for Better Writing

1. Check the essay from which each anecdote is taken and explain why the story does or does not accomplish its task.
2. How does each transitional sentence link the story to the rest of the essay?
3. Find the introductory anecdotes on pages **213** and **237**, and explain why each is effective.

Personal Narrative

In the following narrative, student writer Miguel Surieno tells about one event that was part of a painful episode in his family's life.

Dad

The opening introduces characters and sets the scene.

It was noon, and my mom sat slumped in a chair by the kitchen table. *1* Her eyes lifted only briefly when I entered the house. Her cheeks were streaked with tears, and Mr. Marshall, the high school vice-principal, sat in a chair across from her as she sniveled.

"Odd," I thought. "I didn't know they were close." I assumed that Mom *2* wasn't feeling well, but thought little of her crying—it wasn't uncommon. Because I didn't want to intrude, and because my buddy's Grand Am was honking in the driveway, I headed back out the door, pausing to grab my wallet and tell her that we were going downtown and would probably catch a movie. As an afterthought, I popped my head back in and asked, "Where's Dad?"

"He's in Atlanta for a meeting," she choked. Such trips weren't unusual. *3* He'd meet with other principals or go to assessment seminars—guess I'd forgotten about this trip. At least his absence somewhat explained Mr. Marshall's being there.

But she had lied, not wanting to ruin my day off from school. *4*

A transition indicates a shift in the action.

About 11:30 that night, my friend dropped me off. We had had a good *5* time, and I was tired. As usual, I walked in the front door and plopped down on the blue love seat in our living room. I knew that Mom would be there waiting for me, and I was ready to study the ivy-wallpaper pattern while enduring the interrogation.

"What movie did you watch?" *6*

"I forget." *7*

"Who was there?" *8*

"The usual." *9*

"Who's the usual?" *10*

However, this late night was different. Mom sat across from me, her *11* legs tucked under her as she parked on the end of the couch where most of her evenings were spent reading. But instead of asking the usual questions, she just looked at me and said softly, "Your father is in St. Joseph's Hospital."

She paused. I stared straight ahead. *12*

Dialogue provides background information.

"This morning he left the house with a gun, ready to take his own life." *13* My mother's eyes, already red and swollen, began to water over. "He's done some stupid stuff, and we need to forgive him for that."

"What are you talking about?" I needed an explanation. *14*

"You know Mrs. Corado?" She went on, not waiting for my response. *15* "Your father has had an affair with her over the past year, and her husband threatened to go public today. It's a real mess. Dad thought that he was going to lose us all. He thought . . . that it would be better to end his life than to live without you kids."

Silence.   *16*

I was a statue on that love seat, staring at the spot on the carpet near   *17* the chair. My face buzzed, and my vision became speckled, black and white. The room spun and twirled. My throat tightened, and I tried to breathe but couldn't. Slowly one tear rolled down my cheek, then another, with more following, until they streamed. I sniffed occasionally but didn't try to stop them.

"How could he do this?" was all I could think. My dad was the high   *18* school principal—somebody people respected, a role model. He was even an officer in our church. My parents loved each other—didn't they?

"Come here," Mom's voice called from across the room. I obeyed,   *19* crawling over the carpet and curling up, a 6' 2" four-year-old in my mother's arms.

She held me, and I cried. ■   *20*

> The writer concludes by showing how he felt.

Reading for Better Writing

1. The first three paragraphs introduce the narrative. What do they tell you about the father, mother, and narrator?

2. In the middle of the narrative, the writer includes a short dialogue that he anticipates between himself and his mother. What does the dialogue tell you about their relationship?

3. In a sentence or two, what theme or thesis is implied in this brief narrative?

audio

Personal Narrative

In this essay, student writer Jacqui Nyangi Owitti recalls an important personal experience in her life that taught her the pain of loss.

Mzee Owitti

The opening sets the scene and gives background information.

1   I am about 12 years old. We are en route from Nairobi, the capital city, to the rural area of Kisumu on the eastern shores of Lake Victoria in western Kenya where my grandparents live. My five brothers and I are traveling with Mum on the overnight train. I am not particularly sad, though I know what has happened. I base my reactions on my mother's and, since she appears to be handling the whole thing well, I am determined to do the same. You see, my grandfather has died. My dad's dad.

2   We reach the town of my ancestry just as dawn lazily turns into early morning. We buy snacks and hire a car for the last leg of the journey. We then meander through a bewildering maze of mud huts, sisal scrub, and sandy clay grassland, until we come within sight of my grandfather's land, the place where my father grew up.

The narrator describes what she sees and how she feels.

3   The first thing I notice is a crude "tent" made by sticking four poles in the ground, crisscrossing the top with long branches, and covering that with thatch. Despite the early hour, the place is filled with dignitaries, guests, and people like my mother's parents who have traveled far to honor our family. I am struck by the stillness and all-pervading silence. Everything seems frozen. Time itself seems to mourn, and even the wind is still. The car stops a short distance from the property, and we sit motionless and quiet.

Verbs in present tense describe the action.

4   I turn to my mother, questioning. But she has drawn a handkerchief from somewhere and is climbing out of the car. Almost as an actor on the stage, she releases a sound I have never heard before. It is a moan, a scream, and a sob that is deep-throated, guttural, and high-pitched all at the same time. This sudden transformation from a calm, chipper person to a stricken stranger strikes in me a fear that I will long remember. Holding her handkerchief to her face, she breaks into a shuffling run. I sit in the car petrified, watching the drama unfold.

The last sentence explains the women's actions.

5   Out of seemingly nowhere, wailing answers my mother's cry. Other women appear at a run, heading for my mother, hands fluttering from the tops of their heads, to their waists, to their feet. Their heads are thrown back and from side to side in restless anguish. Their bodies are half-bent forward, and their feet are in constant motion even though no distance is covered. My aunts and close female relatives weep, letting loose high-pitched ululating moaning in support of my mother. As the wife of the first child and only son, she commands a high place, and she must not grieve alone.

In the confusion, one lady is knocked down, and she seems to rock ₆ with her legs separated in a way that in other circumstances would be inappropriate and humiliating. Oddly, the people in the tent, mostly male, appear to have seen and heard nothing. They continue silent and still. The whole scene seems unreal. Seeing my fear and confusion, the driver talks soothingly, explaining what is going on.

A paragraph describes one segment of the ceremony.

The wailing and mourning continue intermittently for a couple of days. ₇ Then the time comes for my grandfather to be taken from the mortuary in Kisumu to his final resting place. We all travel to the mortuary. He is dressed in his best suit and then taken to church, where his soul is committed to God. Afterward, the procession starts for home. On the way we are met by the other mourners, who, according to tradition, will accompany the hearse on foot, driving along the cows that are a symbol of wealth in life and a testament to a good life, respectability, and honor in death. Being city kids unable to jog for an hour with the mourners and cows, we ride in a car.

A transition word indicates a shift.

Finally, we are back at the homestead. My grandfather is put in the ₈ house where he spent the latter part of his life. The crying and mourning are now nearly at a feverish pitch, and the sense of loss is palpable. However, before people may enter the house to pay their last respects, one—they call him "Ratego"—must lead the way to say his good-byes. Suddenly, there is a commotion, and I stare in disbelief as a big bull, taller than my tall-for-your-age twelve-year-old height and wider than the doorway, is led toward

Precise words tell what the narrator sees and smells.

my grandfather's house. Long, thick horns stick out of the colossal head. The body, pungent with an ammonia-laced, grassy smell, is a mosaic of black and brown—an odorous, pulsing mountain.

The bull's wild, staring eyes seem fixed on me. An old, barefoot man, ₉ dressed in a worn, too-short jacket and dusty black pants, leads this bull with a frayed rope. He waves his rod, yelling and leaping in syncopation with the bull's snorting and pawing. Dust puffs dance around their feet. The bull is a symbol of high honor for my grandfather, and only the largest bull in the land can embody this deep respect. Although I do not fully comprehend its significance, I know that it is the biggest animal I have ever seen. I step back as people try to get the bull into the house to pay its respects to my grandfather. After much yelling, shoving, and cries of pain from those whose feet the bull steps on, the effort is abandoned. Ratego is much too big.

The narrative approaches its climax.

As the bull is led away into the *boma*, people enter the room that has ₁₀ been emptied of furniture. I squeeze through the heaving, weeping mass, almost suffocating in the process. The room is surprisingly cool and dim, unlike the hot and bright sun outside. I approach curiously and cautiously, not knowing what to expect. At last I stand before the casket and look at my grandfather. He does not look dead. In fact, he is smiling! He looks like the person I remember, who always had a smile and an unshared secret lurking in the depths of his eyes.

A flashback adds depth to the present.

I peer into his face, recalling a time when I was four and he caught me doing something that deserved a reprimand. I had thought no one had seen me. However, my grandfather, on one of his rare visits to the city, had seen. Standing in front of his casket, I again hear him laugh. I remember how his kind, brown eyes had twinkled, and his white mustache, white teeth, and rich bitter-chocolate face had broken into an all-knowing, but-you-can-trust-me smile. I remember how the deep love that radiated from him assured me that I was his no matter what. And I remember how I had responded to his love by laughing happily and then skipping away, his answering laugh reverberating in my ears.

11

The narrator describes a pivotal point in the story.

That is my grandfather. Death cannot possibly touch him! Then I look closer and realize that the white streak breaking up his face is not the white teeth I remember. It is, instead, cotton stuffed into his mouth, as white as his teeth had been, making a mockery of my memories. At that moment, my granddaddy dies.

12

The last sentence offers a powerful image.

Until this point the whole has been a drama played out before my stunned, wide-eyed gaze. Rich in ancestry and tradition, its very nature and continuity are a celebration of life rather than death, fostering in me a keen sense of identity and a strong desire to keep the ancestral torch burning brightly, fiercely, and with pride. Now, however, Grandpa is dead. It is now that I cry. I am grieving. My granddaddy is gone, and the weighted arrow of sorrow pierces home. The pain is personal, unrelenting, and merciless. I stare at him and cannot tear myself away. I weep, saying over and over that he is smiling, he is smiling. My heartbreak and tears echo the refrain. He is smiling—a radiant, unforgettable smile. ■

13

write

Reading for Better Writing

1. The writer uses verbs in the present tense to tell her story. How does this choice affect (a) the clarity of the plot, (b) the tension in the episode about the bull, and (c) your empathy with the narrator in the closing?

2. Choose a paragraph containing a particularly vivid description. How do the word choice, sentence structure, and punctuation affect your ability to sense the action?

3. In a conversation with an editor of this book, Jacqui Nyangi Owitti described her love for her grandfather and her pride in her heritage. Does the story reflect that love and pride? Explain.

Personal Narrative

Asiya S. Tschannerl is a professional writer. In the essay below, she recalls a pivotal time in her life, and she reflects on how the events impacted her development and worldview.

One Remembers Most What One Loves

The opening describes the writer's memories.

I have often been commended for my memory. I can even remember being held when I was adopted at three months of age. Perhaps one only recalls events that profoundly change one's life.

I remember my youth very clearly. How the seasons would change! September would bring its chilly air and a nervous start of a new school year. November would be full of excitement, with its strong gusts of wind and swirling sandstorms. It was amazing to look at a grain of sand and know that it had come from over 2,000 miles away, from the Gobi desert. I remember leaning back against that wind and not being able to fall. I can still see that stream of bicycles going to the city, every head clad with a thin scarf to protect against the sand. . . .

She reflects on why and how she remembers.

Perhaps my memory is fostered by the countless nights I spent memorizing Chinese characters, stroke after stroke. In any case, I cannot forget. I love my childhood. I love Beijing.

Bei sha tan nong ji xue yuan. This is the name of the Chinese compound we lived in, an agricultural mechanization institute on the outskirts of Beijing. During the day, my father worked there while I would accompany my mother into the city. My mother taught sociology at the Beijing Foreign Languages Institute, and I attended its adjoining Chinese elementary school. At age nine, I was in a country I had not lived in since I was a toddler, and my Chinese was very poor. Hence, I entered first grade having already had four years of American grade school.

I remember my apprehension when my teacher introduced me on the first day of school. A hush fell over the classroom as forty pairs of wide eyes beheld for the first time a person of African descent. After what seemed a long time, class went on as usual, and finding myself amidst a maze of unintelligible dialogue, I took out my coloring pencils and began to draw. The children around me smiled shyly at me, curious to see what I was drawing. Such was the beginning of enduring friendships.

A transition indicates a shift in the story.

As the months rolled by, the sea of gibberish slowly became a wealth of vocabulary. I never knew that a language could describe things so precisely—but this is not to be wondered at when one considers the 15,000 characters that comprise the Chinese language, of which one must know at least 3,000 to be literate. . . .

Chinese class would involve reading passages from our textbooks and learning new characters. Breaks between every class would be used to clean the classroom—sprinkling water on the concrete floor to dampen the famous Beijing dust before sweeping, washing the blackboards with wet cloths, and neatening up the teacher's desk. One of these breaks was used for everyone to massage their heads while relaxing music wafted down from the announcement speaker attached to the ceiling. In the middle of the day, everybody went home to eat lunch and nap for a few hours, after which classes would continue till four in the afternoon. . . .

> The writer gives examples of classroom activity.

At first I found the idea of Saturday classes repelling, but I soon forgot that I ever had a two-day weekend. Sundays I looked forward to the hour of Disney cartoons in Chinese. Every other weekend I visited a nearby cow farm and helped feed the cows and calves. I remember talking at length with a milkmaid who had never before heard of the African slave trade, and her subsequent wishful disbelief. *8*

> She describes what she did and how she felt.

I remember the proud feeling of putting on my red scarf for the first time. By then, I had read a lot about Chairman Mao and talked to people about the history of China. I felt a nationalist pride wearing this scarf, as the Little Red Guards had forty years ago in helping to defeat the Japanese militarists. The red scarf meant that one was committed to helping all those in difficulty and I proceeded to do this with great zeal—picking up watermelons for a man whose wheelbarrow wheels had split, helping old people across busy roads, etc. . . . *9*

I can still see the faces of shopkeepers who had had their backs turned when I had asked for an item and, when they turned around, were astounded to see a little black kid speaking perfect Mandarin. I think I even delighted in shocking people, purposefully going on a raid of the local shops. But I found that people were genuinely touched that I had taken the time to study their difficult language. I was warmly embraced as one of their children. *10*

> The writer introduces a pivotal event.

Fourth grade brought the Tiananmen massacre. Before the shootings, my mother and I had gone every day to visit her students and friends at the square. My heart felt like it was bursting with love, so strong was the feeling of community. There were so many people there that every part of your body was in contact with someone else. Once I looked triumphantly at my mother and exclaimed, "See? When you're with the people, you can't fall!" I remember drawing an analogy between the people and the November winds I could lean back against. Of course, it was also a political statement. *11*

> The quotation reflects irony.

The night of the massacre, I could hear the firings of guns from our home. My mother, who had been in the square at the time, managed to get back safely. The silence the next day pervaded the whole city, and the sadness was unbearable. I remember feeling betrayed. How could this happen to my people? For the first time in forty years, the army had gone against its people. The young said that this was what socialism had come to, but the elders, recognizing that this was a form of fascism, muttered softly that this would never have happened under Chairman Mao. *12*

The vision of black marks on the roads made from burning vehicles is engraved in my mind. The pools of blood were quickly washed away, bullet *13* holes patched, and death tolls revised. Near our institute there was the distinct scent of decomposing bodies brought from the city. These may have been buried or set fire to—no one knew, no one asked or verified. No one dared to speak, but in everyone was a mixture of anger, anguish, and horror.

A transition is used to indicate a shift in the story.

My parents' following separation accentuated the sadness. I spent 14 months trying to heal our broken family, almost believing that that achievement would heal the outside world as well. Fourth grade ended early, and I longed to get away from the sadness. It was at this point that my mother decided to return to the U.S. I dreaded leaving, but I anticipated the change of atmosphere. I was in for a surprise.

For more than a year, I experienced culture shock. Everything was 15 familiar but new—the clothes, hairstyles, houses, toilets. People had so many things they never used or took for granted, and yet they considered themselves not to be well-off. I was incensed at how little respect my peers had for their parents and elders. How anyone could hear what the teachers were saying when classes were so noisy was beyond me. Everyone seemed arrogant and ignorant of other cultures. Kids wouldn't believe I was American because they thought I "spoke weird." They asked me, "Why can't you talk normal?" I grew tired of explaining. Even African Americans thought I was from elsewhere. The pride I had felt when I represented Black America in China suffered a pang. I was disgusted by the racism against the Orient that I discovered to be rampant. I found myself pining for the comfortable existence I had come from.

The writer reflects on her entire experience.

Seven years later, I still like to surprise Chinese people with my 16 knowledge of the language when I happen to meet them. I think it is important to show that cultural gaps can be crossed, and without much difficulty as long as there is an open mind. I go back to China when money is available—I visit Beijing and the cow farm, reliving old memories and making new ones. Perhaps one remembers most what one loves. ■

write

Reading for Better Writing

1. What is the main idea of the essay? How is that idea introduced in the opening, supported in the middle, and reinforced in the conclusion?

2. Choose a paragraph that you find engaging. How do the writer's word choice and sentence structure help communicate the paragraph's main idea?

3. Like most narratives, this narrative relies on chronological organization. Trace how the writer orders the events and how much weight and attention she gives to each. How effectively does the writer organize her narrative?

Guidelines
Writing a Personal Narrative

1. **Select a topic.** Think about your own past experiences. Sort through the stories you recall and choose a story that is important enough to share with others. Think of a way to approach this past experience in a personal narrative.

    TIP: If you can't think of an interesting story off the top of your head, try writing in response to the following statement: *Remember a time when you first discovered that the world was (a) stranger, (b) more wonderful, or (c) more complex than you had thought as a child.* Think about how that experience prepared you to be who you are today.

2. **Narrow your focus.** Once you have chosen an experience to write about, begin to narrow your topic by focusing on a specific moment or outcome. The following questions help you find a clear focus:

    - What is the key moment—the significant point or climax—in the story?
    - What led up to this key moment? What resulted from it?
    - What was really going on?
    - How did others experience the event?
    - What has time taught you about this experience?
    - What would you have changed?

3. **Determine your purpose.** After you have a specific focus, decide why you are telling your story. Personal narratives can serve one of many purposes, or several at once. Consider these:

    - To entertain
    - To warn
    - To celebrate
    - To illustrate
    - To remind
    - To gain sympathy

4. **Gather details.** Gather material that will serve your purpose. Try sorting through photo albums, home videos, and letters. Interview someone who shared your experience or saw you through it. Consult your journal or diary.

5. **Collaborate.** Tell somebody your story out loud; then ask for comments and questions. Based on the feedback you receive, create a basic writing plan. Your plan can be anything from a simple list to a detailed outline.

6. **Write your first draft.** As you write, keep in mind your specific focus and your overall purpose for telling this story. Use the following strategies as you create your first draft:

   Set the stage. ■ Show where things happened and exactly what it was like there. Describe the atmosphere, the people, and the events by using precise details that appeal to the five senses. If appropriate, use comparisons and metaphors to make the descriptions hit home.

   Include dialogue. ■ Recall and create conversations between the people in your story to infuse your narrative with a sense of reality.

   TIP: Use dialogue to enhance a key scene or to explain the relationship between people. But be selective—don't let dialogue dribble on for its own sake.

   Build the plot. ■ Arouse and sustain interest by establishing conflict, building suspense, highlighting the main point, and showing the outcome.

   Express your feelings. ■ It may help to include both past and present thoughts and feelings—those you had during the experience and those you have now, looking back on the past.

   Use transitions. ■ Words like *as, before, meanwhile,* and *later* show where your story is leading. (See page **70**.)

   Select verbs carefully. ■ Verbs affect the movement and voice of your story. Choose active, strong verbs, and make sure tenses accurately reflect time sequences and relationships.

7. **Share your story.** Show your draft to someone. What main point does this reader see in your story? What suggestions or questions does the reader have?

8. **Revise your writing.** Carefully review and revise your writing. Remember that your goal is to re-create an interesting incident or event for your readers. Ask yourself the following questions:
   - Does the writing focus on a specific incident or event?
   - Does the writing contain effective details, descriptions, and dialogue?
   - Does the narrative effectively state or imply a theme, thesis, or point of significance?
   - Does the writing sound sincere and natural?
   - Will readers appreciate the way the story is told?

9. **Edit and proofread.** (See the checklist on page **88**.)

10. **Prepare your final copy.** Use an appropriate type font and size. Leave the right margin ragged (uneven). Avoid placing the first line of a new paragraph at the very bottom of a page. Print your final copy on quality paper.

Writing Checklist

Use these six traits to check the quality of your writing; then revise as needed:

____ The **ideas** focus on a specific experience or event and present an engaging picture of the action and people involved.

____ The **organization** pattern adds to the clarity of the piece and includes a clear beginning that pulls readers in.

____ The **voice** shows that the writer is truly interested in the subject by speaking knowledgeably and enthusiastically.

____ The **words** *show* instead of *tell about*; they appeal to the senses and evoke pictures in the reader's mind.

____ The **sentences** are clear, varied in structure, and smooth.

____ The **copy** is correct, is clean, and follows assigned guidelines for format.

write

Writing Activities

1. Review "Dad" and "Mzee Owitti," observing how the writers help you share their experiences by presenting vivid details in an open, honest way. List a few of your own experiences that you would like to explore and share. Then choose one that would be an appropriate subject for a personal narrative. Write the narrative, perhaps using some of the same organizational strategies employed in these models.

2. In "One Remembers Most What One Loves," the writer recalls a critical time in her life and notes how it permanently affected her outlook. Brainstorm to create a list of such events in your own life. Choose one to write about; make sure that you include some reflections on how that time ultimately changed your attitude.

3. Write a personal narrative based on a memory from your childhood. Write it from the point of view of the child who had that experience, without the benefit of the hindsight you now have. Try to remember how your experience was shaped by all of your senses.

4. In ten years, how will your life differ from your life today? Write a personal narrative from the future, describing one of the events that led to your (future) position in life. Remember to include characters and their reactions to the experience.

Chapter 10
Personal Reflection

audio

It is human nature to reflect. On this score, eighteenth-century poet Robert Burns thought mice luckier than people. In his poem "To a Mouse," Burns noted that mice worry only about the present, whereas humans worried about past, present, and future woes. Whether reflecting on the past is unique to humans or not, we do know that this human trait brings joy, regret, and a thousand variations of those feelings to both young and old.

A personal reflection is often written to draw wisdom from past experiences. Accordingly, you may want to explore an earlier time in your life and reflect on why you felt as you did when you suffered a stinging setback or won a glorious victory.

In this chapter, you'll find topics to consider, model essays, and guidelines that will help you develop your own personal reflection.

What's Ahead

- Overview: Personal Reflection
    - Student Models
    - Professional Model
- Guidelines
- Writing Checklist and Activities

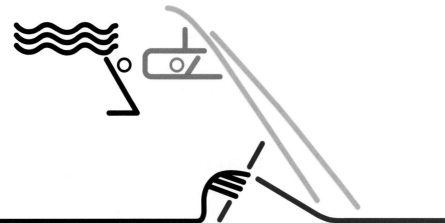

Overview
Writing a Personal Reflection

Writer's Goal

Your goal is to write an essay in which you share one or more past experiences and reflect on their importance for your life.

Keys for Success

Recall precise details. ■ To understand and appreciate your reflections, readers first have to grasp exactly what you experienced. For that reason, you must describe those key details (sights, smells, tastes) that make the experience memorable to you—and worth reflecting on. Often you will find these details in the hardly-noticed-at-the-time part of your memory.

Probe the topic. ■ The mind-searching aspect of writing this essay happens while asking *so-why* questions: *So why does this picture still make me smile?* or *Why does his comment still hurt?* or *Why did I do that when I knew better—or did I know better?* Your answers will help explain why this memory is important to you.

Tell what you find. ■ Your readers need to experience what you experienced, so don't hide what's embarrassing, or painful, or still unclear. Show them the details clearly, explain your insights honestly, and then trust readers to respond with sensitivity, appreciation, and respect.

Topics to Consider

The most promising topics are experiences that gave you insights into yourself, and possibly into others as well. Often such an experience will have led you or others to change patterns of thinking, feeling, or behavior. To identify such topics, consider the categories and then list whatever experiences come to mind:

- Times when you felt *secure, hopeful, distraught, appreciated, confident, frightened, exploited,* or *misunderstood.*
- Times when you made a decision about *lifestyles, careers, education, politics, religion, leaving home,* or *getting an education.*
- Events that tested your *will, patience, self-concept,* or *goals.*
- Events that changed or confirmed your assessment of a *person, group, institution, religious belief, political conviction,* or *philosophical worldview.*

Next Step Read the model essays and perform the activities that follow. As you read, note how the writers help you grasp *what* they experienced, and *why* their experiences are important.

Personal Reflection

In this reflective essay, student writer Jessie Cooper relates a story of pain inflicted by catty classmates on her first day at a new school.

audio

School Style

SCHOOL STYLE: Although it's not one of those textbook terms that *1* you have to memorize like *metamorphosis* or *immigration* or *mitosis*, it is a concept usually learned in school.

"Hurry up, Jess!" my mom called to me from the kitchen. "The bus'll *2* be here soon."

"Yeah, okay," I called back, glancing once more in the mirror. "PER- *3* FECT!" I thought. I looked *exactly* the way I wanted to.

> **The writer invites us to visualize the setting.**

It was my first day in fifth grade at my new school. My family had *4* moved again, this time from Chicago to Milwaukee, and I was nervous about making my debut. But I was prepared—dressed for comfort and confidence in my favorite shirt. It was long sleeved and plain white with pink flowers scattered across the top. In the front, a small white fringe hung just below the flowers. This shirt was my favorite because it reminded me of Tennessee, the place where I was born. The day before, I had made sure that my shirt was washed; and the night before, I carefully set it out, along with my best jeans and tennis shoes. As I went to bed that night, the shirt made me less fearful of getting on a new school bus and going to a new school.

When the bus pulled in front of our house the next morning, I climbed *5* on board for the short ride to the school's front door. When the bus stopped, I grabbed my backpack, walked into the building, wandered down a long hallway, and stepped into a classroom that was already filled with students. It was early morning (much too early, I thought), the sun was just starting to peek through the open windows, and a warm breeze brought in

> **She describes how students fail to respond to her.**

the smell of fall in Wisconsin. While no one said "Hi" to me, the students' unfriendliness didn't bother me then—I was just relieved to be in the right room when the bell rang.

After looking around the room for a while, I found the desk with *6* "Jessie Cooper" taped in large letters across the top. There I set my backpack on the floor and began unloading the supplies that my mom and I had bought the previous week. Each item felt and smelled new as I carefully placed it in just the right spot. While I worked, I sensed that some students were watching me, and that made me uneasy. But then I remembered what

> **She cites what gives her confidence.**

I was wearing. Glancing down at my favorite shirt, I felt a wave of confidence: in that shirt, I could handle anything! As my fingertips straightened its fringe, I smiled at my newly sharpened pencils.

It was then that I noticed the three girls standing next to the chalk- $_7$
board on the other side of the room. They stared, nodded in my direction
now and then, and talked to each other in hushed whispers. Being new, I
wasn't surprised by their curiosity, and I smiled when one girl, who I later
learned was Laura, walked toward me. She was tall for fifth grade and wore
her long, brown hair pulled back into a ponytail. She had on a short-sleeved
red shirt with GAP printed boldly above her arms, which she crossed tightly
in front of her. Thinking that she was coming to say hello, I got ready to
respond.

**The writer
builds toward
the climax.**

"Um," Laura began, looking down at me as disdainfully as a ten-year- $_8$
old can, "I don't know where you're from, but around here, we don't wear
shirts like that." As my smile faded, she turned with a flick of her ponytail
and walked back to her friends. She hadn't even asked me my name. When
I got home that afternoon, I angrily pulled off my now least-favorite shirt,
crumpled it up, shoved it to the very bottom of my dresser drawer, and
never wore it again.

**She reflects
on what she
learned her
first day.**

Today, as I think back on my first day in fifth grade, I remember the $_9$
events—and the lesson—very well. I had wanted to go to school to fit in
and to be liked. But what I did instead was learn the meaning of school
style: school style means pressure to conform; it means sacrificing your own
tastes to earn the acceptance of others. ■

write

Reading for Better Writing

1. What does the writer reveal about her character in the first long
   paragraph?
2. In what ways is the experience unique to the writer? In what ways is it
   universal?
3. The writer is looking back on a childhood experience. What were her
   feelings at the time? What perspective does she have now?
4. Reflect on a time when you tried to conform (or not to conform) in dress
   or behavior to a school style. At what age, if any, do people outgrow such
   pressures?

Personal Reflection

In this essay, student writer Rebecca Babagian discusses her dilemma as a female athlete: become "manly" and succeed, or follow her feminine instincts and risk failure. Notice how the writer reflects on her days as an athlete and the perspective she now has about that time in her life.

Like a Girl

The opening provides a vivid anecdote introducing the dilemma.

"Okay, everybody, line up on the gray line and face me!" Chuck [1] ordered. He knew that his presence commanded our attention—an all-girl class of seven-year-old gymnasts. After all, he owned the gymnastics program, and that alone made him the most revered man in the gym. But it was Chuck's tall stature, thick chest, and resounding voice that made him intimidating. When Chuck spoke, you listened.

"Now, all of you know how running helps you in the floor exercises [2] and vaulting, right?" he asked. Clad in our leotards, we stood quietly nodding our heads and looking back into the cool blue eyes behind the thick, rectangular glasses.

"Good," he said, "because many of you [3] are doing a lot of this kind of running . . ." and he proceeded to jog in front of us with his arms flopping loosely at his sides like strands of spaghetti. We laughed as he pranced around in a circle. But when he paused suddenly, squared his shoulders, and stepped toward us—our giggling stopped.

And so it was that at age seven, I stopped running like a girl.

"There is no room for that kind of [4] running in gymnastics. You've got to stop running like girls. Make fists with your hands and pump your arms—don't let 'em flop around. You have to learn to run correctly!" he said.

The writer gives the reader a broader view.

And so it was that at age seven, I stopped running like a girl. A few [5] years later, I quit gymnastics, but Chuck's instructions still influenced my running—I felt ashamed to run girl-like. Eventually I started basketball, and in the ninth grade, I learned additional requirements for female athleticism. I learned to change not only my female style, but my female tendencies as well. I became my coach's instrument on the court. I was tuned to his commands, and the quality of my performance hinged on his judgment.

The writer reflects on the compromises she felt forced to make.

My goal became losing myself in the sport so the coach could reform [6] my behavior. I learned to accept the furious locker-room spiels at half-time when defending myself was forbidden. I learned to subordinate my will to the will of a coach who tried to transform us girls with discipline and mandates. We had mandates for everything: weight training, team dinners, extra-large jerseys, men's basketball shoes, men's basketball shorts, men's everything. I'm amazed the word "lady" was even associated with the sport.

The writer puts her past experience in a present perspective.

It's only in retrospect that I can see how I struggled to merge "successful athlete" and "evolving woman." To succeed on the court and to satisfy the coach, I had to learn new practices, a new philosophy, and even new values. Pleasing him would make me fulfilled, wouldn't it?

To please the coach, our team understood that we had to make a 7
choice. One choice was joining the girls who bulked up to the point that their clothes fit tight and boys would gawk at the thunderous thighs that shot out of their shorts. I hated that, though I worked out with this group. The other choice was joining the girls who wouldn't hit the court until their makeup was flawless. But no one took those girls too seriously, certainly not the coach. As a seven-year-old gymnast, I had to stop "running like a girl." As a high school basketball player, I had to stop "thinking like a girl."

She restates a key idea to sharpen her point.

In other words, I had to change who I wanted to be. I had to show 8
toughness and aggression in response to disappointment, pain, and even injuries. I had to accept bruises and multicolored contusions as honorable signs of hard work and success. In contrast, I had to reject displaying emotion—particularly crying—because it was a sign of weakness and "acting like a girl."

She captures the tension with images and contrast.

However, instead of being proud of my muscles, battle scars, and 9
aggression, I started hiding myself in baggy clothes, ashamed of the brute that I felt I had become. I found it hard feeling feminine while constantly having to be tough. While "being an athlete" was the reward, self-esteem was the sacrifice. Under my sweaty jersey, I was still a girl who sometimes preferred putting on makeup, a pretty dress, and going to the Winter Formal—more than putting on a uniform and playing in a basketball tournament. I struggled to balance the demands of being masculine on the court and feminine off of it.

The writer explains how she restored her sense of worth.

In time I learned that my own sense of worth could not be determined 10
by anyone but me. My experiences made me reevaluate the qualities that I saw in myself and that I wanted to develop. I learned to be confident about what I felt and thought. I learned that I could find my confidence away from the dictates of others who criticized or condemned my instinctual tendencies as a woman. I could be true to myself without concealing anything.

Unfortunately, I didn't arrive at this point until my basketball career 11
had ended. At times I wonder how this new self-assurance would have affected my success as an athlete during those years.

> **The writer shares a significant moment and a vision of what could be.**

I remember the day during my senior year when basketball season was over. I threw my man-sized, man-style basketball shoes into the garbage, along with my extra-long socks. I had my hair styled at the beauty parlor, and I purchased wildly feminine undergarments for the first time in my life. I looked toward the future, toward the great unknown, beyond the years when confusion blurred my sense of womanhood. I thought about the kind of woman that I wanted to become. I envisioned myself running . . . freely, confidently, . . . my hair flying every which way. I pushed forward, carefree. Freed from constraint, I ran like Rebecca. I ran like me. ■

12

write

Reading for Better Writing

1. In the opening four paragraphs, the writer describes how the gymnastics coach imitated the girls' running. Is this opening anecdote effective? Why or why not?

2. In paragraphs five and six, the writer describes how she gave up "female tendencies" to succeed in sports. What does this passage suggest about her current view of the coach, basketball, and herself?

3. In paragraph nine, the writer reflects on how it was difficult to feel feminine while constantly having to be tough. Explain what she found difficult, and what insight she gained by thinking about these issues.

4. The writer closes by reflecting on how her experience in sports helped her choose to run "like me." Explain how that phrase does or does not fit the writer's experience, personality, and goals.

Personal Reflection

In the following essay, author Richard Rodriguez reflects on his experiences with affirmative action and how these experiences caused him guilt and confusion.

None of This Is Fair

My plan to become a professor of English—my ambition during long years in college at Stanford, then in graduate school at Columbia and Berkeley—was complicated by feelings of embarrassment and guilt. So many times I would see other Mexican Americans and know we were alike only in race. And yet, simply because our race was the same, I was, during the last years of my schooling, the beneficiary of their situation. Affirmative-action programs had made it all possible. The disadvantages of others permitted my promotion: the absence of many Mexican Americans from academic life allowed my designation as a "minority student."

For me, opportunities had been extravagant. There were fellowships, summer research grants, and teaching assistantships. After only two years in graduate school, I was offered teaching jobs by several colleges. Invitations to Washington conferences arrived, and I had the chance to travel abroad as a "Mexican American representative." The benefits were often, however, too gaudy to please. In three published essays, in conversations with teachers, in letters to politicians, and at conferences, I worried about the issue of affirmative action. Often I proposed contradictory opinions. Though consistent was the admission that—because of an early, excellent education—I was no longer a principal victim of racism or any other social oppression. I said that, but still I continued to indicate on applications for financial aid that I was a Hispanic American. It didn't really occur to me to say anything else, or to leave the question unanswered.

Thus I complied with and encouraged the odd bureaucratic logic of affirmative action. I let government officials treat the disadvantaged condition of many Mexican Americans with my advancement. Each fall my presence was noted by Health, Education, and Welfare Department statisticians. As I pursued advanced literary studies and learned the skill of reading Spenser and Wordsworth and Empson, I would hear myself numbered among the culturally disadvantaged. Still, silent, I didn't object.

But the irony cut deep. And guilt would not be evaded by averting my glance when I confronted a face like my own in a crowd. By late 1975, nearing the completion of my graduate studies at Berkeley, I was so wary of the benefits of affirmative action that I feared my inevitable success as an applicant for a teaching position. The months of fall—traditionally that time of academic job-searching—passed without my applying to a single school. When one of my professors chanced to learn this in late November, he was astonished, then furious. He yelled at me: Did I think that because I was a minority student jobs would just come looking for me? What was I

The writer introduces a problem in his experience.

He summarizes his experiences and his struggle.

Recalling feelings of guilt, he reflects on the irony of his situation.

1

2

3

4

The writer summarizes an encounter.

thinking? Did I realize that he and several other faculty members had already written letters on my behalf? Was I going to start acting like some other minority students he had known? They struggled for success and then, when it was almost within reach, grew strangely afraid and let it pass. Was that it? Was I determined to fail?

I did not respond to his questions. I didn't want to admit to him, and 5 thus to myself, the reason I delayed.

I merely agreed to write to several schools. (In my letter I wrote: 6 "I cannot claim to represent disadvantaged Mexican Americans. The very fact that I am in a position to apply for this job should make that clear.") After two or three days, there were telegrams and phone calls, invitations to interviews, then airplane trips. A blur of faces and the murmur of their soft questions. And, over someone's shoulder, the sight of campus buildings shadowing pictures I had seen years before when I leafed through Ivy League catalogues with great expectations. At the end of each visit, interviewers would smile and wonder if I had any questions. A few times I quietly wondered what advantage my race had given me over other applicants. But that was an impossible question for them to answer without embarrassing me. Quickly, several persons insisted that my ethnic identity had given me no more than a "foot in the door"; at most, I had a "slight edge" over other applicants. "We just looked at your dossier with extra care and we liked what we saw. There was never any question of having to alter our standards. You can be certain of that."

He narrows the focus to his job-search experience.

In the early part of January, offers arrived on stiffly elegant stationery. 7 Most schools promised terms appropriate for any new assistant professor. A few made matters worse—and almost more tempting—by offering more: the use of university housing; an unusually large starting salary; a reduced teaching schedule. As the stack of letters mounted, my hesitation increased. I started calling department chairmen to ask for another week, then ten more days—"more time to reach a decision"—to avoid the decision I would need to make.

At school, meantime, some students hadn't received a single job offer. 8 One man, probably the best student in the department, did not even get a request for his dossier. He and I met outside a classroom one day, and he asked about my opportunities. He seemed happy for me. Faculty members beamed. They said they had expected it. "After all, not many schools are going to pass up getting a Chicano with a Ph.D. in Renaissance literature," somebody said, laughing. Friends wanted to know which of the offers I was going to accept. But I couldn't make up my mind. February came and I was running out of time and excuses. (One chairman guessed my delay was a bargaining ploy and increased his offer with each of my calls.) I had to promise a decision by the 10th—the 12th at the very latest.

As the search proceeds, the pressure and tension mount for the writer.

On the 18th of February, late in the afternoon, I was in the office I 9 shared with several other teaching assistants. Another graduate student was sitting across the room at his desk. When I got up to leave, he looked over to say in an uneventful voice that he had some big news. He had finally decided to accept a position at a faraway university. It was not a job he especially wanted, he admitted. He felt trapped, and depressed, since his job would separate him from his young daughter.

I tried to encourage him by remarking that he was lucky at least to have found a job. So many others hadn't been able to get anything. But before I finished speaking, I realized that I had said the wrong thing. And I anticipated his next question.   10

"What are your plans?" he wanted to know. "Is it true you've gotten an offer from Yale?"   11

I said that it was. "Only, I still haven't made up my mind."   12

He stared at me as I put on my jacket. And smiling, then unsmiling, he asked if I knew that he, too, had written to Yale. In his case, however, no one had bothered to acknowledge his letter with even a postcard. What did I think of that?   13

He gave me no time to answer.   14

"Damn!" he said sharply, and his chair rasped the floor as he pushed himself back. Suddenly, it was to me that he was complaining. "It's just not right, Richard. None of this is fair. You've done some good work, but so have I. I'll bet our records are just about equal. But when we look for jobs this year, it's a different story. You get all the breaks."   15

To evade his criticism, I wanted to side with him. I was about to admit the injustice of affirmative action. But he went on, his voice hard with accusation. "It's all very simple this year. You're a Chicano. And I am a Jew. That's the only real difference between us."   16

His words stung me: there was nothing he was telling me that I didn't know. I admitted everything already. But to hear someone else say these things, and in such an accusing tone, was suddenly hard to take. In a deceptively calm voice, I responded that he had simplified the whole issue. The phrases came like bubbles to the tip of my tongue: "new blood"; "the importance of cultural diversity"; "the goal of racial integration." These were all the arguments I proposed several years ago—and had long since abandoned. Of course, the offers were unjustifiable. I knew that. All I was saying amounted to a frantic self-defense. I tried to find an end to a sentence. My voice faltered to a stop.   17

"Yeah, sure," he said. "I've heard all that before. Nothing you say really changes the fact that affirmative action is unfair. You see that, don't you? There isn't any way for me to compete with you. Once there were quotas to keep my parents out of certain schools; now there are quotas to get you in, and the effect on me is the same as it was for them."   18

I listened to every word he spoke. But my mind was really on something else. I knew at that moment that I would reject all of the offers. I stood there silently surprised by what an easy conclusion it was. Having prepared for so many years to teach, having trained myself to do nothing   19

The writer details an especially important encounter.

Narration and quotation build the episode's intensity.

The narrative leads to a crisis of conscience.

He reveals the resolution of the crisis.

else, I had hesitated out of practical fear. But now that it was made, the decision came with relief. I immediately knew I had made the right choice.

The writer broadens the discussion.

My colleague continued talking, and I realized that he was simply right. 20 Affirmative-action programs are unfair to white students. But as I listened to him assert his rights, I thought of the seriously disadvantaged. How different they were from white, middle-class students who come armed with the testimony of their grades and aptitude scores and self-confidence to complain about the unequal treatment they now receive. I listen to them. I do not want to be careless about what they say. Their rights are important to protect. But inevitably when I hear them or their lawyers, I think about the most seriously disadvantaged, not simply Mexican Americans, but all those who do not ever imagine themselves going to college or becoming doctors: white, black, brown. Always poor. Silent. They are not plaintiffs before the court or against the misdirection of affirmative action. They lack the confidence (my confidence!) to assure their right to a good education. They lack the confidence and skills that a good primary and secondary education provides and that are prerequisites for informed public life. They remain silent.

He closes with a strong image.

The debate drones on and surrounds them in stillness. They are dis- 21 tant, faraway figures like the boys I have seen peering down from freeway overpasses in some other part of town. ■

Reading for Better Writing

1. The writer shares several experiences over several years. Trace these experiences. Describe the methods he uses to present them, and explain why he uses these methods.

2. He says that his life differed from the lives of those for whom affirmative action was intended. How does he support that point? Is the claim believable? Why?

3. The writer relates a key exchange with a Jewish classmate. Why are this classmate and his story especially important to the writer?

4. What role does reflection play in the essay? How does the writer weave his past and present thoughts and feelings into his experiences?

Guidelines
Writing a Personal Reflection

1. **Select a topic.** Choose an experience or experiences that influenced you in some key way—either confirming what you thought or planned at that time or changing those thoughts or plans. (Revisit the "Topics to Consider" on page 150 for additional ideas.)

   TIP: If you can't think of any experiences, try listing topics in response to the following statement: *Reflect on times when you first discovered that the world was one of the following—strange, wonderful, complex, frightening, boring, small, uncaring, like you, unlike you, full, or empty.* How did these experiences affect who you are today?

2. **Get the big picture.** Once you have chosen one or more experiences to write about, gather your thoughts by reflecting on the questions below through brainstorming or by freewriting.
   - What are the key moments—the pivotal points—in your experiences?
   - What led to these key moments? Why? What resulted from them?
   - What was going on from your perspective?
   - How did others experience the events?
   - What did you learn from this experience?
   - Did these experiences end as you had hoped? Why or why not?
   - What themes, conflicts, and insights arise from these experiences?
   - How do your feelings now differ from your feelings then?

   TIP: To find out more details about the event or people involved, sort through photo albums and home videos to trigger memories, talk to someone who shared your experiences or saw you through them, or consult your journal, diary, old letters, and saved e-mail.

3. **Get organized.**
   - Review your brainstorming or freewriting, and highlight key details, quotations, or episodes that you want to include in your writing.
   - Draft a brief outline that shows where key information fits into the big picture.
   - List the main events in chronological order or use a cluster to help you gather details related to your experiences.

4. **Write the first draft.** Review your outline and then rough out the first draft in one sitting. Then test your reflection for its significance. Does it answer these questions: what happened, how did the experience affect you, and how do you feel about it now?

5. **Review and revise.** After drafting the essay, take a break. Then read your document again for accuracy and completeness. Look first at the entire piece. Does it *say* what you wanted to say? Does it include any gaps or weak spots? Check your outline to make sure all key details are covered and in the right sequence. (See the checklist on page **76**.)

6. **Test your reflection.** Review what you say about the experiences:
   - Does the tone—whether sarcastic, humorous, regretful, or meditative—fit the content of the reflection?
   - Have you established a viewpoint, and is the reflection built on this point of view?
   - Will the intended readers appreciate the treatment of the subject?

7. **Get feedback.** Ask a classmate or someone in the writing center to read your paper, looking for the following:
   - An opening that pulls the reader into the reflection.
   - Experiences that are portrayed clearly and vividly.
   - An explanation of how you've changed that is woven naturally into the experiences.
   - Transitions that connect paragraphs effectively.
   - A conclusion that restates the point of the reflection clearly and succinctly.

8. **Edit and proofread your essay.** Once you have revised the content, organization, and voice of your personal reflection, polish it. Carefully check your choice of words, the clarity of your sentences, and your grammar, usage, and mechanics.

9. **Publish your writing by doing one or more of the following:**
   - Share your essay with friends and family.
   - Publish it in a journal or on a Web site.
   - Place a copy in your professional portfolio.
   - Submit a copy to your instructor.

Writing Checklist

Use these six traits to check the quality of your writing; then revise as needed:

____ The **ideas** (the topic being reflected upon) provide the reader with an interesting look at your experience.

____ The **organization** pattern effectively blends narration and reflection.

____ The **voice** is reflective, and characters and events are treated respectfully.

____ The **words** are precise and clear; descriptions help the reader experience what you experienced.

____ The **sentences** are smooth and natural.

____ The **copy** is correct and in a format appropriate for your assignment.

write

Writing Activities

1. In "School Style," the writer reflects on an experience that taught her a negative lesson. What negative lesson have you received from an experience? Have you been able to grow out of that lesson? Choose one experience and shape your personal reflection around it.

2. In "Like a Girl," the writer relates the tension she felt over her identity—being pulled in two directions. When have you experienced an "identity crisis"? What was the result? Shape your personal reflection around your own experiences when you felt pressure to be "like _____."

3. In "None of This Is Fair," the writer reflects on his individual relationship to his community. When have you learned a lesson about what it means to be a part of *or* outside a community? When did you learn about unfair advantage and disadvantage? Write a personal reflection essay based on these experiences.

4. Nature or nurture? A common debate about the forces that shape people focuses on whether people are more strongly influenced by genetics or by their environment, upbringing, and education. Reflect on these forces in your own life. What have you inherited from your family line? What factors in your environment have influenced you?

Chapter 11
Personal Description

audio

A personal description examines a subject that the writer finds meaningful. That subject may be an influential person, a distinctive place, a valuable object, or even an animal that crossed the writer's path. For example, in this chapter, you'll find descriptions of a high school teacher, a childhood stream, a Mayan village, a ghost town, and migrating butterflies.

Writing a personal description is like making a multisensory film. First, you want readers to vividly sense the subject—all the sights, sounds, smells, tastes, and textures that make this subject come alive. Second, you want to select and develop details that create a dominant impression of the subject—a sense of the whole. And third, you need to either directly state or clearly imply why the subject is meaningful to you.

Developing your description can be a rich experience. Because the writing process will press you to examine the subject closely, you'll learn something valuable about your subject and about your connection with it. In addition, readers may see connections between your description and their own lives.

What's Ahead

- Overview: Personal Description
  - Student Models
  - Professional Model
- Guidelines
- Writing Checklist and Activities

Overview
Writing a Personal Description

Writer's Goal

Your goal is to describe a subject (a person, place, object, animal, or combination of these) so clearly and richly that the reader can step into the subject and experience its meaning.

Keys for Success

Be curious. ■ Set out to learn more about your subject than you know now. Review easy-to-recall memories, but then dig out those hard-to-grasp details that hide in the shadows. If possible, examine the subject up close by looking at photos, interviewing the person, or touring the site.

Be bold. ■ Describe what you see—blemishes and all. Help the reader smell both the roses and the rubbish. Strive to create a powerful dominant impression—a strong sense of the subject's essential nature, overall value, or personal meaning.

Be precise. ■ Reading a description that uses almost-the-right words is as disappointing as looking through slightly out-of-focus binoculars. Both keep you from seeing what you want to see. Choose nouns, verbs, and modifiers that put details in focus for the reader.

Be vivid. ■ Use a variety of techniques to make your description lively, beginning with your senses. Also develop comparisons that clarify the unfamiliar by likening it to something familiar. For example, a simile compares things using *like* or *as:* "A monarch in flight looks like an autumn leaf with a will." A metaphor establishes an identity between two unlike things, without using *like* or *as:* "Time itself was a scroll unraveled."

Topics to Consider

Choose a subject that means something special to you, one that you want to share with readers.

- **People who influenced you:** parents, grandparents, siblings, uncles, aunts, friends, neighbors, teachers, cousins, colleagues, employers, or employees
- **Places with special significance:** childhood hiding place, teenage hangout, favorite place to read, vacation spot, park, restaurant, or graveyard
- **Objects, creatures, and occasions:** a special gift, the tools of your trade, an animal encounter, a storm and its damage, a party, a play, a sports event

Next Step Read the model essays and perform the activities that follow. As you read, notice the writers' topics and writing strategies. Consider choosing a parallel topic or using similar strategies.

Description of a Person

Rosie Reid is an English major who plans to become a high school teacher. In the essay below, she describes a teacher who understood his students and knew how to teach.

He Knew

The writer starts with an anecdote.

Everybody was in on it, all 36 members of our class. Never before and never since have I witnessed such unity among a more eclectic group. The jocks, the Future Farmers of America, the hippies, the surfers, the self-named "Jesus Freaks," the upper crust, the science fair winners, the Pomo Indians—we all worked on this one. Joanie, always the leader, had conducted formal-but-secret meetings for weeks. She took inventory of our artillery, delegated assignments, and meticulously went over the plan, again and again. No silly misunderstanding was going to botch this job!

She describes the setting.

Finally the right night came. It was a Saturday, as I have found right nights tend to be, and it was late November—air chilly, sky moonless. After parking our cars a quarter of a mile from our target, our whole bunch crept through the forest. With hardly a giggle or a whisper, we moved through the trees to Mr. Tromp's house.

Thanks to Joanie, we knew our roles. Willy, Judy, and I got his car, the Anders twins hit the chicken coop, the six Hugheys conquered the toolshed, and we all worked on the house. Together we danced our silent ballet—unrolling and spreading, unrolling and spreading, unrolling and spreading—until the entire property was laced in white from the 200-plus rolls of toilet paper that we had been stealing from our families' bathrooms for months. Quickly we crept back to our cars—smiling and satisfied with the best T-P job in our school's history.

A transition signals a shift in focus.

However, back in school the following Monday morning, we were less cocky. Though still unified and ready to learn our fate, we were tense. Then fourth period arrived, and we filed into Mr. Tromp's civics class, glancing at each other anxiously and speaking little. We awaited his verdict. He must have known that his sitting silently like that—ankles crossed up on his desk, fingers interlaced behind his head, expression unreadable—would scare the pee out of us.

The quotation suggests the teacher's personality.

Finally, when the pressure in the room made our ears pop, Mr. Tromp said, "Not baaaad . . . but I must say, I'd have at least thrown some rotten eggs in the mailbox!"

We exploded in laughter, breathing out the fear that had nagged us all morning and breathing in our victory. Mr. Tromp knew us too well. He knew that it was our class, not the freshmen, sophomores, or seniors. He knew that we needed him to speak when he did, lest someone buckle. And he knew that for him to remain our favorite teacher, he had to take our prank in good humor. Once again, Mr. Tromp batted a thousand.

During sixth hour that afternoon, I returned to Mr. Tromp's classroom 7
to put in my time as his teaching assistant. Whereas most TAs ran errands and did homework, I liked to talk—to get the skinny on him: lovelife, complaints, political opinions, stories from his days as a lawyer or as a Peace Corps volunteer in Nepal. He'd offer advice on everything: family, friends, boys. He understood teenagers. When someone came to class crying, he would excuse her (it was always a her in high school) to go read some Jane Austen on the steps outside. Perhaps Mr. Tromp understood our tears, mostly love-induced, because he had his own love problems. He complained about the lack of available women in our town: "Every decent woman my age is married!"

Mr. Tromp encouraged us to get out of town. "Go from this place," 8
he'd advise. "See the world, get an education, then find a honey and come back here to raise your brood. No more marrying at 18!"

He seemed to advocate college more for romantic reasons than for academic or economic ones. But we listened because he spoke to us as real people. I, too, listened, but I didn't really hear until one day Mr. Tromp asked me which colleges I was applying to. Sheepishly, I replied, "I can't go to college. At our house we can't afford doctor visits, much less college." 9

> *"So that means I can't go to college!" I explained in my are-you-mental voice.*

"So?" 10

"So that means I can't go to college!" I 11
explained in my are-you-mental voice.

Mr. Tromp took me to his computer and showed me how to surf the 12
Net for college profiles. "Spend the hour looking," he said. "Tomorrow I'll give you a letter of recommendation." Unenthusiastically I did as I was told, sure that my time was wasted.

The next day Mr. Tromp brought me the letter, and when I read it, I 13
cried. Never before had I thought of myself so positively, so marketable, so worthy of the "So?" that he pushed us to take. That afternoon I continued my search for colleges and scholarships, and I allowed myself to think—for the first time—that college was possible.

Five years later at Westmont College in southern California, I looked at 14
Jean Valjean in *Les Misérables* as an example of an altruistic man. While thinking about his good heart and good works, I thought of Mr. Tromp. I

thought of his giving up law to teach, of his hosting our senior BBQ at his house (the one we mummified), of his writing the letter, of his giving me a copy of *The Catcher in the Rye* and telling me to swear with Holden on the days when nobody understood. Mr. Tromp remembered being seventeen.

During one of our sixth-period chats, I asked Mr. Tromp, "Were you *15* even a little mad that our class T-P'd your house?"

He laughed and replied, "Of course not. If I minded, I would have told *16* you to knock it off."

Dumbfounded, I stared at him. "You knew we were out there?" *17*

"Knew?" he snorted. "You were about as quiet as elephants!" *18*

The conclusion mirrors the opening.

"Then why didn't you stop us?" *19*

"I saw that you were having fun. And I also knew that you wouldn't *20* have come all the way out to my house if you didn't love me."

True. ■ *21*

write

Reading for Better Writing

1. In a sentence, what is the dominant impression that this essay creates of Mr. Tromp?

2. The writer opens and closes her essay by referring to the same event. Why? What does the event reveal about the teacher and about the writer? Does the strategy unify the essay? Why or why not?

3. Why is "He Knew" an effective title? Precisely what did the teacher know about the T-P event? About his students? About teaching? About the writer herself?

4. A writer can describe a person vividly by using techniques such as comparisons, anecdotes, or quotations. Find examples of these techniques in the essay. Are the techniques used effectively?

5. Paragraph 14 includes a reference to Jean Valjean in *Les Miserables*. Find out more about this character. Is the analogy effective? Why?

audio

Description of a Place

Nicole Suurdt is a student from Ontario, Canada. In this essay, she describes a time and place that she loved as a child and yearns for as an adult.

The Stream in the Ravine

Behind my childhood home is a small ravine, and through it runs the seasonal overflow of a little pond deep within the woods. It's a noisy stream, just narrow enough for an eight-year-old to take one stretching step across and reach the other side with dry shoes. And when I was eight, this stream was everything to me. [1]

> The writer introduces the topic and then gives background information.

You see, for most of my childhood, I lived on a small hobby farm in Ontario, Canada, where rolling pasture and croplands surrounded my home. The pasture fenced in Scottish Highland cattle with terrifying horns, unbroken horses with skittish hooves, and one half-blind, unpredictable donkey. These creatures separated me from the woods just beyond the pasture. But when I was little, it wasn't simply my fear of these fitful animals that penned me in on my side of the fence—it was a fear of what lay beyond the shadowy barrier of maples and pines. [2]

> Description of the visits builds tension.

It's not that I'd never been to the woods before. I had, twice. The first time, my brother took me in search of the tallest tree in the forest and got us lost for a couple of hours. My second visit was a dark winter journey. Dad dragged the family into the woods late one night in search of a missing cow. We found her half-devoured body lying in bloodstained snow, packed down by wolves' paws. [3]

> A transition signals a shift in the action.

But eventually, curiosity overpowered my fears. One spring day when I was eight, armed with a staff, I skirted the pasture and headed for the forest. I approached the fence that my dad had put up to ward off the woods. Quickly I scaled the fence, but then stood some time holding on to its boards, figuring that if a wolf came along, I could scramble back to the other side. However, after five minutes passed and no wolf appeared, I calmed down, let go of the fence, and stepped into the forest—lured on by the sound of chipmunks, birds, wind through trees, and snapping twigs. [4]

Drawn forward, I discovered rocky burrows of unknown creatures. I chased chipmunks. I sang. I passed a hunter's fort perched high in a pine, deserted after last fall's deer-hunting season. I passed under an archway of tall cedars. I waded through the muck and mire surrounding a small swamp and plodded my mud-caked shoes up a small rise, thick with the faded, crumbled leaves of last year's fall. One particular sound kept pulling me forward—the gurgle of running water. [5]

> The writer describes the stream and shares its personal importance.

Standing at the peak of the rise, with brown leaves stuck to my muddy sneakers, I found the source. Below me, within its shallow bed, ran a tiny stream, little more than a trickle, really. But to me it was a beautiful, rushing brook, my own source of clear, cold water protected by oak, maple, and [6] pine sentries. That day I spent hours scooping decaying leaves out of my stream's bed and sitting by her side to watch the water spill over the rocks and roots. She was my own discovery, my own territory, my own secret place. From that day on, the little stream past the hunter's fort, under the cedar archway, through the muck and the mire, and over the rocky rise became my quiet, private place.

But I never could keep a secret for long. During dinner one Sunday, I told my parents about my stream. I figured that it needed a bridge, something only Dad could help me build. And so, that afternoon, I led Mom and Dad over the fence, into the woods, and up to my secret stream. Together, we built a bridge using the fallen branches lying about. Mom took a picture of Dad and me sitting on our homemade, lopsided bridge, the water washing over the toes of the big rubber boots that she had insisted we wear.

My parents separated eight years after that picture was taken, and I haven't gone back to my stream since, though I think of it often. Somewhere, tucked away in Mom's photo albums, is the picture of a little girl in her dreamland, her dad beside her, his big feet hanging near her small ones. Her mom stands in the water just a few feet away behind the camera lens.

Sometimes, I want to go back there, back into that photo. I want to step into a time when life seemed safe, and a tiny stream gave us all that we needed. In that picture, our smiles last, our hearts are calm, and we hear only quiet voices, forest sounds, and my bubbling stream. Bitter words are silenced and tears held back by the click and whir of a camera.

I've been thinking about making the journey again past the hunter's fort, under the stand of cedars, through the muck and mire, and over the rocky rise. But it's been a long summer, and the small, seasonal stream running out of the overflow of the pond has probably dried up. ■

The picture shows the father, the daughter, and their bridge.

The writer yearns for life as shown in the photo.

Reading for Better Writing

1. Three times in the essay, the writer mentions four sites (hunter's fort, cedar archway, muck and mire, rocky rise) along her route. What do the references to these sites contribute to the description?

2. How does the writer organize her description? Develop a paragraph-by-paragraph outline. Then identify the strategies used and discuss their effectiveness.

3. Review the references to the photograph taken by the mother, and describe what the photo shows. What does the writer mean when she says, "Sometimes, I want to go back there, back into that photo"?

4. Reread the opening and closing paragraphs, comparing how the writer describes the stream in each paragraph. Are the details and voices of the two passages different? Give examples.

Description of a Place and People

Student writer David Bani wrote the following essay about his trip to the Mayan village of Yaxhachen.

Beyond the End of the Road

The writer describes the sights he sees outside the van.

Our van moves slowly down the narrow, winding roads that lead to Yaxhachen. Like a carnival ride, these roads swing from side to side and up and down. We drive through fields of *henequen*, and under the red *flamboyan* and gold *lluvia de oro* trees. We pass through small villages, ride over *topes* (speed bumps), dodge tricycle taxis, and bounce through potholes. Field workers are making their way home on bicycles, their *coas* or machetes strapped to their backs.

Our van, carrying only my dad, mom, two sisters, and me, passes through Oxkubskab, a center where orchard owners take their produce. All types of fruit grown in Yucatan can be found here, and the smells are powerful variations of sweet ripeness. On the way back, we'll pick up some bags of oranges and mandarins, one or two papayas, plus anything else that looks good. But right now we're getting near our destination.

He uses a parenthetical phrase to define a Spanish word.

Next, we enter Xul, the end of the road. It's the end of the road both in name (*xul* is Maya for the end of the road) and in reality—the pavement ends here. Beyond this point, only a serpentine, dirt trail leads on, and its boulders and rocks make traveling even slower. Though we must drive only about 12 miles, the journey takes over half an hour.

He shows details about the village and its people.

Finally, we arrive at Yaxhachen. The first one to welcome us to this Mayan village is a pig, but once we reach the center of town, people begin to gather. We get out of the van, stretch, and then walk around the town square and down side streets. While some streets were paved at one time, the pavement has long since crumbled. We explore the area with no fear of getting lost. All streets eventually meander back to the center of town.

While walking through town, I feel a little self-conscious because we are the only white people here. For most residents, whites are a rare sight, but for some small children at least, we are a novelty. Yet everyone, young and old, treats us kindly. Some children shyly peek at us from over stone walls and giggle, while others follow us at a distance. Old men and women, sitting on logs in front of their houses, nod pleasantly.

A question signals a shift in focus.

Everything in the village smells earthy and sweaty, including us. In this climate you can't help sweating, and you don't mind it because it feels right. Why are we here? One of Dad's hobbies is helping people in outlying villages find sources for clean water. He already has some pump equipment out and is looking at the control box for the submersible pump. A few years ago, he installed this pump, and another one on the edge of town.

The words "dusk" and "cool" suggest a shift in time.

Dusk starts to settle in, and the air begins to cool. Dad is just finishing his repairs when one of the church elders invites us to have supper at his

The description moves inside.

house—a cluster of stick and thatch huts. We sit down on anything our host can find, like some wooden folding chairs from the church. We eat by ourselves—partly because there isn't enough room around the tables for both his family and us, but mostly because serving us separately is the Mayan way of showing respect. As we eat, our host sits nearby to make pleasant talk and to order one of his children to get us more tortillas, or whatever else he sees we need. To honor us, he serves us "city food," which is Spam, scrambled eggs, and soft drinks. But the better food is the hand-made tortillas and refried beans.

The writer uses details to describe the Mayan people.

When it's dark enough, we walk to the church and set up the projector   9
outside in the cool night air. A large crowd gathers because any film is a rare event, and because this film (which tells the story of Jesus) is one of the few movies in the Mayan language. In fact, the first time that Dad showed the film to a Mayan audience, he didn't explain that it was in Maya, and the people were both surprised and pleased. They marveled that the voices in the film spoke their language, even though they shyly tried to hide their amazement. Tonight, some people are not dressed for the cold, and many cannot find a place to sit, but still they come. The young men sit on the stone wall in the back so that they can talk as they watch the movie.

He concludes by repeating the title.

By the time the film is finished, it's too late for us to leave Yaxhachen,   10
so we set up hammocks in the church. We take everything off the floor, and we secure the door to prevent small animals from entering the building. Then, feeling well-fed, welcome, and tired, we sleep soundly in this village beyond the end of the road. ■

write

Reading for Better Writing

1. In a sentence, state the dominant impression this essay creates of Yaxhachen.

2. Review the descriptive details in the first six paragraphs. To what senses do these details appeal? Do the details help you imagine the sites? Give examples of strong or weak word choices.

3. The writer uses verbs in the present tense. Is this a good choice? Why or why not? Choose a paragraph and explain how its impact would be different if the verbs were in the past tense.

4. Cite words and phrases that communicate the writer's attitude toward the people and scenes that he describes. Why is this place meaningful to the writer?

5. The writer does not comment on his reasons for describing these scenes. Is he contented simply to remember details, or does he seem to have an unexpressed purpose?

Description of a Place and Occasion

James C. Schaap is a writer and college professor. In this essay he describes the place where he took his writing students on a particularly memorable day. The essay was first published in *The Des Moines Register*.

That Morning on the Prairie

The writer introduces the setting.

On some beautiful early fall days out here on the emerald cusp of the Great Plains, it's hard to believe that we are where we are. Warm southern breezes swing up from Texas, the sun smiles with a gentleness not seen since June, and the spacious sky reigns over everything in azure glory.　*1*

Early on exactly that kind of fall morning, I like to take my writing classes to a ghost town, Highland, Iowa, ten miles west and two south, as they say out here on the square-cut prairie. Likely as not, Highland fell victim to a century-old phenomenon in the Upper Midwest: 100 years ago, land was cut into 160-acre chunks, most had homesteads, and small towns thrived. Today, when the portions are ten times bigger, fewer people live out here, and many towns have died out.　*2*

He details the location.

What's left of Highland is a stand of pines circled around no more than twenty gravestones, and an old carved sign with hand-drawn figures detailing what was home for some people—a couple of Protestant churches, a couple of horse barns, and a blacksmith shop, little else. The town of Highland once flourished atop this swell of land at the confluence of a pair of nondescript gravel roads that still float out in four distinct directions like dusky ribbons over undulating prairie. But mostly, today, it's gone.　*3*

He explains why he takes students to Highland— and how they respond.

I like to take my students to Highland because what's not there never fails to silence them. Maybe it's the emaciated cemetery; maybe it's the south wind's low moan through that stand of pines, a sound you don't hear often on the plains; maybe it's some variant of culture shock—they stumble sleepily out of their cubicle dorm rooms and wake up suddenly in a place with no walls.　*4*

I'm lying. I know why they fall into psychic shock. It's the sheer immensity of the land that unfurls before them, the horizon only seemingly there where earth weaves effortlessly into sky; it's the vastness of rolling landscape William Cullen Bryant once claimed looked like an ocean stopped in time. It seems as if there's nothing here, and everything, and that's what stuns them into silence. That September morning, on those gravel roads, no cars passed. We were alone—20 of us, all alone and vulnerable on a high-ground swath of prairie once called Highland, surrounded by nothing but startling openness.　*5*

The topic sentence indicates a transition.

That's where I was—and that's where they were—on September 11, 2001. We left for Highland about the same time Mohamed Atta and his friends were commandeering American Airlines Flight 11 into the north tower of the World Trade Center, so we knew absolutely nothing about what　*6* had happened until we returned. While the rest of the world watched in horror, my students, notebooks and pens in hand, looked over a landscape so immense only God could live there—and were silent.

They found it hard to leave, but then no one can stay on retreat forever, so when we returned we heard the horrible news. All over campus and all over town, TVs blared. 7

I like to think that maybe on our campus that morning my students were best prepared for the horror everyone felt—prepared, not by having been warned, but by having been awed. 8

The writer reflects on the trip's impact on students.

Every year it's a joy for me to sit at Highland with a new group of students, all of us trying to define and describe the beauty of what seems characterless prairie. But this year our being there on the morning of September 11 was more than a joy—it was also a kind of blessing. ■ 9

write

Reading for Better Writing

1. In the first three paragraphs of his essay, the writer describes Highland. Cite passages that do or do not help you see the setting. What mood or feeling does the description evoke?

2. James C. Schaap, himself a writer, takes his students to Highland where he asks them to use the setting as a writing prompt. What could students learn from the experience? Why?

3. Schaap concludes the essay by saying that his students' presence in Highland on September 11 was "a kind of a blessing." What does he mean?

4. What do you think the writer is trying to say in the last several lines?

Description of an Animal and Occasion

The following passage is from "Northing," a chapter in Annie Dillard's *Pilgrim at Tinker Creek*. Here, the author vividly describes monarch butterflies and their migration.

Northing

The writer introduces the subject.

A few days later the monarchs hit. I saw one, and then another, and then others all day long, before I consciously understood that I was witnessing a migration, and it wasn't until another two weeks had passed that I realized the enormity of what I had seen. 1

She describes how the monarchs hatched.

Each of these butterflies, the fruit of two or three broods of this summer, had hatched successfully from one of those emerald cases that Teale's caterpillar had been about to form when the parasitic larvae snapped it limp, eating their way out of its side. They had hatched, many of them, just before a thunderstorm, when winds lifted the silver leaves of trees and birds sought the shelter of shrubbery, uttering cries. They were butterflies, going south to the Gulf states or farther, and some of them had come from Hudson's Bay. 2

She describes how they flew.

Monarchs were everywhere. They skittered and bobbed, rested in the air, lolled on the dust—but with none of their usual insouciance. They had but one unwearying thought: South. I watched from my study window: three, four . . . eighteen, nineteen, one every few seconds, and some in tandem. They came fanning straight toward my window from the northwest, and from the northeast, materializing from behind the tips of high hemlocks, where Polaris hangs by night. They appeared as Indian horsemen appear in movies: first dotted, then massed, silent, at the rim of a hill. 3

Using color, shape, texture, motion, and comparisons, she describes their bodies.

Each monarch butterfly had a brittle black body and deep orange wings limned and looped in black bands. A monarch at rest looks like a fleck of tiger, stilled and wide-eyed. A monarch in flight looks like an autumn leaf with a will, vitalized and cast upon the air from which it seems to suck some thin sugar of energy, some leaf-life or sap. As each one climbed up the air outside my window, I could see the more delicate, ventral surfaces of its wings, and I had a sense of bunched legs and straining thorax, but I could never focus well into the flapping and jerking before it vaulted up past the window and out of sight over my head. 4

An anecdote deepens the description.

I walked out and saw a monarch do a wonderful thing: it climbed a hill without twitching a muscle. I was standing at the bridge over Tinker Creek, at the southern foot of a very steep hill. The monarch beat its way beside me over the bridge at eye level, and then, flailing its wings exhaustedly, ascended straight up in the air. It rose vertically to the enormous height of 5 a bankside sycamore's crown. Then, fixing its wings at a precise angle, it glided up the steep road, losing altitude extremely slowly, climbing by checking its fall, until it came to rest at a puddle in front of the house at the top of the hill.

I followed. It panted, skirmished briefly westward, and then, returning to the puddle, began its assault on the house. It struggled almost straight up the air next to the two-story brick wall, and then scaled the roof. Wasting no effort, it followed the roof's own slope, from a distance of two inches. Puff, and it was out of sight. I wondered how many more hills and houses it would have to climb before it could rest. From the force of its will it would seem it could flutter through the walls.

The writer describes their flight patterns and provides scientific background.

Monarchs are "tough and powerful, as butterflies go." They fly over Lake Superior without resting; in fact, observers there have discovered a curious thing. Instead of flying directly south, the monarchs crossing high over the water take an inexplicable turn toward the east. Then when they reach an invisible point, they all veer south again. Each successive swarm repeats this mysterious dogleg movement, year after year. Entomologists actually think that the butterflies might be "remembering" the position of a long-gone, looming glacier. In another book I read that geologists think that Lake Superior marks the site of the highest mountain that ever existed on this continent. I don't know. I'd like to see it. Or I'd like to be it, to feel when to turn. At night on land migrating monarchs slumber on certain trees, hung in festoons with wings folded together, thick on the trees and shaggy as bearskin.

She speculates about their taste.

Monarchs have always been assumed to taste terribly bitter, because of the acrid milkweed on which the caterpillars feed. You always run into monarchs and viceroys when you read about mimicry: viceroys look enough like monarchs that keen-eyed birds who have tasted monarchs once will avoid the viceroys as well. New studies indicate that milkweed-fed monarchs are not so much evil-tasting as literally nauseating, since milkweed contains "heart poisons similar to digitalis" that make the bird ill. Personally, I like an experiment performed by an entomologist with real spirit. He had heard all his life, as I have, that monarchs taste unforgettably bitter, so he tried some. "To conduct what was in fact a field experiment the doctor first went South, and he ate a number of monarchs in the field. . . . The monarch butterfly, Dr. Urquhart learned, has no more flavor than dried toast." Dried toast? It was hard for me, throughout the monarch migration, in the middle of all that beauty and real splendor, to fight down the thought that what I was really seeing in the air was a vast fluttering tea tray for shut-ins.

She describes a specific butterfly's movement, appearance, and grip.

It is easy to coax a dying or exhausted butterfly onto your finger. I saw a monarch walking across a gas station lot; it was walking south. I placed my index finger in its path, and it clambered aboard and let me lift it to my face. Its wings were faded but unmarked by hazard; a veneer of velvet caught the light and hinted at the frailest depth of lapped scales. It was a male; his legs clutching my finger were short and atrophied; they clasped my finger with a spread fragility, a fineness as of some low note of emotion or pure strain of spirit, scarcely perceived. And I knew that those feet were actually tasting me, sipping with sensitive organs the vapor of my finger's skin: butterflies taste with their feet. All the time he held me, he opened and closed his glorious wings, senselessly, as if sighing.

The closing of his wings fanned an almost imperceptible redolence   10 at my face, and I leaned closer. I could barely scent a sweetness, I could almost name it . . . fireflies, sparklers—honeysuckle. He smelled like honeysuckle; I couldn't believe it. I knew that many male butterflies exuded distinctive odors from special scent glands, but I thought that only laboratory instruments could detect those odors compounded of many, many butterflies. I had read a list of the improbable scents of butterflies: sandalwood, chocolate, heliotrope, sweet pea. Now this live creature here on my finger had an odor that even I could sense—this flap actually smelled, this chip that actually took its temperature from the air like any envelope or hammer, this programmed wisp of spread horn. And he smelled of honeysuckle. Why not caribou hoof or Labrador tea, tundra lichen or dwarf willow, the brine of Hudson's Bay or the vapor of rivers milky with fine-ground glacial silt? This honeysuckle was an odor already only half-remembered, as breath of the summer past, the Lucas cliffs and overgrown fence by Tinker Creek, a drugged sweetness that had almost cloyed on those moisture-laden nights, now refined to a wary trickle in the air, a distillation pure and rare, scarcely known and mostly lost, and heading south.

> **She describes its surprising odor.**

I walked him across the gas station lot and lowered him into a field.   11 He took to the air, pulsing and gliding; he lighted on sassafras, and I lost him.

For weeks I found paired monarch wings, bodiless, on the grass or on   12 the road. I collected one such wing and freed it of its scales; first I rubbed it between my fingers, and then I stroked it gently with the tip of an infant's silver spoon. What I had at the end of this delicate labor is lying here on this study desk: a kind of resilient scaffolding, like the webbing over a hot-air balloon, black veins stretching the merest something across the nothingness it plies. The integument itself is perfectly transparent; through it I can read the smallest print. It is as thin as the skin peeled from sunburn, and as tough as a parchment of fleeced buffalo hide. The butterflies that were eaten

> **The writer describes the monarch's wings.**

here in the valley, leaving us their wings, were, however, few: most lived to follow the valley south.

She shares how the migration affected her.

The migration lasted in full force for five days. For those five days I was *13* inundated, drained. The air was alive and unwinding. Time itself was a scroll unraveled, curved and still quivering on a table or altar stone. The monarchs clattered in the air, burnished like throngs of pennies, here's one, and here's one, and more, and more. They flapped and floundered; they thrust, splitting the air like the keels of canoes, quickened and fleet. It looked as though the leaves of the autumn forest had taken flight, and were pouring down the valley like a waterfall, like a tidal wave, all the leaves of hardwoods from here to Hudson's Bay. It was as if the season's color were draining away like lifeblood, as if the year were molting and shedding. The year was rolling down, and a vital curve had been reached, the lift that gives way to headlong rush. And when the monarchs had passed and were gone, the skies were vacant, the air poised. The dark night into which the year was plunging was not a sleep but an awakening, a new and necessary austerity, the sparer climate for which I longed. The shed trees were brittle and still, the creek light and cold, and my spirit holding its breath. ■

She describes the monarchs' departure and her reaction.

write

Reading for Better Writing

1. Review the first paragraph in which Annie Dillard introduces her topic by saying, "It wasn't until another two weeks had passed that I realized the enormity of what I had seen." What does she mean by "enormity"? Why is the migration meaningful to the writer? What dominant impression does it create?

2. List the monarch's traits that Dillard describes. Choose one or two passages that you find particularly effective, and explain why.

3. Throughout the description, Dillard uses comparisons—similes and metaphors. Examine the comparisons in two paragraphs: What do these comparisons contribute to the description of the butterflies?

4. Describe the writer's voice and attitude toward her subject. Cite passages to support your answer.

5. Trace the organization of this description. Comment on the effectiveness of the order.

6. Summarize the closing paragraph and explain why it is effective.

Guidelines
Writing a Personal Description

1. **Select a topic.** Starting with the "Topics to Consider" ideas on page **164**, brainstorm lists of people, places, objects, and animals that have been personally meaningful to you. From these lists, choose the topic that will reward your descriptive energies, prove rich in significance, and interest readers.

2. **Get the big picture.** Establish the big picture first by answering these questions about your topic:
   - What are your topic's names? What words are associated with the topic?
   - What is this person, place, object, or animal all about? What is its character, heart, or essence?
   - What is this topic's meaning for you, and why is it meaningful? What is your relationship to it?
   - What are the dimensions, elements, or parts of this person, place, object, or animal?
   - What is the topic's history?

3. **Tap the senses.** List sensory details:
   - Colors, shapes, and movements that you saw
   - Sounds that you heard
   - Smells, tastes, and textures that you remember

4. **Consider all sides.** If you're writing about a person, consider what he or she is like at different times, in different moods, with different people, and in different settings. If you're writing about a place or an object, think about how it looks from all sides—top to bottom, right side in, and inside out.

5. **Deepen the description.** Experiment with a number of strategies that will help make your description vivid and memorable:
   - Develop comparisons for your topic. Play with similes, metaphors, and analogies that might help readers see your topic more clearly and understand it more fully.
   - Develop anecdotes about your topic. What stories characterize this place or object? What behaviors, events, and activities define this person or creature? Through freewriting, flesh out these anecdotes. When appropriate, include quotations or dialogue.

6. **Choose a dominant impression.** At this point, tentatively decide which overall idea, theme, and/or emotion you want to convey through description. What truth about the topic and your relationship with it do you want to share?

7. **Think organization.** If you're ready to write, go for it. But it may also be good to think through how best to organize and build your description—moving from general overview to specific parts, from distant view to close-up, from context to detail, from left to right, from top to bottom, from front to back—or the reverse. Consider how to start and how to finish.

8. **Write your first draft.** If the words flow freely, rough out the entire essay. But if you get stuck, go back to the material that you developed for steps 2 through 7 and consider where you could insert an item, describe a trait, or include additional details. If you're still blocked, choose one trait or detail, and freewrite for a few minutes, letting the writing take you wherever it wants to go.

9. **Revise the writing.** Read the draft by asking questions like the following:
   - Is the dominant impression created the one you want to create?
   - Does the organizational pattern work, leading the reader effectively through parts of the topic?
   - Does the opening grab the reader's attention and set up what follows?
   - Do the middle paragraphs give helpful pictures of the subject—each revealing a new facet of the person, place, object, or creature?
   - Is the description filled with vivid details, enlightening anecdotes, and sharp comparisons?
   - Does the closing complete the word picture and unify the essay?

10. **Get feedback.** Ask someone to read both your assignment and your essay, using the following questions:
    - Does the essay accomplish the assigned task? What dominant impression does it create?
    - Is the description vivid, suggestive, clear, engaging, and complete?
    - Does it read easily, with smooth sentences and clear transitions between paragraphs?

11. **Edit the essay for clarity and correctness.** Check the following:
    - Are verbs vivid and nouns precise?
    - Are adverbs and adjectives used effectively to clarify verbs and nouns?
    - Do sentences read smoothly? In particular, do transitions like *above*, *beneath*, and *near* guide readers through the description? (See page **70**.)
    - Are capitalization, usage, and spelling correct?
    - Does the format follow guidelines in the assignment or this book?

12. **Publish the essay.** Share your essay with a broad audience:
    - Publish the essay on appropriate Web sites (including your own).
    - Submit the essay for competition in a writing contest.
    - Give copies to family members and friends.

Writing Checklist

Use these six traits to check your essay, then revise as needed:

____ The **ideas** give insights into the identity, complexity, and personal significance of the topic. The dominant impression is clear and insightful.

____ The **organization** includes an engaging opening that leads smoothly into the description of the topic. Paragraphs follow a clear and logical order, signaled by smooth transitions. The closing completes and unifies the essay.

____ The **voice** is informed, inviting, reflective, and lively.

____ The **words** include strong verbs and precise nouns. Adverbs and adjectives are used to refine the description.

____ The **sentences** are clear, vary in structure, and read smoothly. Transitions between sentences (especially spatial transitions) help unify paragraphs.

____ The **copy** is correct and follows assigned guidelines for format.

write

Writing Activities

1. Review "He Knew" and "The Stream in the Ravine," noting how each writer invites you into her close relationship with a person or a place. List similar topics from your life. Then choose one that you're willing to revisit and share with readers. Write the essay by imitating organizational strategies used in a model or by developing your own strategy.

2. Review "Beyond the End of the Road" and "That Morning on the Prairie," noting how both essays describe a journey and a destination. Consider how the journey in each essay distances the writer from his home or workplace and helps him reflect on the place he describes. What faraway or nearby places help you gather your thoughts, reflect, and find insight or peace? Choose a place, think about related people, and then describe the place.

3. Select a few paragraphs from "Northing," noticing how the writer's precise word choice and comparisons help you see what she sees. Then choose one of your favorite things and write a descriptive essay that helps your reader see what you see.

4. Describe a person or place related to one of your courses, to your major, or to your career plans. For example, you could describe a person or place related to a class project, field trip, experiment, or internship.

Analytical Writing

CONTENTS

Chapter 12
Cause and Effect

audio

Now why did that happen? We ask this question every day at home, in college, and on the job. But why do we ask, "Why"?

We ask it to understand and cope with things that happen in our lives. For example, knowing why our car overheated will help us avoid that problem in the future. Knowing what causes a disease like diabetes—or knowing its effects—helps us understand and control the condition. In other words, cause-and-effect reasoning helps us deal with everyday issues.

In a cause-and-effect essay, the writer develops the thesis through cause-and-effect reasoning. That is, he or she analyzes and explains the causes, the effects, or both the causes and the effects of a phenomenon.

Are you ready to write—to analyze and explain the causes and/or effects of one of life's "happenings"? This chapter will help you do so.

What's Ahead

- Overview: Cause-and-Effect Essay
    Student Models
    Professional Model
- Guidelines
- Writing Checklist and Activities

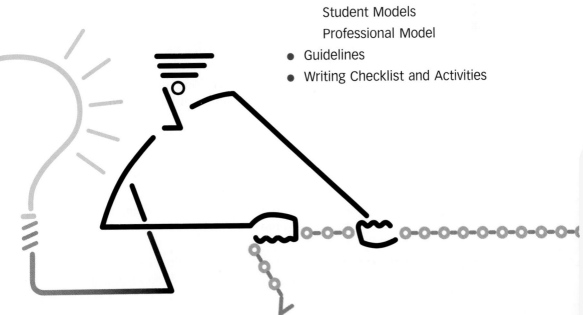

Overview
Writing a Cause-and-Effect Essay

Writer's Goal

Your goal is to analyze and explain the causes, the effects, or both the causes and the effects of some phenomenon (fact, occurrence, or circumstance).

Keys for Success

Know your readers. ■ Consider what your readers know and think about your subject. Are they aware of the cause/effect connection associated with it? Do they accept it? Why or why not? If they deny that the connection exists or is relevant, what arguments support their position? Are these arguments strong?

Think logically. ■ Linking cause to effect, or vice versa, requires clear, logical thinking supported by strong evidence. To practice this kind of reasoning, (1) research the topic for evidence connecting a specific cause and/or effect to a specific phenomenon, (2) draft a working thesis stating that connection, and (3) explain the connection in language that your readers will understand.

Test your thinking. ■ Check your main points for clarity, your supporting points for relevance, and your overall argument for logic. Use the list of logical fallacies to identify common weaknesses. (See pages **261–264**, especially "False Cause" on page **263**.)

Topics to Consider

Choose a topic that you care about. Begin by thinking about categories such as the ones given below. Then brainstorm a list of phenomena related to each category. From this list, choose a topic and prove its causes, effects, or both.

- **Family life:** adult children living with parents, increasing number of stay-at-home dads, families choosing to simplify their lifestyles, more people squeezed by needs of children and parents, older women having babies
- **Politics:** decreasing number of student voters, increasing support for oil exploration, increased interest in third-party politics, tension between political-action groups
- **Society:** nursing shortage, security concerns, nursing-care facilities, immigrant-advocacy groups, shifting ethnic balances
- **Environment:** common water pollutants, new water-purification technology, effects of a community's recycling program
- **Workplace:** decreasing power of unions, more businesses providing child-care services, need for on-the-job training in technology

> **Next Step** Read the model essays and do the activities that follow. As you read, note how the writers develop their theses by using cause-and-effect reasoning.

Cause and Effect

Sarah Hanley is a college student living on a U.S. military base in Germany. In the essay below, she uses both research and her military experience to identify the causes and effects of adrenaline highs.

Adrenaline Junkies

The writer introduces the topic by asking a series of questions.

What do you picture when you hear the phrase "adrenaline junkie"? Evel Knievel soaring through the air on a motorcycle? Tom Cruise rappelling down the side of a mountain? An excited retiree stuffing quarters in a slot machine? Actually, all three qualify as adrenaline junkies if they do the activities to get their adrenaline highs. But what, exactly, is an adrenaline high, what causes it, what are its effects, and are the effects positive? *1*

She describes the causes and effects of an adrenaline high.

Adrenaline (also called epinephrine) is a hormone linked to the two adrenal glands located on top of the kidneys. Each gland has two parts: the outer portion called the cortex, and the inner portion called the medulla. When a person experiences an unusual exertion or a crisis situation, his or her brain triggers the medullas, which release little packets of adrenaline into the bloodstream (Nathan). The rush of adrenaline in the blood leads to increased blood pressure, heart rate, sugar metabolism, oxygen intake, and muscle strength. All these phenomena cause an adrenaline high: feeling highly alert and very energetic (Scheuller 2). *2*

However, while all healthy people experience adrenaline highs, different people need different levels of stimulus to trigger the highs. The level of stimulus that a person needs depends on the amount of protein in his or her medullas. In other words, the medullas release adrenaline through channels containing a certain protein. If the channels contain a large amount of the protein, they release adrenaline more easily than channels containing less protein. Therefore, a person with a higher level of protein in the channels of his or her medullas experiences an adrenaline release more easily than someone with a lower level of the protein (Scheuller 4). *3*

She uses an illustration to clarify a point.

To illustrate this difference, we'll call the people with a higher level of protein (and a more easily stimulated output of adrenaline) Type N, for nervous; the others we'll call Type C, for calm. Because Type N people release adrenaline more easily than Type C people do, Type N's require a lesser stimulus to trigger an adrenaline release. For example, a Type N person may get an adrenaline high from finishing his research paper on time, whereas a Type C person will get a similar buzz when she parachutes from a plane at 10,000 feet! *4*

While different people get their adrenaline highs differently, any person's highs can be channeled for healthy or harmful effects. For example, the Type N person who gets a rush from finishing the research project could do good work as a junkie research technician in a science lab. As long as he avoids becoming a workaholic, seeking the highs won't threaten his health, and the work may contribute to the overall welfare of society. Similarly, the *5*

Type C person who gets her highs by jumping out of airplanes could do good work as a junkie fire-fighter or a junkie brain surgeon. As long as she gets periodic relief from the tension, the highs won't hurt her health, and the work could help her community.

> **An introductory phrase signals a shift in focus.**

On the other hand, pursuing the wrong type of adrenaline high, or seeking too many highs, can be destructive. Examples of this kind of behavior include compulsive gambling, drug use, careless risk taking in sports, and win-at-all-cost business practices. Destructive pursuits have many high-cost results including bankruptcy, broken relationships, physical injury, drug addiction, and death (Lyons 3).

6

Because adrenaline highs can lead to positive results, maybe we waste time worrying about becoming adrenaline junkies. Instead, we should ask ourselves how to pursue those highs positively. In other words, the proteins, hormones, and chemical processes that produce adrenaline highs are, themselves, very good—and they can be used for good. In fact, someday we may figure out how to bottle the stuff and put it on the market! ∎

7

> **The writer concludes by reviewing her main points.**

Note: The Works Cited page is not shown.

write

Reading for Better Writing

1. Name two or more ways that the opening paragraph engages you and effectively introduces the topic and thesis.

2. Paragraphs three and four explain how different people need different levels of stimulus to trigger adrenaline highs. Is this explanation clear and believable? Why or why not?

3. In one sentence, summarize the writer's argument regarding the causes and effects of an adrenaline high. Explain why you do or do not find this argument convincing.

4. The writer concludes the essay with a playful sentence suggesting that someday adrenaline may be bottled and sold. Explain why you think the sentence is or is not an effective closing.

Cause and Effect

In the essay below, student writer Tiffany Boyett analyzes the causes and effects of stress in our lives.

Life-Threatening Stress

The writer uses an illustration to introduce the topic.

It was 8:00 a.m., her husband, Lance, had left for work without filling the tank on the Mazda, and her daughter, Gina, had gotten on the school bus without her show-and-tell bunny. "Great," thought Jan, "now I have to get gas at Demler's, stop by Gina's school, and drop Alex off at day care—all before my 9:30 class!" Quickly she grabbed the diaper bag, picked up the baby, and headed for the door. At 9:35, with her heart pounding and hands sweating, she scrambled into the classroom, found an open seat, and was hurriedly pulling out her psych notes when the prof asked, "So . . . precisely what does Jung mean by 'collective unconscious'—Jan?"

"Uh . . . what was the question?" she responded.

Does the scene sound familiar—too much work, too little time, and too much stress? Actually, periods of excessive stress are just part of life in college—or out of college, for that matter. Normally, stress (the response to a perceived threat) is a powerful, life-saving force, but when stress becomes excessive, it is a life-threatening condition. So what do we do—simply accept stress as one more cost of living?

She states the thesis.

While accepting some stress is inescapable, for our own health and for the well-being of others, we have to do more. We have to understand what stress is—both its causes and its effects. In addition, to avoid the negative effects, we have to learn how to manage the stress in our lives.

She explains the symptoms of stress with an example.

So what is stress? Actually, the physiological characteristics of stress are some of the body's potentially good self-defense mechanisms. Take, for example, a man who is crossing a street when he spots an oncoming car. Immediately his brain signals his adrenal glands to release a flood of adrenaline into his bloodstream. As a result, his muscles contract, his eyes dilate, his heart pounds faster, his breathing quickens, and his blood clots more readily. Each one of these responses helps the man leap out of the car's path. His muscles contract to give him exceptional strength. His eyes dilate so that he can see more clearly. His heart pumps more blood and his lungs exchange more air—both to increase his metabolism. If the man were injured, his blood would clot faster, ensuring a smaller amount of blood loss. In this situation and many more like it, stress symptoms are good (Curtis 25–26).

A question indicates a transition.

So when is stress dangerous? The danger comes when stress responses are triggered too frequently in a short period of time, or when they are triggered constantly over a longer period of time. While everyday stressors are not life-threatening by themselves, when these stressors happen so frequently that the body lacks time to relax, the normal effects of stress compound. One result is that certain body hormones, such as adrenaline and cortisol, are elevated. If the levels of these two hormones are elevated over an extended period of time, several life-threatening conditions can result.

An effect of prolonged stress is described.

One of the most immediate results of prolonged stress is a decrease in 7 the body's natural immune function. The release of cortisol into the bloodstream inhibits a protective hormone released during the immune response and thereby suppresses immune reactions. During periods of stress, the immune system becomes compromised, and the body experiences increased susceptibility to disease (Dombrowski 128). For example, some studies have proved that when medical students prepare for board exams, they experience more stress and get sick more often than when they prepare for less stressful exams.

The writer explains the effects of elevated stress.

How do elevated stress levels affect one's health? According to the U.S. 8 Census Bureau, the most common cause of death in America is heart disease (90). Elevated levels of adrenaline and cortisol in the bloodstream trigger the release of fatty acids, triglycerides, and cholesterol. These substances contribute to the blockage of arteries in the heart, and the blockages lead to heart attacks (Dombrowski 126). Excessive production of cortisol also produces a sustained level of elevated blood pressure or hypertension. If a person is under stress for a long period of time, his or her blood pressure will remain high, forcing the heart to work harder and, consequently, wear out sooner (Wickrama 527).

She shows that stress is linked to specific illnesses.

But stress-induced illnesses include more than head colds, flu, and 9 heart disease. According to the U.S. Census Bureau, the second most common cause of death in America is cancer, and recent studies have linked stress with an increased risk of developing cancer. Increased levels of cortisol associated with stress reduce the efficacy of the immune system, allowing cancer cells to multiply more easily, and thus lead to full-blown cancer (Eysenck 223).

According to the U.S. Census Bureau, the third most common cause of 10 death in America is stroke. A new study released by the University of Michigan claims that stress is linked to increased risk of stroke in middle-aged white men (Chande 1771). Increased blood pressure from higher adrenaline levels, along with the blood's increased clotting ability associated with stress, results in a higher risk that blood clots will develop in the brain and cause a stroke.

Another example is given.

Diabetes is another illness that has recently been linked to stress. 11 Adrenaline in the bloodstream causes the liver to release glucose, the increased glucose raises the level of blood sugar, and increased blood sugar causes the pancreas to secrete insulin. In addition, because cortisol released into the bloodstream actually decreases the effectiveness of insulin, the pancreas must release even greater amounts of insulin. As a result of the high insulin levels, the insulin receptors become less sensitive to insulin, making it harder for the cells to take up sugar, even when there are no stressors. This decrease in the receptors' sensitivity is the basis for type II diabetes (Dombrowski 127).

The writer inserts a qualifier to refine the focus of the sentence.

However, excessive stress is dangerous not only because of its link to serious illnesses, but also because of its very nature. In other words, stress is a nonspecific response: although stress may vary in degree, its nature is the same no matter what sort of threat is perceived. In fact, the threat doesn't even have to be real! As long as a person perceives a threat, he or she will experience stress. For example, someone who is afraid of poisonous spiders may undergo great stress even when in the presence of a harmless spider. In addition, the nonspecific nature of stress works the other way. Someone who is in real danger, but doesn't perceive the danger, will experience no stress. Finally, stress's nonspecific nature makes stress particularly dangerous for those people who perceive threats very readily. These individuals experience stress more commonly—and often more intensely—than others.

12

She reuses her opening illustration to close and unify the essay.

Because stress is so common, many people fail to recognize its potential danger. For example, Jan, the student described earlier, was certainly aware that she experienced stress while bustling through her busy morning. However, if she is like most of us, she wasn't aware that excessive stress could lead to serious illness and early death. Learning about stress's causes and effects is an important first step that we all must take. After that, we'll be ready for the second step—learning how to manage our life-threatening stress. ■

13

Note: The Works Cited page is not shown.

Reading for Better Writing

1. The writer uses an illustration to open and close the essay. Explain why the illustration is or is not effective.

2. List the causes of stress described in the essay. Are they described objectively? Cite examples to support your answer.

3. The writer distinguishes between—and describes the effects of—three forms of stress: normal stress, prolonged stress, and elevated (or excessive) stress. Examine the thinking she uses to link each form to specific effects. Is the logic clear? Is it believable? Why or why not?

4. The writer states her purpose as follows: "We have to understand what stress is—both its causes and its effects." Does she convince you that understanding and managing stress are important? Cite examples to support your answer.

Cause and Effect

In the following passage from "A New Vision for America," author Carl Rowan argues against legalizing drug use. Notice how the writer supports his argument by using cause-and-effect reasoning midway through the passage.

A New Vision for America

There is no area of urban life that causes more well-meaning people to say "we give up" than the proliferating curse of drug abuse. In my city, children are killing children, peddlers are wiping out nonpaying junkies, girls are bartering their bodies for dope, entire neighborhoods are imprisoned in fear of the gunshots that deliver more than a corpse a day. In my suburb, the teenagers and young adults of affluent white families are taking in tens of thousands of dollars per night selling crack, marijuana, and other illicit substances. In the rural areas hardly an hour from my home, country boys are running labs that produce, not the moonshine of two generations ago, but Quaaludes, PCP, and a deadly assortment of mind-bending, life-shortening drugs.

> *The writer introduces the subject and gives examples.*

Still, a destructive notion that we ought to legalize the drugs that are devouring America creeps slowly into the minds of more and more "important" people—judges, journalists, mayors, a former secretary of state. *Surrender* is becoming the American password.

> *He describes the argument that he opposes.*

Legalization advocates, like Nobel Prize-winning economist Milton Friedman and Mayor Kurt Schmoke of Baltimore, seem to think that with legalization some cosmic market forces would take over, the profit incentives for the Colombian and other cartels would vanish, and drug-related crime would become a term of the past.

> *He uses cause-and-effect reasoning to predict the effects of legalizing drugs.*

Legalization is bound to lead millions more Americans to try, and get hooked on, crack, cocaine, heroin, and other mind-altering drugs. Who's going to supply all the drugs needed to meet the demand? You can bet your sweet bulletproof vest that if the Medellin cartels of Colombia, the gangs of Los Angeles, and the mobsters of Washington, D.C., do not remain the suppliers, they will aim their automatic guns and target their car and truck bombs on anyone else who seeks to grab the market.

The new druggies will shoplift, rob convenience stores, sell sex (and intensify the problems of AIDS, syphilis, and other venereal diseases in the process). Those on horrible drugs like PCP will commit more gruesome crimes.

Legalization of these drugs will give America a crime problem beyond anything it has experienced. Those arguing for legalization want to stop fighting in the belief that we have "lost the war." The truth is that there hasn't been any real war against the drug merchants, and especially not against the armies of illicit drug users across this land. A handful of prominent people are cloaking cowardice in intellectualism and asking you and me to cave in.

The writer argues that demand for drugs is the core problem.

I know that I, as a liberal or civil libertarian of sorts, am not expected to write this truth: The only way America will ever escape the abominations of imported and locally produced designer drugs is to wipe out the U.S. demand for such dope. And that requires medical help and education for the lower-class kids who are vulnerable day to day, and a draconian sledge-hammer wielded against the middle-class and wealthy Americans whose drug purchases enrich and embolden the Medellín and Cali cartels of Colombia and the drug lords of New York, Los Angeles, Detroit, Washington, D.C., Miami, and a dismaying number of other cities. . . .

The seemingly insatiable American demand for marijuana, crack, heroin, cocaine, and other drugs is the overriding abomination. The American demand is so high that farmers will grow poppies and coca, cartels will kill to protect their production facilities, and U.S. sheriffs, bankers, street cops, judges, and others will take bribes.

He summarizes to conclude his argument.

The Feds and other antidrug law enforcers could lock up ten million drug purchasers tomorrow, and I would never write a word saying that they have some constitutional right to subsidize the drug culture that is devouring so many children and weakening America in so many critical ways. So I have a vision of an America where rich people use their money to give hope to children at risk rather than allow them to commit to chemical suicide. ■

write

Reading for Better Writing

1. Carl Rowan introduces his essay by describing the effects of drug use. Explain why this choice does or does not strengthen his argument against legalizing drugs.

2. In the fourth, fifth, and sixth paragraphs, Rowan uses cause-and-effect thinking to argue against legalization. Explain why this logic is or is not convincing.

3. What is Rowan's purpose for writing, and who might his intended readers be? Is the essay's voice appropriate for this purpose and audience? Explain.

Guidelines
Writing a Cause-and-Effect Essay

1. **Select a topic.** Look again at the list of facts, occurrences, or circumstances mentioned under "Topics to Consider" on page 184. Expand the list by jotting down additional items for each category, or listing new categories, along with related items. From this finished list, choose a topic and prove its causes, its effects, or both.

   TIP: If your professor approves, you could write an essay contradicting the logic in another writer's cause-and-effect essay. For an example, see "An Apology for the Life of Ms. Barbie D. Doll" on pages 302–303.

2. **Narrow and research the topic.** Write down or type your topic. Below it, brainstorm a list of related causes and effects in two columns. Next, do preliminary research to expand the list and distinguish primary causes and effects from secondary ones. Revise your topic as needed to address only primary causes and/or effects that research links to a specific phenomenon.

Cause/Effect Topic: (state topic)	
Causes (Because of . . .)	Effect (. . . these conditions resulted)
1.	1.
2.	2.
3.	3.
4.	4.

3. **Draft and test your thesis.** Based on your preliminary research, draft a working thesis (you may revise it later) that introduces the topic, along with the causes and/or effects that you intend to discuss. Limit your argument to only those points that you can prove.

4. **Gather and analyze information.** Research your topic, looking for clear evidence that links specific causes to specific effects. At the same time, avoid arguments mistaking a coincidence for a cause/effect relationship. Use the list of logical fallacies (see pages 261–264) to weed out common errors in logic. For example, finding chemical pollutants in a stream running beside a chemical plant does not "prove" that the plant caused the pollutants.

5. **Get organized.** Develop an outline that lays out your thesis and argument in a clear pattern. Under each main point asserting a cause/effect connection, list details from your research that support the connection.

   Thesis: _____

   Point #1
   - Supporting details
   - Supporting details
   - Supporting details

   Point #2
   - Supporting details
   - Supporting details
   - Supporting details

   Point #3
   - Supporting details
   - Supporting details
   - Supporting details

6. **Use your outline to draft the essay.** Try to rough out the overall argument before you attempt to revise it. As you write, show how each specific cause led to each specific effect, citing examples as needed. To indicate those cause/effect relationships, use transitional words like the following:

- accordingly
- as a result
- because
- consequently
- for this purpose
- or this reason
- hence
- just as
- since
- so
- such as
- thereby
- therefore
- thus
- to illustrate
- whereas

7. **Revise the essay.** Whether your essay presents causes, effects, or both, use the checklist below to trace and refine your argument.

____ The thesis and introduction clearly identify the causes and/or effects.

____ All major causes and/or effects are addressed.

____ Statements regarding causes and/or effects are sufficiently limited and focused.

____ Supporting details are researched, relevant, and strong.

____ Links between causes and effects are clear and logical.

____ The conclusion restates the main argument and unifies the essay.

8. **Get feedback.** Ask a peer reviewer or someone from the college's writing center to read your essay for the following:

- An engaging opening
- A clear and logical thesis
- Clear and convincing reasoning that links specific causes to specific effects
- A closing that wraps up the argument, leaving no loose ends

9. **Edit the essay for clarity and correctness.** Check for the following:

- Precise, appropriate word choice
- Complete, smooth sentences
- Clear transitions between paragraphs
- Correct names, dates, and supporting details
- Correct mechanics, usage, and grammar

10. **Publish your essay.** Share your writing with others as follows:

- Submit it to your instructor
- Post it on the class's or department's Web site
- Submit the essay for presentation at an appropriate conference
- Send it as a service to relevant nonprofit agencies
- Share the essay with family and friends

Writing Checklist

Use these six traits to check the quality of your writing, then revise as needed:

____ The **ideas** explain the causes and/or effects of the topic in a clear, well-reasoned argument supported by credible information.

____ The **organization** helps the reader understand the cause/effect relationship. The links between main points and supporting points are clear.

____ The **voice** is informed, polite, and professional.

____ The **words** are precise and clear. Technical or scientific terms are defined. Causes are linked to effects with transitional words and phrases such as *therefore, as a result,* and *for this reason.*

____ The **sentences** are clear, varied in structure, and smooth.

____ The **copy** is correct, is clean, and follows assigned guidelines for format.

Writing Activities

1. In "Life-Threatening Stress," the writer argues that one cause of stress is a fast-paced lifestyle. Brainstorm a list of other effects that lifestyle choices may cause. Choose one lifestyle/effect pair. Research the topic and write an essay proving that the lifestyle choice does or does not cause the phenomenon.

2. In "Adrenaline Junkies" and "A New Vision for America," each writer describes a form of addiction: adrenaline highs and drug use. List other addictions, choose one, and write an essay proving its causes and/or effects.

3. List several phenomena in your family life or work life, and then choose a topic that you would like to examine. Next, research the topic's causes and/or effects by (a) listing your own experiences and insights, (b) interviewing family members or co-workers, and (c) studying library and Web resources. Finally, write an essay on the topic. Consider sharing the finished paper with family members or co-workers.

4. Choose a phenomenon that is related to your program or major and discussed in the news media. Write an essay that analyzes and explains either its causes, its effects, or both. Consider submitting the essay to your adviser, asking for feedback, and then polishing the piece for inclusion in your professional portfolio.

Chapter 13
Comparison and Contrast

audio

In his plays, William Shakespeare includes characters, families, and even plot lines that mirror each other. As a result, we see Hamlet in relation to Laertes and the Montagues in relation to the Capulets. In the process, we do precisely what the writer wants us to do—we compare and contrast the subjects. The result is clarity and insight: by thinking about both subjects, we understand each one more clearly.

In this chapter, four writers use compare-and-contrast organization: one to discuss lightbulbs, another to distinguish literary characters, a third to weigh two tragedies, and a fourth to describe ethnic groups. Elsewhere in this book, you will find writers working in the natural sciences, social sciences, and the humanities— all comparing and contrasting two or more subjects with the goal of helping their readers understand the topics.

What's the point? Comparing and contrasting is a writing-and-thinking strategy used across the curriculum. You are about to write an essay using this strategy. What you learn in the process will help you succeed both in other courses and in your career.

What's Ahead

- Overview: Comparison-and-Contrast Essay
  - Student Models
  - Professional Model
- Guidelines
- Writing Checklist and Activities

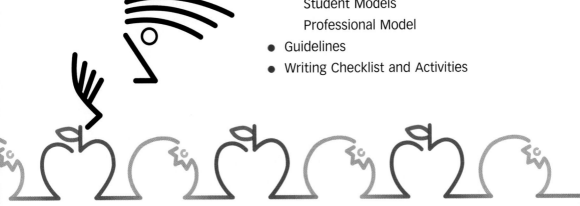

Overview
Writing a Comparison-and-Contrast Essay

Writer's Goal

Your goal is to write an essay that (1) sets two or more subjects side by side, (2) shows the reader how they are similar and/or different, and (3) draws conclusions or makes some point based on what you have shown.

Keys for Success

Think about your readers. ▪ What do they know about the subject? What should they know? Why should they care? Answering these questions will help you understand both your readers and your purpose for writing.

Know your purpose. ▪ What do you want your essay to do? Inform? Explain? Persuade? Some combination of these? Knowing your purpose will help you decide what to include (and not include) in the essay, how to organize it, and how to help readers use the information.

Be logical. ▪ Comparing and contrasting is a logical process that helps you understand your subjects more fully and explain them more clearly. Begin by determining the basis of your comparison: how are the subjects related? Then decide whether to compare, to contrast, or both. When *comparing* subjects, show how they are similar. When *contrasting* them, show how they are different. When *comparing* and *contrasting* subjects, show how they are both similar and different. To choose which of the three patterns to follow, think about your purpose. Which pattern will help your essay accomplish what you want it to do?

Topics to Consider

Choose subjects that are related in some important way. To get started, think about pairs of objects, events, places, processes, people, ideas, beliefs, and so on. For more inspiration, read the four models in this chapter and scan the models listed below. Each of these essays uses compare/contrast strategies. List topics similar to those in the models.

- "Three Family Cancers," pages 213–215
- "Four Ways to Talk About Literature," pages 216–217
- "The Effects of Temperature and Inhibitors . . . ," pages 361–364

Next Step Read the model essays and perform the activities that follow. As you read, note whether the writer compares, contrasts, or both. Also note the pattern used to organize the essay: subject by subject, trait by trait, and so on. (For more on these patterns, see "Get Organized" on page 206.)

Comparison

The following essay by David Zupp compares two lightbulbs. Having researched *Consumer Reports*, checked an encyclopedia, and visited a hardware store, the writer points out differences between the bulbs and gives advice about which is the better buy.

Seeing the Light

The writer introduces his topic and purpose.

All lightbulbs make light, so they're all the same, right? Not quite. You *1* have many choices regarding how to light up your life. Two types of lightbulbs are the traditional incandescent and the newer compact fluorescent. By checking out how they're different, you can better choose which one to buy.

He compares and contrasts the lightbulbs, trait by trait.

While either incandescent or compact fluorescent bulbs can help *2* you read or find the bathroom at night, these bulbs make light differently. In an incandescent bulb, electricity heats up a tungsten filament (thin wire) to 450 degrees, causing it to glow with a warm, yellow light. A compact fluorescent is a glass tube filled with mercury vapor and argon gas. Electricity causes the mercury to give off ultraviolet radiation. That radiation then causes phosphors coating the inside of the tube to give off light.

"Both" signals a similarity; "on the other hand" signals a difference.

Both types of bulbs come in many shapes, sizes, and brightnesses, but *3* compacts have some restrictions. Because of their odd shape, compacts may not fit in a lamp well. Compacts also may not work well in very cold temperatures, and they can't be used with a dimmer switch.

On the other hand, while compact fluorescents are less flexible than *4* incandescents, compacts are four times more efficient. For example, a 15-watt compact produces as many lumens of light as a 60-watt incandescent. Why? Incandescents turn only about 5 percent of electricity into light and give off the other 95 percent as heat.

But are compacts less expensive than incandescents? In the short run, *5* no. A compact costs about fifteen dollars while an incandescent costs only a dollar. However, because compacts burn less electricity—and last 7 to 10 times longer—in the long run, compacts are less expensive.

The conclusion restates the main points.

Now that you're no longer in the dark about lightbulbs, take a look at *6* the lamp you're using to read this essay. Think about the watts (electricity used), lumens (light produced), efficiency, purchase price, and lamplife. Then decide how to light up your life in the future. ∎

write

Reading for Better Writing

1. Does the introduction adequately introduce the essay's topic and purpose? Explain why or why not.

2. The writer organizes his message trait by trait. Explain how this choice does or does not help him accomplish his purpose.

3. Are the transitional words or phrases used effectively? Why or why not?

Comparison

In this essay, Janae Sebranek compares the fate of two tragic literary characters, Bigger in *Native Son* and Alan in *Equus*. The student writer makes a trait-by-trait comparison, exploring the effects of work, religion, and the media on the characters' lives.

Beyond Control

The writer introduces her topic, main points of comparison, and thesis.

Most children, no matter what their personal or family situation, lead more or less controlled lives. As they grow, they begin to sense the pressure of controlling factors in their lives, and start struggling to take control themselves. This can be a difficult process. In the works *Native Son* and *Equus*, Richard Wright and Peter Shaffer, respectively, create two characters who must deal with this struggle. Bigger in *Native Son* and Alan in *Equus* are both entering adulthood and have come to realize that they are controlled by work, religion, and the media. In the midst of these characters' efforts to gain control, each character falls into a tragic situation. [1]

She describes one of the traits of the first character.

We find Alan experiencing the pressure of working as a clerk at Bryson's appliance store. The customers are demanding, and the many products and brand names are confusing. He finds that he cannot function in this work environment. Later, under hypnosis, he admits to Dr. Dysart that his "foes" are the myriad of brand names he is challenged to locate and explain to the customers—"The Hosts of Hoover. The Hosts of Philco. Those Hosts of Pifco. The House of Remington and all its tribe!" (73). However, by recognizing the demands of this job, Alan attempts to take some control over his life. [2]

Alan exercises further control when he decides to look for another job. He likes being around horses, so he pursues and lands a job with Mr. Dalton, a stable owner. He enjoys his job and begins to deal more effectively with the whole concept of work. [3]

She describes a parallel trait of the second character and then contrasts the traits.

Bigger must also struggle with the pressure and anxiety of his first job. Because of his family's desperate financial situation, he is forced to take the one job he is offered, coincidentally, by a Mr. Dalton. He works as a chauffeur for Mr. Dalton's wealthy suburban family. Bigger cannot relate to them. He sees himself as a foreigner, forced to live and work among the privileged. The Daltons tell him where, when, and even how to drive. Bigger struggles; but, like Alan, he cannot deal with the extreme discomfort he is feeling. He quits after only two days on the job. Unlike Alan, however, he does not have the option of getting a job that interests him. [4]

Alan and Bigger also find religion to be a controlling factor in their lives. Alan's mother, Dora, "doses [religion] down the boy's throat" as she whispers "that Bible to him hour after hour, up there in his room" (33). Obviously, Alan's mother believes that he needs the controlling force of religion in his life, so she preaches to him every night. For a time, he is fascinated by the Bible's imagery and ideas. Eventually, though, this fascination begins to fade. [5]

She notes a contrast.

Bigger's mother does not push the issue of religion to the extreme that Alan's mother does. Instead, she tries to make her son see its value with daily comments such as "You'll regret how you living someday" (13). She offers her advice by singing religious songs from behind a curtain in their one-room apartment. She tries to show Bigger that religion is a valid way of dealing with a world out of control. But Bigger refuses to accept her religion, and he is left with no spiritual footing or direction. 6

She introduces her last point of comparison.

Finally, we find the media playing a tormenting, controlling role in both Alan's and Bigger's lives. Alan's father calls television a "dangerous drug" (27) that can control the mind. Alan still manages to watch television, but only because his mother "used to let him slip off in the afternoons to a friend next door" (31) to watch. Later, while he is under psychiatric care, he watches television every night and eventually finds himself becoming controlled by the medium. 7

Bigger, in a more tragic way, is also controlled by the media. He reads about himself in the newspapers and begins to believe certain things that have no valid basis. He is referred to as a "Negro killer" who looks "as if about to spring upon you at any moment" (260). The papers remark that Bigger "seems a beast utterly untouched" (260) by and out of place in the white man's world. Unfortunately, he has no control over what is printed or over what other people believe about him. 8

She summarizes her argument and restates the thesis.

Bigger's ultimate fate is clearly beyond his control. He is falsely accused of raping and killing a woman, and he cannot convince anyone of the truth. Bigger's identity is too closely linked with the descriptions given in the newspapers. And this identity tragically leads to his death. Alan's fate is different, although tragic in its own right. While in the psychiatric ward, he gains a certain control with the help of therapy and medication. However, he loses his passion for life: "Passion, you see, can be destroyed by a doctor. It cannot be created" (108). This is Alan's personal tragedy. 9

Ultimately, both Alan and Bigger fail to gain real control over the outside forces in their lives. Alan forfeits his interest in life, and Bigger forfeits life itself. They, like so many people, become victims of the world in which they live. ■ 10

Note: The Works Cited page is not shown.

write

Reading for Better Writing

1. Do the opening paragraphs adequately introduce the topic and thesis? Why or why not?

2. This essay is organized trait by trait. Is this strategy used effectively? Explain.

3. Does the writer focus on similarities, differences, or both? Is her choice effective?

Comparison and Contrast

One week after the attack on the World Trade Center, when the causes and consequences were still unclear, Canadian student Anita Brinkman wrote this editorial. To make her point, she compares the attack to other significant tragedies.

A Fear Born of Sorrow

The writer cites statistics that introduce her topic.

More than 100 people were killed in the tragic bombing of the *1* Oklahoma Federal Building in 1995. About 6,000 die in Africa each day of AIDS. Between 8,000 and 10,000 people worldwide die of starvation daily. Tragedies occur all around us, and we accept them out of necessity as a part of life. But sometimes the horror of a tragedy affects us in a new way: it overwhelms a nation and stuns the international community. This is what happened last week when two hijacked passenger planes hit the Twin Towers of the World Trade Center, and their resulting collapse killed thousands of people from several countries. News of the tragedy flashed around the globe. Everywhere, it seemed, people in uncomprehending horror listened to reports on their radios or watched endless replays on their televisions. Several countries declared days of mourning and scheduled services of remembrance. Now, one week after the attack, tokens of grief and letters of condolence still flood U.S. embassies and government offices worldwide.

She states her thesis as a question.

But why is the outpouring of grief so much deeper for this tragedy than for others? Why isn't the attack considered just a large-scale repeat of the Oklahoma bombing? Could it be that our grief is more than sorrow, and that our loss is much more than what lies in the rubble?

Two parallel events are compared and contrasted.

The Oklahoma bombing was grievous and alarming, but localized. The *2* bomber was soon arrested, his motives deduced, and justice served. While lives were changed and a nation was shaken, the world community remained composed. However, the September 11 attack unsettled us more, in part because the World Trade Center stood for so much more than the Oklahoma Federal Building did. The Twin Towers symbolized American domination of world finances: they were a major center for the Internet, a hub for international business, and an emblem of American life. The fall of the towers struck violently at the nation's psyche, and the manner in which they were destroyed—with America's own airplanes filled with passengers—has raised questions about America's security and future. Threatened to their core, Americans have demanded retaliation—but against whom? The terrorists' identity is not clear, and evidence seems elusive. In a sense, an unknown offender has injured Americans, and they beat the air in the dark. In such a case, terrorism is aptly named, for America's outcry expresses more than sorrow—it also expresses fear.

The word "fear" links this paragraph with the next one.

The fear that Americans feel comes partly from the uncertainty related ³ to this attack. The attackers demonstrated technical and planning skills that have surprised Americans, making them question their safety and fear future attacks. Air travel, long considered safe, now includes security measures like armed guards, luggage searches, and bomb-sniffing dogs—all strategies to achieve safety. As Americans struggle to find answers in the shattered peace, nations are forming alliances, war seems imminent, and the whole world waits anxiously to see where it all will lead.

The writer contrasts the 9-11 and Pearl Harbor attacks.

Fear and uncertainty are new to Americans living today because ⁴ America has not been attacked in this way since Britain ruled her as a colony. While the bombing of Pearl Harbor awoke many to the fact that America could be targeted, the Japanese bombers hit Hawaii—then a U.S. territory, not a state, and not the mainland. Following World War II, many in the world community again thought of America as the invulnerable Land of Opportunity. However, this belief is now shattered, and many citizens of the global village fear that what was lost last week includes more than what lies in the rubble.

She shows how the events differ.

On September 11, 2001, America, along with its Western allies, lost its ⁵ aura of invincibility. As the whole world watched, the towers fell, and we stumbled in shock and pain. Moreover, as time passes, America may fail to identify its enemy and to understand the attack. If this happens, the oppressed people of the world—to some extent victims of Western culture—will take notice.

She restates her thesis.

It is now one week since the towers fell, and the world still grieves. ⁶ However, mingled with this grief is the fear that we may be mourning not only for the lives lost, but also for our lost way of life. ∎

write

Reading for Better Writing

1. Review the title and explain how it does or does not forecast the essay's main idea.

2. The writer compares and contrasts the September 11 attack with the Oklahoma City and Pearl Harbor attacks. What does she conclude from each comparison? Explain why you do or do not agree with her.

3. Review the essay's final paragraph and explain why it is or is not an effective closing.

Comparison and Contrast

Author Gary Soto describes falling in love against his family's advice with a girl who is not Mexican. In doing so, he draws a number of comparisons.

Like Mexicans

The title forecasts a comparison.

My grandmother gave me bad advice and good advice when I was in my early teens. For the bad advice, she said that I should become a barber because they made good money and listened to the radio all day. "Honey, they don't work como burros," she would say every time I visited her. She made the sound of donkeys braying. "Like that, Honey!" For good advice, she said that I should marry a Mexican girl. "No Okies, hijo"—she would say—"Look, my son. He marry one and they fight every day about I don't know what and I don't know what." For her, everyone who wasn't Mexican, black, or Asian was an Okie. The French were Okies, the Italians in suits were Okies. When I asked about Jews, whom I had read about, she asked for a picture. I rode home on my bicycle and returned with a calendar depicting the important races of the world. "Pues si, son Okies también!" she said, nodding her head. She waved the calendar away and we went to the living room, where she lectured me on the virtues of the Mexican girl: first, she could cook and, second, she acted like a woman, not a man, in her husband's home. She said she would tell me about a third when I got a little older.

An anecdote introduces the topic.

I asked my mother about it—becoming a barber and marrying Mexican. She was in the kitchen. Steam curled from a pot of boiling beans, the radio was on, looking as squat as a loaf of bread. "Well, if you want to be a barber—they say they make good money." She slapped a round steak with a knife, her glasses slipping down with each strike. She stopped and looked up. "If you find a good Mexican girl, marry her, of course." She returned to slapping the meat, and I went to the backyard where my brother and David King were sitting on the lawn feeling the inside of their cheeks.

The writer subtly compares his grandmother's and mother's responses.

"This is what girls feel like," my brother said, rubbing the inside of his cheek. David put three fingers inside his mouth and scratched. I ignored them and climbed the back fence to see my best friend, Scott, a second-generation Okie. I had called him and his mother pointed to the side of the house where his bedroom was, a small aluminum trailer, the kind you gawk at when they're flipped over on the freeway, wheels spinning in the air. I went around to find Scott pitching horseshoes.

I picked up a set of rusty ones and joined him. While we played, we talked about school and friends and record albums. The horseshoes scuffed up dirt, sometimes ringing the iron that threw out a meager shadow like a sundial. After three argued-over games we pulled two oranges apiece from his tree and started down the alley still talking school and friends and record albums. We pulled more oranges from the alley and talked about who we would marry. "No offense, Scott," I said with an orange slice in my mouth, "but I would never marry an Okie." We walked in step, almost touching, with a sled of shadows dragging behind us. "No offense, Gary," Scott said, "but I would *never* marry a Mexican." I looked at him: a fang of orange slice showed from his munching mouth. I didn't think anything of it. He had his girl and I had mine. But our seventh-grade vision was the same: to marry, get jobs, buy cars and maybe a house if we had money left over.

We talked about our future lives until, to our surprise, we were on the downtown mall, two miles from home. We bought a bag of popcorn at Penneys and sat on a bench near the fountain watching Mexican and Okie girls pass. "That one's mine," I pointed with my chin when a girl with eyebrows arched into black rainbows ambled by. "She's cute," Scott said about a girl with yellow hair and mouthful of gum. We dreamed aloud, our chins busy pointing out girls. We agreed that we couldn't wait to become men and lift them onto our laps.

"But" signals a surprise, a difference.

But the woman I married was not Mexican but Japanese. It was a surprise to me. For years, I went about wide-eyed in my search for the brown girl in a white dress at a dance. I searched the playground at the baseball diamond. When the girls raced for grounders, their hair bounced like something that couldn't be caught. When they sat together in the lunchroom, heads pressed together, I knew they were talking about us Mexican guys. I saw them and dreamed them. I threw my face into my pillow, making up sentences that were as good as in the movies.

> *For years, I went about wide-eyed in my search for the brown girl in a white dress at a dance.*

The writer contrasts his original fantasies with reality.

But when I was twenty, I fell in love with this other girl who worried my mother, who had my grandmother asking once again to see the calendar of the Important Races of the World. I told her I had thrown it away many years before. I took a much-glanced-at snapshot from my wallet. We looked at it together, in silence. Then Grandma reclined in her chair, lit a cigarette, and said, "Es pretty." She blew and asked with all her worry pushed up to her forehead: "Chinese?"

I was in love and there was no looking back. She was the one. I told my mother who was slapping hamburger into patties. "Well, sure if you want to marry her," she said. But the more I talked, the more concerned she became. Later I began to worry. Was it all a mistake? "Marry a Mexican girl," I heard my mother say in my mind. I heard it at breakfast. I heard it over math problems, between Western Civilization and cultural geography. But then one afternoon while I was hitchhiking home from school, it struck me like a baseball in the back: my mother wanted me to marry someone of my own social class—a poor girl. I considered my fiancee, Carolyn, and she didn't look poor, though I knew she came from a family of farm workers and pull-yourself-up-by-your-bootstraps ranchers. I asked my brother who was marrying Mexican poor that fall, if I should marry a poor girl. He screamed "Yeah" above this terrible guitar playing in his bedroom. I considered my sister who had married Mexican. Cousins were dating Mexicans. Uncles were remarrying poor women. I asked Scott, who was still my best friend, and he said, "She's too good for you, so you better not."

I worried about it until Carolyn took me home to meet her parents. 9 We drove in their Plymouth until the houses gave way to farms and ranches and finally her house fifty feet from the highway. We pulled into the drive, I panicked and begged Carolyn to make a U-turn and go back so we could talk about it over a soda. She pinched my cheek, calling me a "silly boy." I felt better, though, when I got out of the car and saw the house: the chipped paint, a cracked window, boards for a walk to the back door. There were rusting cars near the barn. A tractor with a net of spiderwebs under a mulberry. A field. A bale of barbed wire like children's scribbling leaning against an empty chicken coop. Carolyn took my hand and pulled me to my future mother-in-law, who was coming out to greet us.

We had lunch: sandwiches, potato chips, and iced tea. Carolyn and 10 her mother talked mostly about neighbors and the congregation at the Japanese Methodist Church in West Fresno. Her father, who was in khaki work clothes, excused himself with a wave that was almost a salute and went outside. I heard a truck start, a dog bark, and then the truck rattle away.

Carolyn's mother offered another sandwich, but I declined with a shake 11 of my head and a smile. I looked around when I could, when I was not saying over and over that I was a college student, hinting that I could take care of her daughter. I shifted my chair, I saw newspapers piled in corners, dusty cereal boxes and vinegar bottles in corners. The wallpaper was bubbled from rain that had come in from a bad roof. Dust. Dust lay on lamp shades and windowsills. These people are just like Mexicans, I thought. Poor people.

Carolyn's mother asked me through Carolyn if I would like a *sushi*. A 12 plate of black and white things was held in front of me. I took one, wide-eyed, and turned it over like a foreign coin. I was biting into one when I saw a kitten crawl up the window screen over the sink. I chewed and the kitten opened its mouth of terror as she crawled higher, wanting to paw the leftovers from our plates. I looked at Carolyn, who said that the cat was just showing off. I looked up in time to see it fall. It crawled up, then fell again.

We talked for an hour and had apple pie and coffee, slowly. Finally, *13* we got up with Carolyn taking my hand. Slightly embarrassed, I tried to pull away but her grip held me. I let her have her way as she led me down the hallway with her mother right behind me. When I opened the door, I was startled by a kitten clinging to the screen door, its mouth screaming "cat food, dog biscuits, *sushi* . . . ." I opened the door and the kitten, still holding on, whined in the language of hungry animals. When I got into Carolyn's car, I looked back: the cat was still clinging. I asked Carolyn if it were possibly hungry, but she said the cat was being silly. She started the car, waved to her mother, and bounced over the rain-poked drive, patting my thigh for being her lover baby. Carolyn waved again. I looked back, waving, then gawking at a window screen where there were now three kittens clawing and screaming to get in. Like Mexicans, I thought. I remembered the Molinas and how the cats clung to their screens—cats they shot down with squirt guns. On the highway, I felt happy, pleased by it all. I patted Carolyn's thigh. Her people were like Mexicans, only different. ∎

> He again focuses on a cat and begins his comparison.

> The writer compares Japanese and Mexican people by comparing their cats.

Reading for Better Writing

1. Briefly explain what the title, "Like Mexicans," signifies.
2. List the items that the writer either directly or indirectly compares (for example, two kitchens, two mothers). Do these comparisons add to or detract from the essay's main point? Explain your answer.
3. Explain how the essay is organized. Is the organization effective? Why or why not?
4. The writer describes cats three times. How is the climbing of cats on screens related to his main point?

Guidelines
Writing a Comparison-and-Contrast Essay

1. **Select a topic.** List subjects that are similar and/or different in ways that you find interesting, perplexing, disgusting, infuriating, charming, or informing. Then choose two subjects whose comparison and/or contrast gives the reader some insight into who or what they are. For example, you could explain how two chemicals that appear to be similar are actually different—and how that difference makes one more explosive, poisonous, or edible.

2. **Get the big picture.** Using a computer or a paper and pen, create three columns as shown below. Brainstorm a list of traits under each heading. (Also see the Venn diagram on page **46**.)

   Traits of Subject #1   *Shared Traits*   *Traits of Subject #2*

3. **Gather information.** Review your list of traits, highlighting those that could provide insight into one or both subjects. Research the subjects, using hands-on analysis when possible. Consider writing your research notes in the three-column format shown above.

4. **Draft a working thesis.** Review your expanded list of traits and eliminate those that now seem unimportant. Write a sentence stating the core of what you learned about the subjects and whether you are comparing, contrasting, or both. If you're stuck, try completing the sentence below. (Switch around the terms "similar" and "different" if you wish to stress similarities.)

   While _____ and _____ seem similar, they are different in several ways, and the differences are important because _____.

5. **Get organized.** Decide how to organize your essay. Generally, *subject by subject* works best for short, simple comparisons. *Trait by trait* works best for longer, more complex comparisons.

Subject by Subject:	Trait by Trait:
Introduction	Introduction
Subject #1	Trait A
• Trait A	• Subject #1
• Trait B	• Subject #2
• Trait C	Trait B
Subject #2	• Subject #1
• Trait A	• Subject #2
• Trait B	Trait C
• Trait C	• Subject #1
	• Subject #2

6. **Draft the essay.** Review your outline and then write your first draft in one sitting if possible. Check your outline for details and integrate them into the text.
   Subject-by-subject pattern:
   - **Opening**—get readers' attention and introduce the two subjects and thesis.
   - **Middle**—describe one "package" of traits representing the first subject and a parallel set of traits representing the second subject.
   - **Conclusion**—point out similarities and/or differences, note their significance, and restate your main point.

   Trait-by-trait pattern:
   - **Opening**—get readers' attention and introduce the two subjects and thesis.
   - **Middle**—compare and/or contrast the two subjects trait by trait (include transitions that help readers look back and forth between the two subjects).
   - **Conclusion**—summarize the key relationships, note their significance, and restate your main point.

7. **Revise the essay.** Check the essay for the following:
   - Balanced comparisons and contrasts of comparable traits
   - Complete and thoughtful treatment of each subject
   - Genuine and objective voice
   - Clear, smooth sentences with varied structure
   - Title and introduction that spark interest
   - Thoughtful, unifying conclusion

8. **Get feedback.** Ask a classmate or someone in the writing center to read your paper, looking for the following:
   - A clear, interesting thesis
   - An engaging and informative introduction
   - A middle that compares and/or contrasts significant, parallel traits
   - Ideas that offer insight into the subject
   - A conclusion that restates the main point and unifies the essay

9. **Edit your essay.** Look for the following:
   - Transitions that signal comparisons and link paragraphs: *on the other hand, in contrast, similarly, also, both, even though, in the same way.*
   - Correct quotations and documentation
   - Correct spelling, punctuation, usage, and grammar

10. **Publish your essay.** Share your writing with others:
    - Submit it to your instructor
    - Share it with other students or publish it on a Web site

Writing Checklist

Use these six traits to check the quality of your writing, then revise as needed:

____ The **ideas** (points made or conclusions drawn from comparing and contrasting) provide insight into who or what both subjects are and why they are important. The basis for comparison is clear.

____ The **organization** pattern (subject by subject, trait by trait) helps readers grasp the similarities and differences between the subjects.

____ The **voice** is informed, involved, and genuine.

____ The **words** are precise and clear. Technical or scientific terms are defined. Links between subjects are communicated with transitions such as these:

- Although
- Either one
- In contrast
- Neither
- As a result
- For this reason
- In the same way
- On the other hand
- Both
- However
- Likewise
- Therefore

____ The **sentences** are clear, well-reasoned, varied in structure, and smooth.

____ The **copy** is correct, clean, and properly formatted.

Writing Activities

1. At first glance, the topic of "Seeing the Light" (two lightbulbs) may seem trivial. The topic becomes interesting, however, as we learn more about these common objects. List other common classroom, lab, household, or workplace objects that would be interesting topics to research and compare/contrast.

2. In "Beyond Control," the writer uses compare-and-contrast strategies to describe and analyze two literary characters. List other pairs of characters from literature, film, or TV. Choose a pair and write a compare-and-contrast essay that helps readers understand these characters.

3. In "A Fear Born of Sorrow," the writer analyzes the effects of the September 11 attacks by comparing and contrasting them with other historical attacks. Identify key people or events in the news this week. Choose a current-events topic and explain its significance by comparing and/or contrasting it with one or more parallel topics from history.

4. In "Like Mexicans," Gary Soto compares two ethnic groups who are part of his family. List related pairs that are part of your life (siblings, uncles, homes, family conflicts, educational experiences, teachers, neighbors, and so on). Choose a topic that you and your readers would find interesting. Write an essay in which you compare and/or contrast the subjects to gain insight into your life.

Chapter 14
Classification

audio

Classification is an organizational strategy that helps writers make sense of large or complex sets of things. A writer who is using this strategy looks at a topic and then breaks it into components that can be sorted into clearly distinguishable subgroups. For example, if writing about the types of residents who might live in assisted-care facilities, a nursing student might classify possible residents into subgroups according to various physical and/or mental limitations.

By sorting the residents in this way, the writer can discuss them as individuals, as representatives of a subgroup, or as members of the group as a whole. By using an additional strategy like compare/contrast, he or she can show both similarities and differences between one subgroup and another, or between individuals within a subgroup. By using classification, the writer helps readers understand both individual components of the topic and relationships among the components.

For help as you write a classification essay, read the instructions and models in this chapter.

What's Ahead

- Overview: Classification Essay
    Student Models
    Professional Model
- Guidelines
- Writing Checklist and Activities

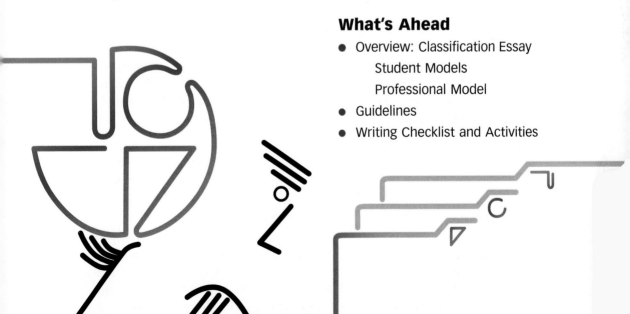

Web

Overview
Writing a Classification Essay

Writer's Goal

Your goal is to divide a group of people, places, things, or concepts into subgroups, and then to write an essay that helps readers understand each component, the subgroups, and the topic as a whole.

Keys for Success

Choose classification criteria that fit the topic. ■ Use classification criteria to distinguish one subgroup from another. For example, to explain her family's experience with cancer, student writer Kim Brouwer examines three types of cancer (*type* is a basis for classification). Because cancer is a complex illness, grouping by type fits her subject (see "Three Family Cancers," pages **213–215**).

Choose classification criteria that fit your purpose. ■ Use criteria that help you achieve your goal. For example, Caitlin Eisenhart classifies weight lifters according to their reasons for weight lifting (a criterion). Because her purpose is to show the variety of people who lift weights, grouping weight lifters based on why they lift weights fits her purpose (see "Why We Lift," pages **211–212**).

Follow classification principles. ■ Sort items into subgroups according to these principles:

- **Consistency:** Use the same criteria in the same way when deciding which individual items to place in which subgroups. For example, Caitlin classifies all weight lifters according to their motivation (one criterion); she does not classify some according to motivation and others according to age (a different criterion).

- **Exclusivity:** Establish distinct subgroups so that each one differs from the others. For example, in "Three Family Cancers," the writer explains three distinct—or exclusive—types of cancer. While the three types share some traits, each type is distinct.

Topics to Consider

To choose a topic, start by writing a half-dozen general headings like the academic headings below; then list two or three related topics under each heading. Finally, pick a topic that can best be explained by breaking it into subgroups.

Engineering	Biology	Social Work	Education
• Branches	• Whales	• Child welfare	• Learning styles
• Bridges	• Fruits	• Organizations	• Testing methods

Next Step Read the model essays and do the activities that follow. As you read, note how the classification strategy helps writers address complex topics.

Classification

Caitlin Eisenhart wrote the following essay about the people she has met while working out in a university's weight room.

The writer introduces the topic, gives her criterion for classifying (why they lift), and identifies subgroups.

She describes the first subgroup.

She describes the second subgroup.

She describes the third subgroup and notes a trait common to all weight lifters.

Why We Lift

I'd heard rumors about it before I ever left for college, and once I 1 moved into the dorm, I realized it was not just a rumor. I needed a way to combat the "freshman fifteen," that dreaded poundage resulting from a combination of late-night pizzas, care-package cookies, and cafeteria cheesecakes. So, my roommate and I headed to the university gym, where the weight-training rooms are filled with student "chain gangs" sweating and clanging their way through a series of mechanical monsters. As I looked around, it became obvious that people work out for quite different reasons. Health enthusiasts, toning devotees, athletes, and bodybuilders seem to be the main categories of those lifting weights.

Some students lift weights as part of an exercise program aimed at 2 maintaining or improving health. They've heard how strong abdominals reduce lower-back problems. They've learned that improved flexibility can help to reduce tension buildup and prevent the headaches and other problems related to prolonged periods of sitting or studying. They know that combining weights with aerobic exercise is an efficient way to lose weight. A person who exercises can lose weight while continuing to eat well because increased muscle mass burns more calories. Typical weight-lifting routines for health enthusiasts are around 20 minutes a day, three times a week.

The toners' routine is different because they want smoothly defined 3 muscles. Not surprisingly, this group includes many young women. Lifting weights can target problem spots and help shape up the body. To develop solid arms, these people use dumbbells and a bench press. Other equipment focuses on achieving toned legs, abdominals, and buttocks. Toning workouts must be done more often than three times a week. I talked to a few young women who lift weights (after aerobic activity of some kind) for about 30 minutes, five times a week.

Athletes also lift weights. Volleyball, rowing, basketball, football—all of 4 these sports require weight training. It may seem obvious that a football player needs to be muscular and strong, but how do other athletes benefit from weight lifting? Muscles are a lot like brains; the more they are used, the more they can do. Strong muscles can increase a person's speed, flexibility, endurance, and coordination. Consider the competition required in various sports—different muscle groups matter more to different athletes. For example, while runners, especially sprinters, need bulging thighs for quick starts and speed, basketball players need powerful arms and shoulders for endless shots and passes. And while gymnasts want overall muscle strength for balance and coordination, football players develop the large muscles for strength, speed, and agility. For all members of this group, however, weight lifting is a vital part of their training.

She describes the last subgroup.

One last group that can't be ignored are the people who lift weights to become as big and as strong as possible. I worked out with a guy who is about 6 feet 2 inches and weighs more than 200 pounds. He bench-presses more than I weigh. In a room devoted to dumbbells and barbells (also known as free weights), bodybuilders roar bulk-boosting battle cries as they struggle to lift superheavy bars. After only a short time in this grunt room, it's clear that the goal is not simply to be healthy, toned, or strong. These lifters want muscles for both strength and show—muscles that lift and bulge. For this reason, many participants spend little time on aerobic activity and most of their time lifting very heavy weights that build bulk and strength. My partner works out for an hour or more, five days a week.

The conclusion, like the opening, includes a personal note.

Not everyone fits neatly into these four categories. I work out to be healthy and toned, and find that I can benefit from lifting only three times a week. Weight lifting has become more and more popular among college students who appreciate exercise as a great stress reliever. And for me, the gym proved to be the best place to combat that dreaded "freshman fifteen." ∎

Reading for Better Writing

1. The writer opens and closes her essay by describing her own interest in weight lifting. Explain why this strategy is or is not effective.

2. The writer classifies weight lifters according to their reasons for weight lifting. Does this criterion fit the topic? What other criteria could be used?

3. Based on your own knowledge of the topic, does the essay accurately describe the people who work out in a weight room? In other words, is the classification consistent, exclusive, and complete? Explain.

audio

Classification

In the essay below, Kim Brouwer reports on her family's experience with cancer. To do so, she distinguishes among three types of cancer, each of which caused the death of one of her grandparents.

Three Family Cancers

The writer introduces the topic with an anecdote.

One day back in fourth grade, my teacher said, "Use your imagination and make an invention—something new and useful." I grumped all the way home from school. An invention? For what, I thought. What could I invent that we could use? "What about a cure for cancer?" Mom asked. [1]

A few weeks earlier my family had learned that Grandpa DeRonde had cancer, so I went to work imagining my very own miracle cure. I drew a picture of a medicine bottle, similar to a bottle of cough syrup, with a drop of liquid coming out of it. I called my masterpiece, "The Cure for Cancer." [2]

She gives her criterion for classifying ("different forms") and identifies subgroups.

I can remember those school days pretty well, but I can't say the same for three of my grandparents—Grandma and Grandpa DeRonde and Grandpa Vernooy. Before I could grow up and get to know them, their lives were invaded, taken over, and destroyed by different forms of cancer—multiple myeloma, prostate cancer, and lung cancer. Now, years later, I am a college freshman, faced with another assignment that gives me a chance to think about cancer: What is it and what causes it? And what were these illnesses like for my grandparents? To get some answers, I checked out some research on cancer and talked with my mother. [3]

She explains what all forms of cancer have in common.

Cancer, as my family learned firsthand, is a serious killer. In fact, it's the second leading cause of death in the United States. Each year, the disease kills about 500,000 Americans, and doctors discover more than one million new cases (Microsoft Encarta). Cancer is so powerful because it's not one illness, but rather many diseases attacking many parts of the body. All cancers are basically body cells gone crazy—cells that develop abnormally. These cells then clone themselves using an enzyme called telomerase. As they multiply like creatures in a sci-fi horror movie, the cells build into tumors, which are tissues that can "invade and destroy other tissues" (Microsoft Encarta). [4]

The writer categorizes carcinogens.

Researchers aren't exactly sure what triggers these cancerous growths, but they think that 80 percent of cancers happen because people come into regular contact with carcinogens—cancer-causing agents. Carcinogens are classified into three groups: chemicals, radiation, and viruses (Compton's). People can be exposed to these carcinogens in many ways and situations. One study showed that 5 percent of cancers could be traced to environmental pollution, including carcinogens in the workplace. Radiation, for [5] example, devastated the population of Chernobyl, Russia, after the nuclear power plant meltdown. But carcinogens don't cause cancer overnight—even from exposure in a terrible accident. The cancer may take 30 to 40 years to develop (Compton's).

She describes the first subgroup.

I don't know what carcinogens attacked my Grandma DeRonde, but I do know the result: she developed multiple myeloma. For a multiple-myeloma patient, the average period of survival is 20 months to 10 years (Madden 108). When I talked with my mother, she said that my family doesn't really know when Grandma came down with multiple myeloma, but she lived for two years after learning that she had it. For two years, she suffered through radiation and chemotherapy treatments, and life seemed measured by the spaces between appointments to check her white blood cell count.

She gives distinguishing details.

What causes multiple myeloma remains a mystery, though its effects are well known. This cancer involves a malignant growth of cells in the bone marrow that makes holes in the skeleton. The holes develop mostly in the ribs, vertebrae, and pelvis. Because the holes make the bones brittle, the victim cannot do simple things like drive and cook. In the end, patients fracture bones and die from infection and pneumonia (Madden 108). It was this weakening of the bones, along with the chemotherapy treatments, that made my grandmother suffer.

She describes the second subgroup.

My Grandpa DeRonde was diagnosed with prostate cancer several years after my grandma died. The doctors began radiation therapy right away, and my family was hopeful because the cancer was caught in its early stages. At first, the cancer seemed to go into remission, but cancer cells were actually invading other sites in his body. Because the cancer spread, the doctors couldn't treat all of it through radiation or surgery. Grandpa lived for only two years after learning he was ill, and during that time he had many chemotherapy treatments and spent a lot of time in the hospital. On his death certificate, the doctor wrote that Grandpa died of cardiac arrest and carcinoma of the lung, with metastasis.

Like multiple myeloma, prostate cancer is a powerful killer. Even though many technological changes help doctors catch this cancer at an early stage, the number of deaths per year is still going up. Prostate cancer is the second most common cancer in the United States, and experts believe that it can be found in about 25 million men over the age of 50 (Fintor).

Prostate cancer is a tumor (called a carcinoma) lining the inside of the organ—in this case, the prostate gland. Many factors trigger this form of cancer: age, diet, environmental conditions, or maybe just having a cancer-prone family ("Prostate Cancer Trends" 183). A survey of more than 51,000 American men showed that eating a lot of fat, found mostly in red meat, can lead to advanced prostate cancer. On the other hand, researchers concluded that fats from vegetables, fish, and many dairy products are probably not linked to the growth of a carcinoma (Cowley 77).

She describes the third subgroup. ----- My second grandfather died from a different carcinoma—lung cancer. *11* Doctors found a tumor in the lower lobe of Grandpa Vernooy's right lung, recommended surgery, and removed the lung. The next winter, he weakened, got pneumonia, and died. His doctors believed that his smoking habit caused the cancer. Smoking, in fact, remains the most important factor in developing lung cancer ("Family Ties" 109). The truth is that cigarette smoking causes almost half of all cancer cases, even though only one out of ten smokers actually comes down with this disease (Compton's).

She cites distinguishing details. ----- One study concluded that genetics may play a role in whether a person *12* develops lung cancer. Research suggests that if a person is missing positive genes called tumor-suppressor genes, it's bad news. If these genes weren't inherited, or if smoking destroyed them, then cancer-related genes are free to do their damage (Edwards 358). Another study identified a special gene that is inherited from one or both parents and that metabolizes chemicals from cigarette smoke. In this case, if the gene is there, the cancer risk goes up, especially for smokers ("Family Ties" 109).

She closes by reviewing the subgroups and reflecting on the opening anecdote. I still wish I could cure cancer with a magic miracle liquid in a medicine bottle. But today I understand that cancer is a complicated disease. *13* My grandparents died from three types of the disease—multiple myeloma, prostate cancer, and lung cancer. If it hadn't been for cancerous tumors taking over their bodies, my grandparents might still be alive, and I'd have many more memories of them. Maybe I'd even be sharing with them stories about my first year at college. On the other hand, perhaps this paper is a cure of a different type—while it can't change what happened, it can help me understand it. ■

Note: The Works Cited page is not shown.

Reading for Better Writing

1. The writer opens and closes the essay with a personal anecdote. Explain why this story does or does not strengthen the essay.

2. For each subgroup (type of cancer), the writer uses a grandparent as an example. Explain how her use of examples does or does not help clarify the subject.

3. Where in the essay does the writer compare and contrast different forms of cancer? Is the comparison and contrast effective? Why or why not?

4. Writing about a scientific topic like cancer nearly always requires technical terminology. Cite two terms used in this essay, and explain how the writer clarifies each term's meaning.

Classification

In this essay John Van Rys, a college professor, classifies four basic approaches to literary criticism. His essay is intended to help college freshmen interpret literature.

Four Ways to Talk About Literature

The writer introduces the topic and criterion for creating four subgroups.

Have you ever been in a conversation where you suddenly felt lost—out of the loop? Perhaps you feel that way in your literature class. You may think a poem or short story means one thing, and then your instructor suddenly pulls out the "hidden meaning." Joining the conversation about literature—in class or in an essay—may indeed seem daunting, but you can do it if you know what to look for, and what to talk about. There are four main perspectives, or approaches, that you can use to converse about literature. *1*

He describes the first subgroup and gives an example.

Text-centered approaches focus on the literary piece itself. Often called *formalist criticism,* such approaches claim that the structure of a work and the rules of its genre are crucial to its meaning. The formalist critic determines how various elements (plot, character, language, and so on) reinforce the meaning and unify the work. For example, the formalist may ask the following questions concerning Robert Browning's poem "My Last Duchess": How do the main elements in the poem—irony, symbolism, and verse form—help develop the main theme (deception)? How does Browning use the dramatic monologue genre in this poem? *2*

He describes the second subgroup and gives an example.

Audience-centered approaches focus on the "transaction" between text and reader—the dynamic way the reader interacts with the text. Often called *rhetorical* or *reader-response criticism,* these approaches see the text not as an object to be analyzed, but as an activity that is different for each reader. A reader-response critic might ask these questions of "My Last Duchess": How does the reader become aware of the duke's true nature, if it's never actually stated? Do men and women read the poem differently? Who were Browning's original readers? *3*

He describes the third subgroup and gives examples.

Author-centered approaches focus on the origins of a text (the writer and the historical background). For example, an author-centered study examines the writer's life—showing connections, contrasts, and conflicts between his or her life and the writing. Broader historical studies explore social and intellectual currents, showing links between an author's work and the ideas, events, and institutions of that period. Finally, the literary historian may make connections between the text in question and earlier and later literary works. The author-centered critic might ask these questions of "My Last Duchess": What were Browning's views of marriage, men and women, art, class, and wealth? As an institution, what was marriage like in Victorian England (Browning's era) or Renaissance Italy (the duke's era)? Who was the historical Duke of Ferrara? *4*

He describes
the fourth
approach and
gives
examples
of each
subgroup
in it.

The fourth approach to criticism applies ideas outside of literature to 5 literary works. Because literature mirrors life, argue these critics, disciplines that explore human life can help us understand literature. Some critics, for example, apply psychological theories to literary works by exploring dreams, symbolic meanings, and motivation. Myth or archetype criticism uses insights from psychology, cultural anthropology, and classical studies to explore a text's universal appeal. Moral criticism, rooted in religious studies and ethics, explores the moral dilemmas literary works raise. Marxist, feminist, and minority criticism are, broadly speaking, sociological approaches to interpretation. While the Marxist examines the themes of class struggle, economic power, and social justice in texts, the feminist critic explores the just and unjust treatment of women as well as the effect of gender on language, reading, and the literary canon. The critic interested in race and ethnic identity explores similar issues, with the focus shifted to a specific cultural group.

He cites
sample
questions.

Such ideological criticism might ask a wide variety of questions about 6 "My Last Duchess": What does the poem reveal about the duke's psychological state and his personality? How does the reference to Neptune deepen the poem? What does the poem suggest about the nature of evil and injustice? In what ways are the Duke's motives class-based and economic? How does the poem present the duke's power and the duchess's weakness? What is the status of women in this society?

If you look at the variety of questions critics might ask about "My Last 7 Duchess," you see both the diversity of critical approaches and the common ground between them. In fact, interpretive methods actually share important characteristics: (1) a close attention to literary elements such as character, plot, symbolism, and metaphor; (2) a desire not to distort the work; and (3) a sincere concern for increasing interest and understanding in a text. In actual practice, critics may develop a hybrid approach to criticism, one that matches their individual questions and concerns about a text. Now that you're familiar with some of the questions defining literary criticism, exercise your own curiosity (and join the ongoing literary dialogue) by discussing a text that genuinely interests you. ■

The closing
presents
qualities
shared by
all four
approaches.

write

Reading for Better Writing

1. Explain how the writer introduces the subject and attempts to engage the reader. Is this strategy effective? Why or why not?

2. The writer uses the same poem to illustrate how each of the four critical approaches works. Explain why this strategy is or is not effective.

3. Review the last paragraph and explain why it does or does not unify the essay.

Guidelines
Writing a Classification Essay

1. **Select a topic.** Review the list of headings and topics that you developed in response to "Topics to Consider" on page 210. Choose a topic that you find interesting and can explain well using classification strategies. If you need more choices, develop a new list of headings and topics.

2. **Look at the big picture.** Do preliminary research to get an overview of your topic. Review your purpose (to explain, persuade, inform, and so on), and consider what classification criteria will help you divide the subject into distinct, understandable subgroups.

3. **Choose and test your criterion.** Choose a criterion for creating subgroups. Make sure it produces subgroups that are consistent (all members fit the criterion), exclusive (subgroups are distinct—no member of the group fits into more than one subgroup), and complete (each member fits into a subgroup with no member left over).

   TIP: To better visualize how you are dividing your topic and classifying its members, take a few minutes to fill out a graphic organizer like the one shown below. (Also see the graphic organizer on page 46.)

4. **Gather and organize information.** Gather information from library and Web resources, as well as interviews. To take notes and organize your information, consider using a classification grid like the one shown below. Set up the grid by listing the classification criteria down the left column and listing the subgroups in the top row of the columns. Then fill in the grid with appropriate details. (The following grid lists the classification criterion and subgroups used in "Four Ways to Talk About Literature," pages 216–217.)

Classification Criteria	Subgroup #1	Subgroup #2	Subgroup #3	Subgroup #4
	Text-centered approach	*Audience-centered approach*	*Author-centered approach*	*Ideas outside literature*
Focus of the critical approach	• Trait #1 • Trait #2 • Trait #3	• Trait #1 • Trait #2 • Trait #3	• Trait #1 • Trait #2 • Trait #3	• Trait #1 • Trait #2 • Trait #3

Note: If you do not use a grid similar to this one, construct an outline to help organize your thoughts.

5. **Draft a thesis.** Draft a working thesis (you can revise it later as needed) that states your topic and main point. Include language introducing your criteria for classifying subgroups.

6. **Draft the essay.** Write your first draft, using either the organizational pattern in the classification grid or an outline.

   Opening: Get the readers' attention, introduce the subject and thesis, and give your criteria for dividing the subject into subgroups.

   Middle: Develop the thesis by discussing each subgroup, explaining its traits, and showing how it is distinct from the other subgroups. For example, in the middle section of "Four Ways to Talk About Literature," the writer first shows the unique focus of each of the four approaches to literary criticism, and then illustrates each approach by applying it to the same poem, "My Last Duchess."

   Closing: While the opening and middle of the essay separate the subject into components and subgroups, the closing brings the components and subgroups back together. For example, in "Four Ways to Talk About Literature," the writer closes by identifying three characteristics that the four subgroups share in common (see page **217**).

7. **Get feedback.** Ask a classmate or someone from the writing center to read your essay looking for the following:

   - An engaging opening that introduces the subject, thesis, and criteria for classifying
   - A well-organized middle that distinguishes subgroups, shows why each subgroup is unique, and includes adequate details
   - A clear closing that reaches some sort of conclusion

8. **Revise the essay.** Check the essay for the following:

   - Subgroups that are consistent, exclusive, and complete
   - Organization that helps the reader understand the subject
   - Appropriate examples that clarify the nature and function of each subgroup
   - A unifying conclusion

9. **Edit the essay.** Check for the following:

   - An informed, reader-friendly voice
   - Clear, complete sentences
   - Unified paragraphs linked with appropriate transitions
   - Correct usage, grammar, punctuation, and spelling

10. **Publish the essay.** Share your writing by doing the following:

    - Offer copies to classmates and friends
    - Publish it in a journal or on a Web site
    - Place a copy in your professional portfolio

Writing Checklist

Use these six traits to check the quality of your writing, then revise as needed:

____ The **ideas** in the classification criteria are logical and clear. The criteria result in subgroups that are consistent, exclusive, and complete.

____ The **organization** of the essay helps the reader understand the components, the subgroups, and the subject as a whole. Paragraphs form cohesive units of thought.

____ The **voice** is informed, courteous, and professional.

____ The **words** are precise, descriptive, and appropriate for the subject. Terms used in classifications are employed in the same way throughout the essay.

____ The **sentences** are complete, varied, and easy to read. Appropriate transitions link sentences and paragraphs.

____ The finished **copy** follows documentation and formatting rules.

write

Writing Activities

1. Review "Why We Lift," noting how classifying weight lifters helps readers get to know them as individuals—not as a homogeneous group. Choose another set of people whom your readers may know only as a group (bikers, artists, salespeople). Write an essay in which you classify the members so readers get to know them better.

2. Kim Brouwer wrote "Three Family Cancers" to better understand a series of painful experiences in her family's life. List painful (or pleasant) experiences in your family's life, and select a topic that you can clarify by classifying. Write an essay using classification strategies that explain the topic.

3. "Four Ways to Talk About Literature" examines four approaches to reading and understanding a piece of literature. Identify a similar group of approaches to analysis or problem solving in your program or major. Write an essay in which you break your topic into subgroups, sort the subgroups, and explain the topic to the reader.

4. Develop a list of social, economic, or political topics in the news. Choose one, research it, classify its components, and then write an essay that explains the topic.

Chapter 15
Process Writing

audio

Process writing is practical writing that answers the kinds of questions that we face every day at home, in college, or on the job: "How do I remove these ugly stains?" or "How does cancer spread?" or "How do I install this software?" Writing that answers these types of questions analyzes the process in which we're interested, breaks it into steps, and shows how the process works.

The three basic forms of process writing include *describing* a process, *explaining* a process, and giving *instructions*. This chapter distinguishes between these forms and shows how to write each. In addition, the chapter includes models showing how writers have used the forms to accomplish their writing goals.

Study this chapter for tips that will help you choose a topic, break it into steps, and explain it clearly in writing.

What's Ahead

- Overview: Writing About a Process
  - Student Models
  - Professional Model
- Guidelines
- Writing Checklist and Activities

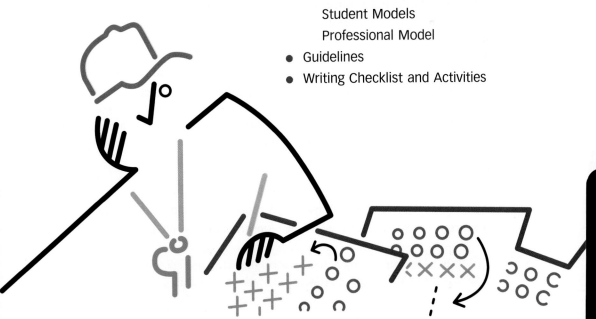

Overview
Writing About a Process

Writer's Goal

Your goal is to analyze a process, break it into specific steps, and write about it using one of the following forms: a *description* of a process, an *explanation* of the process, or *instructions* on how to carry out the process.

Keys for Success

Think logically. ■ To write one of these forms, you must study the process until you understand it, and then write clearly about it. In other words, you must know—and show—how each step leads *logically* to the next, and how all the steps together complete the process.

Know your purpose and your audience. ■ Decide what your writing should do and choose the form that fits your purpose and audience:

- To inform a broad audience how something happens naturally, *describe* the process in an essay that tells how the process unfolds (for example, how cancer cells multiply, how hair grows).
- To help readers who want to know how something is done or made, *explain* the process in an essay that tells how someone would complete each step (for example, how surfers enter the curling point of the wave).
- To help readers who wish to perform the process themselves, provide how-to information in brief, clear *instructions* (for example, how to perform the task of opening a college library each day).
  Note: While descriptions and explanations are usually formatted as essays, instructions are formatted somewhat differently. Instructions include a summary of the process, a list of materials and tools, and a numbered list of steps organized chronologically and stated using clear, command-like verbs.

Consider *all* of your readers. ■ Regardless of the form that you choose, make your writing accessible to all your readers by addressing the reader who knows the least about your topic. Include all the information that this person needs to have, and use language that everyone can understand.

Topics to Consider

- A course-related process
- A process that keeps you healthy
- A process that you've mastered
- A process in the news
- A process that helps you get a job
- A process in your planned occupation

Next Step Read the model essays and perform the activities that follow. As you read, observe how each writer approaches the task of explaining, describing, or instructing.

Describing a Process

Student writer Kerri Mertz wrote this essay (a description of a process) to help nonscientists understand how cancer cells multiply and affect the body.

audio

Wayward Cells

The writer uses the title and an analogy to introduce the topic.

Imagine a room containing a large group of people all working hard toward the same goal. Each person knows his or her job, does it carefully, and cooperates with other group members. Together, they function efficiently and smoothly—like a well-oiled machine.

Then something goes wrong. One guy suddenly drops his task, steps into another person's workstation, grabs the material that she's working with, and begins something very different—he uses the material to make little reproductions of himself, thousands of them. These look-alikes imitate him—grabbing material and making reproductions of themselves. Soon the bunch gets so big that they spill into other people's workstations, getting in their way, and interrupting their work. As the number of look-alikes grows, the work group's activity slows, stutters, and finally stops.

She uses a simile to explain the analogy.

A human body is like this room, and the body's cells are like these workers. If the body is healthy, each cell has a necessary job and does it correctly. For example, right now red blood cells are running throughout your body carrying oxygen to each body part. Other cells are digesting that steak sandwich that you had for lunch, and others are patching up that cut on your left hand. Each cell knows what to do because its genetic code—or DNA—tells it what to do. When a cell begins to function abnormally, it can initiate a process that results in cancer.

She describes the first step in the process and cites a potential cause.

The problem starts when one cell "forgets" what it should do. Scientists call this "undifferentiating"—meaning that the cell loses its identity within the body (Pierce 75). Just like the guy in the group who decided to do his own thing, the cell forgets its job. Why this happens is somewhat unclear. The problem could be caused by a defect in the cell's DNA code or by something in the environment, such as cigarette smoke or asbestos (German 21). Causes from inside the body are called genetic, whereas causes from outside the body are called carcinogens, meaning "any substance that causes cancer" (Neufeldt and Sparks 90). In either case, an undifferentiated cell can disrupt the function of healthy cells in two ways: by not doing its job as specified in its DNA and by not reproducing at the rate noted in its DNA.

She describes the next step and its result.

Most healthy cells reproduce rather quickly, but their reproduction rate is controlled. For example, your blood cells completely die off and replace themselves within a matter of weeks, but existing cells make only as many new cells as the body needs. The DNA codes in healthy cells tell them how

1

2

3

4

5

many new cells to produce. However, cancer cells don't have this control, so they reproduce quickly with no stopping point, a characteristic called "autonomy" (Braun 3). What's more, all their "offspring" have the same qualities as their messed-up parents, and the resulting overpopulation produces growths called tumors.

She describes the third step— how tumors damage the body.

Tumor cells can hurt the body in a number of ways. First, a tumor can 6 grow so big that it takes up space needed by other organs. Second, some cells may detach from the original tumor and spread throughout the body, creating new tumors elsewhere. This happens with lymphatic cancer—a cancer that's hard to control because it spreads so quickly. A third way that tumor cells can hurt the body is by doing work not called for in their DNA. For example, a gland cell's DNA code may tell the cell to produce a necessary hormone in the endocrine system. However, if cancer damages or distorts that code, sick cells may produce more of the hormone than the body can use—or even tolerate (Braun 4). Cancer cells seem to have minds of their own, and this is why cancer is such a serious disease.

A transition signals a shift in focus from the illness to treatments.

Fortunately, there is hope. Scientific research is already helping doctors 7 do amazing things for people suffering with cancer. One treatment that has been used for some time is chemotherapy, or the use of chemicals to kill off all fast-growing cells, including cancer cells. (Unfortunately, chemotherapy can't distinguish between healthy and unhealthy cells, so it may cause negative side effects such as damaging fast-growing hair follicles, resulting in hair loss.) Another common treatment is radiation, or the use of light rays to kill cancer cells. One of the newest and most promising treatments is gene therapy—an effort to identify and treat chromosomes that carry a "wrong code" in their DNA. A treatment like gene therapy is promising because it treats the cause of cancer, not just the effect. Year by year, research is helping doctors better understand what cancer is and how to treat it.

The writer reuses the analogy to review main points.

Much of life involves dealing with problems like wayward workers, 8 broken machines, or dysfunctional organizations. Dealing with wayward cells is just another problem. While the problem is painful and deadly, there is hope. Medical specialists and other scientists are making progress, and some day they will help us win our battle against wayward cells. ■

Works Cited

Braun, Armin C. *The Biology of Cancer.* Boston: Addison-Wesley, 1994.

German, James. *Chromosomes and Cancer.* New York: John Wiley & Sons, 1998.

Neufeldt, Victoria, and Andrew N. Sparks, eds. *Webster's New World Dictionary.* New York: Warner Books. 2001.

Pierce, G. Barry. *Cancer: A Problem of Developmental Biology.* Upper Saddle River: Prentice Hall, 1998.

write

Reading for Better Writing

1. Review the opening four paragraphs in which the writer uses an analogy to introduce and describe the process. Explain why the analogy is or is not effective.

2. Review the three steps cited by the writer, and describe the transitions that she uses to lead into and out of each step. Explain why the transitions are or are not effective.

3. Review the guidelines on page **232** to identify and list traits of a *description* of a process. Explain why this essay does or does not exemplify these traits.

4. At times, the writer uses cause-and-effect reasoning to describe the process. Find an example and explain why this reasoning is or is not effective.

Explaining a Process

California student Luke Sunukjian wrote the following essay (an explanation of a process) to show readers how to enter the "green room."

Entering the "Green Room"

The writer introduces the subject, explains its importance, and defines two terms.

Learning how to surf is really pretty easy; it's actually doing it that presents a challenge. For instance, it's very important to learn how to get "tubed" (to place yourself under the curl of the wave) before going surfing. Major consequences await those who try to get tubed improperly. You may get caught too far behind the wave's lip or get sucked to the top of the wave. Or you may be thrown down the wave's face, knocked unconscious, or worse. Do not let this dangerous situation stop you from learning how to get tubed. There is nothing to fear if you follow my explanation of how to enter the "green room," the curling part of the wave.

He explains the first step.

Before you enter the green room, you must first learn how to stand up on your board. To get to your feet, put your hands on the rails (sides) of the board and push your body up as though you are doing a push-up. Then swing your feet underneath your body. You are now ready to place yourself on the correct part of the wave.

A transitional phrase introduces the second step.

As you get to your feet, you will be dropping down the wave's face (the front of the water rolling toward shore) and will need to prepare for the bottom turn. Your feet should be spread apart near the tail (back) of the board, facing perpendicular to the direction in which you are moving. Put your weight on your back foot to avoid sinking the nose into the water. After dropping past the bottom of the wave, lean toward the face of the wave while continuing to put pressure on the tail of the board. This action will turn the board toward the face of the wave and accelerate you alongside the wave.

The writer explains the third step and defines two terms.

At this point you are slightly ahead of the barreling part of the wave, and you need to "stall," or slow yourself, to get into the tube. There are three methods of stalling used in different situations. If you are slightly ahead of the tube, you can drag your inside hand along the water to stall. If you are a couple of feet in front of the barrel, apply all your weight to your back foot and sink the tail into the water. This is known as a "tail stall" for obvious reasons, and its purpose is to decrease your board speed. If you are moving faster than the wave is breaking, you need to do what is called a "wrap-around." To accomplish this maneuver, lean back away from the wave while applying pressure on the tail. This shifts your forward momentum away from the wave and slows you down. When the wave comes, turn toward the wave and place yourself in the barrel.

He explains the fourth and fifth steps.

While surfing in the barrel, your body position is key. Duck your head 5 (unless the wave is over ten feet) and lean toward the face of the wave so the lip does not crash on your body. You want the breaking part of the wave to completely cover you without the water touching your body. Be careful not to get too close to the face of it because the wave will pull the board upward, causing you to be hurled off. To avoid this scenario, position your board a foot's distance away from the wave's face.

The final step in completing a tube ride is coming out of the tube, and 6 there are two ways to do this. You can increase your board speed to move faster than the wave is breaking. Or you can have the wave "spit" you out. The latter option refers to the barreling wave creating so much air pressure inside the tube that some of the air is forced out. The air being spit out of the barrel hits your back, forcing you out of the wave.

He closes by describing the impact of the process.

Once you complete your first tube ride, you will be hooked, and will 7 come back again and again, always in search of the perfect table, always looking for that twenty-foot wave with a curl that looks like a giant hollow cylinder. Nothing you ever do in life will match the thrill of entering and exiting the perfect "green room." ■

write

Reading for Better Writing

1. The writer appeals to fear to introduce his topic and get the reader's attention. Explain why the appeal is or is not effective.

2. To explain how to enter the "green room," the writer breaks the process into six steps. What transitions move the reader into and out of each step?

3. List the traits of an *explanation* of a process. Explain why this essay does or does not exemplify these traits.

Giving Instructions

Librarian Sheryl Sheeres Taylor wrote the following instructions for students who open the Central College Library each morning. Notice how she uses lists to make things easy to follow and how carefully she explains each step in the process.

The title and first paragraph clearly state the topic.

Instructions for Opening the CCL

Arrive at the library at least one hour before its scheduled opening time with your personal library key and this instruction sheet. To open the Central College Library and prepare it for use, follow the steps below.

The writer lists tools and materials.

Materials

You will need the following six keys:

- Your personal key for the front doors
- Allen key (in the key cupboard behind the circulation desk)
- Workroom key (labeled and in the key cupboard)
- Copy-machine key (labeled and in the key cupboard)
- Cash-drawer key (labeled and in the workroom security box)
- Book-drop key (labeled and in the key cupboard)

Steps

Follow the steps below and call the maintenance department if you experience problems:

She numbers steps and lists them in chronological order.

1. Unlock the front doors using your personal key and fasten the door latches open using the Allen wrench.

2. Unlock the workroom.

3. Shut off the porch lights (switch is in the electrical panel by the workroom door).

She states each step succinctly using verbs in the imperative (command) mood.

4. Turn on the lights in the following areas:
   - Main areas on the first and second floors (switches in the electrical panel by the workroom door)
   - Reference Room (switch on the east end of the south wall)
   - N-PT Room (switch on the south end of the east wall)
   - Q-Z Room (switch in the middle of the east wall)
   - Archives and Demonstration Room (switches in the electrical panel outside the main entrance)

5. Prepare the copy machines:
   - Turn on the four copy machines (two upstairs, one downstairs, and one in the workroom), and add paper in each paper carriage as needed.
   - Using the copy-machine key, open the door in front of the machine, turn the machine on, and lock the door.
   - Get paper from the supply closet in the workroom.

6. Unlock the cash drawer using the cash-drawer key.

7. Change the dates on the two book stamps:

   OUT—set two weeks ahead of the current date

   IN—set for the current date

8. Turn on the PCs, printers, and terminals in the main area of the second floor and in the Learning Resource Center.

9. Turn on the computer on the Public-Service Desk and log in.

10. Open the book drop (using the book-drop key), and check in items using the "book-drop" function on the computer.

11. Get the daily newspapers from the book drop and place them in the news rack.

   After finishing all tasks, return all keys to their proper places. ■

> She states a follow-up activity in the last sentence.

write

Reading for Better Writing

1. Describe how the writer introduces the topic, and explain why the introduction is or is not clear.

2. Note the following formatting strategies: opening-sentence summary, boldfaced title and headings, numbered tasks, and supporting details stated in bulleted phrases. Explain how each strategy does or does not help the employee complete the library-opening process.

3. Some steps contain one action, whereas other steps contain two or three actions. What logic is used to break the process into steps?

4. Would the description of the process have been easier to follow if it had been written entirely in paragraph form?

Describing a Process

Verne Meyer, an educator and a contributing editor, wrote this description of a process to help nonscientists understand how hair grows.

Hair Today, Gone Tomorrow

The writer uses an analogy to introduce the process and distinguish its steps.

Imagine a pitcher's mound covered with two layers of soil: first a layer of clay, and on top of that a layer of rich, black dirt. Then imagine that 100,000 little holes have been poked through the black dirt and into the clay, and at the bottom of each hole lies one grass seed. *1*

Slowly each seed produces a stem that grows up through the clay, out of the dirt, and up toward the sky above. Now and then every stem stops for awhile, rests, and then starts growing again. At any time about 90 percent of the stems are growing and the others are resting. Because the mound gets shaggy, sometimes a gardener comes along and cuts the grass. *2*

He explains the analogy.

Your skull is like that pitcher's mound, and your scalp (common skin) is like the two layers of soil. The top layer of the scalp is the epidermis, and the bottom layer is the dermis. About 100,000 tiny holes (called follicles) extend through the epidermis into the dermis. *3*

An illustration shows parts of a hair stem.

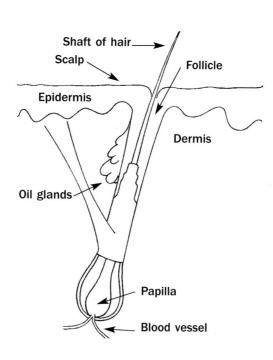

The writer explains steps analogous to those in the illustration.

At the base of each follicle lies a seed-like thing called a papilla. At the bottom of the papilla, a small blood vessel drops like a root into the dermis. This vessel carries food through the dermis into the papilla, which works like a little factory using the food to build hair cells. As the papilla makes cells, a hair strand grows up through the dermis past an oil gland. The oil gland greases the strand with a coating that keeps the hair soft and moist. 4

When the strand reaches the top of the dermis, it continues up through the epidermis into the open air above. Now and then the papilla stops making new cells, rests awhile, and then goes back to work again. 5

Most of the hairs on your scalp grow about one-half inch each month. If a strand stays healthy, doesn't break off, and no barber snips it, the hair will grow about 25 inches in four years. At that point hair strands turn brittle and fall out. Every day between 25 and 250 hairs fall out of your follicles, but nearly every follicle grows a new one. 6

He closes with a brief summary and humor.

Around the clock, day after day, this process goes on . . . unless your papillas decide to retire. In that case you reach the stage in your life—let's call it "maturity"—that others call "baldness." ■ 7

write

Reading for Better Writing

1. The writer uses a baseball analogy to describe the process of how hair grows. List elements of the analogy, along with corresponding elements of the process. Then explain why the analogy is or is not effective.

2. The writer uses an illustration to show parts of a hair stem. Study the illustration and explain why it does or does not help clarify the message.

3. Review the introduction to the essay, noting the author's purpose for writing. Then describe his voice and explain why it does or does not help achieve his purpose.

Guidelines
Writing About a Process

1. **Select a topic.** Choose a topic from the list that you generated under "Topics to Consider" on page 222. If you're stuck, review your notes and textbooks to generate more course-related topics.

2. **Review the process.** Use your present knowledge of the topic to fill out an organizer like the one on the right. List the subject at the top, each of the steps in chronological order, and the outcome at the bottom. Review the organizer to identify issues that you need to research.

   > **Process Analysis**
   > Subject:
   > • Step #1
   > • Step #2
   > • Step #3
   > Outcome:

3. **Research as needed.** Find information that spells out the process: what it is, what steps are required, what order the steps should follow, how to do the steps, what outcome the process should produce, and what safety precautions are needed. If possible, observe the process in action or perform it yourself. Carefully record correct names, materials, tools, and safety or legal issues.

4. **Organize information.** After conducting your research, revise the organizer by adding or reordering steps as needed. Then develop an outline, including steps listed in the organizer as well as supporting details from your research.

5. **Draft the document.** Write the essay or instructions using the guidelines below.

Describing a Process	Explaining a Process	Writing Instructions
Opening: Introduce the topic, stating its importance and giving an overview of the steps.	**Opening:** Introduce the topic and give an overview of the process.	**Opening:** Name the process in the title; then summarize the process and list any materials and tools needed.
Middle: Describe each step clearly (usually in separate paragraphs), and link steps with transitions like *first, second, next, finally,* and *while.* Describe the outcome and its importance.	**Middle:** Explain what each step involves and how to do it (typically using a separate paragraph for each). Use transitions like first, second, and next to link the steps. Explain the outcome.	**Middle:** Present each step in a separate— usually one- or two-sentence— paragraph. Number the steps and state each clearly, using commands directed to the reader.
Closing: Describe the process as a whole and restate key points.	**Closing:** Explain follow-up activity and restate key points.	**Closing:** In a short paragraph, explain any follow-up action.

6. **Revise the writing.** Check for the following and revise as needed:
   - A clear opening that identifies the process
   - Steps that are stated clearly and in the correct order

     For explanations and instructions:
     - Clear details explaining how to perform each step
     - A closing that includes necessary follow-up activity

     For instructions:
     - Clear and correct safety cautions in boldfaced type

7. **Test the writing.** Read the writing for organization and completeness. For *explanations* and *instructions*, perform the process yourself using the writing as a guide. For each step, do only *what* you're told to do and *how* you're told to do it. Note where the writing is incomplete, out of order, or lacking adequate safety precautions. Revise as needed.

8. **Get feedback.** Ask a classmate who is unfamiliar with the process to read the writing for clarity, completeness, and correctness. For *instructions*, have the person use the writing as a guide to perform the process, noting where details are incomplete or unclear, and noting where word choice is either imprecise or too technical. Use the feedback to guide further revision.

9. **Edit the writing by looking for the following:**
   - Word choice appropriate for your least-informed reader
   - Clear transitions between steps
   - Consistent verb tense in all steps
   - For *instructions*—verbs that give clear commands
   - Correct, consistent terminology
   - Informed, respectful voice
   - Proper format (particularly for *instructions*—adequate white space)

10. **Publish the essay.** Share your writing with others:
    - Offer it to instructors or students working with the process
    - Offer explanations and instructions to people on campus or at nonprofit agencies who can use the writing to do their work
    - Post the writing on a suitable Web site

Writing Checklist

Use these six traits to check your essay, then revise as needed:

____ The **ideas** describe or explain the process clearly and completely.

____ The **organization** sequence helps clarify the process. In explanations and instructions, the organization is chronological and helps the reader work through the process.

____ The **voice** matches the writer's purpose. Cautions regarding safety or legal issues sound serious but are not alarming.

____ The **words** are precise, and technical terms are defined.

____ The **sentences** are smooth, varied in structure, and engaging. In instructions, sentences are shaped as clear, brief, no-nonsense commands.

____ The **copy** is formatted properly as an essay or set of instructions.

write

Writing Activities

1. Review the topics that you listed under "Topics to Consider" on page **222.** Choose a topic and write about it, letting the writing take any one of these forms: *description, explanation,* or *instructions.*

2. Review the "Wayward Cells" and "Hair Today, Gone Tomorrow" models. List similar scientific or technical processes that interest you. Choose one and write about it as a *description.*

3. Review "Entering the 'Green Room.'" List similar nontechnical processes that you enjoy. Choose one and write about it as a *description, explanation,* or set of *instructions.*

4. Review "Instructions for Opening the CCL." Write *instructions* for a similar process that could be used by people on your campus or in your community.

Chapter 16
Definition

audio

Whether you're writing a persuasive essay, a lab report, or a project proposal, defining key terms helps you distinguish the boundaries of your subject.

In most writing situations, you will include short definitions of terms consisting of one or two sentences or one or two paragraphs. While this chapter includes information that will enable you to write such brief definitions, its main purpose is to help you write longer, essay-length pieces sometimes called *extended definitions*.

When you write an extended definition, study this chapter, which will guide you through every step in the writing process—from choosing the term to refining the definition. When reading the model essays, look closely at the strategies that each writer uses "to peel the onion"—that is, to unfold and examine each layer of a word's meaning until finally reaching the core.

What's Ahead

- Overview: Definition Essay
    Student Models
    Professional Model
- Guidelines
- Writing Checklist and Activities

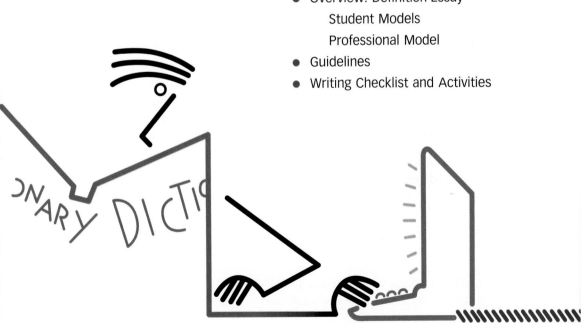

Overview
Writing a Definition Essay

Writer's Goal

Your goal is to choose a word or phrase that interests you, explore what it means (and doesn't mean), and write an essay that helps readers better understand that term.

Keys for Success

Know your purpose. ■ Decide what you want your writing to do: entertain, inform, explain, persuade readers to act, or a combination of these.

Choose appropriate writing strategies. ■ Select strategies that help you accomplish your purpose. For example, the writers whose essays are included in this chapter make the following choices:

- To explore a personal experience with *gullible*, Mary Beth Bruins examines a dictionary definition, an encyclopedia explanation, the word's etymology (or history), and quotations from three professional writers.

- To explain her fascination with *eclectic*, Kirsten Zinser first quotes a dictionary definition, and then playfully examines how the word feels in her mouth and how it does—and does not—describe her.

- To show readers how to treat patients with *dementia*, Sarah Anne Morelos defines the term using anecdotes and details gathered through research.

- To entertain and instruct people listening to his radio program, David Schelhaas examines the word *deft* by first sharing a personal anecdote, and then comparing and contrasting the definitions and etymologies of *deft* and *daft*.

- To help readers understand the emergency-medical condition *code blue*, Abraham Verghese, a physician, defines the term by writing a narrative.

Present fresh information. ■ Choose details that help readers understand the word's denotations (literal meanings) as well as its connotations (associated meanings). For example, one denotation of *cute* is *attractive*. Depending on the context, however, the associations of this word may be positive or negative.

Topics to Consider

Beneath headings like the following, list words that you'd like to explore.

Words that are related to an art or sport:	Words that are (or should be) in the news:	Words that are over-used, unused, or abused:	Words that make you chuckle, frown, or fret:	Words that do— or do not— describe you:

Next Step Read the model essays and notice the writing strategies these writers used; think about how you might use them in your essays.

audio

Definition

In this essay, student writer Mary Beth Bruins describes how she earned the name "Gullible" and what the name means to most people—and specifically what it means to her. Notice the variety of sources the writer uses to fully define and illustrate the meaning of the word.

The Gullible Family

The writer uses the title and an anecdote to introduce the topic.

The other day, my friend Loris fell for the oldest trick in the book: "Hey, somebody wrote 'gullible' on the ceiling!" Shortly after mocking "Gullible Loris" for looking up, I swallowed the news that Wal-Mart sells popcorn that pops into the shapes of cartoon characters. And so, as "Gullible Mary," I decided to explore what our name means, and who else belongs to the Gullible family. What I learned is that our family includes both people and birds, related to each other by our willingness to "swallow."

She gives an example and the word's Germanic root.

A gullible person will swallow an idea or argument without questioning its truth. Similarly, the *gull* (a long-winged, web-footed bird) will swallow just about anything thrown to it. In fact, the word *gullible* comes from *gull*, and this word can be traced back to the Germanic word *gwel* (to swallow). Both *gull* and *gwel* are linked to the modern word *gulp*, which means, "to swallow greedily or rapidly in large amounts." It's not surprising then that Loris and I, sisters in the Gullible family, both eagerly gulped (like gulls) the false statements thrown to us.

> "Hey, somebody wrote 'gullible' on the ceiling!"

She cites details from an encyclopedia.

Swallowing things so quickly isn't too bright, and *gull* (when referring to a bird or a person) implies that the swallower is immature and foolish. For example, *gull* refers to an "unfledged" fowl, which the *Grolier Encyclopedia* describes as either "an immature bird still lacking flight feathers" or something that is "inexperienced, immature, or untried." These words describe someone who is fooled easily, and that's why *gull*, when referring to a human, means "dupe" or "simpleton." In fact, since 1550, *gullet*, which means "throat," has also meant "fooled."

She quotes two writers.

To illustrate this usage, the *Oxford English Dictionary* quotes two authors who use *gull* as a verb meaning *to fool*. "Nothing is so easy as to *gull* the public, if you only set up a prodigy," writes Washington Irving. William Dean Howells uses the word similarly when he writes, "You are perfectly safe to go on and *gull* imbeciles to the end of time, for all I care."

She closes with a playful, positive spin.

Both of these authors are pretty critical of gullible people, but does *gullible* have only negative connotations? Is there no hope for Gullibles like Loris and me? C. O. Sylvester Marson's comments about *gullible* may give us some comfort. He links *gullible* to "credulous, confiding, and easily deceived." At first, these adjectives also sound negative, but *credulous* does mean "to follow implicitly." And the word *credit* comes from the Latin word *credo* (meaning "I believe"). So what's bad about that? In other words, isn't *wanting to believe* other people a good thing? Why shouldn't Loris and I be proud of at least that aspect of our gull blood? We want to be positive—and we don't want to be cynics! ■

write

Reading for Better Writing

1. The writer tells anecdotes about herself and Loris. Find each anecdotal reference and explain how it does or does not help define *gullible*.

2. Review each paragraph and explain whether and how it strengthens the definition.

3. Describe the writer's voice and explain why it does or does not fit the topic.

4. The writer uses "family" as a metaphor for a group that includes both birds and people. Explain why this metaphor is or is not effective.

Definition

Words mean different things to different people. In this essay, student writer Kirsten Zinser takes a whimsical approach to defining the word *eclectic*. The personal approach she uses tells us as much about her as it does about the word that she defines.

A Few of My Favorite Things

The writer opens with examples of eclectic.

Purple cows, purple bruises, boxes on skateboards, dresses with bells, a dog named Tootsie, a neighbor named Scott, a song about meatballs, a certain good-night kiss, a broken swing. What have all these to do with each other? Nothing.

She identifies the word.

Go-carting, Handel's *Messiah*, a blue bike, pump organs, box cities, tenth grade . . . "But what do these have to do with each other?" you wonder. As I said, nothing. My memories, like the things I enjoy, can only be described in one way: *eclectic*, a word I find endlessly fascinating.

She explains how the word sounds and feels.

Ec-lec-tic. Say it out loud, savoring each syllable—*ec . . . lec . . . tic.* Notice the different positions of your tongue. Odd how a word made of nothing more than clicking noises conveys meaning. I love to say the word. The lips do absolutely no work.

Now try saying it with your lips separated as little as possible. It still works. All the action is done on the inside, a dance of the muscular tongue on the teeth. If I were a ventriloquist, I would use the word as often as possible. Notice how the sound emerges as you form the letters. *E*—here it comes right down the center, *cl*—out from either side, *e*—an open corridor, *c*—the sound cut off, *ti*—the sound explodes past the tongue and over the teeth until pinched off with the last—*c*.

She cites a dictionary definition and responds to it.

Webster defines *eclectic* as selecting or choosing elements from different sources or systems. *Eclectic* implies variety. But what a grand way of saying variety. *Variety* sounds so generic, so discount. But *eclectic* is rich with imaginative sound.

She imagines the word's form.

I think if I could get inside the word, I would find air so pure it would sting my lungs. I imagine the space inside the walls of the word to be like a long hallway that differs in shape every few feet. At one point, the distance between the walls would offer so much space, you could run and jump with little caution. In the next few feet, the walls would be so close together that you would need to walk sideways to squeeze through. A few feet later, open space again, and so on. You would need to be limber to move through the many different-shaped spaces within the word.

For me, *eclectic* is one of those words that isn't simply used to describe something. It is a word that fits my soul. When I was young and first heard the word, I said it all the time, though I did not really understand its meaning. Then, as I began to internalize its definition, something inside me vowed allegiance. I knew that this word would become not only a part of my vocabulary, but also a part of my life.

She lists eclectic examples.

And so I pledge my loyalty to the variety of life. To enjoy theater, music, science, the outdoors, sports, philosophy, everything—this is my strategy. I want to be mature enough to carry on a conversation at elite restaurants, and young enough to squish my toes in thick mud. I want to be wild enough to walk on top of tall fences, and wise enough to be afraid of falling. 8

When I have a house of my own, I want an eclectic house—an old lamp here, a new dresser there, a vintage couch with a knitted afghan. The walls crowded with paintings, pictures, and stencils. Wild plants that fill a yard with tall, fragrant grass, but also pop up in unexpected places in the gravel driveway. Or perhaps I'll ditch the possession thing and root myself in the poetry of life, soaking in everything by osmosis, but being owned by nothing. I'll adopt a policy of "no policy." I won't be eclectic based on the things I possess, but on the experiences that I have. 9

She closes by restating her opening.

Purple cows, purple bruises, boxes on skateboards, dresses with bells, a dog named Tootsie, a neighbor named Scott, a song about meatballs, a certain good-night kiss, a broken swing. "But these have nothing to do with each other," you say. Precisely. ■ 10

write

Reading for Better Writing

1. Summarize the writer's main point. Cite three strategies that she uses to communicate her point.

2. Review how the essay is organized, and explain why this organization is or is not effective.

3. Describe the writer's voice, and explain why it does or does not fit the topic.

4. Review the opening and closing, and explain how they work.

Definition

Based on research and her experience as a nursing home employee, student writer Sarah Anne Morelos defines a class (or group) of illnesses known as dementia.

Understanding Dementia

<table>
<tr><td>

The writer uses the title and an anecdote to introduce the topic.

</td><td>

"Hello, Jenny! It's Sarah . . . I'm going to clean your room." Saying her name assured her that I knew who she was and that I was friendly. As I made her bed, I asked, "How are you doing this morning, Jenny?"

"Oh, I'm good," she said. Then, after a pause, she added, "My husband, Charlie, died in this room, you know."

</td></tr>
</table>

1

2

I looked in her face and saw the familiar tears. "I'm so sorry, Jenny," I answered. Then I held her hand and listened to the same details of Charlie's death that I had heard every week for the past year. Suddenly Jenny stopped her story, looked up, and asked, "Who are you?" She didn't even remember my entering her room. 3

Jenny has dementia, a disease that affects many people over 80 years old. When I first started work as a nursing home housekeeper, the patients experiencing this illness frightened me. I didn't understand their words or behavior. Now that I understand more about the patients and their illness, I am better able to respond to them in a helpful way. 4

> *"You took it! You rotten thief!" she screamed.*

She defines the word and distinguishes the class (dementia) from illnesses within that class.

It is now estimated that more than half of the nursing home residents in the United States have dementia. But what, exactly, is this disease? Dementia is a broad term that refers to a number of health problems, including Alzheimer's disease, brain tumors, arteriosclerosis, and hardening of arteries to the heart. The outward symptoms of dementia are often disturbing, as this disease affects both the language skills and the behavior of the patient. 5

She describes symptoms.

The most common and noticeable symptom is memory loss. Patients in the early stages of dementia first experience short-term memory loss; as the illness advances, they also experience long-term memory loss. For example, Jenny demonstrated short-term loss. While she could remember countless details about Charlie's death, an event that had happened ten years earlier, she could not remember my name—or even that I had entered the room. Another sign of memory loss is repetitiveness: patients like Jenny retell their stories over and over. 6

She uses an anecdote.

In addition to forgetting information and repeating stories, people with dementia may express strange beliefs or fears. At one point, a resident 7 named Wilma accused me of stealing from her. "You took it! You rotten thief!" she screamed.

"What are you missing, Wilma?" I asked. She started to tell me, but 8 then couldn't remember. Soon she had forgotten the episode altogether, although she was still flustered and very angry. This irrationality may be caused by bouts of schizophrenia.

Another symptom of dementia is diminished language skills. While 9 adults with healthy minds easily recall thousands of vocabulary words, patients with dementia struggle to name even the most common things and most familiar people in their lives. For example, a woman in the middle stages of the illness may recognize her son, but not be able to recall his name. However, as the illness advances, she will lose the ability to recognize his face as well.

> **For each symptom, the writer provides examples and/or anecdotes.**

Patients with dementia also show behavioral changes. One common 10 change is forgetting how to do simple tasks like washing dishes. Another change is forgetting to do basic things like shutting off the stove. Other behavioral changes signal a shift in personality. For example, 15 years ago, Wilma was my friendly next-door neighbor who occasionally brought my family cookies. Today, Wilma is one of the dementia patients whom I take care of. As a neighbor, she was mild-mannered, but as a patient she gets very angry with anyone who enters her room. "Get out of here!" she yells with arms flailing. "You're not allowed in here!"

Not surprisingly, dementia can also leave people unable to care for 11 themselves. They may have trouble dressing, bathing, or even using the bathroom. This level of neediness causes two problems. First, the individual cannot do the activity, and second, he or she often suffers from related depression.

> **A question signals a transition.**

What's the solution to dementia? Sadly, there is no cure. While nursing 12 home staff can help patients with activities, and medication helps them cope with depression, nothing can stop the illness. Both the disease and its symptoms get worse.

> **The writer gives another example.**

Steve is a good example. When he entered the nursing home just six 13 months ago, he was experiencing the early stages of dementia. Today, however, his illness is much more advanced. The stress of moving into this new environment and leaving his wife at home alone affected Steve deeply. When he first arrived, Steve often cried and begged to be taken home. "I'll give you $20—please just take me home," he'd plead.

Painfully, I would explain, "Steve, this is your home." After some time, 14 the situation got so bad that he would not sleep or eat. He was depressed, and he cried often, thinking that no one cared about him. Eventually, Steve was given stronger drugs to help with the depression. For a few months, the medication seemed to work—he laughed at jokes and occasionally told one himself. But then Steve's dementia advanced again. Soon he was asking his same sad questions: "Where am I?" and "Do you know what I'm doing here?"

She closes by encouraging readers to show understanding and kindness.

So what is the best "medication" for people with dementia? While no 15 treatment can stop the illness, understanding the disease and its symptoms is the key to helping people cope. Doctors who understand the science of dementia can prescribe medicine. However, all of us who understand the heartbreaking symptoms and effects of the disease can provide another, possibly more effective treatment. We can respond to the victim of dementia with patience, kindness, and love. ■

write

Reading for Better Writing

1. Describe how the writer introduces the topic, and explain why the introduction is or is not effective.

2. Describe how the writer distinguishes the class (dementia) from specific illnesses within that class. How are illnesses within the class defined and explained?

3. The writer extends her definition by focusing largely on the symptoms of the disease. Examine her strategies for doing so, and explain whether you find them effective.

4. Review how the writer closes with an appeal to readers. Is the closing fitting? Why or why not?

Definition

Professor David Schelhaas delivered the following definition on his weekly radio program, *What's the Good Word?*

Deft or Daft

The writer introduces the topic with an anecdote.

The other day, my wife, watching our son-in-law with his large hands gracefully tie the shoelaces of his little daughter, remarked, "You really are deft." Ever the cynic, I remarked, "He's not only deft, he's daft." I talk that sort of nonsense frequently, but as I said this, I began to wonder. What if *deft* and *daft* come from the same root and once meant the same thing? A quick trip to the dictionary showed that, indeed, they did once mean the same thing (though my wife thought me daft when I first suggested it). *1*

He describes the history of *daft*.

Let me see if I can explain the original meaning and also how *daft* and *deft* came to part company. *Daft* originally meant mild or gentle. The Middle English *dafte* comes from the Old English *gadaefte,* which has as its underlying sense *fit* or *suitable.* Quite likely, mild or gentle people were seen as behaving in a way that was fit and suitable. *2*

Gradually, however, the mild, gentle meaning descended in connotation to mean crazy or foolish. First, animals were described as daft—that is, without reason—and eventually people also. The word *silly,* which once meant happy or blessed, slid down the same slope. So that explains where *daft* got its present meaning. *3*

He compares and contrasts the two words.

But how does *deft,* meaning skillful or dexterous, fit into the picture? Again, if we start with the Old English meaning of *fit* or *suitable,* we can see a connection to skillful. In fact, the root of *gadaefte,* which is *dhabh,* to fit, carries with it the sense of a joiner or an artisan, someone who skillfully made the ends or corners of a cupboard or piece of furniture fit neatly together. From *fit* to *skillful* to *dexterous.* Thus we see how one root word meaning *fit* or *suitable* went in two different directions—one meaning crazy, the other meaning skillful. *4*

He closes with a reflection, and his usual sign-off.

These days it is usually considered much better to be deft than to be daft. But don't be too sure. It is good to remind ourselves that one person's deftness might very well appear as daftness to another. *5*

This is David Schelhaas asking, "What's the Good Word?" ■ *6*

write

Reading for Better Writing

1. Explain how the opening attempts to engage the reader. In what ways does it succeed?

2. Describe how the writer shows that the meanings of the words have changed. Is his explanation clear? Why or why not?

3. Describe the writer's tone and explain why it is or is not effective for a radio program.

Definition

Abraham Verghese is a physician who writes about scientific topics for a general audience. To define the emergency-medical condition "code blue," he wrote the following story.

Code Blue: The Story

The writer uses the title to introduce the topic.

In the early evening of August 11, 1985, he was rolled into the emergency room (ER) of the Johnson City Medical Center—the "Miracle Center," as we referred to it when we were interns. Puffing like an overheated steam engine, he was squeezing in forty-five breaths a minute. Or so Claire Bellamy, the nurse, told me later. It shocked her to see a thirty-two-year-old man in such severe respiratory distress.

He describes a patient about to experience code blue.

He sat bolt upright on the stretcher, his arms propped behind him like struts that braced his heaving chest. His blond hair was wet and stuck to his forehead; his skin, Claire recalled, was gunmetal gray, his lips and nail beds blue.

She had slapped an oxygen mask on him and hollered for someone to pull the duty physician away from the wound he was suturing. A genuine emergency was at hand, something she realized, even as it overtook her, she was not fully comprehending. She knew what it was not; it was not severe asthma, status asthmaticus; it was not a heart attack. She could not stop to take it all in. Everything was happening too quickly.

He describes visible symptoms.

With every breath he sucked in, his nostrils flared. The strap muscles of his back stood out like cables. He pursed his lips when he exhaled, as if he was loath to let the oxygen go, hanging on to it as long as he could.

> ... a monitor showed his heart fluttering at a desperate 160 beats per minute.

Electrodes placed on his chest and hooked to a monitor showed his heart fluttering at a desperate 160 beats per minute. On his chest X-ray, the lungs that should have been dark as the night were instead whited out by a veritable snowstorm.

He tells how hospital personnel treat the patient.

My friend Ray, a pulmonary physician, was immediately summoned. While Ray listened to his chest, the phlebotomist drew blood for serum electrolytes and red and whole blood cell counts. The respiratory therapist punctured the radial artery at the wrist to measure blood oxygen levels. Claire started an intravenous line. And the young man slumped on the stretcher. He stopped breathing.

Claire punched the "Code Blue" button on the cubicle wall and an operator's voice sounded through the six-story hospital building: "Code Blue, emergency room!"

He extends the definition for "code blue." The code team—an intern, a senior resident, two intensive care unit nurses, a respiratory therapist, a pharmacist—thundered down the hallway. Patients in their rooms watching TV sat up in their beds; visitors froze in place in the corridors. 8

More doctors arrived; some came in street clothes, having heard the call as they headed for the parking lot. Others came in scrub suits. Ray was "running" the code; he called for boluses of bicarbonate and epinephrine, for a second intravenous line to be secured, and for Claire to increase the vigor but slow down the rate of her chest compressions. 9

A new paragraph signals a shift in the action. The code team took their positions. The beefy intern with Nautilus shoulders took off his jacket and climbed onto a step stool. He moved in just as Claire stepped back, picking up the rhythm of chest compression without missing a beat, calling the cadence out loud. With locked elbows, one palm over the back of the other, he squished the heart between breastbone and spine, trying to squirt enough blood out of it to supply the brain. 10

The writer describes each step in the process. The ER physician unbuttoned the young man's pants and cut away the underwear, now soiled with urine. His fingers reached for the groin feeling for the femoral artery to assess the adequacy of the chest compressions. 11

A "crash cart" stocked with ampules of every variety, its defibrillator paddles charged and ready, stood at the foot of the bed as the pharmacist recorded each medication given and the exact time it was administered. 12

The clock above the stretcher had been automatically zeroed when the Code Blue was called. A code nurse called out the lapsed time at thirty-second intervals. The resident and another nurse from the code team probed with a needle for a vein to establish the second "line." 13

He uses and defines a technical term. Ray "bagged" the patient with a tight-fitting mask and hand-held squeeze bag as the respiratory therapists readied an endotracheal tube and laryngoscope. 14

At a signal from Ray, the players froze in midair while he bent the young man's head back over the edge of the stretcher. Ray slid the laryngoscope in between tongue and palate and heaved up with his left hand, pulling the base of the tongue up and forward until the lead-shaped epiglottis appeared. 15

He describes what the physician saw and did. Behind it, the light at the tip of the laryngoscope showed glimpses of the voice box and vocal cords. With his right hand, Ray felt the endotracheal tube alongside the laryngoscope, down the back of the throat, past the epiglottis, and past the vocal cords—this part done almost blindly with a prayer—and into the trachea. Then he connected the squeeze bag to the end of the endotracheal tube and watched the chest rise as he pumped air into the lungs. He nodded, giving the signal for the action to resume. 16

Now Ray listened with his stethoscope over both sides of the chest as the respiratory therapist bagged the limp young man. He listened for the muffled whoosh of air, listened to see if it was equally loud over both lungs. 17

He heard sounds only over the right lung. The tube had gone down 18
the right main bronchus, a straighter shot than the left.

He pulled the tube back an inch, listened again, and heard air entering 19
both sides. The tube was sitting above the carina, above the point where
the trachea bifurcates. He called for another chest X-ray; a radiopaque
marker at the end of the tube would confirm its exact position.

With a syringe he inflated the balloon cuff at the end of the 20
endotracheal tube that would keep it snugly in the trachea. Claire wound
tape around the tube and plastered it down across the young man's cheeks
and behind his neck.

The blue in the young man's skin began to wash out and a faint pink 21
appeared in his cheeks. The ECG machine, which had spewed paper into a
curly mound on the floor, now showed the original rapid heart rhythm
restored.

At this point the young man was alive again, but just barely. The Code 22
Blue had been a success. ∎

He describes the treatment and its effect.

He concludes by describing the outcome.

Reading for Better Writing

1. The author is a physician who wrote this narrative to define an
emergency-medical condition to nonscientists. Explain why the
narrative form is or is not effective.

2. The writer uses technical terms in his narrative. Find examples and
explain how he does or does not clarify their meaning.

3. Explain why specific details are effective.

4. The writer concludes the story abruptly by signaling that the patient is
alive. Explain why this closing does or does not fit the writer's purpose.

Guidelines
Writing a Definition Essay

1. **Select a topic.** Review the words that you listed under "Topics to Consider" page 236, and choose one that you want to explore. If you're stuck, list words similar to those defined in the five models.

   TIP: The best topics are abstract nouns (like *totalitarianism, individualism,* or *terrorism*), complex terms (like *code blue, dementia, spousal abuse,* or *Italian opera*), or adjectives connected to a personal experience (like the words defined in the models *gullible, eclectic, deft* and *daft*).

2. **Identify what you know.** To discern what you already know about the topic, write freely about the word, letting your writing go where it chooses. Explore both your personal and academic connections with the word.

3. **Gather information.** To find information about the word's history, grammatical form, and usage, use strategies like the following:

   - Consult a general dictionary, including an unabridged dictionary; list both denotative (literal) and connotative (associated) meanings for the word.
   - Consult specialized dictionaries that define words related to specific disciplines or occupations: music, literature, law, medicine, and so on.
   - If appropriate, interview experts on your topic or poll students about the topic.
   - Check books like *Bartlett's Famous Quotations* to see how famous speakers and writers have used the word.
   - Research the word's etymology and usage by consulting appropriate Web sources like <dictionary.com>, <m-w.com>, or <xrefer.com>.
   - Do a general search on the Web to see where the word pops up in titles of songs, books, or films; company names, products, and ads; nonprofit organizations' names, campaigns, and programs; and topics in the news.
   - List synonyms (words meaning the same—or nearly the same) and antonyms (words meaning the opposite).

4. **Compress what you know.** Based on your freewriting and research, try writing a formal, one-sentence definition that satisfies the following equation:

   Equation: **Term = larger class + distinguishing characteristics**
   Examples: **Swedish pimple** = fishing lure + silver surface, tubular body, three hooks
   melodrama = stage play + flat characters, contrived plot, moralistic theme
   Alzheimer's = dementia + increasing loss of memory, hygiene, social skills

5. **Get organized.** To organize the information that you have, and to identify details that you may want to add, fill out a graphic organizer like the one on page 47.

   TIP: Although you can draft your essay directly from the organizer, you may save time by writing a traditional outline that lists your main points, subpoints, and supporting details.

6. **Draft the essay.** Review your outline as needed to write the first draft.

   Opening: Get the reader's attention and introduce the term. If you're organizing the essay from general to specific, consider using an anecdote, illustration, or quotation to set the context for what follows. If you're organizing it from specific to general, consider including an interesting detail from the word's history or usage. Wherever you use a dictionary definition, do so with a fresh slant and avoid the dusty phrase "According to Webster . . ."

   Middle: Show your reader precisely what the word does or does not mean. Build the definition in unified paragraphs, each of which addresses distinct aspects of the word: common definitions, etymology, usage by professional writers, and so on. Link paragraphs so that the essay unfolds the word's meaning one layer after another.

   Closing: Review your main point and close your essay. (You might, for example, conclude by encouraging readers to use—or not use—the word.)

7. **Get feedback.** Ask a classmate or someone from the college's writing center to read your essay for the following:

   - **Engaging opening**—Does the introduction identify the word and set the context for what follows?
   - **Clarity**—Is each facet of the definition clear, showing precisely what the word does and does not mean?
   - **Continuity**—Is each paragraph unified, and is each one linked to the paragraphs that precede it and follow it? Is the essay focused and unified?
   - **Completeness**—Is the definition complete, telling the reader all that he or she needs in order to understand and use the word?
   - **Fitting closing**—Does the conclusion wrap up the message and refocus on the word's core meaning?

8. **Revise and edit the essay.** Use the feedback to revise the essay. If necessary, do additional research to find information that answers your reader's questions. Edit the essay for correctness by looking for clear sentences; correct quotations; specific, appropriate words; and correct grammar, spelling, usage, and punctuation.

9. **Publish the essay.** Share your writing with interested readers, including friends, family, and classmates. Submit the essay to your instructor.

Writing Checklist

Use these six traits to check your essay, then revise as needed:

____ The **ideas** in the definition clearly distinguish what the word does and does not mean. Supporting details strengthen main points where needed.

____ The **organizational** pattern is logical and appropriate for the definition's content. Paragraphs are unified and ordered to build a clear pattern of thought.

____ The **voice** is informed, engaging, and courteous.

____ The **words** are precise and appropriate, and complex or technical terms are defined. Transitional words and phrases link paragraphs smoothly and logically.

____ The **sentences** are complete, clear, varied in structure, and readable.

____ The **copy** is formatted correctly and includes no errors in spelling, punctuation, or grammar.

write

Writing Activities

1. Review "The Gullible Family" and think about similar situations when you and your friends played with a particular word or phrase. Choose one of the words you used, research its meaning, and write an essay that defines the word.

2. Review "A Few of My Favorite Things," noting how the writer defines a word that describes her. List words that describe you or someone you know, then choose one of the words, and write an essay that defines it.

3. Review "Understanding Dementia" and choose a similarly complex health or social condition. Research the topic and write an essay defining it.

4. Review "Deft or Daft" and choose a pair of words that similarly mirror each other's meaning. Research the words, and write an essay comparing and contrasting their etymologies and meanings.

5. Reread "Code Blue: The Story" and identify a similarly complex situation or problem. Research the topic and write a story that defines it.

6. Write an essay defining a word or phrase that is understood by people in a particular field of study but not by "outsiders." Write for the audience of outsiders.

Persuasive Writing

CONTENTS

Chapter 17
Strategies for Argumentation and Persuasion

audio

"I wasn't convinced. I just didn't buy it." Maybe you've said something similar while watching a political debate, viewing a TV ad, or discussing an issue in class or at work. You simply didn't find the argument logical, believable, or persuasive.

In a sense, college is a place where big issues get argued out. Your courses aim to strengthen your reasoning abilities so that you can construct persuasive arguments. Your goal as a persuasive writer is to reason effectively with your readers or listeners and to motivate them to believe, change, or act.

This chapter is a resource on reasoning. It explains the foundations of argumentation and persuasion and introduces four related forms—taking a position, persuading readers to act, arguing against a claim, and proposing a solution.

What's Ahead

- Building Persuasive Arguments
- Preparing Your Argument
- Making and Qualifying Claims
- Supporting Your Claims
- Identifying Logical Fallacies
- Engaging the Opposition
- Using Appropriate Appeals
- Writing Activities

Building Persuasive Arguments

What is an argument?

Formally, an *argument* is a series of statements arranged in a logical sequence, supported with sound evidence, and expressed powerfully so as to sway your reader or listener. Arguments appear in a variety of places:

- A research paper about e-mail surveillance by the FBI
- An analysis of *Beloved* (the novel) or *The Lord of the Rings* (the film)
- A debate about the ethics of transferring copyrighted music over the Internet

How do you build a persuasive argument?

Step 1: **Prepare your argument.**

- **Identify your audience and purpose.** Who is your audience and what is your goal? Do you want to take a position, to persuade readers to act, to counter an argument, or to offer a solution?
- **Generate ideas and gather solid evidence.** You can't base an argument on opinions. Find accurate, pertinent information about the issue and uncover all viewpoints on it.
- **Develop a line of reasoning.** To be effective, you need to link your ideas into a clear, logical sequence.

Step 2: **Make and qualify your claim.**

- **Draw reasonable conclusions from the evidence.** State your proposition—the central point for which you will argue. Claim, for example, that something is true, has value, or should be done.
- **Add qualifiers.** Words such as "typically" and "sometimes" soften your claim, making it more reasonable and acceptable.

Step 3: **Support your claim.**

- **Support each point** in your claim with solid evidence.
- **Identify logical fallacies.** Test your thinking for errors in logic. (See pages 261–264.)

Step 4: **Engage the opposition.**

- **Make concessions,** if needed, by granting points to the opposition.
- **Develop rebuttals,** whenever possible, that expose the weaknesses of the opposition's position.
- **Use appropriate appeals**—emotional "tugs" that ethically and logically help readers see your argument as convincing.

Preparing Your Argument

An argument is a reason or chain of reasons used to support a claim. To use argumentation well, you need to know how to draw logical conclusions from sound evidence. Preparing an effective argument involves a number of specific steps, starting with those discussed below.

Consider the situation.

- **Clearly identify your purpose and audience.** This step is essential for all writing, but especially true when building an argument. (See page **29**.)
- **Consider a range of ideas** to broaden your understanding of the issue and to help focus your thinking on a particular viewpoint. (See page **41**.)
- **Gather sound evidence** to support your viewpoint. (See pages **258–260**.)

Develop a line of reasoning.

In argumentative writing, it's crucial that you develop a clear line of reasoning. Each point you make should clearly support your argument. This line of reasoning might develop naturally as you study the issue, or you may need to adopt a more formal approach. Use either of the following outlines as a guide to structuring your argument.

Outline 1: **Present your supporting arguments, then address counterarguments, and conclude with the strongest argument.**

    Introduction: question, concern, or claim
      1. Strong argument supporting claim
         • Discussion and support
      2. Other arguments supporting claim
         • Discussion of and support for each argument
      3. Objections, concerns, and counterarguments
         • Discussion, concessions, answers, and rebuttals
      4. Strongest argument supporting claim
         • Discussion and support
    Conclusion: argument consolidated—claim reinforced

Outline 2: **Address the arguments and counterarguments point by point.**

    Introduction: question, concern, or claim
      1. Strong argument supporting claim
         • Discussion and support
         • Counterarguments, concessions, and rebuttals
      2. Other arguments supporting claim
         • For each argument, discussion and support
         • For each argument, counterarguments, concessions, and rebuttals
      3. Strongest argument supporting claim
         • Discussion and support
         • Counterarguments, concessions, and rebuttals
    Conclusion: argument consolidated—claim reinforced

Making and Qualifying Claims

An argument centers on a claim—a debatable statement. That claim is the thesis, or key point you wish to explain and defend so well that readers agree with it. A strong claim has the following traits:

- **It's clearly arguable**—it can be vigorously debated.
- **It's defendable**—it can be supported with sufficient arguments and evidence.
- **It's responsible**—it takes an ethically sound position.
- **It's understandable**—it uses clear terms and defines key words.
- **It's interesting**—it is challenging and worth discussing, not bland and easily accepted.

Distinguish claims from facts and opinions.

A claim is a conclusion drawn from logical thought and reliable evidence. A fact, in contrast, is a statement that can be checked for accuracy. An opinion is a personally held taste or attitude. While a claim can be debated, a fact or opinion cannot.

Fact: The Fellowship of the Ring is the first book in J. R. R. Tolkien's trilogy The Lord of the Rings.

Opinion: I liked the movie almost as much as the book.

Claim: While the film version of The Fellowship of the Ring does not completely follow the novel's plot, it does faithfully capture the spirit of Tolkien's novel.

Distinguish three types of claims.

Truth, value, and policy—these types of claims are made in an argument. The differences between them are important because each type has a distinct goal.

Claims of truth state that something is or is not the case. As a writer, you want readers to accept your claim as trustworthy.

➤ **The Arctic ice cap will begin to disappear as early as 2050.**
The cholesterol in eggs is not as dangerous as previously feared.

Comment: Avoid statements that are (1) obviously true or (2) impossible to prove. Also, truth claims must be argued carefully because accepting them (or not) can have serious consequences.

Sample Essay: "An Apology for the Life of Ms. Barbie D. Doll," pages 302–303.

Claims of value state that something does or does not have worth. As a writer, you want readers to accept your judgment.

➤ **Volunteer reading tutors provide a valuable service.**
Many music videos fail to present positive images of women.

Comment: Claims of value must be supported by referring to a known standard or by establishing an agreed-upon standard. They should not be statements simply of personal taste or preference. Because value claims are rooted in beliefs, such claims risk emotional bias. To avoid a bias, base your judgments on the known standard, not on your feelings.

Sample Essay: "Tanning Beds in Health Clubs: Marriage or Mismatch?," pages **272–273**.

Claims of policy state that something ought or ought not to be done. As a writer, you want readers to approve your course of action.

➤ **Special taxes should be placed on gas-guzzling SUVs.**
The developer should not be allowed to fill in the pond where the endangered tiger salamander lives.

Comment: Policy claims focus on action. To arrive at them, you must often first establish certain truths and values; thus, an argument over policy may include truth and value claims.

Sample Essay: "Practical Wildlife Management," pages **315–316**.

Develop a supportable claim.

An effective claim balances confidence with common sense. To find that balance, follow these tips:

Avoid all-or-nothing, extreme claims. Propositions containing words that are overly positive or negative—such as *all, best, never,* and *worst*—may be difficult to support. Statements that leave no room for exceptions are easy to attack.

Extreme Claim: All people charged even once for DUI should never be allowed to drive again.

Make a truly meaningful claim. Avoid claims that are obvious, trivial, or unsupportable. None is worth the energy needed to argue the point.

Obvious Claim: College athletes sometimes receive special treatment.
Trivial Claim: The College Rec Center is a good place to get fit.
Unsupportable Claim: Athletics are irrelevant to college life.

Use qualifiers to temper your claims. Qualifiers are words or phrases that make claims more reasonable. Notice the difference between these two claims:

Unqualified: All star athletes take far too many academic shortcuts.
Qualified: Some star athletes take improper academic shortcuts to get through their courses.

Note: The "qualified" claim is easier to defend because it narrows the focus and leaves room for exceptions. Use qualifier words like these:

• almost	• many	• often	• tends to
• frequently	• maybe	• probably	• typically
• likely	• might	• some	• usually

Supporting Your Claims

A claim stands or falls on its support. It's not the popular strength of your claim that matters, but rather the strength of your reasoning and evidence. To develop strong support, consider how to select and use evidence.

Gather evidence.

Several types of evidence can support claims. To make good choices, review each type as well as its strengths and weaknesses.

Observations and anecdotes share what people (including you) have seen, heard, smelled, touched, tasted, and experienced. Such evidence offers an "eye witness" perspective shaped by the observer's viewpoint, which can be powerful but may also prove narrow and subjective.

➤ **Most of us have closets full of clothes: jeans, sweaters, khakis, T-shirts, and shoes for every occasion.**

Statistics offer concrete numbers about a topic. Numbers don't "speak for themselves," however. They need to be interpreted and compared properly—not slanted or taken out of context. They also need to be up-to-date, relevant, and accurate.

➤ **Pennsylvania spends $30 million annually in deer-related costs. Wisconsin has an estimated annual loss of $37 million for crop damage alone.**

Tests and experiments provide hard data developed through the scientific method, data that must nevertheless be carefully studied and properly interpreted.

➤ **According to the two scientists, the rats with unlimited access to the functional running wheel ran each day, and gradually increased the amount of running; in addition, they started to eat less.**

Graphics provide information in visual form—from simple tables to more complex charts, maps, drawings, and photographs. When poorly done, however, graphics can distort the truth.

➤ **See the line graph in the experiment report on page 363 and the drawing in "Hair Today, Gone Tomorrow" on page 230.**

Analogies compare two things, creating clarity by drawing parallels. However, every analogy breaks down if pushed too far.

➤ **It is obvious today that America has defaulted on this promissory note insofar as her citizens of color are concerned. Instead of honoring this sacred obligation, America has given the Negro people a bad check; a check which has come back marked "insufficient funds." But we refuse to believe that the bank of justice is bankrupt.**

—Martin Luther King, Jr.

Expert testimony offers insights from an authority on the topic. Such testimony always has limits: experts don't know it all, and they work from distinct perspectives, which means that they can disagree.

- ► **One specialist opposed to drilling is David Klein, a professor at the Institute of Arctic Biology at the University of Alaska–Fairbanks. Klein argues that if the oil industry opens up the ANWR for drilling, the number of caribou will likely decrease because the calving locations will change.**

Illustrations, examples, and demonstrations support general claims with specific instances, making such statements seem concrete and observable. Of course, an example may not be your best support if it isn't familiar.

- ► **Think about how differently one can frame Rosa Parks' historic action. In prevailing myth, Parks—a holy innocent—acts almost on whim. . . . The real story is more empowering: It suggests that change is the product of deliberate, incremental action.**

Analyses examine parts of a topic through thought patterns—cause/effect, compare/contrast, classification, process, or definition. Such analysis helps make sense of a topic's complexity, but muddles the topic when poorly done.

- ► **A girl's interest in romance is no more Barbie's fault than the fault of books like *On the Shores of Silver Lake*. Fashion magazines targeted at adolescents are the cause of far more anorexia cases than is Barbie.**

Predictions offer insights into possible outcomes or consequences by forecasting what might happen under certain conditions. Like weather forecasting, predicting can be tricky. To be plausible, a prediction must be rooted in a logical analysis of present facts.

- ► **While agroterrorist diseases would have little direct effect on people's health, they would be devastating to the agricultural economy, in part because of the many different diseases that could be used in an attack.**

Use evidence.

Finding evidence is one thing; using it well is another. To marshal evidence in support of your claim, follow three guidelines:

1. **Go for quality and variety, not just quantity.** More evidence is not necessarily better. Instead, support your points with sound evidence in different forms. Quality evidence is
   - *accurate:* correct and verifiable in each detail.
   - *complete:* filled with pertinent facts.
   - *concrete:* filled with specifics.
   - *relevant:* clearly related to the claim.
   - *current:* reliably up-to-date.
   - *authoritative:* backed by expertise, training, and knowledge.
   - *appealing:* able to influence readers.

2. Use inductive and deductive patterns of logic. Depending on your purpose, use inductive or deductive reasoning. (See page **7**.)

Induction: Inductive reasoning works from the particular toward general conclusions. In a persuasive essay using induction, look at facts first, find a pattern in them, and then lead the reader to your conclusion.

Sample Essay: **In "To Drill or Not to Drill," Rebecca Pasok first details specific threats to the environment before arriving at her claim that drilling for oil in an Alaskan wilderness refuge is not our best option.** (See pages **304–306**.)

Deduction: Deductive reasoning—the opposite of inductive reasoning—starts from accepted truths and applies them to a new situation so as to reach a conclusion about it. For deduction to be sound, be sure the starting principles or facts are true, the new situation is accurately described, and the application is logical.

Sample Essay: **In "Education Through Application," Jeff Bulthuis starts with the general idea that students learn best through application. He then uses that idea to support his claim that students should be given the opportunity to substitute work-study programs for classroom study.** (See page **271**.)

3. Reason using valid warrants. To make sense, claims and evidence must have a logical connection. That connection is called the *warrant*—the often unspoken thinking used to relate the evidence to the claim. If warrants are good, arguments hold water; if warrants are faulty, then arguments break down. In other words, beware of faulty assumptions.

Check the short argument outlined below. Which of the warrants seem reasonable and strong, and which seem weak? Where does the argument fail?

Evidence: **If current trends in water usage continue, the reservoir will be empty in two years.**

Claim: **Therefore, Emeryville should immediately shut down its public swimming pools.**

Unstated Warrants or Assumptions:
- It is not good for the reservoir to be empty.
- The swimming pools draw significant amounts of water from the reservoir.
- Emptying the pools would help raise the level of the reservoir.
- No other action would better prevent the reservoir from emptying.
- It is worse to have an empty reservoir than an empty swimming pool.

INSIGHT: An argument is no stronger than its warrants. Examine the assumptions in your own arguments and in others' arguments before you allow yourself to be persuaded.

Identifying Logical Fallacies

Fallacies are false arguments—that is, bits of fuzzy, dishonest, or incomplete thinking. They may crop up in your own thinking, in your opposition's thinking, or in such public "arguments" as ads, political appeals, and talk shows. Because fallacies may sway an unsuspecting audience, they are dangerously persuasive. By learning to recognize fallacies, however, you may identify them in opposing arguments and eliminate them from your own writing. In this section, logical fallacies are grouped according to how they falsify an argument.

Distorting the Issue

The following fallacies falsify an argument by twisting the issue out of a logical framework.

Bare Assertion ◆ The most basic way to distort an issue is to deny that it exists. This fallacy claims, "That's just how it is."
- **The private ownership of handguns is a constitutional right.**
  (*Objection:* The claim shuts off discussion of the U.S. Constitution or the reasons for regulation.)

Begging the Question ◆ Also known as circular reasoning, this fallacy arises from assuming in the basis of your argument the very point you need to prove.
- **We don't need a useless film series when every third student owns a DVD player or VCR.** (*Objection:* There may be uses for a public film series that private video viewing can't provide. The word "useless" begs the question.)

Oversimplification ◆ This fallacy reduces complexity to simplicity. Beware of phrases like "It's a simple question of." Serious issues are rarely simple.
- **Capital punishment is a simple question of protecting society.**

Either-Or Thinking ◆ Also known as black-and-white thinking, this fallacy reduces all options to two extremes. Frequently, it derives from a clear bias.
- **Either this community develops light-rail transportation or it will be impossible to grow in the future.** (*Objection:* The claim ignores the possibility that growth may occur through other means.)

Complex Question ◆ Sometimes by phrasing a question a certain way, a person ignores or covers up a more basic question.
- **Why can't we bring down the prices that corrupt gas stations are charging?** (*Objection:* This question ignores a more basic question—"Are gas stations really corrupt?")

Straw Man ◆ In this fallacy, the writer argues against a claim that is easily refuted. Typically, such a claim exaggerates or misrepresents the opponents' actual arguments.
- **Those who oppose euthanasia must believe that the terminally ill deserve to suffer.**

Sabotaging the Argument

These fallacies falsify the argument by twisting it. They destroy reason and replace it with something hollow or misleading.

Red Herring ◆ This strange term comes from the practice of dragging a stinky fish across a trail to throw tracking dogs off the scent. When a person puts forth a volatile idea that pulls readers away from the real issue, readers become distracted. Suppose the argument addresses drilling for oil in the ANWR of Alaska, and the writer begins with this statement:

- **In 1989, the infamous oil spill of the *Exxon Valdez* led to massive animal deaths and enormous environmental degradation of the coastline.**
  (*Objection:* Introducing this notorious oil spill distracts from the real issue—how oil drilling will impact the ANWR.)

Misuse of Humor ◆ Jokes, satire, and irony can lighten the mood and highlight a truth; when humor distracts or mocks, however, it undercuts the argument. What effect would the mocking tone of this statement have in an argument about tanning beds in health clubs?

- **People who use tanning beds will just turn into wrinkled old prunes or leathery sun-dried tomatoes!**

Appeal to Pity ◆ This fallacy engages in a misleading tug on the heartstrings. Instead of using a measured emotional appeal, it seeks to manipulate the audience into agreement.

- **Affirmative action policies ruined this young man's life. Because of them, he was denied admission to Centerville College.**

Use of Threats ◆ A simple but unethical way of sabotaging an argument is to threaten opponents. More often than not, a threat is merely implied: "If you don't accept my argument, you'll regret it."

- **If we don't immediately start drilling for oil in the ANWR, you will soon face hour-long lines at gas stations from New York to California.**

Bandwagon Mentality ◆ Someone implies that a claim cannot be true because a majority of people are opposed to it, or it must be true because a majority support it. (History shows that people in the minority have often had the better argument.) At its worst, such an appeal manipulates people's desire to belong or be accepted.

- **It's obvious to intelligent people that cockroaches live only in the apartments of dirty people.** (*Objection:* Based on popular opinion, the claim appeals to a kind of prejudice and ignores scientific evidence about cockroaches.)

Appeal to Popular Sentiment ◆ This fallacy consists of associating your position with something popularly loved: the American flag, baseball, apple pie. Appeals to popular sentiment sidestep thought to play on feelings.

- **Anyone who has seen *Bambi* could never condone hunting deer.**

Drawing Faulty Conclusions from the Evidence

This group of fallacies falsifies the argument by short-circuiting proper logic in favor of assumptions or faulty thinking.

Appeal to Ignorance ◆ This fallacy suggests that because no one has proved a particular claim, it must be false; or, because no one has disproved a claim, it must be true. Appeals to ignorance unfairly shift the burden of proof onto someone else.

➤ **Flying saucers are real. No scientific explanation has ruled them out.**

Hasty or Broad Generalization ◆ Such a claim is based on too little evidence or allows no exceptions. In jumping to a conclusion, the writer may use intensifiers like *all, every,* or *never.*

➤ **Today's voters spend too little time reading and too much time being taken in by 30-second sound bites.** (*Objection:* Quite a few voters may, in fact, spend too little time reading about the issues, but it is unfair to suggest that this is true of everyone.)

False Cause ◆ This well-known fallacy confuses sequence with causation: If *A* comes before *B, A* must have caused *B.* However, *A* may be one of several causes, or *A* and *B* may be only loosely related, or the connection between *A* and *B* may be entirely coincidental.

➤ **Since that new school opened, drug use among young people has skyrocketed. Better that the school had never been built.**

Slippery Slope ◆ This fallacy argues that a single step will start an unstoppable chain of events. While such a slide may occur, the prediction lacks real evidence.

➤ **If we legalize marijuana, it's only a matter of time before hard drugs follow and America becomes a nation of junkies and addicts.**

Misusing Evidence

These fallacies falsify the argument by abusing or distorting the evidence.

Impressing with Numbers ◆ In this case, the writer drowns readers in statistics and numbers that overwhelm them into agreement. In addition, the numbers haven't been properly interpreted.

➤ **At 35 ppm, CO levels factory-wide are only 10 ppm above the OSHA recommendation, which is 25 ppm. Clearly, that 10 ppm is insignificant in the big picture, and the occasional readings in some areas of between 40 and 80 ppm are aberrations that can safely be ignored.** (*Objection:* The 10 ppm may be significant, and higher readings may indicate real danger.)

Half-Truths ◆ A half-truth contains part of, but not the whole truth. Because it leaves out "the rest of the story," it is both true and false simultaneously.

➤ **The new welfare bill is good because it will get people off the public dole.** (*Objection:* This may be true, but the bill may also cause undue suffering for some truly needy individuals.)

Unreliable Testimonial ◆ An appeal to authority has force only if the authority is qualified in the proper field. If he or she is not, the testimony is irrelevant. Note that fame is not the same thing as authority.

- ➤ **On her talk show, Alberta Magnus recently claimed that most pork sold in the United States is tainted.** (*Objection:* While Magnus may be an articulate talk show host, she is not an expert on food safety.)

Attack Against the Person ◆ This fallacy directs attention to a person's character, lifestyle, or beliefs rather than to the issue.

- ➤ **Would you accept the opinion of a candidate who experimented with drugs in college?**

Hypothesis Contrary to Fact ◆ This fallacy relies on "if only" thinking. It bases the claim on an assumption of what would have happened if something else had, or had not, happened. Being pure speculation, such a claim cannot be tested.

- ➤ **If only multiculturalists hadn't pushed through affirmative action, the U.S. would be a united nation.**

False Analogy ◆ Sometimes a person will argue that *X* is good (or bad) because it is like *Y*. Such an analogy may be valid, but it weakens the argument if the grounds for the comparison are vague or unrelated.

- ➤ **Don't bother voting in this election; it's a stinking quagmire.** (*Objection:* Comparing the election to a "stinking quagmire" is unclear and exaggerated.)

Misusing Language

Essentially, all logical fallacies misuse language. However, three fallacies falsify the argument especially by the misleading use of words.

Obfuscation ◆ This fallacy involves using fuzzy terms like *throughput* and *downlink* to muddy the issue. These words may make simple ideas sound more profound than they really are, or they may make false ideas sound true.

- ➤ **Through the fully functional developmental process of a streamlined target refractory system, the U.S. military will successfully reprioritize its data throughputs.** (*Objection:* What does this sentence mean?)

Ambiguity ◆ Ambiguous statements can be interpreted in two or more opposite ways. While ambiguity can result from unintentional careless thinking, writers sometimes use ambiguity to obscure a position.

- ➤ **Many women need to work to support their children through school, but they would be better off at home.** (*Objection:* Does *they* refer to *children* or *women*? What does *better off* mean? These words and phrases can be interpreted in opposite ways.)

Slanted Language ◆ By choosing words with strong positive or negative connotations, a writer can draw readers away from the true logic of the argument. Here is an example of three synonyms for the word *stubborn* that the philosopher Bertrand Russell once used to illustrate the bias in slanted language:

- ➤ **I am firm. You are obstinate. He is pigheaded.**

Engaging the Opposition

Think of an argument as an intelligent, lively dialogue with readers. Anticipate their questions, concerns, objections, and counterarguments. Then follow these guidelines.

Make concessions.

By offering concessions—recognizing points scored by the other side—you acknowledge your argument's limits and the truth of other positions. Paradoxically, such concessions strengthen your overall argument by making it seem more credible. Concede your points graciously, using words like the following:

Admittedly	Granted	I agree that	I cannot argue with
It is true that	You're right	I accept	No doubt
Of course	I concede that	Perhaps	Certainly it's the case

➤ **Granted, Barbie's physical appearance isn't realistic. As Motz explains . . .**

Develop rebuttals.

Even when you concede a point, you can often answer that objection by rebutting it. A good rebuttal is a small, tactful argument aimed at a weak spot in the opposing argument. Try these strategies:

1. **Point out the counterargument's limits** by putting the opposing point in a larger context. Show that the counterargument leaves something important out of the picture.

2. **Tell the other side of the story.** Offer an opposing interpretation of the evidence, or counter with stronger, more reliable, more convincing evidence.

3. **Address logical fallacies** in the counterargument. Check for faulty reasoning or emotional manipulation. For example, if the counterargument forces the issue into an either-or straightjacket, show that other options exist.

   ➤ **Granted, Barbie's physical appearance isn't realistic. As Motz explains . . . I say, so what? While the only "real" version of Barbie's body would be a long-limbed 13-year-old with breast implants, who cares? Arguing that Barbie's bod isn't realistic and that the lack of realism hurts girls' self-esteem is weak logic. Children have had dolls for ages. For example . . .**

Consolidate your claim.

After making concessions and rebutting objections, you may need to regroup. Restate your claim so carefully that the weight of your whole argument can rest on it.

➤ **Playing with Barbies need not be an unimaginative, antisocial activity that promotes conformity, materialism, and superficial ideals.**

Using Appropriate Appeals

For your argument to be persuasive, it must not only be logical, but also "feel right." It must treat readers as real people by appealing to their common sense, hopes, pride, and sense of right and wrong. How do you appeal to all these concerns? Do the following: (1) build credibility, (2) make logical appeals, and (3) focus on readers' needs.

Build credibility.

A persuasive argument is credible—so trustworthy that readers can change their minds painlessly. To build credibility, observe these rules:

Be thoroughly honest. ■ Demonstrate integrity toward the topic—don't falsify data, spin evidence, or ignore facts. Document your sources and cite them wherever appropriate.

Make realistic claims, projections, and promises. ■ Avoid emotionally charged statements, pie-in-the-sky forecasts, and undeliverable deals.

Develop and maintain trust. ■ From your first word to your last, develop trust—in your attitude toward the topic, treatment of readers, and respect for opposing viewpoints.

Make logical appeals.

Arguments stand or fall on their logical strength, but your readers' acceptance of those arguments is often affected more by the emotional appeal of your ideas and evidence. To avoid overly emotional appeals, follow these guidelines:

Engage readers positively. ■ Appeal to their better natures—to their sense of honor, justice, social commitment, altruism, and enlightened self-interest. Avoid appeals geared toward ignorance, prejudice, selfishness, or fear.

Use a fitting tone—one that is appropriate for the topic, purpose, situation, and audience.

Aim to motivate, not manipulate, readers. ■ While you do want them to accept your viewpoint, it's not a win-at-all-costs situation. Avoid bullying, guilt-tripping, and exaggerated tugs on heartstrings.

Don't trash-talk the opposition. ■ Show tact, respect, and understanding. Focus on issues, not personalities.

Use arguments and evidence that readers can understand and appreciate. ■ If readers find your thinking too complex, too simple, or too strange, you've lost them.

INSIGHT: Remember the time-honored adage—the best argument is one that sounds like an explanation.

Focus on readers' needs.

Instead of playing on readers' emotions, connect your argument with readers' needs and values. Follow these guidelines:

Know your real readers. ■ Who are they—peers, professors, or fellow citizens? What are their allegiances, their worries, their dreams?

Picture readers as resistant. ■ Accept that your readers, including even those inclined to agree with you, need convincing. Think of them as alert, cautious, and demanding—but also interested.

Use appeals that match needs and values. ■ Your argument may support or challenge readers' needs and values. To understand these needs, study the table below, which is based loosely on the thinking of psychologist Abraham Maslow. Maslow's hierarchy of needs ranks people's needs on a scale from most basic to most complex needs. The table begins at the bottom with *having necessities* (a basic need) and ends at the top with *helping others* (a more complex need).

For example, if you're writing to argue for more affordable housing for the elderly, you'd argue differently to legislators (whose focus is on *helping others*) than to the elderly who need the housing (whose focus is on *having necessities*). Follow these guidelines:

- Use appeals that match the foremost needs and values of your readers.
- If appropriate, constructively challenge those needs and values.
- Whenever possible, phrase your appeals in positive terms.
- After analyzing the readers' needs, choose a persuasive theme for your argument—a positive benefit, advantage, or outcome that readers can expect if they accept your claim. Use this theme to bring readers to care about your claims.

Reader needs . . .	Persuasive appeals . . .
To make the world better by • *Helping others*	To values and social obligations
To achieve by • *Being good at something* • *Getting recognition*	To self-fulfillment, status To appreciation
To belong by • *Being part of a group*	To group identity, acceptance
To survive by • *Avoiding threats* • *Having necessities*	To safety, security To physical needs

write

Writing Activities

1. Select an essay from one of these chapters: "Taking a Position," "Persuading Readers to Act," "Arguing Against a Claim," or "Proposing a Solution." Read the essay carefully. Then describe and evaluate the argumentative strategies used by the writer, answering the specific questions below:

   ■ *What is the main claim that the writer makes? Is it a claim of truth, value, or policy?*

   ■ *Is the claim arguable—that is, is it supportable, appropriately qualified, and effectively phrased?*

   ■ *What arguments does the writer develop in support of the claim? Are these arguments logical?*

   ■ *What types of evidence does the writer provide to support his or her discussion? Is the evidence valid, sufficient, and accurate?*

   ■ *Does the writer effectively address questions, alternatives, objections, and counterarguments?*

2. Examine the essay that you read for the first activity for its persuasive strategies. Answer the following questions:

   ■ *Describe the writer's tone. Does it effectively engage readers? Why or why not?*

   ■ *Does the argument seem credible and authoritative? Explain.*

   ■ *Identify ways that the writer connects with readers' needs and values.*
   How does he or she develop a persuasive theme that appeals to those needs and stresses reader benefits?

3. Examine an ad in a newspaper or magazine, on TV, or on the Internet. What kind of persuasive appeals (pages 266–267) does the ad use? Are they used effectively and appropriately? Explain.

4. Find a letter to the editor on a current, controversial issue. Examine the strengths and weaknesses of the writer's argument, and construct your own argument on this issue in the form of a letter to the same editor.

5. What are some of the key academic journals in your field of study? With help from a librarian or instructor in your discipline, find a quality article in a respected journal. Read the article and then answer these questions: What forms of reasoning, appeals, and evidence does the author use? What types of reasoning, appeals, and evidence does he or she avoid?

Chapter 18
Taking a Position

audio

Sometimes you just have to take a stand. An issue comes up that hits you where you live, gets your blood flowing, or challenges your thinking. In response, you say, "Okay, this is what I believe, and this is why I believe it."

Writing a position paper gives you the opportunity to take a stand. It's a chance, in other words, to refine what you think and feel, to clarify and deepen your perspective on an issue that you find meaningful—from tanning beds to the treatment of animals in experiments. The list of debate-worthy issues is endless. In fact, each discipline in college has its own controversial issues that press scholars and students to test one another's positions.

Because a position paper articulates what you profess to believe about an issue, such writing requires commitment. Use the position paper, then, as an opportunity to take a stand, to debate those who hold different positions, and to explore what you are willing to risk.

What's Ahead

- Overview: Taking a Position
    Student Models
    Professional Model
- Guidelines
- Writing Checklist and Activities

Overview
Taking a Position

Writer's Goal

Your goal is to take a stand on a controversial issue. Aim to explain what you believe and why you believe it. Be thoughtful but bold, encouraging readers to respect and even adopt your position.

Keys for Success

Explore all positions. ■ Before settling firmly on a position, study the pluses and minuses of all possible stands that could be taken on the issue.

Go beyond pure opinion. ■ Opinions and positions are different. Whereas an opinion may be uninformed and inherited, you *think* your way into a position. A position carries weight because of tested reasoning and reliable evidence. It shows mature thinking—thinking that is lively and concrete, not clichéd.

Take a measured stance. ■ Instead of taking a defend-at-all-costs approach, be reasonable. Concede points to your opponents, and address objections to your view. If necessary, soften your stance with qualifiers. Let the evidence weigh in favor of your position—not verbal aggression, bluster, or the fever of your feelings.

Topics to Consider

What topics work well for a position paper? Debatable ones, of course—ideas on which thoughtful people can reasonably disagree.

- **Current Affairs:** Explore recent trends, new laws, major changes, and emerging controversies discussed in the news media, journals, or online discussion groups.

- **Burning Issues:** What issues related to family, work, education, recreation, technology, the environment, or popular culture do you care about? Which issue do you want to confront?

- **Dividing Lines:** What dividing lines characterize the communities to which you belong—what issues set people against one another? Religion, gender, money, class, sports? Think about these broad subjects, and then identify a focused issue in one of them.

- **Fresh Fare:** Sometimes an unexpected topic, like barbed versus smooth fishing hooks, offers the most potential. Avoid tired issues, unless you can revive them with a fresh perspective.

Next Step Read the model essays and perform the activities that follow. As you read, think of similar issues on which you could take a stand. What position would you take, and how would you defend it?

Taking a Position

In this editorial, student writer Jeff Bulthuis promotes work-study programs as valuable learning experiences. He supports his claim very effectively by sharing his own experiences as a volunteer in a local hospital.

Education Through Application

The opening paragraph establishes an engaging personal tone.

Rather than spend my senior year taking a lot of elective courses, I wanted to get involved in a special work-study program where I could volunteer my services at the local hospital. My proposal was accepted without complaint by the high school principal, the dean of students, and the superintendent. It's the best decision I ever made.

As students, we aren't always able to retain information in our classes because we hardly ever see it applied in everyday life. We are taught a new concept one day, and the next day we have no recollection of what the teacher was even talking about. Studies have shown that students become more knowledgeable through visual aids. If the learning process can be greatly improved by seeing concepts in the classroom, imagine the possibilities of retaining new information by experiencing it in real-life situations. I know firsthand how valuable such experience can be.

Specific examples support the writer's claim.

I learned a lesson in faithfulness when I met Tommy, a father who has visited his comatose daughter in the hospital three times a week for the past 14 years. I came to appreciate my Spanish classes when I invited Antonio, a Hispanic American struggling through rehab, to the chapel service in the hospital. I came to value the strength of human contact when I held another patient's hand while a doctor made his examination. I also learned about the importance of choosing a career that I really like, because on many occasions, doctors told me, "Don't ever become a doctor; it's not worth all of the stress."

In the closing, the writer strongly restates his position and its benefits.

I have seen time and time again the beneficial results of learning through experience. My high school gave me a firm foundation in education, but it was only through application that I truly learned. All students should have the opportunity to volunteer at places that interest them. I was given the chance, and every day I reap the rewards of that experience. ∎

Reading for Better Writing

1. In this editorial, the writer argues that work-study programs are valuable educational experiences. What is his main argument in asserting their value?

2. What evidence does he provide to support that argument? Is the evidence convincing? Why?

3. Explain why the type of evidence used is or is not appropriate in an editorial.

audio

Taking a Position

In this essay, student writer Tanya Laarman takes a position on the tanning-bed controversy. A well-developed position paper gives reasons for the writer's point of view and may also mention opposing positions.

Tanning Beds in Health Clubs: Marriage or Mismatch?

The opening introduces the controversy through questions.

1 What does a healthy body look like? Are you thinking fit and trim . . . and tan? In magazines and on TV, a healthy person is often a bronzed person who has spent a lot of time in the sun. Because many people connect healthy with tan, it's not surprising that many health and fitness centers have tanning beds. The local Midtown Fitness Center even offers a package deal for fitness classes and tanning. But do tanning beds even belong in health clubs?

The writer explores one possible position, conceding points when needed.

2 Obviously, many health club owners think so. Having tanning beds is an additional service for their clients and an additional source of income for themselves. Besides, say these owners, tanning beds have something in common with their physical fitness equipment—both help people look good. I agree—trim and tan bodies are attractive.

3 Some health club owners even claim that a tanning-bed tan is healthy. For example, Connie Alexander, owner of Midtown Fitness Center, says that using a tanning bed creates a base tan that can protect you from sunburn. Many of her clients use the beds before going on beach vacations. Some tanning-bed operators also say that using the bed is safer than sunbathing because the tanning booth is a controlled environment: sessions are usually limited to 20 minutes.

Showing understanding of the opposition, she begins her own position.

4 In fact, these owners would probably be annoyed that I'm even asking the question: Do tanning beds belong in health clubs? After all, they could argue that the beds are legal and regulated by the state. So if the beds are legal, why shouldn't club owners be free to rent them, and adults be free to use them?

5 It's hard to argue with owners' freedom to rent the beds. But one could ask owners what the purpose of their health club is. Do tanning beds really help their clients achieve good looks and good health?

She uses a variety of arguments to develop her own position.

6 If the purpose is for clients to look good, tanning is a short-term answer with long-term consequences. People who have spent a lot of time exposed to ultraviolet rays, especially between the ages of birth and 18, will eventually experience premature-aging wrinkles (Donald 7). The effects of overexposure may not be obvious right away but will appear in the future.

7 It's also doubtful whether a tanning-bed tan is "healthy" in terms of providing a protective base tan for future exposure to the sun. The ultra-

violet rays used in tanning booths turn the skin brown but don't create a thick, tough layer that protects lower layers of skin. So users may feel secure and protected from sunburn when they're really still at risk.

8 Skin specialists and cancer researchers say that any kind of tanning is a health risk. Incidents of skin cancer have greatly increased in the last couple of decades. The American Cancer Society estimates that 700,000 Americans will develop skin cancer each year, plus 32,000 will be diagnosed with melanoma, the deadliest form of skin cancer. Researchers blame the increase in skin cancer on the diminishing ozone layer and overexposure to ultraviolet rays (Donald 9–10).

She uses scientific studies to stress the seriousness of the danger.

9 Even though the ultraviolet rays used in tanning beds are different from the sun's, they're still dangerous. A recent study in Sweden showed that heavy use of tanning lamps increases a person's risk of melanoma, especially for people under 30. The study showed that anyone who had ever used sunlamps or sun beds faced a 30 percent greater risk of melanoma than those who had never used such devices. People under 20 who "fake-baked" more than 10 times a year were eight times more likely to develop melanoma than nonusers ("Facts on Cancer").

10 Finally, while cancer is serious, it's not the only health problem associated with the use of sunlamps. For example, tanners using salons in several states need to sign a paper warning them of potential eye injury (such as increased chance of developing cataracts), activation of some viral conditions such as cold sores, and allergic reactions.

The writer concludes by directly stating her position.

11 So do tanning beds belong in health clubs? Sure, owners are free to rent the beds—no law prevents them. But the flip side of freedom is responsibility. If health club owners feel responsible for their clients' health, they'll use their money and space for exercise equipment, not tanning beds. ■

Note: The Works Cited page is not shown.

write

Reading for Better Writing

1. In this essay, the writer builds up to her position rather than stating it immediately. Why does she treat opposing positions first? Is this an effective strategy?

2. Describe the writer's treatment of the opposition. Is it effective? Explain.

3. What logic and evidence does the writer provide to support her position about tanning beds? Are her reasoning and her research sound? Explain.

4. Look closely at the opening and closing paragraphs. Are they effective? Why or why not?

Taking a Position

In this essay, student writer David DeHaan takes a position in favor of banning barbed hooks from sport fishing. Notice that his measured approach to the issue seems reasonable and sensible throughout.

Evening the Odds

The writer opens with a vivid picture, a concern, and a position statement.

A new breed of hunter dwells among North America's hidden waterways. Armed with a $100 rod and reel, $75 hip waders, and a wide array of lures ranging from glowing gadgets to old-fashioned worms, today's fisherman has improved his arsenal well beyond the bent nail and old twine that Huck Finn used for jigging. But most modern fishermen still carry one piece of equipment that is outdated: the barbed hook, which is still added to almost every lure produced commercially. This mechanism continues to plague the sport of fishing by damaging young fish stocks. Barbed hooks should be banned from lure fishing to protect fish that are not yet ready for anglers to keep.

Through strong contrasts, he spells out arguments for his position.

A smooth (barbless) fishing hook is much easier to remove from a fish's mouth than a barbed hook. A smooth hook comes out cleanly, leaving only a small puncture, and giving fishermen the opportunity to release undamaged fish. A properly set barbed hook, on the other hand, often inflicts serious injury to the jaw of the fish. While this is not a problem for the larger keepers, it does have serious consequences for smaller fish that should be released back into the waterway. Many of these small fish are kept because the anglers know that releasing them would be inhumane, while others are released with portions of their jaws missing, unable to feed properly. By improving the angler's chances of safely releasing unwanted fish, barbless hooks help to preserve our limited fish stocks.

The writer addresses questions, concerns, and objections.

Supporters of barbed fishing hooks say that banning the hooks would decrease the number of fish they are able to land. They claim that enjoyment of the sport would be limited by the increased difficulty of keeping fish on the line. They are at least partially correct; playing a fish is difficult without a barb. However, this does not have to limit the enjoyment of the sport.

He uses historical analysis to support his position.

When sportsmen stop to reflect on why they find fishing so enjoyable, most realize that what they love is the feel of a fish on the end of the line, not necessarily the weight of the fillets in their coolers. Fishing has undergone a slow evolution over the last century. While fishing used to be a way of putting food on the table, most of today's lure fishermen do so only for the relaxation that it provides. The barbed hook was invented to increase the quantity of fish a person could land so as to better feed his or her family. This need no longer exists, and so barbed hooks are no longer necessary.

The writer summarizes expert testimony.

According to some anglers who use smooth hooks, their lures perform 5 better than barbed lures as long as they maintain a constant tension on the line. Smooth hooks can bite deeper than barbed hooks, actually providing a stronger hold on the fish. These anglers testify that switching from barbed hooks has not noticeably reduced the number of fish that they are able to land. In their experience, and in my own, enjoyment of the sport is actually heightened by adding another challenge to playing the fish (maintaining line tension).

He raises and answers a second objection.

Some people have argued that replacing all of the barbed hooks in their 6 tackle would be a costly operation. While this is certainly a concern, barbed hooks do not necessarily require replacement. With a simple set of pliers, the barbs on most conventional hooks can be bent down, providing a cost-free method of modifying one's existing tackle. These modified hooks are also much safer to use. Young children who are just learning to fish often pose a certain danger using fishhooks. While the possibility of snagging someone still remains with a smooth hook, the hook is much easier to remove from skin, clothing, and branches.

He restates his position and drives it home with a comparison.

The gradual evolution of fishing for food into fishing for sport has 7 outdated the need for barbed hooks. Just as in any other sport, enjoyment comes from being able to achieve a goal despite considerable difficulty. If anglers chose their equipment solely on the quantity of fish they were able to land, we would all be fishing with dragnets. While everyone agrees that nets take the sport out of fishing, they must realize that barbed hooks do the same thing. Fishing with smooth hooks is a way of caring for and conserving our fish stocks while still maintaining the enjoyment of sport fishing for the angler. ■

write

Reading for Better Writing

1. Examine the opening carefully. How does it prepare us for the position statement in the last sentence of the essay? Is the position statement formulated effectively? Why or why not?

2. In writing, trace the author's thinking—point by point. What lines of reasoning does he establish? How does he support his reasoning?

3. To whom is he writing? How does he appeal to these readers?

4. How does the closing repeat the opening? Does the ending add anything new?

Taking a Position

In this article, Meg Greenfield explains her position on a highly emotional issue — animal rights. As you will see, she places herself in a philosophically vulnerable position, a position she believes many of her readers will share.

In Defense of the Animals

The writer states her position immediately, forcefully, and simply.

I might as well come right out with it. Contrary to some of my most cherished prejudices, the animal-rights people have begun to get to me. I think that in some part of what they say, they are right. [1]

I never thought it would come to this. As distinct from the old-style animal rescue, protection, and shelter organizations, the more aggressive newcomers . . . have earned a reputation in the world I live in as fanatics, and just plain kooks. And even with my own recently (relatively) raised consciousness, there remains a good deal in both their critique and their prescription for the virtuous life that I reject, being not just a practicing carnivore, a wearer of shoe leather, and so forth, but also a supporter of certain indisputably agonizing procedures visited upon innocent animals in the furtherance of human welfare, especially experiments undertaken to improve human health. [2]

She shares her difficulty at taking this stand.

So, viewed from the pure position, I am probably only marginally better than the worst of my kind, if that: I don't buy the complete "speciesist" analysis or even the fundamental language of animal "rights" and continue to find a large part of what is done in the name of that cause harmful and extreme. But I also think, patronizing as it must sound, that zealots are required early on in any movement if it is to succeed in altering the sensibility of the leaden masses, such as me. Eventually they get your attention. And eventually you at least feel obliged to weigh their arguments and think about whether there may not be something there. [3]

While criticizing the extremes of a movement, she concedes its force.

It is true that this end has often been achieved—as in my case—by means of vivid, cringe-inducing photographs, not by an appeal to reason or values so much as by an assault on squeamishness. From the famous 1970s photo of the newly skinned baby seal to the videos of animals being raised in the most dark, miserable, stunting environment as they are readied for their life's sole fulfillment as frozen patties and cutlets, these sights have had their effect. . . . [4]

She refers to "our" to draw readers into the debate.

The objection to our being confronted with these dramatic, disturbing pictures is first that they tend to provoke a misplaced, uncritical, and highly emotional concern for animal life at the direct expense of a more suitable concern for human suffering. What goes into the animals' account, the reasoning goes, necessarily comes out of ours. But I think it is possible to remain stalwart in our view that the human claim comes first, and in your acceptance of the use of animals for human betterment, and still to believe that there are some human interests that should not take precedence. For [5]

She refines and expands her position statement.

we have become far too self-indulgent, hardened, careless, and cruel in the pain we routinely inflict upon these creatures for the most frivolous, unworthy purposes. And I also think that the more justifiable purposes, such as medical research, are shamelessly used as cover for other activities that are wanton.

She clarifies a key point with an example.

For instance, not all of the painful and crippling experimentation that 6 is undertaken in the lab is being conducted for the sake of medical knowledge or other purposes related to basic human well-being and health. Much of it is being conducted for the sake of super-refinements in the cosmetic and other frill industries, the noble goal being to contrive yet another fragrance or hair tint or commercially competitive variation on all the daft, fizzy, multicolored "personal care" products for the medicine cabinet and dressing table, a firmer-holding hair spray, that sort of thing. . . .

This strikes me as decadent. My problem is that it also causes me to 7 reach a position that is, on its face, philosophically vulnerable, if not absurd—the muddled, middling, inconsistent place where finally you are saying it's all right to kill them for some purposes, but not to hurt them gratuitously in doing it or to make them suffer horribly for one's own trivial whims.

Acknowledging her muddled position, the writer defends it vigorously and ends positively.

I would feel more humiliated to have fetched up on this exposed 8 rock, if I didn't suspect I had so much company. When you see pictures of people laboriously trying to clean the Exxon gunk off sea otters even knowing that they will be able to help out only a very few, you see this same outlook in action. And I think it can be defended. For to me the biggest cop-out is the one that says that if you don't buy the whole absolutist, extreme position it is pointless and even hypocritical to concern yourself with lesser mercies and ameliorations. The pressure of the animal-protection groups has already had some impact in improving the way various creatures are treated by researchers, trainers, and food producers. There is much more in this vein to be done. We are talking about rejecting wanton, pointless cruelty here. The position may be philosophically absurd, but the outcome is the right one. ■

write

Reading for Better Writing

1. If Greenfield is actually defending animal rights, why does she spend so much time criticizing the animal-rights movement?

2. Describe Greenfield's tone. Is it effective for this topic and this audience? Why or why not?

3. After stating her position simply in the opening, how does Greenfield proceed to explain, clarify, and expand that stand? Note where she explicitly restates her position and look closely at her concluding paragraph.

Guidelines
Taking a Position

Note: For in-depth help on developing persuasive arguments, see pages **253–268**.

1. **Select and narrow a topic.** Through reading, viewing, or surfing the Internet, explore current issues on which people can take different, well-reasoned positions. Select an issue that you care about, and carve that topic down to size by considering a specific angle on it.

2. **Take stock.** Before you dig into your topic, assess your starting point. What is your current position on the topic? Why? What evidence do you have?

3. **Get inside the issue.** To take a defensible position, study the issue carefully. The following strategies will help you measure and develop what you know:
   - Investigate all possible positions on the issue. Through brainstorming and research, think through all arguments and issues on all sides.
   - Consider doing firsthand research that will help you speak with authority and passion.
   - Write your position at the top of a page. Below it, set up "Pro" and "Con" columns. List arguments in each column and then modify your position.
   - Develop a line of reasoning supporting your position. Then test that reasoning for two things:
     First, no logical fallacies, such as broad generalization, either-or thinking, oversimplification, and slanted language. (See pages **261–264**.)
     Second, an effective range of support: statistics, observations, expert testimony, comparisons, experiences, and analysis. (See pages **258–260**.)

4. **Refine your position.** By now, you may have sharpened or radically changed your starting position. Before you organize and draft your essay, clarify your position. If it helps, use this formula:

   I believe this to be true about _____ :

   _____ .

5. **Organize your development and support.** Now you've committed yourself to a position. Before drafting, review these organizational options:
   - **Traditional Pattern:** Introduce the issue, state your position, support it, address and refute opposition, and restate your position.
   - **Blatant Confession:** Place your position statement in the first sentence—boldly displayed for your reader to chew on.
   - **Delayed Gratification:** In the first part of your essay, explore the various positions available on the topic; compare and contrast them, and then defend your position.

- **Changed Mind:** If your research changed your mind on the topic, build that shift into the essay itself. Readers may respond positively to such honesty.
- **Winning Over:** If your readers may strongly oppose your position, then focus on that opposition. Defend your position by anticipating and answering each question, concern, and objection.

6. **Write your first draft.** If helpful, set aside your notes and get your position and support down on paper. If you prefer, work closely from your outline. Here are some possible strategies:

   Opening: Seize the reader's imagination. Raise concern for the issue with a dramatic story, a pointed example, a vivid picture, a thought-provoking question, or a personal confession. Supply background information that readers need to understand the issue.

   Development: Deepen, clarify, and support your position statement, using solid logic and reliable support. A clear, well-reasoned defense will help readers accept your position.

   Closing: End on a lively, thoughtful note that stresses your commitment. If appropriate, make a direct or indirect plea to readers to adopt your position.

   Title: Choose a bold title that offers a choice or stresses a stand.

7. **Share your position.** At this point, feedback from a peer or a tutor in the writing center might help. Does your reviewer accept your position? Why or why not?

8. **Revise your writing.** Consider your reviewer's comments and review the draft yourself. Cut, change, and/or add material with the following questions in mind:
   - Is the position clearly stated? Is it effectively qualified and refined?
   - Have you shown how your stand affects yourself and others?
   - Are the reasoning and support sound, or do they need further development?
   - Does the essay show awareness of questions, concerns, and other positions?
   - Do the ideas flow smoothly?
   - Is the tone confident and sincere, not bullying, cocky, or apologetic?

9. **Edit and proofread.** See page **87** for guidelines, but check especially that your writing is free of slogans, clichés, platitudes, insults, and mystifying jargon. Make your language lively, concrete, and energetic.

10. **Prepare and publish your final essay.** Submit your position paper according to your instructor's requirements. In addition, seek a forum for your position—with peers in a discussion group, with relatives, or online.

Writing Checklist

Use these six traits to check your essay, then revise as needed:

____ The **ideas** establish and defend a stand on a debatable issue. The essay provides sound reasoning and support that help the reader understand and appreciate the position.

____ The **organization** includes an engaging opening that raises the issue, a carefully sequenced development and defense of the position, and a reflective closing.

____ The **voice** is thoughtful, measured, committed, convincing, and knowledgeable. The feelings expressed are appropriately strong.

____ The **words** used are precise, concrete, and lively. Jargon, clichés, platitudes, and insults are avoided.

____ The **sentences** flow smoothly. Their lengths are varied: short sentences make snappy points, while longer sentences develop thoughtful points.

____ The **copy** follows rules of grammar, format, and documentation.

write

Writing Activities

1. Two of the model essays in this chapter are position papers on environmental issues: fish hooks and fish stocks, and animal rights and medical research. In your position paper, discuss a similar environmental issue that you care about.

2. The essay "Tanning Beds in Health Clubs: Marriage or Mismatch?" takes a stand on a health issue. Think of other controversial health issues, and then take a position on one.

3. Throughout history, people have been jailed, beaten, or killed rather than recant a position they have defended. Do you hold a position that you would die for? What are your commitments and convictions? Brainstorm two lists: one of things that you are for, and one of things that you are against. Select a topic from one of these lists.

4. Reflect on hot topics in your major—check textbooks, talk to professors or experts, and review journals in the field. Then take a position on a controversial issue.

5. What controversies have you experienced at work? What issues do workers debate? Select one of these debates, and write a position paper geared toward an appropriate workplace audience.

Chapter 19
Persuading Readers to Act

audio

Persuasion is an art. Especially when you wish to influence readers' behavior and actions, it requires that you artfully "charm" your readers by convincing them to believe you, rethink their own perspectives, and take a concrete step. In the end, you want them to change their minds and actions.

In an essay persuading readers to act, you seek to change readers' opinions on a debatable, complex, and timely issue about which you deeply care—worn-out words, excessive consumer spending, or the problem of racism, for example. In addition, your essay presses for the next logical step—*motivating* readers to act. You achieve that goal with sound logic, reliable support, and fitting appeals. In a sense, you say to readers, "Come, let us reason together."

What do you feel strongly about, and what actions do you want to influence? This chapter will help you write in a way that stirs people to action.

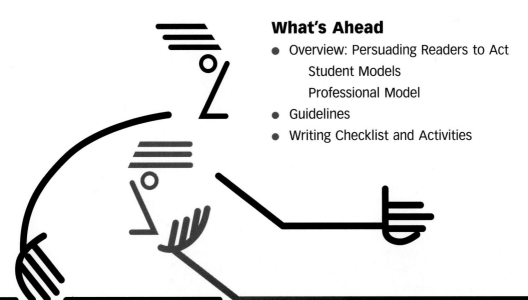

What's Ahead

- Overview: Persuading Readers to Act
    - Student Models
    - Professional Model
- Guidelines
- Writing Checklist and Activities

Overview
Persuading Readers to Act

Writer's Goal

Your goal is to urge individual readers to change their behavior or to take action on an issue. To accomplish this goal, you need to change the minds of those who disagree with you, and give encouragement to those who do agree with you.

Keys for Success

Know your readers. ▪ When you seek to persuade, you assume that your reader will have some opposition or resistance to your viewpoint. To motivate resistant readers to act, you must know who they are—whether they are peers, professors, the college community, or your nation. Consider their knowledge of and attitudes toward the topic so that you can address their concerns.

Promote your cause—not a quarrel. ▪ Your goal is to motivate your readers to act, not to manipulate them so that you win an argument. Study the topic from all sides. Bottom line: know your subject.

Be reasonable. ▪ Make logical claims about your topic, testing them to make sure that they can be supported with sufficient evidence. Review your thinking to identify any logical fallacies as well. Moreover, fine-tune the essay's voice until it is passionate, thoughtful, and sincere.

Topics to Consider

Choose a debate-worthy, timely issue that you care about. Consider topics in these categories:

- **Personal experiences:** What personal experiences have raised questions or concerns for you?
- **Personal ideas:** What issues often prey on your mind? What do you stew about or fear? What makes you say, "Something should be done"?
- **Community concerns:** Think about the different "communities" to which you belong—family, college, race, ethnic group, or gender. What issues concern each group, and why?
- **National or international affairs:** What national or global issues are discussed in your circle of friends, your college community, or the news?
- **"No comment" topics:** Consider issues about which you don't have an opinion. Would you like to develop a strong stance on one of these topics?

Next Step Read the model essays and perform the activities that follow. As you read, think of parallel issues that interest you. Why do these issues intrigue you? How could you communicate that interest to readers and challenge them to take action?

Persuasive Action

In the essay below, student writer Sarah Den Boer shares a pet peeve—the use of the worn-out word *cute*—and tries to convince readers to drop the word from their vocabularies.

audio

Let's Kill *Cute*

The writer states her claim forcefully but playfully.

1 If there's one word that deserves to be hauled into a back alley and dismembered letter by letter, it's *CUTE*. Just looking at the word brings up images of pink, frilly dresses, *Veggie Tales*, and helpless puppies. And the word brings up my breakfast. But why do I want to deface pictures of babies sitting in flowers? Why do I want to smash Precious Moments figurines into smithereens? And why do I want to put big black X's over stylized hearts?

Each word used as a word appears in italics.

2 For as long as I can remember, *cute* has inspired nothing in me but contempt. It's a cop-out descriptor. Whenever I hear it, I think, "What? Can you find no better adjective? With so many options, how could you choose *cute*?" Because *cute* is used so often and so carelessly, it means so little.

3 "Your shirt is sooo cute!"

4 "They make such a cute couple!"

5 "What a cute idea!"

6 "Look—that house—it's so cute!"

7 Soon we'll be calling Jesse Ventura cute, or Fidel Castro, or nuclear warfare. Just recently I heard a girl squeal about a plain-faced education prof, "Oh, Dr. O'Reilly is so cute!" Get me a bucket so I can throw up. Cutely, of course.

The writer uses humor to connect readers with her argument.

8 The word's nebulous nature isn't all that bothers me. I also dislike the meaning—suggesting naïve innocence. The meaning is false. For example, the pink, frilly dresses (mentioned earlier) are undoubtedly 100 percent polyester. *Veggie Tales* tells ridiculous stories about annoying little vegetables that have somehow acquired souls. And the helpless puppies probably have rabies.

9 The worst thing anyone can call me is cute. Why? Because the word is wrong, implying qualities that are not me. In fact, these qualities indicate what I *don't* want to be. *Cute* makes me sound like I'm sweet. But I'm not— I can be nasty. *Cute* makes me sound weak. But I'm not—I'm independent. *Cute* makes me sound childish.

10 What I dislike most about *cute* is that people using the word aren't taking their subjects seriously. I want to be taken seriously, and when someone says that I'm cute, I feel that my important qualities have been ignored. Barney may be cute, but you can't take him seriously. And whoever heard of a cute feminist?

She uses a personal anecdote to express her feelings.

My worst run-in with *cuteness* happened about a year ago. I was home 11 for Christmas and my friend Lisa said, "Do you know what my sister said about you? She said, 'You know, when I think of Sarah, I think of a bunny— all cute and cuddly.' "

I grimaced. After that, bunnies plagued me. They popped up every- 12 where, hopping across the road, scampering through our yard. Every time I saw one, I remembered those insulting words.

One day I was talking with another friend who knows how I feel about 13 bunnies, and he said, "Last night I had a dream about you. I dreamt that you were searching everywhere for bunnies."

I groaned, positive that I knew what was coming. 14

"And then you found some, and together we herded them into the 15 Too-Cute-To-Live Crematorium."

I let out a contented sigh. Finally, a happy ending. 16

We need to find an equally happy ending for *cute*, a word that has out- 17 lived its usefulness. But how should we get rid of it? One option is burying *cute* in the Dead-Words Graveyard where it can rot into frilly dust. A better choice is tossing *cute* in the Waste-Words Blender and pureeing it out of our lives! But maybe the best choice is thought. Before you ever use the word again, think—precisely what do I mean by *cute*? Because you can't answer that question, *cute* will die from obsolescence. ■

The ending presses readers to take action.

write

Reading for Better Writing

1. Describe the tone of this essay, pointing to specific passages. Is the tone appropriate for the topic? Why or why not?

2. The writer uses several examples, quotations, and illustrations. Identify four or five of them and explain whether they are or are not effective persuasive strategies.

3. While this essay focuses on the word *cute*, the writer doesn't offer a dictionary definition of the term. Is this choice a weakness?

4. This persuasive essay is very personal: the writer reveals much about herself. Is that strategy effective?

5. What action does the essay call for? Given the argument, is the call to action persuasive? Explain.

Persuasive Action

In the essay below, student writer Allison Young tries to persuade readers to rethink their spending habits. She argues that what we buy and the amount we buy say a great deal about who we are and what we want to be.

If We Are What We Wear, What Are We?

The writer starts with a personal story with which readers may identify.

I've always loved new clothes. When I was younger, I loved going to the mall each fall to buy school clothes: new shirts and jeans and shoes. Now I have a job and buy my own clothing; when I want something new, I go shopping with friends to find those clearanced jeans or funky shoes. [1]

In fact, most of us have closets full of clothes: jeans, sweaters, khakis, T-shirts, and shoes for every occasion. We love having a variety of clothes that look good on us and express our personalities. To keep up with the trends, however, we buy and buy and buy—usually getting new clothes long before our old ones wear out. [2]

The problem is introduced and explored with thoughtful quotes and questions.

In his article, "Trapped in the Cult of the Next Thing," Mark Buchanan argues that our urge to consume the latest and best traps us in this mind-set: "Crave and spend, for the Kingdom of Stuff is here." As a result, we're driven to possess as much new, fashionable stuff as possible—including clothing. It's part of the American dream, this feeling that we need to have more and more. But what does this craving really cost? [3]

Statistics help the writer make a comparison/ contrast point.

To have more, we need to spend more. According to the U.S. Census Bureau, in 1995 Americans spent more than $323 billion on clothing and accessories. That same source lists the 1995 gross national product (GNP) of 66 countries: 54 of those countries had a GNP of less than $323 billion, and 32 had a GNP of less than $100 billion. [4]

I have contributed my share to that $323 billion. In my closet I have 12 T-shirts, 23 short-sleeved shirts, and 26 long-sleeved shirts. I have six pairs of jeans (only four of which I wear), two pairs of khakis, five pairs of shorts, three pairs of pajama pants, and a pair of tear-away pants. I have 12 pairs of shoes, nine skirts, and four dresses. And I know I'm not the only "poor college kid" to have a plethora of clothing. I have so much—and I like having so much. [5]

The writer digs deeper into opposing perspectives.

The American excuse for owning multiples is that clothing styles change so rapidly. At the end of the '80s, trends in high fashion changed every two and a half months (Durning 95). Even for those of us who don't keep up with high fashion, styles change often enough that our clothing itself lasts much longer than the current trend. Perhaps this is one of the reasons the average American spent $997 on clothing in 1996 (U.S. Department of Commerce). [6]

While Americans are spending a thousand or more dollars a year on clothing, people in Ethiopia make an average of only $96 a year, those in Bangladesh make $280, and the average Filipino worker makes $1,052 [7] annually (United Nations Statistics Division). I, on the other hand, made more than $5,000 last year, and that job was only part-time. When an American college student can earn more money at her part-time job than three billion people each make for a living, it's time to question our culture and ask, as Alan Durning did, "How much is enough?"

A relevant quotation advances the writer's argument.

"Enough is never enough," claims Dolores Curran in "There Is a Lot to Be Said for Less." Soon, she adds, we become "possessed by our possessions." But what does our passion for having more of "the latest" reveal about our culture? Are we so accustomed to this way of life, to having closets full of fashionable clothes, that we don't see the flaws in our lifestyle? And even if we become aware of the problems, how should we respond? 8

Possible responses and changes are introduced and explored.

One solution is to take G. K. Chesterton's advice: "There are two ways to get enough. One is to accumulate more. The other is to need less" (qtd. in Buchanan). But too often Americans choose to accumulate more to please—or to impress—those around them. As Dolores Curran explains, "What we once considered luxuries we come to regard as necessities, and eventually we become dependent upon the things we acquire." Instead of being content with a generic-brand sweater, we pay three times as much for a Tommy Hilfiger label because we think that we are what we wear. 9

If that's true, then what are we? If our identity is so intertwined with what we wear, then what do our appetites for clothing make us? A name-brand label? A trend? A style decided by others? If so, are we saying that we're willing to be what others want us to be? Have we become imitation human beings, superficial replicas of other people? 10

In closing, the writer presses readers to change their thinking and behavior.

Clothing, varied and fun though it can be, is ultimately superficial. What if we dared to reach for more? What if we chose to define ourselves not by what we have, but by what we do? To do more, whether in our own communities or throughout the world, we would have to share more. One way to share our resources is to need less, buy less for ourselves, and give more to others. We can use our resources to help needy people, not only in America, but in other countries as well. ■ 11

Note: The Works Cited page is not shown.

write

Reading for Better Writing

1. Why does the topic of clothing matter to the writer? Is clothing the real issue? How does she encourage her readers to care about the issue?

2. Note the questions asked by the writer. Why does she use this strategy at certain points in the essay?

3. Trace the writer's use of evidence to support her claims. What types of evidence does she use, and does she use each type persuasively? Explain.

4. How does the writer want readers to change? What does she want them to do? Is the call to action convincing? Why or why not?

Persuasive Action

Paul Rogat Loeb is a freelance writer and university lecturer trained in social research. In the excerpt below from his 1999 book, *Soul of a Citizen*, Loeb argues that ordinary people can bring about social change.

Soul of a Citizen: Living with Conviction in a Cynical Time

Loeb starts with a positive general claim, but raises a related problem and a question.

Most Americans are thoughtful, caring, generous. We try to do our best by family and friends. We'll even stop to help a fellow driver stranded by a roadside breakdown or give spare change to a stranger. But increasingly, a wall separates each of us from the world outside, and from others who have taken refuge in their own private sanctuaries. How can we renew the public participation that's the very soul of democratic citizenship? 1

Noting concerns, he concedes problems through powerful contrasts. He then offers readers an alternative vision.

To be sure, the issues we face are complex. It's hard to comprehend the moral implications of a world in which Nike pays Michael Jordan millions to appear in its ads while workers at its foreign shoe factories toil away for pennies a day. The 500 richest people on the planet now control more wealth than the poorest three billion, half the human population. Is it possible even to grasp this extraordinary imbalance? And, more important, how do we begin to redress it? 2

Certainly we need to decide for ourselves whether particular causes are wise or foolish. But we also need to believe that our individual involvement is worthwhile, that what we might do in the public sphere will not be in vain. The challenge is as much psychological as political. As the Ethiopian proverb says, "He who conceals his disease cannot be cured." 3

We need to understand our cultural diseases—callousness, short-sightedness, denial—and learn what it will take to heal our society and our souls. How did so many of us become convinced that we can do nothing to affect the future our children and grandchildren will inherit? And how have others managed to work powerfully for change? 4

Key questions introduce a story that illustrates his argument.

Pete Knutson is one of my oldest friends. During 25 years as a commercial fisherman in Washington and Alaska, he has been forced to respond to the steady degradation of salmon spawning grounds. He could have accepted this as fate and focused on getting a maximum share of the dwindling fish populations. Instead, he gradually built an alliance between Washington fishermen, environmentalists, and Native American tribes, and persuaded them to demand that this habitat be preserved and restored. 5

Cooperation didn't come easily. Washington's fisherman are historically individualistic and politically mistrustful. But with their new allies, they pushed for cleaner spawning streams, preservation of the Endangered Species Act, and increased water flow over regional dams to help boost salmon runs. Fearing that these measures would raise electricity costs or restrict development opportunities, aluminum companies and other large 6 industrial interests bankrolled a statewide referendum, Initiative 640, to regulate fishing nets in a way that would eliminate small family operations.

The example shows that successful action is possible.

At first, those who opposed 640 thought they had no chance of success: They were outspent, outstaffed, outfunded. Similar initiatives backed by similar corporate interests had already passed in Florida, Louisiana, and Texas. But the opponents refused to give up. Pete and his co-workers enlisted major environmental groups to campaign against the initiative. They worked with the media to explain the larger issues at stake and focus public attention on the measure's powerful financial backers. On election day in November 1995, Initiative 640 was defeated. White fishermen, Native American activists, and Friends of the Earth staffers threw their arms around each other in victory. "I'm really proud of you, Dad," Pete's twelve-year-old son kept repeating. Pete was stunned. *7*

He analyzes the anecdote, using a quotation for support and insight.

We often think of social involvement as noble but impractical. Yet it can serve enlightened self-interest and the interests of others simultaneously, giving us a sense of connection and purpose nearly impossible to find in private life. "It takes energy to act," says Pete. "But it's more draining to bury your anger, convince yourself you're powerless, and swallow whatever's handed to you." *8*

We often don't know where to start. Most of us would like to see people treated more justly and the earth accorded the respect it deserves, but we mistrust our own ability to make a difference. The magnitude of the issues at hand has led too many of us to conclude that social involvement isn't worth the cost. *9*

Such resignation isn't innate or inevitable. It's what psychologists call learned helplessness, a systematic way of ignoring the ills we see and leaving them for others to handle. We find it unsettling even to think about crises as profound as the extinction of species, depletion of the ozone layer, destruction of the rainforests, and desperate urban poverty. We're taught to doubt our voices, to feel that we lack either the time to learn about and articulate the issues or the standing to speak out and be heard. To get socially involved, we believe, requires almost saintlike judgment, confidence, and character—standards we can never meet. Our impulses toward involvement are dampened by a culture that demands idealism, enshrines cynicism, and makes us feel naïve for caring about our fellow human beings or the planet we inhabit. *10*

Anticipating objections, the writer defines a key concept. He then uses a second, well-known example for support.

A few years ago, on Martin Luther King Day, I was interviewed on CNN along with Rosa Parks. "Rosa Parks was the woman who wouldn't go to the back of the bus," said the host. "That set in motion the yearlong bus boycott in Montgomery. It earned Rosa Parks the title of 'mother of the civil rights movement.'" *11*

The host's description—the standard rendition of the story— stripped the boycott of its context. Before refusing to give up her seat to a white person, Parks had spent 12 years helping to lead the local NAACP chapter. The summer before, she had attended a 10-day training session at the Highlander Center, Tennessee's labor and civil rights organizing school, *12* where she'd met older activists and discussed the Supreme Court decision banning "separate but equal" schools. Parks had become familiar with previous challenges to segregation: another Montgomery bus boycott, 50 years earlier; a bus boycott in Baton Rouge two years before Parks was arrested; and an NAACP dilemma the previous spring, when a young Montgomery woman had also refused to move to the back of the bus. The NAACP had considered a legal challenge but decided the unmarried, pregnant woman would be a poor symbol for a campaign.

> **Loeb describes the complexity of true social action.**

In short, Parks didn't make a spur-of-the-moment decision. She was 13 part of a movement for change at a time when success was far from certain. This in no way diminishes her historical importance, but it reminds us that this powerful act might never have taken place without the humble, frustrating work that preceded it.

> **He contrasts familiar and anonymous heroism. He explains the costs of inaction.**

We elevate a few people to hero status—especially during times of 14 armed conflict—but most of us know next to nothing of the battles ordinary men and women fought to preserve freedom, expand democracy, and create a more just society. Many have remarked on America's historical amnesia, but its implications are hard to appreciate without recognizing how much identity dissolves in the absence of memory. We lose the mechanisms that grassroots social movements have used successfully to shift public sentiment and challenge entrenched institutional power. Equally lost are the means by which participants eventually managed to prevail.

Think about how differently one can frame Rosa Parks' historic action. 15 In prevailing myth, Parks—a holy innocent—acts almost on a whim, in isolation. The lesson seems to be that if any of us suddenly got the urge to do something heroic, that would be great. Of course, most of us wait our entire lives for the ideal moment.

> **Ending positively, the writer challenges readers.**

The real story is more empowering: It suggests that change is the product 16 of deliberate, incremental action. When we join together to shape a better world, sometimes our struggles will fail or bear only modest fruits. Other times they will trigger miraculous outpourings of courage and heart. We can never know beforehand what the consequences of our actions will be. ∎

write

Reading for Better Writing

1. What is the writer arguing for and against? What does he want readers to do? Look at the question in the opening paragraph. What answer does Loeb present?

2. What efforts does Loeb make to address readers' questions, concerns, and opposing arguments? Are these efforts successful? Explain.

3. Examine the examples that Loeb uses: Pete Knutson and Rosa Parks. Do these examples work as support for the writer's claims? Why or why not?

4. Broadly speaking, what is the author's view of life, and how does that perspective come through in the essay?

Persuasive Action

Dr. Martin Luther King, Jr., was a leader in the Civil Rights Movement during the 1950s and 1960s. On August 28, 1963, he delivered this persuasive speech to a crowd of 250,000 people gathered at the Lincoln Memorial in Washington.

I Have a Dream

King starts with a tragic contrast.

Five score years ago, a great American, in whose symbolic shadow we stand, signed the Emancipation Proclamation. This momentous decree came as a great beacon light of hope to millions of Negro slaves who had been seared in the flames of withering injustice. It came as a joyous daybreak to end the long night of captivity. [1]

He uses figurative language to describe the present situation.

But one hundred years later, we must face the tragic fact that the Negro is still not free. One hundred years later, the life of the Negro is still sadly crippled by the manacles of segregation and the chains of discrimination. One hundred years later, the Negro lives on a lonely island of poverty in the midst of a vast ocean of material prosperity. One hundred years later, the Negro is still languishing in the corners of American society and finds himself an exile in his own land. So we have come here today to dramatize an appalling condition. [2]

An analogy clarifies the problem.

In a sense we have come to our nation's Capitol to cash a check. When the architects of our republic wrote the magnificent words of the Constitution and the Declaration of Independence, they were signing a promissory note to which every American was to fall heir. This note was a promise that all men would be guaranteed the unalienable rights of life, liberty, and the pursuit of happiness. [3]

It is obvious today that America has defaulted on this promissory note insofar as her citizens of color are concerned. Instead of honoring this sacred obligation, America has given the Negro people a bad check; a check which has come back marked "insufficient funds." But we refuse to believe that the bank of justice is bankrupt. We refuse to believe that there are insufficient funds in the great vaults of opportunity of this nation. So we have come to cash this check—a check that will give us upon demand the riches of freedom and the security of justice. We have also come to this hallowed spot to remind America of the fierce urgency of *now*. This is no time to engage in the luxury of cooling off or to take the tranquilizing drug of gradualism. *Now* is the time to make real the promises of Democracy. *Now* is the time to rise from the dark and desolate valley of segregation to the sunlit path of racial justice. *Now* is the time to open the doors of opportunity to all of God's children. *Now* is the time to lift our nation from the quicksands of racial injustice to the solid rock of brotherhood. [4]

Repeated words and phrases create urgency.

It would be fatal for the nation to overlook the urgency of the moment and to underestimate the determination of the Negro. This sweltering summer of the Negro's legitimate discontent will not pass until there is an [5] invigorating autumn of freedom and equality. 1963 is not an end, but a beginning. Those who hope that the Negro needed to blow off steam and will now be content will have a rude awakening if the nation returns to business as usual. There will be neither rest nor tranquility in America until the Negro is granted his citizenship rights. The whirlwinds of revolt will continue to shake the foundations of our nation until the bright day of justice emerges.

King addresses specific audiences in turn.

But there is something I must say to my people who stand on the warm threshold which leads into the palace of justice. In the process of gaining our rightful place we must not be guilty of wrongful deeds. Let us not seek to satisfy our thirst for freedom by drinking from the cup of bitterness and hatred. We must forever conduct our struggle on the high plane of dignity and discipline. We must not allow our creative protest to degenerate into physical violence. Again and again we must rise to the majestic heights of meeting physical force with soul force. The marvelous new militancy which has engulfed the Negro community must not lead us to a distrust of all white people, for many of our white brothers, as evidenced by their presence here today, have come to realize that their destiny is tied up with our destiny and their freedom is inextricably bound to our freedom. We cannot walk alone.

The writer responds to the arguments of opponents.

And as we talk, we must make the pledge that we shall march ahead. We cannot turn back. There are those who are asking the devotees of civil rights, "When will you be satisfied?" We can never be satisfied as long as the Negro is the victim of the unspeakable horrors of police brutality. We can never be satisfied as long as our bodies, heaving with the fatigue of travel, cannot gain lodging in the motels of the highways and the hotels of the cities. We cannot be satisfied as long as the Negro's basic mobility is from a smaller ghetto to a larger one. We can never be satisfied as long as a Negro in Mississippi cannot vote and a Negro in New York believes he has nothing for which to vote. No, no, we are not satisfied, and we will not be satisfied until justice rolls down like waters and righteousness like a mighty stream.

Appropriate emotional appeals are used in the context of suffering.

I am not unmindful that some of you have come here out of great trials and tribulations. Some of you have come fresh from narrow jail cells. Some of you have come from areas where your quest for freedom left you battered by the storms of persecution and staggered by the winds of police brutality. You have been the veterans of creative suffering. Continue to work with the faith that unearned suffering is redemptive.

Go back to Mississippi, go back to Alabama, go back to South Carolina, go back to Georgia, go back to Louisiana, go back to the slums and ghettos of our northern cities, knowing that somehow this situation can and will be changed. Let us not wallow in the valley of despair.

I say to you today, my friends, that in spite of the difficulties and frustrations of the moment I still have a dream. It is a dream deeply rooted in the American dream.

I have a dream that one day this nation will rise up and live out the 11 true meaning of its creed: "We hold these truths to be self-evident; that all men are created equal."

I have a dream that one day on the red hills of Georgia the sons of 12 former slaves and the sons of former slaveowners will be able to sit down together at the table of brotherhood.

The repetition of key phrases becomes a persuasive refrain.

I have a dream that the state of Mississippi, a desert state sweltering 13 with the heat of injustice and oppression, will be transformed into an oasis of freedom and justice.

I have a dream that my four little children will one day live in a nation 14 where they will not be judged by the color to their skin but by the content of their character.

I have a dream today. 15

I have a dream that the state of Alabama, whose governor's lips are 16 presently dripping with the words of interposition and nullification, will be transformed into a situation where little black boys and black girls will be able to join hands with little white boys and girls and walk together as sisters and brothers.

I have a dream today. 17

The writer's vision offers hope and motivates readers to change society.

I have a dream that one day every valley shall be exalted, every hill and 18 mountain shall be made low, the rough places will be made plain, and the crooked places will be made straight, and the glory of the Lord shall be revealed, and all flesh shall see it together.

This is our hope. This is the faith with which I return to the South. 19 With this faith we will be able to hew out of the mountain of despair a stone of hope. With this faith we will be able to transform the jangling discords of our nation into a beautiful symphony of brotherhood. With this faith we will be able to work together, to pray together, to struggle together, to go to jail together, to stand up for freedom together, knowing that we will be free one day.

This will be the day when all God's children will be able to sing with 20 new meaning.

King appeals to ideals and to humanity's better nature, ending with a vision of a just society.

My country 'tis of thee 21
Sweet land of liberty,
Of thee I sing,
Land where my fathers died,
Land of the pilgrims' pride,
From every mountainside
Let freedom ring.

And if America is to be a great nation this must become true. So let 22 freedom ring from the prodigious hilltops of New Hampshire. Let freedom ring from the mighty mountains of New York. Let freedom ring from the heightening Alleghenies of Pennsylvania!

Let freedom ring from the snow-capped Rockies of Colorado! *23*
Let freedom ring from the curvaceous peaks of California! *24*
But not only that; let freedom ring from Stone Mountain of Georgia! *25*
Let freedom ring from Lookout Mountain of Tennessee! *26*
Let freedom ring from every hill and molehill of Mississippi! From *27* every mountainside, let freedom ring.

When we let freedom ring, when we let it ring from every village and *28* every hamlet, from every state and every city, we will be able to speed up that day when all of God's children, black men and white men, Jews and Gentiles, Protestants and Catholics, will be able to join hands and sing in the words of the old Negro spiritual, "Free at last! Free at last! Thank God almighty, we are free at last!" ■

> The closing urges readers to work for a better future.

write

Reading for Better Writing

1. King is actually speaking to several audiences at the same time. Who are these different audiences? How does King address each?

2. For what specific changes does King call? What does he want his listeners to do?

3. Explore the writer's style. How does he use religious imagery, comparisons, and analogies? How does repetition function as a persuasive technique?

4. In a sense, King's speech addresses a gap between reality and an ideal. How does he present this gap?

Guidelines
Persuading Readers to Act

Note: For in-depth help on developing persuasive arguments, see pages **253–268**.

1. **Select a topic.** List issues about which you feel passionately, issues where you see a need for change. (See "Topics to Consider" on page **282**.) Then choose a topic that meets these criteria: the topic is debatable, significant, current, and manageable.

Not Debatable	*Debatable*
Statistics on spending practices	The injustice of consumerism
The existence of racism	Solutions to racism

2. **Choose and analyze your readers.** Think about who your readers are. Make a list of words and phrases describing their perspectives on the issue.

3. **Narrow your focus and determine your purpose.** Consider what you can achieve within the assignment's constraints. Should you focus on one aspect of the issue or all of it? What patterns of thinking and behavior can you try to change? With these readers, what actions can you call for?

4. **Generate ideas and support.** Use prewriting strategies like those below to develop your thinking and gather support:

   - Set up "opposing viewpoints" columns. In one column, take one side; in the other column, take the other side.
   - Construct a dialogue between two people—yourself and someone who doesn't support your position.
   - Talk to others about the issue. How do peers, friends, co-workers, and relatives respond to your ideas?
   - Research the issue to find current, reliable sources from a variety of perspectives. Consider interviewing an expert.
   - Consider what outcome or results you want.

5. **Organize your thinking.** Get your thoughts in order so that you can step confidently into your first draft. Consider the following strategies:

   - Make a sharp claim about the issue, a claim that points toward action. Try this basic pattern:

     On the issue of _____ , *I believe* _____ .
     Therefore, we must change _____ .

● Review the evidence, and develop your line of reasoning by generating an outline or using a graphic organizer.

Simple Outline: **Introduction: claim**
Supporting point 1
Supporting point 2
Supporting point 3
Conclusion: call to action

6. **Write your first draft.** As you write, remember your persuasive goal and your specific readers. Here are some possible strategies:

Opening: Gain the reader's attention, raise the issue, help the reader care about it, and state your claim.

Development: Follow your outline but feel free to explore new ideas that arise. Decide where to place your most persuasive supporting argument: first or last. Anticipate readers' questions and objections, and use appropriate logical and emotional appeals to overcome their resistance.

Closing: Do one or more of the following: restate your claim, summarize your support, encourage readers to take the action you want.

Title: Develop a thoughtful, energetic working title that stresses a vision or change. (For ideas, scan the titles of the sample essays in this chapter.)

7. **Share your essay.** Try out your thinking and persuasive appeals on a real reader. Does he or she find your argument convincing? Why or why not?

8. **Revise your writing.** Think about your reviewer's comments, and then ask these questions of your draft:

● Does your argument flow effectively? Consider shuffling points to make the sequence more persuasive. Add transitions if necessary.

● Is the evidence credible and persuasive? Does your logic have gaps? Do you need to qualify some points and strengthen others?

● Do images, examples, and analogies help readers understand and identify with your cause? Do these elements urge readers to act?

● Is the voice fitting—energetic but controlled, confident but reasonable? Will your tone persuade readers, or start a quarrel?

9. **Edit and proofread.** See page **87** for guidelines, but check especially for appropriate word choice and clear sentences. Avoid clichés and jargon.

10. **Prepare and publish your final essay.** Submit your essay according to your instructor's format and documentation requirements. If appropriate, "publish" your essay and solicit feedback from your audience—perhaps on a Web site, in the school newspaper, or with an appropriate discussion group.

Writing Checklist

Use these six traits to check the quality of your essay, then revise as needed:

____ The **ideas** in your essay prompt readers to change their thinking and behavior. The essay has a clear opinion statement, effective reasoning, good support, and a clear call to action.

____ The **organization** is logical and includes an engaging opening that raises the issue, a clearly sequenced argument, and a convincing conclusion focused on change and action.

____ The **voice** is thoughtful, caring, and convincing.

____ The **words** are precise, concrete, and easily understood (or defined as needed). The language is free of clichés and glib phrases.

____ The **sentences** flow smoothly, with effective transitions and logical connections.

____ The **copy** follows correct format, documentation, and rules of writing.

write

Writing Activities

1. In "Let's Kill *Cute*," the writer explores a pet peeve—something that really bothers her. What are your pet peeves? Make a list, choose one, and write an essay persuading readers to get peeved and take action.

2. Three essays in this chapter address significant social issues—consumerism, democratic participation, and racism. Brainstorm a list of other social issues that you find significant, choose one, and then write an essay that persuades readers to do something related to the issue.

3. If you are a natural sciences major, consider debatable issues that are central to studying and applying the sciences—environmental, medical, biotechnical, and agricultural issues, for example. If you are a social science or humanities major, do the same brainstorming in your area.

4. Focus on an issue that directly affects you. Which college, community, or state policies should be strengthened or changed? Select an issue, write a persuasive essay, and submit your work as an editorial to a news publication.

5. Consider the workplace. What issues have come up in your job? Contemplate issues such as pay equity, equal opportunity, management policies, and unsafe work conditions. Then write a persuasive report to a decision maker or fellow employees.

Chapter 20
Arguing Against a Claim

audio

What do you imagine when you hear the word "argument"—an unfriendly squabble, a family fight, or a heated shouting match? All too often, "argument" has these negative connotations.

In college, written arguments are meant to be positive and productive. They are opportunities to debate controversial issues, to arrive at logical conclusions, and perhaps even to achieve agreement. Sometimes, however, you must focus on disagreement. That's the purpose behind an essay arguing against a claim. You take issue with a currently held view or a specific opponent and then make your case against that position. In the end, you may argue for an alternative.

When well written, an argument enlightens readers, helping them make informed decisions about the issue. It wins agreement through persuasion, not belligerence. Such writing helps you develop your thinking skills, refine your perspective on life, and prepare for debates at work, at school, and in the public square. In the end, argumentative writing just might help you avoid a shouting match or two.

What's Ahead

- Overview: Arguing Against a Claim
  - Student Models
  - Professional Model
- Guidelines
- Writing Checklist and Activities

Overview
Arguing Against a Claim

Writer's Goal

Your goal is to examine a specific claim and argue against it. Aim to analyze the main point, evaluate key evidence, weigh alternative claims, and construct an effective counterargument.

Keys for Success

Respect the claim. ■ Ground your argument in a thorough understanding of the opposition's stance. Is the claim a general, unexamined belief held by many people? Or is it an argument put forward by a distinct group or individual? Why do others hold this position? Make your disagreement respectful and informed.

Develop a credible counterargument. ■ To persuade readers, you must both critique the claim and offer a valid alternative. What shortcomings, blind spots, and fallacies do you find at work in the claim? What new evidence and counterclaims can you bring to the discussion?

Provide quality evidence. ■ Thoroughly research the issue, the claim, and alternatives. To convince readers to reject a claim they may hold themselves, put forth varied support—from statistics to expert testimony. Let the evidence carry the weight of your counterargument.

Claims to Consider

To find a claim that you want to debate, review the following categories and generate topics within them:

- **Common beliefs and values:** What views, beliefs, positions, and policies do people seem to accept blindly? What recent events have challenged what you or others hold dear?

- **Expert claims:** In the news, on talk shows, in books, and in magazines, what claims do experts and spokespersons for causes make about controversial issues?

- **Community controversies:** In your communities (city, neighborhood, club, and so on), what seem to be the prevailing views on various controversial issues? Are those views right?

- **Political policies:** In your city, state, or nation, what topics are liberals and conservatives debating? With which side do you disagree? Why?

> **Next Step** Read the model essays and perform the activities that follow. As you read, consider the claims and counterarguments presented. Identify similar types of claims and opposition strategies to use in your own writing.

Arguing Against a Claim

In the essay below, student writer Stephanie Lems argues against the common belief that a lot of exercise is a good thing. She argues that one serious exception exists.

Too Much of a Good Thing

The writer uses a personal anecdote to raise and question a common belief.

Dressed in shorts, a T-shirt, and well-worn running shoes, I was *1* halfway through my warm-up stretches when I asked myself, "Why do I run?" To keep in shape? To lose weight? To have fun? "Running is a good thing," I decided, "and I do it for fun." Then I looked down at my shoes that were new only three months earlier, saw their worn edges, and wondered, "So I run just for fun . . . really?"

Earlier in the week I had done some reading about people who exercise *2* compulsively. One writer had argued that a person in a good exercise program works out regularly to get fit and stay that way. However, exercise becomes compulsive if a person repeatedly works out beyond the requirements for good health, feels driven to work out, experiences guilt about not working out, or lets exercise control his or her life.

To counter the common belief, she links exercise and anorexia.

Another writer described girls who are both anorexic and addicted to *3* exercise. As I stretched, I thought about the girls I knew who run to lose weight, and I wondered whether the writer was right—whether anorexia and exercise addiction could be connected. After I finished my run, and after I researched the topic, I decided that the two are linked at least to this extent: in an anorexic's life, a large decrease in eating often correlates with progressively more exercise. I also decided that when the two are linked, both are very dangerous.

She defines a key term and clarifies an important distinction.

Anorexia nervosa, commonly called anorexia, is a syndrome character- *4* ized by extreme weight loss. Because they fear being fat or have distorted images of their own bodies, people with anorexia starve themselves to lose weight. This starvation becomes an addiction so strong that an individual can control it only with a tremendous personal effort and the help of others.

She supports the thesis with expert testimony, quoting directly.

Although most people with anorexia try to control their weight by *5* controlling their food intake, many also use exercise to burn up the calories in what they do eat. One expert, Marvel Harrison, Ph.D., R.D., is the national director of Life Balance, a program for people who suffer from eating disorders. She comments on how women with anorexia use exercise: "Women are devoting an incredible amount of energy to controlling their bodies through exercise and diet, obsessing about calories consumed and burned" (qtd. in Despres 3). They exercise excessively not only to burn calories, but also to relieve stress or to get in shape. However, no matter what the motive for excessive exercise, these workouts can become a serious—and sometimes deadly—disease, especially if anorexia is involved.

A number of scientific studies have found a connection between 6
anorexia and excessive exercise. Researchers David Pierce and Frank Epling
from the University of Alberta did one of the studies, and they used rats to
explore the topic. Pierce and Epling placed rats in two cages. The rats in the
first cage were given a functional running wheel, along with a reduced diet
of one meal per day. The rats in the second cage were given a nonfunctional
running wheel, but they also received a reduced diet of one meal per day.
According to the two scientists, the rats with unlimited access to the functional running wheel ran each day, and gradually increased the amount of
running; in addition, they started to eat less. At the end of one week, some
rats in the first group stopped eating altogether and ran themselves to death.
On the other hand, rats in the second group had a happier ending. Because
their running wheel did not function, these rats did not run, soon adapted
to their reduced diet, and stayed healthy. Pierce and Epling concluded that
given the opportunity to run, rats on a reduced diet would exercise to the
point of hurting their health (McGovern 1–2).

> *The writer supports her claim with scientific research on both rats and people.*

Clive Long and Jenny Smith, from the Department of Clinical 7
Psychology at St. Andrew's Hospital in Northampton, England, did another
study. They studied how the attitudes and exercise behavior of anorexic
females compare with the attitudes and exercise behavior of non-anorexic
females. For two weeks, twenty-one anorexic females and forty-five non-
anorexic females participated in the study. Throughout this time, each
person recorded details concerning how long she exercised, when she exercised, whether she exercised secretly, and what eating habits she practiced.
The participants also evaluated their motives for exercising.

The results of the study were enlightening. By comparing the anorexic 8
females with the non-anorexic females, Long and Smith determined that
those with anorexia exercised considerably more often, were more likely to
exercise every day, often exercised secretly, and participated in more sports
(Long and Smith 3). The researchers also found that the individuals with
anorexia continued their exercise program even if health issues interfered.
Finally, the people with anorexia were more hyperactive than those without
anorexia, even though the anorexic group ate less food than the other
group. The anorexic participants were constantly on the move trying to
burn off as many calories as possible.

> *She summarizes the studies and links them with a key concept pointing to a cause/effect relationship.*

Researchers involved in both studies identified a new disease called 9
"activity anorexia." David Pierce of the Sociology and Neuroscience
Department at the University of Alberta defined activity anorexia as "a
problematic behavior pattern in which a drastic decrease in eating causes
progressively more exercise, which further reduces eating, in a vicious cycle"
(qtd. in Dess 1). Among other findings, Pierce and Epling determined that
people who are driven to exercise, and who constantly obsess over it, are
most likely to develop either anorexia or another type of eating disorder.

> *For support, she uses the experiences of an activity anorexic.*

Individuals struggling with activity anorexia use exercise not to sustain 10
their health but to control their weight. Renee Despres, author of "Burn,

Baby, Burn," makes that point when she describes her own struggle with exercise disorder: "I welcomed the chance to burn the calories—400 of them, if I had measured and calculated everything right—in last night's salad. To make sure every last calorie had been burned, I ran for an hour and a half" (5). Activity anorexics assess the exact number of calories in the food they consume, and then they try to exercise enough to burn off all or most of them. They exercise not for fun, nor for health, but for control.

To close, the writer stresses the issue's seriousness, uses "we" to pull readers into the discussion, and promotes awareness and action.

The bad news is that activity anorexia is a significant problem today, *11* but the good news is that we can do something about it. We can learn about the illness and use that information to help others. In addition, we can muster the courage to ask ourselves honestly, "Why do I exercise?" Our answers to that question will help us better understand ourselves and our health. Our goal must be twofold. First, we must accept ourselves for who we are—every bone, muscle, nerve, and fat molecule. And second, we must use food and exercise—both very good things—enough, but not too much. ■

Note: The Works Cited page is not shown.

write

Reading for Better Writing

1. Precisely what is this writer arguing against? What does she argue for?
2. In a list, trace the writer's reasoning. Does that reasoning create a convincing "line" or sequence of ideas? Why or why not?
3. Examine the types of supporting evidence provided. Is that evidence convincing? Why or why not?
4. This essay begins with personal reflection and ends with a direct appeal to readers. Are these two strategies effective? Explain.

Arguing Against a Claim

Rita Isakson is an English major who read an article in which the writer asserts that Barbie dolls harm young girls' development. In this essay, Isakson uses logic and her own experience to build a counterargument.

An Apology for the Life of Ms. Barbie D. Doll

The writer states her opponent's arguments and disagrees with them.

Barbie's boobs and spacious mansion helped cause the decay of today's youth, supposed experts say. For example, in her article, "'I Want to Be a Barbie Doll When I Grow Up': The Cultural Significance of the Barbie Doll," Marilyn Ferris Motz argues the following: Barbie dolls encourage young girls to be conformists focused on "leisure activities, personal appearance, popularity and the consumption of materials" (125). Barbie's skinny waist, huge bosom, and narrow hips entice girls into poor diets and eating disorders. Barbie-play trains girls to depend on Ken-figures (or other males) to achieve self-worth. Barbie's All-American-Girl values teach conformity; and Barbie's racy cars, plush houses, and chic outfits cause materialism (128–132). But I don't buy Motz's "reasons." They sound fake—like the theories of somebody who lacks first-hand experience. I had Barbie dolls—twelve of them, in fact, and the Barbie Mansion and Soda Shop to boot—but I don't consider myself an anorexic, dependent, conforming, materialistic girl, at least no more than I would be had I foregone the Barbie experience.

Her tone is forceful and playful, but thoughtful.

She concedes a point but rebuts the argument.

Granted, Barbie's physical appearance isn't realistic. As Motz explains, "If Barbie stood five feet nine inches tall, her bust measurement would be 33 inches, her waist a meager 18 inches, and her hips only 28 1/2 inches" (128). In addition, Motz says, "Barbie's arms are extremely thin and her hands disproportionately small. Her legs are much too long . . ." (128–129). I say, so what? While the only "real" version of Barbie's body would be a long-limbed 13-year-old with breast implants, who cares? Arguing that Barbie's bod isn't realistic and that the lack of realism hurts girls' self-esteem is weak logic. Children have had dolls for ages. For example, in Pompeii, the preserved remains of a 3,000-year-old doll are displayed. That doll has an egghead, a ratty cloth for a dress, no limbs, and a body that looks like a thick, shapeless rock. If Barbie's unrealistic proportions hurt modern girls' self-esteem, I pity antiquity's girls who had these lumps for models!

Her own experience adds support.

Motz says that the average age of girls who play with Barbie is six, and that girls this age imitate the doll's values, like her preoccupation with appearance (127). However, while I was about six when I played with Barbie, I didn't imitate her. At age seven, I had a bowl haircut that was constantly snarled because I wouldn't take time to brush it. I didn't care about my own appearance, while fixing Barbie's was fun. I didn't fuss over my own hair and weight until I was in high school, and fashion mags were scripture. In other words, Motz's theory that girls' preoccupation with Barbie's appearance leads to later preoccupation with their own, simply

1

2

3

doesn't reflect my experience. Nor does her theory reflect the experiences of many other girls, including my two roommates.

The writer rebuts each point in turn, often quoting directly from the article.

In response to Motz's idea that Barbies make girls dependent on males, I say, "Phooey." I played with Barbies until every last cow came home, and am now a happy single girl. In fact, I have often been single, free from all romantic attachments. True, I've had boyfriends, but I never felt compelled to sacrifice my needs or identity to keep a boyfriend. And I am not an exception to Motz's rule! I know many girls whose primary concerns are their friends, family, and/or schoolwork. Admittedly, there are probably an equal number of girls who live only for their beaus; however, their behavior doesn't prove that Barbie causes female dependency. For example, my own interest in boys was prompted most by "good" TV shows and books—like Laura Ingalls Wilder's *On the Shores of Silver Lake.* It was stories like these—about teenage girls in love—that encouraged me to crave romance.   4

She summarizes her disagreement and offers alternative explanations.

In other words, Motz uses Barbie as a scapegoat for problems that have complex causes. For example, a girl's interest in romance is no more Barbie's fault than the fault of books like *On the Shores of Silver Lake.* Fashion magazines targeted at adolescents are the cause of far more anorexia cases than is Barbie. Mothers who encourage daughters to find security in men teach female dependency, but Barbie doesn't. In fact, Motz herself points out that when "the Barbie doll was created, many parents hailed the doll as a model of wholesome teenage behavior and appearance" (130). I would add that today, many parents still hail Barbie as a model for wholesome behavior. But it is more the manner in which parents give toys to their children—the parents' ideas and instructions about how to play—that determine whether Barbie-play is good or bad.   5

Speaking directly to the opposition, the writer shares an anecdote and restates her counterclaim.

To Motz and similar "experts," I say this: some of my finest childhood memories are of my best friend, Solara, coming over to my house with her pink carry-on suitcase stuffed with Barbies and their accoutrements. For hours we would play with them, giving haircuts, filling mixing bowls to make swimming pools, and creating small "campfires" so Barbie could make s'mores. Sometimes we dressed her in store-bought clothes, and sometimes we designed clothing for her. Other times we turned Barbie into the heroines in our books, and she helped us act out the plots. Playing with Barbies need not be an unimaginative, antisocial activity that promotes conformity, materialism, and superficial ideals. I played with Barbies and I'm fine. Take that, Motz! ■   6

write

Reading for Better Writing

1. The word *apology* can mean *defense*, as well as a statement of regret for wrongdoing. Is the use of the word fitting in the title? Why or why not?

2. This essay is a counterargument that relies heavily on logic and personal experience for support. How does the writer treat the original source? How do concessions and rebuttals function in the argument?

Arguing Against a Claim

Rebecca Pasok is an environmental studies major who wrote this essay to argue against a policy position in favor of drilling for oil in the Arctic National Wildlife Refuge.

To Drill or Not to Drill

The opening provides background information before raising the controversial position.

Known as "America's Last Frontier," the Arctic National Wildlife Refuge (ANWR) is located in the northeast corner of Alaska, right along the Beaufort Sea. President Dwight D. Eisenhower established the refuge in 1960, and today its 19 million acres make it one of the biggest refuges in the United States, and home to a wide variety of wildlife such as eagles, wolves, moose, grizzly bear, polar bear, and caribou. During the last few years, however, the security of that home has been threatened by those who want to use one section of the ANWR to drill for oil. That section—named Area 1002—encompasses 1.5 million acres of pristine land near the coast.

The writer starts with a strong argument against drilling but then maps out why others support it.

One of the strongest arguments against oil drilling anywhere in the refuge is that the environmental impact of drilling conflicts with the very purpose of the ANWR. The primary mandate for the ANWR, as laid out by the U.S. Fish and Wildlife Service that administers the refuge, is "to protect the wildlife and habitats of the area for the benefit of people now and in the future." The question then is whether drilling for oil supports, or is in conflict with, this mandate. President George W. Bush and others argue that oil drilling does not conflict with the mandate because new oil-drilling techniques cause only minimal damage to the environment. These techniques include drilling fewer wells, placing wells closer together, and building pipelines above ground so as not to disturb the animals (McCarthy).

She counters the position with expert testimony for the other side.

Some environmental experts support the argument that the new techniques will not hurt wildlife. While these individuals acknowledge that some land disturbance will result, they argue that animals such as caribou will not suffer. One expert taking this position is Pat Valkenberg, a research coordinator with the Alaska Department of Fish and Game; he maintains that the caribou population is thriving and should continue to thrive. To support this point, Valkenberg notes that between 1997 and 2000, the caribou population actually grew from 19,700 to 27,128 (*Petroleum News*).

Other experts challenge those statistics with information about the caribou's birthing patterns. These experts point to herds like the Porcupine caribou that live in the ANWR and move along the coast of the Beaufort Sea in the United States and also into Canada. A majority of the females in this herd wear radio collars that have been tracked to Area 1002 during calving season. Experts who argue against drilling note that the calves born on ANWR's coastal plain have a greater chance of surviving than those that are born in the foothills where many of their predators live (*U.S. Fish and Wildlife*). This difference in survival ratios, argue anti-drilling experts, may not be accounted for in the statistics used by pro-drilling advocates like Valkenberg.

One specialist opposed to drilling is David Klein, a professor at the Institute of Arctic Biology at the University of Alaska–Fairbanks. Klein argues that if the oil industry opens up the ANWR for drilling, the number of caribou will likely decrease because the calving locations would change. He points out that oil-industry work in the Prudhoe oil field (also in Alaska) has already split up the Central Arctic herd of caribou, so it is likely that drilling in Area 1002 will similarly affect the Porcupine herd (McCarthy).

> **The writer strongly states her thesis—that she agrees with opponents of drilling.**

But caribou are not the only wildlife that would be affected by drilling in Area 1002. Musk oxen, polar bear, and grizzly bear could be driven out of the refuge and possibly into regions where people live, thereby threatening their safety. Clearly, the bottom line in this debate is that drilling in Area 1002 will destroy at least some of the ecological integrity that makes ANWR a natural treasure. Environmentalists say that "just as there is no way to be half-pregnant, there is no 'sensitive' way to drill in a wilderness" (McCarthy). They are right.

> **By looking at effects on people, the writer expands her opposition.**

However, oil drilling in ANWR will hurt more than the environment and wildlife; the drilling also will hurt at least one of the two Inuit tribes living in Alaska—the Inupiat Eskimos and the Gwich'in Indians. The Inupiat is the larger group, and they favor drilling. Money generated by the oil industry, say the Inupiat, will help them improve a variety of tribal services such as education and health care. On the other hand, the Gwich'in tribe depend on the Porcupine Caribou for food. As a result, if oil drilling displaces such as animals, the people will suffer. Not only do they need the caribou to survive, but they also need them to retain the tribe's dignity and way of life. In other words, while oil drilling in ANWR may give some residents more money, others clearly will pay the price.

> **A question serves as a transition to a key counterargument.**

So if oil drilling in ANWR would have so many negative effects, what is driving the argument for drilling? Unfortunately, nothing more than a shortsighted, ill-informed effort to satisfy America's excessive appetite for oil: to continue using too much, we want to produce more. But is drilling in the ANWR the answer to our consumption problem?

At best, getting more oil from Alaska is a shortsighted solution: ANWR's reserves are simply too small to provide a long-term solution. A 1998 study by the U.S. Geological Survey concluded that the total amount of accessible oil in the ANWR is 5.7 to 16 billion barrels, with an expected amount of 10.4 billion barrels (*Arctic Power*). But while these figures are considered the official estimate, the National Resources Defense Council (a group of lawyers, scientists, and environmentalists) disagrees. It estimates the accessible amount to be 3.2 billion barrels—a resource the United States would use up in just six months! In the meantime, using the ANWR oil would do nothing to ease our dependence on Middle Eastern countries for oil. There has to be a better choice.

The writer redirects the discussion to the root of the problem.

And there is. The question is not whether drilling should take place in the ANWR, but how to provide energy for everyone, now and in the future. A poll taken by *The Christian Science Monitor* shows that voters believe that the best option for Americans is to develop new technologies (Dillan). Finding new energy sources, they say, is more important than finding new oil reserves. 10

There are two main problems with relying primarily on oil for our energy: oil supplies are limited, and oil-use pollutes. Democratic Representative Rosa DeLauro of Connecticut made this point well when she said the following: 11

A closing quotation focuses and supports the writer's objections; the quotation is indented ten spaces.

We need a serious energy policy in the United States. Drilling in the Arctic National Wildlife Refuge is not the solution. We should look to increase domestic production while balancing our desire for a cleaner environment. We must also look at ways to reduce our dependency on fossil fuels themselves, a smart and necessary step that will lead to a cleaner environment. (qtd. in Urban) 12

While reducing our use of fossil fuels will not be easy, it is possible if we do two things: (1) develop energy-saving technologies, and (2) make lifestyle choices that conserve energy. Unlike the short-term (and short-sighted) solution of drilling in the ANWR, these strategies will help save the environment. In addition, the strategies will help people both now and in the future. ■ 13

Note: The Works Cited page is not shown.

write

Reading for Better Writing

1. The writer describes both positions on drilling before stating her opposition explicitly. Is this strategy effective?

2. The writer uses the testimony of experts extensively. Why?

3. What does the writer do to acknowledge, concede points to, and refute support for drilling?

4. Review pages **258–260** about types of support. Then trace the types of evidence provided in this essay. Evaluate the quality and completeness of the evidence.

5. Does the last paragraph offer an effective closing to the writer's counterargument? Why or why not?

Arguing Against a Claim

Writer Linda Chavez's essay, which was published in 1994, argues against the "advance of multiculturalism" in the United States. Chavez speaks confidently and assertively throughout the essay—conceding little to the opposition.

Demystifying Multiculturalism

The writer portrays the current trends, questions these trends, and raises the alarm.

Multiculturalism is on the advance, everywhere from President Clinton's cabinet to corporate boardrooms to public-school classrooms. If you believe the multiculturalists' propaganda, whites are on the verge of becoming a minority in the United States. The multiculturalists predict that this demographic shift will fundamentally change American culture—indeed destroy the very idea that America has a single, unified culture. They aren't taking any chances, however. They have enlisted the help of government, corporate leaders, the media, and the education establishment in waging a cultural revolution. But has America truly become a multicultural nation? And if not, will those who capitulate to these demands create a self-fulfilling prophecy?

The essay presents arguments for multiculturalism, along with counter-arguments.

At the heart of the argument is the assumption that the white population is rapidly declining in relation to the nonwhite population. A 1987 Hudson Institute report helped catapult this claim to national prominence. The study, *Workforce 2000,* estimated that by the turn of the century only 15 percent of new workers would be white males. The figure was widely interpreted to mean that whites were about to become a minority in the workplace—and in the country.

Statistics support the writer's claims.

In fact, white males will still constitute about 45 percent—a plurality—of the workforce in the year 2000. The proportion of white men in the workforce *is* declining—it was nearly 51 percent in 1980—but primarily because the proportion of white women is growing. They will make up 39 percent of the workforce within 10 years, according to government projections, up from 36 percent in 1980. Together, white men and women will account for 84 percent of all workers by 2000—hardly a minority share. . . .

Multiculturalists insist on treating race and ethnicity as if they were synonymous with culture. They presume that skin color and national origin, which are immutable traits, determine values, mores, language, and other cultural attributes, which, of course, are learned. In the multiculturalists' world view, African Americans, Puerto Ricans, or Chinese Americans living in New York City have more in common with persons of their ancestral group living in Lagos or San Juan or Hong Kong than they do with other New Yorkers who are white. Culture becomes a fixed entity, transmitted, as it were, in the genes, rather than through experience. . . .

The writer questions the opposition's logic.

Such convictions lead multiculturalists to conclude that "[T]here is no 5 common American culture." The logic is simple, but wrongheaded: Since Americans (or more often, their forebears) hail from many different places, each of which has its own specific culture, the argument goes, America must be multicultural. And it is becoming more so every day as new immigrants bring their cultures with them.

Indeed, multiculturalists hope to ride the immigrant wave to greater 6 power and influence. They have certainly done so in education. Some 2.3 million children who cannot speak English well now attend public schools, an increase of 1 million in the last seven years. Multicultural advocates cite the presence of such children to demand bilingual education and other multicultural services. The Los Angeles Unified School District alone currently offers instruction in Spanish, Armenian, Korean, Cantonese, Tagalog, Japanese, and Russian. Federal and state governments now spend literally billions of dollars on these programs.

She probes opposing arguments and exposes ironies.

Ironically, the multiculturalists' emphasis on education undercuts their 7 argument that culture is inextricable from race or national origin. They are acutely aware of just how fragile cultural identification is; why else are they so adamant about reinforcing it? Multiculturalists insist on teaching immigrant children in their native language, instructing them in the history and customs of their native land, and imbuing them with reverence for their ancestral heroes, lest these youngsters be seduced by American culture.

She analyzes multicultural proponents.

The impetus for multiculturalism is not coming from immigrants, but 8 from their more affluent and assimilated native-born counterparts. The proponents are most often the elite—the best educated and most successful members of their respective racial and ethnic groups. College campuses, where the most radical displays of multiculturalism take place, are fertile recruiting grounds. Last May, for example, a group of Mexican American students at UCLA, frustrated that the university would not elevate the school's 23-year-old Chicano studies program to full department status, stormed the faculty center, breaking windows and furniture and causing half a million dollars in damage. The same month, a group of Asian American students at UC–Irvine went on a hunger strike to pressure administrators into hiring more professors of Asian American studies. These were not immigrants or even, by and large, disadvantaged students, but middle-class beneficiaries of their parents' or grandparents' successful assimilation into the American mainstream.

She uses statistics to describe those who support multicultural policies.

Whatever their newfound victim status, these students look amazingly 9 like other Americans on most indices. For example, the median family income of Mexican American students at Berkeley in 1989 was $32,500, slightly above the national median for all Americans that year, $32,191; and 17 percent of those students came from families that earned more than $75,000 a year, even though they were admitted to the university under affirmative-action programs (presumably because they suffered some educational disadvantage attributed to their ethnicity).

> **A critical point about the source of multiculturalism is saved for the end.**

Multiculturalism is not a grassroots movement. It was created, nurtured, and expanded through government policy. Without the expenditure of vast sums of public money, it would wither away and die. That is not to say that ethnic communities would disappear from the American scene or that groups would not retain some attachment to their ancestral roots. American assimilation has always entailed some give-and-take, and American culture has been enriched by what individual groups brought to it. The distinguishing characteristic of American culture is its ability to incorporate so many disparate groups, creating a new whole from the many parts. Lately, we have nearly reversed course, treating each group, new and old, as if what is most important is to preserve its separate identity and space.

10

> **The writer presses readers to question policies and closes with a provocative question.**

It is easy to blame the ideologues and radicals who are pushing the "disuniting of America," to use Arthur Schlesinger's phrase, but the real culprits are those who provide multiculturalists with the money and the access to press their cause. Without the acquiescence of policy makers and ordinary citizens, multiculturalism would be no threat. Unfortunately, most major institutions have little stomach for resisting the multicultural impulse—and many seem eager to comply with whatever demands the multiculturalists make. Americans should have learned by now that policy matters. We have only to look at the failure of our welfare and crime policies to know that providing perverse incentives can change the way individuals behave—for the worse. Who is to say that if we pour enough money into dividing Americans, we won't succeed? ∎

11

Reading for Better Writing

1. In a nutshell, what is Chavez arguing against, and why?

2. How would you describe her attitudes toward the topic, her readers, and her opposition?

3. Trace the writer's argument in outline form. How effectively does Chavez use counterarguments? Does she put forward her own argument, or does she simply imply it?

Guidelines
Arguing Against a Claim

Note: For in-depth help on developing an argument, see pages **253–268**.

1. **Find a topic and claim.** For ideas on how to find a topic and claim, review "Claims to Consider" on page **298**. Once you've found a claim to argue against, test it by asking these questions:
   - Is the claim stated fairly and honestly? Or is it a "straw man"—a claim that simplifies or exaggerates the opposition's position? (See page **261**.)
   - Do you care about the issue? Does the claim bother you? Does it have an effect on you, others you care about, or something you value?

2. **Interrogate the claim.** State the claim—either as you originally encountered it or as you understand it. Then analyze the claim:
   - What is actually true or acceptable about this claim?
   - Who supports this claim, and why? Where does it come from? What is its basis? What evidence is marshalled to support it?
   - What is false or misguided about the claim? What are its assumptions, limits, blind spots, and fallacies?

3. **Consider your readers.** Productively disagree by meeting your readers part way. Answer these questions:
   - Will you write directly to those who strongly support the claim or to an audience whose members perhaps haven't thought much about the issue?
   - Is your goal to be provocative or primarily educational?
   - What persuasive strategies will convince readers to take your opposition seriously?

4. **Develop your counterargument.** If helpful, list arguments supporting the claim in one column and then develop counterarguments in a second column. Thoroughly research the issue, doing justice to all sides. Pay careful attention to authoritative sources. Critique the arguments, examine the evidence, and deepen your own perspective. Share your counterarguments in three ways:
   - Where appropriate, make concessions to advocates of the opposing claim and point out your specific disagreement.
   - Share your opposition as a rebuttal (see page **265**). Show how the argument is faulty or partial.
   - Develop an alternative. Based on your thinking and research, state the truth of the matter. Share a counterclaim that makes more sense.

5. **Commit yourself to a working thesis.** Build both your disagreement and your alternative into your thesis, considering how to phrase it. Do you want to stress an error or simply a limit, a sensible modification or the outright rejection of the claim? Try the following pattern:

    *(**The claim**) is faulty because (**main reason**). Instead, the truth is (**alternative or counterclaim**).*

6. **Outline your essay.** Organize your counterargument by considering your working thesis, goal, and readers. What line of reasoning will persuasively make your case? Here are three options to consider:

    - If a claim is a general belief or value, briefly describe it and then fully develop your objections and alternative. See "Too Much of a Good Thing" (pages **299–301**).
    - If the claim is controversial, present the argument in detail before countering with your opposition and alternative. See "To Drill or Not to Drill" (pages **304–306**).
    - If the claim is complex, present and counter the argument point by point. See "An Apology for the Life of Ms. Barbie D. Doll" (pages **302–303**) and "Demystifying Multiculturalism" (pages **307–309**).

7. **Write your first draft.** If possible, get your argument on paper in a single sitting, working from your outline but freely exploring ideas as they develop.
    Opening: Raise the issue by getting readers' attention with a question, dilemma, story, or contradiction. State your thesis, if appropriate.
    Middle: Logically develop and support your opposition to the claim and your preference for a counterclaim.
    Closing: Restate your opposition, clarify your counterclaim, and offer food for thought. If appropriate, challenge readers to adopt your position.

8. **Share your draft and revise it as needed.** Test the clarity and strength of your counterarguments. Ask a tutor in the writing center or a peer to answer these questions: Is your opposition clearly stated? Is the original claim treated fairly? Is your support convincing? Is the tone polite but confident?

9. **Edit and proofread.** Check the quality of the writing:

    - Have you chosen words carefully and defined terms when necessary?
    - Do sentences flow smoothly? Do you use logical transition words such as *however, furthermore, instead of, but,* and *so* to show a turn of thought?
    - Is your essay free of grammar, usage, punctuation, spelling, and format errors? Have you documented your sources?

10. **Prepare and share your final essay.** Submit a final version to your instructor, but also seek ways to share your writing with others.

Writing Checklist

Use these six traits to check the quality of your essay, then revise as needed:

____ The **ideas** offer reasonable, powerful opposition to a claim. The conclusions are valid, following logically from evidence that is varied and convincing.

____ The **organization** offers an easy-to-follow line of reasoning that lays out the opposition's stance and offers an alternative. Both the opening and closing are engaging and thoughtful.

____ The **voice** is consistently judicious, responsible, and lively.

____ The **words** are well chosen. Unfamiliar terms are defined and used correctly. The prose contains specific nouns, vivid verbs, and fitting modifiers—not clichés, platitudes, and slanted language.

____ The **sentences** have varied lengths and openings. Logical transitions such as *and, therefore, nevertheless, but,* and *however* signal the argument's flow.

____ The **copy** follows rules for correct writing, format, and documentation.

write

Writing Activities

1. In "Too Much of a Good Thing," the writer counters a common faith in the benefits of exercise by presenting a discussion of exercise addiction. In what other areas of life do you see "too much" of something? Develop a counterargument against a form of excess.

2. In "An Apology for the Life of Ms. Barbie D. Doll," the writer debates an expert about the effects of playing with Barbie dolls. Through reading, find an expert opinion concerning a topic that you care about and construct a similar counterargument.

3. In "To Drill or Not to Drill," the writer expresses her opposition on an environmental and public-policy issue. Take a side in a similar debate that inspires you, focusing your efforts on arguing against the opposing viewpoint.

4. "Demystifying Multiculturalism" focuses on exposing what the writer sees as a harmful sociological practice, condition, or movement. List social practices that you believe are harmful, choose one, and develop an opposing viewpoint.

Chapter 21
Proposing a Solution

Proposals are prescriptions for change. As such, they challenge readers to care about a problem, accept a solution, and act upon it. A strong proposal offers a logical, practical, and creative argument that leads toward positive change, whether it's controlling deer overpopulation, defending against terrorism, reducing levels of carbon monoxide in a factory, or adding to the debate on cloning.

Proposal writers argue for such remedies in all areas of life. In your college courses, you'll be challenged to map out solutions to many difficult problems. In your community, you may participate in policy making and civic development. In the workplace, you may write proposals that justify expenditures, sell products, or troubleshoot problems. In each situation, you'll be challenged to clearly explain the problem, offer a solution, and argue for adopting that solution.

This chapter will walk you through the challenge of writing such proposals, from selecting a problem to submitting your plan.

Note: Some problem-solution writing can be primarily explanatory, rather than persuasive.

What's Ahead
- Overview: Proposing a Solution
    Student Models
    Professional Model
- Guidelines
- Writing Checklist and Activities

Overview
Proposing a Solution

Writer's Goal

Your goal is to argue for a positive change, convincing readers to accept and contribute to that change. To accomplish this goal, aim to describe a problem, analyze its causes and effects, argue for one solution among several options, defend that solution against objections, and prove the solution both feasible and desirable.

Keys for Success

Show passion for change. ■ Proposal writing requires a willingness to challenge the status quo and a mind that is open to creative possibilities. Dare to ask, "What's really wrong here, and how can we fix it?"

Avoid Band-Aid solutions. ■ Whatever solution you choose, base it on a concrete and personal understanding of the problem and a bold exploration of all possible solutions. Choose the best solution only after weighing each option against sensible criteria for solving the problem, comparing and contrasting its strengths and weaknesses. Consider especially how well solutions attack root causes, bring about real benefits, and prove workable.

Know your readers. ■ Who can bring about the change you envision—specific decision makers (the city council, college administrators, a department manager) or a broader community affected by the problem? What are their allegiances and alliances? Knowing your readers will help you speak convincingly to them, build a spirit of teamwork, and persuasively challenge readers to change.

Conduct quality research. ■ Your proposal will stand or fall on the quality of both your reasoning and its support. To build that quality, conduct primary research (observations and interviews, for example), but also check journals, books, and Internet sources to understand the problem, explore possible solutions, and garner support for the solution you choose.

Problems to Consider

- **People problems:** Consider generations—your own or a relative's. What problems does this generation face?
- **College problems:** List the top ten problems faced by college students. In your major, what problems are experts trying to solve?
- **Social problems:** What problems do our communities and country face? Where do you see suffering, injustice, waste, or harm?
- **Workplace problems:** What challenges do you encounter at work?

Next Step Read the model essays and perform the activities that follow. As you read, consider the problems presented and the solutions offered. What similar problems do you care about?

Proposing a Solution

In this essay, student writer Gilbert Angelino proposes a solution to the problem of a growing deer population that is encroaching on urban areas and upsetting the ecosystem.

Practical Wildlife Management

One of the most pressing wildlife management issues is that of growing deer populations in many parts of the country. Deer populations have risen nationally from 500,000 at the turn of the century to more than 20 million today. According to Cathy Blumig in an article in the September 1995 issue of *Deer and Deer Hunting*, Pennsylvania spends $30 million annually in deer-related costs. Wisconsin has an estimated annual cost of $37 million for crop damage alone. Conservative estimates place auto/deer collisions at 500,000 yearly in the United States. Furthermore, Lyme disease, an infectious human disease that is carried by the deer tick, now trails only AIDS as the fastest-growing infectious disease in the United States.

Much of the conflict between humans and deer has been caused by humans moving into the deer's forest habitat and developing it for housing. Modern suburbs sometimes divide the woods into five-acre plots, and after the houses are built, the plots have an area of woods bordering an open meadow like a feeding area. This is perfect whitetail habitat. The food is at the deer's front door for nocturnal feeding; they simply step back into the woods for cover when daylight comes.

Due to the close proximity of houses in suburbs, most of these areas banned hunting in the mid-1970s. In the ensuing 20 years there was a deer population boom, and now the deer are eating forests and private shrubbery alike. People who moved to these suburbs for the beauty of nature are experiencing the drawbacks of living too close to nature. Some even call the deer "rats with hooves."

One attempt at controlling the deer population has been an intensive study of birth control for deer, but there are several problems with this method. One major problem is cost—from $500 to $1,000 per deer sterilized per year. To maintain or reduce the deer population, 50 percent or more of the does must not give birth. If this program were implemented in place of hunting in Iowa, for example, it would cost from $22.5 to $45 million to keep the deer from overpopulating.

Another question is whether it is safe for humans to consume deer that have been vaccinated with an immunocontraceptive (ICC). Since millions of Americans eat venison, the drug would have to be tested and approved by the Food and Drug Administration. Deer transitory movements could also nullify the effects of ICCs. Deer do not stay in one area long enough to be certain that 50 percent of the does have been sterilized. Even in urban areas, deer move up to 25 miles in their eight-year life span.

Another concern about ICCs is the chance of other animals ingesting 6
the contraceptives by eating the bait or by preying or scavenging on deer.
This is an obvious danger to the ecosystem. Considering those negative
facts, deer contraceptives may be safely used in zoos, but not in the wild.

Some suburbs have tried to trap deer and release them in other areas 7
of the country. However, according to Bill Gordon in the November issue of
North American Hunter, this method results in a 25 percent mortality rate.
Additionally, there are scarcely any areas that want more deer. This method,
therefore, has proved to be inviable.

The writer introduces and argues for his solution.

The best and most effective solution to controlling deer populations is 8
to stay as close to nature's ways as possible. Game management by hunting
meets this criterion. Since we have eliminated the natural predators, we
must provide others—hunters. The strongest animals have the best chance
of escaping hunters, so natural selection is implemented.

He supports his solution with an example.

Hunting with guns in the suburbs is impractical and dangerous. 9
However, bow hunting is a viable alternative. In Fox Chapel Borough,
Pennsylvania, a town of 5,600 residents, 45 deer were being killed each year
by autos, and deer were destroying greenery. The town implemented a deer
management program that matched an experienced bow hunter with a private landowner. Rules were implemented to provide safety for humans and
humane treatment of the deer. During the 1993 season, there were no
shooting accidents, no wounded deer escaped, and 128 deer were harvested
with a bow. In the 1994 hunt, 185 deer were taken by bow. Since the deer
herd numbers around 4,300, Fox Chapel Borough still has some deer to
cull, but they are on their way to an effective deer management program.

He closes by stressing the benefits of his solution.

Of all the methods tried or considered to rid urban and suburban areas 10
of unwanted deer, this last one holds the most promise. It is practical,
efficient, safe, and humane; and while the sentimentalist may not want to
see deer dispatched in any way, it is actually in the long-term interest of the
deer population that they be managed. In this way we can keep a heritage
alive for many generations and minimize the damage to humans and the
ecosystem. ■

write

Reading for Better Writing

1. What strategies does the writer use to help readers understand and care
about the problem? Are these strategies effective? Explain.

2. The writer raises and dismisses alternative solutions before presenting his
own solution. Does this organization work? Explain.

3. Does the writer address the concerns of both those who support hunting
and those who oppose hunting? Is the tone effective for the essay's readers?

4. The closing focuses on benefits of the solution, rather than a specific
action to be taken by readers. Does this approach strengthen or weaken
the proposal?

Proposing a Solution

In this essay, student writer Brian Ley defines agroterrorism, predicts that it could become a serious problem, and proposes a multifaceted solution.

Preparing for Agroterror

The writer opens by illustrating the problem.

An Al Quaeda terrorist in Africa obtains a sample of fluid from a cow infected with foot-and-mouth disease, and he sends the fluid to an accomplice in a small, rural American town. This terrorist takes the sample and rides around the country, stopping at several points to place small amounts of the fluid on objects that animals are likely to touch. When he is finished, he calmly drives to the nearest airport and leaves the country unnoticed. 1

Cows, pigs, and sheep then come into contact with this highly contagious disease. Over the next few days, farmers see blisters on the feet and mouths of their animals. Thinking that the animals have a bacterial infection, the farmers administer antibiotics and wait for improvement. However, because antibiotics can't kill a virus, the animals get sicker. Meanwhile, the virus is spreading by means of wind and the movement of animals and humans. Within a few weeks, the virus is out of control. 2

While the story above is hypothetical, it is also very possible. People used to think of terrorists as men in ski masks blowing up embassies and taking hostages. But after the events of September 11, 2001, and the subsequent anthrax scares, we realize that more kinds of terrorism are possible. 3

He defines the problem and presents expert testimony.

One type that we rarely consider is agroterrorism, which involves using diseases as weapons to attack a country's agriculture industry in order to attack the country itself. The agroterrorist's weapons of choice are those diseases that affect plants, animals, and even humans. Professor Peter Chalk of the RAND Corporation, an expert on transnational terrorism, believes that agroterrorism should be a huge concern for Americans because it has many advantages from a terrorist's point of view. 4

He analyzes why the problem could become serious.

First of all, an attack on the agricultural sector of the United States would be quite easy. The diseases needed to kill large populations of animals can be obtained with little difficulty; the most devastating ones are ready for use in their natural form. These samples pose little risk to the terrorist because many of the diseases are harmless to humans. 5

In addition, doing agroterrorism is less risky in terms of getting caught and getting punished. Agroterrorism is hard to trace, especially because Americans have assumed that all animal epidemics are natural in origin and that American livestock contract such diseases only by accident. Consequences for those caught inflicting a disease on animals are also less severe than for terrorists who harm humans. In fact, because agroterrorism first affects the health of plants and animals rather than humans, those few terrorists with consciences can even escape some guilt for their actions. 6

Using
specific
details, he
outlines the
problem's
potential
effects.

However, while agroterrorist diseases would have little direct effect on   7
people's health, they would be devastating to the agricultural economy, in
part because of the many different diseases that could be used in an attack.
One of the most devastating is foot-and-mouth disease. This illness hurts
all infected animals by impeding their weight gain, and it hurts dairy cows
in particular by decreasing their milk production. Because the disease
is highly contagious, all infected animals, along with any cloven-hoofed
animals within about 50 miles of the infection site, must be killed.

While foot-and-mouth disease is not dangerous to humans, other ani-   8
mal diseases are. One of these is bovine spongiform encephalopathy, better
known as mad-cow disease. This illness is not easily spread, but a few cases
in the United States would send people into a panic. Meat consumption
would drop sharply, and the agricultural economy would be deeply shaken.

Another disease that could be used as a weapon is West Nile encephali-   9
tis. This virus can be spread by insects and can even cross species, affecting
horses, birds, pigs, and humans. It is a fatal illness without a vaccination or
a cure. These diseases plus more are likely candidates for use in an agroterrorist attack.

The agricultural community is particularly susceptible to a terrorist   10
attack. Unlike "typical" terrorist targets in metropolitan areas, farms do not
have sophisticated security systems to protect against intruders. The average
farmer's security system includes a mean dog and a shotgun: the dog for
humans and the gun for animal pests. If terrorists wanted to infect a dairy,
swine operation, or even a large-scale cattle-finishing operation, they would
encounter few obstacles. The terrorists merely have to place a piece of
infected food in an area with livestock. This single action could start an
epidemic.

Agroterrorism is a threat that demands our response. Several actions   11
can be taken to discourage terrorism as well as to deal with its consequences.
One of the first steps is convincing all citizens—farmers and nonfarmers
alike—that agroterrorism could happen, and that it could cause horrific
consequences. Farmers must realize that they are susceptible to an attack
even though they may live far from large metropolitan areas. Nonfarmers
must realize how an attack could affect them. If nonfarmers know that an
attack could create panic, drive up food prices, and possibly eliminate food
sources, they will look out for suspicious activity and report it.

The writer
proposes a
multifaceted
solution.

Preventive action on farms is needed to ensure the safety of our food   12
supply. For example, the South Dakota Animal Industry Board recently
published a newsletter outlining several precautions that farmers can take.
Farms should have better security, especially in areas where animals are
kept. These security measures include allowing only authorized persons to
have access to farm buildings and animals, and keeping all key farm buildings locked.

Farmers also need training to detect the diseases that terrorists might   13
use, and to know what actions can contain and decontaminate an infected
area. For example, if a farmer discovers that cows have blisters on their

tongues and noses, and that they are behaving abnormally, the owner should immediately call a veterinarian to assess the situation. Because the disease might be foot-and-mouth, no cattle should leave the farm until a diagnosis has been made.

In addition, public authorities need a plan for responding to an identified agroterrorism attack. For example, thousands of animals may have to be killed and disposed of—an action with significant environmental concerns. Moreover, public money should be used for continued research of the diseases that may be spread by agroterrorists. Vaccines and treatments may be produced that would stop diseases or limit them from becoming epidemic. 14

> **The closing stresses the problem's seriousness and calls for action.**

Agroterrorism has not yet been used on a large scale anywhere on the globe. However, its use seems inevitable. The United States is a prime target for terrorism of this sort because we have the largest, most efficiently raised food supply in the world. Destroying part of this supply would affect not only our own country but also all those countries with whom we trade. Because we are prime targets, we must act now to develop our defenses against agroterrorism. If we wait until an attack happens, people may become ill, our overall economy could be damaged, and our agricultural economy may never recover. ■ 15

Note: The Works Cited page is not shown.

Reading for Better Writing

1. This essay predicts that a problem may develop. Is the writer's prediction persuasive? Why or why not?

2. What tactics does the writer use to get readers concerned about the problem? Are these strategies successful?

3. The solution proposed is multifaceted. Briefly list who must do what. Is this solution persuasive? Is it workable? Does it get at root causes?

4. A strong proposal provides strong evidence about both the problem and the solution. Trace the evidence used in this essay. Are the types of evidence convincing? Do any gaps need to be filled?

Proposing a Solution

The workplace report below is a troubleshooting proposal. In it, engineer Nick Jeffries addresses a problem with air quality and proposes a workable solution.

Rankin Manufacturing
MEMO

Date: February 19, 2002

To: John Cameron

From: Nick Jeffries

The subject line points to a positive change.

Subject: Reducing Levels of Carbon Monoxide in the Factory

As you requested, I have investigated the high levels of carbon monoxide we have been experiencing in the factory. The following proposal (1) explains the problem's source and (2) details a plan for attacking the problem.

Problem: Emission from Lift Trucks

The writer explains the problem, detailing its effects and seriousness.

Since November 2000, we have been recording high levels of carbon monoxide (CO) in the factory, particularly in Area 3, during winter months (November–March). General CO levels in the factory have exceeded 35 ppm, and many office spaces have experienced levels of 40–80 ppm, when the OSHA recommendation is 25 ppm.

These CO levels are a concern for three reasons:

   1. They range from 10 to 55 ppm above OSHA recommendations and could bring a substantial fine.

   2. High CO levels make people ill, with sick leave, lower productivity, and dangerous conditions resulting.

   3. Using summer exhaust fans in winter reduces relative humidity, shrinking wood used for manufacturing.

He outlines the problem's cause.

To determine the cause of the high CO levels, I investigated all sources of combustion in the factory. I concluded that the excess CO is caused by lift trucks, particularly those operating in Area 3.

I then checked all the lift trucks to see if they were producing more CO than normal. All lifts were in good working condition and were being used properly.

Proposal: Phase Out Shipping Department Internal-Combustion Lifts

He identifies criteria that any solution must meet.

Ideally, any solution implemented should accomplish the following in a timely and cost-effective manner:

    1. Bring down CO levels so that they are consistently at or below 25 ppm.

    2. Maintain the relative humidity of the factory air to ensure product quality.

He lists two possible solutions.

Given these criteria, we could continue using the exhaust fans and install humidifying equipment, but such a renovation would cost $32,000. (See attached estimate.) Or we could replace all internal-combustion lift trucks in Area 3 immediately with electric lift trucks for $175,000.

He shows that his solution is workable.

Instead, I propose that we gradually replace the internal-combustion lifts in the Shipping Department with electric lift trucks, for these reasons:

• The Shipping Department currently has 14 lift trucks that operate almost 24 hours per day. These lifts are clearly the highest source of CO in Area 3.

• The Shipping area also shows the best potential for using electric lift trucks. Shipping lift trucks do not have to travel long distances or use ramps.

• The pros of purchasing electric lift trucks outweigh the cons. While electric lifts have a higher initial cost, they do have a lower operating and maintenance cost. A five-year cost analysis shows that the costs of owning and operating both types of lift are similar. (See attachment.) In fact, after five years, electric lifts save money. (Electric lifts do require, however, that operators be involved in daily charging and maintenance of batteries.)

Implementation: Phase in Electric Lifts Through Regular Purchases

He maps out steps needed to implement the solution.

Rankin buys an average of four lift trucks annually. The switch to electric lifts in Shipping can take place through purchasing only electric ones for the next four years. Here's how the process would work:

1. An area requests replacement of an existing lift truck.

2. Management approves the request and purchases a new electric lift truck.

3. The new electric lift truck goes to the Shipping Department.

4. The newest internal-combustion lift truck in Shipping is transferred to the area that requested the new lift truck.

Through this process, each lift truck in Shipping is transferred to the area that requested the new lift truck.

Conclusion

> He restates his solution, emphasizes its benefits, and calls for action.

Gradually replacing the internal-combustion lifts in Shipping with electric lifts will involve a higher initial cost but will reap two important benefits: (1) CO levels will go down below 25 ppm, reaching OSHA standards, ensuring the safety of Rankin employees, and guarding product quality; and (2) the electric lifts will prove less costly to own and operate in the long run.

Therefore, I recommend that Rankin management approve this switch, to be phased in over the next four years as outlined above. Safety, quality, and total operating costs over the long run outweigh the initial costs. If you wish to discuss this proposal, please call me at extension 1449.

Attachments (2) ∎

write

Reading for Better Writing

1. This proposal is a workplace report. How is this model similar to and different from the essay proposals in this chapter?

2. The proposal's introduction indicates that the reader is aware of the problem. How does the writer use that awareness to shape his proposal?

3. What kinds of evidence does the writer provide in discussing the problem? Is the evidence convincing? Why or why not?

4. What strategies does the writer use to present and support his solution? Are these strategies convincing? Why or why not?

Proposing a Solution

Leigh Turner works at the Hastings Center, a nonprofit research institute in Garrison, New York. In the following essay, he explains why the current debate on cloning is a problem, and he proposes a three-part solution.

The Media and the Ethics of Cloning

The writer introduces the topic with an analogy from popular culture.

If the contemporary debate on cloning has a patron saint, surely it is Andy Warhol. Not only did Warhol assert that everyone would have 15 minutes of fame—witness the lawyers, philosophers, theologians, and bioethicists who found their expertise in hot demand on the nightly morality plays of network television following Ian Wilmut's cloning of the sheep Dolly—but he also placed "clones," multiple copies of the same phenomenon, at the heart of popular culture. Instead of multiple images of Marilyn Monroe and Campbell's soup cans, we now have cloned sheep. Regrettably, it is Warhol's capacity for hyperbole rather than his intelligence and ironic vision that permeates the current debate on cloning.

He identifies and outlines the problem.

It would be unfair to judge hastily written op-ed pieces, popular talk shows, and late-night radio programs by the same standards that one would apply to a sustained piece of philosophical or legal analysis. But the popular media could do more to foster thoughtful public debate on the legal, moral, political, medical, and scientific dimensions of the cloning of humans and nonhuman animals.

Instead of multiple images of Marilyn Monroe and Campbell's soup cans, we now have cloned sheep.

An example illustrates the problem.

As did many of my colleagues at the Hastings Center, I participated in several interviews with the media following Ian Wilmut's announcement in *Nature* that he had succeeded in cloning Dolly from a mammary cell of an adult sheep. After clearly stating to one Los Angeles radio broadcaster before our interview that I was not a theologian and did not represent a religious organization, I was rather breathlessly asked during the taping what God's view on cloning is and whether cloning is "against creation." Predictably, the broadcaster didn't want to discuss how religious ethicists are contributing to the nascent public discourse about the ethics of cloning. Instead, he wanted me to provide a dramatic response that would get the radio station's phones ringing with calls from atheists, agnostics, and religious believers of all stripes.

In addition to inundating the public with hyperbolic sound bites and their print equivalents, the media have overwhelmingly emphasized the issues involved in cloning humans, paying almost no attention to the moral implications of cloning nonhuman animals. While the ethics of cloning humans clearly need to be debated, the cloning of nonhuman animals has already taken place and deserves to be treated as a meaningful moral concern. [4]

A transition signals a shift in focus.

Although I suspect that a compelling argument for the cloning of animals can be made, we should not ignore the difference between actually formulating such arguments and merely presuming that nonhuman cloning is altogether unproblematic. Admittedly, humans already consider non-human animals as commodities in many ways, including as a source of food. Yet perhaps cloning animals with the intent of using them as "pharmaceutical factories" to produce insulin and other substances to treat human illnesses should raise questions about how far such an attitude ought to extend. What moral obligations should extend to humans' use of other species? Do the potential medical benefits for humans outweigh the dangers of encouraging people to think of nonhuman animals as machines to be manipulated to fulfill human goals? These kinds of questions deserve to be part of the public discussion about cloning. Given some people's concerns about the use of traps to catch wild animals, the living conditions of farm animals, and the treatment of animals used in medical and pharmaceutical research, I find this gap in public discourse perplexing. [5]

The writer identifies a key facet of the problem and gives an example.

But perhaps the most significant problem with the media hyperbole concerning cloning is the easy assumption that humans simply are a product of their genes—a view usually called "genetic essentialism." Television hosts and radio personalities have asked whether it would be possible to stock an entire basketball team with clones of Michael Jordan. In response, philosophers, theologians, and other experts have reiterated wearily that, although human behavior undeniably has a genetic component, a host of other factors—including uterine environment, family dynamics, social setting, diet, and other personal history—play important roles in an individual's development. Consequently, a clone produced from the DNA of an outstanding athlete might not even be interested in sports. [6]

While this more sophisticated message has received some media attention, we continue to see stories emphasizing that the wealthy might some day be able to produce copies of themselves, or that couples with a dying infant might create an identical copy of the child. The popular media seem to remain transfixed by what Dorothy Nelkin, the New York University sociologist of science, refers to as "DNA as destiny." [7]

He explains another facet of the problem.

What's more, the cloning issue reveals the way in which the mass media   8
foster attitudes of technological and scientific determinism by implying that
scientific "progress" cannot be halted. Of course, many scientists share these
attitudes, and, too often, they refuse to accept moral responsibility for their
participation in research that may contribute to human suffering. But scientists should not merely ply their craft, leaving moral reasoning to others.
They should participate in public debates about whether certain scientific
projects are harmful and should not be allowed to continue because they
have unjustifiable, dehumanizing implications. A good model is the out-
spoken criticism of nuclear weapons by many nuclear physicists, who have
helped limit research intended to produce more effective nuclear devices.

Scientists are not riding a juggernaut capable of crushing everything in   9
its path simply because mass cloning of animals, and possibly eventually
humans, may be technically possible. There is no reason to think that scientific research has a mandate that somehow enables it to proceed outside
the web of moral concerns that govern all other human endeavors; it does
not exist above the law or outside the rest of society. To think otherwise is
to succumb to a technological determinism that denies the responsibilities
and obligations of citizenship.

He introduces his three-part solution.

Despite the media's oversimplifications, citizens have an obligation to   10
scrutinize carefully all of the issues involved and, if necessary, to regulate
cloning through laws, professional codes of behavior, and institutional
policies. I want to suggest three ways that scholars, policy makers, and concerned citizens can, in fact, work to improve public debate about ethical
issues related to new developments in science and technology.

Recognize Moral Implications

Part one— scientists must address the ethical issues related to their work.

First, scientists and ethicists need a fuller understanding of each other's   11
work. Scientists must recognize the moral implications of their research and
address those implications when they discuss the research in public. The
formal education of most scientists does not encourage them to consider
ethical issues. Whereas courses in bioethics are now found in most schools
of medicine and nursing, graduate students in such disciplines as human
genetics, biochemistry, and animal physiology are not encouraged to grap-
ple with the ethical aspects of their research. Similarly, most ethicists have
very little knowledge of science, although many of them feel perfectly
entitled to comment on the moral issues of new scientific discoveries.

The writer gives examples.

This gap in understanding fosters an inaccurate, unrealistic conception   12
of what the most pressing ethical issues are. For example, the real challenges
for researchers today involve the cloning of nonhuman animals for use in
developing pharmaceutical products. Sustained study of nonhuman clones
will be needed before researchers can even begin to seriously consider

research involving human subjects. Rather than encouraging the media's interest in cloning humans, ethicists more knowledgeable about the science involved might have been able to shift the public debate toward the moral questions raised by cloning sheep, pigs, and other animals, questions that need immediate public debate.

Thus, we need to include more courses in various scientific depart- 13 ments on the ethics of contemporary scientific research; offer courses for ethicists on the basics of human genetics, anatomy, and physiology; and establish continuing-education courses and forums that bring together scientists and scholars in the humanities.

Present Concerns of Ethicists

Part two—ethicists must address ethical issues more effectively.

Second, ethicists need to do a better job of presenting their concerns in 14 the popular media. Scientific journals written for a popular audience—such as *Scientific American, New Scientist, Discover*, and *The Sciences*—provide excellent popular accounts of scientific research and technological developments, but they rarely specifically address the moral implications of the discoveries they report. Regrettably, most of the academic journals that do address the ethical aspects of scientific topics—such as the *Hastings Center Report*, the *Journal of Medical Ethics*, and the *Cambridge Quarterly of Healthcare Ethics*—lack the broad readership of the popular-science magazines. Right now, perhaps the best "popular" source of sustained ethical analysis of science, medicine, and health care is *The New York Times Magazine*.

The writer gives examples.

If ethicists hope to reach larger audiences with more than trivial sound 15 bites, they need to establish and promote appropriate outlets for their concerns. For example, Arthur Caplan, director of the Center for Bioethics at the University of Pennsylvania, wrote a regular weekly newspaper column for the *St. Paul Pioneer Press* when he directed a bioethics center at the University of Minnesota. His column addressed the ethical implications of medical and scientific research. Other scholars have yet to follow his example—perhaps, in part, because many academics feel that writing for the mass media is unworthy of their time. They are wrong.

One way of improving public debate on these important issues is for 16 universities to encourage their faculty members to write for newspapers, popular magazines, and even community newsletters. Such forms of communication should be viewed as an important complement to other forms of published research. Leon Kass's writing on cloning in *The New Republic* and Michael Walzer's and Michael Sandel's writing on assisted suicide in the same publication should not be considered any less significant simply because the work appears in a magazine intended for a wide audience. After all, if universities are to retain their public support, they must consistently be seen as important players in society, and one easy way to do this is to encourage their faculty members to contribute regularly to public discussion.

Expand Public Debate

Part three—scientists and ethicists must engage others in the debate.

Finally, we need to expand public debate about ethical issues in science *17* beyond the mass media. To complement the activities of the National Bioethics Advisory Commission and the projects on ethics at universities and research centers, we should create forums at which academics and citizens from all walks of life could meet to debate the issues. Instead of merely providing a gathering place for scholars pursuing research projects, institutions such as the Hastings Center, Georgetown University's Kennedy Institute of Ethics, and the University of Pennsylvania's Center for Bioethics need to foster outreach programs and community-discussion groups that include nonspecialists. My experience suggests that members of civic organizations and community-health groups, such as the New York Citizens' Committee on Health Care Decisions, are quite eager to discuss the topic of cloning.

The writer closes by summarizing his solution.

What we need are fewer commentaries by self-promoting experts on *18* network television, and more intelligent discussions by scholars and citizens in local media, including local public-television stations. We need creative alternatives to the onslaught of talking heads, all saying much the same thing (as though they themselves were clones) to docile, sheep-like audiences waiting for others to address the most pressing moral issues of the day. ∎

write

Reading for Better Writing

1. The writer introduces the topic by using Andy Warhol as an analogy. Explain why the analogy is or is not effective.

2. Reread the first two pages in which the writer states and explains the problem. Summarize what he says, and explain why his presentation is or is not clear.

3. Summarize the author's three-part solution, and explain why this part of the essay is or is not effective.

4. Reread the conclusion, and explain whether it effectively unifies the essay.

Guidelines
Proposing a Solution

Note: For in-depth help on developing persuasive arguments, see pages **253–268**.

1. **Select and narrow a topic.** Choose a problem from "Problems to Consider" on page **314**, or search for one in periodicals, on news programs, or on the Internet. Then test your topic:
   - Is the problem real, serious, and fairly complex? Does it show brokenness, danger, or disadvantage? Does it predict future harm?
   - Do you care about this problem and believe that it must be solved?
   - Can you offer a workable solution? Should you narrow the focus to part of the problem or a local angle?

2. **Identify and analyze your readers.** Potentially, you could have three audiences: decision makers with the power to deliver change, people affected by the problem, and a public that needs to learn about the problem and get behind a solution. Once you've determined your audience, study them:
   - What do they know about the problem? What are their attitudes toward it, their likely questions, and their potential concerns?
   - Why might they accept or resist change? Would they prefer a specific solution?
   - Does the problem affect them directly or indirectly? What can and can't they do about the problem?
   - What arguments and evidence would convince them to agree that the problem exists, care about it, and take action?
   - What common ground do you and your readers share?

3. **Probe the problem.** If helpful, use the graphic organizer on page 47.
   Define the problem. ■ What is it exactly? What are its parts or dimensions?
   Determine the problem's seriousness. ■ Why should it be fixed? Who is affected and how? What are its immediate, long-term, and potential effects?
   Analyze causes. ■ What are its root causes and contributing factors?
   Explore context. ■ What is the problem's background, history, and connection to other problems? What solutions have been tried in the past? Who, if anyone, benefits from the problem's existence?
   Think creatively. ■ Take a look at the problem from other perspectives— other states and countries, both genders, different races and ethnic groups, and other generations.

4. **Brainstorm possible solutions.** List all imaginable solutions—both modest and radical fixes. Then evaluate the alternatives:
   - List criteria that any solution should meet. These measurements indicate a solution's effectiveness at resolving the problem: The solution must . . .
   - Compare and contrast alternatives by examining strengths, weaknesses, and workability.

5. **Choose the best solution and map out support.** In a sentence, state the solution that best solves the problem—a workable plan that attacks causes and treats effects. Try this pattern for your thesis: Given [the problem—its seriousness, effects, or causes], we must [the solution]." Next, identify support for your solution. Compared with alternatives, why is it preferable? Is it more thorough, beneficial, and practical?

6. **Outline your proposal and complete a first draft.** A proposal's structure is quite simple: describe the problem, offer a solution, and defend the solution. However, what you do in each section can become complicated. Choose strategies that fit your purpose and audience.
   - **The problem:** Consider whether readers understand the problem and accept its seriousness. Inform and/or persuade them about the problem by using appropriate background information, cause/effect analysis, examples, analogies, parallel cases, visuals, and expert testimony.
   - **The solution:** If necessary, first argue against alternative solutions. Then present your solution. State clearly what should happen, who should be involved, and why. For a complex solution, lay out the different stages.
   - **The support:** Show how the solution solves the problem. Use facts and analysis to argue that your solution is feasible and to address objections. You may choose to accept some objections, while refuting others.

7. **Get feedback and revise the draft.** Share your draft with a peer or a tutor in the writing center, getting answers to the following questions:
   - Does the solution fit the problem? Is the proposal precise, well reasoned, realistic, and complete? Does it address all possible objections?
   - Is the evidence credible, compelling, clear, and well documented?
   - Does the voice fit the problem's seriousness and treat the opposition tactfully?
   - Is the opening engaging? Is the closing thoughtful, forceful, and clear?

8. **Edit and proofread.** Check for accurate word choice and helpful definitions; smooth, energetic sentences; and correct grammar, spelling, and format.

9. **Prepare and share your final essay.** Submit your proposal to your instructor, but also consider posting it on the Web.

Writing Checklist

Use these six traits to check your essay, then revise as needed:

____ The **ideas** show a thorough understanding of the problem and present a workable solution. The proposal uses strong reasoning and well-researched evidence.

____ The **organization** convincingly moves from problem to solution to support. Each part is effectively ordered using strategies such as cause/effect, compare/contrast, and process.

____ The **voice** is positive, confident, objective, and sensitive to opposing viewpoints. The tone fits the seriousness of the problem.

____ The **words** are precise and effectively defined.

____ The **sentences** read smoothly, with effective variations and logical transitions.

____ The **copy** follows rules of grammar, format, and documentation.

Writing Activities

1. In "Practical Wildlife Management," the student writer tackles an environmental problem. What environmental problems concern you? Select one, research it, and develop a workable solution.

2. "Preparing for Agroterror" predicts that a problem may develop. Thinking about current conditions and trends, forecast a problem, and write a proposal explaining how to prepare for or prevent it.

3. Write a proposal that identifies a problem faced by families today, or by people of your generation, another generation, your race, another race, your community, or another community.

4. In "The Media and the Ethics of Cloning," the writer focuses on the ethical and cultural problems related to the scientific pursuit of cloning. Select a scientific or technological advance that concerns you. Then propose ways to counter its negatives.

5. What are some challenges facing the planet Earth and the human race in the foreseeable future? Find a focused challenge and write a proposal.

6. The proposal on eliminating carbon monoxide from the factory tackles a workplace problem. Consider workplaces famililar to you. Do you see a need for change? Write a proposal to an appropriate supervisor or manager.

Report Writing

CONTENTS

Chapter 22
Observation Report

audio

Observant people are insightful people. What others overlook, they notice, and they use these observations to expand and deepen their understanding of life. For such people, observing comes naturally.

Learning to observe lies at the heart of an observation report. In addition, writing such a report challenges you to effectively re-create an observed world and share it with readers. Whether the report profiles a beach or a bus terminal, it's a documentary formed in words and built upon your sensory impressions—and sometimes your thoughts and feelings, too.

Such observation is part of many college courses. An education student visiting a kindergarten classroom, a biology student observing white-tailed deer, and a theater student studying a production of *Othello* are all observing to learn. Even in the workplace, observations are shaped into reports about site inspections, incidents, and trips. This chapter will get you started on developing the observation skills and writing abilities needed to construct reports in college and at work.

What's Ahead

- Overview: Observation Report
    Student Models
    Professional Model
- Guidelines
- Writing Checklist and
    Activities

Overview
Writing an Observation Report

Writer's Goal

Your goal is to powerfully re-create your observations of a location and/or an event. Aim to share your sensory impressions so clearly that your reader gets an accurate, rich sense of the site.

Keys for Success

Determine your vantage point. ▨ First, identify your purpose: Is it to understand the site, discover surprises, or answer a question? Second, choose a perspective: Should you observe passively, or interact? Should you observe objectively, or add thoughts and feelings? Should you observe from one position, or several?

Plan your observation. ▨ To observe well, you must prepare. Consider these issues: permission, safety, background research, timing, transportation, clothing, and equipment.

Show rather than tell. ▨ Describe what you see, hear, smell, feel, and taste. Provide concrete details, not generalities.

Develop a theme. ▨ Tie together the details of your observation with an idea or mood that is stated or implied.

Sites to Consider

Use the headings below to generate a list of good observation sites.

- **Natural sites:** Select an interesting location in nature—a state park, garden, zoo, or lake.
- **People sites:** Try a location brimming with people doing interesting activities—a sports arena, a community center, a theater, or a market.
- **Unfamiliar sites:** Choose a peculiar or unfamiliar site—a different neighborhood, a work site, or an ethnic or gender-specific event.
- **Serene sites:** Try a quiet spot requiring subtle observation—a night scene, an empty building, a quiet park, or a cathedral.
- **Coursework-related sites:** For example, if you are taking a course in early childhood education, visit a day care center or kindergarten classroom.
- **Border sites:** As a margin between two worlds, a border is often a busy site. Consider lines between city and suburb, town and country, land and water, or field and forest.

Next Step Read the model essays and perform the activities that follow. As you read, think about what makes these locations good observation sites. List similar places that you could observe.

Observation Report

Laura Apol is a student who traveled to western Washington to explore a short span of shoreline on the Straits of Juan de Fuca. This essay is her report on what she observed.

The Beach

The writer opens with a contrast, context, the location, and a theme.

Where I live in eastern Washington, water is irrigation, wildlife is rattlesnakes and coyotes, and hills are a blanket of sagebrush. But western Washington, where my grandfather lives, is different. His house sits across the road from a small beach running along the Straits of Juan de Fuca. Last March I took some friends along to visit my grandfather. I wanted to show them the Straits and its strange ocean-side world.

The focus moves from large to small.

The first day of our visit was dreary, but we crossed the road and pushed through the tall, damp weeds to the beach. The fog-filled air made the entire sky a palette of mixed grays so thick that we could barely see the distant shore of Vancouver Island. The biting breeze made my eyes water and penetrated my T-shirt and jeans. The beach itself stretched only 50 yards to either side, accepting the tame waves that every few seconds rolled up on its sand and rocks. Littered with driftwood and seaweed, the beach looked dirty and stank of dead fish.

She appeals to multiple senses: sight, sound, and touch.

The water's grayness matched the sky, and the buoys that bobbed atop the small waves marked a path for barges. As the waves came ashore, they carried with them small, smooth rocks that made clacking noises as they shuffled over the larger rocks half-buried in the sand. Each wave swirled around the rocks, disturbing the tide pools between them and pushing the driftwood a little farther up the beach. The wood—once live tree limbs— was smooth, as if rubbed with fine sandpaper that wore the branches down to nubs.

Kelp was strewn over the beach like giant worms, their hollow insides filled with debris collected from the water. When I stepped on one, it oozed black muck onto the sand. My stomach turned and I walked away.

She uses precise nouns, vivid verbs, and strong modifiers.

I flipped over a rock sticking out of the water. Where the rock had been, the water suddenly rippled and the sand stirred with life. With a stick, I gingerly prodded the sand and neighboring rocks, trying to coax the creature out; but when it emerged, it was little more than a shell with spindly legs. One of my friends identified the creature as a hermit crab. Grabbing its shell and turning it upside down, he showed me the little crab stuffed inside. Repulsed, I watched the crab retreat into its shell as a turtle might have, pulling its head and legs inside.

In another tide pool, I found a bumpy, greenish-black, jelly-like lump attached to a rock. Extended a few inches from this lump were thin, cloudy-white tentacles with bright pink suckers. The tentacles swayed with the current, as if they were feeling the water for something to grab. Slowly, I

The writer shares her curiosity and describes how she became involved in the scene.

extended my finger into the water toward the tentacles. When we touched, the tentacles sucked hard against my skin. Surprised, I jerked my hand out of the water and then stared down at the tentacles that waved back, un-affected. My finger didn't hurt, but it tingled. Again, I brushed my finger across hundreds of tentacles. They sucked again, but then let go when I pulled my finger away. Wondering what this creature did when its tentacles caught something edible, I spotted a shell stuck to a rock and pulled it off. I looked inside, and the shiny black thing living within hid deeper. I dropped the shell into the water beside the lump. Within seconds the lump's tentacles closed around the shell before pulling it into the creature's center, where the shell disappeared.

I looked for more creatures, eventually spotting a starfish nearly hidden under a rock. Putting my fingers near the base of the arms, I pulled lightly on the starfish's body, but it didn't budge. Nor did it budge when I pulled again with all my strength. So I called a friend, and together we used a stick to pry the starfish off the rock and out of the water. Its arms didn't flop, as I had expected, but stayed stiff. Instead of being soft, the creature was as hard as the rock that it had clung to—and just as bumpy. I turned the starfish over to see thousands of tiny tentacles lining each arm like a fingerprint. Some tentacles stretched out farther than others, reaching for something to hold on to. Thinking that I could get the starfish to conform to my hand, as it had to the rock, I put it on the back of my hand and watched. But it moved so slowly that I lacked the patience to wait. So I picked it off my hand—and then yelled in pain! The creature's tiny tentacles had grabbed onto the hair on the back of my hand! 7

The closing contrasts a stereotype with reality and offers reflection.

I stooped down and gently placed the starfish back onto its rock. Then I stood up again, looked over the beach, and thought. What I saw were no miles of white tropical sand, and no crashing, majestic waves—just 100 yards of kelp-covered, seaweed-littered sand and rocks. Yet this was an amazing place, and its thousands of inhabitants were amazing creatures! In fact, I thought, they and I have something in common: just as I claim eastern Washington—a small spot on the globe—my home, so these strange creatures call this nameless beach theirs. ■ 8

write

Reading for Better Writing

1. In the introduction, the writer describes the location as a "strange ocean-side world." How does this phrase function as a theme for this report?

2. What sensory impressions does the writer share, and how does she do so? Select one paragraph from the body of the essay, list sensory details, and explore their effectiveness.

3. Describe the essay's tone. Is it fitting?

4. At certain points, the writer observes by comparing and contrasting. Locate these examples, and comment on their effectiveness.

Observation Report

Joel Sorensen is a student who traveled to Santo Domingo to complete a service-learning project. In this essay he reports on what he observed, what he learned about the local people, and what he learned about himself.

Revelation in Santo Domingo

The writer establishes time, location, and conditions.

1   It is nearly January and the evening temperature in Santo Domingo is a sticky 85 degrees. We wait two hours in the airport for our ride, trying to catch the quick Spanish phrases and brush off men who want to carry our luggage. I expect these things. What I don't expect are the Burger Kings, Lexus dealerships, Wells Blue Bunny ice cream shops, and Marlboro billboards. I have come with fourteen college friends to do a service-learning project for the poor of the Dominican Republic, and I want to see some poverty.

2   And poverty I get.

He uses present tense to create immediacy.

3   As I stare out the windows of our van, I soon realize that the wealth does not run deep. Behind large apartment buildings are shoddily constructed shacks housing people who can only dream of living in the castles in front of them. A block from a sprawling car dealership, people hang out on street corners, unable to buy liquor for their New Year's Eve celebrations. Clusters of people, worn out by want, walk along the highway next to the beautiful expanse of ocean. We pass a city dump overflowing with rubble from Hurricane George. The farther we drive from the airport, the worse the poverty.

A key question offers a theme for the report.

4   How can such extremes of poverty and wealth, such beauty and ugliness, exist side by side? I can do nothing but stare. Nothing I see seems real.

With suggestive details and contrasts, the writer records his first impressions.

5   Soon, we enter Los Alcarizos, the suburb of Santo Domingo that will be our home for the next two weeks. Los Alcarizos has a population of about 400,000 people, many of whom are former farmers who squatted here hoping to make a living in the city, but failed. Our large Ford van crawls along the dirt streets, weaving back and forth to avoid giant potholes. The homes are small and cramped together, only slightly larger than the backyard sheds that house the rakes and lawn mowers of North America's middle class. People sit in front of the shacks, drinking, talking, enjoying each other and the night. Mopeds, driven by young and old, swerve around us. Groups of friends walk along the side of the road. In some shops resembling outdoor newsstands, large speakers blaring merengue music sit on shelves otherwise reserved for alcohol. Other shops have a TV around which men huddle. People are everywhere. We pass two young men along the side of the road, urinating on a tree. Suddenly, I am struck by the fact that these people are real.

The observation deepens with quotations, snapshots of people, and images of buildings.

In the morning, our interpreter Eli brings our group outside the eight-foot cement walls of our camp into the barrio we passed through the night before. Walking the streets of Los Alcarizos feels like a stroll through a film designed to encourage Sunday-school offerings. Rusted tin roofs pop through the trees. Children who see us point and yell, "*Americanos! Americanos!*" A wide-eyed boy stops, looks at me, and exclaims, "*Americano es muy grande!*" Some children raise their hands to their eyes and pretend to snap pictures. Others tug on cameras hanging from our necks, begging to be photographed. A member of our group raises his camera and children scramble to be included. A group of men sit nearby, laughing at their children—and the Americans. A woman breast-feeds her child. We try to talk to those we meet but seldom get past "*Hola, como esta?*" to which we receive an automatic, "*Bien, gracias.*" A boy wearing nothing but a long, red T-shirt with Michael Jordan's number 23 dangles from the branch of a tree. He looks down at us warily while other children—some wearing only underwear, some shorts, some nothing—play underneath.

The writer pauses to explain and reflect on his observations.

Many of the homes we pass are partially constructed of cinder block, tin, and wood. Our interpreter explains that the Dominicans buy block when they can afford it and construct the rest of their homes out of whatever they can find. Many homes are pale brown or gray and seem to have bubbled up out of the mud. Other homes are covered by cracked and peeling paint—brilliant pinks, blues, greens, and yellows. In many homes, women mop and sweep with straw brooms. Their effort to clean seems futile given the piles of garbage that surround them—in the streets, in a creek that runs parallel to the road, and in the remnants of a broken-down brick building that has somehow been leveled down to its windows. Small dogs run by and pick through the trash but find nothing to eat.

Vivid images offer sights, sounds, smells, textures, and tastes.

As the morning heat begins to rise, we enter the business district of Los Alcarizos. A building like the homes that we have passed is full of chickens. In front of the chicken house, working in a swarm of flies, a butcher chops up chickens for the women who wait to buy them. To the left of the chicken house is a small green pharmacy where a glass case holds pill bottles, squirt guns, and other trinkets. Another store advertises Pepsis for five pesos. On one corner sits a green building with "DISCO" splashed across it in bright blue letters. Across the street, a yellow building, unlike the homes that we pass, has two stories. In front of it dangles a purple and green sign that reads, "Hotel New Jersey."

The writer contrasts a new site with the previous one.

The world that we see on our morning stroll through the streets of Los Alcarizos contrasts sharply with the world that we encounter on our afternoon visit to the beach. Here we still see signs of poverty—vendors selling fried fish (eyeballs and all), children selling brightly colored shells, and adults hawking sunglasses and necklaces. "Cheap, cheap," they all cry out. However, at the beach the poor are only a part of the landscape. The scenery also includes deep blue water, long white beaches, 20-story hotels, pricey restaurants, and beautiful homes of the upper class. Tourists are everywhere: fat men in Speedos, topless European women with leathery tans, American families playing Frisbee and trying not to look at the Europeans, kids building sand castles, and retirees sipping Diet Pepsis.

He closes with reflection and self-reflection.

Feeling angry and self-righteous, I want to grab the tourists in their   10 stupid straw hats. I want to yell, "You just don't get it, do you? Can't you see that there are people in this country who are starving?" I want to tell the tourists that they disgust me. I want to lecture them about how their money could help the poor in Los Alcarizos. I want to demand that they see the real Dominican Republic.

And then I realize something. I have seen a family of five that sleeps in   11 a house half the size of my dorm room. I have seen naked, starving children. I have seen men who struggle to provide one meal a day for their families. But the truth is, I don't get it either.

No matter how hard I look, the poverty of Los Alcarizos is not real to   12 me. Real poverty can't be escaped, but this evening, after I finish work, I will escape. I will eat my third meal of the day, while outside the walls of our camp many will struggle for their first. At night, I will lie down under the protection of an armed guard. Then, after two weeks, I will return home to my life as a "poor" college kid, just as the tourists will return to theirs. ■

Reading for Better Writing

1. This report focuses on a cross-cultural experience. With that focus in mind, identify the theme of the writer's observations. What does he conclude? Is that conclusion valid?

2. Explore how the report appeals to different senses. What patterns percolate up through these details?

3. What organizational strategies order the wealth of details included in the report? Are these strategies effective? Would you use different methods?

4. The writer sprinkles his thoughts and feelings throughout the report. Review these moments. Are they effective? Why or why not?

Observation Report

Professional writer Randall VanderMey bases this report on the observations he recorded while waiting for a bus in a Greyhound station. As you will see, this report is much more than an as-it-happened record of what the writer saw and heard. It is also a brief documentary of a particular slice of American life.

"Scab!"

The opening establishes a tense context and tone.

The driver of the airport shuttle bus had to drop me off on the street so as not to cross the line of Greyhound drivers marching with their picket signs in the dusk. The picketers were angry. Had he turned in at the driveway to the terminal, they would have spat on him and yelled "Scab!" or "Strikebreaker!" Newspapers and TV had carried stories of rocks and bottles being thrown at passenger-filled buses by disgruntled Greyhound drivers whose demands for decent wages had not been heard. Most of the drivers in other unions were honoring the picket lines. Someday, they knew, they might be in the same fix.   *1*

The writer locates himself in the scene.

Inside the terminal I sat with my feet on my suitcase. I didn't want to pay four quarters for a storage box and didn't want to turn my back on my belongings. In the strange, tense atmosphere of the bus depot, I wondered if I was better off there or on a bus. Writing notes became my shield.   *2*

Switching to present tense, he describes what he senses.

A Hispanic couple behind me plays Spanish music for everyone in the terminal to hear. Men go in the men's room and stay there for a strangely long time, punching the button on the electric blow dryer over and over as if to cover up their talk. Near me an old man in a blue baseball cap and blue nylon jacket mumbles to himself as he paces the floor slowly. I hear him say, "My children is all grown up." Another man in a white yachting cap strides around the terminal making a sliding, streaking sound with a metal heel protector that's working its way loose. He seems to like the sound because he keeps walking around on the hard tile floors, over to the video-game room, over to the cafeteria, over to the bathroom, over to the ticket window, around and around in the open spaces in front of the nuns, college kids, young black girls with children, and Texas farmers waiting for their bus to Dallas. I know where the man in the yachting cap is without even looking up.   *3*

He describes the terminal and the people, including snippets of dialogue.

A tiny boy, curiosity in a red sweater, is twirling around. Everybody who sees him smiles. A while ago I saw an older man teasing him, saying "Hey, I'm gonna get you" and trying to slip a 10-gallon straw cowboy hat over his ears.   *4*

A policeman with his hair shaved off all over his round, bumpy head takes his drawn nightstick into the men's room and brings out, by the elbow, a young black man who doesn't seem to know where he is. He cradles a radio in his arm that blasts its music to everyone's discomfort. The cop says,   *5*

"Didn't I throw you out of here last night? Come on with me." The guy looks dazed and says, "Where we going?" The cop says, "We're just going to have a little talk." Turning off the blaring radio, he walks the young man toward the entrance.

| He records what he sees, hears, and smells.

Something weird is in the air, as if drugs are being dealt in the bathrooms, though the place remains calm and well lit. The odor of french fries and cleaning solutions fills the air.   6

The Hispanic music plays much more softly now, and I hear the dyed-blond lady break out of her Spanish to say to her husband or boyfriend, "Thang you very mush."   7

| The writer briefly reflects on the scene.

The iron screen benches are starting to lay a print in my back and rear end, so I shift and squirm. When I bought my ticket at the front counter, I asked the lady who took my money what I'd have to do for two hours and a half. She had laughed and said, "Look at the walls," and she had been right.   8

| By comparing, he deepens the observation's meaning.

The man in the blue baseball cap is mumbling again. But now I see that he's reading the newspaper and seems not to be able to read unless he pronounces the words aloud. I hear him say, "That's a liquidation sale."   9

The man with the metal heel protector is back again, clicking and shrieking across the tile floor, carrying a blue nylon satchel. Out of the video-game room come noises like echoes in a long hollow pipe. A kid behind the cash register in the cafeteria has neatly combed hair and glasses. He keeps smiling all the time, looking comfortingly sane. Overhead in there, the ceiling-fan blades turn hardly faster than the second hand on a clock.   10

| To conclude, the writer returns to the opening, putting his experience into perspective.

It has taken me some time to realize fully how I felt on that hard metal bench for two and a half hours among so many different kinds of people harboring so many different purposes. I said not a word to anyone. Only wrote and wrote. With my eyes and ears I broke into their lives while giving nothing of myself. I got in and got away without any real contact.   11

I hope the drivers get their money. But I'm not sure my being there helped. I felt like a scab. ■   12

write

Reading for Better Writing

1. This observation report is filled with tension. What is the source of this tension, and how does it create a theme for the report?

2. Locate where the writer shifts verb tenses from past to present, and then to past again. What is the effect of these shifts?

3. How does the writer make his observations vivid? Trace sights, sounds, smells, textures, and tastes. Do these details create patterns or themes?

4. The writer is both present in and separate from what he observes. Explore the strengths and limitations of the writer's uneasy position.

Guidelines
Writing an Observation Report

1. **Select a site.** Check the list of sites you generated with "Sites to Consider" on page **334**. Choose a site that will prove rich in sensory appeal.

2. **Consider your purpose and your readers.** What do you want to learn from observing this site? Should you stand back, or become involved in the scene? Who are your readers, what do they know about the site, and what could they gain from your observations?

3. **Prepare to observe.** Test your readiness with the checklist below:

   ___ I understand my goal for observing and have listed what to look for.

   ___ I've done necessary background research.

   ___ If the site isn't public, I've gotten permission to observe.

   ___ My timing is right: I have (1) chosen a good time to observe, (2) set aside enough time, and (3) planned multiple visits, if needed.

   ___ I have appropriate transportation and clothing, considering the site and weather.

   ___ I've gathered helpful equipment (pens, notebook, maps, measuring tools, sample containers, laptop, flashlight, camera, video recorder).

4. **Actively observe.** When on site, record the details of your visit.
   - Patiently follow your purpose and plan, but be open to surprises.
   - Identify your position. Where are you in the site? What is your angle? More broadly, what is your frame of mind—are you an insider or an outsider here?
   - Focus on all five senses, recording impressions freely and thoroughly as they happen.
     - **Sights**—record colors, shapes, and appearance; see the big picture and the little details.
     - **Sounds**—listen for loud and subtle, harsh and pleasant, natural and mechanical sounds; if people are present, record relevant conversations.
     - **Smells**—check out both pleasant and unpleasant odors: what's sweet, spicy, sweaty, pungent, sour, rancid, and so on.
     - **Textures**—safely test things for temperature, smoothness, roughness, thickness, and so on.
     - **Tastes**—if your site permits (a restaurant, a ball park), taste for sweet, sour, bitter, and so on.
   - Explore your sixth sense. Record thoughts, feelings, and associations.
   - If appropriate, collect samples, take photos, or record sounds.

5. **Organize your observations.** Soon after the visit, review your notes and other material you collected. Add details and clarify points, if necessary. Then outline your report:

   - Consider a theme, perhaps an insight based on your observations. What's the site's heart, its identity? What patterns bubbled to the surface? What surprised you?
   - Arrange points and supporting details to develop the theme. For example, you could move from the big picture to small details, from a wide angle to a close-up, from first impressions to second looks, from neutral observation to involvement. Alternatively, you could present observations chronologically, relating your sensory perceptions as they happened.

6. **Write the first draft.** Consider when to use past and present verb tenses, and whether to combine reflection with observation. Follow these tips:

   Opening: Offer a vivid detail, identify the site, supply background, indicate your position, and establish your theme.

   Middle: Present vital, well-organized details. Make observations vivid, but also make sure that all the details fit together coherently.

   Conclusion: Remind readers of your theme. Stress the observation's value, along with broader insights. Perhaps explain how the observation expanded your world.

   Working Title: Develop a title that identifies the site and/or hints at your theme.

7. **Get feedback and revise your draft.** Get a fresh perspective from a peer or a tutor in the writing center. Improve the draft by using their responses to the following questions:

   - Are the place, time, and purpose of the observation clear?
   - Does the report vividly appeal to multiple senses and create a strong sense of the site?
   - Does the report flow naturally and build to a conclusion?
   - Are insights logically related to the observations themselves?
   - Does the tone fit the site, the situation, and the theme?

8. **Edit and proofread.** Work through your report sentence by sentence:

   - Replace vague nouns, bland verbs, and weak modifiers.
   - Rewrite tired, predictable sentences. Check verb tenses for consistency.
   - Proofread for typos, grammar errors, spelling mistakes, and correct format.

9. **Prepare and share the final essay.** Find ways to communicate your observations. Besides submitting the report to your instructor, turn it into a presentation, post it on the class's Web site, or share it with family and friends.

Writing Checklist

Use these six traits to check the quality of your writing, then revise as needed:

____ The **ideas** share insights derived from what you observed. The report brings the site to life.

____ The **organization** follows an effective flow, whether chronological or theme-driven.

____ The **voice** fits the purpose. The tone is appropriately objective or subjective, relaxed or tense, matter-of-fact or surprised.

____ The **words** are powerful: precise nouns, vivid verbs, and sharp modifiers.

____ The **sentences** are smooth and varied. Past and present verb tenses are used correctly and consistently.

____ The **copy** is clean, correct, and attractive.

write

Writing Activities

1. In "The Beach," the student writer observes a natural border where land and water meet. What other natural borders exist? Select one, observe it, and write up your borderland report.

2. In "Revelation in Santo Domingo" and "Scab!," the writers (both white, middle-class males) observe sites that contain cross-cultural elements. Given your own ethnic identity, what cross-cultural sites could you visit? Select one, observe it, and write a cross-cultural report.

3. It's time to (safely) step outside your comfort zone. What places or events do you find uncomfortably strange? Select one and write an "it's-a-strange-world" report.

4. List a variety of familiar locations and events, select one, and observe it closely so that you can go beyond the obvious (the familiar). Then write a "fresh-look" report.

5. Is careful observation important in your major? Research what things get observed, what experts look for, and how they report their observations. Then perform such an observation yourself.

6. In the workplace, observation is often used in site or trip reports. Observe a site or event related to your work (or future work), and write a report for a real (or imagined) supervisor.

Chapter 23
Interview Report

audio

The idea of an interview is simple. You talk with someone—an expert on a topic, a client, or a case-study subject—to gain insights into the topic and/or person. As a question-and-answer session, an interview can generate primary information to supplement other research, or it can provide the information and focus for an entire piece of writing such as an interview report.

The idea of an interview may be simple, but conducting a good interview and writing a good report can be tough. That's because a good interview must be carefully planned and executed to become a productive conversation. Planning gives you background information and helps you develop questions that produce solid data, interesting details, and lively quotations. Poor interviewing leads to flat facts, irrelevant tangents, and bland generalities.

This chapter focuses on developing meaningful interview reports. The overview, guidelines, and models that follow will help you carry out your interviews and write your reports.

What's Ahead

- Overview: Interview Report
    Student Models
    Professional Model
- Guidelines
- Writing Checklist and Activities

Overview
Writing an Interview Report

Writer's Goal

Your goal is to gain insights by interviewing someone and then to share those revelations with readers. Aim to ask the right questions, record answers accurately, and report results clearly.

Keys for Success

Plan carefully. ■ An interview needs to be properly prepared, conducted, and processed. Give yourself enough time, and respect your interviewee by being on time, efficient, informed, and courteous.

Ask clear, relevant questions. ■ Clear questions yield useful information— insights into the topic or person that peek below the factual surface. Getting quality information depends on the art of interviewing—planning relevant questions, listening well, following up with sensible responses, and being open to surprises.

Respect the interviewee's voice. ■ Know the person's identity, story, and values. In the interview, listen much more than you talk. In the report, present the person's words and thoughts clearly and honestly. Consider sharing the report with the interview subject before you "go public."

Analyze and synthesize the results. ■ Analysis helps you understand pieces of information, and synthesis helps you pull together separate facts to show relationships. To write an interview report, you must both analyze and synthesize the results of your interview to discover a meaningful theme. Shape the discussion so that the report hangs together, means something, and goes somewhere.

People to Consider

Choose an interviewee from one of the following categories:

- **The expert:** Who is an authority on your topic? Could you find such an expert in your college or community, through local organizations or businesses, or on the Internet?

- **The experienced:** Who has had unique, direct experiences with the topic? Who has participated in, witnessed, or been affected by the situation?

- **The person:** If your purpose is to focus on a person rather than a topic, choose someone intriguing—someone from a particular background, generation, ethnicity, nationality, or occupation.

Next Step Read the model essays and perform the activities that follow. As you read, think about the interview subjects chosen and the strategies used to report on these interviews. Consider how to use similar strategies.

Interview Report

Student writer Marsha Lee was assigned an interview on a personal career-related issue. In the report below, she relates how the interview led her to an important decision.

Dramatic Learning

The writer gives background information.

As a first-semester freshman last fall, I arrived on campus with my career track as clear in my head as the highlighted road map that guided me to Reese College. From kindergarten through high school, I liked reading, writing, and doing school plays, so choosing a major was easy—I'd become an English teacher. Imagine, I thought, people will pay me to do that stuff! What I didn't know is which courses would help me reach my goal.

She introduces her topic and identifies her interviewee.

Then two week ago, on the same day I was assigned this interview report, I got an e-mail message from my adviser saying that it was time to choose courses for my sophomore year. So I decided to hit two targets with one stone by interviewing Dr. Angela Wit in the Theater Department. She could tell me which theater courses would help me as an English teacher, and reporting on the interview would help me finish my assignment.

Just before noon the following morning, I entered Dr. Wit's office and introduced myself. She asked me to sit down, and then started to talk.

The writer uses quotations that reflect Wit's ideas and personality.

"Marsha," she said, "you've made a good choice! Middle school students need English teachers who can help them read and write, but they also need English teachers who can help them produce quality plays. Taking theater courses will help you learn that."

"How many courses?" I asked.

"Enough to be a professional educator," she replied.

"And how many is that?" I asked.

Dr. Wit smiled, leaned back in her chair, and asked, "Have you thought about taking a fifth year?" She then delivered a five-minute monologue on how teachers must be professional practitioners in their fields of study. "For you," she said, "that means getting a firm grasp of both the academic and technical aspects of theater. To do that, you should stay a fifth year and finish a theater major, along with your English major." She closed by describing her past student, Mike Krause, an "outstanding young professional" who teaches history and directs first-rate plays at Sylvan Middle School in nearby Jonesburg.

She shares her response and introduces the second interview.

I went back to my dorm room a bit depressed. During our talk, Dr. Wit had given me enough raw material to draft a report, but she gave me no help selecting courses. Besides, I wanted to be out of college in three years! So after a good pout, I decided to do a second interview—this time with the middle school teacher whom Dr. Wit mentioned, Mike Krause.

The next afternoon I arrived at Sylvan at 1:55, just in time to get caught   *10*
in the stream of kids heading for their last-hour classes. When I found Mr.
Krause—sitting in front of a puppet stage in the back corner of his classroom—he responded like we knew each other. "Hey, Marsha, over here!"
he called. I walked over and he introduced me to five bubbly kids with
scissors, colored paper, cloth, and glue. "They're making costumes for a play
they wrote about the Lewis and Clark expedition," he said, "and they need
your help." Then he walked away.

> **She summarizes what happened.**

The next hour was a whirlwind. I helped make a dress for Sacagawea,   *11*
rehearsed a dialogue as Martha Washington, and responded to a poem
about Sally Hemings and Thomas Jefferson.

After the bell rang and the last student left, Mr. Krause slid into a   *12*
student's chair and pointed to one nearby. "Take a seat," he said. "On the
phone you said that you want to talk about theater courses."

"Yes," I said, "and I'd like your ideas."

> **She uses a long quote that captures Krause's main point.**

"I've already given you my best shot," he replied. Mr. Krause then   *13*
explained why he invited me to visit his class. "I direct school plays at
Sylvan," he said, "but the stage isn't where the real theater takes place. The
real stuff happens in classrooms like mine where students do theater activities that help them learn history, or science, or whatever. The key to
choosing theater courses that will help you teach English is knowing what
you need to learn. Today you learned that you already know a lot about
helping kids put on plays. So maybe you should focus on what English
teachers must teach, and then select only those theater courses that help you
teach that stuff."

> **She reflects on both interviews and describes what she learned.**

That evening I thought about both interviews. Dr. Wit told me that I   *14*
have to be a professional in my field, and I agree. But Mr. Krause taught me
that my *profession* is education.

Last Monday I met with my adviser to choose my courses for next fall,   *15*
and the choice was easy. Three years from now, I'm going to graduate and
get a job as an English teacher. Between now and then, I'll finish the
prescribed courses and take a few electives like creative dramatics and
acting. Oh yes, and for one of the required field experiences in education, I
definitely plan to spend a few weeks observing Mr. Krause! ■

write

Reading for Better Writing

1. Explain why the writer does or does not succeed in communicating the ideas and voices of Dr. Wit and Mr. Krause.

2. Identify the report's theme and explain how the quotations do or do not develop that idea.

3. Reread the conclusion. Does the writer's voice show honest reflection about the two interviews? Explain.

Interview Report

Because of a disturbing childhood experience, college student Benjamin Meyer toured a funeral home and interviewed the director. In the following essay, Benjamin reports on what he learned.

The Dead Business

The writer starts with background information that creates a personal theme.

"You're going to tour a what?" *1*

"A funeral home." *2*

My friends were shocked. They laughed while describing scenes from *3*
Night of the Living Dead and *The Shining*.

But their stories didn't frighten me—I feared something else. When I *4*
was ten, my grandmother died, and my family drove to the funeral home to
view the body. As we entered the place, I noticed the funeral director standing in the corner looking like a too-eager-to-please salesman who'd made a
deal he didn't deserve. The guy's thin-lipped smile seemed unnatural—
almost glib. Like a ghoul in a business suit, he didn't seem to care that a
stroke had stopped my grandmother's beating heart midway through the
doxology that concluded the Sunday-evening church service. He didn't seem
to care that she and I would share no more cookies, no more coloring
books, no more Rook games, no more laughing, no more. I was ten, very
sad, and he didn't seem to care.

Freely using "I," the writer tells the story of his visit and interview.

Now a college student, I wanted to tour a different funeral home to *5*
work through my earlier experience. While I no longer feared ghouls, I was
still nervous while driving to the Vander Ploeg Furniture Store/Funeral
Home. I remembered the thin-lipped smile.

I walked inside not knowing what to expect. Suddenly, a man from *6*
behind a desk hopped out of his chair and said, "Hi, I'm Howard Beernink."

I looked at the tall, smiling guy, paused a moment, and glanced back at *7*
the door. His partner had stepped in front of the exit while scribbling on
tags that dangled from Lazy Boy rockers. I realized that this interview was
something I had to do . . . like getting a tetanus shot.

He describes the setting.

Howard led me into a room full of furniture where he found a soft, *8*
purple couch. We sat down, and he described how the business started.

He relates the early history of the business.

In 1892, pioneers established the town of Sioux Center, Iowa. Winter *9*
storms and disease pummeled the tiny community, and soon residents
needed someone to bury the dead. A funeral director wasn't available, but a
furniture maker was. The furniture maker was the only person with the
tools, hardwood, and knowledge to build coffins. As a result, the Vander
Ploeg Furniture Store/Funeral Home was born.

The writer
summarizes,
paraphrases,
and quotes
from the
interview.

Today, starting a funeral home isn't that easy. For example, a funeral *10* home requires the services of an embalmer, and an embalmer must be certified by the state. To get a certificate, the person must complete two years of college, one year of embalming school, and one year of apprentice work. After that, the individual must pass a state exam every year to retain certification.

"But why a funeral home director?" I was baffled. Why would anyone *11* embalm dead bodies for a living?

"Because it's a family business." Howard smiled as if he expected my *12* question. "Vander Ploegs and Beerninks have run this place for generations. Today it's difficult to start a funeral home because there are so many of them with long histories and good reputations."

He narrates what happened during the interview.

After he answered the rest of my questions, Howard asked if I wanted *13* to see the embalming room.

"Okay," I said, tentatively. *14*

He led me through doors, down hallways, up a staircase, and into a *15* well-lighted display room containing several coffins. Finally, we entered a small, cold room containing a row of cupboards, a large ceramic table, and a small machine that resembled a bottled-water cooler.

"We like to keep the room cold when we're not using it," Howard said. *16*

"What is all this stuff?" I asked. *17*

Howard described why embalming is done and what it involves. The *18* purpose of embalming is to extend the period for viewing the body, and the process includes replacing body fluids with embalming fluid. He opened a cupboard, pulled out a bottle of fluid and said, "Here . . . smell."

The writer shares surprises and what he learned.

"Smells like Pepto-Bismol," I replied. *19*

After he embalms the body, Howard applies makeup so the face *20* appears "more natural." He gets his cosmetics (common powders and tints) from the local Avon lady.

"But sometimes we also have to use this," Howard said, pulling out *21* another bottle.

"Tissue builder?" I asked, squinting at the label. *22*

"It's like silicon implants," he answered. "We inject it into sunken *23* cheeks, like the cheeks of cancer victims."

When the body is ready for burial, the funeral director must show a *24* price list to the family of the deceased. The Funeral Rule, adopted in 1984 by the Federal Trade Commission, requires that a price list be shown to the family before they see caskets, cement boxes, and vaults. The purpose of the Funeral Rule is to prevent unethical funeral directors from manipulating customers with comments like, "But that's a pauper's casket; you don't want to bury your mother in that. Bury her in this beauty over here."

Unfortunately, only a third of the country's 22,000 funeral homes abide by the Funeral Rule.

"After showing customers where the caskets are, I step away so they can talk among themselves," said Howard. "It's unethical to bother the family at this difficult time." 25

Before burying a casket, Howard and his partner place it in either a cement box or a vault. A cement box is a container that's neither sealed nor waterproofed, whereas a vault is both sealed and waterproofed. Howard explained, "Years ago, cemeteries began to sink and cave in on spots, so state authorities demanded containers. Containers make the cemetery look nicer." 26

He ends the report with a strong quotation and personal reflection.

After the tour, I asked Howard, "How has this job affected your life?" 27

He glanced at the ceiling, smiled, and said, "It's very fulfilling. My partner and I comfort people during a stressful time in their lives, and it strengthens our bond with them." 28

As I drove back to the college, I thought again about Howard's comment, and about my childhood fear. Howard was right. He doesn't exploit people. Instead, he comforts them and helps them move on. And while I still fear the pain of saying goodbye to someone I love, I don't fear funeral directors anymore. They're just people who provide services that a community needs. ■ 29

write

Reading for Better Writing

1. This report centers on the writer's own story, reflections, and needs. Discuss how these elements are woven into the report. Are they effective? Why or why not?

2. Examine the opening and the closing of the essay. Do they work well together? Do they effectively share a theme for the report? Explain.

3. Describe how the writer organizes the interview's results. Is the organization effective? Explain.

4. Look carefully at the writer's use of summary and paraphrase on the one hand and quotation on the other hand. Are the strategies effective? Explain.

Interview Report

Writer David Thome based the following report on interviews with his subject, the owner of a limousine business. The result is a personal, interesting, and informative account of one young woman's ride to success.

Lambie's Limousines

To open, the writer introduces the interviewee and her company.

Many entrepreneurs continue working for someone else until a new *1* venture gets established. Although Shiela Lambie cut back from three jobs to one while getting Lambie's Luxury Limousines off and rolling, her new business didn't shift into full gear until she made it a full-time priority.

"I get my entrepreneurial drive from my mother," Lambie says. "She's *2* the person who pushed me into how I do things. She always told me that there's nothing you can't do if you put your heart into it, and that whatever you do, do it to the best of your ability."

The day after graduating from high school, Lambie went to work in the *3* business department of the Kenosha Public Library, where she did general secretarial work and some bookkeeping. She says she liked the job, but she wasn't sure where she wanted her career path to lead. So she took classes at Gateway Technical Institute to fill the core requirements for a degree.

The writer tells the interviewee's story through summary, paraphrase, and quotation.

She never received a degree, but instead took a job in the service *4* department of Vigansky's TV and Appliance, where she did secretarial work and served as a dispatcher.

She stayed with Vigansky's for four years, working up to manager of *5* the parts department.

"I left after the birth of my first child, thinking I'd never work again," *6* she says. "I had this idea of being a wonderful, perfect mother who stayed home all the time. Within two weeks, I was back at Vigansky's."

She ended up working three jobs to support herself and her two chil- *7* dren after a divorce in the early '80s. A few years later she became engaged to Al Lambie, an over-the-road trucker who was growing tired of making the long hauls. Vigansky's, hurt by the recession and the closing of Kenosha's AMC plant, began to cut back Lambie's hours. At the same time Lambie's sister, Sherri, and her husband, John, bought a limousine so they could make extra money chauffeuring wedding parties on weekends. But with John's job as a sheriff's deputy, the couple found it increasingly difficult to continue moonlighting.

A quotation stresses a key point.

Lambie recognized an opportunity in this confluence of events. "It was *8* incredibly good timing," Lambie says. "Sherri and John wanted to get rid of the limo, and Al and I thought a limo service could be a good business if you did things a certain way."

The writer supplies precise, interesting details.

Shiela and Al bought a house and used the home equity to buy the limo for $9,000. At first, they too limited the limo service to weekends, while Al kept his job and Shiela quit Vigansky's to open a kiosk for Total Furniture in the Kenosha Factory Outlet Centre. They soon found that with the cost of gas, repairs, insurance, phone calls, advertising, and hiring an answering service, the limousine service did little to enhance their income. 9

"In fact, we were losing money," Lambie says. "I was taking my entire paycheck and putting it into the limo business. We weren't getting the results we wanted, so we decided we had to make a commitment." Lambie quit her job in 1985 to devote her energies to the limo service. Business doubled the first month and tripled again in the second. 10

Transitions smoothly link parts of the report.

At first, most of Lambie's business came from weddings. "Our biggest competition was funeral homes," she recalls. "Of course, they all had black cars, so rather than go head-to-head with them, I had only white cars." 11

To expand her business, Lambie placed ads in the Yellow Pages and *Happenings* magazine. She did some prospecting. And, by approaching businesses about driving executives and clients to and from airports, she hit upon a rich vein that had been largely untapped in this locality. 12

Today, transporting corporate executives and guests has supplanted weddings, dances, and funerals as Lambie's bread and butter. . . . 13

The closing focuses on the future and offers a strong quotation.

Lambie said that in spite of the rising cost of cars, insurance, repairs, and gas, she expects her business to grow over the next few years. She should know: Lambie's has already grown from $5,000 in sales in 1985 to nearly $500,000 in 1991. She has two simple secrets for success: work hard and keep in touch. 14

"You work three times as hard when you work for yourself as you do working for someone else," she says. "An employee can punch a clock and go home. When you work for yourself, you can't do that. The business becomes part of your life. . . ." ∎ 15

write

Reading for Better Writing

1. This report focuses on a specific person and her life. What does the writer do to portray that person and tell her story?

2. What is the theme of the report? (Note that the theme may not be directly stated but merely implied.)

3. To share the interview results, the writer uses summaries, paraphrases, and quotations from the interview. Choose two examples and explain why they are or are not effective.

4. In this report, the writer takes an objective stance—one in which he doesn't offer his own opinions. Is this stance appropriate for this report? Explain.

5. Describe how this report is organized. Is this method appropriate and effective? Explain.

Guidelines
Writing an Interview Report

1. **Choose a person to interview.** Review "People to Consider" on page 346 to find an interviewee. Also, consider a community or campus leader.

2. **Plan the interview.** As soon as possible, take care of the details:
   - Determine your goal—what you want the interview to accomplish, and what information and insights you want to gather.
   - Choose a sensible recording method (pen and paper, tape recorder) and a medium (face-to-face, telephone, e-mail).
   - Consider what you know about the topic and the interviewee. Then figure out what you must know to ask meaningful questions. If necessary, do some research on the interview subject.
   - Contact the interviewee and politely request an interview. Explain who you are, why you need the interview, and how you will use it. Schedule a time and place convenient for the interviewee. If you wish to record the interview, ask permission.
   - Gather and test tools and equipment: a notebook, pens, and perhaps recording equipment (tape, video, digital camera).

3. **Prepare questions.** Do the following to help you structure the interview:
   - Consider types of questions to ask—the five *W*'s and *H* (*who, what, when, where, why,* and *how*).
   - Understand open and closed questions. Closed questions ask for simple, factual answers; open questions ask for detailed explanations.
       Closed: How many months did you spend in Vietnam?
       Open: Can you describe your most vivid memory of Vietnam?
   - Avoid slanted questions pressuring readers to give a specific answer.
       Slanted: Aren't you really angry that draft dodgers didn't do their duty?
       Neutral: How do you feel about those who avoided the draft?
   - Think about specific topics to cover and write questions for each one. Start with a simple question that establishes rapport and groundwork. Plan target questions—ones that you must ask.
   - Put questions on the left side of the page with room for notes on the right. Rehearse your questions, visualizing how the interview should go.

4. **Conduct the interview.** Arrive on time and be professional:
   - Introduce yourself, reminding the interviewee why you've come.
   - If you have permission to record the interview, set up equipment off to the side so that it doesn't interfere with the conversation. However, even if you're recording, take notes on key facts and quotations.

- Listen actively by including nods and eye contact. Pay attention to the interviewee's body language.
- Be flexible. If the person looks puzzled by a question, rephrase it or ask another. Ask one of these questions if an answer needs to be amplified:

  Clarifying: "Do you mean this or that?"
  Explanatory: "What do you mean by that?"
  Detailing: "What happened exactly? Can you describe that?"
  Analytical: "Did that happen by stages? What were the causes? The outcomes?"
  Probing: "What do you think that meant?"
  Comparative: "Did that remind you of anything?"
  Contextual: "What else was going on then? Who else was involved?"
  Summarizing: "Overall, what was your response? What was the net effect?"

- Be tactful. If the person avoids a question, politely rephrase it. Don't react negatively or forcefully invade the interviewee's private territory.
- Listen "between the lines" for what the interviewee seems to want to say.
- Expect important points to come up late in the interview, and give the interviewee a chance to add any final thoughts.

5. **Follow up.** As soon as possible, review your notes and fill in the blanks. By phone or in writing, clarify points and thank the interviewee.

6. **Organize and draft the report.** Shape the opening to seize interest, the middle to sustain interest, and the closing to reward interest:
   - Analyze and interpret the interview results. Locate the heart or theme of your report, and then develop an outline supporting the theme.
   - Start with background, along with a point that gains readers' interest.
   - Summarize and paraphrase material from the interview (see pages 460–462). Use quotations selectively to share the interviewee's character or stress a point.
   - If appropriate, weave your thoughts and reflections into the report.

7. **Get feedback and revise the report.** Ask someone to answer these questions: Does the report supply complete, satisfying insights? Is the organization effective, with an engaging opening and closing? Is the writing lively, fair, and respectful?

8. **Edit and proofread.** Review your report for precise word choice, smooth sentences, and correct grammar. In particular, make sure that quotations are integrated smoothly (see page 468).

9. **Prepare a final copy.** Submit a clean copy to your instructor (and perhaps the interviewee), but also look for ways to publish your report—as a Web page with digital photos and sound clips, or as a presentation for classmates.

Writing Checklist

Use these traits to check the quality of your writing, then revise as needed:

____ The **ideas** share the heart of the interview—the interviewee's insights—through summary, paraphrase, and quotation.

____ The **organization** centers on a theme and creates, sustains, and rewards interest.

____ The **voice** sounds genuine and interested. The interviewee's voice is respected.

____ The **words** are precise and understandable. Quotations reflect the interviewee's ideas and personality.

____ The **sentences** are smooth, with quotations effectively integrated. Transitional words link sentences and sections.

____ The **copy** is correct in terms of its grammar, punctuation, usage, spelling, and format.

write

Writing Activities

1. "Dramatic Learning" shares the writer's exploration of issues related to her studies and career choices. Consider your own career choices. Learn more by interviewing someone at your college or in a workplace.

2. "The Dead Business" recounts the writer's exploration of a topic that caused him discomfort and sadness. What similar issues affect you? Would an interview help you work through the issue? Write your own reflective interview report.

3. In "Lambie's Limousines," the writer develops a "venture" report based on interviews—a report that details how a person developed a particular business or organization. Do you know any venturous people? What industries interest you? Write your own venture report.

4. Do you know someone who has led a fascinating life? Someone who on the surface seems to have led an ordinary life? Someone serving others in inspiring ways? Write that person's life story—an extended biography.

5. Is there a particular issue in your community that concerns you—a public debate, a college problem, a program being cut back? Who has insights into the issue? Who are people on different sides? Whose lives are affected? Who has the power to change things? Select one or more people to interview, and then write a report on the issue.

Chapter 24
Experiment, Lab, and Field Reports

audio

Good science writing is rooted in good science—the careful study of phenomena through observation and experiment. Social scientists seek to understand human behavior and societies, whereas natural scientists investigate the physical world.

As a student, you may be asked to do scientific research in a whole range of courses. In labs and in the field, you may perform experiments, gather data, and interpret results and then share your insights with fellow students and members of the scientific community. Such experiences provide valuable preparation for a variety of careers in the sciences.

When you do science, you share your research story. Whether you are studying the nature of hydrochloric acid or factors affecting fermentation rates in ethanol, your report shares what you did, why you did it, and what you learned. This chapter will help you put your experiments and field research into writing—and your good writing into science.

What's Ahead

- Overview: Experiment, Lab, or Field Reports
  - Student Models
  - Professional Model
- Guidelines
- Writing Checklist and Activities

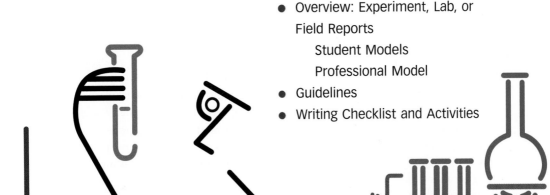

Web

Overview
Writing an Experiment, Lab, or Field Report

Writer's Goal

Your goal is to accurately record and thoughtfully interpret the results of a scientific study or experiment—so clearly that others could repeat your experiment.

Keys for Success

Follow the scientific method. ■ Science focuses on measured observations aimed at understanding. Experiments are set up to test hypotheses about why things happen. However, experiments don't prove hypotheses correct: experimental results can merely "agree with" or disprove a hypothesis. Overall, the method moves from observation to explanation as you do the following:

1. Observe something interesting, often while looking for something else.
2. Check whether other scientists have explained the same observation.
3. Summarize your observations and turn that generalization into a testable hypothesis—a working theory explaining the phenomenon.
4. Design research to test the hypothesis, paying attention to variables and controls.
5. Based on the results of your experiment, accept, reject, or modify your hypothesis.
6. Repeat steps 3 through 5 until you understand the phenomenon. Then write up your research so that others can respond to your work.

Follow the standard format. ■ To model scientific thinking, lab and field reports include an introduction establishing the problem, a methods section detailing procedures, a results section providing the data, and a discussion that interprets the data.

Distinctions to Consider

Whatever your assignment, you need to understand these distinctions:

- **Distinguish facts from possibilities.** Facts are the data you collect. Possibilities are your interpretations of the data. Don't confuse the two.
- **Distinguish experiments from studies.** Experiments test hypotheses by manipulating variables. Studies observe what's there—counting, measuring, sampling, and so on. In this chapter, the report on fermentation is an experiment; the field report on cockroaches is a study.

Next Step Read the model reports and perform the activities that follow. As you read, examine how the reports follow the scientific method so that you can use that method in your own reports.

Lab Report

Student Coby Williams wrote the basic lab report below to describe a chemical compound and inform readers about its nature.

audio

Working with Hydrochloric Acid

The writer identifies the chemical compound and states its nature.

Overview and Purpose

The goal in writing this report is to educate others on the dangers of using and storing hydrochloric acid in the lab (HCl) and in the home (muriatic acid). In addition, this report will provide a list of appropriate ways to protect against burns when using HCl as well as ways to dispose of it properly.

Characteristics

Hydrochloric acid (HCl), which is made from hydrogen gas and chlorine gas, is a clear, colorless to slightly yellow, fuming liquid with a sharp, irritating odor. HCl is a strong, highly corrosive acid, soluble in water and alcohol. Other characteristics include the following:

✔ The chemical reaction is: $H_2 + Cl_2 = 2HCl$.

✔ Its molecular weight is 36.45.

✔ Its boiling point is 85°C.

✔ Its specific gravity is 1.16.

Hydrochloric acid is commercially known as muriatic acid, a substance used to manufacture dyes and plastics or to acidize (activate) petroleum wells. It is also used in the food processing of corn, syrup, and sodium glutamate, and is an ingredient in many household and industrial cleaners.

Safety Procedures

Hydrochloric acid is highly corrosive and can severely burn skin. Whenever HCl is used, it must be handled according to the following precaution:

Storage

- Keep hydrochloric acid in tightly-capped bottles back from the edge of the shelf or table.
- Keep bottles away from metals. Contact will corrode metals and could release hydrogen gas, which is highly explosive.

Protection

He organizes details in distinct categories.

- Always wear safety glasses to protect your eyes.
- Wear latex gloves and old clothes when using concentrated HCl—not short-sleeved shirts, shorts, or sandals.
- Do not breathe the fumes, which can cause fainting.

- If acid spills on skin or splashes in someone's eyes, rinse the area with water for 5 minutes. Treat burns appropriately. In each case, get medical help immediately.

Usage

In the lab, hydrochloric acid is either diluted or titrated.

- When diluting, always pour the acid into the water. Doing the reverse can cause boiling, splashing, and burning.
- When titrating, carefully measure the HCl needed. Then react the HCl with a sample that has a base such as sodium hydroxide to get an accurate measurement of the base in the sample.

Disposal

- To dispose of HCl, neutralize it by mixing the acid with a sodium hydroxide solution. Flush the neutralized solution down the drain.
- If you spill HCl, cover the spill with baking soda. After the fizzing stops, sweep up the soda and flush it down the drain. ■

write

Reading for Better Writing

1. Who would the main audience for this type of report be? What evidence can you point to support your analysis?

2. List the strategies used to organize the report. Are these strategies effective? Explain.

3. How does this report demonstrate scientific thinking?

Experiment Report

In this report, student writer Andrea Pizano shares the results of a lab experiment that she completed to explore how different factors affect fermentation.

The Effects of Temperature and Inhibitors on the Fermentation Process for Ethanol

Andrea Pizano
January 29, 2002

Introduction

The opening creates context and explains concepts.

Alcoholic liquids were made and used for centuries before scientists fully understood the process by which alcohol developed. An Egyptian papyrus dated 3500 B.C.E. mentions wine making, although alcoholic spirits like gin and brandy started only about a thousand years ago. From beverages such as beer and wine to fuel additives such as ethanol, alcohol has been used by people for recreation, religious rites, medical purposes, energy, and industry. Even today people are surprised to learn that it is ethanol—a by-product of yeast growth—that makes bread smell good. Studying the process by which alcohol is made can help make the process more efficient and successful. [1]

Generally, alcohol can be made by fermenting different types of sugars, including sucrose, glucose, and fructose. Fermentation is a process that creates heat and changes the properties of a substance through a leaven or fermenting agent. For the fermentation process to succeed, certain enzymes must function as catalysts. These enzymes are present in yeast, the fermenting agent. While useful as catalysts, these enzymes are sensitive to temperature changes and inhibitors. [2]

The writer describes the experiment and states her hypotheses.

In this experiment, ethanol—a specific type of alcohol—was synthesized from sucrose in the presence of yeast. The effects of extreme temperatures and of inhibitors on the rate of fermentation were tested quantitatively. The factors below were tested, and the outcomes below were anticipated. First, extremely high temperatures denature enzymes. Therefore, fermentation in the sample was expected to stop. Second, extremely cool temperatures reduce the kinetic energy of molecules. Therefore, the reaction rate in the sample was expected to drastically slow. Third, sodium fluoride can inhibit one of the enzymes needed in the fermentation process. Therefore, the presence of sodium fluoride was expected to effectively stop the reaction. Fourth, normal fermentation usually delivers a maximum of up to 15% ethanol. Through distillation, a 95% concentration of ethanol can be obtained. However, the presence of [3] concentrated ethanol kills the yeast cells and also acts as a negative feedback mechanism to the enzymes necessary for the fermentation process. Therefore, concentrated ethanol was expected to effectively stop the reaction.

Method

To test each of these hypotheses, the following procedure was followed *4* in this experiment:

> **She details the procedure using numbered steps and precise terms.**

1. 200 mg of yeast was mixed with 1.25 ml of warm water in a 5-ml round-bottomed, long-necked flask. The mixture was shaken until the yeast was well distributed.

2. 9 mg of disodium hydrogen phosphate, 1.30 g sucrose, and 3.75 ml warm water were added to the flask. This mixture was left for 15 minutes—until the fermentation was proceeding at a vigorous rate.

3. The fermentation mixture was then divided equally into 5 reaction tubes.
   - To tube 1, 1.0 ml of water was added.
   - To tube 2, 1.0 ml of 95% ethanol was added.
   - To tube 3, 1.0 ml of 0.5 M sodium fluoride solution was added.
   - To each of tubes 4 and 5, 1.0 ml of water was added.

4. The bubbles produced in a reaction tube filled with water were counted. A septum was first fit over the neck of each reaction tube. Then some polyethylene tubing was connected from the septum to the water-filled reaction tube. In this way, the reaction rate could be quantitatively measured by counting the number of gas bubbles that were released into the water each minute for 5 minutes.

5. Test tube 4 was heated for 5 minutes in boiling water. Then it was cooled to room temperature, and the fermentation rate was measured as explained in step 4.

6. Test tube 5 was put on ice for 5 minutes, and then the fermentation rate was measured as explained in step 4, while the reaction tube was kept on ice to maintain the low temperature.

7. After the experiment was completed, the solutions were washed down the drain as waste.

Results

The reaction rates of the 5 reaction conditions are plotted on Figure 1 *5* below.

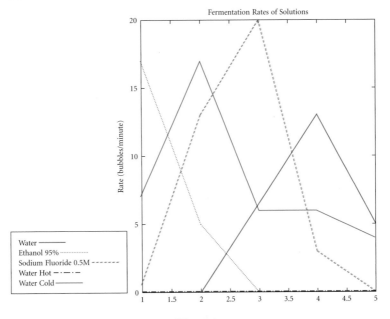

Figure 1

With the sample containing water at room temperature, the fermenta- *6* tion rate peaked at 13 bubbles/minute at minute 4. The fermentation rate of the sample with 95% ethanol started at 17 bubbles/minute, but within 2 minutes the rate quickly slowed to 5 bubbles/minute. By 3 minutes, the rate was 0 bubbles/minute. In the sample with sodium fluoride, the fermenta- tion increased to 20 bubbles/minute after 3 minutes, but then quickly reached 0 bubbles/minute after 5 minutes. In the sample that was boiled, the fermentation rate was consistently 0 bubbles/minute. In the sample placed on ice, the fermentation rate increased to 17 bubbles/minute after 2 minutes, but then gradually slowed to 4 bubbles/minute after 5 minutes.

Discussion

Many different factors affect fermentation rates. For example, when *7* ethanol concentration is very high, yeast usually dies. So when 95% ethanol is added to a fermenting sugar and yeast mixture, one would expect the fer- mentation rate to decline sharply. The experiment's data support this hypothesis. After 3 minutes, the fermentation had completely stopped.

In addition, sodium fluoride inhibits the action of a specific enzyme in *8* yeast, an enzyme needed for the fermentation process. Therefore, when sodium fluoride is added to a fermenting mixture, one would expect a halted fermentation rate. However, the reaction rate initially increased to 20 bubbles/minute when sodium fluoride was added. This increase may have occurred because not all of the enzymes were inhibited at first. Perhaps the fermentation rate declined to 0 bubbles/minute only when the sodium fluoride became evenly distributed. This measurement occurred after 5 minutes.

She explores possible explanations for unexpected results and suggests further research.

Temperature is a third factor affecting fermentation. On the one hand, high temperatures denature many enzymes; therefore, when a fermenting mixture is placed in boiling water for 5 minutes, one would expect the fermentation rate to stop because no enzymes are present anymore to carry out the fermentation process. This hypothesis is supported by the data, as no fermentation occurred in the hot mixture. On the other hand, cold temperatures reduce the kinetic energy of molecules. As a result, the speed decreases, and the likelihood of the enzymes making contact with the substrate decreases exponentially in relation to the temperature. One would expect that the reaction rate would slow down drastically after the mixture has been cooled. This hypothesis is somewhat supported by the data. After an initial increase in the reaction rate to 17 bubbles/minute, the reaction rate slowed to 4 bubbles/minute after 5 minutes. A repeat of the experiment would be needed to clarify this result. Moreover, because the measuring method was somewhat unsophisticated (as indicated by the spikes in the line graph), perhaps a new experiment could be designed to measure fermentation-rate changes more sensitively.

The closing summarizes the experiment's value.

This experiment helped quantify the effects that various factors such as temperature, inhibitors, and high ethanol concentration have on fermentation rates. Even though the measuring apparatus was fairly basic, the experiment largely supported the hypotheses. Such data are helpful for determining methods of efficient and successful fermentation. Further research testing other factors and other inhibitors would add to this knowledge. ■

Reading for Better Writing

1. Where does the writer discuss the experiment's purpose and value? Are her efforts convincing?

2. In the "Method" section, what strategies does the writer use to ensure that the experiment can be repeated?

3. In the "Results" section, what is the relationship between the line graph and the paragraph?

4. In the "Discussion" section, the writer addresses results that did and did not support the hypotheses. Are her interpretations and conclusions sound?

Field Report

In the following workplace report, a team of writers investigates the causes and effects of cockroach infestation in an apartment complex. In the study, they use their findings to recommend solutions.

SOMMERVILLE DEVELOPMENT CORPORATION

Date: September 20, 2002

To: Bert Richardson, VP of Tenant Relations

From: Hue Nguyen, Cherryhill Complex Manager
Sandra Kao, Building Superintendent
Roger Primgarr, Tenant Relations
Juan Alexander, Tenant Representative

The subject line functions as a title.

Subject: Investigation of Cockroach Infestation at 5690 Cherryhill

The opening clarifies the study's purpose and goals.

During the month of July 2002, 26 tenants of the 400-unit building at 5690 Cherryhill informed the building superintendent that they had found cockroaches in their units. On August 8, the management-tenant committee authorized us to investigate these questions: [1]

1. How extensive is the cockroach infestation?
2. How can the cockroach population best be controlled?

We monitored this problem from August 9 to September 8, 2002. This report contains a summary, an overview of our research methods, and findings, conclusions, and recommendations. [2]

SUMMARY

The summary focuses on outcomes.

The 5690 Cherryhill building has a moderate infestation of German cockroaches. Only an integrated control program can manage this infestation. Pesticide fumigations address only the symptoms, not the causes. We recommend that Sommerville adopt a comprehensive program that includes (1) education, (2) cooperation, (3) habitat modification, (4) treatment, and (5) ongoing monitoring. [3]

RESEARCH METHODS AND FINDINGS

Overview of Research

We researched the problem in the following ways: 4

1. Contacted the Department of Agriculture, the Ecology Action Center, and Ecological Agriculture Projects.
2. Consulted three exterminators.
3. Inspected 5690 Cherryhill building, from ground to roof.
4. Placed pheromone traps in all units to monitor cockroach population.

Research methods are described.

The Cockroach Population

Pheromone traps revealed German cockroaches, a common variety. Of the   5
400 units, 112 units (28 percent) showed roaches. Based on the numbers, the infestation is rated moderate.

Results are categorized logically.

The German Cockroach

Research shows that these roaches thrive in apartment buildings.   6

- Populations thrive when food, water, shelter, and migration routes are available. They prefer dark, humid conditions near food sources.

- The cockroach seeks shelter in spaces that allow its back and underside to remain in constant contact with a solid surface.

Methods of Control

Sources we consulted stressed the need for an integrated program of   7
cockroach control involving sanitation, habitat modification, and non-toxic treatments that attack causes. Here are the facts:

Findings are presented clearly and concisely.

- The German cockroach is immune to many chemicals.

- Roaches detect most pesticides before direct contact.

- Spot-spraying simply causes roaches to move to unsprayed units.

- Habitat modification through (1) eliminating food and water sources, (2) caulking cracks and crevices, (3) lowering humidity, and (4) increasing light and airflow makes life difficult for cockroaches.

CONCLUSIONS

Based on our findings, we conclude the following: 8

1. A single method of treatment, especially chemical, will be ineffective.
2. A comprehensive program of sanitation, habitat modification, and nontoxic treatments will eliminate the German cockroach.

Conclusions follow logically from the findings.

RECOMMENDATIONS

We recommend that Sommerville Development adopt an Integrated Program of Cockroach Prevention and Control for its 5690 Cherryhill building. Management would assign the following tasks to appropriate personnel: 9

Education: (1) Give tenants information on sanitation, prevention, and home remedies; and (2) hold tenant meetings to answer questions.   10

Habitat Modification: Revise the maintenance program and renovation schedule to give priority to the following: 11

- Apply residual insecticides before sealing cracks.
- Caulk cracks and crevices (baseboards, cupboards, pipes, sinks). Insert steel wool in large cavities (plumbing, electrical columns).
- Repair leaking pipes and faucets. Insulate pipes to eliminate condensation.
- Schedule weekly cleaning of common garbage areas.

Treatment: In addition to improving sanitation and prevention through education, attack the roach population through these methods: 12

- Use home remedies, traps, and hotels.
- Use borax or boric-acid powder formulations as residual, relatively nontoxic pesticides.
- Use chemical controls on an emergency basis.
- Ensure safety by arranging for a Health Department representative to make unannounced visits to the building.

Monitoring: Monitor cockroach population in the following ways: 13
1. Every six months, use traps to check on activity in all units.
2. Keep good records on the degree of occurrence, population density, and control methods used.

We believe that this comprehensive program will solve the cockroach problem. We recommend that Sommerville adopt this program for 5690 Cherryhill and consider implementing it in all its buildings.   14

Recommendations apply what was learned in the study.

The closing stresses the value and benefits of the study.

write

Reading for Better Writing

1. Examine the report's format and organizational strategies. How is this workplace report similar to and different from the other lab and experiment reports in this chapter?

2. Describe the tone of the report. What does this tone accomplish?

3. This report depends extensively on cause/effect thinking. Where do the writers use cause/effect thinking, and how effective is it?

Guidelines
Experiment, Lab, or Field Reports

1. **Review the lab manual and any handouts.** In most science courses, studies and experiments are assigned through textbooks, manuals, and handouts. Study those materials to understand what you must do and why. Read background information on the topic in textbooks and other sources.

2. **Use a field or lab notebook.** Accurate, complete recordkeeping is crucial to doing good scientific research. Use the notebook to plan research, record what you do, collect data, make drawings, and reflect on results. For each notebook entry, record the date and your goal.

3. **Plan and complete your study or experiment.** For a productive study, do the following:
   ● Develop your key research questions. If you are conducting an experiment, not just a study, then state your hypotheses and design procedures for testing them.
   ● Gather the proper tools, equipment, and materials required to conduct your study.
   ● Carefully and alertly conduct your tests and perform your observations.
   ● Take copious notes, being especially careful to record data accurately, clearly, and completely. If helpful, use a data collection sheet.

4. **Relying on your notebook, draft the report.** Wrestle with your data. What do they mean? Were results expected or unexpected? What factors could explain those results? What further research might be necessary? Once you have conducted this analysis, draft parts of the report in the sequence outlined below:
   ● **Methods:** Start by explaining what you did to study the topic or test the hypothesis. Supply essential details, factors, and explanations. Be so clear that someone else could repeat the steps you took.
   ● **Results:** Using two strategies, present the data you collected. First, share data in graphical forms—as tables, line charts, bar graphs, photographs, and so on. While the correct design of graphics and the proper presentation of statistical data are beyond the scope of this book, follow this basic rule: make your graphic be independent of the written text by giving it a descriptive title, clear headings and labels, units of measurement, and footnotes. Readers should be able to study your graphics and see the "story" of your study. Second, draw attention to the major observations and key trends available in the data. However, do not interpret the data here or give your reactions to them.

- **Discussion:** Interpret the results by relating the data to your original questions and hypotheses, offering conclusions, and supporting each conclusion with details. Essentially, answer the question, "What does it all mean?" Explain which hypotheses were supported, and why. Also explore un-expected results, and suggest possible explanations. Conclude by reemphasizing the value of what you learned.
- **Introduction:** Once you have mapped out the methods, results, and discussion, write an introduction that creates a framework for the report. Explain why you undertook the study, provide background information and any needed definitions, and raise your key questions and/or hypotheses.
- **Summary or abstract:** If required, write a summary of your study's purpose, methods, results, and conclusions. An abstract is a one-paragraph summary that allows readers to (1) get the report in a nutshell, and (2) determine whether reading the study would be worthwhile.
- **Title:** Develop a precise title that captures the "story" of your study. Worry less about the length of the title and more about its clarity.
- **Front and end matter:** If required, add a title page, references page, and appendixes.

5. **Share and revise the draft.** Once you have roughed out the report, show it to a peer or a tutor in the writing center. Ask these questions:
   - Are the report's purpose, hypotheses, conclusions, and support clear and complete?
   - Is the traditional structure of a lab or field report followed effectively?
   - Is the voice objective, curious, and informed?

6. **Edit and proofread.** Carefully examine the style of your report, checking for these conventions of science writing:
   - **Measured use of passive voice:** generally, use passive voice only when needed—usually to keep the focus on the action and the receiver, not the actor. (See page **633.1**.)
   - **Past and present tenses of verbs:** generally, use past tense in your report. However, present tense may be appropriate when discussing published work, established theories, and your conclusions.
   - **Objectivity:** make sure that your writing is precise (not ambiguous), specific (not vague), concise (not wordy).
   - **Mechanics:** follow the conventions in the discipline with respect to capitalization, abbreviations, numbers, and symbols.

7. **Prepare and share your report.** Following the format and documentation conventions of the discipline, submit a polished report to your instructor. Also find ways to share your study with the scientific community.

Writing Checklist

Use these six traits to check your report, then revise as needed:

___ The **ideas** provide scientifically sound conclusions about accurate data.

___ The **organization** effectively follows the standard structure: introduction, methods, results, and discussion.

___ The **voice** demonstrates interest and curiosity, yet remains objective.

___ The **words** are used accurately. The language of the discipline is used precisely.

___ The **sentences** flow smoothly from point to point. Passive voice constructions are used only when necessary.

___ The **copy** is correct in terms of its format, grammar, punctuation, usage, and spelling.

Writing Activities

1. The report on hydrochloric acid describes a chemical compound. In your discipline, what are the main objects of study? Write a report that introduces that topic to students new to the discipline.

2. The lab experiment on fermentation describes careful research that should be repeatable. With appropriate supervision, repeat the lab experiment and compare results.

3. The field report objectively researches the problem of cockroach infestation. What campus or community problems could you research in a similar manner? Develop a research plan, get approval from your instructor, and complete your study.

4. What issues, problems, or puzzles exist in your area of study? With help from an instructor in your major, write a proposal to conduct a lab experiment or field research.

Special Forms
of Writing

CONTENTS

Chapter 25
Writing About Literature and the Arts

In one way or another, people respond to the arts. Audiences may applaud a dancer, gripe about a film or play, or give a standing ovation to a musician. Often writers are moved to respond even more precisely, by analyzing one actor's portrayal while criticizing another's performance, or praising the script of a film but questioning camera angles or lighting.

Because the arts are complex, writing about them requires careful listening, reading, or viewing. For example, you may analyze a film or play in terms of the acting, the casting, or the directing. Similarly, you may analyze a poem or story by looking at its form, its diction, or the insights it provides. In other words, to write effectively about the arts, you need a good ear, a keen eye, and an open mind.

This chapter includes model essays, guidelines, literary terms, and assignments to help you evaluate a variety of art forms.

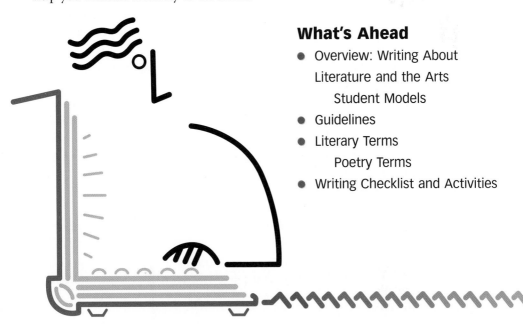

What's Ahead
- Overview: Writing About Literature and the Arts
    Student Models
- Guidelines
- Literary Terms
    Poetry Terms
- Writing Checklist and Activities

Web

Overview
Writing About Literature and the Arts

Writer's Goal

Your goal is to experience an artwork or performance, understand its elements, and then write an essay analyzing the work and perhaps evaluating it.

Keys for Success

Know your subject. ■ Read the poem, view the film or painting, or listen to the concert more than once, if necessary on tape. Be sure you understand what the artist/writer is trying to do, noting specific choices and their effects.

Analyze the work's key elements. ■ In works of fiction, for example, consider issues of point of view, plot, character, setting, and theme. (See the list of literary terms on pages **384–387** for other elements to think about.)

Compare it. ■ If this work of art reminds you of some other piece, review the second work and note similarities and differences.

Form your own insights and opinions. ■ If others have written about this work of art, do not read what they wrote until you have experienced the work yourself and developed your own insights and opinions.

Topics to Consider

Choose a piece of literature, a film, a concert, or a play that has meaning for you or has aroused your curiosity.

- **Poems:** You could choose one of thousands of great poems from literature or poetry anthologies. Poems from literary magazines, college classmates or relatives, or a Web site may also be analyzed if they merit your time and your readers' attention.

- **Short stories:** Like poems, short stories from literature anthologies, literary or popular magazines, or Web sites are easy to access.

- **Films:** While you could write about a current big-name film, consider analyzing a classic film or a film never shown in your area theaters. Choosing a film on video will enable you to replay the entire film or just specific scenes.

- **Concerts:** You could write about a major concert in your city or on campus, but consider analyzing the music played by lesser-known artists performing in student recitals or backstreet theaters.

- **Plays:** Any play may invite an analysis (big-name touring shows, for instance), but consider writing about campus productions or plays staged in your community. You might also analyze a play based on your reading of it.

Next Step Read the model essays and perform the activities that follow, noting strategies that help you understand an artwork and write about it.

Writing About Literature

In this essay, Jacqueline Williams examines a novel about the Vietnam War called *The Things They Carried* by Tim O'Brien. Williams approaches this novel (and her analysis) with some skepticism because so much has already been written about this tragic time. As you will see, she still concludes that O'Brien's book is a valuable addition to the literature about the Vietnam experience.

The Truth in Tim O'Brien's
The Things They Carried

The writer relates how the book affected her.

Unlike the traditional college student, I come to Vietnam-era movies and novels with skepticism . . . and annoyance. Having been a college sophomore when the Vietnam conflict finally ended (or at least U.S. involvement in it), I know what Vietnam was like. My husband was in the army from 1970 to 1974, and I had several friends whose brothers served in Nam. I know it was awful. I know how kids' minds were messed up by the whole ordeal, if not their bodies. Nearly 30 years have passed since the war, and I just do not want to relive or deal with it anymore. Even the title of O'Brien's novel bothered me, *The Things They Carried*, because it obviously refers to the emotional and psychological effects of Vietnam.

She describes its episodic form and some of the characters.

Those were my feelings as I began to read this book. To my surprise, by the time I had finished O'Brien's work, I had a broader and deeper understanding of how Vietnam affected those who fought in it. Although I grimaced when reading his graphic descriptions of the horrible acts committed, I knew that the author was not embellishing the story with gore or using obscenities gratuitously. O'Brien, I think, tells these stories for therapeutic purposes—his and ours: he confronts his own personal ghosts, and he forces readers to face them as well.

She shows us characters who were warped forever by the war.

The novel is actually a collection of interrelated tales about men and women who experienced Vietnam directly or indirectly. Many of the stories tell of the brutal realities of death and how soldiers meet it and deal with it. There's Ted Lavender, shot in the head after relieving himself, "zapped while zipping," as the other soldiers put it. There's Curt Lemon, blown up into a tree, remembered gruesomely by one soldier in singing the song "Lemon Tree." There's Kiowa, sucked down into a "_____ field." And there's the Vietcong soldier that the narrator himself kills. With each of these deaths, O'Brien holds back no punches—showing us the horror, tragedy, and related black humor of war.

He shows us how Vietnam changes the living. One strange story, for example, tells about Mary Anne Bell, an all-American girl smuggled into Nam by her boyfriend. In a horrifying way, she gets swallowed up by the war; in fact, this "Barbie Doll" seems to thrive on it. Another powerful change happens to Norman Bowker, who goes home eaten by guilt for

1

2

3

4

Kiowa's death. All he can do, trapped in his hometown, is drive the loop around the lake over and over . . . until he kills himself. But maybe the biggest change happens to the narrator himself. Early in the novel, we see him struggle with his draft notice. He is all idealism and innocence. By the end of the novel, we see that the war has cost him both, and that they have been replaced only by personal loss, and knowledge of his own capacity for evil.

The truth O'Brien seeks is not in the events that he details, but in the emotions, attitudes, and feelings that his stories project. The stories look at courage and fear and how the imagination helps us understand and shape the truth. The novel is an illustration of how "story truth is truer than happening truth." As a fiction writer who experienced Vietnam, O'Brien wants to confront us with the imaginative truth of it all, not just the hard facts.   5

Tim O'Brien convinced me, even when I didn't want him to. Thirty years later, Vietnam is still an important daily reality for millions of Americans, and really for the whole nation. The tales in *The Things They Carried* drive home that truth. In fact, they give the reader a "truth goose," as the narrator puts it. ■   6

> **She says O'Brien helps readers confront the hard truth of war.**

Reading for Better Writing

1. The writer opens by commenting about herself and her husband. Explain why her comments are or are not fitting.

2. The writer says that O'Brien tells us the war stories for "therapeutic purposes—his and ours." Why would veterans *and* nonveterans need "therapy" for the Vietnam War?

3. Review the details of war cited in paragraph three, as well as the writer's comment: "With each of these deaths, O'Brien . . . [shows] us the horror, tragedy, and related black humor of war." What is she implying about this book's effects on the reader?

4. Why does the reviewer conclude saying, "Tim O'Brien convinced me, even when I didn't want him to"? Do you think novelists usually try to "convince" readers? Is this statement fitting in this essay? Why?

Writing About a Poem

In the essay below, student writer David Koza analyzes "The Darkling Thrush" by Thomas Hardy.

audio

The writer introduces the poet, his poem, and its focus.

Brooding on "The Darkling Thrush"

The close of a century often brings mixed feelings. Loud celebrations   *1*
often hide a deeper sadness or fear brought on by a sense of loss. Through
imagery, rhythm, and rhyme, poems often capture these strong emotions.
One such poem is "The Darkling Thrush," written by Thomas Hardy at the
end of the nineteenth century. This poem powerfully expressed the poet's
gloomy outlook as one century dies and another is born.

He focuses on the poem's imagery.

From beginning to end, "The Darkling Thrush" is filled with dismal   *2*
natural images and dark comparisons that create the mood of pessimism.
For example, the speaker compares the world he inhabits to the dying day
and the winter season. The "weakening eye of day" is upon them, and "all
mankind that haunted nigh / Had sought their household fires" (7, 8). Day
is dying, winter has driven everyone to seek warmth, and the speaker himself is "fervourless." Even the speaker's past successes seem buried beneath
the sky:

> The land's sharp features seemed to be
>   The Century's corpse outleant,
> His crypt the cloudy canopy,
>   The wind his death-lament. (9–12)

Lines 5 and 6 tell us that "The tangled bine-stems scored the sky / Like
strings of broken lyres" (5, 6). The music of nature is dead. But lines 9–12
above show death to be pervasive; it includes the land and even the century.

He notes a startling, unexpected contrast.

Perhaps even more striking are the lines suggesting that the very soil   *3*
has lost its power to give life to seeds: "The ancient pulse of germ and
birth / Was shrunken hard and dry" (13, 14). If fertility is gone, what's
left? Nothing that Hardy can see.

But then surprise! Above him he sees a "darkling thrush" singing "a   *4*
full-hearted evensong." This bird, an "aged thrush, frail, gaunt, and small /
In blast-beruffled plume," is singing joyfully in the darkness and deadness
of the earth. The speaker is dumbfounded.

He reflects on the speaker's mood and emotions.

One might expect the speaker would change his mind—see that his   *5*
gloom was perhaps premature. But no, his gloom is too deep to be bright-
ened by this bird's cheerful song. There is no fickle mood change. Instead
the speaker concludes that the bird must know something he does not. But
though he sees no cause for caroling, there may be a wistfulness in the
speaker's wonder. He envies the bird of its joy.

The "caroling" suggests that the bird may be aware of a long-lost God   *6*
that the speaker vaguely remembers but can't recover. He is not happy to
have lost this God, nor free of a yearning for him. He is "free" only of what

the thrush seems to know: "Some blessed Hope." Thus the poem expresses a deep loss of faith that no bird's song can cure. His gloom is not from one bad day but from one lost hope. Like his contemporary Matthew Arnold in "Dover Beach," Hardy seems to be lamenting that the "Sea of Faith" is no longer full.

Two other facts deepen our sense of the poem's gloom. First, the poem was printed a couple of days before the end of the nineteenth century. Later Hardy affixed a date, December 31, 1900, to the poem. Lines 9–10 show Hardy's direct reference to the departing century: "The land's sharp features seemed to be / The Century's corpse outleant" (9, 10). Second, the meter that Hardy uses is a common meter, the meter of hymns. Writing a hymn to a dying century would seem to be a poet's duty, but a hymn is usually a song of praise. Yet the bleak landscape laid out as the corpse of the nineteenth century does not receive praise but a lament. *7*

> The closing stresses the poem's continuing power.

"The Darkling Thrush," with its dark vision of life, challenges readers to understand a bleak world. The impressions, the irony, and the questioning that this poem stirs up are probably the reason that a century later—at the close of the twentieth century—readers still feel drawn to the poem. ■ *8*

Reading for Better Writing

1. Review the opening and closing paragraphs of the essay. How do they create a framework for the writer's analysis of the poem?

2. Why does the writer focus on the poem's images and comparisons?

3. Why does he devote a full paragraph to the bird's song?

4. Why does he focus on the effect of the song on the speaker?

Writing About a Performance

In the essay below, student writer Annie Moore reviews the performance of a rock music group, Sigur Ros. She praises several qualities of their experimental music.

Sigur Ros, *Agaetis Byrjun*

The writer states the accomplishments of the group.

Sigur Ros, an experimental noise quartet hailing from Reykjavik, is the biggest thing since Bjork. Those Icelandic folk must know something we don't. Never before has a rock/pop album captured the beauty and quiet strength that pervades *Agaetis Byrjun,* the band's sophomore release. *1*

She describes the quality of their sound.

The album flows seamlessly as a single stream of consciousness. Jonsi Birgisson's ethereal vocals are divine as his falsetto effortlessly rides the sweeping melodies. Tension builds from the delicate intros, gathers fury, and then explodes in a burst of percussion and crashing guitars hammered by violin bow. The storm ends, a quiet lull follows, and then the cycle begins again. Added pianos, muted horns, and the strings of the Icelandic Symphony Orchestra give the songs of *Agaetis Byrjun* the essence of a twentieth-century classic. *2*

She describes their effect on the audience.

Although the lyrics are impossibly cryptic, written entirely in Icelandic, they are sung with an emotion and urgency so intense they are not merely perceived, but *felt.* The full force of the music resonates deep in the souls of listeners. It is exactly this "inarticulate speech of the heart" of which Van Morrison once spoke that gives *Agaetis Byrjun* its heart-wrenching sense of sincerity. *3*

With impeccable musicianship and a skillful mix of the traditional and innovative, Sigur Ros will change the world of music. Or perhaps they already have. ■ *4*

Reading for Better Writing

1. What characteristics of the vocalists does she cite? Why?

2. What other instrumental sounds does she cite?

3. Why does she tell us of the effect on the audience?

Writing About a Film

In the essay below, student writer Jennifer Berkompas explains what she likes in *The Lord of the Rings: The Fellowship of the Ring* and what she thinks her readers might like as well.

Wonder of Wonders: *The Lord of the Rings*

I have only one problem with Peter Jackson's film *The Lord of the Rings: The Fellowship of the Ring:* His elves don't laugh.

As fans of J. R. R. Tolkien's *Middle Earth* know, elves (immortal creatures) live alongside men, dwarves, hobbits, and wizards. Powerful, wise, and dignified, they also laugh musically, dance passionately, tell all-night stories, and sing of their homeland. The movie elves are powerful, wise, and dignified, and have a wry sense of humor, but they don't laugh.

The writer cites the problem.

True, there is little to laugh about in their circumstances. An evil lord is gaining power in the South, and what he needs to plunge the world into slavery has fallen into the hands of a hobbit. Hobbits are silly and sociable, like eating, but don't like excitement. The future looks grim.

> *Tolkien fans, be warned: the movie doesn't try to follow the book scene by scene or character by character.*

She notes who must solve the problem.

But this hobbit, Frodo Baggins (played by Elijah Wood) has spirit, has common sense, and knows what he must do: take the ring that will darken the whole earth back to the heart of the dark lord's kingdom, Mordor, to destroy the ring and the kingdom.

On his quest he is joined by eight other adventurers, including Aragorn, a mysterious wanderer who happens to be Gondor's long-lost king.

She alerts those who have read the book.

Tolkien fans, be warned: the movie doesn't try to follow the book scene by scene or character by character. If you are fond of Tom Bombadil or elf lord Glorfindel, you won't find them. But the movie does stay close in spirit to the books. The director read the books often to prepare for filming, reading key scenes several times as he shot them. The martial power of Numenoreans, the rustic naivete of the Shire, the peace and beauty of Rivendell and Lothlorien, the presence of evil, the persistence of good and camaraderie, the pain, the power—it's all there.

Having read the books and seen the movie four times, I recommend that you look at the movie with an open mind. Admire the halls of Moria, the bridge of Khazad-dûm, the river of Rivendell, the towering kings, the

Argonath—all incredible scenes. Enjoy what Jackson imagines a hobbit or a Numenorean or a wizard to look like.

She assures those who have not read the book.

If you haven't read the books, you can still enjoy the movie for its scenery, gripping plot, good acting, good role models, fight scenes, compelling characters, and chivalric romance and honor rarely seen today in film or life. Peter Jackson and crew capture Tolkien well.   *8*

A note of caution: Evil forces in this film are portrayed powerfully. We see war, and war is violent. Some scenes you won't want kids under ten to see.   *9*

For more information, visit <lordoftherings.net>. ■   *10*

write

Reading for Better Writing

1. What one drawback does the writer see in the film?

2. Reread what she says about Frodo Baggins, and explain how the comments do or do not support the main point of her review.

3. The writer describes what the director did to catch the spirit of Tolkien. How do these observations strengthen or weaken the review?

Guidelines
Writing About Literature and the Arts

1. **Select a topic.** Choose an art form or performance with which you are familiar or are willing to learn about. For ideas, review "Topics to Consider" on page **374**.

2. **Understand the work.** Experience it thoughtfully (two or three times, if possible), looking carefully at its content, form, and overall effect.

   - For plays and films, examine the plot, setting, characters, dialogue, lighting, costumes, sound effects, music, acting, and directing.
   - For novels and short stories, focus on point of view, plot, setting, characters, style, and theme.
   - For poems, examine diction, simile, tone, sound, figures of speech, symbolism, irony, form, and theme.
   - For music, focus on harmonic and rhythmic qualities, dynamics, melodic lines, lyrics, and interpretation.

3. **Gather information.** Take notes on what you experienced, using the list above to guide your thoughts. Seek to understand the whole work before you analyze the parts. Consider freewriting briefly on one or more aspects of the work to explore your response and dig more deeply into the work. If analyzing a written text, annotate it.

4. **Organize your thoughts.** Review the notes that you took as you analyzed the work. What key insight about the work has your analysis led you to see? Make that insight or judgment your thesis, and then order supporting points logically in a scratch or full outline.

5. **Write the first draft.**
   Opening: Use ideas like the following to gain your readers' attention, identify your topic, narrow the focus, and state your thesis:

   - Summarize your subject briefly. Include the title, the author, and the literary form or performance.
     Example: **"The Darkling Thrush," a poem written at the end of the nineteenth century, expresses Thomas Hardy's gloomy outlook.**
   - Start with a quotation from the film, story, or poem and then comment on its importance.
   - Explain the artist's purpose and how well he or she achieves it.
   - Open with a general statement about life that relates to the focus of your analysis.
     Example: **"Hardy compares the world to the dying day and winter."**

- Begin with a general statement about the literature or performance. (See page **380**.)
  Example: **"I have only one problem with Peter Jackson's film *The Lord of the Rings: The Fellowship of the Rings*: His elves don't laugh."**
- Assert your thesis. State the key insight about the work that your analysis has revealed—that is, the insight that your essay will seek to support.

Middle: Develop or support your focus by following this pattern:

- State the main points, relating them clearly to the focus of your essay.
- Support each main point with specific details or direct quotations.
- Explain how these details prove your point.

Conclusion: Tie key points together to focus your analysis. Assert your thesis or evaluation in a fresh way, leaving readers with a sense of the larger significance of your analysis.

6. **Review and revise.** Once you have a first draft written, relax for a time, and then reread your essay for its logic and completeness. Check whether you have supported each of your observations with evidence from the poem, story, film, or other artwork. Test your analysis with questions like these:

   - Did you fully understand the performance, the reasons for the acting or costuming, the lyrics of the song, or whatever is central to the work?
   - Did you explore the ironies, if present, or any important images, vocal nuances, dramatic action, or shift in setting, or symbolism?
   - Did you bring your analysis to a clear conclusion?

7. **Get feedback.** Ask a knowledgeable classmate, friend, or tutor to read your essay, looking for the following:

   ____ An analytical thesis statement supported by evidence (such as quotations)
   ____ Key insights into both content or meaning on the one hand and form or style on the other hand
   ____ Clear transitions between sentences and paragraphs
   ____ A tone that is respectful and honest

8. **Edit and proofread.** Once you have revised your appraisal, clarified your transitions, and checked your evidence, polish the phrasing and diction. Make certain your paper is free of awkward syntax or errors in usage, punctuation, spelling, or grammar. In particular, check that you have used the special terms of the literary genre or art form clearly and accurately.

9. **Publish your essay.**

   - Share your essay with friends and family.
   - Publish it in a journal or on a Web site.
   - Place a copy in your personal or professional portfolio.

Literary Terms

Your analysis of novels, poems, plays, and films will be deeper and more sophisticated if you understand the most common literary terms.

Allusion is a reference to a person, place, or event in history or literature.

Analogy is a comparison of two or more similar objects, suggesting that if they are alike in certain respects, they will probably be alike in other ways, too.

Anecdote is a short summary of an interesting or humorous, often biographical incident or event.

Antagonist is the person or thing working against the protagonist, or hero, of the work.

Climax is the turning point, an intense moment characterized by a key event.

Conflict is the problem or struggle in a story that triggers the action. There are five basic types of conflict:

Person vs. person: One character in a story is in conflict with one or more of the other characters.

Person vs. society: A character is in conflict with some element of society: the school, the law, the accepted way of doing things, and so on.

Person vs. self: A character faces conflicting inner choice.

Person vs. nature: A character is in conflict with some natural happening: a snowstorm, an avalanche, the bitter cold, or any other element of nature.

Person vs. fate: A character must battle what seems to be an uncontrollable problem. Whenever the conflict is a strange or unbelievable coincidence, it can be attributed to fate.

Denouement is the outcome of a play or story. See "**Resolution.**"

Diction is an author's choice of words based on their correctness or effectiveness.

Archaic words are old-fashioned and no longer sound natural when used, such as "I believe thee not" for "I don't believe you."

Colloquialism is an expression that is usually accepted in informal situations and certain locations, as in "He really grinds my beans."

Heightened language uses vocabulary and sentence constructions that produce a stylized effect unlike that of standard speech or writing, as in much poetry and poetic prose.

Profanity is language that shows disrespect for someone or something regarded as holy or sacred.

Slang is the everyday language used by a particular group among themselves.

Trite expressions lack depth or originality, or are overworked or not worth mentioning in the first place.

Vulgarity is language that is generally considered common, crude, gross, and, at times, offensive. It is sometimes used in fiction, plays, and films to add realism.

Exposition is the introductory section of a story or play. Typically, the setting, main characters, and themes are introduced, and the action is initiated.

Falling action is the action of a play or story that follows the climax and shows the characters dealing with the climactic event or decision.

Figure of speech is a literary device used to create a special effect or to describe something in a fresh way. The most common types are *antithesis, hyperbole, metaphor, metonymy, personification, simile,* and *understatement.*

    Antithesis is an opposition, or contrast, of ideas.

> "It was the best of times, it was the worst of times, it was the age of wisdom, it was the age of foolishness . . ." — Charles Dickens, *A Tale of Two Cities*

    Hyperbole (hi-pur´ ba-lee) is an extreme exaggeration or overstatement.

> "I have seen this river so wide it had only one bank." —Mark Twain, *Life on the Mississippi*

    Metaphor is a comparison of two unlike things in which no word of comparison (*as* or *like*) is used: "Life is a banquet."

    Metonymy (ma-ton´a-mee) is the substituting of one term for another that is closely related to it, but not a literal restatement.

> "Friends, Romans, countrymen, lend me your ears." (The request is for the *attention* of those assembled, not literally their *ears.*)

    Personification is a literary device in which the author speaks of or describes an animal, object, or idea as if it were a person: "The rock stubbornly refused to move."

    Simile is a comparison of two unlike things in which a word of comparison (*like* or *as*) is used.

> "She stood in front of the altar, shaking like a freshly caught trout." —Maya Angelou, *I Know Why the Caged Bird Sings*

    Understatement is stating an idea with restraint, often for humorous effect. Mark Twain described Aunt Polly as being "prejudiced against snakes." Because she hated snakes, this way of saying so is *understatement.*

Genre refers to a category or type of literature based on its style, form, and content. The mystery novel is a literary *genre.*

Imagery refers to the words or phrases that a writer selects to appeal to the reader's senses.

> "The sky was dark and gloomy, the air was damp and raw, the streets were wet and sloppy." —Charles Dickens, *The Pickwick Papers*

Irony is a deliberate discrepancy in meaning or in the way something is understood. There are three kinds of irony:

    Dramatic irony, in which the reader or the audience sees a character's mistakes or misunderstandings, but the character does not.

    Verbal irony, in which the writer says one thing and means another ("The best substitute for experience is being sixteen").

    Irony of situation, in which there is a great difference between the purpose of a particular action and the result.

Mood is the feeling that a piece of literature arouses in the reader: *happiness, sadness, peacefulness, anxiety,* and so forth.

Paradox is a statement that seems contrary to common sense yet may, in fact, be true: "The coach considered this a good loss."

Plot is the action or sequence of events in a story. It is usually a series of related incidents that build upon one another as the story develops. There are five basic elements in a plot line: *exposition, rising action, climax, falling action,* and *resolution.*

Point of view is the vantage point from which the story unfolds.
In the **first-person** point of view, the story is told by one of the characters: "I stepped into the darkened room and felt myself go cold."
In the **third-person** point of view, the story is told by someone outside the story: "He stepped into the darkened room and felt himself go cold."
Third-person narrations can be *omniscient,* meaning that the narrator has access to the thoughts of all the characters, or *limited,* meaning that the narrator focuses on the inner life of one central character.

Protagonist is the main character or hero of the story.

Resolution (or denouement) is the portion of the play or story in which the problem is solved. It comes after the climax and falling action and is intended to bring the story to a satisfactory end.

Rising action is the series of conflicts or struggles that build a story or play toward a climax.

Satire is a literary tone used to ridicule or make fun of human vice or weakness, often with the intent of correcting, or changing, the subject of the satiric attack.

Setting is the time and place in which the action of a literary work occurs.

Structure is the form or organization that a writer uses for her or his literary work. A great number of possible forms are used regularly in literature: parable, fable, romance, satire, farce, slapstick, and so on.

Style refers to how the author uses words, phrases, and sentences to form his or her ideas. Style is also thought of as the qualities and characteristics that distinguish one writer's work from the work of others.

Symbol is a person, place, thing, or event used to represent something else. For example, the dove is a symbol of peace.

Theme is the statement about life that a particular work shares with readers. In stories written for children, the theme is often spelled out clearly at the end. In more complex literature, the theme will often be more complex and will be implied, not stated.

Tone is the overall feeling, or effect, created by a writer's use of words. This feeling may be serious, mock-serious, humorous, satiric, and so on.

Poetry Terms

Alliteration is the repetition of initial consonant sounds in words such as "rough and ready." An example of alliteration is underlined below:

"Our gang paces the pier like an old myth . . ."

—Anne-Marie Oomen, "Runaway Warning"

Assonance is repetition of vowel sounds without repetition of consonants.

"My words like silent rain drops fell . . ." —Paul Simon, "Sounds of Silence"

Blank verse is an unrhymed form of poetry. Each line normally consists of ten syllables in which every other syllable, beginning with the second, is stressed. As blank verse is often used in very long poems, it may depart from the strict pattern from time to time.

Consonance is the repetition of consonant sounds. Although it is similar to alliteration, consonance is not limited to the first letters of words:

" . . . and high school girls with clear skin smiles . . . "

—Janis Ian, "At Seventeen"

Foot is the smallest repeated pattern of stressed and unstressed syllables in a poetic line. (See "**Verse**.")

Iambic: an unstressed followed by a stressed syllable (re-peat´)
Anapestic: two unstressed followed by a stressed syllable (in-ter-rupt´)
Trochaic: a stressed followed by an unstressed syllable (old´-er)
Dactylic: a stressed followed by two unstressed syllables (o´-pen-ly)
Spondaic: two stressed syllables (heart´-break´)
Pyrrhic: two unstressed syllables (Pyrrhic seldom appears by itself.)

Onomatopoeia is the use of a word whose sound suggests its meaning, as in *clang, buzz,* and *twang.*

Refrain is the repetition of a line or phrase of a poem at regular intervals, especially at the end of each stanza. A song's refrain may be called the *chorus.*

Rhythm is the ordered or free occurrences of sound in poetry. Ordered or regular rhythm is called *meter.* Free occurrence of sound is called *free verse.*

Stanza is a division of poetry named for the number of lines it contains:

Couplet: two-line stanza   **Sestet:** six-line stanza
Triplet: three-line stanza   **Septet:** seven-line stanza
Quatrain: four-line stanza   **Octave:** eight-line stanza
Quintet: five-line stanza

Verse is a metric line of poetry. It is named according to the kind and number of feet composing it: *iambic pentameter, anapestic tetrameter,* and so on. (See "**Foot**.")

Monometer: one foot   **Pentameter:** five feet
Dimeter: two feet   **Hexameter:** six feet
Trimeter: three feet   **Heptameter:** seven feet
Tetrameter: four feet   **Octometer:** eight feet

Writing Checklist

Use these six traits to check your writing, then revise as needed:

____ The **ideas** offer insight into what the literature or art means and how it communicates.

____ The **organization** of the essay flows logically and provides an easy-to-follow pattern.

____ The **voice** is positive, confident, objective, and sensitive to opposing viewpoints. The tone fits the literature or art being discussed.

____ The **words** are precise and effectively defined.

____ The **sentences** read smoothly, with effective variations and logical transitions.

____ The **copy** follows rules of grammar, format, and documentation.

write

Writing Activities

1. In his essay on "The Darkling Thrush," the writer cites the mood of the poem and the images that create the mood. Find a poem in which mood or tone is essential to the overall meaning or impact. Write an essay describing how images or words work to make the poem effective.

2. Jennifer Berkompas reviews the film *The Lord of the Rings: The Fellowship of the Rings,* which, she notes, does "stay close in spirit to the book." Write an essay about a movie based on a book. Explain how it does or does not "stay close in spirit to the book" upon which it is based.

3. Attend a concert. Respond to the style of the music, to the performance of the singer or group, and to the content of the lyrics. Note also the age of the audience, its response, and the way in which the performance is or is not affected by that response. Explain your own response as well.

4. Visit an art gallery. Find an exhibit that engages you. Explain what in this exhibit you find appealing or intriguing. Also explain what value this exhibit might have to society or to you personally, and why.

Chapter 26
Writing Across the Curriculum

In college, instructors in nearly all departments assign writing. Why? Because they know that writing helps you in two ways: (1) to learn course content, and (2) to learn how to carry on a written dialogue with others in your field. In other words, writing enables you to learn course material today, but also prepares you to succeed in the future. The purpose of this chapter is to show you three things about writing across the curriculum:

- What kinds of writing you can expect to do in all courses
- Where to find information in this book that will help you do this writing
- How writing skills required in one class are linked to skills required in another

What's Ahead
- Three Curricular Divisions
- Types of Writing in Each Division
- Traits of Writing Across the Curriculum
- Preparing to Write Well
- Writing Activities

Three Curricular Divisions

Based on each department's area of study and focus, the college curriculum is generally divided into three groups: Humanities, Social Sciences, and Natural and Applied Sciences. These groups are then subdivided into specific departments, such as Biology, Chemistry, and Physics. Below you will find an explanation of each division, along with its more common departments.

Humanities

Scholars within this division study human culture, both past and present. They examine topics such as the history of civilization, cultural trends and institutions, religious beliefs and practices, languages and their use, and artwork and performance skills. Some departments within this division include the following:

• Art	• Film Studies	• Philosophy	• Theology
• Dance	• Graphic Design	• Photography	• Women's Studies
• English	• History	• Religion	• World Languages
• Ethnic Studies	• Music	• Theater Arts	

Social Sciences

Scholars in this division study human behavior and societies using research strategies adapted from the natural sciences. For example, a researcher may develop a hypothesis regarding a topic or phenomenon, and then devise an experiment to test that hypothesis. Students study topics such as economic systems, correctional programs, and personality disorders. Departments in this division include the following:

• Anthropology	• Economics	• Geophysics	• Psychology
• Business	• Education	• Government	• Social Work
• Communication	• Genetics	• Physical Education	• Sociology
• Criminology	• Geography	• Political Science	• Urban Planning

Natural and Applied Sciences

The natural sciences (such as biology, zoology, and chemistry) focus on specific aspects of nature such as animal life, plant life, and molecular structures. In contrast, the applied sciences (such as mathematics, computer science, and engineering) consider how to use scientifically based information or practices to understand concepts and develop ideas. Here are some of the departments in this division:

• Agriculture	• Biology	• Environment	• Physics
• Agronomy	• Botany	• Forestry	• Physiology
• Anatomy	• Chemistry	• Mathematics	• Public Health
• Architecture	• Computer Science	• Nutrition	• Space Science
• Astronomy	• Engineering	• Oceanography	• Zoology

Types of Writing in Each Division

Listed below are the types of writing commonly assigned in the three academic divisions. Often instructors in different divisions will assign the same type of essay—but with a different purpose or focus. When an assigned form differs from the one shown in the book, adapt the guidelines in the book to the form stated in the assignment.

Humanities

Arguing Against a Claim (302–303)

Cause and Effect (190–191)

Classification (216–217)

College Essay (127–129)

Comparison (198–199)

Definition (239–240)

Description of a Place (168–169)

Essay Test (401–403)

Interview Report (352–353)

Observation Report (340–341)

Personal Narrative (138–139, 140–142)

Personal Reflection (151–152)

Persuading Readers to Act (290–293)

Explaining a Process (226–227)

Proposing a Solution (317–319)

Research Paper (525–534)

Taking a Position (272–273)

Writing About a Performance (379)

Social Sciences

Arguing Against a Claim (307–309)

Cause and Effect (190–191)

Classification (211–212)

Comparison and Contrast (200–201)

Definition (237–238)

Description of a Place (170–171)

Essay Test (401-403)

Field Report (365–367)

Interview Report (347–348)

Observation Report (337–339)

Personal Reflection (153–155, 156–159)

Persuasive Action (285–286)

Describing a Process (223–225)

Proposing a Solution (317–319)

Research Paper (555–566)

Taking a Position (272–273)

Natural and Applied Sciences

Arguing Against a Claim (304–306)

Cause and Effect (185–189)

Classification (213–215)

Comparison (197)

Definition (241–243)

Description (174–177)

Essay Test (401–403)

Experiment Report (361–364)

Field Report (365–367)

Lab Report (359–360)

Observation Report (335–336)

Persuasive Action (285–286)

Describing a Process (223–225, 230–231)

Proposing a Solution (320–322, 323–327)

Research Paper (555–566)

Taking a Position (274–275)

Traits of Writing Across the Curriculum

Below are listed the more common writing tasks in each of the three divisions, along with six traits that distinguish good writing for each task. Compare and contrast the traits of writing tasks within a division, and between divisions.

Humanities

Idea: **Personal writing:** explores the writer's ideas, experiences, and feelings.
Organization: Narratives—usually chronological; others follow varied patterns.
Voice: Narratives—engaging, fits the story; others—honest, reflective, direct.
Sentences: Narratives—appropriate for dialogue and description; others use varied forms.
Word Choice: Words are precise and fit the writer's topic, purpose, audience, and characters.
Correctness: Documentation and format follow MLA style.

Idea: **Analyze a work of art:** describes the work and analyzes its quality.
Organization: Appropriate for the artwork and the writer's focus.
Voice: Honest appraisal and analysis, supported by evidence.
Sentences: Varied in length and structure, with clear transitions.
Word Choice: Appropriate for the art form; technical terms explained in the text.
Correctness: Documentation and format follow MLA style.

Idea: **Argue a point:** persuades reader regarding the point's meaning and context.
Organization: Order fits the topic and purpose: cause/effect, compare/contrast, and so on.
Voice: Informed, impartial, inviting.
Sentences: Tend to be longer; complexity fits the topic, discipline, and audience.
Word Choice: Precise, often including scholarly terms used in the discipline.
Correctness: Documentation and format follow MLA style.

Idea: **Analyze a phenomenon:** explains its meaning in relation to its historical context.
Organization: Often combines cause/effect, compare/contrast, and examples.
Voice: Scholarly, fair, informed, balanced.
Sentences: Tend to be longer; complexity fits the topic, discipline, and audience.
Word Choice: Precise, often including scholarly terms used in the discipline.
Correctness: Documentation and format follow MLA style.

Social Sciences

Idea: **Case study:** describes and analyzes the topic, identifies methodology, gives results.
Organization: Gives overview, presents steps chronologically, analyzes outcome.
Voice: Impartial reporting; respectful, thoughtful analysis.
Sentences: Medium-length sentences with clear structures and transitions.
Word Choice: Statistical and discipline-related terms; precise, nonpejorative words.
Correctness: Documentation and format follow APA style.

Idea: **Literature review:** summarizes literature on a topic and evaluates the literature.
Organization: Each article discussed separately followed by conclusions.
Voice: Unbiased reporting, formal tone, logical analysis.
Sentences: Shorter sentences and paragraphs with clear transitions.
Word Choice: Includes technical terms and statistics; precise, nonpejorative words.
Correctness: Documentation and format follow APA style.

      Idea: **Analyze a policy or project:** analyzes the topic, its history, and its effects.
Organization: Analysis often uses cause/effect, classification, and compare/contrast.
     Voice: Impartial, informed, concerned, thoughtful.
   Sentences: Sentences are varied in length and structure, with clear transitions.
Word Choice: Includes technical terms and statistics; words are clear, descriptive, and precise.
Correctness: Documentation and format follow APA style.

      Idea: **Describe a process:** describes materials, steps in the process, and its importance.
Organization: Usually states topic and outcome, gives steps chronologically, closes.
     Voice: Experienced, objective, concerned about effectiveness and safety.
   Sentences: Description of a process—sentences vary in form; instructions—short, direct.
Word Choice: Precise, often including technical terms associated with the process.
Correctness: Description follows APA style; instructions follow a workplace form.

Natural and Applied Sciences

      Idea: **Lab or experiment report:** includes clear data, logical analysis, unbiased reporting.
Organization: States problem, methods with procedure, results with data, discussion.
     Voice: Interested, curious, impartial, logical, meticulous.
   Sentences: Medium length, smooth, logical, passive voice only when needed.
Word Choice: Precise, often including scientific and technical terms.
Correctness: Documentation and format follow CBE or APA style.

      Idea: **Field report:** includes clear data and unbiased interpretation and reporting.
Organization: States problem, methods with procedure, results with data, discussion.
     Voice: Interested, curious, logical, meticulous.
   Sentences: Medium length, smooth, logical, passive voice only when needed.
Word Choice: Precise, often including scientific and technical terms.
Correctness: Documentation and format follow CBE or APA style.

      Idea: **Literature review:** summarizes literature on a topic and evaluates the literature.
Organization: Each article discussed separately, followed by conclusions.
     Voice: Equitable reporting, formal tone, logical, clear analysis.
   Sentences: Shorter sentences and paragraphs with clear transitions.
Word Choice: Includes technical scientific terms and concepts; first person rarely used.
Correctness: Documentation and format follow CBE or APA style.

      Idea: **Explain a process:** describes materials, steps in process, and its importance.
Organization: Usually states topic, gives steps chronologically, closes.
     Voice: Experienced, impartial, concerned about effectiveness and safety.
   Sentences: Description of a process—sentences vary in form; instructions—short, direct.
Word Choice: Precise, often including scientific and technical terms.
Correctness: Description follows CBE or APA style; instructions follow a workplace form.

MLA Modern Language Association <www.mla.org>
APA American Psychological Association <www.apa.org>
CMS Chicago Manual of Style <www.press.uchicago.edu>
CBE Council of Biology Editors <www.cbe.org>

Note: The Council of Biology Editors was recently renamed the Council of Science Editors <councilscienceeditors.org>.

Preparing to Write Well

While learning to write well in any discipline is challenging, the task can be made easier if you follow these five guidelines:

1. Study the literature in your field. Your assignments will require that you read textbooks, journals, reference works, and Web documents. As you read, study the content—but also study the writing itself by asking questions like these:

- **Idea:** What topics do the writers address? What do they consider a strong idea, and why? How do they state their theses and support them? What kinds of research do they use, and how do they use it?

- **Organization:** How do writers introduce topics and project where the writing is headed? How do they signal shifts in focus or topics? How do they shape openings, middles, and closings?

- **Voice:** How do writers treat their topics, the writing task, and their readers? Does the writing feel inviting, impartial, and informed?

- **Sentence fluency:** Are the sentences long or short, simple or complex? Which sentences are clearest, and why? How are sentences linked?

- **Word choice:** Are the writers' words formal or informal, common or scholarly, general or technical? How do writers clarify or define words?

- **Correctness:** How do writers format and document their writing (MLA, APA, and so on)? How do they indicate quotations, use tables, or list sources?

2. Develop your professional vocabulary. As you read and listen, list key terms related to your field of study in a notebook, review them periodically, and use them in appropriate conversations and writing.

3. Test your writing. Whenever possible, share your writing and get feedback. Use your writing center and peer editors, and publish your writing.

4. Take shortcuts. All the guidelines, models, checklists, and tips in this book are shortcuts to good writing. Use them to save work and time.

5. Trust the writing process. Work through the steps of prewriting, drafting, revising, editing, and proofreading. This process will help you write well.

Writing Activities

1. Choose a current reading assignment and analyze the writer's strategies by answering the questions under #1 above.

2. Choose a current writing assignment and find a listing in "Types of Writing in Each Division" (page **391**) that resembles your assignment. Find relevant models, guidelines, and tips to help you complete the work.

3. Read "Traits of Writing Across the Curriculum" (pages **392–393**) and find two assignments that you must do this semester. Identify similarities among those assignments, and list ways in which work on one could help you with another assignment.

Chapter 27
Taking Essay Tests

audio

There is nothing more disheartening than sitting down to take a test for which you're not prepared. The results are predictable—and they're not pretty. Conversely, there is nothing more exhilarating than walking out of a classroom after nailing a test. This is especially true in a college setting, where tests count for so much and second chances and extra credit are rare.

Many of the skills in writing that you've already developed should serve you well in writing essay tests. Read the instructions for an essay test carefully, and you'll find requests for describing, analyzing, classifying, persuading, and more.

This chapter will help you write better essay answers. As a bonus, it shows a variety of other helpful ways to improve your test-taking skills.

What's Ahead

- Reviewing for Tests
- Forming a Study Group
- Mnemonics and Other Memory Guides
- Taking the Essay Test
- Taking an Objective Test

Reviewing for Tests

Do you consider yourself a "bad" test taker? Do you know the material, yet somehow perform poorly on tests? Do you feel overwhelmed by all the information you have to cover when studying for a test? Does even the thought of studying so much material make you nervous? What you need is a positive mental attitude—and good study habits. Together they can make the difference between "spacing" during a test and "acing" an exam.

Daily Reviews

Why Daily? Begin your reviews on the first day of class; if you miss a day, dust yourself off and start over again. Daily reviews are especially good because you tend to forget new information rapidly. Reviewing while the material is fresh in your mind helps to move it from your short-term memory into your long-term memory.

How Much Time? Even 5–10 minutes before or after each class will pay big dividends. Depending on the day's class, you may read through (or talk through) your notes, look over the headings in a reading assignment, skim any summaries you have, or put information into graphic organizers.

What To Do

- Put "Daily review of . . ." on your "To Do" list, calendar, or date book.
- Use the buddy system. Make a pact with a classmate and review together.
- Put your subconscious to work by reviewing material before you go to sleep.

Weekly Reviews

Why Weekly? More than anything else, repetition helps anchor memory. You can cram a lot of data into your brain the night before an exam, but a day or two later you won't remember much of anything. And when final exam time comes, you'll have to learn the material all over again.

How Much Time? Plan to spend about one hour per week for each class. (This review can either take place by yourself or with a study group.) Remember that repetition is the single most important factor in learning anything.

What To Do

- Make mind maps and flash cards of important information.
- Practice answering review questions by saying them out loud and by writing out short answers.
- Test your understanding of a subject by teaching or explaining it to someone else.
- Create mnemonics. (See page **398**.)
- Organize a study group. (See page **397**.)

Forming a Study Group

A study group can keep you interested in a subject, force you to keep up with classwork, and increase your retention of study material. Group energy can be more powerful than individual energy. You will hear other points of view and other ways to approach a subject that you may never have thought of on your own. If you use a chat room, you can meet with others via a computer. To get started, follow these guidelines.

1. Find five to six people.
- Consider people who seem highly motivated and collaborative.
- Ask your instructor to inform the class about the opportunity.

2. Consider a chat room.
- Check first with your instructor and student services about the availability of chat rooms on your campus.
- Go to any search engine (Yahoo!, Google, Excite, Internet Explorer) and enter the term "chat room." For example, Yahoo! provides both private and public chat rooms ("clubs") free of charge.
- Follow the guidelines below for forming a study group.

3. Arrange a time and place.
- Plan one session. (It may become obvious at the first meeting that your group won't work out.)
- Agree on a time limit for the initial session.
- Choose somebody in the group to keep everyone on task (or rotate this duty) and agree to accept any prodding and nudging with good humor.

4. Set realistic goals and decide on a plan of action.
- Discuss what the group needs to accomplish and what your goals are.
- Agree to practice "people skills" (listening, observing, cooperating, responding, and clarifying).
- Decide which part of the course work you will review (lectures? labs? texts? exam questions?).

5. Evaluate at the end of the first session.
- Honestly and tactfully discuss any problems that arose.
- Ask who wants to continue.
- Choose a time (and place) for your next session.
- Determine an agenda for the next session.
- Exchange necessary information such as phone numbers, e-mail addresses, chat room passwords, and so forth.

Mnemonics and Other Memory Guides

Mnemonics is the art of improving memory by using key words, formulas, or other aids to create "file tabs" in your brain that help you pull out hard-to-remember information.

Acronyms ◆ Use the first letter in each word to form a new word. Everyone learns a few acronyms during their school years, but feel free to make up your own.

➤ HOMES (the Great Lakes—Huron, Ontario, Michigan, Erie, Superior)

Acrostics ◆ Form a phrase or silly sentence in which the first letter of each word helps you remember the items in a series.

➤ **Z**oe **C**ooks **C**howder **I**n **P**ink **P**ots **I**n **M**iami. (essential minerals—**z**inc, **c**alcium, **c**hromium, **i**ron, **p**otassium, **p**hosphorus, **i**odine, **m**agnesium)

Categories ◆ Organize your information into categories for easier recall.

➤ Types of joints in body (immovable, slightly movable, freely movable)

Peg Words ◆ Create a chain of associations with objects in a room, a sequence of events, or a pattern with which you are familiar (such as the positions on a baseball diamond).

➤ To remember a sequence of Civil War battles, you might "peg" them to the positions on a baseball field—for example, Shiloh to home plate (think of the "high" and "low" balls); the Battle of Bull Run to the pitcher's mound (think of the pitcher's battle for no runs); and so on.

Rhymes ◆ Make up rhymes or puns.

➤ *Brown* v. *Board of Education* / ended public-school segregation.

---

tips TO IMPROVE YOUR MEMORY

- **Intend to remember.** Scientists say that our brains never forget anything: It's our recall that is at fault. Who forgets that they have tickets to a concert? We remember the things that are important to us.

- **Link new information** to things you already know.

- **Organize your material.** Understand the big picture and then divide the information you need to know into smaller, more manageable categories.

- **Review new material as soon as possible.** The sooner you review, the more likely you'll remember.

Taking the Essay Test

Your teachers expect you to include all the right information, and they expect you to organize it in a clear, well-thought-out way. In addition, they expect you to evaluate, synthesize, predict, analyze, and write a worthwhile answer.

Key Words

Key words help you define your task. Pay special attention to them when you read questions. Key words tell you how to present all the information needed to write an essay answer.

Following is a list of key terms, along with a definition and an example of how each is used. Studying these terms carefully is the first step in writing worthwhile answers to essay questions.

Analyze ◆ To analyze is to break down a problem or situation into separate parts of relationships.

➤ Analyze the major difficulties found at urban housing projects.

Classify ◆ To classify is to place persons or things (especially animals and plants) together in a group because they share similar characteristics. Science uses a special classification or group order: phylum, class, order, family, genus, species, and variety.

➤ Classify three kinds of trees found in the rainforests of Costa Rica.

Compare ◆ To compare is to use examples to show how things are similar and different, placing the greater emphasis on similarities.

➤ Compare the vegetation in the rainforests of Puerto Rico with the vegetation in the rainforests of Costa Rica.

Contrast ◆ To contrast is to use examples to show how things are different in one or more important ways.

➤ Contrast the views of George Washington and Harry S. Truman regarding the involvement of the United States in world affairs.

Compare and contrast ◆ To compare and contrast is to use examples that show the major similarities and differences between two things (or people, events, ideas, and so forth). In other words, two things are used to clarify each other.

➤ Compare and contrast people-centered leadership with task-centered leadership.

Define ◆ To define is to give the meaning for a term. Generally, it involves identifying the class to which a term belongs and telling how it differs from other things in that class.

➤ Define the term "emotional intelligence" as it pertains to humans.

Describe ◆ To describe is to give a detailed sketch or impression of a topic.
- Describe how the Euro tunnel (the Chunnel) was built.

Diagram ◆ To diagram is to explain with lines or pictures—a flowchart, a map, or other graphic device. Generally, a diagram will label the important points or parts.
- Diagram the parts of a DNA molecule.

Discuss ◆ To discuss is to review an issue from all sides. A discussion answer must be carefully organized to stay on track.
- Discuss how Rosa Parks's refusal to move to the back of the bus affected the civil rights movement.

Evaluate ◆ To evaluate is to make a value judgment by giving the pluses and minuses along with supporting evidence.
- Evaluate the efforts of mid-sized cities to improve public transportation services.

Explain ◆ To explain is to bring out into the open, to make clear, and to analyze. This term is similar to *discuss* but places more emphasis on cause/effect relationships or step-by-step sequences.
- Explain the effects of global warming on a coastal city like New Orleans.

Justify ◆ To justify is to tell why a position or point of view is good or right. A justification should be mostly positive—that is, the advantages are stressed over the disadvantages.
- Justify the use of antilock brakes in automobiles.

Outline ◆ To outline is to organize a set of facts or ideas by listing main points and subpoints. A good outline shows at a glance how topics or ideas fit together or relate to one another.
- Outline the events that caused the United States to enter World War II.

Prove ◆ To prove is to bring out the truth by giving evidence to back up a point.
- Prove that Atticus Finch in *To Kill a Mockingbird* provided an adequate defense for his client.

Review ◆ To review is to reexamine or to summarize the key characteristics or major points of the topic. Generally speaking, a review presents material in the order in which it happened or in decreasing order of importance.
- Review the events since 1976 that have led to the current hip-hop culture.

State ◆ To state is to present a concise statement of a position, fact, or point of view.
- State your reasons for voting in the last national election.

Summarize ◆ To summarize is to present the main points of an issue in a shortened form. Details, illustrations, and examples are usually omitted.
- Summarize the primary responsibilities of a school in a democracy.

Trace ◆ To trace is to present—in a step-by-step sequence—a series of facts that are somehow related. Usually the facts are presented in chronological order.
- Trace the events that led to the fall of the United Soviet Socialist Republic.

Planning and Writing the Essay-Test Answer

In addition to a basic understanding of the key words, you must understand the process of writing the essay answer.

1. **Reread the question several times.** (Pay special attention to any key words used in the question.)

2. **Rephrase the question into a topic sentence/thesis statement** with a clear point.

> *Question:* **Explain why public housing was built in Chicago in the 1960s.**

> *Thesis statement:* **Public housing was built in Chicago because of the Great Migration, the name given to the movement of African Americans from the South to the North.**

3. **Outline the main points you plan to cover in your answer.** Time will probably not allow you to include all supporting details in your outline.

4. **Write your essay (or paragraph).** Begin with your thesis statement (or topic sentence). Add whatever background information may be needed, and then follow your outline, writing as clearly as possible.

ONE-PARAGRAPH ANSWER

If you feel that only one paragraph is needed to answer the question, use the main points of your outline as supporting details for your thesis statement.

> *Question:* **Explain why public housing was built in Chicago in the 1960s.**

Topic sentence ------ Public housing was built in Chicago because of the Great Migration, the name given to the movement of African Americans from the South to the North. The mechanical cotton picker, introduced in the 1920s, replaced field hands in the cotton fields of the South. At that time Chicago's factories and stockyards were hiring workers. In addition, Jim Crow laws caused hardships and provided reasons for African Americans to move north. Finally, some African Americans had family and relatives in Chicago who had migrated earlier and who, it was thought, could provide a home base

Supporting details for the new migrants until they could get work and housing. According to the U.S. Census Reports, there were 109,000 African Americans in Chicago in 1920. By 1960, there were more than 800,000. However, this increase in population could have been handled except that the public wanted to keep the African Americans in the Black Belt, an area in South Chicago. Reluctant lending agencies and realtors made it possible for speculators to

Conclusion operate. Speculators increased the cost of houses by 75 percent. All of these factors led to a housing shortage for African Americans, which public housing filled.

MULTI-PARAGRAPH ANSWER

If the question is too complex to be handled in one paragraph, your opening paragraph should include your thesis statement and any essential background information. Begin your second paragraph by rephrasing one of the main points from your outline into a suitable topic sentence. Support this topic sentence with examples, reasons, or other appropriate details. Handle additional paragraphs in the same manner. If time permits, add a summary or concluding paragraph to bring all of your thoughts to a logical close.

Question: **Explain the advantages and disadvantages of wind energy.**
Thesis: **Wind energy has an equal number of advantages and disadvantages.**

Outline
I. Advantages of wind energy
   A. Renewable
   B. Economical
   C. Nonpolluting
II. Disadvantages of wind energy
   A. Intermittent
   B. Unsightly
   C. A danger to some wildlife

The introductory paragraph sets up the essay's organization.

1   Wind energy has an equal number of advantages and disadvantages. It is renewable, economical, and nonpolluting; but it is also intermittent, unsightly, and a danger to the bird population.

2   Wind energy is renewable. No matter how much wind energy is used today, there will still be a supply tomorrow. As evidence indicates that wind energy was used to propel boats along the Nile River about 5000 B.C.E., it can be said that wind is an eternal, renewable resource.

3   Wind energy is economical. The fuel (wind) is free, but the initial cost for wind turbines is higher than for fossil-fueled generators. However, wind energy costs do not include fuel purchases and only minimal operating expenses. Wind power reduces the amount of foreign oil the United States imports and reduces health and environmental costs caused by pollution. Is it possible to sell excess power? The Public Utilities Regulatory Policy Act of 1978 (PURPA) states that a local electric company must buy any excess power produced by a qualifying individual. This act encourages the use of wind power.

Each paragraph follows a point in the outline.

4   Wind energy does not pollute. Whether one wind turbine is used by an individual or a wind farm supplies energy to many people, no air pollutants or greenhouse gases are emitted. California reports that 2.5 billion pounds

of carbon dioxide and 15 million pounds of other pollutants have *not* entered the air thanks to wind energy.

How unfortunate is it that wind energy is intermittent? If a wind does   *5* not blow, there is little or no electrical power. One way to resolve this dilemma is to store the energy that wind produces in batteries. The word *intermittent* also refers to the fact that wind power is not always available at the places where it is most needed. Often the sites that offer the greatest winds are located in remote locations far from the cities that demand great electrical power.

Specific details explain the main point.

Are wind turbines unsightly? A home-sized wind machine rises about   *6* 30 feet with rotors between 8 and 25 feet in diameter. The largest machine in Hawaii stands about 20 stories high with rotors a little longer than the length of a football field. It supplies electricity to 1,400 homes. Does a single wind turbine upset the aesthetics of a community as much as a wind farm? The old adage "Beauty is in the eye of the beholder" holds up wherever wind turbines rotate. If ongoing electrical costs are almost nil, that wind turbine may look beautiful.

Questions help the reader understand the issue.

How serious is the issue of bird safety? The main questions are: *7* (1) Why do birds come near wind turbines? (2) What, if any, are the effects of wind development on bird populations? (3) What can be done to lessen the problem? If even one bird of a protected species is killed, the Endangered Species Act has been violated. If wind turbines kill migratory birds, the Migratory Bird Treaty Act has been violated. As a result, many countries and agencies are studying the problem carefully.

The ending makes a final conclusion.

The advantages of wind energy seem to outweigh the disadvantages.   *8* The wind energy industry has been growing steadily in the United States and around the world. The new wind turbines are reliable and efficient. People's attitudes toward wind energy are mostly positive. Many manufacturers and government agencies are now cooperating to expand wind energy, making it the fastest-growing source of electricity in the world. ∎

write

Reading for Better Writing

1. How does the writer provide a clear focus and logical organization in the essay answer? How soon are the focus and organization provided? What advantages does this approach offer the writer? The reader?

2. How do the sentences used to introduce the advantages differ from the sentences used to introduce the disadvantages? How does this technique aid the reader?

3. Why must the paragraphs in the body contain specific facts and examples? What facts and examples does this writer use?

Taking the Essay Test

QUICK GUIDE

■ **Make sure you are ready for the test both mentally and physically.**

■ **Listen to or carefully read the instructions.**
  - How much time do you have to complete the test?
  - Do all the essay questions count equally?
  - Can you use any aids, such as a dictionary or handbook?
  - Are there any corrections, changes, or additions to the test?

■ **Begin the test immediately and watch the time.** Don't spend so much time answering one question that you run out of time before answering the others.

■ **Read all the essay questions carefully,** paying special attention to the key words. (See pages **399–400**.)

■ **Ask the instructor for clarification** if you don't understand something.

■ **Rephrase each question into a controlling idea for your essay answer.** (This idea becomes your thesis statement.)

■ **Think before you write.** Jot down all the important information and work it into a brief outline. Do this on the back of the test sheet or on a piece of scrap paper.

■ **Use a logical pattern of organization and a strong topic sentence for each paragraph.** Tie your points together with clear, logical transitions.

■ **Write concisely.** Don't, however, use abbreviations or nonstandard language.

■ **Be efficient.** Write about those areas of the subject of which you are most certain first; then work on other areas as time permits.

■ **Keep your test paper neat and use reasonable margins.** Neatness is always important, and readability is a must, especially on an essay exam.

■ **Revise and proofread.** Read through your essay as carefully and completely as time permits.

Taking an Objective Test

Even though objective tests are generally straightforward and clear, following some tips can help you avoid making any foolish mistakes.

True/False Test

- Read the entire question before answering. Often the first half of a statement will be true or false, while the second half is just the opposite. For an answer to be true, the entire statement must be true.
- Read each word and number. Pay special attention to names, dates, and numbers that are similar and could easily be confused.
- Beware of true/false statements that contain words like *all, every, always,* and *never.* Very often these statements will be false.
- Watch for statements that contain more than one negative word. Remember: Two negatives make a positive. (*Example:* It is unlikely ice will not melt when the temperature rises above 32 degrees F.)

Matching Test

- Read through both lists quickly before you begin answering. Note any descriptions that are similar and pay special attention to the differences.
- When matching a word to a word, determine the part of speech of each word. If the word is a verb, for example, match it with another verb.
- When matching a word to a phrase, read the phrase first and look for the word it describes.
- Cross out each answer as you find it—unless you are told that the answer can be used more than once.
- Use capital letters rather than lowercase letters because they are less likely to be misread by the person correcting the test.

Multiple-Choice Test

- Read the directions to determine whether you are looking for the correct answer or the best answer. Also, check whether some questions can have two (or more) correct answers.
- Read the first part of the question, looking for negative words like *not, never, except,* and *unless.*
- Try to answer the question in your mind before looking at the choices.
- Read all the choices before selecting your answer. This step is especially important on tests in which you must select the best answer, or on tests where one of your choices is a combination of two or more answers. (*Example:* d. Both a and b / e. All of the above / f. None of the above)

tips FOR COPING WITH TEST ANXIETY

You might consider the following advice:

■ **Study smart**. Use a variety of study and memory techniques to help you see your coursework from several different angles.

■ **Review with others.** Join a study group and prepare with them. Also, ask a classmate or family member to put you to the test.

■ **Prepare yourself both physically and mentally.** Get a good night's sleep and eat a healthful, light meal before the test (doughnuts and coffee are not a healthful, light meal).

■ **Get some exercise.** Aerobic exercise (running, swimming, walking, aerobics) is a great way to relieve stress, and it has also been proven to help you think quicker and more clearly.

■ **Hit the shower.** Hot water is relaxing, cold water is stimulating, and warm water is soothing. Take your pick.

■ **Get to class early . . . but not too early!** Hurrying increases anxiety, but so does waiting.

■ **Relax.** Take a few deep breaths, close your eyes, and think positive thoughts. The more relaxed you are, the better your memory will serve you.

■ **Glance through the entire test**. Then plan your time, and pace yourself accordingly. You don't want to discover with only 5 minutes of class time left that the last question is an essay that counts for 50 percent of your grade.

■ **Begin by filling in all the answers you know.** This process relieves anxiety and helps to trigger answers for other questions that you may not know immediately. Also, jot down important facts and formulas that you know you will need later on.

■ **Don't panic.** If other people start handing in their papers long before you are finished, don't worry. They may have given up or rushed through the exam. Often, the best students finish last.

Bottom Line ─

The better you prepare for a test—mentally and physically—the less likely you'll suffer serious test anxiety.

Chapter 28
Writing for the Workplace

audio

One thing you already know about writing in college is that you have to do a lot of it—and it has to be good. Nothing does more to help you make a good impression than writing well. You also know that college is very much like real life, in that you have to take care of business in and out of class. There are bills to pay, letters to write, memos to fax, and messages to e-mail. It's your personal responsibility to get each of these jobs done clearly, concisely, and on time.

This chapter should aid you in taking care of the business at hand. Sample letters and memos will help you communicate effectively with people ranging from the registrar to scholarship committees. The sample applications and résumés will help you make a favorable impression when you apply for a job or internship. There's even a special set of guidelines to help you master e-mail messages so that you can "take care of business," no matter where in the world it may be.

What's Ahead

- Writing the Business Letter
- Writing Memos and E-Mail
- Applying for a Job
- Preparing a Résumé

Writing the Business Letter

Business letters do many things—for example, share ideas, promote products, or ask for help. Putting a message in writing gives you time to think about, organize, and edit what you want to say. In addition, a written message serves as a record of important details for both the sender and the recipient.

Parts of the Business Letter

Heading: The heading gives the writer's complete address, either in the letterhead (company stationery) or typed out, followed by the date.

Inside Address: The inside address gives the reader's name and address.

- If you're not sure which person to address or how to spell someone's name, you could call the company for the information.
- If the person's title is a single word, place it after the name and a comma (Mary Johnson, President). A longer title goes on a separate line.

Salutation: The salutation begins with *Dear* and ends with a colon, not a comma.

- Use *Mr.* or *Ms.* plus the person's last name, unless you are well acquainted. Do not guess at *Miss* or *Mrs.*
- If you can't get the person's name, replace the salutation with *Dear* or *Attention* followed by the title of an appropriate reader.
  (*Examples:* Dear Dean of Students: or Attention: Personnel Manager)

Note: See pages **84–86** for a complete list of "unbiased" ways to refer to an individual or a particular group.

Body: The body should consist of single-spaced paragraphs with double spacing between paragraphs. (Do not indent the paragraphs.)

- If the body goes to a second page, put the reader's name at the top left, the number 2 in the center, and the date at the right margin.

Complimentary Closing: For the complimentary closing, use *Sincerely, Yours sincerely,* or *Yours truly* followed by a comma; use *Best wishes* if you know the person well.

Signature: The signature includes both the writer's handwritten and typed name.

Initials: When someone types the letter for the writer, that person's initials appear (in lowercase) after the writer's initials (in capitals) and a colon.

Enclosure: If a document (brochure, form, copy, or other form) is enclosed with the letter, the word *Enclosure* or *Encl.* appears below the initials.

Copies: If a copy of the letter is sent elsewhere, type the letter *c:* beneath the enclosure line, followed by the person's or department's name.

Model Letter

Heading

Box 143
Balliole College
Eugene, OR 97440-5125
August 29, 2002

Four to Seven Spaces

Inside address

Ms. Ada Overlie
Ogg Hall, Room 222
Balliole College
Eugene, OR 97440-0222

Double Space

Salutation

Dear Ms. Overlie:

Double Space

As the president of the Earth Care Club, I welcome you to Balliole Community College. I hope the year will be a great learning experience both inside and outside the classroom.

Double Space

That learning experience is the reason I'm writing—to encourage you to join the Earth Care Club. As a member, you could participate in the educational and action-oriented mission of the club. The club has most recently been involved in the following:

Body

- Organizing a reduce, reuse, recycle program on campus
- Promoting cloth rather than plastic bag use among students
- Giving input to the college administration on landscaping, renovating, and building for energy efficiency
- Putting together the annual Earth Day celebration

Double Space

What environmental concerns and activities would you like to focus on? Bring them with you to the Earth Care Club. Simply complete the enclosed form and return it by September 8. Then watch the campus news for details on our first meeting.

Double Space

Complimentary closing and signature

Yours sincerely,

Four Spaces

Dave Wetland

Dave Wetland
President

Double Space

Initials Enclosure Copies

DW:kr
Encl. membership form
c: Esther du Toit, membership committee

Writing Memos and E-Mail

A memorandum is a written message sent from one person to one or more other people, usually within the same organization. As such, it is less formal than a letter. A memo can vary in length from a sentence or two to a four- or five-page report. It can be delivered in person, dropped in a mailbox, or sent via e-mail.

Memos are written to create a flow of information within an organization—asking and answering questions, describing procedures and policies, reminding people about appointments and meetings. Here are some guidelines:

- Write memos only when necessary, and only to those people who need them.
- Distribute them via appropriate media—mail, fax, bulletin boards, kiosk, or e-mail.
- Make your subject line precise so that the topic is clear and the memo is easy to file.
- Get to the point: (1) state the subject, (2) give necessary details, and (3) state the response you want.

Date:	September 27, 2002
To:	All Users of the Bascom Hill Writing Lab
From:	Kerri Kelley, Coordinator
Subject:	New Hours/New Equipment

The subject line clarifies the memo's purpose.

The main point is stated immediately.

Beginning October 15, the Bascom Hill Writing Lab will expand its weekend hours as follows: Fridays, 7:00 A.M.–11:00 P.M.; Saturdays, 8:00 A.M.–11:00 P.M.

Also, six additional computers will be installed next week, making it easier to get computer time. We hope these changes will help meet the increased demand for time and assistance we've experienced this fall. Remember, it's still a good idea to sign up in advance. To reserve time, call the lab at 462-7722 or leave your request at bhill@madwis.edu.

Readers are asked to take note of a few final facts.

Finally, long-range planners, mark your calendars. The lab will be closed on Thanksgiving Day morning and open from 1:00 P.M.–11:00 P.M. We will also be closed on Christmas and New Year's Day. We will post our semester-break hours sometime next month.

Sending E-Mail

With e-mail, people can correspond through computer networks around the globe. E-mail allows you to do the following:

- Send, forward, and receive many messages quickly and efficiently, making it ideal for group projects and other forms of collaboration
- Set up mailing lists (specific groups of e-mail addresses) so that you can easily send the same message to several people at the same time
- Organize messages in "folders" for later reference, and reply to messages

tips FOR E-MAIL

- **Revise and edit messages for clarity and correctness before sending them.** Confusing sentences, grammatical errors, and typos limit your ability to communicate on a computer screen just as they do on paper.

- **Use e-mail maturely.** Sooner or later you will send e-mail to the wrong person. Keep this possibility in mind at all times, and never write anything that would embarrass you if the wrong party received it.

- **Make messages easy to read and understand.** (1) Provide a clear subject line so readers will scan it and decide whether to read or delete the message. (2) Type short paragraphs, with line lengths of no more than 65 characters.

From:	"Sherry West" <SWEST@stgeorge.edu>
To:	outreach@stgeorge.edu
Date sent:	Mon, 23 Sept 2002 14:13:06 CST
Subject:	Agenda for Student Outreach Committee Meeting

Just a reminder that our next meeting is this Wednesday, Sept. 25, at 8:00 p.m. in SUB Room 201. We'll discuss the following agenda items:

1. The minutes of our Sept. 16 meeting
2. A proposal from SADD about Alcohol Awareness Week
3. A progress report on the Habitat for Humanity project

Before the meeting, review the minutes and the SADD proposal attached to this message.

Applying for a Job

When you apply for some jobs, you have to do nothing more than fill out an application form. With other jobs, it's a different story. You may be required to write a letter of application, gather letters of recommendation, put together a résumé, and write an application essay. The following pages provide models to fit nearly every occasion.

Web

The Letter of Application

Your letter of application (or cover letter) introduces you to an employer and often highlights information on an accompanying résumé. Your goal in writing this letter is to convince the employer to invite you for an interview.

Ogg Hall, Room 222
Balliole College
Eugene, OR 97440-0222
April 17, 2002

Address a specific person, if possible.

Professor Edward Mahaffy
Greenhouse Coordinator
Balliole College
Eugene, OR 97440-0316

Dear Professor Mahaffy:

State the desired position and your chief qualification.

I recently talked with Ms. Sierra Arbor in the Financial Aid Office about work-study jobs for 2002–2003. She told me about the Greenhouse Assistant position and gave me a job description. As a full-time Balliole student, I'm writing to apply for this position. I believe that my experience qualifies me for the job.

Focus on how your skills meet the reader's needs.

As you can see from my résumé, I spent two summers working in a raspberry operation, doing basic plant care and carrying out quality-control lab tests on the fruit. Also, as I was growing up, I learned a great deal by helping with a large farm garden. In high school and college, I studied botany. Because of my interest in this field, I'm enrolled in the Environmental Studies program at Balliole.

Request an interview and thank the reader.

I am available for an interview. You may phone me any time at 341-3611 (and leave a message on my machine) or e-mail me at dvrl@balliole.edu. Thank you for considering my application.

Yours sincerely,

Ada Overlie

Ada Overlie

Encl. résumé

The Recommendation Request Letter

When you apply for a job or program, it helps to present references or recommendations to show your fitness for the position. To get the support you need from people familiar with your work (instructors and employers), you need to ask for that support. You can do so in person or by phone, but a courteous and clear letter or e-mail message makes your request official and helps the person complete the recommendation effectively. Here is a suggested outline:

Situation: Remind the reader of your relationship to him or her; then ask the person to write a recommendation or to serve as a reference for you.

Explanation: Describe the work you did for the reader and the type of job, position, or program for which you are applying.

Action: Explain what form the recommendation should take, to whom it should be addressed, and where and when it needs to be sent.

2456 Charles Street
Lexington, KY 40588-8321
March 21, 2002

Dr. Rosa Perez
271 University Boulevard
University of Kentucky
Lexington, KY 40506-1440

Dear Dr. Perez:

The situation
As we discussed on the phone, I would appreciate your writing a recommendation letter for me. You know the quality of my academic work, my qualities as a person, and my potential for working in the medical field.

The explanation
As my professor for Biology 201 and 202, you are familiar with my grades and work habits. As my adviser, you know my career plans and should have a good sense of whether I have the qualities needed to succeed in the medical profession. I am asking you for your recommendation because I am applying for summer employment with the Lexington Ambulance Service. I recently received my Emergency Medical Technician (Basic) license to prepare for such work.

The action
Please send your letter to Rick Falk, EMT Coordinator, at the University Placement Office by April 8. Thank you for your help. Let me know if you need any other information (phone 231-6700; e-mail jnwllms@ukentucky.edu).

Yours sincerely,

Jon Williams

Jon Williams

The Application Essay

For some applications, you may be asked to submit an essay, a personal statement, or a response paper. For example, you might be applying for admission to an academic program (social work, engineering, optometry school) or for an internship, a scholarship, or a research grant. Whatever the situation, what you write and how well you write it will be important factors in the success of your application.

On the facing page is a model application essay. Jessy Jezowski wrote this essay as part of her application to a college social work program.

tips FOR AN APPLICATION ESSAY

- Understand what you are being asked to write and why. How does the essay fit into the entire application? Who will read your essay? What will they look for?

- Focus on the instructions for writing the essay. What type of question is it? What topics are you asked to write about? What hints do the directions give about possible organization, emphasis, style, length, and method of submitting the essay?

- Be honest with yourself and your readers. Don't try to write only what you think readers want to hear.

- Develop your essay using the following organization (if the instructions allow for it):
  - An introduction with a fresh, interesting opening statement and a clear focus or theme
  - A body that develops the focus or theme clearly and concisely—with some details and examples—in a way appropriate to the instructions
  - A conclusion that stresses a positive point and looks forward to participating in the program, internship, organization, or other position

- Write in a style that is personal but professional. Use words that fit the subject and the readers. Avoid clichés, and balance generalizations with concrete examples and details.

- Refine your first draft into a polished piece. First, get feedback from another student or, if appropriate, a professor, and revise the essay. Second, edit the final version thoroughly: you don't want typos and grammar errors to derail your application.

Model Application Essay

audio

February 28, 2002
Jessy Jezowski

Personal Statement

The opening provides a clear focus for the essay.

While growing up in Chicago, I would see people hanging out on street corners, by grocery stores, and in parks—with no home and barely any belongings. Poverty and its related problems are all around us, and yet most people walk by them with blinders on. I have found myself quick to assume that someone else will help the poor man on the corner, the woman trapped in an abusive relationship, or the teenager suffering from an eating disorder. But I know in my heart that all members of society are responsible to and for each other. Social welfare issues affect every member of society—including me.

The writer demonstrates knowledge of the field and explains what she hopes to learn.

Because these issues are serious and difficult to solve, I wish to major in social work and eventually become a social worker. In the major, I want to gain the knowledge, skills, and attitudes that will make me part of the solution, not part of the problem. By studying social work institutions, the practices of social work, and the theory and history behind social work, I hope to learn how to help people help themselves. When that pregnant teenager comes to me, I want to have strong, practical advice—and be part of an effective social work agency that can help implement that advice.

Two concrete examples help back up her general statements.

I am especially interested at this point in working with families and teenagers, in either a community counseling or school setting. Two experiences have created this interest. First, a woman in my church who works for an adoption agency, Ms. Lesage, has modeled for me what it means to care for individuals and families within a community and around the world. Second, I was involved in a peer counseling program in high school. As counselors, we received training in interpersonal relationships and the nature of helping. In a concrete way, I experienced the complex challenges of helping others.

The conclusion summarizes her goals for the future.

I believe strongly in the value of all people and am interested in the well-being of others. As a social worker, I would strive to make society better (for individuals, families, and communities) by serving those in need, whatever their problems.

1

2

3

4

Preparing a Résumé

A strong résumé isn't generic—a ho-hum, fill-in-the-blanker. Rather, it's a vivid word picture of your skills, knowledge, and past responsibilities. It says exactly who you are by providing the kind of information listed below.

Personal Data: name, address, phone number, e-mail address (enough for the reader to identify you and to reach you easily).

Job Objective: the type of position you want and the type of organization for which you want to work.

Skills Summary: the key qualities and skills you bring to a position, listed with supporting details. Here are some skill areas that you might consider for your own résumé:

- Communication
- Organization
- Problem solving
- Computer
- Management (people, money, other resources)
- Working with people, counseling, training
- Sales, marketing, public relations
- Languages

Experience: positions you've held (where and when), and your specific duties and accomplishments.

Education: degrees, courses, and special projects.

Other Experiences: volunteer work, awards, achievements, tutoring jobs, extra-curricular activities (related to your job objective), licenses, and certifications.

tips FOR RÉSUMÉ WRITING

- Design each résumé to fit the particular job.
- Be specific—use numbers, dates, and names.
- Present information first that is the most impressive and/or important to the job for which you are applying. This guideline will help you determine whether to put your experience or your education first.
- Use everyday language and short, concise phrases.
- Be parallel—list similar items using similar structures.
- Use boldface type, underlining, white space, and indentations to make your résumé more readable.
- Get someone else's reaction; then revise and proofread the résumé.

Sample Résumé

Ada Overlie

Home
451 Wiser Lake Road
Ferndale, WA 98248-8941
(360) 354-5916

School
Ogg Hall, Room 222
Balliole College
Eugene, OR 97440-0222
Phone: (503) 341-3611
E-mail: dvrl@balliole.edu

Job Objective: Part-time assistant in a nursery or greenhouse.

Skills Summary:

Horticultural Skills: Familiar with garden planting, care, and
  harvesting practices—planning, timing, companion planting,
  fertilizing.

Lab Skills: Familiar with procedures for taking fruit
  samples, pureeing them, checking for foreign objects, and
  testing sugar content.

Work Experience:

Summer 2001 and 2002: Lab Technician.
  Mayberry Farms and Processing Plant, Ferndale, WA.
  Worked in Quality Control testing raspberries to make sure
  they met company standards.

Summer 1999 and 2000: Camp Counselor.
  Emerald Lake Summer Camp, Hillsboro, WA.
  Supervised 12-year-olds in many camp activities, including
  nature hikes in which we identified plants and trees.

Education:

August 2002 to present: Balliole College, Eugene, OR.
  Environmental Studies and Communication major.
  Courses completed and in progress include environmental
  studies and general botany. First semester GPA 3.7.

August 1998 to June 2002: Ferndale High School, Ferndale, WA.
  Courses included biology, agriculture, U.S. government, and
  economics.

  Special Projects: Completed research papers on
  clean-water legislation and organic farming practices.

References available upon request.

Sample Electronic Résumé

To find employees, companies often use computer programs to search electronic résumés for key words (especially nouns) found in job descriptions or ads. Anticipating such a search, Jonathan Greenlind identified key words and inserted them into his job description and résumé.

Jonathan L. Greenlind
806 5th Avenue
Waterloo, Iowa 50701
Telephone: 319.268.6955
E-mail: grnlnd@aol.com

OBJECTIVE

Position as hydraulics supervisor that calls for hydraulics expertise, technical skills, mechanical knowledge, reliability, and enthusiasm.

SKILLS

Operation and repair specialist in main and auxiliary power systems, subsystems, landing gears, brakes and pneumatic systems, hydraulic motors, reservoirs, actuators, pumps and cylinders from six types of hydraulic systems.

Dependable, resourceful, strong leader, team worker.

EXPERIENCE

Aviation Hydraulics Technician

United States Navy (1996–present)
- Repair, test, and maintain basic hydraulics, distribution systems, and aircraft structural hydraulics systems.
- Manufacture low-, medium-, and high-pressure rubber and Teflon hydraulic hoses, and aluminum stainless-steel tubing.
- Perform preflight, postflight, and other periodic aircraft inspections.
- Operate ground-support equipment.
- Supervise personnel.

Aircraft Mechanic

Sioux Falls International Airport (1994–1996)
Sioux Falls, South Dakota
- Performed fueling, engine overhauls, minor repairs, and tire and oil changes of various aircraft.

EDUCATION
- United States Navy (1996–2000).
- Certificate in Hydraulic Technical School "A", GPA 3.8/4.0.
- Certificate in Hydraulic, Pneumatic Test Stand School, GPA 3.9/4.0.
- Courses in Corrosion Control, Hydraulic Tube Bender, Aviation Structural Mechanics.
- Equivalent of 10 semester hours in Hydraulic Systems Maintenance and Structural Repair.

References available upon request.

Chapter 29
Writing for the Web

   While the Internet is still relatively young, it has rapidly become a fixture in our culture. For many people, the Net is already the first tool used for research. E-mail and instant messaging have emerged as common means of communication. And the public nature of the World Wide Web means that anyone with Internet access (even at a public library) can publish pages online.

   Using the Net effectively requires specialized writing skills—from phrasing search requests to crafting e-mail messages to creating Web pages. This chapter provides guidelines for writing e-mail and related messages, and for creating Web pages. To learn more about search requests, see Chapter 32.

What's Ahead

- Writing for E-Mail, List Servers, and Message Boards
- Creating Web Pages and Web Sites
- Other Writing Environments on the Net

Writing for E-Mail, List Servers, and Message Boards

List servers (or listservs, or mailing lists) provide the means to quickly send messages to a group of subscribers. Message boards allow for message posting to a Web page where any visitor can read and respond to it. Despite the immediacy of these systems, it still takes time to write a clear, effective message in the first place. Consider the guidelines below as you write.

Planning

1. **Consider Your Audience.** Think about who your readers are and your purpose for sending a message to them.
2. **Gather Details.** Make sure you include all the details your readers need to know. (If your message is a response to an earlier message, don't assume that your readers will remember the earlier content. Instead, include a reminder of the original message.)

Drafting and Revising

3. **Organize the Message.** Organize your message into three parts:
   Beginning: Address the message header according to the e-mail program or message board guidelines. Always include a precise subject line to identify the message.
   Middle: Fill in the details of your message, using short, concise paragraphs. Double-space between paragraphs, and use numbers, lists, and headings to organize your content.
   Ending: Identify any response you expect from your readers. Then end politely.
4. **Check Your Writing.** Before you send or post your message, read it again and consider the following questions:
   - Is the message complete and clear? (If readers need to write back for clarification, they may ignore the message altogether.)
   - Is the tone right for your audience? Online, a friendly but serious tone is generally best. Your text must stand alone, without visual or vocal cues to its meaning. Also, remember your Netiquette. (See page 500.)
   - Is your message concise? Brief messages are easiest to read and comprehend. Also, because many people pay for their Internet connection by the minute, they don't want to download long-winded messages.

Editing and Proofreading

5. **Check for Style and Accuracy.** Although e-mail and message board postings are often casual, your message will be more effective if its terminology, spelling, and punctuation are accurate.

Sample E-Mail

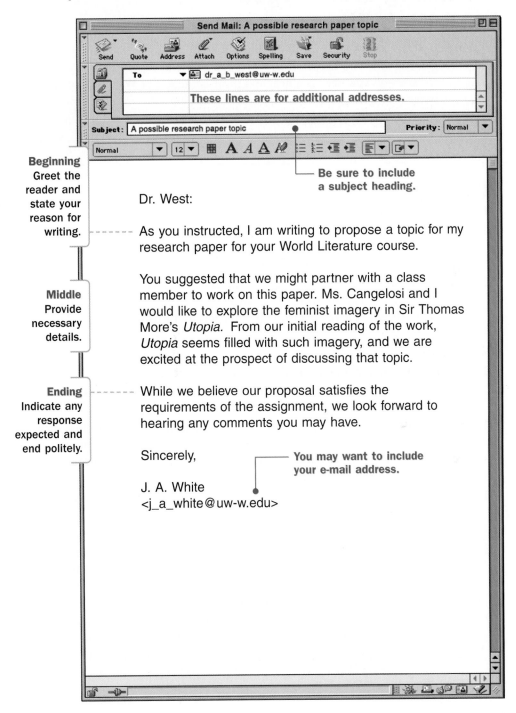

Beginning
Greet the reader and state your reason for writing.

Middle
Provide necessary details.

Ending
Indicate any response expected and end politely.

Send Mail: A possible research paper topic

Send   Quote   Address   Attach   Options   Spelling   Save   Security   Stop

To ▼ dr_a_b_west@uw-w.edu

These lines are for additional addresses.

Subject: A possible research paper topic   Priority: Normal ▼

Normal ▼ 12 ▼ A A A 𝒜 ≡ ⅙ ⁖ ⁖ ☰ ▼ ⧉ ▼

— Be sure to include a subject heading.

Dr. West:

As you instructed, I am writing to propose a topic for my research paper for your World Literature course.

You suggested that we might partner with a class member to work on this paper. Ms. Cangelosi and I would like to explore the feminist imagery in Sir Thomas More's *Utopia.* From our initial reading of the work, *Utopia* seems filled with such imagery, and we are excited at the prospect of discussing that topic.

While we believe our proposal satisfies the requirements of the assignment, we look forward to hearing any comments you may have.

Sincerely,

— **You may want to include your e-mail address.**

J. A. White
<j_a_white@uw-w.edu>

Web

Creating Web Pages and Web Sites

A Web page is a single document on the Web. A Web site is a collection of linked pages. Anyone with access to the Web can create and publish a Web page or Web site—all you need is a host and some content. For Web hosting, ask your Internet service provider, or type "free host" into any search site to find other resources. When creating your content, consider the following guidelines.

Planning

1. **Gather Information**. Decide what content your site will include. Draft a mission statement defining its purpose. (Many people post their own essays, fiction, poetry, artwork, and photos on their Web sites.) Collect any writing you plan to post, and begin thinking about how to organize it.

2. **Develop a Site Plan**. Consider the arrangement of pages on sites you visit often; then draw a map showing the arrangement of your own pages. This step is critical to ensure that visitors won't become lost and frustrated.

Drafting

3. **Identify the Site**. Working from your mission statement, write an introductory sentence or brief paragraph for your site's home page. Let your visitors know immediately the site's purpose.

4. **Provide Clear Links**. Create links for your pages, using clear descriptors such as "Original Poetry." (Avoid phrases such as "Click here for poetry.") If necessary, add a descriptive sentence to further identify the link. Let your visitors know exactly where each link will take them.

5. **Introduce Each Page**. Search sites may deliver some visitors to a page other than your home page. Give each page its own brief introduction to clearly identify it. Also, remember to provide a link back to your home page.

6. **Use Effective Page Design**. Dense text is even more difficult to read on-screen than on paper, so use short paragraphs when you can. Most sites use double-spacing between paragraphs. Add headings to identify sections, and include illustrations and other graphics where possible.

7. **Save the Page as HTML**. To be viewed in a Web browser, your pages must be formatted in Hypertext Markup Language (HTML). Your word processor may have a "Save As HTML" or "Save As Web Page" option. Many HTML editing programs are also available on the Web. Type "HTML" into a search site for more details.

Revising

8. Check the Site. Open your home page from your Web browser. Does the site make sense? Can you navigate it easily? Make any needed changes.

9. Ask for Peer Review. Ask a few friends to test your site. Watch them navigate it and take notes about any confusion. Make any needed changes.

10. Provide a Feedback Link. Provide an e-mail address on your site, inviting visitors to contact you with any comments or suggestions after the site goes "live."

Editing and Proofreading

11. Check the Text. Reread all the text on your site. Trim wherever possible (the shorter, the better online), and check all spelling and punctuation.

Publishing

12. Post the Site. Upload the site to your hosting space. (Check your host's instructions for doing so.) Add the posting date to each page, and update it each time you change a page.

13. Announce the Site. Advertise your site in e-mails. Submit it to search sites. Consider joining a "webring" of similar sites to draw more traffic. Let colleagues, friends, and family know about your site.

Sample Home Page

Other Writing Environments on the Net

The Internet is a complex construct made up of much more than Web pages and e-mail. Other writing venues on the Net are described below.

Newsgroups ◆ Like listservs, newsgroups allow users to send and receive text messages among a specific group of people interested in a particular subject. Unlike listserv messages, however, newsgroup messages are stored so that their contents can later be retrieved. Newsgroups have been around since the early days of the Internet, and thousands upon thousands of them currently exist. Some are excellent sources of specialized information; others are pure frivolity. Many e-mail programs allow access to newsgroups.

> *Example:* Google Groups <groups.google.com)

OWLs ◆ Your university or college probably has a writing lab where you can seek help with your writing assignments. It may also have a Web-based OWL (online writing lab) where you can access help via an Internet connection. OWLs post answers to questions you may have about writing, and they often allow for e-mail or instant message communications with a writing tutor. Before contacting an OWL tutor, take the time to read any instructions posted on the site.

> *Example:* Purdue University OWL <owl.english.purdue.edu>

MUDs, MOOs, and MUSHes ◆ Some instructors hold classes online in a MUD. A MUD (multiuser dimension) is a text-based "world" that people can share. (MOOs and MUSHes are variant types of MUDs.) MUDs have virtual rooms to explore and virtual objects to examine and handle. To use a MUD, you must learn the text commands for interacting with it. Most MUDs require software for a Telnet connection, but some are accessible via Telnet-enabled Web pages.

> *Example:* Diversity University MOO <www.marshall.edu/commdis/moo>

Chat Servers ◆ A chat server provides a place on the Net where you can type a message that other people will see instantly. They can then respond with text messages of their own. Some teachers and tutors may use a chat room to confer with students or to hold a class discussion online. Although some chat servers require special software, many are available as Web pages.

> *Example:* Yahoo!Chat <chat.yahoo.com>

Instant Messaging Services ◆ Instant messaging (IM) services are a relatively recent development on the Internet. Each IM is a software program installed on your computer, allowing you to type and send a message instantaneously to friends and colleagues who use the same software. Most IMs allow users to send computer files to one another. (Just be careful not to pass a computer virus this way.)

> *Example:* ICQ <web.icq.com>

Chapter 30
Preparing Oral Presentations

audio

In college—and in life—you will use your speaking skills every day to accomplish one of the following activities:

- Talking one-on-one with students, instructors, and workers inside the classroom and on the job
- Interviewing people to get information and ideas about a topic you're researching, or being interviewed for an internship, assistantship, or job
- Giving oral reports on work-related projects or classroom assignments

This chapter provides guidelines on becoming a better speaker and all-around communicator.

What's Ahead

- Planning Your Presentation
- Writing Your Presentation
- Preparing Your Presentation Script
- Rehearsing and Presenting
- Presentation Checklist

Planning Your Presentation

Planning an oral presentation is a lot like planning an essay. You need to pay close attention to your purpose, subject, audience, and the details of your topic. The following guidelines will help you plan a successful presentation.

Determine your purpose.

There are three main reasons for making a presentation: to inform, to persuade, and to demonstrate.

- **Informing:** If your purpose is to inform or to educate, you are preparing an informative presentation. (Collecting plenty of details is essential. See pages **35–37.**)
- **Persuading:** If your purpose is to argue for or against something, you are preparing a persuasive presentation. (Developing a convincing and logical argument is your main job. See pages **254–268.**)
- **Demonstrating:** If your purpose is to show how to do something or to show how something works, you are preparing a demonstration presentation. (Composing a clear, step-by-step explanation is the key.)

Select a topic.

A good presentation starts with a good topic—one that truly interests both you and your audience. Here are some important points to consider.

- **Choose the right topic.** Make sure that your topic meets the requirements (and purpose) of the assignment.
- **Know your topic.** Make sure that you know your topic well or that you can learn about it in the time you have to prepare.
- **Choose a specific topic.** Make sure that your topic is specific enough to cover in the allotted time. (See the chart below.)

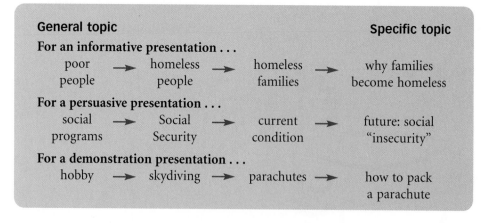

General topic			Specific topic
For an informative presentation . . .			
poor people →	homeless people →	homeless families →	why families become homeless
For a persuasive presentation . . .			
social programs →	Social Security →	current condition →	future: social "insecurity"
For a demonstration presentation . . .			
hobby →	skydiving →	parachutes →	how to pack a parachute

Consider your audience.

You will want to think about your audience at each step in the process. Here are some suggestions you can follow.

- **Choose your topic carefully.** Show that you care about your audience by choosing an interesting topic.

- **Be clear.** Organize the presentation so clearly that listeners get the point immediately.

- **Anticipate questions.** Try to think of questions your audience might have, and answer them in your presentation.

- **Make it enjoyable.** Use thought-provoking quotations, interesting anecdotes, and a little humor (when appropriate).

- **Be brief.** Speak only as long as you must to make your point.

Note: After you've considered your purpose, topic, and audience, you may want to write a thesis or purpose statement for your presentation. (See page **41**.)

Collect interesting details.

Now it's time to start collecting information. Listed below are different sources of information that you can refer to for your presentation. Always consult as many sources as time permits.

- **Tap your memory.** If your presentation is based on an experience, write down the facts, details, and feelings as you remember them.

- **Talk with people.** Discuss your subject with a variety of people who may be able to provide details from their own experiences.

- **Interview an expert.** Questioning and listening to an expert who has specific information can provide key facts, quotations, and impressions.

- **Get firsthand experience.** Experiencing (or trying out) your subject is especially important for demonstrations.

- **Search the library.** Check a variety of library resources, including books, magazines, pamphlets, and videos.

- **Explore the Internet.** Check out appropriate Web sites and newsgroups for information.

- **Visit a bookstore.** See whether any books about your topic have been recently published.

Look for photographs, maps, models, artifacts, charts, objects, and other graphics. Showing such items can help make any presentation clearer and more interesting, especially a demonstration speech. Consider creating your own graphics or charts as well.

Writing Your Presentation

After you've completed your basic planning, you need to select your best details and organize them into an effective presentation. The way you organize your details and write them down depends primarily on (1) the kind of presentation you are giving and (2) the kind of "script" or notes you plan to use. (See pages **432–433** for a sample script.)

For a short demonstration, you may need only a few notes (note cards). If you plan to inform your audience, you may want to speak from a well-organized list (outline). If you are giving a persuasive presentation, you may want to use a word-for-word script (manuscript). Whatever approach you choose, you need to be well prepared with an effective introduction, body, and conclusion.

Begin strong.

A good introduction sets the tone and direction of your presentation by getting the attention of your audience, introducing your topic, and stating your central idea or purpose.

Start-Up Ideas: To get the audience's attention and help them focus on your topic, begin your presentation with one or more of the following ideas:

- Ask a thought-provoking question.
- Tell a funny story or anecdote.
- Give a short demonstration or use an attention-getting visual aid.
- Make a strong statement about why the topic is important to you and to your audience.
- Share an appropriate quotation related to your topic.

Stating Your Thesis

After you've considered your purpose, topic, and audience (and gathered some information), you need to write a thesis statement to focus your planning efforts. Begin the statement with "My purpose is . . ." and finish it with your specific presentation topic. If you choose to include your thesis statement in your introduction, you will want to reword it so that it sounds natural and sincere.

"My purpose is to persuade my classmates that we cannot depend on the Social Security system for our retirement funds, so we need to start our own savings plans now."

Organize and support your main points.

As you write the body of your presentation, turn each fact or detail into an interesting, connected thought. Explain or describe each part of your topic clearly so that your audience can follow along easily. If you are giving your opinion about something, support your point of view with enough logical reasons to convince your listeners. Organize your details as effectively as possible. Here are six popular ways to do that, plus speech ideas that would use such a type of organization:

Order of Importance ◆ Arrange information according to its importance: least to greatest, or greatest to least.

➤ A persuasive speech on using wind power to generate electricity

Chronological Order ◆ Arrange information according to time—the order in which events take place.

➤ A how-to speech about sending e-mail messages

Comparison/Contrast ◆ Give information about subjects by comparing them (showing similarities) and contrasting them (showing differences).

➤ An explanatory speech about choosing one Internet provider rather than another one

Cause and Effect ◆ Give information about a situation, a problem, or a process by sharing its causes and effects.

➤ A report on what causes high prices for prescription drugs and what the effects are for the elderly

Order of Location ◆ Arrange information about subjects according to where things are located in relation to other items.

➤ An informational speech about the "anatomy" of the Statue of Liberty

Problem/Solution ◆ Describe a problem and then present a solution.

➤ A persuasive speech about how warm-ups prevent muscle strain in athletes

Make a lasting impression.

The conclusion of your presentation ought to leave your audience focused on the most important points of your message. A good conclusion helps your audience understand what they have heard, why it's important, and what they should do about it. Here are some suggestions to consider:

- **Tell one last interesting fact or story.**
  (This is a good way to end an informative presentation.)

- **Explain why the topic is important.**
  (This is a good way to end a persuasive presentation.)

- **Sum up the most important ideas in your presentation.**
  (This is a good way to end a demonstration presentation.)

Preparing Your Presentation Script

Once you have the general draft written, it's time to prepare the "script." The script is the form you will use when you are giving your presentation. You can use an outline, note cards, or a word-for-word manuscript.

Consider using an outline.

If you outline your presentation, follow these guidelines and model:

1. Write your opening (I) and closing (V) statements in sentence form.

2. Write the main points (II–IV) of the body of your speech as sentences and all supporting points (facts, dates, numbers) as phrases.

3. Add notes [in brackets] to indicate where to use visual aids.

4. Write all quotations out completely.

Save NOW or Pay Later

I. Imagine that you've finished school, gotten a job, worked hard all week, and this dollar bill represents your whole paycheck. [hold up dollar bill]

II. Your employer will have to take out these amounts from your week's earnings. [rip dollar bill]
   A. 20% income tax [show overhead]
   B. 30% Social Security and Medicare
   C. 50% for you (Sen. Simpson's statistics)

III. The problem is that the Social Security System cannot ensure our retirement savings.
   A. Social Security started in 1935 [show overhead]
   B. System failing, 1983 fix—good until 2056
   C. 1992 report—fix good only until 2043
   D. New research predicts system bankrupt by 2029

IV. What can you do about your own "social security"?
   A. Stay informed and vote as soon as you can
   B. Start a savings account [show overhead]

V. What's the solution? We have to start our own savings plans; and the earlier we start, the easier it will be to reach our goals.

Use note cards when appropriate.

If you plan to deliver your presentation using note cards, it's a good idea to write out your entire introduction and conclusion. For the body of your presentation, write one main point (and related details) per card.

①

Introduction

Imagine that you've finished school, gotten a job, worked hard all week, and this dollar bill represents your whole paycheck. [hold up dollar bill] As your employer, I'm about to hand you the check when I stop, tear off about 20% like this, give it to Uncle Sam an

Then I

②

A 50% deduction from your paycheck may soon be a reality.
 - Social Security system failing
 - Out of money by the year 2043?
 - Additional taxes

③

Social Security system began in 1935.
 - "fixed" many times
 - 1983 changes were supposed to last until

④

What can we do about our own social security?
 - Start saving
 - [show graph]

⑤

Conclusion

What's my point? The Social Security system can't promise us financial security when we retire in 2049.

What's the solution? We have to start our own savings plans; and the earlier we start, the easier it will be to reach our goals.

Use a manuscript for formal presentations.

If you use a word-for-word manuscript, make sure that you write to be heard, not read. Also, mark your copy to help you deliver your presentation effectively. (See "Marking Your Presentation" on page 434.) Notice in the manuscript below how Burnette Sawyer, the student writer, uses *italics* to add feeling and **boldface** to add emphasis. In addition, notice how she builds her argument by showing the audience how the problem affects each person.

Save Now or Pay Later

The speaker begins with an anecdote.

Imagine that you've finished school, gotten a job, worked hard all week, 1 and this dollar bill represents your whole paycheck. *[hold up dollar bill]* As your employer, I'm about to hand you the check when I stop, tear off about 20 percent like this, give it to Uncle Sam, and say, "Here's my employee's income tax." Then I tear off another 30 percent like this, give that to Uncle Sam too, and say, "And here's her Medicare and Social Security tax."

She tears the dollar for emphasis.

Finally, I give you this half and say, "Here, hard worker, this is what's 2 left of your *whole paycheck.*"

Does that sound like science fiction? 3

The speaker cites an authority to support her argument.

Senator Alan Simpson doesn't think so. In the magazine *Modern* 4 *Maturity,* he says that unless legislation changes the Social Security system, *our generation* will have to pay 20 percent *[show overhead]* of our paychecks as income tax, and 30 percent as Social Security tax. That means we can keep just **50 percent** of what we earn.

But the news gets **worse**. Remember this 30 percent that we paid to 5 Social Security? *[hold up piece of dollar bill]* Well, that won't be enough money for retired people to live on in the year 2043. Remember that year, 2043—we'll come back to that soon.

The speaker asks questions to involve the audience.

What's the problem? The Social Security system can't ensure our 6 savings for retirement.

What's the solution? We have to start our own savings plans, and the 7 *earlier,* the *better.*

Ever since the Social Security system started back in 1935 *[show over-* 8 *head]*, it has never been *secure.* While the system has been "fixed" a number of times, these fix-it jobs haven't solved the problem. For example, writer Keith Carlson points out that in 1983 Congress raised payroll taxes, extended the retirement age, and said that the system would be in good financial shape until 2056.

But then, says Carlson, *just nine years later,* a report came out saying 9 that Congress had been **wrong**. The report said in 1992 that Social Security money wouldn't even last until 2056—it would run out by 2043. *Remember that year, 2043?* **That's before many of us are** supposed to retire at age 67!

Do you think this news is bad? The *AARP Bulletin* reported on the   *10*
Bipartisan Commission on Entitlement and Tax Reform. This commission
warned that entitlement programs like Social Security are growing so fast
they could "bankrupt the country" by the year 2029—long before we retire!

So what should we do? Next fall we can vote in a presidential election   *11*
for the first time. Both Democrats and Republicans say they have a plan
that will use money from the budget surplus to fix Social Security. What if
we all vote for the presidential candidate with the best plan? Will that save
our retirement funds? **Don't count on it!** As the track record for Social
Security shows, one more fix-it job won't fix the system. We have to start
our own retirement plans—and do it early in our careers.

In fact, in his book *Retirement 101,* Willard Enteman says that we   *12*
should start a personal savings plan the day we get our first paychecks. In
sociology class last week, Mr. Christians made the same point. He gave us
this bar graph *[show overhead]* showing that if our goal is to save $200,000
by age 67, we had better *start early* before saving gets too expensive.

As you can see from the graph, if we start saving when we're 25, we can   *13*
reach $200,000 by saving just $49 a month. If we wait until we're 35, we'll
have to save $113 a month. If we wait until we're 45, we'll have to put away
$279 a month. And if we wait until we're 55, we'll need $832 a month.

Look at the difference. To reach $200,000 by age 67 would cost $49 a   *14*
month if we start at 25, and $832 a month if we start at 55.

What's my point? The Social Security system *can't promise us* financial   *15*
security when we retire in 2049.

What's the solution? We have to start our own savings plans; and the   *16*
earlier we start, the *easier* it will be to reach our goals. ■

> **Throughout the
> speech, she
> uses three
> overheads
> to give her
> listeners
> a clear
> understanding
> of the main
> points.**

> **The closing
> paragraphs
> help readers
> reflect on
> the subject.**

write

Reading for Better Writing

1. How does the writer get the audience's attention? How effective is her
method? Can you think of an approach that would work better?

2. Find the three parts of this speech—introduction, body, and conclusion—
to help you see the sequence of ideas. How does the writer sequence the
ideas? How does the sequence help her listeners understand the speech?

3. Identify the main idea. What kinds of support are used to develop the
main idea?

4. Take a little time to think about the speaker's position. Judge whether the
argument is effective.

5. Does this speech have emotional power? If so, how does the writer-speaker
create the emotional power?

Rehearsing and Presenting

Rehearse your presentation until you're comfortable with it. Ask a family member or friend to listen and give you feedback, or use a tape recorder or video recorder so that you can hear and see yourself. When you rehearse (or give) your presentation, follow the guidelines below.

Before you present . . .

- Check all your equipment and visual aids before you start.
- Check your outline, note cards, or manuscript to be sure everything is in the right order.
- Stand, walk to the front, and face the audience.

As you present . . .

- Speak loudly and clearly.
- Don't rush. Read carefully if you're using a manuscript; glance at your note cards or outline if you're using that approach.
- Think about what you're saying and add feeling to your voice.
- Use appropriate gestures to help you communicate.
- Look at the audience as you speak, and communicate with your facial expressions.

After you present . . .

- Ask if anyone has any questions (if appropriate).
- Conclude the presentation.

Marking Your Presentation

As you rehearse your presentation, decide which words or phrases to emphasize, where to pause, and where to add visual aids. Then use the symbols and text enhancements below to mark the copy of your presentation.

Italic or boldface . . . . for additional feeling or emotion

Underlining . . . . for greater volume or emphasis

Dash, diagonal, ellipsis . . . . for a pause—or / a break
. . . in the flow

Brackets . . . . for actions or [visual aids]

Use visual aids.

While constructing your presentation, think about visual aids that would grab the audience's attention and help them understand the message. For example, in her speech, the student writer Burnette Sawyer used three overheads that helped her audience stay focused on the presentation. To see how she used the overheads, look for the bracketed notes within the text of her speech. (See pages 432–433.)

Sample Overheads

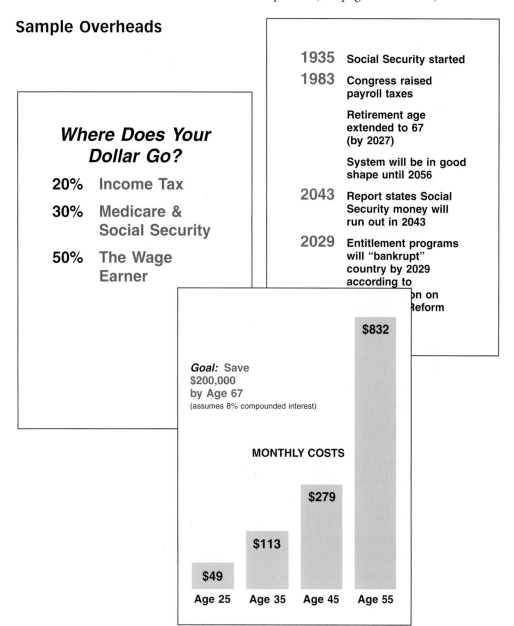

Where Does Your Dollar Go?

20% Income Tax

30% Medicare & Social Security

50% The Wage Earner

1935 Social Security started

1983 Congress raised payroll taxes

Retirement age extended to 67 (by 2027)

System will be in good shape until 2056

2043 Report states Social Security money will run out in 2043

2029 Entitlement programs will "bankrupt" country by 2029 according to on Reform

Goal: Save $200,000 by Age 67
(assumes 8% compounded interest)

MONTHLY COSTS

$832

$279

$113

$49

Age 25   Age 35   Age 45   Age 55

Presentation Checklist

Stimulating Ideas

The presentation . . .

_____ Focuses on an important or interesting topic appropriate for the audience and purpose.

_____ Includes support and details that help develop the topic and bring it to life.

Logical Organization

_____ Includes a clearly developed beginning, middle, and ending.

_____ Introduces the topic in a logical and interesting way.

_____ Presents information in an organized manner.

Engaging Voice

_____ Speaks in a sincere and knowledgeable voice.

_____ Includes appropriate graphs, charts, or other audio/visual aids.

Appropriate Word Choice

_____ Employs an appropriate level of language and explains or defines any unfamiliar terms.

_____ Creates effective analogies and word pictures.

Overall Fluency

_____ Flows smoothly from one idea to the next.

_____ Shows a variety of sentence lengths and beginnings.

Correct, Accurate Copy

_____ Adheres to the rules of grammar, spelling, and punctuation.

_____ Follows the guidelines for format and documentation.

Overall Effectiveness

_____ Incorporates appropriate action, gestures, and eye contact.

_____ Shows enthusiasm and/or concern from start to finish.

_____ Meets overall purpose or goal.

III. Research
Guide

Research and Writing

CONTENTS

Chapter 31
Writing the
Research Paper

In one sense, writing a research paper is simple. You research a topic and analyze what your research shows; then you write up your findings or conclusions in an interesting and persuasive way.

In another sense, the research paper may be your toughest college assignment. Why? Because most research papers are big projects. They take weeks to complete, including hours spent on the trail of facts, figures, and ideas. They require you to organize your tasks in the best possible sequence and to digest the thinking of others while discovering your own perspective.

But the rewards of a research project can be great—new insights into a subject that really interests you, a deepened understanding of your major or profession, knowledge to share with others, and sharpened thinking skills.

What's Ahead

- The Research Paper: Quick Guide
- Basic Research Principles
- Getting Started
- Planning Your Research
- Conducting Research
    - Taking Notes
- Organizing Your Research
- Drafting Your Paper
    - Using Sources
    - Avoiding Plagiarism
- Revising and Editing
- Activities and Assignments

Web

The Research Paper

QUICK GUIDE

When you write a research paper, you ask important questions, look systematically for answers, and share your conclusions with readers. In other words, it's all about curiosity, discovery, and dialogue.

STARTING POINT: The assignment usually relates to a course concept, so consider what your instructor wants you to learn and how your project will be evaluated. Then take ownership of the project by looking for an angle that makes the writing personal.

PURPOSE: The project requires you to do research and share results. Your specific goal is to discover something worth sharing with others.

FORM: The traditional research paper is a fairly long essay (5 to 15 pages), complete with thesis, supporting paragraphs, integrated sources, and careful documentation. However, you may be asked to shape your research into a Web page or multimedia presentation.

AUDIENCE: Traditionally, the research paper addresses "the academic community," a group made up mainly of instructors and students. However, your actual audience may be more specific: addicted smokers, all Floridians, fellow immigrants, and so on.

VOICE: The tone is usually semiformal, but check your instructor's expectations. In any research paper, maintain a thoughtful, confident tone. After all, your research has made you somewhat of an authority on the topic.

POINT OF VIEW: In the past, research writers avoided the pronouns "I" and "you" in order to remain properly objective and academic sounding. Unfortunately, this resulted in an overuse of both the pronoun "one" and the passive voice. Many instructors now encourage students to connect research with experience, meaning that you may use the pronouns "I" and "you" occasionally. Be careful, however, to keep the focus where it belongs—on the topic.

INSIGHT: The best research writing centers on *your* ideas, ideas you develop through thoughtful engagement with sources. In poor research papers, the sources dominate, and the writer's perspective disappears.

Basic Research Principles

Each research project that you tackle is a quest for reliable information. To succeed in that quest, follow these basic guidelines.

1. **Think quality.** Don't use encyclopedias, popular magazines, and flashy Web sites as the foundation of your research. Rely instead on academic books, scholarly articles, and online sources approved by experts. In addition, conduct reliable primary research. For example, you might interview an optometrist about the effects of air pollution on the human eye, but not about the causes of pollution.

2. **Be patient and persistent.** Research can get complicated, so expect occasional dead ends and delays. The book that you want may be checked out, or you may need to get an article through interlibrary loan. Moreover, it takes time to digest sources.

3. **Know what research technology can and cannot do.** An information tool—whether it's a book or a database—becomes useful only with practice. Learn to use each research tool effectively.

4. **Work with the experts.** Information specialists are everywhere—from your library to the Internet. Find the experts you need, and take advantage of their skills.

5. **Master keyword searching.** Select precise keywords and design searches carefully (see pages 486–487).

6. **Use sources to discover more sources.** Pay attention to books, articles, and experts mentioned in reliable sources.

> *One source often points the way to other sources of equal or greater value.*

7. **Keep good records.** Photocopy or print key materials, "bookmark" all important Web sites, and organize your project by using files. Record information about your sources, and take good notes to prevent problems later. Keep track of your project in a research journal.

8. **Evaluate all sources.** Remain open to all sources, including ones that disagree with your opinion, but make sure that all material is accurate and reliable.

9. **Work to develop insights.** Good research creates understanding; it doesn't simply pile up data or seek to win an argument. Synthesize material by linking new information to what you already know.

10. **Fit the research to the subject.** Use the research methods required by your instructor or expected in your subject area (biology, psychology). Present your research in a form that makes sense for the discipline, topic, and readers.

Overview
The Research and Writing Process

Research writing shares much in common with other forms of writing. For example, a research paper is best generated through the full writing process. However, a research project offers special challenges. Some of these challenges are outlined below and on the pages that follow.

Writer's Goal

Research writing inevitably involves discovering information, sharing what you have learned, and using that information to support a key point or issue. Your purpose will generally be either to inform your readers or to persuade them to accept your point of view.

- **Writing to inform:** When your goal is to inform readers, then your motto should be "just the facts, please." In this case, you are writing an expository essay or a research report. You need to provide the descriptions, explanations, statistics, and examples that your readers need to understand your main idea.

- **Writing to persuade:** When your goal is to persuade readers—affecting how they think, behave, or act—then you definitely need more than "just the facts." Position papers, problem-solution essays, and evaluation papers are examples of persuasive writing. You must develop your own position and then use facts, descriptions, explanations, statistics, and examples to support it.

Keys for Success

Plan carefully. ■ Plan your time carefully and break the project into manageable steps with realistic deadlines. Pulling an all-nighter won't result in a good paper, because it doesn't give you the time to research, read, think, write, revise, and polish.

Choose the right resources. ■ To gather reliable information, start by considering these questions:

- Which **primary sources**—observations, interviews, surveys, experiments, documents—will give you the needed information?
- Which **secondary sources**—books, articles, Web sites—offer relevant, reliable data?

Conduct in-depth research. ■ Follow these tips when gathering information:

- Dig for quality sources using the library, the Internet, and primary sources.
- Let each source lead you to other sources.
- Keep an accurate record of your sources.
- Read sources carefully, take good notes, and use the information appropriately in your paper.

Approaches to Consider

Just about anyone can complete a research project and get a passing grade. Excellent research papers, on the other hand, demonstrate real commitment. Check the approaches below and find ways to use them in your research projects.

Research that is I-focused. ■ The I-focused paper records the writer's quest to satisfy his or her curiosity. The student researcher uses primary sources such as visits, observations, and interviews, but checks print sources only when recommended by a primary source. The I-focused paper then becomes the story of the writer's research adventure—telling what the writer wanted to know, where he or she looked, and what he or she discovered. This form relies heavily on the writer's personal findings, which are often recorded in a research journal.

Research that is reader-focused. ■ A good reader-focused paper records the writer's side of a conversation about a topic—a conversation with the readers. Consider these questions:

- What do you want to say about the topic to your readers?
- Is your goal to interest your readers, help them understand, solve their problems, argue a point with them, or persuade them to act?
- What kind of response do you imagine receiving from your readers?

Research that integrates both approaches. ■ Both of the preceding approaches can guide a research paper. Some instructors ask students to include facts about the process that become apparent while the research is being conducted. The results of primary searches may be included, along with any changes in the writer-researcher's perceptions, attitudes, and opinions. Consider these questions:

- What happened as you did your research?
- What did you learn?

INSIGHT: Before you get started on your research paper, pause and review the list of issues below. They offer you some direction to explore in preparation for your own project.

- To get a sense of the whole research process, review the chart on page **446**.
- To study sample research papers, turn to pages **525–534** for an MLA paper or pages **555–566** for an APA paper. (**Note:** Many of the examples in this chapter relate to the sample MLA paper on UN sanctions against Iraq.)
- For in-depth help with conducting primary, library, and Internet research, see Chapter 32 (pages **477–502**).
- Special help with the following key research issues can be found later in this chapter: evaluating sources (page **456**), taking notes (pages **457–462**), integrating sources (pages **467–468**), avoiding plagiarism (pages **471–473**).
- For details of MLA format, see Chapter 33. For APA, see Chapter 34.

The Research Process: A Flowchart

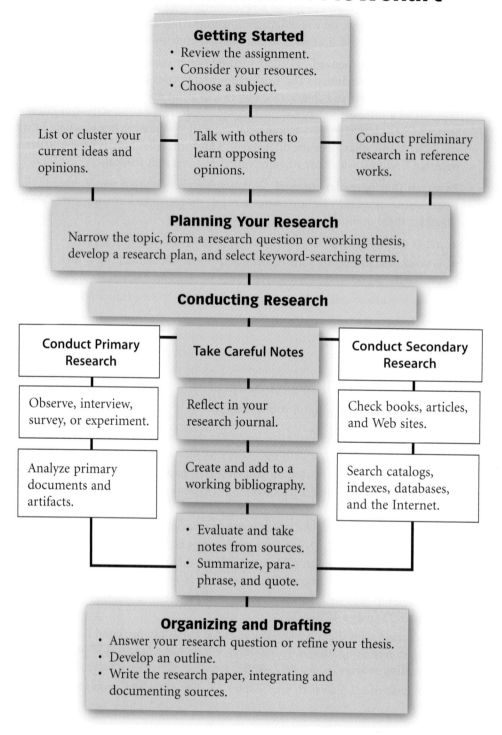

Getting Started
- Review the assignment.
- Consider your resources.
- Choose a subject.

List or cluster your current ideas and opinions.

Talk with others to learn opposing opinions.

Conduct preliminary research in reference works.

Planning Your Research
Narrow the topic, form a research question or working thesis, develop a research plan, and select keyword-searching terms.

Conducting Research

Conduct Primary Research

Take Careful Notes

Conduct Secondary Research

Observe, interview, survey, or experiment.

Reflect in your research journal.

Check books, articles, and Web sites.

Analyze primary documents and artifacts.

Create and add to a working bibliography.

Search catalogs, indexes, databases, and the Internet.

- Evaluate and take notes from sources.
- Summarize, para-phrase, and quote.

Organizing and Drafting
- Answer your research question or refine your thesis.
- Develop an outline.
- Write the research paper, integrating and documenting sources.

Getting Started

video

Understand the assignment.

The assignment you are given should direct your research and set its boundaries. Therefore, understanding the assignment is a crucial first step in conducting effective research. Use the questions below to focus your thinking about the project.

Purpose ◆ What are you being asked to research? Why? What weight does the project carry in the course? How is the assignment related to course goals?

Product ◆ What should result from your research—an essay, a presentation, or a Web site? Consider these issues as well:

- **Length:** number of pages or words required
- **Format:** margins, line spacing, type size, justification, headers, pagination, and documentation methods (MLA, APA)
- **Submission:** what you must turn in (outline, research notes, first draft)
- **Method of evaluation:** how the project will be assessed

Process ◆ What are the stages in the process and when must each be completed?

- **Selecting a topic:** Are there restrictions on what topic you can choose? Do you need an approved thesis statement?
- **Planning:** When do you need to finish the following steps: Working thesis? Outline? Bibliography? First draft? Final project?
- **Writing:** Can you collaborate with a classmate? Where can you obtain help along the way? Who will answer your questions?

Research Expectations ◆ What types of sources are you expected to use?

- **Print sources:** Are you expected to use primarily printed materials, such as books, periodicals, or professional journals?
- **Electronic sources:** Are you limited in the number of Web sources you can use? Should you focus on academic databases?
- **Primary sources:** Are you encouraged to interview people? Make observations? Conduct surveys?

Key Terms ◆ Study the assignment for the following words:

- **Audience words:** terms indicating who your readers are.
- **Subject words:** terms indicating the research subject. What should you research, and what should you avoid?
- **Action words:** terms indicating what to do with the subject. Are you expected to analyze, compare and contrast, predict, or evaluate? (See pages **399–400**.)

Prepare to respond.

A key step in getting started on your research paper is simply preparing to do the research. Take care of the practical details below.

Review any handouts. ▣ Note any special tips, advice, and requirements. If necessary, ask your instructor to clarify the details of the assignment, such as the purpose, audience, research expectations, length, format, and evaluation method. (See "Understand the assignment," page **447**.)

Develop a schedule. ▣ Each situation is different, but generally you should spend about half of your time on research and half on writing. As always, start your project as soon as possible. Sketch out a preliminary schedule of when you will complete each phase of your work: choosing a topic, creating a working thesis, conducting research, developing an outline, completing your first draft, completing the works-cited list, and so on.

Activity	*Due Date*
Choose a topic	April 11
Create a working thesis	April 12
Conduct research	April 22

Select a method of note taking. ▣ Choose from the note-card, double-entry notebook, copy-and-annotate, and research-log methods (pages **457–459**).

Create a recordkeeping system. ▣ Arrange your notes, printouts, photocopies, and drafts in separate folders, binders, or computer files. Having complete notes and records makes it easier to draft the paper, and you'll be ready in case your instructor asks to see your research notes.

Select an interesting topic.

If you have some leeway, choose a topic that you would like to explore. Consider current issues, personal interests, or classroom topics. (See "Selecting a Topic," pages **30–34**.)

- Talk with classmates and family members.
- Consider topics covered in your textbooks or other classes.
- Use freewriting or clustering to explore possibilities.
- Check a variety of Web sites. (Your instructor may suggest some sites.)
- Keep subjects in mind as you read newspapers, study material for other courses, and watch newscasts and documentaries.
- Ask your instructor (or a librarian) for some general topic categories often used in research projects.

Avoid topics that are overused, outdated, too general, too specific, or not important enough to warrant your spending the time required researching them.

Planning Your Research

video

Narrow and focus your topic.

Once you have identified an interesting topic, you need to focus on a specific feature of that topic. You can begin by reading background sources, by checking the *Library of Congress Subject Headings* for narrower topics (see page **486**), and by examining subject directories on the Internet (see page **498**). Try freewriting and brainstorming to discover and explore interesting angles.

Believe it or not, you'll know that you've narrowed your subject enough when you begin to think, "I'll never find enough information on this topic!" To be sure that you've arrived at a manageable topic, use these tests:

- Am I truly interested in this topic?
- Does it meet all the assignment requirements?
- Do I have access to enough information?
- Is a paper on this topic feasible, given the time and page constraints?

Form a working thesis.

Before digging into your research, pause to give your project a sharp sense of direction.

Ask a key research question. ■ Make it a specific question about the topic, a question to which you don't yet have the answer, a question that demands research. Use this question—and the *who, what, when, where, why,* and *how* questions—as you begin to do your actual research. (See pages **100–101**.)

I want to find out *who* . . .

　I want to discover *what* . . .

　　I want to learn *when* . . .

　　　I want to know *where* . . .

　　　　I want to understand *why* and *how* . . .

Record a working thesis. ■ Make a statement that demands, "Prove it!" Don't settle for a simple statement of fact, but choose something that seems debatable or requires an explanation. (See page **450**.)

Bottom Line _

Beginning your research project with a specific topic and thesis spelled out is important. However, you should realize that your working thesis may change as you conduct your research. This change is perfectly acceptable. Always remember that your working thesis is written in sand, not stone.

tips FOR WRITING A THESIS STATEMENT

A good thesis statement tells readers what your topic is and, more important, what angle you plan to take or what point you hope to make. Your thesis also helps you to focus on your topic throughout the research process and to prioritize your research time. It will help you decide whether to thoroughly read a particular book or just skim it, photocopy an article or take a few notes on it, view an entire Web site or search for specific details.

The Process at Work

A thesis statement is usually a single sentence that contains two main parts: a limited topic plus a specific focus. To arrive at a working thesis, you might follow this process:

● **Select a subject.**	UN sanctions
● **Narrow your subject to a limited topic.**	UN sanctions against Iraq
● **Find a specific focus or feature.**	The negative effects of the UN sanctions on the people of Iraq
● **Put your focus in the form of a question.**	How serious are the negative effects of the UN sanctions on the men, women, and children of Iraq?
● **Compose a working thesis statement.**	The suffering of Iraqi men, women, and children is/is not a justifiable side effect of the sanctions against Iraq.

Thesis Checklist

1. **Does your thesis statement focus on a single, limited topic?**
2. **Is your thesis stated in a clear, direct sentence (or sentences)?**
3. **Does your thesis convey your personal perspective about the topic?**
4. **Do you have access to enough good information to support your thesis statement?**
5. **Does your thesis direct you to write a paper that meets all the requirements of the assignment?**

Develop a research plan.

It pays to plan your research. In fact, minutes spent *planning* research can save hours *doing* research. With your topic and working thesis in mind, consider these issues and develop a plan that will take you to valuable resources.

Planning Questions ◆ Before you begin your research, ask yourself the following questions:

_____ What resources are required by the assignment?

_____ What resources will help me answer my research question or support my thesis?

_____ How will I gather material—by signing out library resources, photocopying articles, printing electronic files, or bookmarking Web sites?

_____ How will I organize material—in a project binder, a set of file folders, electronic files, or a research journal?

Background Research ◆ To find information about your topic's history, controversial issues, and key terms, take these steps:

_____ Use the *Library of Congress Subject Headings* (in a library's reference section) to find keywords to use in searching the library catalog, periodical databases, and the Internet.

_____ Conduct a preliminary search to make sure that good resources exist.

_____ Check your textbook for a topic overview, bibliography, or glossary.

_____ Use reference works to find background, definitions, facts, and statistics.

Library Research ◆ Select important library resources.

_____ **Books:** Would scholarly studies (print or e-Book) deal with your topic and provide current information?

_____ **Periodical articles:** Would periodical articles supply reliable information? What kinds of periodicals would be best—newspapers or broadcast transcripts, popular magazines, or scholarly journals?

_____ **Other resources:** Does your library have a documentary, taped interview, or pamphlet on your topic? Look online for government publications.

Internet Research ◆ Plan effective Internet searches by considering the following:

_____ **Search engines and subject guides:** Which tools will lead you to quality resources?

_____ **Librarian guidance:** Which Web sites do librarians recommend?

Field Research ◆ Do some field research if appropriate.

_____ Does an interview or a survey make sense for your project?

_____ How about an experiment or a field observation?

Locate a variety of sources.

Information comes in all shapes and sizes. The chart below provides an overview of what kinds of information are available and where you can find that information. Tap those resources that will be the most useful for your research project.

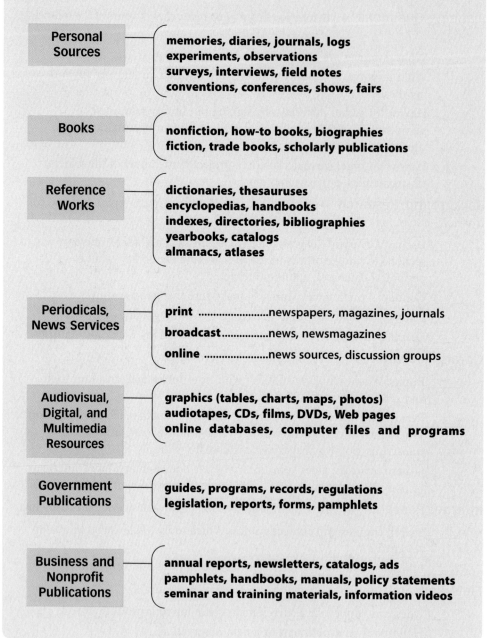

Personal Sources
- memories, diaries, journals, logs
- experiments, observations
- surveys, interviews, field notes
- conventions, conferences, shows, fairs

Books
- nonfiction, how-to books, biographies
- fiction, trade books, scholarly publications

Reference Works
- dictionaries, thesauruses
- encyclopedias, handbooks
- indexes, directories, bibliographies
- yearbooks, catalogs
- almanacs, atlases

Periodicals, News Services
- print ....newspapers, magazines, journals
- broadcast................news, newsmagazines
- online ....news sources, discussion groups

Audiovisual, Digital, and Multimedia Resources
- graphics (tables, charts, maps, photos)
- audiotapes, CDs, films, DVDs, Web pages
- online databases, computer files and programs

Government Publications
- guides, programs, records, regulations
- legislation, reports, forms, pamphlets

Business and Nonprofit Publications
- annual reports, newsletters, catalogs, ads
- pamphlets, handbooks, manuals, policy statements
- seminar and training materials, information videos

Conducting Research

Conduct preliminary research.

video

Explore your working thesis or research question on a variety of fronts, using each source to lead you to other sources.

- Uncover basic facts about your topic through background readings.
- Conduct keyword searches of library catalogs, databases, indexes, and the Internet to locate relevant books, journals, and online resources. (Use the *Library of Congress Subject Headings* to find keywords for your search; also, see pages **486–487**.)
- Skim the sources that you find, and do some field research (for example, interviewing and observing).
- Keep track of answers to your research question or refinements to your working thesis. Let your research guide your thinking.

Take inventory.

Construct a list or complete a graphic overview after you have selected your topic and done some preliminary reading. What information do you already know? Not know? Need to know? Also consider where you will find this information.

Know	Need to Know	Want to Know
Many Iraqi children have starved to death.	How many deaths have been verified?	Have economic sanctions caused this?

Do in-depth research.

At this point, you should be ready to do in-depth research, pursuing answers to your research questions or support for your working thesis. Conduct your research by taking the following steps, which are outlined in more detail on the pages listed below:

1. **Locate a variety of sources.** Consider both primary and secondary resources, and use your college library and the Internet. See "Primary, Library, and Internet Research," pages **477–502**.

2. **Create a working bibliography.** Record essential information about each source. See pages **454–455**.

3. **Evaluate each source.** Make sure sources are current and reliable. See page **456**.

4. **Take careful notes.** Use an efficient note-taking system to summarize, paraphrase, and quote sources clearly and accurately. See pages **457–462**.

Create a working bibliography.

A working bibliography lists sources that you have used or intend to use. It helps you track your research and develop your final bibliography.

Choose an orderly method.

- **Paper note cards:** Use 3" ✕ 5" cards, and record one source per card.
- **Paper notebook:** Use a small, spiral-bound book to record sources.
- **Computer program:** Record source information in electronic form.
  TIP: Giving each source a code number will help you during the drafting, revising, and editing, especially as you document your sources.

Include complete information for each source.

- **Books:** author, title and subtitle, publication details (place, publisher, date)
- **Periodicals:** author, article title, journal name, publication information (volume, number, date), page numbers
- **Online sources:** author (if available), document title, sponsor, database name, publication or posting date, access date, other information
- **Primary or field research:** date conducted, name and/or descriptive title of person interviewed, place observed, survey conducted

Add locating information.

- **Books:** Include the call number.
- **Articles:** Note where and how you accessed them.
- **Field research:** Write down a telephone number or an e-mail address.
- **Web pages:** Carefully record the Internet address.

Annotate the source. Add a note about the source's content, focus, usefulness, and reliability.

Periodical Source Note

Card Number	#5
Source Information	Cortright, David, and George A. Lopez. "Are Sanctions Just? The Problematic Case of Iraq." Journal of International Affairs 52:2 (Spring 1999): 735–755.
Location	Bound periodicals
Annotation	Quality academic source with good discussion of the political and moral issues involved in the sanctions.

Book Source Note

Although this book deals only indirectly with the paper's topic (sanctions), the historical information may be valuable.

Card Number	#2
Source Information	Mackey, Sandra. *The Reckoning: Iraq and the Legacy of Saddam Hussein.* New York: W.W. Norton, 2002.
Location	953.82
Annotation	Author presents case for America not to destroy Hussein. A lot of historical info on Iraq.

Internet Source Note

In this case, obtaining an e-mail address from the Web site led to an interview with the author of the article (see the interview source note below).

Card Number	#3
Source Information	Capaccio, George. "Suffer the Little Children." *Iraq Action Coalition.* 12 March 2002.
Location	http://iraqaction.org/suffer.html
Annotation	Details efforts of relief workers in Iraq.

Interview Source Note

Card Number	#4
Source Information	Capaccio, George. E-mail interview. 7 April 2002.
Location	jsmith@orc.com, 607-763-8855
Annotation	E-mail correspondence with author of article "Suffer the Little Children."

Web

Evaluate each source.

As you work with your sources, test their reliability by asking the questions below. Using trustworthy sources strengthens the credibility of your research paper.

Is the author an expert?

An expert is an authority—someone who has mastered a subject area. Is the author an expert on this topic?

Web test Does a subject directory recommend this site? Who sponsors it? Are the author's name, credentials, and contact information available?

Is the source current?

A five-year-old book on computers may be ancient history, but a book on Abraham Lincoln could be 50 years old and still be the best source available.

Web test When was the site created and last updated? Are links current?

Using trustworthy sources strengthens the credibility of your research paper.

Is the source accurate and logical?

Check for obvious factual errors, analysis that doesn't make sense, and conclusions that don't add up.

Web test Is the material easy to understand, with useful multimedia elements? How are claims backed up? Can you trace the sources used?

Does the source seem complete?

Try to see the whole picture. Does the discussion seem full, or do you sense major gaps? Have you received both sides of the argument?

Web test Does the site seem thin? Review the topics covered, their depth, and the site's internal and external links.

Is the source unbiased?

A bias means, literally, a tilt to one side. Although all sources come from a specific perspective, a biased source may be pushing a particular agenda. Watch for bias toward a region, country, political party, gender, philosophy, religion, industry, or ethnic group. Ask, "Why was this source created?"

Web test Is the site nonprofit (.org), government (.gov), educational (.edu), or commercial (.com)? Is it promoting a cause, product, or belief?

How does the source compare?

Does it conflict with other sources? Do sources disagree on the facts themselves or on how to interpret the facts?

Web test Is it easy to get into and move around in the site? Is the site's information consistent with print sources?

Taking Notes

Accurate, thoughtful notes create a foundation for your research paper. To take good notes, you must be selective—recording only information that is related to your research question or working thesis. The key is to select an efficient note-taking system. A good system will help you to

- Keep accurate records and thereby avoid accidental plagiarism.
- Record summaries, paraphrases, and quotations correctly.
- Explore your own ideas and responses to sources.
- Develop an outline and write a first draft of your paper.

Four systems are outlined below and on the pages that follow. Choose the system that works best for you or combine elements to develop a system of your own.

Use a note-taking system.

An efficient note-taking system will enable you to work with your sources carefully and thoughtfully. Note taking will also make organizing and drafting your paper simpler.

Copy and Annotate

The copy-and-annotate method involves working with electronic texts, photocopies, or print versions of sources.

1. Selectively photocopy or print important articles, chapters, and Web pages. Copy carefully, making sure that you have the full page, including page number. (With electronic texts, copy and paste the material into a word-processing program.)

2. Add identifying information directly on the copy—author, publication details, and date—if you do not yet have a working bibliography. Each source should be easy to identify and trace.

3. As you read, annotate the text and highlight key statements. In the margins (or within your computer file), record your ideas, responses, and questions.

Upside: Copying helps maintain the accuracy of your sources; adding explanations and comments encourages critical thinking and forces you to immediately digest what you have read.

Downside: Organizing material for drafting is inconvenient.

Note: For more information on annotation strategies, see pages 16–17. Also, you may want to check out the new methods of digital note taking now available.

The Computer Notebook or Research Log

The computer notebook or research log method involves note taking on a computer or on sheets of paper. Here's how it works:

1. Establish a central location for your notes—a notebook, a file folder, a binder, or an electronic folder.

2. Take notes on one source at a time, making sure first to identify the source fully. Number your pages.

3. When recording your own thoughts, distinguish them from source material by using your initials or some other symbol.

4. When it's time to outline your paper, use codes to go through your notes and identify which information relates to which topic in your outline.

Upside: Taking lists of notes feels natural without being overly systematic.

Downside: Preparing to draft may require time-consuming reorganization.

Note Cards

Using paper note cards is the traditional method of note taking:

1. Establish one set of cards (3" × 5") for your working bibliography (see pages **454–455**).

2. On a second set of cards (4" × 6"), take notes by following these guidelines:
- Record one point from one source per card.
- Clarify the source: list the author's last name, a shortened title, or a code number from the matching bibliography card. Include a page number.
- Provide a heading, called a *slug*, to help you arrange information.
- Label the note as a summary, paraphrase, or quotation of the original.
- Distinguish between the source's information and your own comments.

Upside: Note cards make outlining and drafting easier.

Downside: Preparing note cards can be tedious.

Slug	*The justice of sanctions* ①
Paraphrase	*The just-war doctrine emphasizes that according to the rules of war, countries cannot target vulnerable populations. (para.) p. 740*
Comments	*TH: important idea about innocent victims, but is the UN "targeting" children? Is the difference important? Possible topic sentence?*

Double-Entry Notebook

When using a double-entry notebook, do the following:

1. Divide the notebook pages in half vertically.

2. In the left column, record bibliographic information and take notes.

3. In the right column, write your responses. Think about what the source is saying, why the point is important, whether you agree with it, and how the point relates to other ideas.

Upside: The double-entry method creates accurate source records while encouraging thoughtful response; also, it can be used on a computer.

Downside: Organizing material for drafting is a challenge.

Cortright, David, and George A. Lopez. "Are Sanctions Just? The Problematic Case of Iraq." Journal of International Affairs 52.2 (1999): 735–755.

Sanctions have become a common UN policy tool for resolving disputes. (735)

"Although often intended to protect human rights, sanctions may contribute to the further deterioration of the human rights situation in a target nation." (735)

The sanctions often affect the average person, not the political leaders causing the problem. (735–736)

Sanctions work as a "middle ground between mere diplomatic protest and ultimate military force." (736)

The sanctions situation is complicated by the way the UN implements them. Sanctions are largely in the hands of the members of the Security Council because they can block changes or push their own agenda. (736–737)

Cortright and Lopez really get to the heart of the problem, which is a terrible irony in a way. The sanctions are an effective way to pressure a nation into stopping terrible behavior.

The problem is that these sanctions often end up hurting some of the people they're meant to help—the average people suffering under unjust governments.

That's the challenge—how to make sanctions work without making the situation worse.

Question: How do sanctions relate to diplomacy and military action?

I didn't realize that the Security Council had so much power, including America. In what ways is power a central issue both in the UN and in Iraq? What are the motives behind the power?

Use quotes, summaries, and paraphrases.

As you work with sources, you need to determine what to put in your notes and how to record it—as a summary, paraphrase, or quotation. The passage below comes from an article that the student writer used in his research paper on UN sanctions (pages **525–534**). After reading the passage, note how the researcher summarizes, paraphrases, and quotes from the source (always recording the page number of the material).

Original Passage

From pages 745–746 of "Are Sanctions Just? The Problematic Case of Iraq," by David Cortright and George A. Lopez, published in the *Journal of International Affairs* (Spring 1999, 52:2): 735–755.

Given Baghdad's opposition to the oil-for-food program, it is not surprising that this project has been unable to relieve the humanitarian crisis in Iraq: nor is it likely to do so in the future. This crisis is simply too vast and the reluctance of the Iraqi government too great to permit the kind of comprehensive, coordinated effort needed to overcome the effects of eight years of sanctions. The Iraqi government has adopted a strategy for resisting UN pressure that redirects the pain of sanctions onto the most vulnerable and allows its people to die as a means of generating sympathy for the lifting of sanctions. The United Nations has been put in an untenable situation. To offer an analogy with warfare, it is as if the opposing army has brought children to the front lines and allowed them to be massacred. Would a military force facing such a diabolical maneuver be justified in attacking? Is the Security Council justified in maintaining comprehensive sanctions against an opponent who is willing to make innocent children the primary victim? A policy designed to exert pressure on an aggressor regime has been perverted by that regime into a virtual attack on innocents. It may be correct to say that responsibility for the humanitarian suffering rests with Saddam Hussein, but this does not solve the practical problem of overcoming injustice. The oil-for-food program may be a sincere attempt to address the injustice caused by sanctions in Iraq, but it is not a sufficient answer and does not acquit the members of the Security Council of the obligation to take further steps to prevent the suffering of innocent civilians. Precisely because it is known that the Iraqi government is victimizing its own population, the United Nations must adjust its policies and find a different approach to achieving its objectives in Iraq.

Quoting

Quoting records the original source word for word, within quotation marks. Quote only statements that are relatively short, well phrased, or authoritative.

1. Note the quotation's context—how it fits in the author's discussion.

2. Copy the phrase, sentence, or passage word for word—carefully. Enclose the original material in clearly visible quotation marks.

3. If you leave out any words, note that omission with an ellipsis [. . .].

4. Integrate the quotation smoothly into your paper. (See pages **467–468**.)

Sample Quotations

"A policy designed to exert pressure on an aggressor regime has been perverted by that regime into a virtual attack on innocents" (745).

Note: The researcher quotes this sentence because it effectively states a tragic irony.

"Precisely because it is known that the Iraqi government is victimizing its own population, the United Nations must adjust its policies and find a different approach to achieving its objectives in Iraq" (746).

Note: This sentence makes a good quotation because it succinctly captures the authors' thesis.

Summarizing

Summarizing condenses only the main points in a passage into your own words. Summarize when a source provides basic ideas or information on your topic.

1. Reread the passage, jotting down the key points or phrases.

2. Without looking back at the original, state the main point in your own words. Add key supporting points, leaving out examples and details.

3. Check your summary against the original, making sure that you have not recorded exact phrases without quotation marks.

Sample Summary

The oil-for-food program hasn't solved the suffering in Iraq, partly because of the Iraqi government's resistance. In fact, Saddam Hussein has used his own people as a weapon against the UN. For this very reason, the UN should rethink and modify sanctions. (745–746)

Paraphrasing

Paraphrasing restates the entire passage in your own words. Paraphrase when you need to clarify a particularly important passage.

1. Quickly review the passage to get a sense of the whole.

2. Go though the passage carefully, sentence by sentence.
  - State the ideas in your own words, using synonyms whenever possible.
  - Consider putting the ideas in a new order, but don't change the meaning.
  - Use simple words instead of technical language, defining words as necessary.
  - Be careful not to borrow phrases directly unless you put them in quotation marks and record page numbers.

3. Check your paraphrase against the original material for accurate tone and meaning.

Sample Paraphrase

As David Cortright and George A. Lopez point out, the Iraqi government has resisted the oil-for-food program, and the suffering of Iraq's people hasn't been resolved. After eight years of sanctions, the problem is just too big. In fact, Iraq's government is using the sanctions to cause suffering for its own people so that public opinion will grow against the sanctions—putting the UN in a no-win situation. Should the Security Council continue to impose sanctions when the Iraqi government is perverting them? While it's true that Hussein carries the main guilt, blaming him doesn't solve the problem. The oil-for-food program, although well intentioned, isn't enough. The Security Council must find a new approach that achieves its objectives while limiting harm to civilians. (745–746)

Reflect on your sources.

Good research goes beyond recording quotations, paraphrases, and summaries. It fully explores the meaning of the facts and figures. As you work with your sources, reflect on them by doing the following:

1. Record and review your reactions. What do the sources make you think and feel about the topic? How do they connect or conflict with your experiences, attitudes, and beliefs?

2. Put each source in context. How does the source relate to your topic? Does this source confirm or counter other material that you have been reading?

3. Consider how you might use this source in your paper. How might the source help you develop and share your ideas?

Organizing Your Research

Establish a method of development.

An organizing pattern for your paper may be built into your assignment. For example, you may be asked specifically to develop a cause/effect or comparison paper. When a pattern is not assigned, one may still evolve quite naturally during your planning. If this evolution doesn't happen, take a careful look at your thesis statement (and supporting information). An effective thesis will often suggest a method of development; if your thesis doesn't, consider changing it.

When you choose a method of development, you are really looking for a basic framework or structure for your paper. Within that general structure, other patterns may come into play. You may, for example, be writing a comparison, but within that structure, you may do some describing or classifying. Or you may be developing an argument, but within that structure, you introduce some of your supporting points using a cause/effect approach.

Types of Patterns

Knowing how these various patterns work will help you plan and organize your writing. Use the chart below to get started. (The numbers refer to writing samples in the book that are organized according to the listed pattern.)

Types	Organizing Principles
Process (How something works)	Chronological Order (pages **226–227**)
Narrative (How something happened)	Chronological Order (pages **138–139**)
Description (How something/ someone appears)	Chronological Order and Spatial Order—Location (pages **168–177**)
Comparison (How two things are alike/different)	Whole vs. Whole Comparison Point-by-Point Comparison (page **197**)
Cause/Effect (How one thing affects something else)	Identify Cause/Explore Effects Identify Effect/Explore Causes (pages **185–186**)
Problem/Solution (How a problem can can be solved)	Study the Problem/Solution(s) (pages **315–316**)
Classification (How something can be categorized)	Use Categories (pages **213–215**)
Argumentation (How a position or an opinion can be asserted and supported)	Assert and Support, Counter the Opposition/ Reassert Position (pages **272–273**)
Explain and Analyze (How something is explained or closely examined)	Move Back and Forth Between Explanation (or Definition) and Analysis (pages **241–243**)

Organize your ideas.

Once you've established a general method of development, you're ready to organize the information (main points, supporting details, and so on) that you expect to cover in your research paper. You can begin by organizing your notes into the best possible order. It may be enough simply to jot down a brief list of ideas from your notes. Alternatively, you may find it helpful to arrange your ideas into a full outline.

Organize Your Notes

Depending on which note-taking system you used, organizing your notes should be fairly straightforward. If you used note cards, sort them by headings and subheadings; then sequence the stacks following the method of development you've chosen for your paper (cause/effect, problem/solution, and so on).

If you used a computer note-taking system, use your program to cut, paste, add, and copy until you have an organized sequence. Then print out your notes and use them to construct your research plan or outline.

If you took notes on paper or used the copy-and-annotate method, you should group information using a code system of key words, letters, or numbers. You may even cut up your notes, but make sure that you can still trace all your sources.

Outline Your Ideas

An outline is an orderly list of related ideas. Begin your work by placing your working thesis at the top of your paper. Use it to stay focused on the job at hand.

Sample Outline

Thesis: The suffering of Iraqi men, women, and children is not a justifiable side effect of the UN sanctions against Iraq.

I. To date, the UN sanctions have not worked.
   A. Iraq has not destroyed its weapons of mass destruction.
   B. The blockade of Iraqi exports is only partially working.
   C. The restriction on Iraqi imports is in disarray.

II. Living conditions are deplorable.
   A. Food is scarce, and a good share of the water is undrinkable.
   B. Health care is very poor.
   C. Housing and education are inadequate.
   D. Child abandonment is on the rise.

III. The UN is looking for solutions.
   A. A "oil-for-food" program went into effect in 1995.
   B. More relief agencies may soon be operating in Iraq.

IV. People disagree with the sanctions.
   A. Present sanctions hurt people.
   B. Need fairer, more effective policy.

Drafting Your Paper

video

Select a drafting method.

Before you begin drafting your paper, refine your research question or working thesis as necessary. Then choose a drafting method that works for you:

Option 1: *Writing Systematically*

- Develop a detailed outline, including supporting evidence.
- Arrange your notes in precise order.
- Write a general statement that covers the first main point.
- Begin writing, referring regularly to your statement, outline, and notes.
- Write another statement that covers the second main point.
- Continue in this way, adding facts, examples, and quotations as needed.
- Cite your sources.

Option 2: *Writing Freely*

- Review your research notes, but then set them aside.
- If you need to, jot down a brief outline.
- Begin writing, getting all of your thoughts down on paper.
- Use your own words as much as possible.
- Go back to your notes and use them to further develop your draft.
- Cite your sources.

Start your draft.

Create a Working Title

Write a working title that captures the topic and spirit of your paper. (You may also wait until you've completed a draft to write a title.)

Draft an Introduction

The introduction should do two things. The first part should say something interesting, surprising, or personal about your subject to gain your readers' attention. The second part should identify the specific focus, or thesis, of your research.

- Start out with a revealing story or quotation.
- Give important background information.
- Offer a series of interesting or surprising facts.
- Provide important definitions.
- Identify your focus or thesis.

Develop your main points.

How do you develop a complete and insightful research paper? How do you add dimension and depth to your writing? For starters, you make sure that you have carefully explored and reflected on your specific topic. You also make sure that you have gathered plenty of compelling evidence to support your thesis.

It's in the main part of your paper—in the body—that you develop your thesis. The process usually works in this way: You present each main point, expand on it by including supporting facts or examples, and offer additional analysis or documentation as needed.

Another way to approach your writing is to envision it as a series of paragraph clusters—one cluster of paragraphs for each main point. As you write, you imagine yourself conversing with your readers, telling them what they need to know, and communicating it as clearly and interestingly as you can.

tips FOR RESEARCH WRITING

As you draft your paper, keep the focus on your own thoughts. You don't want your paper to read like a strung-together series of references to other sources.

- Present your own ideas honestly and clearly. Although you will be considering the research of others, be sure to analyze this information yourself and relate your sources to one another. Work at offering your personal perspective on the topic.
- Your instructor may want your thesis to appear in a specific location (perhaps in the last sentence of your first paragraph). Follow his or her wishes.
- Don't try to cram everything you've learned into your draft. Select material that is truly needed to develop your thesis.
- Avoid overusing one particular source; also avoid overusing direct quotations.
- To avoid accidental plagiarism, indicate the source of all borrowed facts as you write your draft. (See "Avoiding Plagiarism," pages **471–473**.)

Write the conclusion.

An effective closing adds to the readers' understanding of a research paper. The first part of the closing usually reviews (or ties together) important points in the paper, reinforces or reasserts the thesis, and/or draws a conclusion. The closing's final lines may expand the scope of the text by making a connection between the paper and the readers' experience, or between the paper and life in general.

Using Sources

After you've found good sources and taken good notes on them, you want to use that research effectively in your writing. Specifically, you want to show (1) what information you are borrowing, and (2) where you got it. By doing so, you create credibility. This section shows you how to develop credibility by integrating and documenting sources so as to avoid plagiarism and other abuses. *Note:* For a full treatment of documentation, see Chapter 33 (MLA) and Chapter 34 (APA).

Integrate your sources.

From your first word to your last, readers should be able to recognize what material is yours and what facts and ideas come from other sources. To be fair to your sources, follow these strategies.

Start with Accurate, Orderly Notes

If you've taken good notes, integrating source material into your paper will go smoothly.

Use Sources for the Right Reasons

Focus on what you want to say, not on all the source material you've collected. Use sources to do the following:

- Support your point with facts, statistics, and details.
- Give credibility to your point by presenting an expert's supporting statement.
- Bring your point to life with an example, observation, or illustration.
- Address a counterargument or an alternative.

Document All Borrowed Material

Generally, you should credit any information that you have summarized, paraphrased, or quoted from any source, whether it's statistics, facts, graphics, song lyrics, phrases, or sequences of ideas. Your reader can then see what's borrowed and what's yours.

Common Knowledge: Common knowledge (information that is generally known to your readers or easily found in several sources) need not be cited. For example, the fact that Iraq invaded Kuwait in 1991 is common knowledge, whereas the precise content of UN Resolution 687 is not. Still not sure of the difference? When in doubt, document.

Use Quotations Sparingly

In most essays, restrict your quoting to key statements. Quotations, especially long ones, must pull their weight, so paraphrase or summarize material instead.

Integrate Quotations Smoothly

When you use quotations, work them into your writing as smoothly as possible. To do so, you need to pay attention to style, punctuation, and syntax. (See pages 586–587.)

Use enough of the quotation to make your point without changing the meaning of the original. Use quotation marks around key phrases taken from the source.

➤ **Cortright and Lopez show that the Iraqi government has "perverted" the sanctions "into a virtual attack on innocents" (745).**

Integrate All Sources Thoughtfully

Fold source material into your writing as logically and smoothly as you can.

1. State and explain your idea, creating a context for the source.
2. Summarize, paraphrase, or quote the source, documenting as necessary.
3. Identify the source (author and page number) and link it to your writing.
4. Integrate the source effectively by explaining, expanding, or refuting it.

Sample Passage

The passage below, taken from the sample research paper on pages 525–534, demonstrates the principles of integrating and documenting sources.

Writer's ideas

Iraq's people are not responsible for Saddam Hussein's aggression, but they have been forced to suffer under the economic sanctions. In fact, many people believe that the suffering of innocent civilians makes economic sanctions illegal under the just-war doctrine. David Cortright, a

Attributive phrase

researcher for International Peace Studies at the University of Notre Dame, explains that according to the just-war doctrine, warring countries cannot target vulnerable populations, such as the elderly, women, and children.

Paraphrase, quotation, and summary

Cortright goes on to argue that "[i]f decision makers in war are bound by the moral criteria of the just-war doctrine, those imposing economic sanctions must be similarly bound by such constraints. The principle of civilian immunity applies no less in the imposition of economic sanctions

Citation

than in the conduct of war" (Cortright and Lopez 740). In the same way, others argue that economic sanctions place Iraq under a siege that harms civilians much more than it harms the military (Gordon 391). The economic sanctions cripple the most vulnerable people in Iraq while doing

Commentary

little to force Saddam Hussein to follow the United Nations' resolutions. The sanctions must be changed both to relieve people's suffering and to keep Hussein from developing weapons of mass destruction.

Document your sources.
Identify Clearly Where Source Material Begins

An attributive statement tells the reader who is being cited. It may indicate the author's name and credentials, the title of the source, and/or helpful background information. The guidelines and examples below follow MLA style. (See pages 508–511 for more details.)

- **David Cortright, a researcher for International Peace Studies at the University of Notre Dame, explains** that according to the just-war doctrine, warring countries cannot target vulnerable populations, such as the elderly, women, and children (Cortright and Lopez 740).

For additional references to the same source, use a simplified attributive phrase, such as the author's last name.

- **Cortright goes on to argue** that "[i]f decision makers in war are bound by the moral criteria of the just-war doctrine, those imposing economic sanctions must be similarly bound by such constraints" (740).

In some situations, such as quoting facts, skip the attributive phrase.

- **UN Resolution 986, the oil-for-food program passed in 1995, allows Iraq to sell $5.2 billion worth of oil every six months (Cortright and Lopez 742).**

The verb that you use to introduce source material is a key part of the attributive phrase. Use fitting verbs, such as the following:

Sample Attributive Verbs—Synonyms for "Says"			
accepts	considers	explains	rejects
acknowledges	contradicts	highlights	reminds
adds	contrasts	identifies	responds
affirms	criticizes	insists	shares
argues	declares	interprets	shows
asserts	defends	lists	states
believes	denies	maintains	stresses
cautions	describes	outlines	suggests
claims	disagrees	points out	supports
compares	discusses	praises	urges
concludes	emphasizes	proposes	verifies
confirms	enumerates	refutes	warns

Normally, use attributive verbs in the present tense. Use the past tense only when you want to stress the "pastness" of a source.

- **In their 1999 article, "Are Sanctions Just? The Problematic Case of Iraq,"** Cortright and Lopez **argued** that civilians should be just as safe from sanctions as they are from a full war. More recently, they **have elaborated** this principle in their book, *The Sanctions Decade . . .*

Use a Citation to Signal Where Source Material Ends

While documentation systems differ, generally place the citation immediately after a quotation, paraphrase, or summary.

➤ **Denis Halliday, the former UN Humanitarian Coordinator to Iraq,** argues that "sanctions are both directly and indirectly killing approximately six or seven thousand Iraqi children per month" **(77)**, whereas Iraq suffered 40,000 casualties during the war.

At times, it may be smoother to place the citation at the end of a sentence. When you discuss several facts or quotations from the same page in a source, use an attributive phrase at the beginning and a single citation at the end.

➤ **Capaccio** saw evidence that in rural areas only about 50 percent of the water is drinkable, and medicines are not available unless they are bought on the black market **(E-mail).**

Set Off Longer Quotations

Set off quotations of five lines or longer. Introduce the quotation with a sentence and a colon. Indent the quotation one inch (ten spaces) and double-space it, but don't use quotation marks. Put the citation outside the final punctuation mark.

➤ **According to Cortright and Lopez, the UN sanctions against Iraq must be judged according to the standards of the just-war doctrine:**

> **If decision makers in war are bound by the moral criteria of the just-war doctrine, those imposing economic sanctions must similarly be bound by such constraints. The principle of civilian immunity applies no less in the imposition of economic sanctions than in the conduct of war.** (740)

Clearly Indicate Changes to Quotations

You may shorten or change a quotation so that it fits more smoothly into your sentence—but don't alter the original meaning.

Use an ellipsis within square brackets to indicate that you have omitted words from the original. An ellipsis is three periods with a space before and after each period.

➤ **In their analysis of Baghdad's responsibility for the suffering of its own citizens, Cortright and Lopez note "the tragic irony [. . .] that the government has found the resources to [. . .] build a 350-mile river channel through the southern region" (744).**

Use square brackets to indicate a clarification or to change a pronoun or verb tense or to switch around uppercase and lowercase.

➤ **Although Cortright and Lopez do not call for a full lifting of sanctions, they do "agree that a quid pro quo [something for something] response from the Security Council is warranted" (748).**

Web

Avoiding Plagiarism

Plagiarism is improperly using someone's words, ideas, or images (often called "intellectual property") so that they appear to be your own. It is a serious offense, always to be avoided. Effectively integrating and documenting source material will help you avoid plagiarism as well as other forms of source abuse. In addition, study the following tips and examples.

Understand the forms of plagiarism.

Plagiarism refers to a whole range of source abuses—some very obvious, some less readily evident. Read the passage below, which comes from an article used by the writer of the research paper on pages **525–534**. Then review the five types of plagiarism that follow, noting how each misuses the source.

Original Article

The paragraph below is from pages 748–749 of "Are Sanctions Just? The Problematic Case of Iraq," by David Cortright and George A. Lopez, published in the *Journal of International Affairs* (Spring 1999, Volume 52:2): 735–755.

As noted earlier, sanctions can help to encourage a process of dialogue and negotiation, but they cannot by themselves remove a targeted regime or force a drastic change in policy. Sanctions should not be used in a purely punitive manner to starve an opponent into submission. Sanctions work best in combination with incentives and other forms of external influence as part of a carrot-and-stick diplomacy designed to resolve a conflict through negotiation.

Submitting Another Writer's Paper

The most blatant form of plagiarism is taking an entire piece of writing and claiming it as your own work. Here are some examples:

- Downloading an article, reformatting it, and submitting it as your own work.
- Buying an essay from a "paper mill."
- Taking a "free" paper off the Internet.
- Turning in another student's work as your own.

Using Copy-and-Paste

It is unethical to take chunks of material from another source and splice them into your paper without acknowledgment. In the example below, the writer pastes in a sentence from the original article without using quotation marks or a citation. Even if the writer changes some words, it would still be plagiarism.

➤ **For sanctions to work, we need to understand their value and their limits. Sanctions can help to encourage a process of dialogue and negotiation, but they cannot by themselves remove a targeted regime or force a drastic change in policy.**

Failing to Cite a Source

Borrowed material must be documented. Even if you use information accurately and fairly, don't neglect to cite the source. Below, the writer correctly summarizes the passage's idea but offers no citation.

➤ **Sanctions alone do not force unjust governments to change. Instead, sanctions should be combined with other tactics rooted in carrot-and-stick negotiation.**

Neglecting Necessary Quotation Marks

Whether it's a paragraph or a phrase, if you use the exact wording of a source, that material must be enclosed in quotation marks. In the example below, the writer cites the source but doesn't use quotation marks around a phrase taken from the original (boldfaced).

➤ **Sanctions fail when they are used in a purely punitive manner (Cortright and Lopez 749).**

Confusing Borrowed Material with Your Own Ideas

Through carelessness (often in note taking), you may confuse source material with your own thinking. In the passage below, the writer indicates that he borrowed material in the first sentence, but fails to indicate that he also borrowed the next sentence.

➤ **Sanctions work best "to encourage a process of dialogue and negotiation" (Cortright and Lopez 748). By themselves, they cannot remove a targeted regime or force a drastic change in policy.**

 Most schools have their own guidelines and policies regarding plagiarism. Become familiar with those policies so that you don't unknowingly violate them. As always, when in doubt, ask your instructor for clarification. Also check the MLA Web site for more information.

Other Source Abuses

Using Sources Inaccurately ▪ When you get a quotation wrong or paraphrase a source poorly, you misrepresent the original. In the quote below, the writer carelessly drops the important word "not" and replaces "starve" with "bully."

- According to Cortright and Lopez, "sanctions **should be** used in a purely punitive fashion to **bully** an opponent into submission" (749).

Using Source Material Out of Context ▪ By taking a statement out of its original context and forcing it into yours, you can make a source seem to say something that it really didn't. Below, the writer uses part of a statement to say virtually the opposite of the original.

- The example of Iraq proves the failure of **"carrot-and-stick diplomacy designed to resolve a conflict through negotiation"** (Cortright and Lopez 749).

Overusing Source Material ▪ When your paper reads like a string of references, especially a string of quotations, sources dominate your writing so that your own thinking disappears. Below, the writer takes the original passage, chops it up, and splices it together.

- It is important to understand that **"sanctions can help to encourage a process of dialogue and negotiation, but they cannot by themselves remove a targeted regime or force a drastic change in policy."** Moreover, **"sanctions should not be used in a purely punitive manner to starve an opponent into submission."** Instead, say the authors, **"Sanctions work best in combination with incentives and other forms of external influence as part of a carrot-and-stick diplomacy designed to resolve a conflict through negotiation"** (Cortright and Lopez 748–749).

"Plunking" Source Material ▪ When you drop or "plunk" source material, especially quotations, into your paper without comment, the discussion becomes choppy and disconnected. Plunking happens when you fail to prepare for and follow up a source. Below, the writer interrupts the flow of ideas with a quote that appears "out of the blue." In addition, the quote hangs at the end of a paragraph.

- In Iraq, the UN sanctions have failed to bring results. "As noted earlier, sanctions can help to encourage a process of dialogue and negotiation" (Cortright and Lopez 748).
    Saddam Hussein has continued to seek ways to rebuild his military . . .

Using "Blanket" Citations ▪ Your reader shouldn't have to guess where borrowed material begins and ends. For example, if you place a parenthetical citation at the end of a paragraph, does that citation cover the whole paragraph or the last part of the paragraph?

Relying Too Heavily on One Source ▪ If your writing is dominated by one source, readers may doubt the depth and integrity of your research.

Revising

When you've completed your draft, take a break from it. Give it to a class-mate, a tutor in the writing center, or your instructor so that fresh eyes can check the focus, content, organization, voice, and so on.

video

Use a revising checklist.

Focus

- Does the paper meet all the requirements of the assignment?
- Does the paper have a clear thesis and purpose?
- Is the thesis fully and logically supported with accurate, well-researched information?

Content and Organization

- Is the paper organized effectively into a logical chain of ideas with no repetition or gaps?
- Does the introduction emphasize the paper's focus and create enough interest to draw the reader in?
- Does information need to be added? Deleted? Rearranged? Rewritten?
- Does the conclusion flow logically from the body of the paper?

Sources

- Does the paper use a variety of quality sources?
- Are the paragraphs well developed, with sources properly introduced and discussed?
- Are the sources summarized, paraphrased, or quoted appropriately?

Voice

- Does the paper have an engaging voice that communicates interest and knowledge throughout?
- Does the tone of the writing match the purpose and audience?

Fluency

- Does the paper use transitional words or phrases to move clearly from one point to the next?
- Have the sources—especially quotations—been smoothly integrated into the paper?

Editing and Proofreading

When you've finished revising your paper, check it for style, word choice, documentation, and mechanics.

Use an editing and proofreading checklist.

video

Style

- Are the ideas expressed in a fresh and interesting manner?
- Are all sentences clear? Complete? Concise?
- Does the writing move smoothly and naturally from start to finish?

Word Choice

- Does the paper include (or avoid) the use of "I" as prescribed by the instructor?
- Does the paper contain accurate and effective word choices, especially in key concepts and definitions?

Documentation

- Does the paper include correct documentation using the appropriate system (MLA, APA)?
- Are the parenthetical references and bibliographic entries handled correctly?
- Does the paper have a complete, accurate works-cited page or reference list?

Format

- Is the paper formatted properly in terms of its margins, headings, pagination, line spacing, justification, and font size?
- Is the correct identifying information included—writer's name, instructor, course title and number, date, and title of the paper?
- Does the paper include a title page or an outline, if either is required?

Punctuation and Grammar

- Are punctuation and spacing accurate throughout?
- Are all quotation marks and parentheses used properly?
- Is the paper free of all errors, including errors in subject-verb agreement, verb tense, and usage?

Research Activities

1. Reflect on previous research projects, perhaps those that you completed in high school. Have these experiences been positive or negative? Why? List the strengths and weaknesses of your research practice.

2. Review a research paper that you wrote for another class. Based on what you learned in this chapter, list the strengths and weaknesses of the paper.

3. Analyze a sample essay in *The College Writer* for evidence of research. In a paragraph, explain the results of your analysis.

4. Find two articles on the same topic: one from a popular magazine, and one from an academic journal. Compare the articles in terms of their treatment of the topic and approach to research.

5. What types of research writing will you do in your major area of study? To answer this question, interview appropriate instructors and students.

Research Assignments

1. Write a research report about your major area of study. Discuss the types of knowledge that the major explores and the professions to which it leads. Address the paper to students considering this major.

2. Good research papers grow out of a writer's "burning questions." In a 10- to 15-minute brainstorming session, list your burning questions. Use those questions as a starting point for your paper.

3. **Search.** Find and list 15–20 available sources on your topic. Visit libraries to locate books, articles, and so forth. Use a search engine and locate sources on the Web. Finally, list any interviews, observations, surveys, and questionnaires that you might set up.

4. **Evaluate.** Test the reliability of one of your Internet sources. Refer to the "Web test" questions on page **456**, and see if you can answer all of them. Based on your answers, decide whether the source is credible enough to strengthen your paper.

5. **Paraphrase and summarize.** Choose a short article or passage from one of your sources. Restate (paraphrase) what you have read using your own words. Put quotation marks around key words and phrases that you take directly from the text. Next, use the same materials to create a summary. Reduce what you just read to a few important points using your own words.

6. **Reflect.** After you have completed your research paper, write a reflective memo answering these questions: What was the toughest part of the research project? Why? What was the most rewarding part? Why?

Chapter 32
Primary, Library, and Internet Research

audio

Today, conducting research is both easy and difficult. It's easy because research technology is powerful. It's difficult because that technology makes so much information available—the good, the bad, and the ugly.

How do you meet this challenge and do quality research? First, sort out the differences between primary and secondary sources. Second, learn how to use an expert resource—your college library. The library is your gateway to print materials and online resources, including the best information on the Web.

What's Ahead

- The Research Process: A Flowchart
- Conducting Primary Research
- Using the Library
- Using Books and Periodicals
- Researching on the Internet
- Research Activities and Assignments

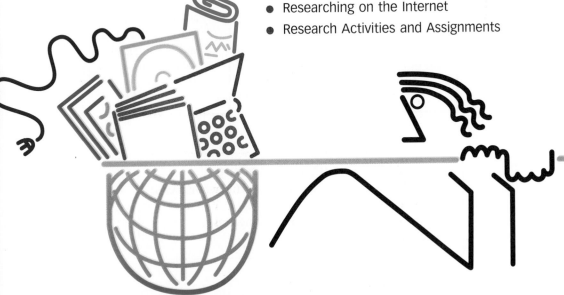

The Research Process: A Flowchart

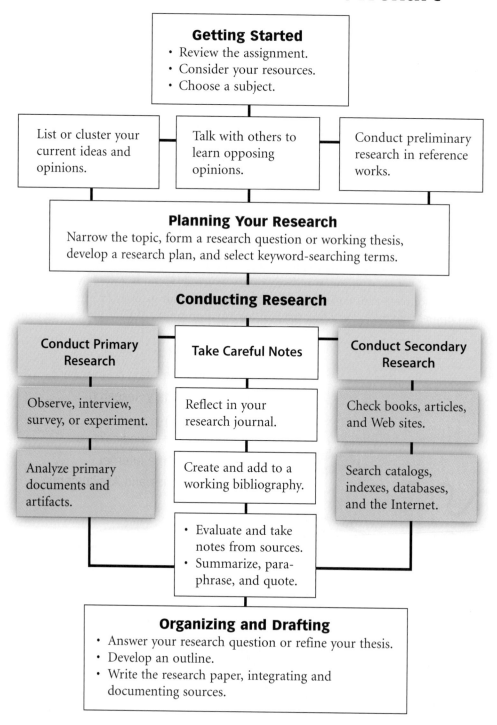

Getting Started
- Review the assignment.
- Consider your resources.
- Choose a subject.

List or cluster your current ideas and opinions.

Talk with others to learn opposing opinions.

Conduct preliminary research in reference works.

Planning Your Research
Narrow the topic, form a research question or working thesis, develop a research plan, and select keyword-searching terms.

Conducting Research

Conduct Primary Research

Take Careful Notes

Conduct Secondary Research

Observe, interview, survey, or experiment.

Reflect in your research journal.

Check books, articles, and Web sites.

Analyze primary documents and artifacts.

Create and add to a working bibliography.

Search catalogs, indexes, databases, and the Internet.

- Evaluate and take notes from sources.
- Summarize, paraphrase, and quote.

Organizing and Drafting
- Answer your research question or refine your thesis.
- Develop an outline.
- Write the research paper, integrating and documenting sources.

Use a variety of information sites.

Where do you go for the information that you need? Consider the options below, remembering that some information sources come in more than one form and can be found in more than one place. A journal article, for instance, may be available both in the library and on the Internet.

People	**experts** (knowledge area, skill, occupation) **population segments or individuals** (with representative or unusual experiences)
Libraries	**general** (public, college, online) **specialized** (legal, medical, government, business)
Computer Resources	**computers:** software, disks, CD-ROMs **networks: local area networks** (LANs), **wide area networks** (WANs), **Internet and other online services** (e-mail, limited-access databases, discussion groups, MUD, chat rooms, Web sites)
Mass Media and Telecommunications	**radio, television** **print** **telephone** (hotlines, recordings, message networks)
Testing, Training, Meeting, and Observation Sites	**museums, galleries, historical sites** **laboratories, research centers, think tanks** **conventions, conferences, seminars** **plants, facilities, field sites**
Municipal, State, and Federal Government Offices	**elected officials, representatives** **offices and agencies** (Government Printing Office) **Web sites** (Census Data Online— <www.census.gov>)
Business, Trade, and Nonprofit Organizations	**computer databases, company files, documents** **electronic bulletin boards, Web sites** **departments** (customer service, public relations)

Consider primary and secondary sources.

Information sources for your research project can be either primary or secondary. Depending on your assignment, you may be expected to use one or both kinds of sources.

Primary Sources

A primary source is an original source, which gives firsthand information on a topic. This source (such as a diary, a person, or an event) informs you directly about the topic, rather than through another person's explanation or interpretation. The most common forms of primary research are observations, interviews, surveys, experiments, and analyses of original documents and artifacts.

Secondary Sources

Secondary sources present secondhand information on your topic—information at least once removed from the original. This information has been compiled, summarized, analyzed, synthesized, interpreted, and evaluated by someone studying primary sources. Journal articles, encyclopedia entries, documentaries, and nonfiction books are typical examples of such secondary sources.

Example: Student writer Troy Holland researched the effects of UN sanctions on Iraq. (See pages **525–534** for his paper.) Below are examples of primary and secondary sources for this topic.

Primary Sources	Secondary Sources
E-mail interview with peace-organization observer who visited Iraq	Journal article discussing the effects of sanctions on Iraq
UN Resolution 687	Newspaper editorial on sanctions
Published statistics about death rates in Iraq	Documentary about the aftermath of the Gulf War
Presidential statement about sanctions	TV news magazine roundtable discussion of administration's position on sanctions

Whether a source is primary or secondary depends on what you are studying. For example, if you were studying American attitudes toward the UN sanctions (and not the effects of the sanctions), then the newspaper editorial and TV roundtable discussion would be primary sources.

Conducting Primary Research

When published sources can't give you the information that you need, consider conducting primary research. However, first weigh its advantages and disadvantages.

Upside of Primary Research

- It produces information precisely tailored to your research needs.
- It gives you direct, hands-on access to your topic.

Downside of Primary Research

- It can take much time and many resources to complete.
- It can require special skills, such as designing surveys and analyzing statistics.

Carry out primary research.

You need to choose the method of primary research that best suits your project. For help, review the following descriptions:

1. **Surveys and questionnaires** gather written responses you can review, tabulate, and analyze. These research tools pull together varied information—from simple facts to personal opinions and attitudes. See "Conduct Surveys," pages **482–483**.

2. **Interviews** involve consulting two types of people. First, you can interview experts for their insights on your topic. Second, you can interview people whose direct experiences with the topic give you their human, personal insights. See "Conduct Interviews," page **484**, and "Interview Reports," pages **345–356**.

3. **Observations, inspections, and field research** require you to examine and analyze people, places, events, and so on. Whether you rely simply on your five senses or use scientific techniques, observing provides insights into the present state of your subject. See "Observation Reports," pages **333–344**.

4. **Experiments** test hypotheses—predictions about why things do what they do—so as to arrive at conclusions that can be accepted and acted upon. Such testing often explores cause/effect relationships. See "Experiment, Lab, and Field Reports," pages **357–370**.

5. **Analysis of documents and artifacts** involves studying original reports, statistics, legislation, literature, artwork, and historical records. Such analysis often provides unique insights into your topic. See "Writing About Literature and the Arts," pages **373–388**.

Conduct surveys.

One source of primary information that you can use for your research projects is a survey or questionnaire. Surveys can collect facts and opinions from a wide range of people about virtually any topic. To get valid information, follow these guidelines:

1. Find a focus.
- Limit the purpose of your survey.
- Target a logical audience.

2. Ask clear questions.
- Phrase questions so that they are easily understood.
- Use words that are objective (not biased or slanted).

3. Match your questions to your purpose.
- Closed questions give respondents easy-answer options, and the answers are easy to tabulate. Closed questions can provide two choices (*yes* or *no*, *true* or *false*), multiple choices, a rating scale (*poor 1 2 3 excellent*), or a blank to fill.
- Open-ended questions bring in a wide variety of responses and more complex information, but they take time to complete and the answers can be difficult to summarize.

4. Organize your survey so that it's easy to complete.
- In the introduction, state who you are and why you need the information. Explain how to complete the survey and when and where to return it.
- Guide readers by providing numbers, instructions, and headings.
- Begin with basic questions and end with any complex, open-ended questions that are necessary. Move in a logical order from one topic to the next.

5. Test your survey before using it.
- Ask a friend or classmate to read your survey and help you revise it before printing it.
- Try your survey out with a small test group.

6. Conduct your survey.
- Distribute the survey to a clearly defined group that won't prejudice the sampling (random or cross section).
- Get responses from a good sample of your target group (10 percent if possible).
- Tabulate responses carefully and objectively.
  Note: To develop statistically valid results, you may need expert help. Check with your instructor.

Sample Survey

Confidential Survey

The introduction includes the essential information about the survey.

My name is Cho Lang, and I'm conducting research about the use of training supplements. I'd like to hear from you, Wabash College's athletes. Please answer the questions below by circling or writing out your responses. Return your survey through campus mail by Friday, April 5. Your responses will remain confidential.

The survey begins with clear, basic questions.

1. Circle your gender. **Male   Female**

2. Circle your year.
   Freshman   Sophomore   Junior   Senior

3. List the sports that you play.

4. Are you presently using a training supplement?
   Yes   No
   Note: If you circled "no," you may turn in your survey at this point.

The survey asks an open-ended question.

5. Describe your supplement use (type, amount, and frequency).

6. Who supervises your use of this training supplement?
   Coach   Trainer   Self   Others

7. How long have you used it?
   Less than 1 month   1–12 months   12+ months

The survey covers the topic thoroughly.

8. How many pounds have you gained while using this supplement?

9. How much has your athletic performance improved?
   None   1   2   3   4   5   Greatly

10. Circle any side effects you've experienced.
    Dehydration   Nausea   Diarrhea

Conduct interviews.

The purpose of an interview is simple. To get information, you talk with someone who has significant experience or someone who is an expert on your topic. Use the guidelines below whenever you conduct an interview. (See also pages 345–356.)

1. **Before the interview,** do your homework about the topic and the person you are planning to interview.

   - Arrange the interview in a thoughtful way. Explain to the interviewee your purpose and the topics to be covered.
   - Think about the specific ideas you want to cover in the interview and write questions for each. Addressing the 5 W's and H (*Who? What? Where? When? Why?* and *How?*) is important for good coverage.
   - Organize your questions in a logical order so that the interview moves smoothly from one subject to the next.
   - Write the questions on the left side of a page. Leave room for quotations, information, and impressions on the right side.

2. **During the interview,** try to relax so that your conversation becomes natural and sincere.

   Based on the interviewee's responses, ask follow-up questions, and don't limit yourself to your planned questions only.

   - Provide some background information about yourself, your project, and your plans for using the interview information.
   - Use recording equipment only with the interviewee's permission.
   - Jot down key facts and quotations.
   - Listen actively. Show that you're listening through your body language—eye contact, nods, smiles. Pay attention not only to what the person says, but also to how he or she says it.
   - Be flexible. If the person looks puzzled by a question, rephrase it. If the discussion gets off track, redirect it. Based on the interviewee's responses, ask follow-up questions, and don't limit yourself to your planned questions only.

3. **After the interview,** do the appropriate follow-up work.

   - As soon as possible, review your notes. Fill in responses you remember but couldn't record at the time.
   - Thank the interviewee with a note, e-mail, or a phone call.
   - If necessary, ask the interviewee to check whether your information and quotations are accurate.
   - Offer to send the interviewee a copy of your writing.

Using the Library

The library door is your gateway to information. Inside, the college library holds a wide range of research resources, from books to periodicals, from reference librarians to electronic databases.

Become familiar with the library.

To improve your ability to succeed at all your research assignments, become familiar with your college library system. Take advantage of tours and orientation sessions to learn its physical layout, resources, and services. Check your library's Web site for policies, tutorials, and research tools. The college library offers a variety of resources for your research projects.

Librarians ◆ Librarians are information experts:

- Librarians manage the library's materials and guide you to resources.
- They help you perform online searches.

Collections ◆ The library collects and houses a variety of materials:

- **Books and electronic materials**—videotapes, CD-ROMs, CDs, and DVDs
- **Periodicals**—journals, magazines, and newspapers (in print or microform)
- **Reference materials**—directories, indexes, handbooks, encyclopedias, and almanacs
- **Special collections**—government publications, historical documents, and artifacts

Research Tools ◆ The library contains many research tools that direct you to materials:

- The online catalog allows you to search everything in the library.
- Print indexes and subscription databases (Lexis-Nexis, EBSCOhost, ProQuest Direct) point you to abstracts and full-text articles.
- Internet access connects you with other library catalogs and online reference help.

Special Services ◆ Special services may also help you to complete research projects:

- Interlibrary loan allows you to obtain books and articles not available in your library.
- "Hold" allows you to request a book that is currently signed out.
- Photocopiers, CD burners, scanners, and presentation software help you perform and share your research.

Web

Conduct keyword searches.

Keyword searching is a vital research skill. With a whole range of research tools available today, what you find and how quickly you find it depends on what keywords you use. Keyword searching helps you find information in several places:

- The library catalog, whether a card or online catalog.
- Print and online databases that index or contain periodicals and reference books.
- Internet resources.

Choose keywords carefully.

Keywords give you "compass points" for navigating through a sea of information. That's why choosing the best keywords is crucial. Consider these tips:

1. Brainstorm a list of possible keywords—topics, titles, and names—based on your current knowledge and/or background reading.

2. Consult the *Library of Congress Subject Headings*. These books contain the keywords that librarians use when classifying materials. For example, if you looked up *immigrants*, you would find the entry below indicating keywords to use, along with narrower, related, and broader terms.

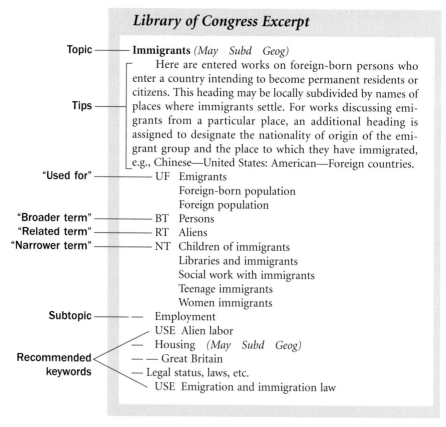

Library of Congress Excerpt

Topic —— **Immigrants** *(May Subd Geog)*

Tips ——
    Here are entered works on foreign-born persons who enter a country intending to become permanent residents or citizens. This heading may be locally subdivided by names of places where immigrants settle. For works discussing emigrants from a particular place, an additional heading is assigned to designate the nationality of origin of the emigrant group and the place to which they have immigrated, e.g., Chinese—United States: American—Foreign countries.

"Used for" —— UF Emigrants
                   Foreign-born population
                   Foreign population

"Broader term" —— BT Persons
"Related term" —— RT Aliens
"Narrower term" —— NT Children of immigrants
                        Libraries and immigrants
                        Social work with immigrants
                        Teenage immigrants
                        Women immigrants

Subtopic —— — Employment
                 USE Alien labor
              — Housing *(May Subd Geog)*
Recommended — — Great Britain
keywords   — Legal status, laws, etc.
                 USE Emigration and immigration law

Use keyword strategies.

The goal of a keyword search is to find quality research sources. To ensure that you identify the best resources available, follow these strategies:

Get to know the database. ■ Look for answers to these questions:

- What material does the database contain? What time frames are included?
- What are you searching—authors, titles, subjects, full text?
- What are the search rules? How can you narrow the search?

Use a shotgun approach. ■ Start with the most likely keyword. If you have no "hits," choose a related term. Once you get some hits, check the citations for clues regarding which words to use as you continue searching.

Use Boolean operators to refine your search. ■ When you combine keywords with Boolean operators—such as those below—you will obtain better results.

Boolean Operators

Narrowing a Search **And, +, not, –** Use when one term gives you too many hits, especially irrelevant ones	buffalo and bison or +buffalo + bison	Searches for citations containing both keywords
	buffalo not water +buffalo –water	Searches for "buffalo" but not "water," so that you eliminate material on water buffalo
Expanding a Search **Or** Combine a term providing few hits with a related word.	buffalo or bison	Searches for citations containing either term
Specifying a Phrase **Quotation marks** Indicate that you wish to search for the exact phrase enclosed	"reclamation project"	Searches for the exact phrase "reclamation project"
Sequencing Operations **Parentheses** Indicate that the operation should be performed before other operations in the search string	(buffalo or bison) and ranching	Searches first for citations containing either "buffalo" or "bison" before checking the resulting citations for "ranching"
Finding Variations **Wild card symbols** Depending on the database, symbols such as $, ?, or # can find variations of a word	ethic# ethic$	Searches for terms like *ethics* and *ethical*

Search the catalog.

Library materials are catalogued so that they are easy to find. In most college libraries, books, videos, and other holdings are catalogued in an electronic database. To find material, use book titles, author names, and keyword searching. (See pages 486–487.)

Sample Electronic Catalog

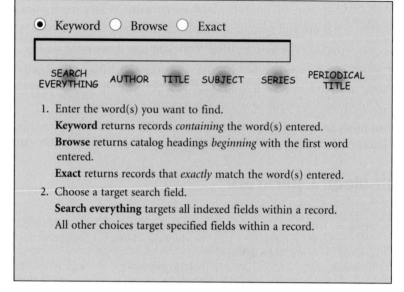

○ Keyword ○ Browse ○ Exact

SEARCH EVERYTHING AUTHOR TITLE SUBJECT SERIES PERIODICAL TITLE

1. Enter the word(s) you want to find.
   Keyword returns records *containing* the word(s) entered.
   Browse returns catalog headings *beginning* with the first word entered.
   Exact returns records that *exactly* match the word(s) entered.
2. Choose a target search field.
   Search everything targets all indexed fields within a record.
   All other choices target specified fields within a record.

When you find a citation for a book or other resource, the result will provide some or all of the following information. Use that information to determine whether the resource is worth exploring further, and to figure out other avenues of research.

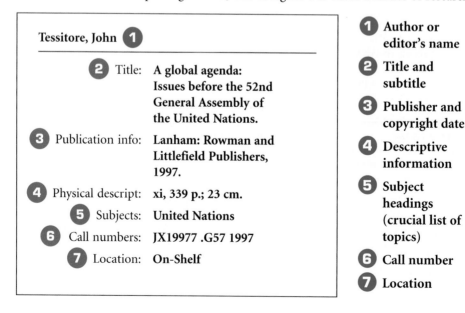

Tessitore, John ❶

❷ Title: **A global agenda: Issues before the 52nd General Assembly of the United Nations.**

❸ Publication info: **Lanham: Rowman and Littlefield Publishers, 1997.**

❹ Physical descript: **xi, 339 p.; 23 cm.**

❺ Subjects: **United Nations**

❻ Call numbers: **JX19977 .G57 1997**

❼ Location: **On-Shelf**

❶ Author or editor's name
❷ Title and subtitle
❸ Publisher and copyright date
❹ Descriptive information
❺ Subject headings (crucial list of topics)
❻ Call number
❼ Location

Web

Locating Resources by Call Numbers

Library of Congress (LC) call numbers combine letters and numbers to specify a resource's broad subject area, topic, and authorship or title. Finding a book, DVD, or other item involves combining both the alphabetical and numerical order. Here is a sample call number for *Arctic Refuge: A Vanishing Wilderness?*

VIDEO QH84.1.A72 1990

subject area (**QH**) topic number (**84**) subtopic number (**1**) cutter number (**A72**)

To find this resource in the library, first note the tab VIDEO. Although not part of the call number, this locator may send you to a specific area of the library. Once there, follow the parts of the call number one at a time:

1. Find the section on natural history containing videos with the "QH" designation.

2. Follow the numbers until you reach "84."

3. Within the "84" items, find those with the subtopic "1."

4. Use the cutter "A72" to locate the resource alphabetically with "A," and numerically with "72."

Note: In the LC system, pay careful attention to the arrangement of subject area letters, topic numbers, and subtopic numbers: Q98 comes before QH84; QH84 before QH8245; QH84.A72 before QH84.1.A72.

Classification Systems

The LC classification system combines letters and numbers. The Dewey decimal system, used in some libraries, uses numbers only. Here is a list of the 20 subject classes for both the LC and Dewey systems.

The Library of Congress and Dewey Decimal Systems

LC Category		Dewey Decimal	LC Category		Dewey Decimal
A	General Works	000–999	K	Law	340–349
B	Philosophy	100–199	L	Education	370–379
	Psychology	150–159	M	Music	780–789
	Religion	200–299	N	Fine Arts	700–799
C	History: Auxiliary Sciences	910–929	P	Language and Literature	800–899
D	History: General and		Q	Science	500–599
	Old World	930–999	R	Medicine	610–619
E–F	History: American	970–979	S	Agriculture	630–639
G	Geography	910–919	T	Technology	600–699
	Anthropology	571–573	U	Military Science	355–359, 623
	Recreation	700–799	V	Naval Science	359, 623
H	Social Sciences	300–399	Z	Bibliography and	010–019
J	Political Science	320–329		Library Science	020–029

Using Books in Research

Your college library contains a whole range of reference books for you to use. Unfortunately, for most research projects, you simply don't have time to read an entire book, and rarely do the entire contents relate to your topic. Instead, use the strategy outlined below to refine your research effort.

Use a research strategy.

1. Check out front and back information.

The title and copyright pages give the book's full title and subtitle, the author's name, and publication information, including publication date and Library of Congress subject headings. The back may contain a note on the author's credentials and other publications.

2. Scan the table of contents.

Examine the contents page to see what the book covers and how it is organized. Ask yourself which chapters have relevance for your project.

3. Using keywords, search the index.

Check the index for coverage and page locations of the topics most closely related to your project. Are there plenty of pages, or just a few? Are these pages concentrated or scattered throughout the book?

4. Skim the preface, foreword, or introduction.

Skimming the opening materials will often indicate the book's perspective, explain its origin, and preview its contents.

5. Check appendices, glossaries, or bibliographies.

These special sections may be a good source of tables, graphics, definitions, statistics, and clues for further research.

6. Carefully read appropriate chapters and sections.

Think through the material you've read and take good notes. (See pages 457–462.) Follow references to authors and other works to do further research on the topic. Study footnotes and endnotes for insights and leads.

Consider these options for working productively with books:

- When you find a helpful book, browse nearby shelves for more books.
- To confirm a book's quality, check *Book Review Digest* for a review.
- If your library subscribes to an eBook service such as NetLibrary, you have access to thousands of books in electronic form. You can conduct electronic searches, browse or check out promising books, and read them online.

Reference Works That Supply Information

Encyclopedias supply facts and overviews for topics arranged alphabetically.

- General encyclopedias cover many fields of knowledge: *Encyclopedia Britannica, Collier's Encyclopedia.*
- Specialized encyclopedias focus on a single topic: *McGraw-Hill Encyclopedia of Science and Technology, Encyclopedia of American Film Comedy.*

Almanacs, yearbooks, and statistical resources, normally published annually, contain diverse facts.

- *The World Almanac and Book of Facts* presents information on politics, history, religion, business, social programs, education, and sports.
- *Statistical Abstract of the United States* provides data on population, geography, politics, employment, business, science, and industry.

Vocabulary resources supply information on languages.

- General dictionaries, such as *American Heritage College Dictionary,* supply definitions and histories for a whole range of words.
- Specialized dictionaries define words common to a field, topic, or group of people: *Dictionary of Engineering, The New Harvard Dictionary of Music.*
- Bilingual dictionaries translate words from one language to another.

Biographical resources supply information about people. General biographies cover a broad range of people. Other biographies focus on people from a specific group. ***Examples:*** *Who's Who in America, Dictionary of Scientific Biography, World Artists 1980–1990.*

Directories supply contact information for people, groups, and organizations. ***Examples:*** *The National Directory of Addresses and Telephone Numbers, USPS ZIP Code Lookup and Address Information* (online), *Official Congressional Directory.*

Reference Works That Are Research Tools

Guides and handbooks help readers explore specific topics. ***Examples:*** *The Handbook of North American Indians, A Guide to Prairie Fauna.*

Indexes point you to useful resources. Some indexes are general, such as *Readers' Guide to Periodical Literature,* while others are specific, such as *Environment Index* or *Business Periodicals Index.* (Many are now available online.)

Bibliographies list resources on a specific topic. A good, current bibliography can be used as an example when you compile your own bibliography on a topic.

Abstracts, like indexes, direct you to articles on a particular topic. But abstracts also summarize those materials so you learn whether a resource is relevant before you invest time in locating and reading it. Abstracts are usually organized into subject areas: *Computer Abstracts, Environmental Abstracts, Social Work Abstracts.* They are incorporated in many online databases.

Web

Using Periodical Articles

Periodicals are publications or broadcasts produced at regular intervals (daily, weekly, monthly, quarterly). Although some periodicals are broad in their subject matter and audience, as a rule, they focus on a narrow range of topics geared toward a particular audience.

- **Daily newspapers and newscasts** provide up-to-date information on current events, opinions, and trends—from politics to natural disasters (*The Wall Street Journal, USA Today, The Newshour*).
- **Weekly and monthly magazines** generally provide more in-depth information on a wide range of topics (*Time, Newsweek, 60 Minutes*).
- **Journals,** generally published quarterly, provide specialized, scholarly information for a narrowly focused audience (*Journal of Labor Economics*).

Use an appropriate research strategy.

Finding Periodical Articles

With thousands of periodicals available, how do you find the articles you need? Begin by asking (1) what search tools your library offers, (2) what periodicals it carries, and (3) how to gain access to those periodicals. The following steps will help:

1. Use an online database to find promising articles.

If your library subscribes to EBSCOhost or a similar service, use keyword searching to find citations on your topic. By studying the citations, you can determine three things:

- Does this article look relevant?
- Is an electronic, full-text version of the article available?
- Does the library have the periodical in its print or microform collection?

Example: A search on EBSCOhost for the terms "Iraqi sanctions" returns a list of articles including information on availability. Below is one citation from the list. Clicking on the title provides an abstract of the article, while clicking on one of the other links leads to the full article.

Economic *Sanctions*, Just War Doctrine, and the 'Fearful Spectacle of the Civilian Dead'. By: Gordon, Joy; Cross Currents, 09/01/99, 14p

Note: This title is NOT available in this library.

 Full Page Image   Full Text   XML Full Text

---

2. Go to specialized indexes.

When a basic search turns up few resources, you can turn to specialized indexes such as ERIC (on education topics) and PsycINFO (on psychology topics). If necessary, work with a librarian to conduct a search through a service such as Dialog.

3. Go to print indexes.

Particularly if you need articles from popular periodicals published before 1985, use *Readers' Guide to Periodical Literature*. Indexes such as *The Humanities Index* or *Social Studies Index* cover only scholarly articles.

- Each bound volume covers one year of periodical publications. Therefore, you may have to search several volumes.
- Articles are listed alphabetically by topic and by author; the title of the article is listed under each of these two entries.
- Some topics are divided into subtopics, with each article being listed under the appropriate subtopic.

4. Record identifying information.

Save, print, or write down key details about promising articles: the periodical's title, the issue and date, and the article's title and page numbers.

5. Check your library's list of periodicals held.

An online citation may indicate that an article is available in your library. Otherwise, you need to check your library's inventory or list of periodicals held, which will be available online and/or in print. Check the list of issues and dates available, the form (print or microform), and the location (current periodicals shelves, bound periodicals shelves, or microfilm cabinets).

6. Locate and obtain the article.

If the full text of an article is available online, simply call it up. If not, follow your library's procedure for using journals. You may have to seek help from a librarian.

Reading Periodical Articles

As with other sources, you must read periodical articles critically and evaluate them carefully. (See page **456**.) But consider especially these issues:

- Examine the periodical's quality. Does it have a record of reliability? Is it a reviewed journal? As a general rule, use periodicals (especially journals) known for careful research. Many newspapers and magazines can't offer an adequate depth of coverage on your topic.
- Recognize the periodical's goals. Which audience does it target? Which perspective does it present?
- Consider the article's date. For some research, you need the most current information. For other research, an older article may provide solid material.

Researching on the Internet

The Internet can be a great resource—or a great waste of time. Consider these benefits and drawbacks:

Benefits

- The Internet contains a wealth of current and specific information.
- Because the information is digital, it can be searched quickly and conveniently, and it can be downloaded, saved, and shared via e-mail.
- The Internet is always open.

Drawbacks

- Because of the quantity of material and its relative disorganization, finding relevant, reliable information can be difficult.
- "Surfing" can encourage shallow research practices.
- The Net changes rapidly—what's here today may be gone, changed, or outdated tomorrow.

Search the Internet.

If you're familiar with the Internet, you already understand the basics of searching this medium. However, the following questions and answers may help you do quality research on the Net.

What Is the Internet?

The Internet is a worldwide network of connected local computers and computer networks, a network that allows computers to share information with one another. For example, your college's network likely gives you access to the library, local resources, and the Internet.

What Is the World Wide Web?

The **Web** provides access to much of the material on the Internet. Millions of Web pages are available because of **hypertext links** that connect Web pages to one another. These links appear as clickable icons or highlighted Web addresses. A **Web site** is a group of related Web pages posted by the same sponsor or organization. A **home page** is a Web site's "entry" page. A **Web browser** such as Netscape or Internet Explorer gives you access to Web resources through a variety of tools, such as directories and search engines. (**Directories** and **search engines** are special Web sites that provide a searchable listing of many services on the Web.)

What Does an Internet Address Mean?

An Internet address is called a URL, or Uniform Resource Locator. The address includes the protocol indicating how the computer file should be accessed—often *http:* or *ftp:* (followed by a double slash); a domain name—often beginning with *www*; and additional path information (following a single slash) to access other pages within a site.

http://www.cnn.com/2002/us/news.html

Directs the browser to use // hypertext to access a site   Domain name   /Path to a particular page within the domain or site

The domain name is a key part of the address because it indicates what type of organization created the site and gives you clues about its goal or purpose. Does the site aim to educate, inform, persuade, sell, and/or entertain? Most sites combine a primary purpose with secondary ones.

- **.com** a commercial organization or business
- **.gov** a government organization—federal, state, or local
- **.edu** an educational institution
- **.org** a nonprofit organization
- **.net** an organization that is part of the Internet's infrastructure
- **.mil** a military site
- **.biz** a business site
- **.info** any site primarily providing information

Note: International Internet addresses include national abbreviations (for example, Canada = **.ca**).

Sample Web Page

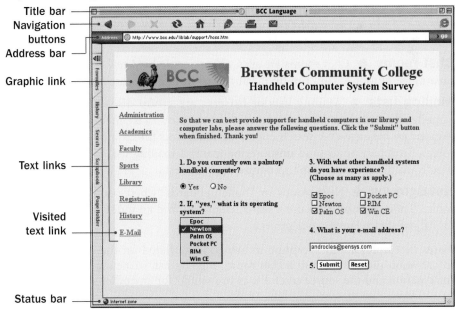

How Can You Save Information?

You must cite Internet sources properly in your writing, and your instructors may ask you to turn in those sources with your project. Save Internet information using these methods:

Bookmark ◆ Your browser can save a site's address through a "bookmark" or "favorites" function on your menu bar.

Printout ◆ If a document looks promising, use the print function to create a hard copy of it. Remember to write down all details needed for citing the source. (While many details will automatically print with the document, some could be missing.)

Save or Download ◆ To keep an electronic copy of material, save the document to a specific drive on your computer. Beware of large files with many graphics: they take up a lot of space. To save just the text, highlight it, copy it, and then paste it into a word-processing program.

E-Mail ◆ If you're not at your own computer, you can e-mail the document's URL to your e-mail address through copy-and-paste.

INSIGHT: To evaluate the quality of Internet information, check "Evaluate Each Source" (page **456**).

How Can You Communicate on the Internet?

As a researcher, you can use the Internet to do more than check out Web pages. Other information on your topic might be available through electronic communities.

E-Mail ◆ Communicating through e-mail can be a useful research strategy. For example, if you get an expert's e-mail address from a Web site or other source, you could follow up with pertinent questions.

Chat rooms ◆ Chat rooms are sites where people hold real-time "conversations" on a range of topics. You can find chat rooms through a search engine.

Mailing lists ◆ Mailing lists or listservs are group discussions of a topic by e-mail, often managed by an automated program. List members can post and respond to messages. A search engine can help you find a mailing list about your topic. To subscribe to (and unsubscribe from) a mailing list, follow the directions exactly, or the program won't recognize your request.

Newsgroups ◆ Newsgroups are "bulletin boards" where people post messages by topic. Thousands exist, so use a search engine to find an index of newsgroups; then visit those that relate to your project.

Note: Be careful about accepting information gathered on the Internet, especially information picked up from a chat room, mailing list, or newsgroup. Evaluate the information and the source carefully, as you would for any other source.

Locating Information on the Internet

Because the Internet contains so much information of varying reliability, you need to become familiar with search tools that locate information you can trust. The key is knowing which search tool to use in which research situation.

Use your library's Web site.

Your library may sponsor a Web site that gives you access to quality Internet resources. For example, it may provide the following assistance:

- Tutorials on using the Internet
- Guides to Internet resources in different disciplines
- Links to online document collections (Project Gutenberg, Etext Archives, New Bartleby Digital Library, and so on)
- Connections to virtual libraries, subscription databases, search engines, directories, government documents, online periodicals, and online reference works

Use a URL.

Finding useful Internet resources can be as easy as typing in a URL:

- If you have a promising Web address, type or copy-and-paste it into the address bar of your Web browser. Then press the Enter or Return key to go to that page.
- If you don't have the exact URL, sometimes you can guess it, especially for an organization (company, government agency, or nonprofit group). Try the organization's name or a logical abbreviation to get the home page.
  Formula: **<www.organization-name-or-abbreviation.domain-name>**
  Examples: **<www.nasa.gov>, <www.honda.com>, <www.ucla.edu>**
- If you find yourself buried deep in a Web site and you want to find the site's home page, keep backspacing on the navigation bar.

Follow helpful links.

Locating information on the Net can involve "surfing" leads:

- If you come across a helpful link (often highlighted in blue), click on the link to visit that new page. Note that the link may take you to another site.
- Your browser keeps a record of the pages that you visit. Click the back arrow to go back one page or the forward arrow to move ahead again.
- If you get lost while on the Net, click the "home" icon on your browser's toolbar to return your browser to its starting place.

Web

Follow the branches of a "subject tree."

A *subject tree*, sometimes called a *subject guide* or *directory*, lists Web sites that have been organized into categories by experts who have reviewed those sites. Use subject trees or directories for the following reasons:

- You need to narrow down a broad topic.
- You want evaluated sites, or desire quality over quantity.

How does a subject tree work? Essentially, it allows you to select from a broad range of subjects or "branches." With each topic choice, you narrow down your selection until you arrive at a list of Web sites, or you can keyword-search a limited number of Web sites.

Check whether your library subscribes to a service such as NetFirst, a database in which subject experts have catalogued Internet resources by topic. Here are some other common subject directories that you can likely access at your library:

WWW Virtual Library	<http://vlib.org/Overview.html>
Argus	<http://www.clearinghouse.net>
Lii	<http://www.lii.org>
Magellan	<http://magellan.excite.com>
LookSmart	<http://looksmart.com>

Use search engines and metasearch tools.

Unlike a subject directory, which is constructed with human input, a search engine is a program that automatically scours a large amount of Internet material for keywords that you submit. A search engine is useful in the following circumstances:

- You have a very narrow topic in mind.
- You have a specific word or phrase to use in your search.
- You want a large number of results.
- You are looking for a specific type of Internet file.
- You have the time to sort the material for reliability.

Be aware that not all search engines are the same. Some search citations of Internet materials, whereas others conduct full-text searches. Choose a search engine that covers a large portion of the Internet, offers quality indexing, and provides high-powered search capabilities. Here's an overview of some popular search engines.

Basic Search Engines: Search millions of Web pages gathered automatically.

Alta Vista	<http://www.altavista.com>
AllTheWeb	<http://www.alltheweb.com>
Google	<http://www.google.com>
HotBot	<http://www.hotbot.com>
Vivísimo	<http://www.vivisimo.com>

Metasearch Tools: Search several basic search engines at once, saving you the time and effort of checking more than one search engine.

Ask Jeeves	<http://www.ask.com>
Dog Pile	<http://www.dogpile.com>
Ixquick	<http://www.ixquick.com>
Northern Light	<http://www.northernlight.com>

"Deep Web" Tools: Check Internet databases and other sources not accessible to basic search engines.

Complete Planet	<http://www.completeplanet.com>
The Invisible Web	<http://www.invisibleweb.com>

INSIGHT: One key to successfully using search engines lies in effective keyword searching (see pages 486–487). To ensure successful searches, it's best to become familiar with a few search engines—what areas of the Internet they search, whether they can access full text, and what rules you must follow.

Observing Netiquette

Although online communication is almost as immediate as speaking face to face, it lacks the visual and vocal cues of in-person communication. To help communication on the Net, a code of conduct called Netiquette has emerged. In essence, it means being considerate of others when you are online.

FAQ ◆ Mailing lists and sites with lots of online traffic often post collections of answers to "Frequently Asked Questions," or FAQ lists. Whenever you have a question about a site or mailing list, check whether it is answered in the FAQs before you consider mailing or posting your question.

Message Clarity ◆ One of the most important parts of Netiquette is being careful as you write. Make your message as clear and concise as possible before you send it. See "Writing E-Mail" on pages **420–421** for more details.

Privacy ◆ Take care to preserve other people's privacy online, as well as your own. Never post someone else's e-mail address in a public forum unless you have that person's express permission. When publicly quoting from someone else's message, be certain he or she won't mind.

Long Messages ◆ If your message is long, add a "Long Message" warning in the subject line, so that readers will be prepared before opening the message itself.

Shouting ◆ On the Net, words in all capital letters are considered SHOUTING. Messages in all capital letters are harder to read, and many people consider them rude. You can safely use all capital letters, however, to represent the title of a book (MOBY DICK, for example) or emphasize a word. For lighter emphasis, bracket a word in asterisks. (Netiquette *is* a virtue.)

Smileys ◆ Often, to add a certain tone to an online message, people use "smileys" (or other "emoticons"). These sideways faces :-) are made up of keyboard characters.

Net Abbreviations ◆ To speed the flow of communication, people on the Net use many abbreviations: LOL for "laughing out loud," TTFN for "ta ta for now," BTW for "by the way," and so on. If you see an abbreviation you don't know, don't be afraid to politely ask the user what it means.

Flaming ◆ Even with the best of Netiquette, misunderstandings sometimes occur. If you receive a message that offends you, give the writer the benefit of the doubt. Chances are, no offense was intended. Never post an angry reply in public. This practice is called "flaming," and experienced Net users should always avoid it.

Accuracy ◆ Don't let the speed of electronic messaging be an excuse for sloppiness. Always proofread your messages for accuracy to help ensure good communication. Be as careful with your own messages as you are forgiving of others'.

Recommended Research Strategies

Virtually any form of writing could require virtually any form of research. However, some forms of writing rely on specific research strategies. Here's an overview of recommended strategies. Use it to plan the research for your next project.

Form of Writing	Research Strategy Recommended
Personal Personal narrative Personal reflection Description of a person, a place, or an event	**Focus on primary research:** • Study your memories. • Study artifacts such as photographs, diaries, old newspapers, and videos. • Observe locations and events. • Interview participants. **Use secondary research** to clarify facts, definitions, and other details.
Report Observation Interview Lab experiment	**Rely on observing, interviewing, and experimenting.** However, consider background research in reference works and other secondary sources to prepare for that primary research.
Analytical Process Illustration Comparison/contrast Definition Classification Cause/effect	**Generally, start with primary research:** • Study documents, maps, objects, events, and videos. • Conduct experiments and tests. **Use secondary research** to support primary research; go to specialized reference works, journal articles, books, and online sources to create a context for and to clarify details of analysis.
Persuasive Taking a position Persuading others to act Arguing against a claim Proposing a solution	**Generally, rely on secondary research:** • Review the literature on your topic. • Find trustworthy information in reference works, journal articles, scholarly books, and reliable Web sites. **Use primary research in a supporting role:** • Conduct interviews and surveys to get other opinions on your topic. • Observe to "see for yourself." • Examine evidence and artifacts to get unbiased, objective information.

Research Activities

1. For the subject "Gender Differences in Toy Preferences," indicate whether the following sources would be considered primary or secondary (P or S):
   ___ a. Observing children in a day-care setting
   ___ b. Journal article about gender-based differences in the brain
   ___ c. Magazine article about a hot new toy
   ___ d. Survey of daycare workers
   ___ e. *Boys' Toys of the Fifties and Sixties* (a book)
   ___ f. Parenting Web site
   ___ g. Interviews of parents

2. Indicate which section of the library would hold each of the following items:
   _____ a. *JAMA (Journal of the American Medical Association)*
   _____ b. *Places Rated Almanac*
   _____ c. *Principles of Corporate Finance* (book)
   _____ d. *Star Trek: Strange New Worlds* (paperback book)
   _____ e. *Merck Index: An Encyclopedia of Chemicals, Drugs, and Biologicals*

Research Assignments

1. List at least five different information sites you could access for information about your chosen research topic.

2. Obtain a map of your college library. Find and highlight the following areas:
   - Computer card catalog(s)
   - Reference books
   - Nonfiction books
   - Journals and magazines
   - Computers for library patrons' use (to access databases or the Internet)
   - Librarian help desk

3. Use a search engine to find one or two online databases you could use for your research topic. Also, access an online subscription service (available at a library), such as EBSCOhost or Academic Search Premier, to obtain one or two pertinent abstracts.

1. *(a.)* P *(b.)* S, *(c.)* S, *(d.)* P, *(e.)* S, *(f.)* S, *(g.)* P
2. *(a.)* periodical collection, *(b.)* reference materials, *(c.)* book section, *(d.)* book section, *(e.)* reference materials

Documentation
and Format Styles

CONTENTS

Chapter 33
MLA Documentation Form

audio

In research papers, it is commonly said, "you are commanded to borrow but forbidden to steal." To borrow ideas while avoiding plagiarism (see pages **471–473**), you must not only mention the sources you borrow from but also document them completely and accurately. You must follow to the last dot the documentation conventions for papers written in your general subject area.

If you are composing a research paper in the humanities, your instructor will most likely require you to follow the conventions established in the style manual of the Modern Language Association (MLA). This chapter provides you with explanations and examples for citing sources in MLA format. An excellent way to learn MLA documentation is to see it in use, so turn to the sample paper demonstrating MLA form on pages **525–534**. Additional information and MLA updates can be found on the Web site for this book: <**www.thecollegewriter.com**>.

What's Ahead

- MLA Research Paper Guidelines
- Parenthetical References
- Works-Cited Entries: Books
- Works-Cited Entries: Periodicals
- Works-Cited Entries: Electronic Sources
- Works-Cited Entries: Other Print and Nonprint Sources
- Sample MLA Research Paper
- Activities

MLAMLAMLAMLAMLAMLAM

MLA Research Paper Guidelines

video

Questions & Answers

Is a separate title page required?

No (unless your instructor requires one, in which case you would format it according to his or her instructions). On the first page of a research paper, type your name, your instructor's name, the course name and number, and the date, one below the other. The title comes next, centered. Then simply begin the text on the next line.

Is the research paper double-spaced?

Yes. Do not single-space anywhere, even in tables, captions, or long quotations.

What about longer quotations?

Verse quotations of more than three lines should be indented one inch (ten spaces) and double-spaced. Do not add quotation marks. Each line of a poem or play begins a new line of the quotation; do not run the lines together. When you are quoting prose that takes more than four typed lines, indent each line of the quotation one inch (ten spaces) from the left margin and double-space it; do not add quotation marks.

To quote two or more paragraphs—in addition to the one inch that you are already indenting for the lengthy quotation—you should indent the first line of each paragraph an extra quarter inch (three spaces). However, if the first sentence quoted does not begin a paragraph in the source, do not make the additional indent. Indent only the first lines of the successive paragraphs.

Are page numbers required?

Yes. Pages should be numbered consecutively in the upper-right corner, one-half inch from the top and flush with the right margin (one inch). Your last name should precede the page number, and no abbreviations or other symbols should be included.

How wide should the margins be?	Top, bottom, left, and right margins should be one inch (except for page numbering). The first word in a paragraph should be indented one-half inch (five spaces). Longer quotations should be set off one inch (ten spaces) from the left margin (see page **470**).
Are references placed in the text?	*Yes.* Indicate only page numbers parenthetically if you identify the author in your text. Give the author's last name in a parenthetical reference if it is not mentioned in the text.
Is a list of sources used in the paper required?	*Yes.* Full citations for all sources used (books, periodicals, etc.) are placed in an alphabetized list labeled "Works Cited" at the end of the paper.
Is an appendix required?	*No.* In MLA style, tables and illustrations are placed as close as possible to the related text.
Is an abstract required?	*No.* An abstract, or summary of your research paper, is not an MLA requirement.
What about headings?	MLA style does not specify a particular format for headings within the text; normally, headings are used only for separate sections of the paper ("Works Cited" or "Notes," for example).
How do I incorporate reference markers if I submit my paper electronically?	Numbering paragraphs is common in electronic publications. Place the paragraph number in brackets. Follow with a space and begin the paragraph. (For other electronic formatting guidelines, check with your instructor.)
Any other special instructions?	Always ask whether your school, department, or instructor has special requirements that may take precedence over those listed here.

Web

MLA Parenthetical References

The MLA Handbook for Writers of Research Papers suggests giving credit for your sources of information in the body of your research paper. To do so, simply insert the appropriate information (usually the author and page number) in parentheses after the words or ideas taken from another source. Place them where a pause would naturally occur to avoid disrupting your writing (usually at the end of a sentence). These parenthetical references refer to sources listed on the "Works Cited" page at the end of your paper. (See page **534**.)

Model Parenthetical References

One Author: Citing a Complete Work

You do not need a parenthetical reference if you identify the author in your text. (See the first entry below.) However, you must give the author's last name in a parenthetical reference if it is not mentioned in the text. (See the second entry.) A parenthetical reference could begin with an editor, a translator, a speaker, or an artist instead of the author if that is how the work is listed in the works-cited section.

WITH AUTHOR IN TEXT (This is the preferred way of citing a complete work.)

In <u>No Need for Hunger</u>, Robert Spitzer recommends that the U.S. government develop a new foreign policy to help Third World countries overcome poverty and hunger.

WITHOUT AUTHOR IN TEXT

<u>No Need for Hunger</u> recommends that the U.S. government develop a new foreign policy to help Third World countries overcome poverty and hunger (Spitzer).

Note: Do not offer page numbers when citing complete works, articles in alphabetized encyclopedias, single-page articles, and unpaginated sources.

One Author: Citing Part of a Work

List the necessary page numbers in parentheses if you borrow words or ideas from a particular source. Leave a space between the author's last name and the page reference. No abbreviation or punctuation is needed.

WITH AUTHOR IN TEXT

Bullough writes that genetic engineering was dubbed "eugenics" by a cousin of Darwin's, Sir Francis Galton, in 1885 (5).

WITHOUT AUTHOR IN TEXT

Genetic engineering was dubbed "eugenics" by a cousin of Darwin's,

Sir Francis Galton, in 1885 (Bullough 5).

Citing Two or More Works by the Same Author(s)

In addition to the author's last name(s) and page number(s), include a shortened version of the title of the work when you are citing two or more works by the same author(s).

WITH AUTHOR IN TEXT

Wallerstein and Blakeslee claim that divorce creates an enduring

identity for children of the marriage (Unexpected Legacy 62).

WITHOUT AUTHOR IN TEXT

They are intensely lonely despite active social lives (Wallerstein and

Blakeslee, Second Chances 51).

Two or Three Authors

Give the last names of every author in the same order that they appear in the works-cited section. (The correct order of the authors' names can be found on the title page of the book.)

Students learned more than a full year's Spanish in ten days using

the complete supermemory method (Ostrander and Schroeder 51).

Four or More Authors

Give the first author's last name as it appears in the works-cited section followed by *et al.* (meaning *and others*).

Communication on the job is more than talking; it is "inseparable

from your total behavior" (Culligan et al. 111).

Note: You may also choose to list all of the authors' last names.

Anonymous Work

When there is no author listed, give the title or a shortened version of the title as it appears in the works-cited section.

Statistics indicate that drinking water can make up 20 percent of a

person's total exposure to lead (*Information* 572).

Corporate Author

If a book or other work was written by a committee or task force, it is said to have a corporate author. If the corporate name is long, include it in the text (rather than in parentheses) to avoid disrupting the flow of your writing. Use a shortened form of the name (common abbreviations are acceptable) in the text and in references after the full name has been used at least once. For example, *Task Force* may be used for *Task Force on Education for Economic Growth*. Be certain to shorten the title in a way that is easily recognized and not confused with another name.

> **The thesis of the Task Force's report is that economic success depends on our ability to improve large-scale education and training as quickly as possible (113–14).**

Note: For inclusive page numbers larger than ninety-nine, give only the two digits of the second number (113–14, not 113–114).

Indirect (or Secondary) Source

If you must cite an indirect source—someone's remarks published in a second source—use the abbreviation *qtd. in* (quoted in) before the indirect source in your reference.

> **Paton improved the conditions in Diepkloof (a prison) by "removing all the more obvious aids to detention. The dormitories are open at night: the great barred gate is gone" (qtd. in Callan xviii).**

Literary Works: Classic Verse Plays and Poems

Cite classic verse plays and poems by division (act, scene, canto, book, part) and line, using Arabic numerals for the various divisions unless your instructor prefers Roman numerals. Use periods to separate the various numbers.

> **In the first act of the play named after him, Hamlet comments, "How weary, stale, flat and unprofitable, / Seem to me all the uses of this world" (1.2.133–134).**

Note: A slash, with a space on each side, shows where each new line of verse begins.

If you are citing lines only, use the word *line* or *lines* in your first reference and numbers only in additional references.

> **In book five of Homer's *Iliad*, the Trojans' fear is evident: "The Trojans were scared when they saw the two sons of Dares, one of them in fright and the other lying dead by his chariot" (lines 22–24).**

Verse quotations of more than three lines should be indented one inch (ten spaces) and double-spaced. Do not add quotation marks. Each line of the poem or play begins a new line of the quotation; do not run the lines together.

> Bin Ramke's poem "A Little Ovid Late in the Day" tells of reading by
>
> the last light of a summer day:
>
>> [T]ales of incest, corruption,
>>
>> any big, mythic vice
>>
>> against the color of the sun,
>>
>> the sweetness of the time of day—
>>
>> I know the story,
>>
>> it is the light I care about. (3–8)

Literary Works: Prose

To cite prose (novels, short stories), list more than the page number if the work is available in several editions. Give the page reference first, and then add a chapter, section, or book number, if appropriate, in abbreviated form after a semicolon.

> In The House of Seven Spirits, Isabel Allende describes Marcos,
>
> "dressed in mechanic's overalls, with huge racer's goggles and an
>
> explorer's helmet" (13; ch. 1).

When you are quoting prose that takes more than four typed lines, indent each line of the quotation one inch (ten spaces) and double-space it; do not add quotation marks. In this case, you put the parenthetical citation (the pages and chapter numbers) outside the end punctuation mark of the quotation itself.

> Allende describes the flying machine that Marcos has assembled:
>
>> The contraption lay with its stomach on terra firma, heavy
>>
>> and sluggish and looking more like a wounded duck than
>>
>> like one of those newfangled airplanes they were starting
>>
>> to produce in the United States. There was nothing in its
>>
>> appearance to suggest that it could move, much less
>>
>> take flight across the snowy peaks. (12; ch. 1)

MLA Works Cited

Web

QUICK GUIDE

The works-cited section lists all of the sources you have cited (referred to) in your text. It does not include any sources you may have read or studied but did not refer to in your paper (that's a bibliography). Begin your list of works cited on a new page (the next page after the text), and number each page, continuing from the number of the last page of the text. The guidelines that follow describe the form of the works-cited section.

1 Type the page number in the upper-right corner, one-half inch from the top of the page, with your last name before it.

2 Center the title *Works Cited* (not in italics or underlined) one inch from the top; then double-space before the first entry.

3 Begin each entry flush with the left margin. If the entry runs more than one line, indent additional lines one-half inch (five spaces) or use the hanging indent function on your computer.

4 Double-space within each entry and between entries.

5 List each entry alphabetically by the author's last name. If there is no author, use the first word of the title (disregard *A, An, The*).

6 A basic entry for a book would be as follows:

> Opie, John. Ogallala: Water for a Dry Land. Lincoln:
>
> U of Nebraska P, 1993.

Note: Use a single space after all punctuation in a works-cited entry.

7 A basic entry for a periodical (a magazine) would be as follows:

> Stearns, Denise Heffernan. "Testing by Design."
>
> Middle Ground Oct. 2000: 21–25.

8 Check the pages that follow for specific information on other kinds of entries. Check the Web site for this book <**www.thecollegewriter.com**> for updates on citing electronic sources. (Also see page **534** for a sample works-cited page.)

video

Works-Cited Entries: Books

The entries that follow illustrate the information needed to cite books, sections of a book, pamphlets, and government publications. The possible components of these entries are listed in order below:

1. **Author's name**
2. **Title of a part of the book**
   (an article in the book or a foreword)
3. **Title of the book**
4. **Name of editor or translator**
5. **Edition**
6. **Number of volume**
7. **Name of series**
8. **Place of publication, publisher, year of publication**
9. **Page numbers, if citation is to only a part**

Note: If any of these components do not apply, they are not listed. In the rare instance that a book does not state publication information, use the following abbreviations in place of information you cannot supply:

n.p.	No place of publication given
n.p.	No publisher given
n.d.	No date of publication given
n. pag.	No pagination given

Additional Guidelines

- List only the city for the place of publication unless it is outside the United States; in this case, add an abbreviation of the country if necessary for clarity. If several cities are listed, give only the first.

- Additionally, note that publishers' names should be shortened by omitting articles (a, an, the), business abbreviations (Co., Inc.), and descriptive words (Books, Press). Cite the surname alone if the publisher's name includes the name of one person; if it includes the names of more than one person, cite only the first of the surnames. Abbreviate *University Press* as *UP.* Also use standard abbreviations whenever possible. (See pages **568** and **602**.)

- Your works-cited section belongs at the end of your paper. Remember the purpose of the works-cited list: it simplifies documentation by allowing you to make only brief references to your sources in the body of your paper.

One Author

Angell, David. The Internet Business Companion: Growing Your Business in the Electronic Age. Reading: Addison-Wesley, 1995.

Two or Three Authors

Bystydzienski, Jill M., and Estelle P. Resnik. Women in Cross-Cultural Transitions. Bloomington: Phi Delta Kappa Educational Foundation, 1994.

Note: List the authors in the same order as they appear on the title page. Reverse only the name of the first author.

Four or More Authors

Schulte-Peevers, Andrea, et al. Germany. Victoria, Austral.: Lonely Planet, 2000.

Note: You may also choose to give all names in full in the order used on the title page.

Two or More Books by the Same Author

List the books alphabetically according to title. After the first entry, substitute three hyphens for the author's name.

Dershowitz, Alan M. Reasonable Doubts: The O. J. Simpson Case and the Criminal Justice System. Thorndike: Thorndike, 1996.

- - - . Supreme Injustice: How the High Court Hijacked Election 2000. Oxford: Oxford UP, 2001.

Single Work from an Anthology

Mitchell, Joseph. "The Bottom of the Harbor." American Sea Writing. Ed. Peter Neill. New York: Library of America, 2000. 584–608.

Note: If you cite a complete anthology, begin the entry with the editor(s).

Neill, Peter, ed. American Sea Writing. New York: Library of America, 2000.

Smith, Rochelle, and Sharon L. Jones, eds. The Prentice Hall Anthology of African American Literature. Upper Saddle River: Prentice Hall, 2000.

Cross-References

To avoid unnecessary repetition when citing two or more entries from a larger collection, you may cite the collection once with complete publication information (see *Forbes* below). The individual entries (see *Joseph* and *MacNeice* below) can then be cross-referenced by listing the author, title of the piece, editor of the collection, and page numbers.

> Forbes, Peter, ed. Scanning the Century. London: Penguin, 2000.
>
> Joseph, Jenny. "Warning." Forbes 335–36.
>
> MacNeice, Louis. "Star-Gazer." Forbes 504.

Corporate Group Author

> Exxon Mobil Corporation. Great Plains 2000. Lincolnwood:
>
> Publications Intl., 2001.

Anonymous Book

> Chase's Calendar of Events 2002. Chicago: Contemporary, 2002.

Note: The Bible is considered an anonymous book. Documentation should read exactly as it is printed on the title page.

> The Jerusalem Bible. Garden City: Doubleday, 1966.

One Volume of a Multivolume Work

> Cooke, Jacob Ernest, and Milton M. Klein, eds. North America in
>
> Colonial Times. Vol. 2. New York: Scribner's, 1998.

Note: If you cite two or more volumes in a multivolume work, give the total number of volumes after each title. Offer specific references to volume and page numbers in the parenthetical reference in your text, like this: (8:112–114).

> Salzman, Jack, David Lionel Smith, and Cornel West. Encyclopedia of
>
> African-American Culture and History. 5 vols. New York: Simon,
>
> 1996.

An Introduction, a Preface, a Foreword, or an Afterword

> Parker, Roger C. Foreword. Looking Good in Presentations. 3rd ed.
>
> By Molly W. Joss. Scottsdale: Coriolis, 1999. xi–xiii.
>
> Barry, Anne. Afterword. Making Room for Students. By Celia Oyler.
>
> New York: Teachers College, 1996.

Republished Book (Reprint)

Give the original publication date after the title.

Atwood, Margaret. Surfacing. 1972. New York: Doubleday, 1998.

Note: New material added to the reprint, such as an introduction, should be cited after the original publication facts: *Introd. C. Becker.*

Book with Multiple Publishers

When a book lists more than one publisher (not just different offices of the same publisher), include all of them in the order given on the book's title page, separated by a semicolon.

Wells, H. G. The Complete Short Stories of H. G. Wells. New York:

St. Martin's; London: A. & C. Black, 1987.

Edition

An edition refers to the particular publication you are citing, as in the third (3rd) edition. The term "edition" also refers to the work of one person that is prepared by another person, an editor.

Shakespeare, William. A Midsummer Night's Dream. Ed. Jane

Bachman. Lincolnwood: NTC, 1994.

Translation

Lebert, Stephan, and Norbert Lebert. My Father's Keeper. Trans.

Julian Evans. Boston: Little, 2001.

Article in a Reference Book

It is not necessary to give full publication information for familiar reference works (encyclopedias and dictionaries). For these titles, list only the edition (if available) and the publication year. If an article is initialed, check the index of authors (in the opening section of each volume) for the author's full name.

"Technical Education." Encyclopedia Americana. 2001 ed.

Lum, P. Andrea. "Computed Tomography." World Book. 2000 ed.

If you use an encyclopedia or other reference book recorded on CD-ROM, use the form below. If available, include publication information for the printed source.

The American Heritage Dictionary of the English Language. 3rd ed.

Boston: Houghton-Mifflin, 1992. CD-ROM. Cambridge: Softkey

Intl., 1994.

Pamphlet

Treat a pamphlet as you would a book.

> Grayson, George W. **The North American Free Trade Agreement.** New
>
> York: Foreign Policy Assn., 1993.

A pamphlet (or a book) with no author or publication information stated is formatted as follows. If known, list the country of publication [in brackets]. Use *n.p.* (no place) if the country or the publisher is unknown and *n.d.* if the date is unknown.

> **Pedestrian Safety.** [United States]: n.p., n.d.

Government Publication

State the name of the government (country, state, and so on) followed by the name of the agency. Most federal publications are published by the Government Printing Office (GPO).

> United States. Dept. of Labor. Bureau of Labor Statistics.
>
> **Occupational Outlook Handbook 2000–2001.** Washington: GPO,
>
> 2000.

When citing the *Congressional Record*, the date and page numbers are all that is required.

> **Cong. Rec.** 5 Feb. 2002: S311–15.

Book in a Series

Give the series name and number (if any) before the publication information.

> Paradis, Adrian A. **Opportunities in Military Careers.** VGM
>
> Opportunities Series. Lincolnwood: VGM Career Horizons, 1999.

Book with a Title Within a Title

If the title contains a title normally in quotation marks, keep the quotation marks and underline the entire title.

> Stuckey-French, Elizabeth. **"The First Paper Girl in Red Oak, Iowa"**
>
> **and Other Stories.** New York: Doubleday, 2000.

Note: If the title contains a title that is normally underlined, do not underline that title in your entry: A Tale of Two Cities as History.

video

Works-Cited Entries: Periodicals

The possible components of these entries are listed in order below:

1. **Author's name**
2. **Title of article**
3. **Name of periodical**
4. **Series number or name, if relevant**
5. **Volume number (for a scholarly journal)**
6. **Issue number**
7. **Date of publication (abbreviate all months but May, June, July)**
8. **Page numbers**

For articles that are continued on a nonconsecutive page, add a plus sign (+) after the first page number. If any of these components do not apply, they are not listed. The entries that follow illustrate the information and arrangement needed to cite periodicals.

Article in a Magazine

> Goodell, Jeff. "The Uneasy Assimilation." Rolling Stone 6–13 Dec. 2001: 63–66.

> "Patent Pamphleteer." Scientific American Dec. 2001: 33.

Article in a Scholarly Journal

> Chu, Wujin. "Costs and Benefits of Hard-Sell." Journal of Marketing Research 32.2 (1995): 97–102.

Note: Journals are usually issued no more than four times per year. The number 32 above refers to the volume. The issue number is not needed if the page numbers in a volume continue from one issue to the next. If the page numbers start over with each issue, then put a period and the issue number right after the volume number, with no intervening space: 32.2.

Printed Interview

Begin with the name of the person interviewed when that's whom you are quoting.

> Cantwell, Maria. "The New Technocrat." By Erika Rasmusson. Working Woman Apr. 2001: 20–21.

Note: If the interview is untitled, *Interview* (no italics) follows the interviewee's name.

Newspaper Article

> Bleakley, Fred R. "Companies' Profits Grew 48% Despite Economy."
>
> Wall Street Journal 1 May 1995, Midwest ed.: 1.

Note: Cite the edition of a major daily newspaper (if given) after the date (1 May 1995, Midwest ed.: 1). If a local paper's name does not include the city of publication, add it in brackets (not underlined) after the name.

To cite an article in a lettered section of the newspaper, list the section and the page number. (For example, A4 would refer to page 4 in section A of the newspaper.) If the sections are numbered, however, use a comma after the year (or the edition); then indicate sec. 1, 2, 3, and so on, followed by a colon and the page number (sec. 1:20).

An unsigned newspaper article follows the same format:

> "Bombs—Real and Threatened—Keep Northern Ireland Edgy."
>
> Chicago Tribune 6 Dec. 2001, sec. 1: 20.

Note: If an article is an editorial, put *Editorial* (no italics) after the title.

Letter to the Editor

> Sory, Forrest. Letter. Discover July 2001: 10.

Review

> Olsen, Jack. "Brains and Industry." Rev. of Land of Opportunity, by
>
> Sarah Marr. New York Times 23 Apr. 1995, sec. 3: 28.

Note: If you cite the review of a work by an editor or a translator, use *ed.* or *trans.* instead of *by*.

Title or Quotation Within an Article's Title

> Morgenstern, Joe. "Sleeper of the Year: In the Bedroom Is Rich Tale
>
> of Tragic Love." Wall Street Journal 23 Nov. 2001: W1.

Note: Use single quotation marks around the shorter title if it is a title normally punctuated with quotation marks.

Article Reprinted in a Loose-Leaf Collection

The entry begins with original publication information and ends with the name of the loose-leaf volume (Youth), editor, volume number, publication information including name of the information service (SIRS), and the article number.

> O'Connell, Loraine. "Busy Teens Feel the Beep." Orlando Sentinel 7
>
> Jan. 1993: E1+. Youth. Ed. Eleanor Goldstein. Vol. 4. Boca
>
> Raton: SIRS, 1993. Art. 41.

video

Works-Cited Entries: Electronic Sources

Citations for online text contain the date of electronic publication as indicated in the source as well as the date on which the site was accessed. URLs are enclosed in angle brackets and identify the complete address, including the access-mode identifier (http, ftp, telnet, and so on). If a URL is quite long and complicated, simply give the site's search page or home page URL. MLA asks for page, paragraph, or section numbers if the document includes them.

1. Author's name
2. Title of article (or Web page)
3. Title of Internet site
4. Site editor's name
5. Version (volume or issue) number
6. Date of electronic publication
7. Name of subscription service
8. Name of list or forum
9. Number range or total number of pages (or other sections)
10. Site sponsor's name
11. Date of access
12. URL

In an entry for online material that has a previous (print or nonprint) version available, document that information first (using the format shown in this chapter for that version), followed by the electronic source reference.

An Entire Site

List the title of the site (underlined), the site's editor (if identified), any electronic publication information available (version number, date of publication or last update, and sponsoring organization), your access date, and the URL.

> Internet Public Library. 2003. University of Michigan. 6 March 2003
> <http://www.ipl.org/>.

A Home Page

Identify the site creator (if available), the title of the department or course (if applicable), and the term *Home page* (preceded by *Course* or *Dept.*, if applicable). Then list the posting date for a personal page, or dates of the course and the department to which it belongs. For a course or department home page, identify the institution, as well. End the citation with your date of access, and the URL.

> Cummings, Ernie. Home page. 13 July 2001
> <http://www.ernie.cummings.net>.

> Laboratory for Integrated Learning and Technology. Dept. home page.
> Illinois State U. 12 May 2003 <http://lilt.ilstu.edu/>.

Online Books

In general, follow the format for printed books. Include publication information for original print version if available. Follow the date of publication with the access date and Web address.

> Simon, Julian L. **The Ultimate Resource II: People, Materials, and**
>
> **Environment. College Park: U of Maryland, 1996. 9 Apr. 2001**
>
> **<http://www.inform.umd.edu/EdRes/Colleges/BMGT/**
>
> **Faculty/JSimon/Ultimate_Resource/>.**

When citing part of an online book, the title (or name of the part, such as **Foreword**) follows the author's name; the title of the book (underlined) is followed by its author's name if different from the first name listed.

> Untermeyer, Louis. **"Author's Apology."** The Donkey of God. 1999.
>
> iUniverse. 7 March 2003 <http://books.iuniverse.com/>.

Article in an Online Periodical

The format for printed periodical matter applies here, with modifications. Begin with the author's name; the article title in quotation marks; and the underlined name of the periodical, its volume or issue number, and date of publication. Include page numbers (or other sections) if numbered. Close with the date of access and URL.

> Dickerson, John. "Nailing Jello." Time.com 5 Nov. 2001. 9 Dec. 2001
>
> <http://www.time.com/time/columnist/dickerson/>.

Note: For an anonymous article from a periodical, begin the citation with the title.

Publication on CD-ROM, Diskette, or Magnetic Tape

Citations for materials published on CD-ROM, diskette, or magnetic tape are similar to those for print sources, with these added considerations: (1) The contents of a work may vary from one medium to another; therefore, the citation should always identify the medium. (2) The publisher and vendor of the publication may be different, in which case both must be identified. (3) Because of periodic updates, multiple versions of the same database may exist, which calls for citation if possible of both the date of the document cited and the date of the database itself.

> Ackley, Patricia. "Jobs of the Twenty-First Century." New Rochelle
>
> Informer 15 Apr. 1994: A4. New Rochelle Informer Ondisc.
>
> CD-ROM. Info-Line. Oct. 1994.
>
> Baker, Anthony. The New Earth Science. Diskette. Cincinnati:
>
> Freeman's P, 1991.

Online Services

When you use a library to access a subscription service, add the name of the database if known (underlined), the service, and the library. Then give the date of access followed by the Internet address for the home page of the service (if known). If no Internet address is given for an entry, add a keyword or path statement in its place, if appropriate. (*Example:* "Keyword: Kiev" or "Path: World Events; Conflicts; Kiev.")

> **Davis, Jerome. "Massacre in Kiev." Washington Post 29 Nov. 1999,**
>
> **final ed.: C12. National Newspapers. ProQuest. Gateway**
>
> **Technical College Elkhorn Campus Library. 30 Nov. 1999**
>
> **<http://proquest.umi.com/pqdweb>.**

Scholarly Project or Information Database

The title of the site is listed first, then the name of the editor (if given). Follow this with the version number (if relevant), the date of publication or update, name of the sponsor, date of access, and URL.

> **Wired Style: Principles of English Usage in the Digital Age. 1994.**
>
> **Wired Digital Inc. 5 Nov. 2001 <http://hotwired.lycos.com/**
>
> **hardwired/wiredstyle/>.**

If you are citing a book that is part of an online scholarly project, first list information about the printed book, followed by publication information for the project. End with the URL of the book.

> **Astell, Mary. Reflections on Marriage. London: Wilkin, 1706. Women**
>
> **Writers Project. Providence: Brown UP, 1999.**
>
> **7 Feb. 2002 <http://www.wwp.brown.edu/texts/astell/**
>
> **marriage.html>.**

E-Mail Communication

> **Barzinji, Atman. "Re: Frog Populations in Wisconsin Wetlands."**
>
> **E-mail to the author. 1 Jan. 2002.**

Online Postings

Follow the author's name and title with *Online posting.* The date that the material was posted is followed by the name of the forum, if known; date of access; and address.

> **Wilcox, G. M. "White Gold Finch." Online posting. 7 Nov. 2001.**
>
> **IN-Bird. 9 Nov. 2001 <http://www.virtualbirder.com/bmail/**
>
> **inbird/latest.html#1>.**

video

Works-Cited Entries: Other Print and Nonprint Sources

The following examples of works-cited entries illustrate how to cite sources such as television or radio programs, films, live performances, works of art, and other miscellaneous nonprint sources.

Manuscript or Typescript

List the author, title or description (such as *Notebook*), form (*ms.* for manuscript or *ts.* for typescript), any identifying number, and name and location of the insitution where this item is held.

> **Smith, L. W. The Visitation. Ts. English Dept., Illinois State U.**

Television or Radio Program

> **"The Ultimate Road Trip: Traveling in Cyberspace." 48 Hours. CBS.**
> **WBBM, Chicago. 13 Apr. 1995.**

Film or Video Recording

The director, distributor, and year of release follow the title. Other information may be included if pertinent.

> **Titanic. Dir. James Cameron. Perf. Leonardo DiCaprio, Kate Winslet.**
> **Paramount Pictures, 1997.**

Cite a filmstrip, slide program, videocassette, or DVD like a film, but include the medium before the name of the distributor.

> **Monet: Shadow & Light. Videocassette. Devine Productions, 1999.**

Sound Recording

If you are not citing a CD, indicate *LP*, *Audiocassette*, or *Audiotape*. If you are citing a specific song on a musical recording, place its title in quotation marks before the title of the recording.

> **O'Higgins, Michael B. Beating the Dow with Bonds. Audiocassette.**
> **Harper Audio, 1999.**

A Painting, Sculpture, or Photograph

> **Titian. The Entombment. The Louvre, Paris.**

Letter or Memo Received by the Author (Yourself)

Thomas, Bob. Letter to the author. 10 Jan. 1999.

Interview by the Author (Yourself)

Brooks, Sarah. Personal interview. 15 Oct. 2002.

Cartoon or Comic Strip

Luckovich, Mike. "The Drawing Board." Cartoon. Time 17 Sept. 2001: 18.

Lecture, Speech, Address, or Reading

If there is a title, use it instead of the descriptive label (for example, *Lecture*).

Annan, Kofi. Lecture. Acceptance of Nobel Peace Prize. Oslo City Hall, Oslo, Norway. 10 Dec. 2001.

Performance

Treat this similarly to a film, adding the location and date of the performance.

Chanticleer. Young Auditorium, Whitewater, Wisconsin. 23 Feb. 2003.

Map or Chart

Follow the format for an anonymous book, adding *Map* or *Chart*.

Wisconsin Territory. Map. Madison: Wisconsin Trails, 1988.

Next Step Study the sample MLA research paper on the pages that follow. In "UN Sanctions and the Suffering of Iraq's People," student writer Troy Holland shows MLA documentation practices in action. As you review the paper, consider the following:

1. Examine how the paper shows sound treatment of sources, as outlined in Chapter 32. How does Troy effectively use sources to advance his own ideas, integrate source material smoothly, and properly document sources?

2. Examine the details of proper MLA format, from pagination to headings, spacing, margins, and so on.

3. Examine the in-text documentation used for various sources and check how those sources are presented in the Works-Cited page.

4. Answer the "Reading for Better Writing" questions on page **535**, as directed by your instructor.

5. Use the "Research Paper Checklist" on page **536** to assess the quality of your own research paper.

Sample MLA Research Paper

The research paper on the following pages is an example of how a paper is put together following MLA guidelines. **The title page and outline are not required for MLA papers,** but if your instructor asks for one or both, use the models and guidelines that follow.

Sample Title Page

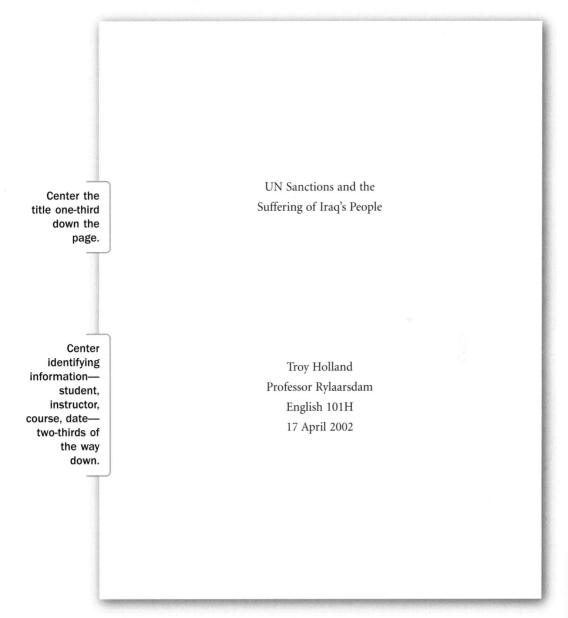

Center the title one-third down the page.

UN Sanctions and the
Suffering of Iraq's People

Center identifying information— student, instructor, course, date— two-thirds of the way down.

Troy Holland
Professor Rylaarsdam
English 101H
17 April 2002

Sample Research-Paper Outline

Center the
title one inch
from the top
of the page.

UN Sanctions and the Suffering of Iraq's People

Introduction—The UN imposed sanctions against Iraq in 1991, after Iraq invaded Kuwait.

I. Ten years later, the sanctions have not brought about the desired results.

   A. The UN's call for the destruction of weapons of mass destruction has not been heeded.

Double-space
throughout.

   B. A blockade of Iraqi exports has not been completely successful.

   C. A restriction on Iraqi imports has fallen short of its goal.

II. Living conditions in Iraq have worsened since 1991.

   A. Iraq's infrastructure has broken down.

   B. Half the water supply is undrinkable.

Use phrases
or complete
sentences
consistently,
as required.

   C. The health care system is inadequate.

   D. Food is in short supply.

III. The children have been most affected.

   A. Sickness and death have increased dramatically.

   B. Health care is minimal.

IV. The UN is searching for solutions.

   A. An "oil-for-food" program was instituted in 1995.

   B. The quota on oil exports has been lifted.

   C. Experts are now debating "targeted" sanctions.

   D. The number of relief agencies allowed in Iraq may be increased.

Set off the
introduction
and the
conclusion.

Conclusion—The present sanctions need to be revamped because they continue to hurt Iraq's most vulnerable citizens without achieving their political goals.

An MLA Research-Paper Model

Troy Holland wrote the following research paper for his freshman composition class. As you review his paper, read the side notes and examine the following:

- The different types of sources used in the paper
- The techniques used to state the thesis and organize the argument
- The methods used to integrate information into the writer's own thinking, including how he cited his sources

Holland 1

The heading (not needed if a title page is used) supplies identifying details.

Troy Holland

Professor Rylaarsdam

English 101H

17 April 2002

UN Sanctions and the Suffering of Iraq's People

The title indicates the topic and theme. The opening introduces the subject and provides background information.

In 1991, the Middle East nation of Iraq, led by Saddam Hussein, attacked its neighbor Kuwait. To protect Kuwait, the United Nations intervened against Iraq, a step that eventually led to the Persian Gulf War. With the military help of the United States, Great Britain, France, and other nations, the UN forced Iraq to withdraw from Kuwait in operation Desert Storm. The United Nations Security Council also placed sanctions on Iraq to enforce Iraq's compliance with UN resolutions and to prevent Hussein from repeating his aggression.

1

Common knowledge is not documented.

More than ten years have passed since the UN implemented these sanctions, the United States is engaged in a war on terrorism, and Saddam Hussein still refuses to cooperate with the United Nations. As a result, the UN, spurred on by the United States, continues to enforce the sanctions. The problem is that these economic sanctions have caused tremendous suffering for average Iraqi people. Many of our elected leaders have argued that because Saddam Hussein seriously threatens world peace, this suffering cannot be avoided. But the decision that such suffering is acceptable should not be made by politicians alone. In a democracy, all citizens share responsibility for the policies that their elected leaders make. In fact, a strong argument can be made that the suffering of Iraqi men, women, and children is not a justifiable side effect of the sanctions against Iraq.

2

The writer states his thesis.

Holland 2

A strong transition leads the reader into the body of the paper.

To understand the issue, we first need to consider what the UN wanted the sanctions to accomplish in Iraq. Following the Gulf War, the UN Security Council passed Resolution 687 on April 3, 1991. This resolution called on Iraq to destroy all its weapons of mass destruction and pay its war debts. The resolution also implemented economic sanctions against Iraq until it complied with the UN's expectations. These sanctions restricted the sale to Iraq of everything from health care supplies to building materials to food. In addition, the sanctions blocked Iraq from exporting all goods except for a limited amount of oil. The money made from the sale of this oil would be used to pay war debts and buy food and medicine. Resolution 687 also set up an organization to monitor the payment of the war debts and make sure that Iraq destroyed all its weapons of mass destruction ("United Nations").

The writer uses a source from the Iraq Action Coalition Web site.

On the one hand, sanctions seem partly to have worked. Some experts argue that sanctions have contained Saddam Hussein's aggression. Hussein does not control all of his own country, he cannot use money from oil sales for weapons, his efforts to secretly build weapons of mass destruction are being thwarted, and he is less of a threat to neighboring countries, such as Kuwait (Yaphe 127). Also, supporters say that food and medicine are allowed into Iraq. For these reasons, many people continue to support sanctions as a way to prevent Hussein from developing weapons of mass destruction, especially in light of the September 11 attacks on the World Trade Towers and the Pentagon.

Both sides of the debate are presented.

On the other hand, sanctions have not been completely successful. Saddam Hussein has been uncooperative from the start, especially about UN inspections of Iraq's weapon sites. He continues to find ways to raise money, and he is still able to acquire weapons by smuggling them (Cortright and Lopez 744). In fact, Hussein also has succeeded at manipulating UN sanctions so that they hurt his own people and raise international opposition. As David Cortright and George Lopez, international peace negotiators at the University of Notre Dame, put it, "[a] policy designed to exert pressure on an aggressor regime has been perverted by that regime into a virtual attack on innocents" (745). While

Holland 3

Hussein continues to follow his own agenda and protect his own power,
the most vulnerable Iraqis suffer.

Instead of forcing Hussein to comply with the disarmament, the
economic sanctions have caused living conditions within Iraq to
deteriorate sharply. Because of Gulf War damages, a lack of funds, a
shortage of building materials, and Hussein's own agenda, Iraq cannot
rebuild; in fact, basic infrastructures have broken down. George Capaccio,
an editor at Houghton Mifflin and a member of relief organizations such
as Conscience International and the Middle East Council of Churches,
traveled to Iraq in March 1997 to witness the conditions firsthand. He
describes these problems:

> In rural areas only about 50 percent of the water is drinkable.
> This is due in large part to the fact that raw sewage continues to
> flow into the major rivers; chlorine for water purification is often
> in short supply; and the network of underground pipes has
> numerous breakages so that waste from sewage lines frequently
> flows into water lines. These conditions can be directly traced to
> the UN sanctions which make spare parts for water and sewage
> treatment plants hard to come by. (E-mail)

Capaccio adds that problems within the health care system, agricultural
sector, and electrical grid have also harmed living conditions for Iraqis. In
other words, because the economic sanctions have restricted imports, the
Iraqi people have not been able to rebuild after the war. And the inability
to rebuild has caused basic services to break down.

One of the most basic needs is food, and the economic sanctions have
cut back Iraq's access to food. Before the sanctions, Iraq imported up to
66 percent of its food; until 1990, Iraq spent an average of $2.5 billion on
food imports each year ("United Nations"). But after the economic
sanctions were put into place, Iraq could no longer import as much food
as it needed. Instead, it has been forced to rely heavily on its own food
production, which is limited because of the desert climate. As a result,
Iraqis have lived with constant food shortages.

The writer indicates a source's credibility before quoting him.

A quotation longer than four lines is introduced with a complete sentence and a colon, and indented ten spaces.

The parenthetical citation is placed two spaces after the period at the end of set-off quotations.

Holland 4

Who has suffered most from these food shortages and the breakdown *8*
in basic services? The children. The economic sanctions have affected
children more severely than other Iraqis because their young bodies break
down more easily under the added strains. These strains lead to both
serious sickness and death. Denis Halliday, the former UN Humanitarian
Coordinator to Iraq, argues that "sanctions are both directly and indirectly
killing approximately six or seven thousand Iraqi children per month"
(77), whereas Iraq suffered 40,000 casualties during the war. Some studies
claim that 237,000 Iraqi children, ages five and younger, have died as a
result of economic sanctions (Gordon 388). At the lowest estimate, the
economic sanctions have caused almost six times more Iraqi deaths than
the Gulf War. This statistic is strong evidence that the sanctions need to be
rethought. Instead of encouraging Saddam Hussein to comply with UN
resolutions, the economic sanctions have caused what Halliday has called
"genocide" (qtd. in Wood).

Iraqi children have been suffering and dying for two main reasons: *9*
malnutrition and poor health care. Hussein's policies have made it hard
for parents to provide for their children, but sanctions make the job even
tougher by restricting imports. The United Nations Children's Fund, or
UNICEF, whose purpose is to protect children's rights, found that in 1997
up to 32 percent of the children, ages five and under, were malnourished.
This number had increased 75 percent from 1991 ("Nearly One Million
Children"). So not only have deaths among children risen sharply since
1991, but the percentage of malnourished children has risen sharply as well.

In addition, most Iraqis have little or no access to health care. *10*
Hospitals have had to deal with shortages of water and power, and often
what water they do have is unclean. In his visit to Iraq, Capaccio
witnessed these shortages, and he remarks that the hospitals in Iraq are in
deplorable shape. Many heating and cooling systems do not work, and
flies travel freely through the hospitals, spreading more disease. Medical
equipment is scarce, including ambulances and diagnostic equipment, and
much of what doctors do have is obsolete. Medicines for diseases such as
leukemia, typhoid, and cholera are not available unless they are bought on

A quotation by an authoritative source (mentioned in the text) is integrated.

The citation indicates that the source was quoted in another source.

The citation lists the title because no author is given.

The writer summarizes a source accurately and fairly.

Holland 5

the black market (E-mail). These conditions are a sharp turnaround from the health care system before the sanctions. The United Nations reports that before 1991, Iraq had a health care system that covered 97 percent of the urban population and 78 percent of the rural population. Iraq also had a welfare system that supported orphans, disabled children, and poor families ("United Nations"). The Iraqi people no longer receive quality health care because of the UN economic sanctions and Saddam Hussein's refusal to comply with UN resolutions.

Iraq's people are not responsible for Saddam Hussein's aggression, but *11* they have been forced to suffer under the economic sanctions. In fact, many people believe that the suffering of innocent civilians makes economic sanctions illegal under the just-war doctrine. David Cortright, a researcher for International Peace Studies at the University of Notre Dame, explains that according to the just-war doctrine, warring countries cannot target vulnerable populations, such as the elderly, women, and children. Cortright goes on to argue that "[i]f decision makers in war are bound by the moral criteria of the just-war doctrine, those imposing economic sanctions must be similarly bound by such constraints. The principle of civilian immunity applies no less in the imposition of economic sanctions than in the conduct of war" (Cortright and Lopez 740). In the same way, others argue that economic sanctions place Iraq under a siege that harms civilians much more than it harms the military (Gordon 391). The economic sanctions cripple the most vulnerable people in Iraq while doing little to force Saddam Hussein to follow the United Nations' resolutions. The sanctions must be changed both to relieve people's suffering and to keep Hussein from developing weapons of mass destruction.

Because of pressure from humanitarian groups, the United Nations *12* has been searching for many years for a solution to the suffering. In 1995, the UN convinced Hussein to accept a temporary solution called the "food for oil program" ("Iraqi Oil Exports"). Under this program, Iraq was allowed to sell a certain amount of oil, and the money from these sales went into an account controlled by the United Nations. The UN then used that money to pay war debts and to allow Iraq to buy food and medicine

---

A quotation is used because of its power and authority.

A change from upper-case in the original to lowercase is shown with brackets.

The writer summarizes the central argument he has been making.

Attempts to solve the problem are explored.

Holland 6

for its people ("Iraqi Oil Exports"). However, these payments were not enough to meet people's needs. Capaccio puts the problem this way:

> The total value of humanitarian supplies that have actually arrived in Iraq is estimated to be 10 billion dollars. Annualized more than four years and divided by a population of 23 million people, this comes to about three dollars per person per month—hardly enough to begin the job of reconstructing an entire society. (E-mail)

Three dollars a month is very little money to support someone who needs food and medicine.

> The writer shows how he has integrated information by commenting on quoted material.

In the past few years, the amount of oil that Iraq can sell has been raised so that there is now no specific limit, and the Iraqi government can use the funds for more than food and medical supplies (Cortright, "Hard Look" 2). However, Hussein continues to find ways to abuse the program and the funds so that innocent Iraqis suffer. Although the oil-for-food program is an excellent idea, it is not enough to stop the malnutrition and poverty. Stronger steps need to be taken to reduce the suffering.

> Strong transitions help readers follow the issues involved.

One step would be to gradually remove the trade restrictions on Iraq. The United Nations could lift sanctions as Saddam Hussein complies with weapons inspections. Until now, the UN's policy has been to keep all sanctions in place until Iraq meets all of the conditions. However, many people believe that Hussein will react better to policies that have a clear end and attached incentives. Russia, France, and China all believe that the economic sanctions must have these qualities to be successful (Yaphe 129–130). As Hussein proves that he is complying with the agreement, the United Nations could gradually increase the imports allowed into Iraq. The priority would be food, health care supplies, and building materials. This change may help Hussein realize the benefits of complying with the United Nations' military requirements.

> The writer builds on others' ideas and qualifies statements to enhance credibility.

For the past year, politicians and experts have been debating "targeted" or "smart" sanctions. On the one hand, these sanctions would apply very tight restrictions to military goods so that Iraq cannot develop its military might. On the other hand, restrictions on peaceful forms of

13

14

15

Holland 7

trade and development would be lifted so that average Iraqis can get on with their lives (Cortright, "Hard Look" 3). In 2001, this idea was defeated in the UN Security Council, but debate continues on its merits. One problem, for example, has been the fuzzy line between military and peaceful goods. If "smart" sanctions passed, the Security Council would have to implement them carefully. While striving to reduce the suffering, Council members must remain firm about blocking Iraq's ability to produce weapons of mass destruction so that the Middle East does not become more unstable than it already is.

Another step that might be very helpful would be to increase the number of relief organizations and relief workers that the United States allows to enter Iraq. Right now, the United States does not allow any American citizens to enter Iraq without official permission (Capaccio, "Suffer"). More relief workers could do a lot to spread aid to more people. This increase in workers would also help to ensure that aid actually reaches the people who need it.

As U.S. citizens, we share responsibility for the policies set by our elected leaders. Madeline Albright, the Secretary of State under former President Clinton, was asked a number of years ago whether the economic sanctions were worth enforcing at such high cost. Her response about the economics being a hard choice but worth the price may have reflected the public opinion at that time. Many people now disagree. They would argue that the present sanctions continue to hurt Iraq's most vulnerable citizens without achieving the political goals. President Bush, the Congress, and the UN must develop a fairer, more effective policy toward Iraq. As citizens concerned about innocent people both at home and abroad, we must take a stand against the suffering of innocent Iraqis. We must press our leaders to rethink the sanctions. If we pledge "liberty and justice for all" in our own land, how can we practice injustice in our foreign policies?

The citation includes both the author and a shortened title because two sources have the same author.

The concluding paragraph summarizes the issue and argument, revisiting ideas in the introduction.

The essay ends with a thought-provoking question.

16

17

Holland 8

Works Cited

Capaccio, George. E-mail interview. 7 April 2002.

Capaccio, George. "Suffer the Little Children." Iraq Action Coalition. May
1997. 12 March 2002 <http://iraqaction.org/suffer.html>.

Cortright, David. "A Hard Look at Iraqi Sanctions." Nation (3 Dec. 2001):
1-3. Academic Search Elite. EBSCOhost. Dordt Coll. Lib., Sioux
Ctr. 12 March 2002 <http://www.ebscohost.com>.

Cortright, David, and George A. Lopez. "Are Sanctions Just? The
Problematic Case of Iraq." Journal of International Affairs 52.2
(1999): 735–755.

Gordon, Joy. "Economic Sanctions, Just War Doctrine, and the Fearful
Spectacle of the Civilian Dead." Cross Currents 49.3 (1999):
387–400.

Halliday, Denis. Interview. "Sanctioned Suffering." Harvard International
Review Winter 1998/99: 76–79.

"Iraqi Oil Exports Surge Once Again." United Nations Office of the Iraq
Program. 13 March 2002 <http://www.un.org/Depts/oip/>.

"Nearly One Million Children Malnourished in Iraq, UNICEF Says."
UNICEF Press Centre. 26 Nov. 1997. 12 March 2002
<http://www.unicef.org/Newsline/97pr60.htm>.

"Resolution 687." United Nations Security Council. 3 Apr. 1991. 4 April
2002 <http://www.un.org/Depts/oip/background/scrsindex.html>.

"United Nations Report on the Current Humanitarian Situation in Iraq."
Iraq Action Coalition. 30 March 1999. 14 March 2002
<http://iraqaction.org/UN1999.html>.

Wood, Douglas S. "Economic Sanctions: Legitimate Diplomatic Tool or
Failed Policy?" CNN.com. 13 March 2002 <http://europe.cnn.com/
SPECIALS/ 2001/ gulf.war/legacy/sanctions/>.

Yaphe, Judith S. "Iraq: The Exception to the Rule." Washington Quarterly
Winter 2001: 126–137. Academic Search Elite. EBSCOhost. Dordt
Coll. Lib., Sioux Ctr. 12 March 2002 <http://www.ebscohost.com>.

The list of works cited begins on a separate page and includes the title, header, and page number.

Sources are listed in alphabetical order by author (or by title if no author is given).

Items are double-spaced throughout. Second and subsequent lines are indented.

Periods separate most items in individual entries but are never underlined.

Internet addresses are indicated between angle brackets.

Reading for Better Writing

1. What do you know about the Gulf War and UN sanctions against Iraq? How does Troy's paper affect your understanding?
2. Do you find the essay engaging? Why or why not?
3. What types of evidence does Troy provide in his writing? Where does he get this evidence?
4. How does Troy distinguish his own ideas from source material? Why are these strategies necessary?
5. Troy's topic is related to the broader subject of U.S. foreign policy. How is his discussion related to other issues, such as terrorism, instability in the Middle East, history, the global economy, and religion?

MLA Documentation Activities

1. Create works-cited entries in correct MLA style for the following publications:

   a. An article in the May 27, 2002, issue (vol. 145, no. 11) of *Fortune* magazine by Joseph Nocera titled "Return of the Raider" (pages 97–114)

   b. Ernest Hemingway's novel *A Farewell to Arms*, published in 1986 by Collier Books, located in New York City

   c. A Web page called "Aruba," part of *The World Factbook 2001* site, sponsored by the Central Intelligence Agency. No author or publication date is listed on the site; it was accessed on March 8, 2002, at <http://www.cia.gov/cia/publications/factbook/index.html>.

2. Using the MLA documentation style, create works-cited entries for three possible sources (one book, one magazine or journal article, and an online source) for a research paper. Have a classmate review your entries.

Research Paper Checklist

Before turning in any research project, check it against the traits of good research writing.

Stimulating Ideas

The writing . . .

_____ Focuses on an important and specific topic, which is expressed in a clear thesis statement.

_____ Effectively develops or supports the thesis with facts and details from a variety of reliable sources.

_____ Creates interest and thoroughly informs readers.

_____ Gives credit, where necessary, for ideas taken from other sources.

Logical Organization

_____ Includes a clearly developed beginning, middle, and ending.

_____ Presents supporting information in a clear, organized manner.

Engaging Voice

_____ Speaks in a sincere and knowledgeable voice.

_____ Shows that the writer is truly interested in the subject.

Appropriate Word Choice

_____ Explains or defines any unfamiliar terms.

_____ Employs an appropriate level of language.

Overall Fluency

_____ Flows smoothly from one idea to the next.

_____ Shows variation in sentence structure.

Design and Appearance

_____ Includes wide margins and double-spaced lines throughout.

_____ Places page headers, page numbers, and headings correctly.

_____ Uses an appropriate typeface and type size.

Correct, Accurate Copy

_____ Adheres to the rules of grammar, spelling, and punctuation.

_____ Follows MLA, APA, or another documentation guide.

Chapter 34
APA Documentation Form

Those who write papers in the social sciences—psychology, sociology, political science, education, journalism, or public health—usually refer to the style guidelines found in the *Publication Manual of the American Psychological Association* (APA). The questions and answers on the next two pages should help you set up a research paper using this style.

APA documentation format is similar to MLA format in two ways: both require (1) parenthetical citations within the text and (2) a final listing of all references cited in the paper. But in the social sciences, the date of publication is often much more crucial than it is in the humanities, so the date is highlighted in in-text citations. APA format also requires a cover page and an abstract. For exact instructions in proper APA documentation style, consult this chapter and the model APA-style research paper on pages 555–566.

What's Ahead
- APA Research Paper Guidelines
- Parenthetical References
- Reference Entries: Books
- Reference Entries: Periodicals
- Reference Entries: Electronic Sources
- Reference Entries: Other Print and Nonprint Sources
- Sample APA Research Paper
- Activities

APAAPAAPAAPAAPAAPAAPAAPA

APA Research Paper Guidelines

video

Questions & Answers

Is a separate title page required?

Yes. Include your paper's title, your name, and the name of your school on three separate lines, double-spaced, centered, and beginning approximately one-third of the way down from the top of the page. Place a shortened title and page number 1 in the top right corner. (See "What about paging?" on the next page.)

What is an abstract and where does it go?

An abstract is required in APA format. An abstract is a 100- to 150-word paragraph summarizing your research paper. (See page **556**.) Place your abstract on a new page and label it "Abstract" (centered); type your short title and page number 2 flush right one-half inch from the top.

Are references placed in the text?

Yes. Include the author and year, separated by a comma; for quotations, add the page number after a comma and "p."

Do you need a bibliography of sources used in the paper?

Yes. Full citations for all sources used (books, periodicals, and so on) are placed in an alphabetized list labeled "References" at the end of the paper.

How are the reference lists to be indented?

Confusion sometimes arises over how the reference lists of APA manuscripts should be indented. Normal paragraph indentation has been called for by APA in the past. However, hanging indentation as shown in this chapter is currently the preferred manuscript form for APA documents, including student papers. As always, ask your instructor if you are in doubt.

Do you need an appendix?

Maybe. Ask your instructor. In student papers, charts, tables, and graphs may sometimes be incorporated at appropriate points in the text, making appendices unnecessary.

What about longer quotations?	Type quotations of 40 or more words in block style (all lines flush left) five spaces in from the left margin. Indent the first lines of any additional paragraphs in the long quotation five spaces in from the quotation margin.
What about margins?	Leave a margin of at least one inch on all four sides (if you are binding your paper, leave one and one-half inches at the left margin); computer users may use a justified right margin, and end-of-line hyphens are acceptable.
What about paging?	Page numbers appear at the top right margin, above the first line of text. Instead of your name, place the short title (first two or three words) either above, or five spaces to the left of, each page number. (See page **557**.)
What about headings?	Headings, like an outline, show the organization of your paper and the importance of each topic. All topics of equal importance should have headings of the same level, or style. Below are the various levels of headings used in APA papers. (In most research papers, only levels 1, 3, and 4 are used.)

LEVEL 1:   Centered Uppercase and Lowercase Heading

LEVEL 2:   *Centered, Italicized, Uppercase and Lowercase Heading*

LEVEL 3: *Flush Left, Italicized, Uppercase and Lowercase Side Heading*

LEVEL 4:   *Indented, italicized, lowercase paragraph heading ending with a period.*

Any other special instructions?	Always ask whether your school or department has special requirements that may take precedence over these guidelines. Web

APA Paper Format

This overview gives formatting guidelines for an APA research paper. Ask your instructor for any special requirements that he or she may have.

Title Page ◆ On the first page, include your paper's title, your name, and your institution's name on three separate lines. Double-space and center the lines beginning approximately one-third of the way down from the top of the page.

Abstract ◆ On the second page, include an abstract—a 100- to 150-word paragraph summarizing your paper. Place the title *Abstract* approximately one inch from the top of the page and center it.

Body ◆ Format the body (which begins on the third page) of your paper as follows:

Margins: Leave a one inch margin on all four sides of each page (one and one-half inches on the left for paper to be bound). A justified right margin and end-of-line hyphens are acceptable.

Line Spacing: Double-space your entire paper, unless your instructor allows single spacing for tables, titles, captions, and so on, for the sake of readability.

Headings: Main headings should be centered, using standard uppercase and lowercase text.

Page Numbers: Place your short title (the first two or three words) and the page number at the upper-right margin of all pages beginning with the title page. The title should be either just above or five spaces to the left of the page number.

Citations ◆ Within your paper, give credit for others' ideas by including the author and year in a citation. For quotations, add the page number(s) to the citation. (See page **541**.) If a quotation runs 40 words or more, type it in block style, five spaces in from the left margin, with all lines flush left along that new margin. If it is more than one paragraph, indent the first line of the second and later paragraphs another five spaces.

References ◆ Place full citations from all sources in an alphabetized list at the end of your paper. Place the title *References* approximately one inch from the top of the page and center it. (See pages **565–566**.)

Appendix ◆ If your instructor requires it, place your charts, tables, and graphs in an appendix. Otherwise, include them within the body of your paper.

video

APA Parenthetical References

In APA style, as in the MLA system, you must cite your source in the text (in parentheses) each time you borrow from it. Each of these parenthetical citations, except for personal communications such as letters, e-mail, or phone conversations, must be matched to an entry in an alphabetized list called "References" at the end of your paper. Each item in the "References" list should, in turn, be cited in the text.

The Form of an Entry

The APA documentation style is sometimes called the "author-date" system because both the author and the date of the publication must be mentioned in the text when citing a source. Both might appear in the flow of the sentence, like this:

> **Only South Africa has more people infected with AIDS than India, according to a 2001 article by Mike Specter.**

If either name or date does not appear in the text, it must be mentioned in parentheses at the most convenient place, like this:

> **According to an article by Mike Specter (2001), only South Africa . . .**

> **According to a recent article (Specter, 2001), only South Africa . . .**

Model Parenthetical References

One Author: Citing a Complete Work

The correct form for a parenthetical reference to a single source by a single author is parenthesis, last name, comma, space, year of publication, parenthesis. Also note that final punctuation should be placed outside the parentheses.

> **. . . and the great majority of Venezuelans live near the Caribbean coast (Anderson, 2001).**

One Author: Citing Part of a Work

When you cite a specific part of a source, give the page number, chapter, or section, using the appropriate abbreviations (*p.* or *pp.*, *chap.*, or *sec.*—for other abbreviations, see page **568**). Always give the page number for a direct quotation.

> **. . . Bush's 2002 budget, passed by Congress, was based on revenue estimates that "now appear to have been far too optimistic" (Lemann, 2001, p. 48).**

One Author: More Than One Publication in the Same Year

If the same author has published two or more articles in the same year, avoid confusion by placing a small letter *a* after the first work listed in the references list, *b* after the next one, and so on. The order of such works is determined alphabetically by title.

PARENTHETICAL CITATION

Coral reefs harbor life forms heretofore unknown (Milius, 2001a, 2001b).

REFERENCES

Milius, D. (2001a). Another world hides inside coral reefs. *Science News,* 160(16), 244.

Milius, D. (2001b). Unknown squids—with elbows—tease science. *Science News,* 160(24), 390.

Two to Five Authors

In APA style, all authors—up to as many as five—must be mentioned in the text citation, like this:

Love changes not just who we are, but who we can become, as well (Lewis, Amini, & Lannon, 2000).

Note: The last two authors' names are always separated by a comma and an ampersand (&) when enclosed in parentheses.

For works with more than two but less than six authors, list all the authors the first time; after that, use only the name of the first author followed by "et al." (the Latin abbreviation for *et alii,* meaning "and others"), like this:

These discoveries lead to the hypothesis that love actually alters the brain's structure (Lewis et al., 2000).

Six or More Authors

If your source has six or more authors, refer to the work by the first author's name followed by "et al.," both for the first reference in the text and all references after that. However, be sure to list all the authors (up to six) in your references list.

Anonymous Book (Work)

If your source lists no author, treat the first two or three words of the title (capitalized normally) as you would an author's last name. A title of an article or a chapter belongs in quotation marks, whereas the titles of books or reports should be italicized:

. . . including a guide to low-stress postures ("How to Do It," 2001).

Group Author

A group author is an organization, association, or agency that claims authorship of a document. Treat the name of the group as if it were the last name of the author. If the name is long and easily abbreviated, provide the abbreviation in square brackets. Use the abbreviation without brackets in subsequent references, as follows:

First text citation: **(National Institute of Mental Health [NIMH], 2002)**

Subsequent citations: **(NIMH, 2002)**

First text citation: **(Occupational Safety and Health Administration [OSHA], 2001)**

Subsequent citations: **(OSHA, 2001)**

Indirect (or Secondary) Source

If you need to cite a source that you have found referred to in another source (a "secondary" source), mention the original source in your text. Then, in your parenthetical citation, cite the secondary source, using the words "as cited in," like this:

. . . theorem given by Ullman (as cited in Hoffman, 1998).

Note: In your references list at the end of the paper, you would write out a full citation for Hoffman (not Ullman).

Two or More Works in a Parenthetical Reference

Sometimes it is necessary to lump several citations into one parenthetical reference. In that case, cite the sources as you usually would, separating the citations with semicolons. Place the citations in alphabetical order, just as they would be ordered in the references list:

These near-death experiences are reported with conviction (Rommer, 2000; Sabom, 1998).

Personal Communications

If you do the kind of personal research recommended elsewhere in *The College Writer,* you may have to cite personal communications that have provided you with some of your knowledge. Personal communications may include personal letters, phone calls, memos, and so forth. Because they are not published in a permanent form, APA style does not place them among the citations in your references list. Instead, cite them only in the text of your paper in parentheses, like this:

. . . according to M. T. Cann (personal communication, April 1, 1999).

. . . by today's standard (M. T. Cann, personal communication, April 1, 1999).

APA References List

QUICK GUIDE

The references section lists all of the sources you have cited in your text. It is found at the end of your research paper. Begin your list on a new page (the next page after the text) and number each page, continuing the numbering from the text. The guidelines that follow describe the form of the references list.

1 Type the short title and page number in the upper-right corner, approximately one-half inch from the top of the page.

2 Center the title, *References,* approximately one inch from the top; then double-space before the first entry.

3 Begin each entry flush with the left margin. If the entry runs more than one line, indent additional lines approximately one-half inch (five to seven spaces).

4 Double-space between all lines on the references page.

5 List each entry alphabetically by the last name of the author, or, if no author is given, by the title (disregarding *A, An,* or *The*).

6 A basic entry for a book would be as follows:

> **Kessler, R. (2000). *The soul of education.* Alexandria,**
>
> **VA: ASCD.**

Note: Leave one space following each word and punctuation mark in an entry. Book titles and article titles are not capitalized in the usual way: only the first letter of the title (and subtitle) and proper nouns are capitalized. Italics for titles of books and periodicals are preferred over underlining. Include the state, province, and/or country in the publisher's location only if the city is not well known for publishing.

7 A basic entry for a periodical (a magazine) would be as follows:

> **Stearns, D. H. (2000, October). Testing by design.**
>
> **Middle Ground, 21–25.**

8 See the following pages for other kinds of entries.

video

Reference Entries: Books

The general form for a book or brochure entry is this:

Author, A. (year). *Title*. Location: Publisher.

For a single chapter of a book, follow this form:

Author, A., & Author, B. (year). Title of chapter. In *Title of*

book (pp. xx–xx). Location: Publisher.

The entries that follow illustrate the information needed to cite books, sections of a book, brochures, and government publications.

One Author

Guttman, J. (1999). *The gift wrapped in sorrow: A mother's quest for*

healing. Palm Springs, CA: JMJ Publishing.

Two or More Authors

Lynn, J., & Harrold, J. (1999). *Handbook for mortals: Guidance for*

people facing serious illness. New York: Oxford University Press.

Note: Follow the first author's name with a comma; then join the two authors' names with an ampersand (&) rather than with the word "and." List up to six authors; abbreviate subsequent authors as "et al."

Anonymous Book

If an author is listed as "Anonymous," treat it as the author's name. Otherwise, follow this format:

Publication manual of the American Psychological Association

(5th ed.). (2001). Washington, DC: American Psychological

Association.

Note: In this title, the words "American Psychological Association" are capitalized because they are a proper name. The word "manual" is not capitalized.

Chapter from a Book

Tattersall, I. (2002). How did we achieve humanity? In *The monkey*

in the mirror (pp. 138–168). New York: Harcourt.

Single Work from an Anthology

> Marshall, P. G. (2002). The impact of the cold war on Asia. In T. O'Neill (Ed.), *The nuclear age* (pp. 162–166). San Diego: Greenhaven Press.

Note: When editors' names appear in the middle of an entry, follow the usual order: initial first, surname last.

One Volume of a Multivolume Edited Work

> Salzman, J., Smith, D. L., & West, C. (Eds.). (1996). *Encyclopedia of African-American culture and history* (Vol. 4). New York: Simon & Schuster Macmillan.

Separately Titled Volume in a Multivolume Work

> The Associated Press. (1995). *Twentieth-Century America: Vol. 8. The crisis of national confidence: 1974–1980.* Danbury, CT: Grolier Educational Corp.

Note: When a work is part of a larger series or collection, as with this example, make a two-part title of the series and the particular volume you are citing.

Group Author as Publisher

> Amnesty International. (2000). *Hidden scandal, secret shame: Torture and ill-treatment of children.* New York: Author.

Note: If the publication is a brochure, identify it as such in brackets after the title.

Edition Other Than the First

> Trimmer, J. (2001). *Writing with a purpose* (13th ed.). Boston: Houghton Mifflin.

Two or More Books by the Same Author

> Dershowitz, A. (2000). *The Genesis of justice: Ten stories of biblical injustice that led to the Ten Commandments and modern law.* New York: Warner Books.
>
> Dershowitz, A. (2002). *Shouting fire: Civil liberties—past, present, and future.* Boston: Little, Brown.

English Translation

> Setha, R. (1998). *Unarmed* (R. Narasimhan, Trans.). Chennai, India: Macmillan. (Original work published 1995)

Note: If you use the original work, cite the original version; the non-English title is followed by its English translation, not italicized, in square brackets.

Article in a Reference Book

> Lewer, N. (1999). Non-lethal weapons. In *World encyclopedia of peace* (pp. 279–280). Oxford: Pergamon Press.

Note: If no author is listed, begin the entry with the title of the article.

Reprint, Different Form

> Albanov, V. (2000). *In the land of white death: An epic story of survival in the Siberian Arctic.* New York: Modern Library. (Original work published 1917)

Note: This work was originally published in Russia in 1917; the 2000 reprint is the first English version. If you are citing a reprint from another source, the parentheses would contain "Reprinted from *Title*, pp. xx–xx, by A. Author, year, Location: Publisher."

Technical or Research Report

> Taylor, B. G., Fitzgerald, N., Hunt, D., Reardon, J. A., & Brownstein, H. H. (2001). *ADAM preliminary 2000 findings on drug use and drug markets: Adult male arrestees.* Washington, DC: National Institute of Justice.

Government Publication

> National Institute on Drug Abuse. (2000). *Inhalant abuse* (NIH Publication No. 00-3818). Rockville, MD: National Clearinghouse on Alcohol and Drug Information.

Note: If the document is not available from the Government Printing Office (GPO), the publisher would be either "Author" or the separate government department that published it.

video

Reference Entries: Periodicals

The general form for a periodical entry is this:

> Author, A. (year). Article title. *Periodical Title*, Volume
>
> Number, page numbers.

Include some other designation with the year (such as a month or season) if a periodical does not use volume numbers. The entries that follow illustrate the information and arrangement needed to cite periodicals.

Article in a Scholarly Journal, Consecutively Paginated

> Epstein, R., & Hundert, E. (2002). Defining and assessing
>
> professional competence. *JAMA, 287*, 226–235.

Note: Pay attention to the features of this basic reference to a scholarly journal: (1) last name and initial(s) as for a book reference, (2) year of publication, (3) title of article in lowercase, except for the first word; title not italicized or in quotations, (4) title and volume number of journal italicized, and (5) inclusive page numbers.

Abstract of a Scholarly Article (from a Secondary Source)

> Shlipak, M. G., Simon, J. A., Grady, O., Lin, F., Wenger, N. K., &
>
> Furberg, C. D. (2001, September). Renal insufficiency and
>
> cardiovascular events in postmenopausal women with coronary
>
> heart disease. *Journal of the American College of Cardiology, 38*,
>
> 705–711. Abstract obtained from *Geriatrics*, 2001, 56(12),
>
> Abstract No. 5645351.

Note: When the dates of the article and the secondary-source abstract differ, the reference in your text would cite both dates, the original first, separated by a slash (2001/2002). When the abstract is obtained from the original source, the description *Abstract* is placed in brackets following the title (but before the period).

Journal Article, Paginated by Issue

> Lewer, N. (1999, summer). Nonlethal weapons. *Forum, 14*(2), 39–45.

Note: When the page numbering of the issue starts with page 1, the issue number (not italicized) is placed in parentheses after the volume number. (Some journals number pages consecutively, from issue to issue, through their whole volume year.)

Journal Article, More Than Six Authors

Wang, X., Zuckerman, B., Pearson, C., Kaufman, G., Chen, C., Wang, G., et al. (2002, January 9). Maternal cigarette smoking, metabolic gene polymorphism, and infant birth weight. *JAMA, 287,* 195–202.

Note: In the text, abbreviate the parenthetical citation as follows: (Wang et al., 2002).

Review

Updike, J. (2001, December 24). Survivor/believer [Review of the book *New and Collected Poems 1931–2001*]. *The New Yorker,* 118–122.

Magazine Article

Silberman, S. (2001, December). The geek syndrome. *Wired, 9*(12), 174–183.

Note: If the article is unsigned, begin the entry with the title of the article.

Tomatoes target toughest cancer. (2002, February). *Prevention, 54*(2), 53.

Newspaper Article

Stolberg, S. C. (2002, January 4). Breakthrough in pig cloning could aid organ transplants. *The New York Times,* pp. 1A, 17A.

AOL to take up to $60 billion charge. (2002, January 8). *Chicago Tribune,* sec. 3, p. 3.

Note: If the article is a letter to the editor, identify it as such in brackets following the title. For newspapers, use "p." or "pp." before the page numbers; if the article is not on continuous pages, give all the page numbers, separated by commas.

Newsletter Article

Newsletter article entries are very similar to newspaper article entries; only a volume number is added.

Teaching mainstreamed special education students. (2002, February). *The Council Chronicle, 11,* 6–8.

video

Reference Entries: Electronic Sources

APA style prefers a reference to the print form of a source, even if the source is available on the Net. If you have read *only* the electronic form of an article's print version, add "Electronic version" in brackets after the title of the article. If an online article has been changed from the print version or has additional information, follow the same general format for the author, date, and title elements of print sources, but follow it with a "retrieved from" statement, citing the date of retrieval and the electronic address.

Periodical, Identical to Print Version

Author, A., & Author, B. (year, month day). Title of article, chapter, or Web page [Electronic version]. *Title of Periodical, volume number or other designation,* inclusive page numbers (if available).

> **Ashley, S. (2001, May). Warp drive underwater [Electronic version].**
>
> *Scientific American (2001, May).*

Periodical, Different from Print Version or Online Only

Author, A., & Author, B. (year, month day). Title of article, chapter, or Web page. *Title of Periodical, volume number,* inclusive page numbers if available. Retrieved Month day, year, from electronic address

> **Nicholas, D., Huntington, P., & Williams, P. (2001, May 23).**
>
> **Comparing web and touch screen transaction log files.** *Journal*
>
> *of Medical Internet Research, 3.* **Retrieved Nov. 15, 2001, from**
>
> **http://www.jmir.org/2001/2/e18/index.htm**

Note: Include an issue number in parentheses following the volume number if each issue of a journal begins on page 1. Use *pp.* (page numbers) in newspapers. Page numbers are often not relevant for online sources. End the citation with a period unless it ends with the electronic address.

Multipage Document Created by Private Organization

> **National Multiple Sclerosis Society. (n.d.)** *About MS: For the newly*
>
> *diagnosed.* **Retrieved May 20, 2002, from**
>
> **http://www.national/mssociety.org**

Note: Use *n.d.* (no date) when a publication date is unavailable. Provide the URL of the home page for an Internet document when its pages have different URLs.

Document from an Online Database

Author, A., & Author, B. (year). Title of article or Web page. *Title of Periodical, volume number,* inclusive page numbers. Retrieved Month day, year, from name of database.

> **Belsie, Laurent. (1999). Progress or peril?** *Christian Science Monitor,*
>
> **91(85), 15. Retrieved September 15, 1999, from DIALOG online**
>
> **database (#97, IAC Business A.R.T.S., Item 07254533).**

Note: If the document cited is an abstract, include *Abstract* before the "retrieved" statement. The item or accession numbers may be included but are not required.

Other Nonperiodical Online Document

Author, A., & Author, B. (year, month day). Title of work. Retrieved Month day, year, from electronic address

> **Boyles, S. (2001, Nov. 14). World diabetes day has people pondering**
>
> **their risk. Retrieved Nov. 16, 2001, from**
>
> **http://my.webmd.com/content/article/1667.51328**

Note: To cite only a chapter or section of an online document, follow the title of the chapter with "In *Title of document* (chap. number)." If the author is not identified, begin with the title of the document. If a date is not identified, put "n.d." in parentheses following the title.

> **Catholic Near East Welfare Association. (2002). Threats to personal**
>
> **security. In** *Report on Christian emigration: Palestine* **(sect. 5)**
>
> **Retrieved May 20, 2002, from http://www.cnewa.org/**
>
> **news-christemigrat-part1.htm**

Document or Abstract Available on University Program or Department Web Site

Author, A., & Author, B. (year). *Title of work.* Retrieved Month day, year, from name of host: electronic address

> **Magill, G. (2001).** *Ethics of stem cell research.* **Retrieved Nov. 23,**
>
> **2001, from St. Louis University, Center for Health Care Ethics**
>
> **Web site: http://www.slu.edu/centers/chce/drummond/**
>
> **magill.html**

Note: The host organization and the relevant program or department are listed before the URL when a document is contained within a large, complex Web site.

Report from a University, Available on Private Organization Web Site

University, Institute. (Year, month). *Title of work.* Retrieved Month day, year, from electronic address

> **Kaiser Family Foundation and University of Wisconsin, Sonderegger Research Center. (2000, July).** *Prescription drug trends— a chartbook.* **Retrieved Nov. 19, 2001, from http://www.kff.org/content/2000/3019/**

Note: If the private organization is not listed as an author, identify it in the "retrieved from" statement.

U.S. Government Report Available on Government Agency Web Site

Name of government agency. (Year, month day). *Title of report.* Retrieved Month day, year, from electronic address

> **United States Department of Commerce, Office of the Inspector General. (2001, March).** *Internal controls over bankcard program need improvement.* **Retrieved July 23, 2001, from http://www.oig.doc.gov/e-library/reports/recent/recent.html**

Note: If no publication date is indicated, use "n.d." in parentheses following the agency name.

Paper Presented at a Symposium or Other Event, Abstract Retrieved from University Web Site

Author, A. (Year, month day). *Title of paper.* Paper presented at name of event. Abstract retrieved Month day, year, from electronic address

> **Smale, S. (2001, Nov. 7).** *Learning and the evolution of language.* **Paper presented at Brains and Machines Seminar Series. Abstract retrieved Nov. 23, 2001, from http://www.ai.mit.edu/ events/talks/brainsMachines/abstracts/F2001/200111071700 _StephenSmale.shtml**

Note: To cite a virtual conference, do not use *Abstract* before the "retrieved from" statement.

E-mail

E-mail is cited only in the text of the paper, not in the references list. See "Personal Communications," on page **543**.

Reference Entries: Other Print and Nonprint Sources

The following citation entries are examples of audiovisual media sources and sources available electronically.

Specialized Computer Software with Limited Distribution

Standard, nonspecialized computer software does not require a reference entry. Treat software as an unauthored work unless an individual has property rights to it.

> Carreau, Stéphane. (2001). Champfoot (Version 3.3) [Computer software]. Saint Mandé, France: Author.

Electronic Copy of Abstract of Journal Article Retrieved from a Database

The following format applies whether the database is on CD, on a Web site, or a university server. The item or accession number is not required, but may be included in parentheses at the end of the retrieval statement.

> Seyler, T. (1994). College-level studies: New memory techniques. *New Century Learners, 30,* 814–822. Abstract retrieved Feb. 1, 1995, from Platinum File: EduPLUS database (40-18421).

Television or Radio Broadcast

> Crystal, L. (Executive Producer). (2002, February 11). *The Newshour with Jim Lehrer* [Television broadcast]. New York and Washington, DC: Public Broadcasting Service.

Television or Radio Series

> Bloch, A. (Producer). (2002). *Thinking allowed* [Television series]. Berkeley: Public Broadcasting Service.

Television or Radio Program (Episode in a Series)

> Berger, Cynthia. (Writer). (2001, December 19). Feederwatch [Radio series program]. In D. Byrd & J. Block (Producers), *Earth & Sky.* Austin, TX: The Production Block.

Audio Recording

> Kim, E. (Author, speaker). (2000). *Ten thousand sorrows* [CD]. New
> York: Random House.

Music Recording

> ARS Femina Ensemble. (Performers). (1998). *Musica de la puebla de
> los angeles: Music by women of baroque Mexico, Cuba, &
> Europe* [CD]. Louisville, KY: Nannerl Recordings.

Note: Give the name and function of the originators or primary contributors. Indicate
the recording medium (CD, record, cassette, and so on) in brackets, immediately
following the title.

Motion Picture

Give the name and function of the director, producer, or both. If its circulation was
limited, provide the distributor's name and complete address in parentheses.

> Jackson, P. (Director). (2001). *The lord of the rings: The fellowship
> of the ring* [Motion picture]. United States: New Line
> Productions, Inc.

Published Interview, Titled, No Author

> Stephen Harper: *The Report* interview. (2002, January 7). *The Report*
> (Alberta, BC), 29, 10–11.

Published Interview, Titled, Single Author

> Fussman, C. (2002, January). What I've learned [Interview with
> Robert McNamara]. *Esquire, 137(1),* 85.

Unpublished Paper Presented at a Meeting

> Lycan, W. (2002, June). *The plurality of consciousness.* Paper
> presented at the meeting of the Society for Philosophy and
> Psychology, New York, NY.

Unpublished Doctoral Dissertation

> Roberts, W. (2001). *Youth crime amidst suburban wealth.*
> Unpublished doctoral dissertation, Bowling Green State
> University, Bowling Green, OH.

Sample APA Research Paper

The research paper on pages 555–566 follows APA guidelines.

Sample Title Page

Place manuscript page headers one-half inch from the top. Put five spaces between the page header and the page number.

Running on Empty   1

Full title, authors, and school name are centered on the page, typed in uppercase and lowercase.

Running on Empty:
The Effects of Food Deprivation on
Concentration and Perseverance
Thomas Delancy and Adam Solberg
Dordt College

Sample Abstract

The abstract summarizes the problem, participants, hypotheses, methods used, results, and conclusions.

Abstract

This study examined the effects of short-term food deprivation on two cognitive abilities—concentration and perseverance. Undergraduate students (N-51) were tested on both a concentration task and a perseverance task after one of three levels of food deprivation: none, 12 hours, or 24 hours. We predicted that food deprivation would impair both concentration scores and perseverance time. Food deprivation had no significant effect on concentration scores, which is consistent with recent research on the effects of food deprivation (Green et al., 1995; Green et al., 1997). However, participants in the 12-hour deprivation group spent significantly less time on the perseverance task than those in both the control and 24-hour deprivation groups, suggesting that short-term deprivation may affect some aspects of cognition and not others.

An APA Research Paper Model

Thomas Delancy and Adam Solberg wrote the following research paper for a psychology class. As you review their paper, read the side notes and examine the following:

- The use and documentation of their numerous sources.
- The background they provide before getting into their own study results.
- The scientific language used when reporting their results.

Center the title one inch from the top. Double-space throughout.

Running on Empty: The Effects of Food Deprivation
on Concentration and Perseverance

Many things interrupt people's ability to focus on a task: distractions, headaches, noisy environments, and even psychological disorders. To some extent, people can control the environmental factors that make it difficult to focus. However, what about internal factors, such as an empty stomach? Can people increase their ability to focus simply by eating regularly?

The introduction states the topic and the main questions to be explored.

One theory that prompted research on how food intake affects the average person was the glucostatic theory. Several researchers in the 1940s and 1950s suggested that the brain regulates food intake in order to maintain a blood-glucose set point. The idea was that people become hungry when their blood-glucose levels drop significantly below their set point and that they become satisfied after eating, when their blood-glucose levels return to that set point. This theory seemed logical because glucose is the brain's primary fuel (Pinel, 2000). The earliest investigation of the general effects of food deprivation found that long-term food deprivation (36 hours and longer) was associated with sluggishness, depression, irritability, reduced heart rate, and inability to concentrate (Keys, Brozek, Henschel, Mickelsen, & Taylor, 1950). Another study found that fasting for several days produced muscular weakness, irritability, and apathy or depression (Kollar, Slater, Palmer, Docter, & Mandell, 1964). Since that time, research has focused mainly on how nutrition affects cognition. However, as Green, Elliman, and Rogers (1995) point out, the effects of food deprivation on cognition have received comparatively less attention in recent years.

The researchers supply background information by discussing past research on the topic.

Extensive referencing establishes support for the discussion.

1

2

The relatively sparse research on food deprivation has left room for $_3$ further research. First, much of the research has focused either on chronic starvation at one end of the continuum or on missing a single meal at the other end (Green et al., 1995). Second, some of the findings have been contradictory. One study found that skipping breakfast impairs certain aspects of cognition, such as problem-solving abilities (Pollitt, Lewis, Garza, & Shulman, 1983). However, other research by M. W. Green, N. A. Elliman, and P. J. Rogers (1995, 1997) has found that food deprivation ranging from missing a single meal to 24 hours without eating does not significantly impair cognition. Third, not all groups of people have been sufficiently studied. Studies have been done on 9–11 year-olds (Pollitt et al., 1983), obese subjects (Crumpton, Wine, & Drenick, 1966), college-age men and women (Green et al., 1995, 1996, 1997), and middle-age males (Kollar et al., 1964). Fourth, not all cognitive aspects have been studied. In 1995 Green, Elliman, and Rogers studied sustained attention, simple reaction time, and immediate memory; in 1996 they studied attentional bias; and in 1997 they studied simple reaction time, two-finger tapping, recognition memory, and free recall. In 1983, another study focused on reaction time and accuracy, intelligence quotient, and problem solving (Pollitt et al.).

According to some researchers, most of the results so far indicate that $_4$ cognitive function is not affected significantly by short-term fasting (Green et al., 1995, p. 246). However, this conclusion seems premature due to the relative lack of research on cognitive functions such as concentration and perseverance. To date, no study has tested perseverance, despite its importance in cognitive functioning. In fact, perseverance may be a better indicator than achievement tests in assessing growth in learning and thinking abilities, as perseverance helps in solving complex problems (Costa, 1984). Another study also recognized that perseverance, better learning techniques, and effort are cognitions worth studying (D'Agostino, 1996). Testing as many aspects of cognition as possible is key because the nature of the task is important when interpreting the link between food deprivation and cognitive performance (Smith & Kendrick, 1992).

The researchers explain how their study will add to past research on the topic.

Clear transitions guide readers through the researchers' reasoning.

The researchers support their decision to focus on concentration and perseverance.

Running on Empty 5

The researchers state their initial hypotheses.

Therefore, the current study helps us understand how short-term food deprivation affects concentration on and perseverance with a difficult task. Specifically, participants deprived of food for 24 hours were expected to perform worse on a concentration test and a perseverance task than those deprived for 12 hours, who in turn were predicted to perform worse than those who were not deprived of food.

Method

Headings and subheadings show the paper's organization.

Participants

Participants included 51 undergraduate-student volunteers (32   5
females, 19 males), some of whom received a small amount of extra credit in a college course. The mean college grade point average (GPA) was 3.19. Potential participants were excluded if they were dieting, menstruating, or taking special medication. Those who were struggling with or had struggled with an eating disorder were excluded, as were potential participants addicted to nicotine or caffeine.

The experiment's method is described, using the terms and acronyms of the discipline.

Materials

Concentration speed and accuracy were measured using an online   6
numbers-matching test (www.psychtests.com/tests/iq/concentration.html) that consisted of 26 lines of 25 numbers each. In 6 minutes, participants were required to find pairs of numbers in each line that added up to 10. Scores were calculated as the percentage of correctly identified pairs out of a possible 120. Perseverance was measured with a puzzle that contained five octagons—each of which included a stencil of a specific object (such

Passive voice is used to emphasize the experiment, not the researchers; otherwise, active voice is used.

as an animal or a flower). The octagons were to be placed on top of each other in a specific way to make the silhouette of a rabbit. However, three of the shapes were slightly altered so that the task was impossible. Perseverance scores were calculated as the number of minutes that a participant spent on the puzzle task before giving up.

Procedure

At an initial meeting, participants gave informed consent. Each   7
consent form contained an assigned identification number and requested the participant's GPA. Students were then informed that they would be notified by e-mail and telephone about their assignment to one of the

three experimental groups. Next, students were given an instruction sheet. These written instructions, which we also read aloud, explained the experimental conditions, clarified guidelines for the food deprivation period, and specified the time and location of testing.

> The experiment is laid out step by step, with time transitions like "then" and "next."

Participants were randomly assigned to one of these conditions using a matched-triplets design based on the GPAs collected at the initial meeting. This design was used to control individual differences in cognitive ability. Two days after the initial meeting, participants were informed of their group assignment and its condition and reminded that, if they were in a food-deprived group, they should not eat anything after 10 a.m. the next day. Participants from the control group were tested at 7:30 p.m. in a designated computer lab on the day the deprivation started. Those in the 12-hour group were tested at 10 p.m. on that same day. Those in the 24-hour group were tested at 10:40 a.m. on the following day.

8

At their assigned time, participants arrived at a computer lab for testing. Each participant was given written testing instructions, which were also read aloud. The online concentration test had already been loaded on the computers for participants before they arrived for testing, so shortly after they arrived they proceeded to complete the test. Immediately after all participants had completed the test and their scores were recorded, participants were each given the silhouette puzzle and instructed how to proceed. In addition, they were told that (1) they would have an unlimited amount of time to complete the task, and (2) they were not to tell any other participant whether they had completed the puzzle or simply given up. This procedure was followed to prevent the group influence of some participants seeing others give up. Any participant still working on the puzzle after 40 minutes was stopped to keep the time of the study manageable. Immediately after each participant stopped working on the puzzle, he/she gave demographic information and completed a few manipulation-check items. We then debriefed and dismissed each participant outside of the lab.

9

> Attention is shown to the control features.

Results

The writers summarize their findings, including problems encountered.

Perseverance data from one control-group participant were   10
eliminated because she had to leave the session early. Concentration data
from another control-group participant were dropped because he did not
complete the test correctly. Three manipulation-check questions indicated
that each participant correctly perceived his or her deprivation condition
and had followed the rules for it. The average concentration score was
77.78 (SD = 14.21), which was very good considering that anything over
50 percent is labeled "good" or "above average." The average time spent on
the puzzle was 24.00 minutes (SD = 10.16), with a maximum of 40
minutes allowed.

"See Figure 1" sends readers to a figure (graph, photograph, chart, or drawing) contained in the paper.

We predicted that participants in the 24-hour deprivation group   11
would perform worse on the concentration test and the perseverance task
than those in the 12-hour group, who in turn would perform worse than
those in the control group. A one-way analysis of variance (ANOVA)
showed no significant effect of deprivation condition on concentration,
F(2,46) = 1.06, p = .36 (see Figure 1). Another one-way ANOVA indicated

All figures and illustrations (other than tables) are numbered in the order that they are first mentioned in the text.

Figure 1.

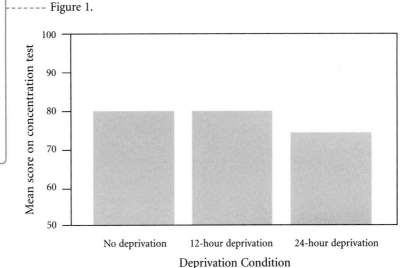

Mean score on concentration test

Deprivation Condition

No deprivation   12-hour deprivation   24-hour deprivation

The researchers restate their hypotheses and the results, and go on to interpret those results.

a significant effect of deprivation condition on perseverance time, $F(2,47)$ = 7.41, p < .05. Post-hoc Tukey tests indicated that the 12-hour deprivation group (M = 17.79, SD = 7.84) spent significantly less time on the perseverance task than either the control group (M = 26.80, SD = 6.20) or the 24-hour group (M = 28.75, SD = 12.11), with no significant difference between the latter two groups (see Figure 2). No significant effect was found for gender either generally or with specific deprivation conditions, Fs < 1.00. Unexpectedly, food deprivation had no significant effect on concentration scores. Overall, we found support for our hypothesis that 12 hours of food deprivation would significantly impair perseverance when compared to no deprivation. Unexpectedly, 24 hours of food deprivation did not significantly affect perseverance relative to the control group. Also unexpectedly, food deprivation did not significantly affect concentration scores.

Figure 2.

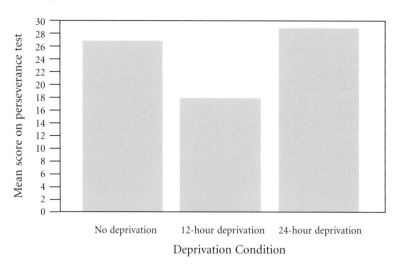

No deprivation   12-hour deprivation   24-hour deprivation

Deprivation Condition

Discussion

The purpose of this study was to test how different levels of food deprivation affect concentration on and perseverance with difficult tasks.

12

Running on Empty   9

We predicted that the longer people had been deprived of food, the lower they would score on the concentration task, and the less time they would spend on the perseverance task. In this study, those deprived of food did give up more quickly on the puzzle, but only in the 12-hour group. Thus, the hypothesis was partially supported for the perseverance task. However, concentration was found to be unaffected by food deprivation, and thus the hypothesis was not supported for that task.

The findings of this study are consistent with those of Green et al. (1995), where short-term food deprivation did not affect some aspects of cognition, including attentional focus. Taken together, these findings suggest that concentration is not significantly impaired by short-term food deprivation. The findings on perseverance, however, are not as easily explained. We surmise that the participants in the 12-hour group gave up more quickly on the perseverance task because of their hunger produced by the food deprivation. But why, then, did those in the 24-hour group fail to yield the same effect? We postulate that this result can be explained by the concept of "learned industriousness," wherein participants who perform one difficult task do better on a subsequent task than the participants who never took the initial task (Eisenberger & Leonard, 1980; Hickman, Stromme, & Lippman, 1998). Because participants had successfully completed 24 hours of fasting already, their tendency to persevere had already been increased, if only temporarily. Another possible explanation is that the motivational state of a participant may be a significant determinant of behavior under testing (Saugstad, 1967). This idea may also explain the short perseverance times in the 12-hour group: because these participants took the tests at 10 p.m., a prime time of the night for conducting business and socializing on a college campus, they may have been less motivated to take the time to work on the puzzle.

Research on food deprivation and cognition could continue in several directions. First, other aspects of cognition may be affected by short-term food deprivation, such as reading comprehension or motivation. With respect to this latter topic, some students in this study reported decreased motivation to complete the tasks because of a desire to eat immediately

The writers speculate on possible explanations for the unexpected results.

13

14

after the testing. In addition, the time of day when the respective groups took the tests may have influenced the results: those in the 24-hour group took the tests in the morning and may have been fresher and more relaxed than those in the 12-hour group, who took the tests at night. Perhaps, then, the motivation level of food-deprived participants could be effectively tested. Second, longer-term food deprivation periods, such as those experienced by people fasting for religious reasons, could be explored. It is possible that cognitive function fluctuates over the duration of deprivation. Studies could ask how long a person can remain focused despite a lack of nutrition. Third, and perhaps most fascinating, studies could explore how food deprivation affects learned industriousness. As stated above, one possible explanation for the better perseverance times in the 24-hour group could be that they spontaneously improved their perseverance faculties by simply forcing themselves not to eat for 24 hours. Therefore, research could study how food deprivation affects the acquisition of perseverance.

The conclusion summarizes the outcomes, stresses the experiment's value, and anticipates further advances on the topic.

In conclusion, the results of this study provide some fascinating insights into the cognitive and physiological effects of skipping meals. Contrary to what we predicted, a person may indeed be very capable of concentrating after not eating for many hours. On the other hand, if one is taking a long test or working long hours at a tedious task that requires perseverance, one may be hindered by not eating for a short time, as shown by the 12-hour group's performance on the perseverance task. Many people—students, working mothers, and those interested in fasting, to mention a few—have to deal with short-term food deprivation, intentional or unintentional. This research and other research to follow will contribute to knowledge of the disadvantages—and possible advantages—of skipping meals. The mixed results of this study suggest that we have much more to learn about short-term food deprivation.

Running on Empty   11

References

Costa, A. L. (1984). Thinking: How do we know students are getting better at it? *Roeper Review, 6,* 197–199.

Crumpton, E., Wine, D. B., & Drenick, E. J. (1966). Starvation: Stress or satisfaction? *Journal of the American Medical Association, 196,* 394–396.

D'Agostino, C. A. F. (1996). Testing a social-cognitive model of achievement motivation. *Dissertation Abstracts International Section A: Humanities & Social Sciences, 57,* 1985.

Eisenberger, R., & Leonard, J. M. (1980). Effects of conceptual task difficulty on generalized persistence. *American Journal of Psychology, 93,* 285–298.

Green, M. W., Elliman, N. A., & Rogers, P. J. (1995). Lack of effect of short-term fasting on cognitive function. *Journal of Psychiatric Research, 29,* 245–253.

Green, M. W., Elliman, N. A., & Rogers, P. J. (1996). Hunger, caloric preloading, and the selective processing of food and body shape words. *British Journal of Clinical Psychology, 35,* 143–151.

Green, M. W., Elliman, N. A., & Rogers, P. J. (1997). The study effects of food deprivation and incentive motivation on blood glucose levels and cognitive function. *Psychopharmacology, 134,* 88–94.

Hickman, K. L., Stromme, C., & Lippman, L. G. (1998). Learned industriousness: Replication in principle. *Journal of General Psychology, 125,* 213–217.

Keys, A., Brozek, J., Henschel, A., Mickelsen, O., & Taylor, H. L. (1950). *The biology of human starvation* (Vol. 2). Minneapolis: University of Minnesota Press.

Kollar, E. J., Slater, G. R., Palmer, J. O., Docter, R. F., & Mandell, A. J. (1964). Measurement of stress in fasting man. *Archives of General Psychology, 11,* 113–125.

Pinel, J. P. (2000). *Biopsychology* (4th ed.). Boston: Allyn and Bacon.

Pollitt, E., Lewis, N. L., Garza, C., & Shulman, R. J. (1982–1983). Fasting and cognitive function. *Journal of Psychiatric Research, 17,* 169–174.

Saugstad, P. (1967). Effect of food deprivation on perception-cognition: A comment [Comment on the article by David L. Wolitzky]. *Psychological Bulletin, 68,* 345–346.

Smith, A. P., & Kendrick, A. M. (1992). Meals and performance. In A. P. Smith & D. M. Jones (Eds.), *Handbook of human performance: Vol. 2, Health and performance* (pp. 1–23). San Diego: Academic Press.

Smith, A. P., Kendrick, A. M., & Maben, A. L. (1992). Effects of breakfast and caffeine on performance and mood in the late morning and after lunch. *Neuropsychobiology, 26,* 198–204.

Reading for Better Writing

1. Before you read Thomas and Adam's paper, what were your expectations about food deprivation's effects on concentration and perseverance? Did the paper confirm or confound your expectations?

2. Did you find the report interesting? Why or why not?

3. What types of evidence did Thomas and Adam use in their paper? Where did they obtain their evidence?

4. How did Thomas and Adam distinguish their own ideas from their sources' ideas? Was it necessary for them to do, and if so, why?

5. Could the results of Thomas and Adam's research be applied to other situations? In other words, how might particular groups interpret these findings?

APA Documentation Activities

1. Create references-list entries in correct APA style for the following sources:

a. An article in the October 2001 issue (vol. 29, no. 2) of *Learning & Leading with Technology* magazine by Bob Albrecht and Paul Davis titled "The Metric Backpack" (pages 29–31, 55)

b. The book *The Playful World: How Technology Is Transforming Our Imagination*, by Mark Pesce, published in 2000 by Ballantine Books, located in New York City

c. A Web page by Roger Fouts called "Frequently Asked Questions," part of *The Chimpanzee and Human Communication Institute* site, sponsored by Central Washington University. No publication date is listed on the site; it was accessed on May 8, 2002, at <http://www.cwu.edu/~cwuchci/quanda.html>.

2. Using the APA documentation style, format references-list entries for three different sources (one book, one magazine or journal article, and an online source) you might use for a research paper. Have a classmate review your entries for correctness—spacing, italics, indenting, and so on.

Research Paper Abbreviations

anon.	anonymous
bk.	book(s)
©	copyright
chap., ch.	chapter(s)
comp.	compiler, compiled, compiled by
ed.	editor(s), edition(s), edited by
e.g.	for example; *exempli gratia*
et al.	and others; *et alii, et aliae*
ex.	example
fig.	figure(s)
GPO	Government Printing Office, Washington, DC
ibid.	in the same place; *ibidem*
i.e.	that is; *id est*
illus.	illustration, illustrated by
introd.	introduction, introduced by
loc. cit.	in the place cited; *loco citato*
ms., mss.	manuscript(s)
narr.	narrated by, narrator(s)
n.d.	no date given
no.	number(s)
n.p.	no place of publication, no publisher given
n. pag.	no pagination
op. cit.	in the work cited; *opere citato*
p., pp.	page(s) (if necessary for clarity)
+	plus the pages that follow
pub. (or publ.)	published by, publication(s), publisher
rev.	revised by, revision, review, reviewed by
rpt.	reprinted by, reprint
sc.	scene
sec. (sect.)	section(s)
sic	thus in the source (used within brackets to indicate an error is that way in the original)
trans. (tr.)	translator, translation
viz.	namely; *videlicet*
vol.	volume(s): capitalize when used with Roman numerals
vs. (v.)	versus (*v.* preferred in legal-case titles)

IV. Handbook

Punctuation, Mechanics, Usage, and Grammar

CONTENTS

Chapter 35
Marking Punctuation

Period

After Sentences

573.1

Use a **period** to end a sentence that makes a statement, requests something, or gives a mild command.

- ► **(Statement)** By 1997 almost 22 percent of females in the United States had received four or more years of college education**.**
- ► **(Request)** Please read the instructions carefully**.**
- ► **(Mild command)** If your topic sentence isn't clear, rewrite it**.**

Note: It is *not* necessary to place a period after a statement that has parentheses around it and is part of another sentence.

- ► Think about joining a club **(the student affairs office has a list of organizations)** for fun and for leadership experience.

After Initials and Abbreviations

573.2

Use a period after an initial and some abbreviations.

► **Mr.**	**Mrs.**	**B.C.E.**	**Ph.D.**	**Sen. Daniel K. Inouye**
Jr.	**Sr.**	**D.D.S.**	**U.S.**	**Booker T. Washington**
Dr.	**M.A.**	**p.m.**	**B.A.**	**A. A. Milne**

When an abbreviation is the last word in a sentence, use only one period at the end of the sentence.

- ► Mikhail eyed each door until he found the name Rosa Lopez, **Ph.D.**

As Decimal Points

573.3

Use a period as a decimal point.

- ► The government spends approximately **$15.5** million each year just to process student loan forms.

Ellipsis

To Show Omitted Words

574.1

Use an **ellipsis** (three periods) to show that one or more words have been omitted in a quotation. When typing, leave one space before and after each period.

➤ **(Original)** We the people of the United States, in order to form a more perfect Union, establish justice, insure domestic tranquility, provide for the common defense, promote the general welfare, and secure the blessings of liberty to ourselves and our posterity, do ordain and establish this Constitution for the United States of America.

—Preamble, U.S. Constitution

➤ **(Quotation)** "We the people . . . in order to form a more perfect Union . . . establish this Constitution for the United States of America."

Note: Omit internal punctuation (a comma, a semicolon, a colon, or a dash) on either side of the ellipsis marks unless it is needed for clarity.

To Use After Sentences

574.2

If words from a quotation are omitted at the end of a sentence, place the ellipsis after the period or other end punctuation.

➤ **(Quotation)** "Five score years ago, a great American, in whose symbolic shadow we stand, signed the Emancipation Proclamation. . . . But one hundred years later, we must face the tragic fact that the Negro is still not free."

—Martin Luther King, Jr., "I Have a Dream"

The first word of a sentence following a period and an ellipsis may be capitalized, even though it was not capitalized in the original.

➤ **(Quotation)** "Five score years ago, a great American . . . signed the Emancipation Proclamation. . . . One hundred years later, . . . the Negro is still not free."

Note: If the quoted material is a complete sentence (even if it was not in the original), use a period, then an ellipsis.

➤ **(Original)** I am tired; my heart is sick and sad. From where the sun now stands I will fight no more forever.

—Chief Joseph of the Nez Percé

➤ **(Quotation)** "I am tired. . . . I will fight no more forever."

To Show Pauses

574.3

Use an ellipsis to indicate a pause or to show unfinished thoughts.

➤ Listen . . . did you hear that?

I can't figure out . . . this number doesn't . . . just how do I apply the equation in this case?

exercise

575.1

Comma

Between Independent Clauses

Use a **comma** between independent clauses that are joined by a coordinating conjunction (*and, but, or, nor, for, yet, so*).

➤ The most expensive film ever made was *Titanic,* **but** the largest makeup budget for any film was $1 million for *Planet of the Apes.*

Note: Do not confuse a compound verb with a compound sentence.

➤ The $1 million makeup budget for *Planet of the Apes* shocked Hollywood **and** made producers uneasy. (compound verb)

The $1 million makeup budget was 17 percent of the film's total production cost, **but** the film became a box-office hit and financial success. (compound sentence)

Between Items in a Series

575.2

Use commas to separate individual words, phrases, or clauses in a series. (A series contains at least three items.)

➤ Many college students must balance studying with **taking care of a family, working a job, getting exercise, and finding time to relax.**

Note: Do *not* use commas when all the items in a series are connected with *or, nor,* or *and.*

➤ Hmm . . . should I study **or** do laundry **or** go out?

To Separate Adjectives

575.3

Use commas to separate adjectives that *equally* modify the same noun. Notice in the examples below that no comma separates the last adjective from the noun.

➤ You should exercise regularly and follow a **sensible, healthful** diet.
A good diet is one that includes lots of **high-protein, low-fat** foods.

video

To Determine Equal Modifiers

To determine whether the adjectives in a sentence modify a noun *equally*, use these two tests.

1 Reverse the order of the adjectives; if the sentence is clear, the adjectives modify equally. (In the example below, *hot* and *crowded* can be reversed, and the sentence is still clear; *short* and *coffee* cannot.)

➤ Matt was tired of working in the **hot, crowded** lab and decided to take a **short coffee** break.

2 Insert *and* between the adjectives; if the sentence reads well, use a comma when *and* is omitted. (The word *and* can be inserted between *hot* and *crowded*, but *and* does not make sense between *short* and *coffee*.)

To Set Off Appositives

576.1

A specific kind of explanatory word or phrase called an **appositive** identifies or renames a preceding noun or pronoun.

➤ Albert Einstein, **the famous mathematician and physicist,** developed the theory of relativity.

Note: Do *not* use commas with *restrictive appositives*. A restrictive appositive is essential to the basic meaning of the sentence.

➤ The famous mathematician and physicist **Albert Einstein** developed the theory of relativity.

To Set Off Clauses

576.2

Use a comma after most introductory clauses functioning as adverbs.

➤ **Although Charlemagne was a great patron of learning,** he never learned to write properly. (adverb clause)

Use a comma if the adverb clause following the main clause is not essential. Clauses beginning with *even though, although, while,* or another conjunction expressing a contrast are usually not needed to complete the meaning of a sentence.

➤ Charlemagne never learned to write properly, **even though he continued to practice.**

Note: A comma is *not* used if the clause following the main clause is needed to complete the meaning of the sentence.

➤ Maybe Charlemagne didn't learn **because he had an empire to run.**

After Introductory Phrases

576.3

Use a comma after introductory phrases.

➤ **In spite of his practicing,** Charlemagne's handwriting remained poor.

Note: A comma is usually omitted if the phrase follows the independent clause.

➤ Charlemagne's handwriting remained poor **in spite of his practicing.**

Also Note: You may omit the comma after a short (four or fewer words) introductory phrase unless it is needed to ensure clarity.

➤ **At 6:00 a.m.** he would rise and practice his penmanship.

To Set Off Transitional Expressions

576.4

Use a comma to set off conjunctive adverbs and transitional phrases. (See 580.2–580.3.)

➤ Handwriting is not, **as a matter of fact,** easy to improve upon later in life; **however,** it can be done if you are determined enough.

Note: If a transitional expression blends smoothly with the rest of the sentence, it does not need to be set off. *Example:* If you are in fact coming, I'll see you there.

A Closer Look
at Nonrestrictive and Restrictive Clauses and Phrases

Use Commas with
Nonrestrictive Clauses and Phrases

577.1

Use commas to enclose **nonrestrictive** (unnecessary) clauses and phrases. A non-restrictive clause or phrase adds information that is not necessary to the basic meaning of the sentence. For example, if the clause or phrase (in **boldface**) were left out of the two examples below, the meaning of the sentences would remain clear. Therefore, commas are used to set them off.

▶ The locker rooms in Swain Hall**, which were painted and updated last summer,** give professors a place to shower. (clause)

Work-study programs**, offered on many campuses,** give students the opportunity to earn tuition money. (phrase)

Don't Use Commas with
Restrictive Clauses and Phrases

577.2

Do *not* use commas to set off **restrictive** (necessary) clauses and phrases. A restrictive clause or phrase adds information that the reader needs in order to understand the sentence. For example, if the clause and phrase (in **boldface**) were dropped from the examples below, the meaning would be unclear.

▶ Only the professors **who run at noon** use the locker rooms in Swain Hall to shower. (clause)

Tuition money **earned through work-study programs** is the only way some students can afford to go to college. (phrase)

Using "That" or "Which"

577.3

Use *that* to introduce restrictive (necessary) clauses; use *which* to introduce non-restrictive (unnecessary) clauses. When the two words are used in this way, the reader can quickly distinguish the necessary information from the unnecessary.

▶ Campus jobs **that are funded by the university** are awarded to students only. (restrictive)

The cafeteria**, which is run by an independent contractor,** can hire nonstudents. (nonrestrictive)

Note: Clauses beginning with *who* can be either restrictive or nonrestrictive.

▶ Students **who pay for their own education** are highly motivated. (restrictive)

The admissions counselor**, who has studied student records,** said that many returning students earn high GPAs in spite of demanding family obligations. (nonrestrictive)

578.1

To Set Off Items in Addresses and Dates

Use commas to set off items in an address and the year in a date.

➤ Send your letter to **1600 Pennsylvania Avenue, Washington, DC 20006, before January 1, 2003,** or send e-mail to president@whitehouse.gov.

Note: *No* comma is placed between the state and ZIP code. Also, *no* comma separates the items if only the month and year are given: January 2002.

578.2

To Set Off Dialogue

Use commas to set off the words of the speaker from the rest of the sentence.

➤ **"Never be afraid to ask for help,"** advised Ms. Kane.

"With the evidence that we now have," Professor Thom said, **"many scientists believe there is life on Mars."**

578.3

To Separate Nouns of Direct Address

Use a comma to separate a noun of direct address from the rest of the sentence.

➤ **Jamie,** would you please stop whistling while I'm trying to work?

578.4

To Separate Interjections

Use a comma to separate a mild interjection from the rest of the sentence.

➤ **Okay,** so now what do I do?

Note: Exclamation points are used after strong interjections: Wow! You're kidding!

578.5

To Set Off Interruptions

Use commas to set off a word, phrase, or clause that interrupts the movement of a sentence. Such expressions usually can be identified through the following tests: (1) They may be omitted without changing the meaning of a sentence; and (2) they may be placed nearly anywhere in the sentence without changing its meaning.

➤ For me**, well,** it was just a good job gone!

—Langston Hughes, "A Good Job Gone"

Lela**, as a general rule,** always comes to class ready for a pop quiz.

578.6

To Separate Numbers

Use commas to separate a series of numbers to distinguish hundreds, thousands, millions, and so on.

➤ Do you know how to write the amount **$2,025** on a check?

25,000   **973,240**   **18,620,197**

To Enclose Explanatory Words

Use commas to enclose an explanatory word or phrase.

➤ Time management, **according to many professionals,** is such an important skill that it should be taught in college.

To Separate Contrasted Elements

Use commas to separate contrasted elements within a sentence.

➤ We work to become, **not to acquire.**   —Eugene Delacroix

Where all think alike, **no one thinks very much.**   —Walter Lippmann

Before Tags

Use a comma before tags, which are short statements or questions at the ends of sentences.

➤ You studied for the test, **right?**

To Enclose Titles or Initials

Use commas to enclose a title or initials and given names that follow a surname.

➤ Until Martin, **Sr.,** was 15, he never had more than three months of schooling in any one year.

—Ed Clayton, *Martin Luther King: The Peaceful Warrior*

The genealogical files included the names Sanders, **L. H.,** and Sanders, **Lucy Hale.**

For Clarity or Emphasis

Use a comma for clarity or for emphasis. There will be times when none of the traditional rules call for a comma, but one will be needed to prevent confusion or to emphasize an important idea.

➤ What she does, does matter to us. (clarity)

It may be those who do most, dream most. (emphasis)   —Stephen Leacock

Avoid Overusing Commas

The commas (in **red**) below are used incorrectly. Do *not* use a comma between the subject and its verb or the verb and its object.

➤ Current periodicals on the subject of psychology, are available at nearly all bookstores.

I think she should read, *Psychology Today*.

Do *not* use a comma before an indirect quotation.

➤ My roommate said, that she doesn't understand the notes I took.

exercise

580.1

Semicolon

To Join Two Independent Clauses

Use a **semicolon** to join two or more closely related independent clauses that are not connected with a coordinating conjunction. In other words, each of the clauses could stand alone as a separate sentence.

➤ I was thrown out of college for cheating on the metaphysics exam**;** I looked into the soul of the boy next to me.

—Woody Allen

580.2

With Conjunctive Adverbs

Use a semicolon before a conjunctive adverb when the word connects two independent clauses in a compound sentence. A comma often follows the conjunctive adverb. Common conjunctive adverbs include *also, besides, however, instead, meanwhile, then,* and *therefore.*

➤ Many college freshmen are on their own for the first time**; however,** others are already independent and even have families.

580.3

With Transitional Phrases

Use a semicolon before a transitional phrase when the phrase connects two independent clauses in a compound sentence. A comma usually follows the transitional phrase.

➤ Pablo was born in the Andes**; as a result,** he loves mountains.

Transitional Phrases

after all	at the same time	in addition	in the first place
as a matter of fact	even so	in conclusion	on the contrary
as a result	for example	in fact	on the other hand
at any rate	for instance	in other words	

580.4

To Separate Independent Clauses

Use a semicolon to separate independent clauses that contain internal commas, even when they are connected by a coordinating conjunction.

➤ Make sure your CD player, computer, bike, and other valuables are covered by a homeowner's insurance policy**;** and be sure to use the locks on your door, bike, and storage area.

580.5

To Separate Items in a Series That Contain Commas

Use a semicolon to separate items in a series that already contain commas.

➤ My favorite foods are pizza with pepperoni, onions, and olives**;** peanut butter and banana sandwiches**;** and liver with bacon, peppers, and onions.

Colon

After Salutations

exercise
581.1

Use a **colon** after the salutation of a business letter.

➤ Dear Mr. Spielberg: Dear Professor Higgins: Dear Members:

Between Numbers Indicating Time or Ratios

581.2

Use a colon between the hours, minutes, and seconds of a number indicating time.

➤ 8:30 p.m.   9:45 a.m.   10:24:55

Use a colon between two numbers in a ratio.

➤ The ratio of computers to students is 1:20. (one to twenty)

For Emphasis

581.3

Use a colon to emphasize a word, a phrase, a clause, or a sentence that explains or adds impact to the main clause.

➤ **I have one goal for myself:** to become the first person in my family to graduate from college.

To Distinguish Parts of Publications

581.4

Use a colon between a title and a subtitle, volume and page, and chapter and verse.

➤ *Ron Brown: An Uncommon Life*   *Britannica* 4: 211   Psalm 23:1–6

To Introduce Quotations

581.5

Use a colon to introduce a quotation following a complete sentence.

➤ **John Locke is credited with this prescription for a good life:** "A sound mind in a sound body."
   Lou Gottlieb, however, offered this version: "A sound mind or a sound body—take your pick."

To Introduce a List

581.6

Use a colon to introduce a list following a complete sentence.

➤ **A college student needs a number of things to succeed:** basic skills, creativity, and determination.

Avoid Colon Errors

Do *not* use a colon between a verb and its object or complement.

➤ Dave likes: comfortable space and time to think. **(Incorrect)**
   Dave likes two things: comfortable space and time to think. **(Correct)**

Hyphen

In Compound Words

Use a **hyphen** to make some compound words.

- great-great-grandfather (noun)   starry-eyed (adjective)
  mother-in-law (noun)   three-year-old (adjective)

Writers sometimes combine words in a new and unexpected way. Such combinations are usually hyphenated.

- And they pried pieces of **baked-too-fast** sunshine cake from the roofs of their mouths and looked once more into the boy's eyes.

—Toni Morrison, *Song of Solomon*

Note: Consult a dictionary to find how it lists a particular compound word. Some compound words (*living room*) do not use a hyphen and are written separately. Some are written solid (*bedroom*). Some do not use a hyphen when the word is a noun (*ice cream*) but do use a hyphen when it is a verb or an adjective (*ice-cream sundae.*)

To Join Letters and Words

Use a hyphen to join a capital letter or a lowercase letter to a noun or a participle.

- T-shirt   U-turn   V-shaped   x-axis

To Join Words in Compound Numbers

Use a hyphen to join the words in compound numbers from *twenty-one* to *ninety-nine* when it is necessary to write them out. (See **599.1**.)

- **Forty-two** people found seats in the cramped classroom.

Between Numbers in Fractions

Use a hyphen between the numerator and denominator of a fraction, but not when one or both of these elements are already hyphenated.

- four-tenths   five-sixteenths   seven thirty-seconds (7/32)

In a Special Series

Use a hyphen when two or more words have a common element that is omitted in all but the last term.

- We have cedar posts in **four-**, **six-**, and **eight-**inch widths.

To Create New Words

Use a hyphen to form new words beginning with the prefixes *self, ex, all,* and *half.* Also use a hyphen to join any prefix to a proper noun, a proper adjective, or the official name of an office.

- post-Depression   mid-May   ex-mayor

To Prevent Confusion

Use a hyphen with prefixes or suffixes to avoid confusion or awkward spelling.

➤ **re-cover** (not *recover*) the sofa   **shell-like** (not *shelllike*) shape

To Join Numbers

Use a hyphen to join numbers indicating a range, a score, or a vote.

➤ Students study **30–40** hours a week.   The final score was **84–82.**

To Divide Words

Use a hyphen to divide a word between syllables at the end of a line of print.

Guidelines for Word Division

1. Leave enough of the word at the end of the line to identify the word.
2. Never divide a one-syllable word: **rained, skills, through.**
3. Avoid dividing a word of five or fewer letters: **paper, study, July.**
4. Never divide a one-letter syllable from the rest of the word: **omit-ted,** not **o-mitted.**
5. Always divide a compound word between its basic units: **sister-in-law,** not **sis-ter-in-law.**
6. Never divide abbreviations or contractions: **shouldn't,** not **should-n't.**
7. When a vowel is a syllable by itself, divide the word after the vowel: **epi-sode,** not **ep-isode.**
8. Avoid dividing a numeral: **1,000,000;** not **1,000,-000.**
9. Avoid dividing the last word in a paragraph.
10. Never divide the last word in more than two lines in a row.
11. Check a dictionary.

To Form Adjectives

Use a hyphen to join two or more words that serve as a single-thought adjective before a noun.

➤ In real life I am a large, **big-boned** woman with rough, **man-working** hands.
—Alice Walker, "Everyday Use"

Most single-thought adjectives are not hyphenated when they come after the noun.

➤ In real life, I am large and **big boned.**

Note: When the first of these words is an adverb ending in *ly,* do *not* use a hyphen. Also, do *not* use a hyphen when a number or a letter is the final element in a single-thought adjective.

➤ fresh**ly** painted barn   grade **A** milk (letter is the final element)

Dash

To Set Off Nonessential Elements

Use a **dash** to set off nonessential elements—explanations, examples, or definitions—when you want to emphasize them.

- Near the semester's end—**and this is not always due to poor planning**—some students may find themselves in academic trouble.

  The term *caveat emptor*—**let the buyer beware**—is especially appropriate to Internet shopping.

Note: A dash is indicated by two hyphens--with no spacing before or after--in typewriter-generated material. Don't use a single hyphen when a dash (two hyphens) is required.

To Set Off an Introductory Series

Use a dash to set off an introductory series from the clause that explains the series.

- **Cereal, coffee, and a newspaper**—without these I can't get going in the morning.

To Show Missing Text

Use a dash to show that words or letters are missing.

- **Mr. —** won't let us marry.

  —Alice Walker, *The Color Purple*

To Show Interrupted Speech

Use a dash (or ellipsis) to show interrupted or faltering speech in dialogue.

- Well, **I—ah—had** this terrible case of the flu, **and—then—ah—the** library closed because of that flash flood, **and—well—the** high humidity jammed my printer.

  —Excuse No. 101

  "You told me to tell her about the—"
  "Oh, just **stop.**"

  Joyce Carol Oates,
  "Why Don't You Come Live With Me It's Time"

For Emphasis

Use a dash in place of a colon to introduce or to emphasize a word, a series, a phrase, or a clause.

- **Jogging**—that's what he lives for.

  Life is like a grindstone—**whether it grinds you down or polishes you up depends on what you're made of.**

  This is how the world moves—**not like an arrow, but a boomerang.**

  —Ralph Ellison

exercise

Question Mark

After Direct Questions

585.1

Use a **question mark** at the end of a direct question.

➤ What can I know**?** What ought I to do**?** What may I hope**?**

—Immanuel Kant

Since when do you have to agree with people to defend them from injustice**?**

—Lillian Hellman

Not After Indirect Questions

585.2

No question mark is used after an indirect question.

➤ After listening to Edgar sing, Mr. Noteworthy asked him if he had ever had formal voice training.

Note: When a single-word question like *how, when,* or *why* is woven into the flow of a sentence, capitalization and special punctuation are not usually required.

➤ The questions we need to address at our next board meeting are not *why* or *whether,* but *how* and *when.*

After Quotations That Are Questions

585.3

When a question ends with a quotation that is also a question, use only one question mark, and place it within the quotation marks.

➤ Do you often ask yourself, "What should I be**?**"

To Show Uncertainty

585.4

Use a question mark within parentheses to show uncertainty about a word or phrase within a sentence.

➤ This July will be the 34th **(?)** anniversary of the first moon walk.

Note: Do *not* use a question mark in this manner for formal writing.

For Questions in Parentheses or Dashes

585.5

A question within parentheses—or a question set off by dashes—is punctuated with a question mark unless the sentence ends with a question mark.

➤ You must consult your handbook **(what choice do you have?)** when you need to know a punctuation rule.

Should I use your charge card (you have one, don't you), or should I pay cash?

Maybe somewhere in the pasts of these humbled people, there were cases of bad mothering or absent fathering or emotional neglect**—what family surviving the '50s was exempt?—**but I couldn't believe these human errors brought the physical changes in Frank.

—Mary Kay Blakely, *Wake Me When It's Over*

Quotation Marks

To Punctuate Titles of Works Within Other Works

586.1

Use **quotation marks** to punctuate some titles. (Also, see **588.2**.)

- "Two Friends" (short story)
  "New Car Designs" (newspaper article)
  "Desperado" (song)
  "Multiculturalism and the Language Battle" (lecture title)
  "The New Admissions Game" (magazine article)
  "Reflections on Advertising" (chapter in a book)
  "Force of Nature" (television episode from *Star Trek: The Next Generation*)
  "Annabel Lee" (short poem)

For Special Words

586.2

Use quotation marks (1) to show that a word is being discussed as a word, (2) to indicate that a word is slang, or (3) to point out that a word is being used in a humorous or ironic way.

1. A commentary on the times is that the word **"honesty"** is now preceded by **"old-fashioned."**
   —Larry Wolters
2. I drank a Dixie and ate bar peanuts and asked the bartender where I could hear **"chanky-chank,"** as Cajuns call their music.
   —William Least Heat-Moon, *Blue Highways*
3. In order to be popular, he works very hard at being **"cute."**

Placement of Periods or Commas

586.3

Always place periods and commas inside quotation marks.

- "Dr. Slaughter wants you to have liquids, Will," Mama said anxiously. "He said not to give you any solid food tonight." —Olive Ann Burns, *Cold Sassy Tree*

Placement of Exclamation Points or Question Marks

586.4

Place an exclamation point or a question mark inside quotation marks when it punctuates both the main sentence and the quotation *or* just the quotation; place it outside when it punctuates the main sentence.

- Do you often ask yourself, "What should I be?"
  I almost croaked when he asked, "That won't be a problem, will it?"
  Did he really say, "Finish this by tomorrow"?

Placement of Semicolons or Colons

586.5

Always place semicolons or colons outside quotation marks.

- I just read "Computers and Creativity"; I now have some different ideas about the role of computers in the arts.

A *Closer Look* at Marking Quoted Material

For Direct Quotations

Use quotation marks before and after a direct quotation—a person's exact words.

➤ Sitting in my one-room apartment, I remember Mom saying, **"Don't go to the party with him."**

Note: Do *not* use quotation marks for *indirect* quotations.

➤ I remember Mom saying **that I should not date him.** (These are not the speaker's exact words.)

For Quoted Passages

Use quotation marks before and after a quoted passage. Any word that is not part of the original quotation must be placed inside brackets.

➤ **(Original)** First of all, it must accept responsibility for providing shelter for the homeless.

➤ **(Quotation)** "First of all, it **[the federal government]** must accept responsibility for providing shelter for the homeless."

Note: If you quote only part of the original passage, be sure to construct a sentence that is both accurate and grammatically correct.

➤ The report goes on to say that the federal government **"must accept responsibility for providing shelter for the homeless."**

For Long Quotations

If more than one paragraph is quoted, quotation marks are placed before each paragraph and at the end of the last paragraph **(Example A)**. Quotations that are five or more lines (MLA style) or forty words or more (APA style) are usually set off from the text by indenting ten spaces from the left margin (a style called "block form"). Do not use quotation marks before or after a block-form quotation **(Example B)**, except in cases where quotation marks appear in the original passage **(Example C)**.

Example A	Example B	Example C

For Quoting Quotations

Use single quotation marks to punctuate quoted material within a quotation.

➤ "I was lucky," said Jane. "The proctor announced, **'Put your pencils down,'** just as I was filling in the last answer."

Italics (Underlining)

In Handwritten and Printed Material

588.1

Italics is a printer's term for a style of type that is slightly slanted. In this sentence, the word *happiness* is printed in italics. In material that is handwritten or typed on a machine that cannot print in italics, underline each word or letter that should be in italics.

➤ In **The Road to Memphis,** racism is a contagious disease.
(typed or handwritten)
Mildred Taylor's **The Road to Memphis** exposes racism. (printed)

In Titles

588.2

Use italics to indicate the titles of magazines, newspapers, books, pamphlets, full-length plays, films, videos, radio and television programs, book-length poems, ballets, operas, lengthy musical compositions, cassettes, CDs, paintings and sculptures, legal cases, Web sites, and the names of ships and aircraft. (Also see **586.1**.)

➤ *Newsweek* (magazine)   *The Nutcracker* (ballet)
New York Times (newspaper)   *Babe* (film)
Sister Carrie (book)   *The Thinker* (sculpture)
Othello (play)   *Nightline* (television program)
Enola Gay (airplane)   *GeoCities* (Web site)
The Joshua Tree (CD)   *College Loans* (pamphlet)
ACLU v. the State of Ohio (legal case)

When one title appears within another title, punctuate as follows:

➤ "The **Fresh Prince of Bel-Air** Rings True" is an article I read.
(title of TV program in an article title)
He wants to watch *Inside the "New York Times"* on PBS tonight.
(title of newspaper in title of TV program)

For Key Terms

588.3

Italics are often used for a key term in a discussion or for a technical term, especially when it is accompanied by its definition. Italicize the term the first time it is used. Thereafter, put the term in Roman type.

➤ This flower has a *zygomorphic* (bilateral symmetry) structure.

For Foreign Words and Scientific Names

588.4

Use italics for foreign words that have not been adopted into the English language; italics are also used to denote scientific names.

➤ Say *arrivederci* to your fears and try new activities. (foreign word)
The voyageurs discovered the shy *Castor canadensis*, or North American beaver. (scientific name)

Parentheses

To Enclose Explanatory or Supplementary Material

589.1

Use **parentheses** to enclose explanatory or supplementary material that interrupts the normal sentence structure.

- The RA **(resident assistant)** became my best friend.

To Set Off Numbers in a List

589.2

Use parentheses to set off numbers used with a series of words or phrases.

- Dr. Beck told us **(1)** plan ahead, **(2)** stay flexible, and **(3)** follow through.

For Parenthetical Sentences

589.3

When using a full "sentence" within another sentence, do not capitalize it or use a period inside the parentheses.

- Your friend doesn't have the assignment **(he was just thinking about calling you),** so you'll have to make a couple more calls.

When the parenthetical sentence comes after the main sentence, capitalize and punctuate it the same way you would any other complete sentence.

- But Mom doesn't say boo to Dad; she's always sweet to him. **(Actually she's sort of sweet to everybody.)** —Norma Fox Mazer, *Up on Fong Mountain*

To Set Off References

589.4

Use parentheses to set off references to authors, titles, pages, and years.

- The statistics are alarming **(see page 9)** and demand action.

Note: For unavoidable parentheses within parentheses (. . . [. . .] . . .), use brackets. Avoid overuse of parentheses by using commas instead.

Diagonal

To Form Fractions or Show Choices

589.5

Use a **diagonal** (also called a *slash*) to form a fraction. Also place a diagonal between two words to indicate that either is acceptable.

- My **walking/running** shoe size is **5 1/2**; my dress shoes are **6 1/2.**

When Quoting Poetry

589.6

When quoting poetry, use a diagonal (with one space before and after) to show where each line ends in the actual poem.

- A dryness is upon the house **/** My father loved and tended. **/** Beyond his firm and sculptured door **/** His light and lease have ended.

    —Gwendolyn Brooks, "In Honor of David Anderson Brooks, My Father"

Brackets

With Words That Clarify

590.1

Use **brackets** before and after words that are added to clarify what another person has said or written.

> "They'd **[the sweat bees]** get into your mouth, ears, eyes, nose. You'd feel them all over you."
> —Marilyn Johnson and Sasha Nyary, "Roosevelts in the Amazon"

Note: The brackets indicate that the words *the sweat bees* are not part of the original quotation but were added for clarification. (See **587.2**.)

Around Comments by Someone Other Than the Author

590.2

Place brackets around comments that have been added by someone other than the author or speaker.

> "In conclusion, *docendo discimus.* Let the school year begin!" **[Huh?]**

Around Editorial Corrections

590.3

Place brackets around an editorial correction.

> "Brooklyn alone has 8 percent of lead poisoning **[victims]** nationwide," said Marjorie Moore.
> —Donna Actie, student writer

Around the Word *Sic*

590.4

Brackets should be placed around the word *sic* (Latin for "so" or "thus") in quoted material; the word indicates that an error appearing in the quoted material was made by the original speaker or writer.

> "There is a higher principal **[sic]** at stake here: Is the school administration aware of the situation?"

Exclamation Point

To Express Strong Feeling

590.5

Use an **exclamation point** to express strong feeling. It may be placed at the end of a sentence (or an elliptical expression that stands for a sentence). Use exclamation points sparingly.

> "That's not the point," said Wangero. "These are all pieces of dresses Grandma used to wear. She did all this stitching by hand. **Imagine!**"
> —Alice Walker, "Everyday Use"

> Su-su-something's crawling up the back of my neck**!**
> —Mark Twain, *Roughing It*

> She was on tiptoe, stretching for an orange, when they heard, "**HEY YOU!**"
> —Beverley Naidoo, *Journey to Jo'burg*

Apostrophe

In Contractions

591.1

Use an **apostrophe** to show that one or more letters have been left out of two words joined to form a contraction.

▶ **don't** → **o** is left out **she'd** → **woul** is left out **it's** → **i** is left out

Note: An apostrophe is also used to show that one or more numerals or letters have been left out of numbers or words.

▶ class of **'02** → **20** is left out good **mornin'** → **g** is left out

To Form Plurals

591.2

Use an apostrophe and an *s* to form the plural of a letter, a number, a sign, or a word discussed as a word.

▶ A → **A's** 8 → **8's** + → **+'s**
  You use too many **and's** in your writing.

Note: If two apostrophes are called for in the same word, omit the second one.

▶ Follow closely the do's and **don'ts** (not **don't's**) on the checklist.

To Form Singular Possessives

591.3

video

The possessive form of singular nouns is usually made by adding an apostrophe and an *s*.

▶ **Spock's** ears my **computer's** memory

Note: When a singular noun of more than one syllable ends with an *s* or a *z* sound, the possessive may be formed by adding just an apostrophe—or an apostrophe and an *s*. When the singular noun is a one-syllable word, however, the possessive is usually formed by adding both an apostrophe and an *s*.

▶ **Dallas'** sports teams (or) **Dallas's** sports teams (two-syllable word)
  Kiss's last concert my **boss's** generosity (one-syllable words)

To Form Plural Possessives

591.4

The possessive form of plural nouns ending in *s* is made by adding just an apostrophe.

▶ the **Joneses'** great-grandfather **bosses'** offices

Note: For plural nouns not ending in *s*, add an apostrophe and *s*.

  women's health issues **children's** program

To Determine Ownership

You will punctuate possessives correctly if you remember that the word that comes immediately before the apostrophe is the owner.

girl's guitar (*girl* is the owner) **girls'** guitar (*girls* are the owners)
boss's office (*boss* is the owner) **bosses'** office (*bosses* are the owners)

592.1

video

To Show Shared Possession

When possession is shared by more than one noun, use the possessive form for the last noun in the series.

➤ Jason, Kamil, and **Elana's** sound system
(All three own the same system.)

Jason's, Kamil's, and Elana's sound systems
(Each owns a separate system.)

592.2

In Compound Nouns

The possessive of a compound noun is formed by placing the possessive ending after the last word.

➤ his **mother-in-law's** name (singular)
the **secretary of state's** career (singular)
their **mothers-in-law's** names (plural)
the **secretaries of state's** careers (plural)

592.3

With Indefinite Pronouns

The possessive form of an indefinite pronoun is made by adding an apostrophe and an *s* to the pronoun. (See **627.4**.)

➤ **everybody's** grades   **no one's** mistake   **one's** choice

In expressions using *else*, add the apostrophe and *s* after the last word.

➤ **anyone else's**   **somebody else's**

592.4

To Show Time or Amount

Use an apostrophe and an *s* with an adjective that is part of an expression indicating time or amount.

➤ **yesterday's** news   a **day's** wage   a **month's** pay

592.5

	Punctuation Marks	
´ (é) **Accent, acute**	: **Colon**	¶ **Paragraph**
` (è) **Accent, grave**	, **Comma**	( ) **Parentheses**
< > **Angle brackets**	† **Dagger**	. **Period**
' **Apostrophe**	— **Dash**	? **Question mark**
* **Asterisk**	¨ (ä) **Dieresis**	" " **Quotation marks**
{ } **Braces**	/ **Diagonal/slash**	§ **Section**
[ ] **Brackets**	... **Ellipsis**	; **Semicolon**
^ **Caret**	! **Exclamation point**	˜ (ñ) **Tilde**
ç **Cedilla**	- **Hyphen**	___ **Underscore**
^ (â) **Circumflex**	..... **Leaders**	

Chapter 36
Checking Mechanics

Capitalization

Proper Nouns and Adjectives

593.1

Capitalize all proper nouns and all proper adjectives (adjectives derived from proper nouns). The chart below provides a quick overview of capitalization rules. The pages following explain specific or special uses of capitalization.

Capitalization at a Glance	
Days of the week	**Sunday, Monday, Tuesday**
Months	**June, July, August**
Holidays, holy days	**Thanksgiving, Easter, Hanukkah**
Periods, events in history	**Middle Ages, World War I**
Special events	**Tate Memorial Dedication Ceremony**
Political parties	**Republican Party, Socialist Party**
Official documents	**the Declaration of Independence**
Trade names	**Oscar Mayer hot dogs, Pontiac Firebird**
Formal epithets	**Alexander the Great**
Official titles	**Mayor John Spitzer, Senator Feinstein**
Official state nicknames	**the Badger State, the Aloha State**
Geographical names	
Planets, heavenly bodies	**Earth, Jupiter, the Milky Way**
Continents	**Australia, South America**
Countries	**Ireland, Grenada, Sri Lanka**
States, provinces	**Ohio, Utah, Nova Scotia**
Cities, towns, villages	**El Paso, Burlington, Wonewoc**
Streets, roads, highways	**Park Avenue, Route 66, Interstate 90**
Sections of the U.S. and the world	**the Southwest, the Far East**
Landforms	**the Rocky Mountains, the Kalahari Desert**
Bodies of water	**Nile and Ural Rivers, Lake Superior, Bee Creek**
Public areas	**Central Park, Yellowstone National Park**

594.1

First Words

Capitalize the first word in every sentence and the first word in a full-sentence direct quotation.

➤ **Attending** the orientation for new students is a good idea.
Max suggested, "**Let's** take the guided tour of the campus first."

594.2

Sentences in Parentheses

Capitalize the first word in a sentence that is enclosed in parentheses if that sentence is not contained within another complete sentence.

➤ The bookstore has the software. (**Now** all I need is the computer.)

Note: Do *not* capitalize a sentence that is enclosed in parentheses and is located in the middle of another sentence.

➤ Your college will probably offer everything (**this** includes general access to a computer) that you'll need for a successful year.

594.3

Sentences Following Colons

Capitalize a complete sentence that follows a colon when that sentence is a formal statement, a quotation, or a sentence that you want to emphasize.

➤ Sydney Harris had this to say about computers: "**The** real danger is not that computers will begin to think like people, but that people will begin to think like computers."

594.4

Salutation and Complimentary Closing

In a letter, capitalize the first and all major words of the salutation. Capitalize only the first word of the complimentary closing.

➤ **Dear Personnel Director:**   **Sincerely** yours,

594.5

Sections of the Country

Words that indicate sections of the country are proper nouns and should be capitalized; words that simply indicate direction are not proper nouns.

➤ Many businesses move to the **South.** (section of the country)
They move **south** to cut fuel costs and other expenses. (direction)

594.6

Languages, Ethnic Groups, Nationalities, and Religions

Capitalize languages, ethnic groups, nationalities, and religions.

African American   **Latino**   **Navajo**   **French**   **Islam**

Nouns that refer to the Supreme Being and holy books are capitalized.

God   **Allah**   **Jehovah**   **the Koran**   **Exodus**   **the Bible**

Titles

595.1

Capitalize the first word of a title, the last word, and every word in between except articles (*a, an, the*), short prepositions, and coordinating conjunctions. Follow this rule for titles of books, newspapers, magazines, poems, plays, songs, articles, films, works of art, and stories.

➤ ***Going to Meet the Man***   ***Chicago Tribune***
  "Nothing Gold Can Stay"   **"Jobs in the Cyber Arena"**
  A Midsummer Night's Dream   ***The War of the Roses***

Note: When citing titles in a bibliography, check the style manual you've been asked to follow. For example, in APA style, only the first word of a title is capitalized.

Organizations

595.2

Capitalize the name of an organization, or a team and its members.

➤ **American Indian Movement**   **Republican Party**
  Tampa Bay Buccaneers   **Tucson Drama Club**

Abbreviations

595.3

Capitalize abbreviations of titles and organizations. (Some other abbreviations are also capitalized. See page **602**.)

➤ **M.D.   Ph.D.   NAACP   C.E.   B.C.E.   GPA**

Letters

595.4

Capitalize letters used to indicate a form or shape.

➤ **U**-turn   **I**-beam   **S**-curve   **V**-shaped   **T**-shirt

Words Used as Names

595.5

Capitalize words like *father, mother, uncle, senator,* and *professor* when they are parts of titles that include a personal name, or when they are substituted for proper nouns (especially in direct address).

➤ Hello, **Senator** Feingold. (*Senator* is part of the name.)
  Our **senator** is an environmentalist.
  Who was your chemistry **professor** last quarter?
  I had **Professor** Williams for Chemistry 101.

Note: To test whether a word is being substituted for a proper noun, simply read the sentence with a proper noun in place of the word. If the proper noun fits in the sentence, the word being tested should be capitalized. Usually the word is not capitalized if it follows a possessive—*my, his, our, your,* and so on.

➤ Did **Dad (Brad)** pack the stereo in the trailer? (*Brad* works in this sentence.)
  Did your **dad (Brad)** pack the stereo in the trailer? (*Brad* does not work in this sentence; the word *dad* follows the possessive *your.*)

596.1
Titles of Courses

Words such as *technology, history,* and *science* are proper nouns when they are included in the titles of specific courses; they are common nouns when they name a field of study.

➤ Who teaches **Art History 202?** (title of a specific course)
   Professor Bunker loves teaching **history.** (a field of study)

Note: The words *freshman, sophomore, junior,* and *senior* are not capitalized unless they are part of an official title.

➤ The **seniors** who maintained high GPAs were honored at the **Mount Mary Senior Honors Banquet.**

596.2
Internet, Web, and E-Mail

The words *Internet, Web,* and *World Wide Web* are always capitalized because they are considered proper nouns. When your writing includes a Web address (URL), capitalize any letters that the site's owner does (on printed materials or on the site itself). Not only is it respectful to reprint it exactly as it appears elsewhere, but, in fact, some Web addresses are case-sensitive and must be entered into a browser's address bar exactly as presented.

➤ When doing research on the **Internet**, be sure to record each site's **Web** address (**URL**) and each contact's **e-mail** address.

Note: Some people include capital letters in their e-mail addresses to make certain features evident. Although e-mail addresses are not case-sensitive, repeat each letter in print just as its owner uses it.

596.3
Avoid Capitalization Errors

Do *not* capitalize any of the following:

- A prefix attached to a proper noun
- Seasons of the year
- Words used to indicate direction or position
- Common nouns and titles that appear near, but are not part of, a proper noun

Capitalize	Do Not Capitalize
American	un-American
January, February	winter, spring
The South is quite conservative.	Turn south at the stop sign.
Duluth City College	a Duluth college
Chancellor John Bohm	John Bohm, our chancellor
President Bush	the president of the United States
Earth (the planet)	earthmover
Internet	e-mail

Plurals

Nouns Ending in a Consonant

Some nouns remain unchanged when used as plurals (*species, moose, halibut,* and so on), but the plurals of most nouns are formed by adding an *s* to the singular form.

- dorm—**dorms**   credit—**credits**   midterm—**midterms**

The plurals of nouns ending in *sh, ch, x, s,* and *z* are made by adding *es* to the singular form.

- lunch—**lunches**   wish—**wishes**   class—**classes**

Nouns Ending in *y*

The plurals of common nouns that end in *y*—preceded by a consonant—are formed by changing the *y* to *i* and adding *es.*

- dormitory—**dormitories**   sorority—**sororities**   duty—**duties**

The plurals of common nouns that end in *y* (preceded by a vowel) are formed by adding only an *s.*

- attorney—**attorneys**   monkey—**monkeys**   toy—**toys**

The plurals of all proper nouns ending in *y* (whether preceded by a consonant or a vowel) are formed by adding an *s.*

- the three **Kathys**   the five **Faheys**

Nouns Ending in *o*

The plurals of words ending in *o* (preceded by a vowel) are formed by adding an *s.*

- radio—**radios**   cameo—**cameos**   studio—**studios**

The plurals of most nouns ending in *o* (preceded by a consonant) are formed by adding *es.*

- echo—**echoes**   hero—**heroes**   tomato—**tomatoes**

Musical terms always form plurals by adding an *s;* check a dictionary for other words of this type.

- alto—**altos**   banjo—**banjos**   solo—**solos**   piano—**pianos**

Nouns Ending in *f* or *fe*

The plurals of nouns that end in *f* or *fe* are formed in one of two ways: If the final *f* sound is still heard in the plural form of the word, simply add *s;* if the final sound is a *v* sound, change the *f* to *ve* and add an *s.*

- **Plural ends with *f* sound:** roof—**roofs**   chief—**chiefs**
  Plural ends with *v* sound: wife—**wives**   loaf—**loaves**

Note: The plurals of some nouns that end in *f* or *fe* can be formed by either adding *s* or changing the *f* to *ve* and adding an *s.*

- **Plural ends with either sound:** hoof—**hoofs, hooves**

Irregular Spelling

598.1

Many foreign words (as well as some of English origin) form a plural by taking on an irregular spelling; others are now acceptable with the commonly used *s* or *es* ending. Take time to check a dictionary.

- child—**children**   alumnus—**alumni**   syllabus—**syllabi, syllabuses**
  goose—**geese**   datum—**data**   radius—**radii, radiuses**

Words Discussed as Words

598.2

The plurals of symbols, letters, figures, and words discussed as words are formed by adding an apostrophe and an *s*.

- Many colleges have now added **A/B's** and **B/C's** as standard grades.

Note: You can choose to omit the apostrophe when the omission does not cause confusion.

   YMCA's or **YMCAs**   **CD's** or **CDs**

Nouns Ending in *ful*

598.3

The plurals of nouns that end with *ful* are formed by adding an *s* at the end of the word.

- three **teaspoonfuls**   two **tankfuls**   four **bagfuls**

Compound Nouns

598.4

The plurals of compound nouns are usually formed by adding an *s* or an *es* to the important word in the compound.

- **brothers**-in-law   **maids** of honor   **secretaries** of state

Collective Nouns

598.5

Collective nouns do not change in form when they are used as plurals.

- **class** (a unit—singular form)
  class (individual members—plural form)

Because the spelling of the collective noun does not change, it is often the pronoun used in place of the collective noun that indicates whether the noun is singular or plural. Use a singular pronoun (**its**) to show that the collective noun is singular. Use a plural pronoun (**their**) to show that the collective noun is plural.

- The class needs to change **its** motto.
  (The writer is thinking of the group as a unit.)
- The class brainstormed with **their** professor.
  (The writer is thinking of the group as individuals.)

esl **Note:** To determine whether a plural requires the article *the*, you must first determine whether it is definite or indefinite. Definite plurals use *the*, whereas indefinite plurals do not require any article. (See **666.3–667.1**.)

Numbers

Numerals or Words

exercise

599.1

Numbers from one to one hundred are usually written as words; numbers 101 and greater are usually written as numerals. Hyphenate numbers written as two words if less than one hundred.

- **two   seven   ten   twenty-five   106   1,079**

The same rule applies to the use of ordinal numbers.

- **second   tenth   twenty-fifth   ninety-eighth   106th   333rd**

If numbers greater than 101 are used infrequently in a piece of writing, you may spell out those that can be written in one or two words.

- **two hundred   fifty thousand   six billion**

You may use a combination of numerals and words for very large numbers.

- **1.5 million   3 billion to 3.2 billion   6 trillion**

Numbers being compared or contrasted should be kept in the same style.

- **8** to **11** years old *or* **eight** to **eleven** years old

Particular decades may be spelled out or written as numerals.

- the **'80s** and **'90s** *or* the **eighties** and **nineties**

Numerals Only

599.2

Use numerals for the following forms: decimals, percentages, pages, chapters (and other parts of a book), addresses, dates, telephone numbers, identification numbers, and statistics.

26.2	**8** percent	Chapter **7**
pages **287–289**	Highway **36**	**(212) 555-1234**
398-55-0000	a vote of **23** to **4**	May **8, 1999**

Note: Abbreviations and symbols are often used in charts, graphs, footnotes, and so forth, but typically are not used in texts.

- He is **five feet one inch** tall and **ten years old.**
  She walked **three and one-half miles** to work through **twelve inches** of snow.

However, abbreviations and symbols may be used in scientific, mathematical, statistical, and technical texts.

- Between **20%** and **23%** of the cultures yielded positive results.
  Your **245B** model requires **220V.**

Always use numerals with abbreviations and symbols.

- **5'4"   8**%   **10** in.   **3** tbsp.   **6** lb. **8** oz.   **90**°F

Use numerals after the name of local branches of labor unions.

- The Office and Professional Employees International Union, Local **8**

600.1 Hyphenated Numbers

Hyphens are used to form compound modifiers indicating measurement. They are also used for inclusive numbers and written-out fractions.

- a **three-mile** trip   the **2001–2005** presidential term
- a **2,500-mile** road trip   **one-sixth** of the pie
- a **thirteen-foot** clearance   **three-eighths** of the book

600.2 Time and Money

If time is expressed with an abbreviation, use numerals; if it is expressed in words, spell out the number.

- **4:00** a.m. or **four** o'clock (not 4 o'clock)
  the **5:15** p.m. train
  a **seven o'clock** wake-up call

If money is expressed with a symbol, use numerals; if the currency is expressed in words, spell out the number.

- **$20** or **twenty** dollars (not 20 dollars)

Abbreviations of time and of money may be used in text.

- The concert begins at **7:00** p.m., and tickets cost $**30.**

600.3 Words Only

Use words to express numbers that begin a sentence.

- **Fourteen** students "forgot" their assignments.
  Three hundred contest entries were received.

Note: Change the sentence structure if this rule creates a clumsy construction.

- **Six hundred thirty-nine** students are new to the campus this fall. (Clumsy)
  This fall, **639** students are new to the campus. (Better)

Use words for numbers that precede a compound modifier that includes a numeral. (If the compound modifier uses a spelled-out number, use numerals in front of it.)

- She sold **twenty 35-millimeter** cameras in one day.
  The chef prepared **24 eight-ounce** filets.

Use words for the names of numbered streets of one hundred or less.

- **Ninth** Avenue
  123 Forty-fourth Street

Use words for the names of buildings if that name is also its address.

- **One Thousand State Street**   **Two Fifty Park Avenue**

Use words for references to particular centuries.

- **the twenty-first century**   **the fourth century B.C.E.**

Abbreviations

An **abbreviation** is the shortened form of a word or a phrase. These abbreviations are always acceptable in both formal and informal writing:

➤ **Mr. Mrs. Ms. Dr. Jr. a.m. (A.M.) p.m. (P.M.)**

Note: In formal writing, do not abbreviate the names of states, countries, months, days, units of measure, or courses of study. Do not abbreviate the words *Street, Road, Avenue, Company,* and similar words when they are part of a proper name. Also, do not use signs or symbols (%, &, #, @) in place of words. (The dollar sign, however, is appropriate when numerals are used to express an amount of money.)

Also Note: When abbreviations are called for (in charts, lists, bibliographies, notes, and indexes, for example), standard abbreviations are preferred. Reserve the postal abbreviations for ZIP code addresses.

Correspondence Abbreviations

States/Territories

	Standard	Postal
Alabama	Ala.	AL
Alaska	Alaska	AK
Arizona	Ariz.	AZ
Arkansas	Ark.	AR
California	Cal.	CA
Colorado	Colo.	CO
Connecticut	Conn.	CT
Delaware	Del.	DE
District of Columbia	D.C.	DC
Florida	Fla.	FL
Georgia	Ga.	GA
Guam	Guam	GU
Hawaii	Hawaii	HI
Idaho	Idaho	ID
Illinois	Ill.	IL
Indiana	Ind.	IN
Iowa	Ia.	IA
Kansas	Kans.	KS
Kentucky	Ky.	KY
Louisiana	La.	LA
Maine	Me.	ME
Maryland	Md.	MD
Massachusetts	Mass.	MA
Michigan	Mich.	MI
Minnesota	Minn.	MN
Mississippi	Miss.	MS
Missouri	Mo.	MO
Montana	Mont.	MT
Nebraska	Neb.	NE
Nevada	Nev.	NV
New Hampshire	N.H.	NH
New Jersey	N.J.	NJ
New Mexico	N.Mex.	NM
New York	N.Y.	NY
North Carolina	N.C.	NC
North Dakota	N.Dak.	ND
Ohio	Ohio	OH

	Standard	Postal
Oklahoma	Okla.	OK
Oregon	Ore.	OR
Pennsylvania	Pa.	PA
Puerto Rico	P.R.	PR
Rhode Island	R.I.	RI
South Carolina	S.C.	SC
South Dakota	S.Dak.	SD
Tennessee	Tenn.	TN
Texas	Tex.	TX
Utah	Utah	UT
Vermont	Vt.	VT
Virginia	Va.	VA
Virgin Islands	V.I.	VI
Washington	Wash.	WA
West Virginia	W.Va.	WV
Wisconsin	Wis.	WI
Wyoming	Wyo.	WY

Canadian Provinces

	Standard	Postal
Alberta	Alta.	AB
British Columbia	B.C.	BC
Labrador	Lab.	LB
Manitoba	Man.	MB
New Brunswick	N.B.	NB
Newfoundland	N.F.	NF
Northwest Territories	N.W.T.	NT
Nova Scotia	N.S.	NS
Nunavut		NU
Ontario	Ont.	ON
Prince Edward Island	P.E.I.	PE
Quebec	Que.	PQ
Saskatchewan	Sask.	SK
Yukon Territory	Y.T.	YT

Address Abbreviations

	Standard	Postal
Apartment	Apt.	APT
Avenue	Ave.	AVE
Boulevard	Blvd.	BLVD
Circle	Cir.	CIR
Court	Ct.	CT
Drive	Dr.	DR
East	E.	E
Expressway	Expy.	EXPY
Freeway	Frwy.	FWY
Heights	Hts.	HTS
Highway	Hwy.	HWY
Hospital	Hosp.	HOSP
Junction	Junc.	JCT
Lake	L.	LK
Lakes	Ls.	LKS
Lane	Ln.	LN
Meadows	Mdws.	MDWS
North	N.	N
Palms	Palms	PLMS
Park	Pk.	PK
Parkway	Pky.	PKY
Place	Pl.	PL
Plaza	Plaza	PLZ
Post Office Box	P.O. Box	PO BOX
Ridge	Rdg.	RDG
River	R.	RV
Road	Rd.	RD
Room	Rm.	RM
Rural	R.	R
Rural Route	R.R.	RR
Shore	Sh.	SH
South	S.	S
Square	Sq.	SQ
Station	Sta.	STA
Street	St.	ST
Suite	Ste.	STE
Terrace	Ter.	TER
Turnpike	Tpke.	TPKE
Union	Un.	UN
View	View	VW
Village	Vil.	VLG

Common Abbreviations

abr. abridged, abridgment
AC, ac alternating current, air-conditioning
ack. acknowledgment
AM amplitude modulation
A.M., a.m. before noon (Latin *ante meridiem*)
AP advanced placement
ASAP as soon as possible
avg., av. average
B.A. bachelor of arts degree
BBB Better Business Bureau
B.C.E. before common era
bibliog. bibliography
biog. biographer, biographical, biography
B.S. bachelor of science degree
C 1. Celsius **2.** centigrade **3.** coulomb
c. 1. *circa* (about) **2.** cup(s)
cc 1. cubic centimeter **2.** carbon copy **3.** community college
CDT, C.D.T. central daylight time
C.E. common era
CEEB College Entrance Examination Board
chap. chapter(s)
cm centimeter(s)
c/o care of
COD, c.o.d. 1. cash on delivery **2.** collect on delivery
co-op cooperative
CST, C.S.T. central standard time
cu 1. cubic **2.** cumulative
D.A. district attorney
d.b.a., d/b/a doing business as
DC, dc direct current
dec. deceased
dept. department
disc. discount
DST, D.S.T. daylight saving time
dup. duplicate
ed. edition, editor
e.g. for example (Latin *exempli gratia*)
EST, E.S.T. eastern standard time
etc. and so forth (Latin *et cetera*)
F Fahrenheit, French, Friday
FM frequency modulation
F.O.B., f.o.b. free on board
FYI for your information
g 1. gravity **2.** gram(s)
gal. gallon(s)
gds. goods
gloss. glossary
GNP gross national product
GPA grade point average
hdqrs. headquarters

HIV human immunodeficiency virus
hp horsepower
Hz hertz
ibid. in the same place (Latin *ibidem*)
id. the same (Latin *idem*)
i.e. that is (Latin *id est*)
illus. illustration
inc. incorporated
IQ, I.Q. intelligence quotient
IRS Internal Revenue Service
ISBN International Standard Book Number
JP, J.P. justice of the peace
K 1. kelvin (temperature unit) **2.** Kelvin (temperature scale)
kc kilocycle(s)
kg kilogram(s)
km kilometer(s)
kn knot(s)
kw kilowatt(s)
l liter(s), lake
lat. latitude
l.c. lowercase
lit. literary; literature
log logarithm, logic
long. longitude
Ltd., ltd. limited
m meter(s)
M.A. master of arts degree
man. manual
Mc, mc megacycle
MC master of ceremonies
M.D. doctor of medicine (Latin *medicinae doctor*)
mdse. merchandise
mfg. manufacture, manufacturing
mg milligram(s)
mi. 1. mile(s) **2.** mill(s) (monetary unit)
misc. miscellaneous
ml milliliter(s)
mm millimeter(s)
mpg, m.p.g. miles per gallon
mph, m.p.h. miles per hour
MS 1. manuscript **2.** multiple sclerosis
Ms. title of courtesy for a woman
M.S. master of science degree
MST, M.S.T. mountain standard time
NE northeast
neg. negative
N.S.F., n.s.f. not sufficient funds
NW northwest
oz, oz. ounce(s)
PA public-address system
pct. percent
pd. paid

PDT, P.D.T. Pacific daylight time
PFC, Pfc. private first class
pg., p. page
Ph.D. doctor of philosophy
P.M., p.m. after noon (Latin *post meridiem*)
POW, P.O.W. prisoner of war
pp. pages
ppd. 1. postpaid **2.** prepaid
PR, P.R. public relations
PSAT Preliminary Scholastic Aptitude Test
psi, p.s.i. pounds per square inch
PST, P.S.T. Pacific standard time
PTA, P.T.A. Parent-Teacher Association
R.A. residence assistant
RF radio frequency
R.P.M., rpm revolutions per minute
R.S.V.P., r.s.v.p. please reply (French *répondez s'il vous plaît*)
SAT Scholastic Aptitude Test
SE southeast
SOS 1. international distress signal **2.** any call for help
Sr. 1. senior (after surname) **2.** sister (religious)
SRO, S.R.O. standing room only
std. standard
SW southwest
syn. synonymous, synonym
tbs., tbsp. tablespoon(s)
TM trademark
UHF, uhf ultrahigh frequency
v 1. physics: velocity **2.** volume
V electricity: volt
VA Veterans Administration
VHF, vhf very high frequency
VIP informal: very important person
vol. 1. volume **2.** volunteer
vs. versus, verse
W 1. electricity: watt(s) **2.** physics: (also **w**) work **3.** west
whse., whs. warehouse
whsle. wholesale
wkly. weekly
w/o without
wt. weight
www World Wide Web

Acronyms and Initialisms

Acronym

603.1

An **acronym** is a word formed from the first (or first few) letters of words in a set phrase. Even though acronyms are abbreviations, they require no periods.

- **radar** radio detecting and ranging
- **CARE** Cooperative for Assistance and Relief Everywhere
- **NASA** National Aeronautics and Space Administration
- **VISTA** Volunteers in Service to America
- **FICA** Federal Insurance Contributions Act

Initialisms

603.2

An **initialism** is similar to an acronym except that the initials used to form this abbreviation are pronounced individually.

- **CIA** Central Intelligence Agency
- **FBI** Federal Bureau of Investigation
- **FHA** Federal Housing Administration

Common Acronyms and Initialisms

603.3

AIDS	acquired immunodeficiency syndrome	**OSHA**	Occupational Safety and Health Administration
APR	annual percentage rate		
CAD	computer-aided design	**PAC**	political action committee
CAM	computer-aided manufacturing	**PIN**	personal identification number
CETA	Comprehensive Employment and Training Act	**POP**	point of purchase
		PSA	public service announcement
FAA	Federal Aviation Administration	**REA**	Rural Electrification Administration
FCC	Federal Communications Commission	**RICO**	Racketeer Influenced and Corrupt Organizations (Act)
FDA	Food and Drug Administration		
FDIC	Federal Deposit Insurance Corporation	**ROTC**	Reserve Officers' Training Corps
		SADD	Students Against Destructive Decisions
FEMA	Federal Emergency Management Agency	**SASE**	self-addressed stamped envelope
		SPOT	satellite positioning and tracking
FHA	Federal Housing Administration	**SSA**	Social Security Administration
FTC	Federal Trade Commission	**SUV**	sport-utility vehicle
IRS	Internal Revenue Service	**SWAT**	Special Weapons and Tactics
MADD	Mothers Against Drunk Driving	**TDD**	telecommunications device for the deaf
NAFTA	North American Free Trade Agreement	**TMJ**	temporomandibular joint
		TVA	Tennessee Valley Authority
NATO	North Atlantic Treaty Organization	**VA**	Veterans Administration
OEO	Office of Economic Opportunity	**WHO**	World Health Organization
ORV	off-road vehicle		

Spelling

A Closer Look at Spelling Rules

Write *i* Before *e*

604.1

Write *i* before *e* except after *c*, or when sounded like *a* as in *neighbor* and *weigh*.

➤ **believe   relief   receive   eight**

Note: This sentence contains eight exceptions:

➤ **Neither sheik** dared **leisurely seize either weird species** of **financiers.**

Words with Consonant Endings

604.2

When a one-syllable word (*bat*) ends in a consonant (*t*) preceded by one vowel (*a*), double the final consonant before adding a suffix that begins with a vowel (*batting*).

➤ sum—**summary**   god—**goddess**

Note: When a multisyllable word (*control*) ends in a consonant (*l*) preceded by one vowel (*o*), the accent is on the last syllable (*con trol′*), and the suffix begins with a vowel (*ing*)—the same rule holds true: double the final consonant (*controlling*).

➤ prefer—**preferred**   begin—**beginning**   gallop—**galloping**
   forget—**forgettable**   admit—**admittance**   hammer—**hammered**

Words with a Final Silent *e*

604.3

If a word ends with a silent *e*, drop the *e* before adding a suffix that begins with a vowel. Do *not* drop the *e* when the suffix begins with a consonant.

➤ state—**stating**—**statement**   like—**liking**—**likeness**
   use—**using**—**useful**   nine—**ninety**—**nineteen**

Note: Exceptions are **judgment, truly, argument, ninth.**

Words Ending in *y*

604.4

When *y* is the last letter in a word and the *y* is preceded by a consonant, change the *y* to *i* before adding any suffix except those beginning with *i*.

➤ fry—**fries, frying**   hurry—**hurried, hurrying**
   lady—**ladies**   ply—**pliable**
   happy—**happiness**   beauty—**beautiful**

Note: When forming the plural of a word that ends with a *y* that is preceded by a vowel, add *s*.

➤ toy—**toys**   play—**plays**   monkey—**monkeys**

TIP: Never trust your spelling to even the best spell checker. Carefully proofread and use a dictionary for words you know your spell checker does not cover.

Commonly Misspelled Words

The commonly misspelled words that follow are hyphenated to show where they would logically be broken at the end of a line.

A

ab-bre-vi-ate
a-brupt
ab-scess
ab-sence
ab-so-lute (-ly)
ab-sorb-ent
ab-surd
a-bun-dance
ac-a-dem-ic
ac-cede
ac-cel-er-ate
ac-cept (-ance)
ac-ces-si-ble
ac-ces-so-ry
ac-ci-den-tal-ly
ac-com-mo-date
ac-com-pa-ny
ac-com-plice
ac-com-plish
ac-cor-dance
ac-cord-ing
ac-count
ac-crued
ac-cu-mu-late
ac-cu-rate
ac-cus-tom (-ed)
ache
a-chieve (-ment)
ac-knowl-edge
ac-quaint-ance
ac-qui-esce
ac-quired
ac-tu-al
a-dapt
ad-di-tion (-al)
ad-dress
ad-e-quate
ad-journed
ad-just-ment
ad-mi-ra-ble
ad-mis-si-ble
ad-mit-tance
ad-van-ta-geous
ad-ver-tise-ment

ad-ver-tis-ing
ad-vice (n.)
ad-vis-able
ad-vise (v.)
ad-vis-er
ae-ri-al
af-fect
af-fi-da-vit
a-gainst
ag-gra-vate
ag-gres-sion
a-gree-able
a-gree-ment
aisle
al-co-hol
a-lign-ment
al-ley
al-lot-ted
al-low-ance
all right
al-most
al-ready
al-though
al-to-geth-er
a-lu-mi-num
al-um-nus
al-ways
am-a-teur
a-mend-ment
a-mong
a-mount
a-nal-y-sis
an-a-lyze
an-cient
an-ec-dote
an-es-thet-ic
an-gle
an-ni-hi-late
an-ni-ver-sa-ry
an-nounce
an-noy-ance
an-nu-al
a-noint
a-non-y-mous
an-swer
ant-arc-tic

an-tic-i-pate
anx-i-ety
anx-ious
a-part-ment
a-pol-o-gize
ap-pa-ra-tus
ap-par-ent (-ly)
ap-peal
ap-pear-ance
ap-pe-tite
ap-pli-ance
ap-pli-ca-ble
ap-pli-ca-tion
ap-point-ment
ap-prais-al
ap-pre-ci-ate
ap-proach
ap-pro-pri-ate
ap-prov-al
ap-prox-i-mate-ly
ap-ti-tude
ar-chi-tect
arc-tic
ar-gu-ment
a-rith-me-tic
a-rouse
ar-range-ment
ar-riv-al
ar-ti-cle
ar-ti-fi-cial
as-cend
as-cer-tain
as-i-nine
as-sas-sin
as-sess (-ment)
as-sign-ment
as-sist-ance
as-so-ci-ate
as-so-ci-a-tion
as-sume
as-sur-ance
as-ter-isk
ath-lete
ath-let-ic
at-tach
at-tack (-ed)

at-tempt
at-tend-ance
at-ten-tion
at-ti-tude
at-tor-ney
at-trac-tive
au-di-ble
au-di-ence
au-dit
au-thor-i-ty
au-to-mo-bile
au-tumn
aux-il-ia-ry
a-vail-a-ble
av-er-age
aw-ful
aw-ful-ly
awk-ward

B

bac-ca-lau-re-ate
bach-e-lor
bag-gage
bal-ance
bal-loon
bal-lot
ba-nan-a
ban-dage
bank-rupt
bar-gain
bar-rel
base-ment
ba-sis
bat-tery
beau-ti-ful
beau-ty
be-com-ing
beg-gar
be-gin-ning
be-hav-ior
be-ing
be-lief
be-lieve
ben-e-fi-cial
ben-e-fit (-ed)
be-tween

bi-cy-cle
bis-cuit
bliz-zard
book-keep-er
bought
bouil-lon
bound-a-ry
break-fast
breath (n.)
breathe (v.)
brief
bril-liant
Brit-ain
bro-chure
brought
bruise
bud-get
bul-le-tin
buoy-ant
bu-reau
bur-glar
bury
busi-ness
busy

C

caf-e-te-ria
caf-feine
cal-en-dar
cam-paign
can-celed
can-di-date
can-is-ter
ca-noe
ca-pac-i-ty
cap-i-tal
cap-i-tol
cap-tain
car-bu-ret-or
ca-reer
car-i-ca-ture
car-riage
cash-ier
cas-se-role
cas-u-al-ty
cat-a-log

ca-tas-tro-phe
caught
cav-al-ry
cel-e-bra-tion
cem-e-ter-y
cen-sus
cen-tu-ry
cer-tain
cer-tif-i-cate
ces-sa-tion
chal-lenge
chan-cel-lor
change-a-ble
char-ac-ter (-is-tic)
chauf-feur
chief
chim-ney
choc-o-late
choice
choose
Chris-tian
cir-cuit
cir-cu-lar
cir-cum-stance
civ-i-li-za-tion
cli-en-tele
cli-mate
climb
clothes
coach
co-coa
co-er-cion
col-lar
col-lat-er-al
col-lege
col-le-giate
col-lo-qui-al
colo-nel
col-or
co-los-sal
col-umn
com-e-dy
com-ing
com-mence
com-mer-cial
com-mis-sion
com-mit
com-mit-ment
com-mit-ted
com-mit-tee
com-mu-ni-cate

com-mu-ni-ty
com-par-a-tive
com-par-i-son
com-pel
com-pe-tent
com-pe-ti-tion
com-pet-i-tive-ly
com-plain
com-ple-ment
com-plete-ly
com-plex-ion
com-pli-ment
com-pro-mise
con-cede
con-ceive
con-cern-ing
con-cert
con-ces-sion
con-clude
con-crete
con-curred
con-cur-rence
con-demn
con-de-scend
con-di-tion
con-fer-ence
con-ferred
con-fi-dence
con-fi-den-tial
con-grat-u-late
con-science
con-sci-en-tious
con-scious
con-sen-sus
con-se-quence
con-ser-va-tive
con-sid-er-ably
con-sign-ment
con-sis-tent
con-sti-tu-tion
con-tempt-ible
con-tin-u-al-ly
con-tin-ue
con-tin-u-ous
con-trol
con-tro-ver-sy
con-ven-ience
con-vince
cool-ly
co-op-er-ate
cor-dial

cor-po-ra-tion
cor-re-late
cor-re-spond
cor-re-spond-
  ence
cor-rob-o-rate
cough
coun-cil
coun-sel
coun-ter-feit
coun-try
cour-age
cou-ra-geous
cour-te-ous
cour-te-sy
cous-in
cov-er-age
cred-i-tor
cri-sis
crit-i-cism
crit-i-cize
cru-el
cu-ri-os-i-ty
cu-ri-ous
cur-rent
cur-ric-u-lum
cus-tom
cus-tom-ary
cus-tom-er
cyl-in-der

D

dai-ly
dair-y
dealt
debt-or
de-ceased
de-ceit-ful
de-ceive
de-cid-ed
de-ci-sion
dec-la-ra-tion
dec-o-rate
de-duct-i-ble
de-fend-ant
de-fense
de-ferred
def-i-cit
def-i-nite (-ly)
def-i-ni-tion

del-e-gate
de-li-cious
de-pend-ent
de-pos-i-tor
de-pot
de-scend
de-scribe
de-scrip-tion
de-sert
de-serve
de-sign
de-sir-able
de-sir-ous
de-spair
des-per-ate
de-spise
des-sert
de-te-ri-o-rate
de-ter-mine
de-vel-op
de-vel-op-ment
de-vice
de-vise
di-a-mond
di-a-phragm
di-ar-rhe-a
dic-tio-nary
dif-fer-ence
dif-fer-ent
dif-fi-cul-ty
di-lap-i-dat-ed
di-lem-ma
din-ing
di-plo-ma
di-rec-tor
dis-agree-able
dis-ap-pear
dis-ap-point
dis-ap-prove
dis-as-trous
dis-ci-pline
dis-cov-er
dis-crep-an-cy
dis-cuss
dis-cus-sion
dis-ease
dis-sat-is-fied
dis-si-pate
dis-tin-guish
dis-trib-ute
di-vide

di-vis-i-ble
di-vi-sion
doc-tor
doesn't
dom-i-nant
dor-mi-to-ry
doubt
drudg-ery
du-pli-cate
dye-ing
dy-ing

E

ea-ger-ly
ear-nest
eco-nom-i-cal
econ-o-my
ec-sta-sy
e-di-tion
ef-fer-ves-cent
ef-fi-ca-cy
ef-fi-cien-cy
eighth
ei-ther
e-lab-o-rate
e-lec-tric-i-ty
el-e-phant
el-i-gi-ble
e-lim-i-nate
el-lipse
em-bar-rass
e-mer-gen-cy
em-i-nent
em-pha-size
em-ploy-ee
em-ploy-ment
e-mul-sion
en-close
en-cour-age
en-deav-or
en-dorse-ment
en-gi-neer
En-glish
e-nor-mous
e-nough
en-ter-prise
en-ter-tain
en-thu-si-as-tic
en-tire-ly
en-trance

en-vel-op (v.)
en-ve-lope (n.)
en-vi-ron-ment
equip-ment
equipped
e-quiv-a-lent
es-pe-cial-ly
es-sen-tial
es-tab-lish
es-teemed
et-i-quette
ev-i-dence
ex-ag-ger-ate
ex-ceed
ex-cel-lent
ex-cept
ex-cep-tion-al-ly
ex-ces-sive
ex-cite
ex-ec-u-tive
ex-er-cise
ex-haust (-ed)
ex-hi-bi-tion
ex-hil-a-ra-tion
ex-is-tence
ex-or-bi-tant
ex-pect
ex-pe-di-tion
ex-pend-i-ture
ex-pen-sive
ex-pe-ri-ence
ex-plain
ex-pla-na-tion
ex-pres-sion
ex-qui-site
ex-ten-sion
ex-tinct
ex-traor-di-nar-y
ex-treme-ly

F

fa-cil-i-ties
fal-la-cy
fa-mil-iar
fa-mous
fas-ci-nate
fash-ion
fa-tigue (-d)
fau-cet
fa-vor-ite

fea-si-ble
fea-ture
Feb-ru-ar-y
fed-er-al
fem-i-nine
fer-tile
fic-ti-tious
field
fierce
fi-ery
fi-nal-ly
fi-nan-cial-ly
fo-li-age
for-ci-ble
for-eign
for-feit
for-go
for-mal-ly
for-mer-ly
for-tu-nate
for-ty
for-ward
foun-tain
fourth
frag-ile
fran-ti-cal-ly
freight
friend
ful-fill
fun-da-men-tal
fur-ther-more
fu-tile

G

gad-get
gan-grene
ga-rage
gas-o-line
gauge
ge-ne-al-o-gy
gen-er-al-ly
gen-er-ous
ge-nius
gen-u-ine
ge-og-ra-phy
ghet-to
ghost
glo-ri-ous
gnaw
go-ril-la

gov-ern-ment
gov-er-nor
gra-cious
grad-u-a-tion
gram-mar
grate-ful
grat-i-tude
grease
grief
griev-ous
gro-cery
grudge
grue-some
guar-an-tee
guard
guard-i-an
guer-ril-la
guess
guid-ance
guide
guilty
gym-na-si-um
gyp-sy
gy-ro-scope

H

hab-i-tat
ham-mer
hand-ker-chief
han-dle (d)
hand-some
hap-haz-ard
hap-pen
hap-pi-ness
ha-rass
har-bor
hast-i-ly
hav-ing
haz-ard-ous
height
hem-or-rhage
hes-i-tate
hin-drance
his-to-ry
hoarse
hol-i-day
hon-or
hop-ing
hop-ping
horde

hor-ri-ble
hos-pi-tal
hu-mor-ous
hur-ried-ly
hy-drau-lic
hy-giene

I

i-am-bic
i-ci-cle
i-den-ti-cal
id-io-syn-cra-sy
il-leg-i-ble
il-lit-er-ate
il-lus-trate
im-ag-i-nary
im-ag-i-na-tive
im-ag-ine
im-i-ta-tion
im-me-di-ate-ly
im-mense
im-mi-grant
im-mor-tal
im-pa-tient
im-per-a-tive
im-por-tance
im-pos-si-ble
im-promp-tu
im-prove-ment
in-al-ien-able
in-ci-den-tal-ly
in-con-ve-nience
in-cred-i-ble
in-curred
in-def-i-nite-ly
in-del-ible
in-de-pend-ence
in-de-pend-ent
in-dict-ment
in-dis-pens-able
in-di-vid-u-al
in-duce-ment
in-dus-tri-al
in-dus-tri-ous
in-ev-i-ta-ble
in-fe-ri-or
in-ferred
in-fi-nite
in-flam-ma-ble
in-flu-en-tial

in-ge-nious
in-gen-u-ous
in-im-i-ta-ble
in-i-tial
ini-ti-a-tion
in-no-cence
in-no-cent
in-oc-u-la-tion
in-quir-y
in-stal-la-tion
in-stance
in-stead
in-sti-tute
in-struc-tor
in-sur-ance
in-tel-lec-tu-al
in-tel-li-gence
in-ten-tion
in-ter-cede
in-ter-est-ing
in-ter-fere
in-ter-mit-tent
in-ter-pret (-ed)
in-ter-rupt
in-ter-view
in-ti-mate
in-va-lid
in-ves-ti-gate
in-ves-tor
in-vi-ta-tion
ir-i-des-cent
ir-rel-e-vant
ir-re-sis-ti-ble
ir-rev-er-ent
ir-ri-gate
is-land
is-sue
i-tem-ized
i-tin-er-ar-y

J

jan-i-tor
jeal-ous (-y)
jeop-ar-dize
jew-el-ry
jour-nal
jour-ney
judg-ment
jus-tice
jus-ti-fi-able

K

kitch-en
knowl-edge
knuck-le

L

la-bel
lab-o-ra-to-ry
lac-quer
lan-guage
laugh
laun-dry
law-yer
league
lec-ture
le-gal
leg-i-ble
leg-is-la-ture
le-git-i-mate
lei-sure
length
let-ter-head
li-a-bil-i-ty
li-a-ble
li-ai-son
lib-er-al
li-brar-y
li-cense
lieu-ten-ant
light-ning
lik-able
like-ly
lin-eage
liq-ue-fy
liq-uid
lis-ten
lit-er-ary
lit-er-a-ture
live-li-hood
log-a-rithm
lone-li-ness
loose
lose
los-ing
lov-able
love-ly
lun-cheon
lux-u-ry

M

ma-chine
mag-a-zine
mag-nif-i-cent
main-tain
main-te-nance
ma-jor-i-ty
mak-ing
man-age-ment
ma-neu-ver
man-u-al
man-u-fac-ture
man-u-script
mar-riage
mar-shal
ma-te-ri-al
math-e-mat-ics
max-i-mum
may-or
mean-ness
meant
mea-sure
med-i-cine
me-di-eval
me-di-o-cre
me-di-um
mem-o-ran-dum
men-us
mer-chan-dise
mer-it
mes-sage
mile-age
mil-lion-aire
min-i-a-ture
min-i-mum
min-ute
mir-ror
mis-cel-la-neous
mis-chief
mis-chie-vous
mis-er-a-ble
mis-ery
mis-sile
mis-sion-ary
mis-spell
mois-ture
mol-e-cule
mo-men-tous
mo-not-o-nous

mon-u-ment
mort-gage
mu-nic-i-pal
mus-cle
mu-si-cian
mus-tache
mys-te-ri-ous

N

na-ive
nat-u-ral-ly
nec-es-sary
ne-ces-si-ty
neg-li-gi-ble
ne-go-ti-ate
neigh-bor-hood
nev-er-the-less
nick-el
niece
nine-teenth
nine-ty
no-tice-able
no-to-ri-ety
nu-cle-ar
nui-sance

O

o-be-di-ence
o-bey
o-blige
ob-sta-cle
oc-ca-sion
oc-ca-sion-al-ly
oc-cu-pant
oc-cur
oc-curred
oc-cur-rence
of-fense
of-fi-cial
of-ten
o-mis-sion
o-mit-ted
op-er-ate
o-pin-ion
op-po-nent
op-por-tu-ni-ty
op-po-site
op-ti-mism
or-di-nance
or-di-nar-i-ly

orig-i-nal
out-ra-geous

P

pag-eant
pam-phlet
par-a-dise
para-graph
par-al-lel
par-a-lyze
pa-ren-the-ses
pa-ren-the-sis
par-lia-ment
par-tial
par-tic-i-pant
par-tic-i-pate
par-tic-u-lar-ly
pas-time
pa-tience
pa-tron-age
pe-cu-liar
per-ceive
per-haps
per-il
per-ma-nent
per-mis-si-ble
per-pen-dic-u-lar
per-se-ver-ance
per-sis-tent
per-son-al (-ly)
per-son-nel
per-spi-ra-tion
per-suade
phase
phe-nom-e-non
phi-los-o-phy
phy-si-cian
piece
planned
pla-teau
plau-si-ble
play-wright
pleas-ant
plea-sure
pneu-mo-nia
pol-i-ti-cian
pos-sess
pos-ses-sion
pos-si-ble
prac-ti-cal-ly

prai-rie
pre-cede
pre-ce-dence
pre-ced-ing
pre-cious
pre-cise-ly
pre-ci-sion
pre-de-ces-sor
pref-er-a-ble
pref-er-ence
pre-ferred
prej-u-dice
pre-lim-i-nar-y
pre-mi-um
prep-a-ra-tion
pres-ence
prev-a-lent
pre-vi-ous
prim-i-tive
prin-ci-pal
prin-ci-ple
pri-or-i-ty
pris-on-er
priv-i-lege
prob-a-bly
pro-ce-dure
pro-ceed
pro-fes-sor
prom-i-nent
pro-nounce
pro-nun-ci-a-tion
pro-pa-gan-da
pros-e-cute
pro-tein
psy-chol-o-gy
pub-lic-ly
pump-kin
pur-chase
pur-sue
pur-su-ing
pur-suit

Q

qual-i-fied
qual-i-ty
quan-ti-ty
quar-ter
ques-tion-naire
quite
quo-tient

R

raise
rap-port
re-al-ize
re-al-ly
re-cede
re-ceipt
re-ceive
re-ceived
rec-i-pe
re-cip-i-ent
rec-og-ni-tion
rec-og-nize
rec-om-mend
re-cur-rence
ref-er-ence
re-ferred
reg-is-tra-tion
re-hearse
reign
re-im-burse
rel-e-vant
re-lieve
re-li-gious
re-mem-ber
re-mem-brance
rem-i-nisce
ren-dez-vous
re-new-al
rep-e-ti-tion
rep-re-sen-ta-tive
req-ui-si-tion
res-er-voir
re-sis-tance
re-spect-a-bly
re-spect-ful-ly
re-spec-tive-ly
re-spon-si-bil-i-ty
res-tau-rant
rheu-ma-tism
rhyme
rhythm
ri-dic-u-lous
route

S

sac-ri-le-gious
safe-ty
sal-a-ry

sand-wich
sat-is-fac-to-ry
Sat-ur-day
scarce-ly
scene
scen-er-y
sched-ule
schol-ar-ship
sci-ence
scis-sors
sec-re-tary
seize
sen-si-ble
sen-tence
sen-ti-nel
sep-a-rate
ser-geant
sev-er-al
se-vere-ly
shep-herd
sher-iff
shin-ing
siege
sig-nif-i-cance
sim-i-lar
si-mul-ta-ne-ous
since
sin-cere-ly
ski-ing
sol-dier
sol-emn
so-phis-ti-cat-ed
soph-o-more
so-ror-i-ty
source
sou-ve-nir
spa-ghet-ti
spe-cif-ic
spec-i-men
speech
sphere
spon-sor
spon-ta-ne-ous
sta-tion-ary
sta-tion-ery
sta-tis-tic
stat-ue
stat-ure
stat-ute
stom-ach
stopped

straight
strat-e-gy
strength
stretched
study-ing
sub-si-dize
sub-stan-tial
sub-sti-tute
sub-tle
suc-ceed
suc-cess
suf-fi-cient
sum-ma-rize
su-per-fi-cial
su-per-in-tend-ent
su-pe-ri-or-i-ty
su-per-sede
sup-ple-ment
sup-pose
sure-ly
sur-prise
sur-veil-lance
sur-vey
sus-cep-ti-ble
sus-pi-cious
sus-te-nance
syl-la-ble
sym-met-ri-cal
sym-pa-thy
sym-pho-ny
symp-tom
syn-chro-nous

T

tar-iff
tech-nique
tele-gram
tem-per-a-ment
tem-per-a-ture
tem-po-rary
ten-den-cy
ten-ta-tive
ter-res-tri-al
ter-ri-ble
ter-ri-to-ry
the-ater
their
there-fore
thief
thor-ough (-ly)

though
through-out
tired
to-bac-co
to-geth-er
to-mor-row
tongue
to-night
touch
tour-na-ment
tour-ni-quet
to-ward
trag-e-dy
trai-tor
tran-quil-iz-er
trans-ferred
trea-sur-er
tru-ly
Tues-day
tu-i-tion
typ-i-cal
typ-ing

U

unan-i-mous
un-con-scious
un-doubt-ed-ly
un-for-tu-nate-ly
unique
u-ni-son
uni-ver-si-ty
un-nec-es-sary
un-prec-e-dent-ed
un-til
up-per
ur-gent
us-able
use-ful
using
usu-al-ly
u-ten-sil
u-til-ize

V

va-can-cies
va-ca-tion
vac-u-um
vague
valu-able
va-ri-ety

var-i-ous
veg-e-ta-ble
ve-hi-cle
veil
ve-loc-i-ty
ven-geance
vi-cin-i-ty
view
vig-i-lance
vil-lain
vi-o-lence
vis-i-bil-i-ty
vis-i-ble
vis-i-tor
voice
vol-ume
vol-un-tary
vol-un-teer

W

wan-der
war-rant
weath-er
Wednes-day
weird
wel-come
wel-fare
where
wheth-er
which
whole
whol-ly
whose
width
wom-en
worth-while
wor-thy
wreck-age
wres-tler
writ-ing
writ-ten
wrought

Y

yel-low
yes-ter-day
yield

Steps to Becoming a Better Speller

1. **Be patient.** Becoming a good speller takes time.

2. **Check the correct pronunciation of each word you are attempting to spell.**

   Knowing the correct pronunciation of each word is important to remembering its spelling.

3. **Note the meaning and history of each word as you are checking the dictionary for the pronunciation.**

   Knowing the meaning and history of a word provides you with a better notion of how the word is properly used, and it can help you remember the word's spelling.

4. **Before you close the dictionary, practice spelling the word.**

   You can do so by looking away from the page and trying to "see" the word in your "mind's eye." Write the word on a piece of paper. Check the spelling in the dictionary and repeat the process until you are able to spell the word correctly.

5. **Learn some spelling rules.**

   The four rules in this handbook (page **604**) are four of the most useful—although there are others.

6. **Make a list of the words that you misspell.**

   Select the first ten words and practice spelling them.

   First: Read each word carefully; then write it on a piece of paper. Look at the written word to see that it's spelled correctly. Repeat the process for those words that you misspelled.

   Then: Ask someone to read the words to you so you can write them again. Then check for misspellings. Repeat both steps with your next ten words.

7. **Write often.**

   As noted educator Frank Smith said,

   > *"There is little point in learning to spell if you have little intention of writing."*

Chapter 37
Using the Right Word

a, an Use *a* as the article before words that begin with consonant sounds and before words that begin with the long vowel sound *u* (yü). Use *an* before words that begin with other vowel sounds.

> ➤ **An** older student showed Kris **an** easier way to get to class.
> **A** uniform is required attire for **a** cafeteria worker.

611.1

a lot, alot, allot *Alot* is not a word; *a lot* (two words) is a vague descriptive phrase that should be used sparingly, especially in formal writing. *Allot* means to give someone a share.

> ➤ Prof Dubi **allots** each of us five spelling errors per semester and he thinks that's **a lot**.

611.2

accept, except The verb *accept* means "to receive or believe"; the preposition *except* means "other than."

> ➤ The instructor **accepted** the student's story about being late, but she wondered why no one **except** him had forgotten about the change to daylight savings time.

611.3

adapt, adopt, adept *Adapt* means "to adjust or change to fit"; *adopt* means "to choose and treat as your own" (a child, an idea). *Adept* is an adjective meaning "proficient or well trained."

> ➤ After much thought and deliberation, we agreed to **adopt** the black Lab from the shelter. Now we have to agree on how to **adapt** our lifestyle to fit our new roommate.

611.4

adverse, averse *Adverse* means "hostile, unfavorable, or harmful." *Averse* means "to have a definite feeling of distaste—disinclined."

> ➤ Groans and other **adverse** reactions were noted as the new students, **averse** to strenuous exercise, were ushered past the X-5000 pump-and-crunch machine.

611.5

advice, advise *Advice* is a noun meaning "information or recommendation"; *advise* is a verb meaning "to recommend."

> ➤ Successful people will often give you sound **advice**, so I **advise** you to listen.

611.6

affect, effect *Affect* means "to influence"; the noun *effect* means "the result."

> ➤ The employment growth in a field will **affect** your chances of getting a job. The **effect** may be a new career choice.

611.7

612.1 **aid, aide** As a verb, *aid* means "to help"; as a noun, *aid* means "the help given." An *aide* is a person who acts as an assistant.

612.2 **all of** *Of* is seldom needed after *all*.

exercise

➤ **All** the reports had an error in them.
All the speakers spoke English.
All of us voted to reschedule the meeting.
(Here *of* is needed for the sentence to make sense.)

612.3 **all right, alright** *Alright* is the incorrect form of *all right*. (**Note:** The following are spelled correctly: *always, altogether, already, almost*.)

612.4 **allude, elude** *Allude* means "to indirectly refer to or hint at something"; *elude* means "to escape attention or understanding altogether."

➤ Ravi often **alluded** to wanting a supper invitation by mentioning the "awful good" smells from the kitchen. These hints never **eluded** Ma's good heart.

612.5 **allusion, illusion** *Allusion* is an indirect reference to something or someone, especially in literature; *illusion* is a false picture or idea.

➤ Did you recognize the **allusion** to David in the reading assignment? Until I read that part, I was under the **illusion** that the young boy would run away from the bully.

612.6 **already, all ready** *Already* is an adverb meaning "before this time" or "by this time." *All ready* is an adjective form meaning "fully prepared." (**Note:** Use *all ready* if you can substitute *ready* alone in the sentence.)

➤ By the time I was a junior in high school, I had **already** taken my SATs. That way, I was **all ready** to apply early to college.

612.7 **altogether, all together** *Altogether* means "entirely." *All together* means "in a group" or "all at once." (**Note:** Use *all together* if you can substitute *together* alone in the sentence.)

➤ **All together** there are 35,000 job titles to choose from. That's **altogether** too many to even think about.

612.8 **among, between** *Among* is typically used when emphasizing distribution throughout a body or a group of three or more; *between* is used when emphasizing distribution to individuals.

➤ There was discontent **among** the relatives after learning that their aunt had divided her entire fortune **between** a canary and a favorite waitress at the local cafe.

612.9 **amoral, immoral** *Amoral* means "neither moral (right) nor immoral (wrong)"; *immoral* means "wrong, or in conflict with traditional values."

➤ Carnivores are **amoral** in their hunt; poachers are **immoral** in theirs.

612.10 **amount, number** *Amount* is used for bulk measurement. *Number* is used to count separate units. (See also "fewer.")

➤ The **number** of new instructors hired next year will depend on the **amount** of revenue raised by the new sales tax.

and etc. Don't use *and* before *etc.*

613.1

➤ Did you remember your textbook, notebook, handout, etc.?

annual, biannual, semiannual, biennial, perennial An *annual* event happens
once every year. A *biannual* event happens twice a year (*semiannual* is the same as
biannual). A *biennial* event happens every two years. A *perennial* event happens
throughout the year, every year.

613.2

anxious, eager Both words mean "looking forward to," but *anxious* also connotes fear
or concern.

613.3

➤ The professor is **eager** to move into the new building, but she's a little **anxious**
that students won't be able to find her new office.

anymore, any more *Anymore* means "any longer"; *any more* means "any additional."

613.4

➤ We won't use that textbook **anymore**; please call if you have **any more**
questions.

any one (of), anyone *Any one* means "any one of a number of people, places, or
things"; *anyone* is a pronoun meaning "any person."

613.5

➤ Choose **any one** of the proposed weekend schedules. **Anyone** wishing to
work on Saturday instead of Sunday may do so.

appraise, apprise *Appraise* means "to determine value." *Apprise* means "to inform."

613.6

➤ Because of the tax assessor's recent **appraisal** of our home, we were **apprised**
of an increase in our property tax.

as Don't use *as* in place of *whether* or *if.*

613.7

➤ I don't know **as** I'll accept the offer. (Incorrect)
I don't know **whether** I'll accept the offer. (Correct)

Don't use *as* when it is unclear whether it means *because* or *when.*

➤ We rowed toward shore **as** it started raining. (Unclear)
We rowed toward shore **because** it started raining. (Correct)

assure, ensure, insure (See "insure.")

bad, badly *Bad* is an adjective, used both before nouns and after linking verbs. *Badly* is
an adverb.

613.8

➤ Christina felt **bad** about serving us **bad** food.
Larisa played **badly** today.

beside, besides *Beside* means "by the side of." *Besides* means "in addition to."

613.9

➤ **Besides** the two suitcases you've already loaded into the trunk, remember the
smaller one **beside** the van.

between, among (See "among.")

bring, take *Bring* suggests the action is directed toward the speaker; *take* suggests the
action is directed away from the speaker.

613.10

➤ If you're not going to **bring** the video to class, **take** it back to the resource
center.

614.1 **can, may** In formal contexts, *can* is used to mean "being able to do"; *may* is used to mean "having permission to do."

- **May** I borrow your bicycle to get to the library? Then I **can** start working on our group project.

614.2 **capital, capitol** The noun *capital* refers to a city or to money. The adjective *capital* means "major or important" or "seat of government." *Capitol* refers to a building.

- The **capitol** is in the **capital** city for a **capital** reason. The city government contributed **capital** for the building expense.

614.3 **cent, sent, scent** *Cent* is a coin; *sent* is the past tense of the verb "send"; *scent* is an odor or a smell.

- For thirty-seven **cents**, I **sent** my friend a love poem in a perfumed envelope. She adored the **scent** but hated the poem.

614.4 **chord, cord** *Chord* may mean "an emotion or a feeling," but it also may mean "the combination of three or more tones sounded at the same time," as with a guitar *chord*. A *cord* is a string or a rope.

- The guitar player strummed the opening **chord**, which struck a responsive **chord** with the audience.

614.5 **chose, choose** *Chose* (chōz) is the past tense of the verb *choose* (chüz).

- For generations, people **chose** their careers based on their parents' careers; now people **choose** their careers based on the job market.

614.6 **climactic, climatic** *Climactic* refers to the climax, or high point, of an event; *climatic* refers to the climate, or weather conditions.

- Because we are using the open-air amphitheater, **climatic** conditions in these foothills will just about guarantee the wind gusts we need for the **climactic** third act.

614.7 **coarse, course** *Coarse* means "of inferior quality, rough, or crude"; *course* means "a direction or a path taken." *Course* also means "a class or a series of studies."

- A basic writing **course** is required of all students.
  Due to years of woodworking, the instructor's hands are rather **coarse**.

614.8 **compare with, compare to** Things in the same category are *compared with* each other; things in different categories are *compared to* each other.

- **Compare** Christopher Marlowe's plays **with** William Shakespeare's plays.
  My brother **compared** reading *The Tempest* **to** visiting another country.

614.9 **complement, compliment** *Complement* means "to complete or go well with." *Compliment* means "to offer an expression of admiration or praise."

- We wanted to **compliment** Zach on his decorating efforts; the bright yellow walls **complement** the purple carpet.

614.10 **comprehensible, comprehensive** *Comprehensible* means "capable of being understood"; *comprehensive* means "covering a broad range, or inclusive."

- The theory is **comprehensible** only to those who have a **comprehensive** knowledge of physics.

comprise, compose *Comprise* means "to contain or consist of"; *compose* means "to create or form by bringing parts together."

615.1

➤ Fruitcake **comprises** a variety of nuts, candied fruit, and spice.
Fruitcake is **composed** of (not *comprised of*) a variety of flavorable ingredients.

conscience, conscious A *conscience* gives one the capacity to know right from wrong. *Conscious* means "awake or alert, not sleeping or comatose."

615.2

➤ Your **conscience** will guide you, but you have to be **conscious** to hear what it's "saying."

continual, continuous *Continual* often implies that something is happening often, recurring; *continuous* usually implies that something keeps happening, uninterrupted.

615.3

➤ The **continuous** loud music during the night gave the building manager not only a headache, but also **continual** phone calls.

counsel, council, consul When used as a noun, *counsel* means "advice"; when used as a verb, *counsel* means "to advise." *Council* refers to a group that advises. A *consul* is a government official appointed to reside in a foreign country.

615.4

➤ The city **council** was asked to **counsel** our student **council** on running an efficient meeting. Their **counsel** was very helpful.

decent, descent, dissent *Decent* means "good." *Descent* is the process of going or stepping downward. *Dissent* means "disagreement."

615.5

➤ The food was **decent**.
The elevator's fast **descent** clogged my ears.
Their **dissent** over the decisions was obvious in their sullen expressions.

desert, dessert *Desert* is barren wilderness. *Dessert* is food served at the end of a meal. The verb *desert* means "to abandon."

615.6

different from, different than Use *different from* in formal writing; use either form in informal or colloquial settings.

615.7

➤ Rafael's interpretation was **different from** Andrea's.

discreet, discrete *Discreet* means "showing good judgment, unobtrusive, modest"; *discrete* means "distinct, separate."

615.8

➤ The essay question had three **discrete** parts.
Her roommate had apparently never heard of quiet, **discreet** conversation.

disinterested, uninterested Both words mean "not interested." However, *disinterested* is also used to mean "unbiased or impartial."

615.9

➤ A person chosen as an arbitrator must be a **disinterested** party.
Professor Eldridge was **uninterested** in our complaints about the assignment.

effect, affect (See "affect.")

elicit, illicit *Elicit* is a verb meaning "to bring out." *Illicit* is an adjective meaning "unlawful."

615.10

➤ It took two quick hand signals from the lookout at the corner to **elicit** the **illicit** exchange of cash for drugs.

616.1   **eminent, imminent**   *Eminent* means "prominent, conspicuous, or famous"; *imminent* means "ready or threatening to happen."

➤ With the island's government about to collapse, assassination attempts on several **eminent** officials seemed **imminent**.

ensure, insure   (See "insure.")

except, accept   (See "accept.")

616.2   **explicit, implicit**   *Explicit* means "expressed directly or clearly defined"; *implicit* means "implied or unstated."

➤ The professor **explicitly** asked that the experiment be wrapped up on Monday, **implicitly** demanding that her lab assistants work on the weekend.

616.3   **farther, further**   *Farther* refers to a physical distance; *further* refers to additional time, quantity, or degree.

➤ **Further** research showed that walking **farther** rather than faster would improve his health.

616.4   **fewer, less**   *Fewer* refers to the number of separate units; *less* refers to bulk quantity.

➤ Because of spell checkers, students can produce papers containing **fewer** errors in **less** time.

616.5   **figuratively, literally**   *Figuratively* means "in a metaphorical or analogous way—describing something by comparing it to something else"; *literally* means "actually."

➤ The lab was **literally** filled with sulfurous gases—**figuratively** speaking, dragon's breath.

616.6   **first, firstly**   Both words are adverbs meaning "before another in time" or "in the first place." However, do not use *firstly*, which is stiff and unnatural sounding.

➤ **Firstly** I want to see the manager. (Incorrect)
First I want to see the manager. (Correct)

Note: When enumerating, use the forms *first, second, third, next, last*—without the *ly*.

616.7   **fiscal, physical**   *Fiscal* means "related to financial matters"; *physical* means "related to material things."

➤ The school's **fiscal** work is handled by its accounting staff.
The **physical** work is handled by its maintenance staff.

616.8   **for, fore, four**   *For* is a conjunction meaning "because," or a preposition used to indicate the object or recipient of something; *fore* means "earlier" or "the front"; *four* is the word for the number 4.

➤ The crew brought treats **for** the barge's **four** dogs, who always enjoy the breeze at the **fore** of the vessel.

616.9   **former, latter**   When two things are being discussed, *former* refers to the first thing, and *latter* to the second.

➤ Our choices are going to a movie or eating at the Pizza Palace: the **former** is too expensive, and the **latter** too fattening.

good, well *Good* is an adjective; *well* is nearly always an adverb. (When used to indicate state of health, *well* is an adjective.) | 617.1
- A **good** job offers opportunities for advancement, especially for those who do their jobs **well.**

heal, heel *Heal* means "to mend or restore to health"; a *heel* is the back part of a human foot. | 617.2

healthful, healthy *Healthful* means "causing or improving health"; *healthy* means "possessing health." | 617.3
- **Healthful** foods and regular exercise build **healthy** bodies.

I, me *I* is a subject pronoun; *me* is used as an object of a preposition, a direct object, or an indirect object. (A good way to know if *I* or *me* should be used in a compound subject is to eliminate the other subject; the sentence should make sense with the pronoun—*I* or *me*—alone.) | 617.4

video

- My roommate and **me** went to the library last night. (Incorrect)
  My roommate and **I** went to the library last night. (Correct: Eliminate "my roommate and"; the sentence still makes sense.)
- Rasheed gave the concert tickets to Erick and **I**. (Incorrect)
  Rasheed gave the concert tickets to Erick and **me**. (Correct: Eliminate "Erick and"; the sentence still makes sense.)

illusion, allusion (See "allusion.")

immigrate (to), emigrate (from) *Immigrate* means "to come into a new country or environment." *Emigrate* means "to go out of one country to live in another." | 617.5
- **Immigrating** to a new country is a challenging experience.
  People **emigrating** from their homelands face unknown challenges.

imminent, eminent (See "eminent.")

imply, infer *Imply* means "to suggest without saying outright"; *infer* means "to draw a conclusion from facts." (A writer or a speaker *implies*; a reader or a listener *infers*.) | 617.6
- Dr. Rufus **implied** I should study more; I **inferred** he meant my grades had to improve or I'd be repeating the class.

ingenious, ingenuous *Ingenious* means "intelligent, discerning, clever"; *ingenuous* means "unassuming, natural, showing childlike innocence and candidness." | 617.7
- Gretchen devised an **ingenious** plan to work and receive college credit for it.
  Ramón displays an **ingenuous** quality that attracts others.

insure, ensure, assure *Insure* means "to secure from financial harm or loss," *ensure* means "to make certain of something," and *assure* means "to put someone's mind at rest." | 617.8
- Plenty of studying generally **ensures** academic success.
  Nicole **assured** her father that she had **insured** her new car.

interstate, intrastate *Interstate* means "existing between two or more states"; *intrastate* means "existing within a state." | 617.9

618.1 **irregardless, regardless** *Irregardless* is the substandard synonym for *regardless*.
➤ **Irregardless** of his circumstance, José is cheerful. (Incorrect)
Regardless of his circumstance, José is cheerful. (Correct)

618.2 **it's, its** *It's* is the contraction of "it is." *Its* is the possessive form of "it."
➤ **It's** not hard to see why my husband feeds that alley cat; **its** pitiful limp and mournful mewing would melt any heart.

618.3 **later, latter** *Later* means "after a period of time." *Latter* refers to the second of two things mentioned.
➤ The **latter** of the two restaurants you mentioned sounds good. Let's meet there **later**.

618.4 **lay, lie** *Lay* means "to place." *Lay* is a transitive verb. (See **630.2**.) Its principal parts are *lay, laid, laid*.
➤ If you **lay** another book on my table, I won't have room for anything else. Yesterday, you **laid** two books on the table. Over the last few days, you must have **laid** at least 20 books there.

exercise

Lie means "to recline." *Lie* is an intransitive verb. (See **630.2**.) Its principal parts are *lie, lay, lain*.
➤ The cat **lies** down anywhere it pleases. It **lay** down yesterday on my tax forms. It has **lain** down many times on the kitchen table.

618.5 **learn, teach** *Learn* means "to acquire information"; *teach* means "to give information."
➤ Sometimes it's easier to **teach** someone else a lesson than it is to **learn** one yourself.

618.6 **leave, let** *Leave* means "to allow something to remain behind." *Let* means "to permit."
➤ Please **let** me help you carry that chair; otherwise, **leave** it for the movers to pick up.

618.7 **lend, borrow** *Lend* means "to give for temporary use"; *borrow* means "to receive for temporary use."
➤ I asked Haddad to **lend** me $15 for a CD, but he said I'd have to find someone else to **borrow** from.

less, fewer (See "fewer.")

618.8 **liable, libel** *Liable* is an adjective meaning "responsible according to the law" or "exposed to an adverse action"; the noun *libel* is a written defamatory statement about someone, and the verb *libel* means "to publish or make such a statement."
➤ Supermarket tabloids, **liable** for ruining many a reputation, make a practice of **libeling** the rich and the famous.

618.9 **liable, likely** *Liable* means "responsible according to the law" or "exposed to an adverse action"; *likely* means "in all probability."
➤ Rain seems **likely** today, but if we cancel the game, we are still **liable** for paying the referees.

like, as *Like* should not be used in place of *as*. *Like* is a preposition, which is followed by a noun, a pronoun, or a noun phrase. *As* is a subordinating conjunction, which introduces a clause. Avoid using *like* as a subordinating conjunction. Use *as* instead.

619.1

➤ You don't know her **like** I do. (Incorrect)

You don't know her **as** I do. (Correct)

Like the others in my study group, I do my work **as** any serious student would—carefully and thoroughly. (Correct)

literally, figuratively (See " figuratively.")

loose, lose, loss The adjective *loose* (lüs) means "free, untied, unrestricted"; the verb *lose* (lüz) means "to misplace or fail to find or control"; the noun *loss* (lòs) means "something that is misplaced and cannot be found."

619.2

➤ Her sadness at the **loss** of her longtime companion caused her to **lose** weight, and her clothes felt uncomfortably **loose**.

may, can (See "can.")

maybe, may be Use *maybe* as an adverb; use *may be* as a verb phrase.

619.3

➤ She **may be** the computer technician we've been looking for. **Maybe** she will upgrade the software and memory.

miner, minor A *miner* digs in the ground for ore. A *minor* is a person who is not legally an adult. The adjective *minor* means "of no great importance."

619.4

➤ The use of **minors** as coal **miners** is no **minor** problem.

number, amount (See "amount.")

oral, verbal *Oral* means "uttered with the mouth"; *verbal* means "relating to or consisting of words and the comprehension of words."

619.5

➤ The actor's **oral** abilities were outstanding, her pronunciation and intonation impeccable, but I doubted the playwright's **verbal** skills after trying to decipher the play's meaning.

OK, okay This expression, spelled either way, is appropriate in informal writing; however, avoid using it in papers, reports, or formal correspondence of any kind.

619.6

➤ Your proposal is satisfactory (not *okay*) on most levels.

passed, past *Passed* is a verb. *Past* can be used as a noun, an adjective, or a preposition.

619.7

➤ That little pickup truck **passed** my 'Vette! (verb)

My stepchildren hold on dearly to the **past**. (noun)

I'm sorry, but my **past** life is not your business. (adjective)

The officer drove **past** us, not noticing our flat tire. (preposition)

peace, piece *Peace* means "tranquility or freedom from war." A *piece* is a part or fragment.

619.8

➤ Someone once observed that **peace** is not a condition, but a process—a process of building goodwill one **piece** at a time.

620.1   **people, person**   Use *people* to refer to human populations, races, or groups; use *person* to refer to an individual or the physical body.

- ➤ What the American **people** need is a good insect repellent.

 The forest ranger recommends that we check our **persons** for wood ticks when we leave the woods.

620.2   **percent, percentage**   *Percent* means "per hundred"; for example, 60 percent of 100 jelly beans would be 60 jelly beans. *Percentage* refers to a portion of the whole. Generally, use the word *percent* when it is preceded by a number. Use *percentage* when no number is used.

exercise

- ➤ Each person's **percentage** of the reward amounted to $125—25 **percent** of the $500 offered by Crime Stoppers.

620.3   **personal, personnel**   *Personal* means "private." *Personnel* are people working at a particular job.

- ➤ Although choosing a major is a **personal** decision, it can be helpful to consult with guidance **personnel**.

620.4   **perspective, prospective**   *Perspective* is a person's point of view or the capacity to view things realistically; *prospective* is an adjective meaning "expected in or related to the future."

- ➤ From my immigrant neighbor's **perspective**, any job is a good job.

 Prospective students wandered the campus on visitors' day.

620.5   **pore, pour, poor**   The noun *pore* is an opening in the skin; the verb *pore* means "to gaze intently." *Pour* means "to move with a continuous flow." *Poor* means "needy or pitiable."

- ➤ **Pour** hot water into a bowl, put your face over it, and let the steam open your **pores**. Your **poor** skin will thank you.

620.6   **precede, proceed**   To *precede* means "to go or come before," while *proceed* means "to move on after having stopped" or "go ahead."

- ➤ Our biology instructor often **preceded** his lecture with these words:

 "OK, sponges, **proceed** to soak up more fascinating facts!"

620.7   **principal, principle**   As an adjective, *principal* means "primary." As a noun, it can mean "a school administrator" or "a sum of money." A *principle* is an idea or a doctrine.

- ➤ His **principal** gripe is lack of freedom. (adjective)

 My son's **principal** expressed his concerns to the teachers. (noun)

 After 20 years, the amount of interest was higher than the **principal**. (noun)

 The **principle** of *caveat emptor* guides most consumer groups.

620.8   **quiet, quit, quite**   *Quiet* is the opposite of noisy. *Quit* means "to stop or give up." *Quite* means "completely" or "to a considerable extent."

- ➤ The meeting remained **quite quiet** when the boss told us he'd **quit**.

620.9   **quote, quotation**   *Quote* is a verb; *quotation* is a noun.

- ➤ The **quotation** I used was from Woody Allen. You may **quote** me on that.

620.10   **real, very, really**   Do not use the adjective *real* in place of the adverbs *very* or *really*.

- ➤ My friend's cake is usually **very** (not *real*) fresh, but this cake is **really** stale.

right, write, wright, rite *Right* means "correct or proper"; it also refers to that which
a person has a legal claim to, as in *copyright*. *Write* means "to inscribe or record." A *wright*
is a person who makes or builds something. *Rite* is a ritual or ceremonial act.

> ➤ Did you **write** that it is the **right** of the **shipwright** to perform the **rite** of
> christening—breaking a bottle of champagne on the bow of the ship?

scene, seen *Scene* refers to the setting or location where something happens; it also
may mean "sight or spectacle." *Seen* is the past participle of the verb "see."

> ➤ An exhibitionist likes to be **seen** making a **scene**.

set, sit *Set* means "to place." *Sit* means "to put the body in a seated position." *Set* is a
transitive verb; *sit* is an intransitive verb.

> ➤ How can you just **sit** there and watch as I **set** the table?

sight, cite, site *Sight* means "the act of seeing" or "something that is seen." *Cite* means
"to quote" or "to summon to court." *Site* means "a place or location" or "to place on a site."

> ➤ After **sighting** the faulty wiring, the inspector **cited** the building contractor for
> breaking two city codes at a downtown work **site**.

some, sum *Some* refers to an unknown thing, an unspecified number, or a part of
something. *Sum* is a certain amount of money or the result of adding numbers together.

> ➤ **Some** of the students answered too quickly and came up with the wrong **sum**.

stationary, stationery *Stationary* means "not movable"; *stationery* refers to the paper
and envelopes used to write letters.

> ➤ Odina uses **stationery** that she can feed through her portable printer. Then she
> drops the mail into a **stationary** mail receptacle at the mall.

take, bring (See "bring.")

teach, learn (See "learn.")

than, then *Than* is used in a comparison; *then* tells when.

> ➤ Study more **than** you think you need to. **Then** you will probably be satisfied
> with your grades.

their, there, they're *Their* is a possessive personal pronoun. *There* is a pronoun used
as a function word to introduce a clause or an adverb used to point out location. *They're*
is the contraction for "they are."

> ➤ Look over **there**.
>
> **There** is a comfortable place for students to study for **their** exams, so **they're**
> more likely to do a good job.

threw, through *Threw* is the past tense of "throw." *Through* means "from one side of
something to the other."

> ➤ In a fit of frustration, Sachiko **threw** his cell phone right **through** the window.

to, too, two *To* is a preposition that can mean "in the direction of." *To* is also used to
form an infinitive. *Too* means "also" or "very." *Two* is the number 2.

> ➤ **Two** causes of eye problems among students are lights that fail **to** illuminate
> properly and computer screens with **too** much glare.

622.1   **vain, vane, vein**   *Vain* means "valueless or fruitless"; it may also mean "holding a high regard for one's self." *Vane* is a flat piece of material set up to show which way the wind blows. *Vein* refers to a blood vessel or a mineral deposit.

➤ The weather **vane** indicates the direction of the wind; the blood **vein** determines the direction of flowing blood; and the **vain** mind moves in no particular direction, content to think only about itself.

622.2   **vary, very**   *Vary* means "to change"; *very* means "to a high degree."

➤ To ensure the **very** best employee relations, the workloads should not **vary** greatly from worker to worker.

verbal, oral   (See "oral.")

622.3   **waist, waste**   *Waist* is the part of the body just above the hips. The verb *waste* means "to squander" or "to wear away, decay"; the noun *waste* refers to material that is unused or useless.

➤ His **waist** is small because he **wastes** no opportunity to exercise.

622.4   **wait, weight**   *Wait* means "to stay somewhere expecting something." *Weight* refers to a degree or unit of heaviness.

➤ The **weight** of sadness eventually lessens; one must simply **wait** for the pain to dissipate.

622.5   **ware, wear, where**   *Ware* refers to a product that is sold; *wear* means "to have on or to carry on one's body"; *where* asks the question "In what place?" or "In what situation?"

➤ The designer boasted, "**Where** can one **wear** my **wares**? Anywhere."

622.6   **weather, whether**   *Weather* refers to the condition of the atmosphere. *Whether* refers to a possibility.

➤ **Weather** conditions affect nearly all of us, **whether** we are farmers, pilots, or plumbers.

well, good   (See "good.")

which, that   (See 577.3.)

622.7   **who, which, that**   *Who* refers to people. *Which* refers to nonliving objects or to animals. (*Which* should never refer to people.) *That* may refer to animals, people, or nonliving objects. (See also 577.3.)

622.8   **who, whom**   *Who* is used as the subject of a verb; *whom* is used as the object of a preposition or as a direct object.

➤ Captain Mather, to **whom** the survivors owe their lives, is the man **who** is being honored today.

622.9   **who's, whose**   *Who's* is the contraction for "who is." *Whose* is a possessive pronoun.

➤ **Whose** car are we using, and **who's** going to pay for the gas?

622.10   **your, you're**   *Your* is a possessive pronoun. *You're* is the contraction for "you are."

➤ If **you're** like most Americans, you will have held eight jobs by **your** 40th birthday.

Chapter 38
Understanding Grammar

audio

Grammar is the study of the structure and features of the language, consisting of rules and standards that are to be followed to produce acceptable writing and speaking. **Parts of speech** refers to the eight different ways words are used in the English language—as *nouns, pronouns, verbs, adjectives, adverbs, prepositions, conjunctions,* or *interjections.*

Noun

623.1

A **noun** is a word that names something: a person, a place, a thing, or an idea.

- **Toni Morrison/author**   ***Lone Star*/film**   **Renaissance/era**
  UC-Davis/university   ***A Congress of Wonders*/book**

esl *Note:* See **665.1, 666.1,** and **666.2** for information on count and noncount nouns.

Classes of Nouns

All nouns are either *proper nouns* or *common nouns.* Nouns may also be classified as *individual* or *collective,* or *concrete* or *abstract.*

Proper Nouns

623.2

A **proper noun**, which is always capitalized, names a person, a place, a thing, or an idea.

- **Rembrandt, Bertrand Russell** (people)
  Stratford-upon-Avon, Tower of London (places)
  ***The Night Watch,* Rosetta Stone** (things)
  New Deal, Christianity (ideas)

Common Nouns

623.3

A **common noun** is a general name for a person, a place, a thing, or an idea. Common nouns are not capitalized.

- **optimist, instructor** (people)   **cafeteria, park** (places)
  computer, chair (things)   **freedom, love** (ideas)

624.1
Collective Nouns

A **collective noun** names a group or a unit.

- ➤ family   audience   crowd   committee   team   class

624.2
Concrete Nouns

A **concrete noun** names a thing that is tangible (can be seen, touched, heard, smelled, or tasted).

- ➤ child   Pearl Jam   gymnasium   village   microwave oven   pizza

624.3
Abstract Nouns

An **abstract noun** names an idea, a condition, or a feeling—in other words, something that cannot be seen, touched, heard, smelled, or tasted.

- ➤ beauty   Jungian psychology   anxiety   agoraphobia   trust

Forms of Nouns

Nouns are grouped according to their *number, gender,* and *case.*

624.4
Number of Nouns

Number indicates whether a noun is singular or plural.

A singular noun refers to one person, place, thing, or idea.

- ➤ student   laboratory   lecture   note   grade   result

A plural noun refers to more than one person, place, thing, or idea.

- ➤ students   laboratories   lectures   notes   grades   results

624.5
Gender of Nouns

Gender indicates whether a noun is masculine, feminine, neuter, or indefinite.
Masculine:
- ➤ father   king   brother   men   colt   rooster

Feminine:
- ➤ mother   queen   sister   women   filly   hen

Neuter (without sex):
- ➤ notebook   monitor   car   printer

Indefinite or **common** (masculine or feminine):
- ➤ professor   customer   children   doctor   people

Case of Nouns

625.1

The **case** of a noun tells how it is related to other words within a sentence. There are three cases: *nominative, possessive,* and *objective.*

Nominative case describes a noun used as a subject. The subject of a sentence tells who or what the sentence is about.

- **Dean Henning** manages the College of Arts and Communication.

Note: A noun is also in the nominative case when it is used as a predicate noun (or predicate nominative). A predicate noun follows a form of the *be* verb (*am, is, are, was, were, be, being, been*) and repeats or renames the subject.

- Either Mr. Cassett or Ms. Yokum is the **person** to talk to about the college's impact in our community.

Possessive case describes a noun that shows possession or ownership.

- Our **president's** willingness to discuss concerns with students has boosted campus morale.

Objective case describes a noun used as an object of the preposition, a direct object, or an indirect object.

- To survive, institutions of higher **learning** sometimes cut budgets in spite of **protests** from **students** and **instructors**.
  (*Learning* is the object of the preposition *of, protests* is the object of the preposition *in spite of,* and *students* and *instructors* are the objects of the preposition *from.*)

A Closer Look
at Direct and Indirect Objects

625.2

A **direct object** is a noun (or pronoun) that identifies what or who receives the action of the verb.

- Budget cutbacks reduced class **choices**.
  (*Choices* is the direct object of *reduced.*)

An **indirect object** is a noun (or pronoun) that identifies the person *to whom* or *for whom* something is done, or the thing *to which* or *for which* something is done. An indirect object is always accompanied by a direct object.

- Recent budget cuts have given **students** fewer class choices.
  (*Choices* is the direct object of *have given; students* is the indirect object.)

esl **Note:** Not every verb can be followed by *both* a direct object and an indirect object. Both can, however, follow *give, send, show, tell, teach, find, sell, ask, offer, pay, pass,* and *hand.*

626.1

Pronoun

A **pronoun** is a word that is used in place of a noun.

➤ Roger was the most interesting 10-year-old **I** ever taught. **He** was a good thinker and thus a good writer. **I** remember **his** paragraph about the cowboy hat **he** received from **his** grandparents. **It** was "too new looking." The brim was not rolled properly. But the hat's imperfections were not the main idea in Roger's writing. No, the main idea was about how **he** was fixing the hat **himself** by wearing **it** when **he** showered.

Antecedents

626.2

An **antecedent** is the noun that the pronoun refers to or replaces. Most pronouns have antecedents, but not all do. (See **627.4.**)

➤ As the wellness **counselor** checked *her* chart, several **students** *who* were waiting *their* turns shifted uncomfortably. (*Counselor* is the antecedent of *her*; *students* is the antecedent of *who* and *their*.)

Note: Each pronoun must agree with its antecedent in number, person, and gender. (See page **655.**)

626.3

Classes of Pronouns

Personal
I, me, my, mine / we, us, our, ours / you, your, yours
they, them, their, theirs / he, him, his, she, her, hers, it, its

Reflexive and Intensive
myself, yourself, himself, herself, itself, ourselves, yourselves, themselves

Relative
who, whose, whom, which, that

Indefinite

all	anything	everybody	most	no one	some
another	both	everyone	much	nothing	somebody
any	each	everything	neither	one	someone
anybody	each one	few	nobody	other	something
anyone	either	many	none	several	such

Interrogative
who, whose, whom, which, what

Demonstrative
this, that, these, those

Reciprocal
each other, one another

Classes of Pronouns

There are several classes of pronouns: *personal, reflexive and intensive, relative, indefinite, interrogative, demonstrative,* and *reciprocal.*

Personal Pronouns

A **personal pronoun** refers to a specific person or thing.

- *Marge* started **her** car; **she** drove the antique *convertible* to Monterey where **she** hoped to sell **it** at an auction.

Reflexive and Intensive Pronouns

A **reflexive pronoun** is formed by adding *-self* or *-selves* to a personal pronoun. A reflexive pronoun can act as a direct object or an indirect object of a verb, an object of a preposition, or a predicate nominative.

- Charles loves **himself.** (direct object of *loves*)
  Charles gives **himself** A's for fashion sense. (indirect object of *gives*)
  Charles smiles at **himself** in store windows. (object of preposition *at*)
  Charles can be **himself** anywhere. (predicate nominative)

An **intensive pronoun** intensifies, or emphasizes, the noun or pronoun it refers to.

- Leo **himself** taught his children to invest their lives in others.
  The lesson was sometimes painful—but they learned it **themselves**.

Relative Pronouns

A **relative pronoun** relates an adjective clause to the noun or pronoun it modifies. (The noun is italicized in each example below; the relative pronoun is in bold.)

- *Freshmen* **who** believe they have a lot to learn are absolutely right.
  Just navigating this *campus*, **which** is huge, can be challenging.

esl **Note:** Make sure you know when to use the relative pronouns *who* or *whom* and *that* or *which*. (See **577.3**, **622.7**, and **622.8**.)

Indefinite Pronouns

An **indefinite pronoun** refers to unnamed or unknown people, places, or things.

- **Everyone** seemed amused when I was searching for my classroom in the student center. (The antecedent of *everyone* is unnamed.)
- **Nothing** is more unnerving than rushing last minute into the wrong room for the wrong class. (The antecedent of *nothing* is unknown.)

esl **Note:** Most indefinite pronouns are singular, so when they are used as subjects, they should have singular verbs.

Interrogative Pronouns

628.1

An **interrogative pronoun** asks a question.

➤ So **which** will it be—highlighting and attaching a campus map to the inside of your backpack, or being lost and late for the first two weeks?

Demonstrative Pronouns

628.2

A **demonstrative pronoun** points out people, places, or things.

➤ We advise **this:** bring along as many maps and schedules as you need. **Those** are useful tools. **That** is the solution.

Note: When a demonstrative pronoun *modifies* a noun (instead of replacing it), it functions as an adjective: *this* teacher, *that* test.

Forms of Personal Pronouns

The **form** of a personal pronoun indicates its *number* (singular or plural), its *person* (first, second, or third), its *case* (nominative, possessive, or objective), and its *gender* (masculine, feminine, neuter, or indefinite).

Number of Pronouns

628.3

A **personal pronoun** is either singular (*I, you, he, she, it*) or plural (*we, you, they*) in number.

➤ **He** should have a budget and stick to it. (singular)
We can help new students learn about budgeting. (plural)

Person of Pronouns

628.4

The **person** of a pronoun indicates whether the person is speaking (first person), is spoken to (second person), or is spoken about (third person).

First person is used to name the speaker(s).

➤ **I** know **I** need to handle **my** stress in a healthful way, especially during exam week; **my** usual chips-and-donuts binge isn't helping. (singular)
We all decided to bike to the tennis court. (plural)

Second person is used to name the person(s) spoken to.

➤ Maria, **you** grab the rackets, okay? (singular)
John and Tanya, can **you** find the water bottles? (plural)

Third person is used to name the person(s) or thing(s) spoken about.

➤ Today's students are interested in wellness issues. **They** are concerned about **their** health, fitness, and nutrition. (plural)
Maria practices yoga and feels **she** is calmer for **her** choice. (singular)
One of the advantages of regular exercise is that **it** raises one's energy level. (singular)

Case of Pronouns

629.1

The **case** of each pronoun tells how it is related to the other words within a sentence. There are three cases: *nominative, possessive,* and *objective.*

Nominative case describes a pronoun used as a subject. The following are nominative forms: *I, you, he, she, it, we, they.*

➤ **He** found an old map in the trunk.

My friend and **I** went biking. (not *me*)

A pronoun is in the nominative case when it is used as a predicate noun (predicate nominative) following a form of the *be* verb (*am, is, are, was, were, be, being, been*).

➤ It was **he** who discovered electricity. (not *him*)

Possessive case describes a pronoun that shows possession or ownership: *my, mine, our, ours, his, her, hers, their, theirs, its, your, yours.*

➤ That coat is **hers.**　This coat is **mine.**　**Your** coat is lost.

Objective case describes a pronoun used as the direct object, indirect object, or object of a preposition: *me, you, him, her, it, us, them.*

➤ Professor Adler hired **her.**
(*Her* is the direct object of the verb *hired.*)

He showed Mary and **me** the language lab.
(*Me* is the indirect object of the verb *showed.*)

He introduced the three of **us**—Mary, Shavonn, and **me**—to the faculty.
(*Us* is the object of the preposition *of; me* is part of the appositive of the object *us.*)

Gender of Pronouns

629.2

The **gender** of a pronoun indicates whether the pronoun is masculine, feminine, neuter, or indefinite. (See page **86** for information on "Addressing Gender.")

Masculine:
➤ he, him, his

Feminine:
➤ she, her, hers

Neuter (without sex):
➤ it, its

Indefinite (masculine or feminine):
➤ they, them, their

Number, Person, and Case of Personal Pronouns

629.3

	Nominative Case	Possessive Case	Objective Case
First Person Singular	I	my, mine	me
Second Person Singular	you	your, yours	you
Third Person Singular	he, she, it	his, her, hers, its	him, her, it
First Person Plural	we	our, ours	us
Second Person Plural	you	your, yours	you
Third Person Plural	they	their, theirs	them

630.1

Verb

A **verb** shows action (*pondered, grins*), links words *(is, seemed)*, or accompanies another action verb as an auxiliary or helping verb *(can, does)*.

➤ Harry **honked** the horn. (shows action)
Harry **is** impatient. (links words)
Harry **was** honking the truck's horn. (accompanies the verb *honking*)

Classes of Verbs

Verbs are classified as action, auxiliary (helping), or linking (state of being).

Action Verbs: Transitive and Intransitive

630.2

As its name implies, an **action verb** shows action. Some action verbs are *transitive*; others are *intransitive*. (The term *action* does not always refer to a physical activity.)

➤ Rain **splashed** the windshield. (transitive verb)
Josie **drove** off the road. (intransitive verb)

Transitive verbs have direct objects that receive the action (**645.5**).

➤ The health care industry **employs** more than 7 million **workers** in the United States. (*Workers* is the direct object of the action verb *employs*.)

Intransitive verbs communicate action that is complete in itself. They do not need an object to receive the action.

➤ My new college roommate **smiles** and **laughs** a lot.

Note: Some verbs can be either transitive or intransitive.

➤ Ms. Hull **teaches** physiology and microbiology. (transitive)
She **teaches** well. (intransitive)

Auxiliary (Helping) Verbs

630.3

Auxiliary verbs (helping verbs) help to form some of the *tenses* (**632.1**), the *mood* (**633.2**), and the *voice* (**633.1**) of the main verb. In the following example, the auxiliary verbs are in **bold**, and the main verbs are in *italics*.

➤ I *believe*, I **have** always *believed*, and I **will** always *believe* in private enterprise as the backbone of economic well-being in America.

—Franklin D. Roosevelt

Common Auxiliary Verbs							
am	been	could	does	have	might	should	will
are	being	did	had	is	must	was	would
be	can	do	has	may	shall	were	

esl **Note:** "Be" auxiliary verbs are always followed by either a verb ending in *ing* or a past participle. Also see "Common Modal Auxiliary Verbs" (**670.2**).

Linking (State of Being) Verbs

A **linking verb** is a special form of intransitive verb that links the subject of a sentence to a noun, a pronoun, or an adjective in the predicate. (See the chart below.)

► The streets **are** flooded. (adjective)   The streets **are** rivers! (noun)

Common Linking Verbs

am   are   be   become   been   being   is   was   were

Additional Linking Verbs

appear   feel   look   seem   sound   grow   remain   smell   taste

Note: The verbs listed as "additional linking verbs" above function as linking verbs when they do not show actual action. An adjective usually follows these linking verbs.

► The thunder **sounded** ominous. (adjective)
My little brother **grew** frightened. (adjective)

Note: When these same words are used as action verbs, an adverb or a direct object may follow them.

► I **looked** carefully at him. (adverb)
My little brother **grew** corn for a science project. (direct object)

Forms of Verbs

A verb's **form** differs depending on its *number* (singular, plural), *person* (first, second, third), *tense* (present, past, future, present perfect, past perfect, future perfect), *voice* (active, passive), and *mood* (indicative, imperative, subjunctive).

Number of a Verb

Number indicates whether a verb is singular or plural. The verb and its subject both must be singular, or they both must be plural. (See "Subject-Verb Agreement," pages **651–654**.)

► My college **enrolls** high schoolers in summer programs. (singular)
Many colleges **enroll** high schoolers in summer courses. (plural)

Person of a Verb

Person indicates whether the subject of the verb is *first, second,* or *third person.* The verb and its subject must be in the same person. Verbs usually have a different form only in **third person singular of the present tense.**

	First Person	Second Person	Third Person
Singular	I think	you think	he/ she/it thinks
Plural	we think	you think	they think

Tense of a Verb

Tense indicates the time of an action or state of being. There are three basic tenses (*past*, *present*, and *future*) and three verbal aspects (*progressive*, *perfect*, and *perfect progressive*).

PRESENT TENSE

Present tense expresses action that is happening at the present time or action that happens continually, regularly.

➤ In the United States, more than 75 percent of workers **hold** service jobs.

Present progressive tense also expresses action that is happening at the present time, but it is always formed by combining *am*, *are*, or *is* and the present participle (ending in *ing*) of the main verb.

➤ More women than ever before **are working** outside the home.

Present perfect tense expresses action that began in the past and has recently been completed or is continuing up to the present time.

➤ My sister **has taken** four years of swimming lessons.

Present perfect progressive tense also expresses an action that began in the past but stresses the continuing nature of the action. Like the present progressive tense, it is formed by combining auxiliary verbs (*have been* or *has been*) and present participles.

➤ She **has been taking** them since she was six years old.

PAST TENSE

Past tense expresses action that is completed at a particular time in the past.

➤ A hundred years ago, more than 75 percent **worked** in agriculture.

Past progressive tense expresses past action that continued over an interval of time. It is formed by combining *was* or *were* with the present participle of the main verb.

➤ A century ago, my great-grandparents **were farming**.

Past perfect tense expresses an action in the past that occurs before another past action or an action that was completed by some specific past time.

➤ By dinnertime my cousins **had eaten** all the olives.

Past perfect progressive tense expresses a past action but stresses the continuing nature of the action. It is formed by using *had been* along with the present participle.

➤ They **had been eating** the olives since they arrived two hours earlier.

FUTURE TENSE

Future tense expresses action that will take place in the future.

➤ Next summer I **will work** as a lifeguard.

Future progressive tense expresses a continuous or repeating future action.

➤ I **will be working** for the park district at North Beach.

Future perfect tense expresses action that will begin in the future and be completed by a specific time in the future.

➤ By 10:00 p.m., I **will have completed** my research project.

Future perfect progressive tense also expresses future action that will be completed by a specific time, but (as with other perfect progressive tenses) stresses the action's continuous nature. It is formed using *will have been* along with the present participle.

➤ I **will have been researching** the project for three weeks by the time it's due.

Voice of a Verb

Voice indicates whether the subject is acting or being acted upon.

Active voice indicates that the subject of the verb is doing something.

➤ People **update** their résumé on a regular basis.
(The subject, *People*, is acting; *résumé* is the direct object.)

Passive voice indicates that the subject of the verb is being acted upon or is receiving the action. A passive verb combines a *be* verb with a past participle.

➤ Your résumé **should be updated** on a regular basis.
(The subject, *résumé*, is receiving the action.)

Using Active Voice

Generally, use active voice rather than passive voice for more direct, energetic writing. To change your passive sentences to active ones, do the following: First, find the noun that is doing the action and make it the subject. Then find the word that had been the subject and use it as either a direct object or an indirect object.

Passive: The winning goal **was scored** by Eva. (The subject, *goal*, is not acting.)

Active: Eva **scored** the winning goal. (The subject, *Eva*, is acting.)

Note: When you want to emphasize the receiver more than the doer—or when the doer is unknown—use the passive voice. (Much technical and scientific writing regularly uses the passive voice.)

Mood of a Verb

The **mood** of a verb indicates the tone or attitude with which a statement is made.

Indicative mood, the most common, is used to state a fact or to ask a question.

➤ **Can** any theme **capture** the essence of the complex 1960s culture? President John F. Kennedy's directive [stated below] **represents** one ideal popular during that decade.

Imperative mood is used to give a command. (The subject of an imperative sentence is *you*, which is usually understood and not stated in the sentence.)

➤ **Ask** not what your country can do for you—**ask** what you can do for your country.
—John F. Kennedy

Subjunctive mood is used to express a wish, an impossibility or unlikely condition, or a necessity. The subjunctive mood is often used with *if* or *that*. The verb forms below create a nontypical subject-verb agreement, forming the subjunctive mood.

➤ If I **were** rich, I would travel for the rest of my life. (a wish)

If each of your brain cells **were** one person, there would be enough people to populate 25 planets. (an impossibility)

The English Department requires that every student **pass** a proficiency test. (a necessity)

634.1 Verbals

A **verbal** is a word that is made from a verb, but it functions as a noun, an adjective, or an adverb. There are three types of verbals: *gerunds, infinitives,* and *participles.*

634.2 Gerunds

A **gerund** ends in *ing* and is used as a noun.

- **Waking** each morning is the first challenge. (subject)

  I start **moving** at about seven o'clock. (direct object)

  I work at **jump-starting** my weary system. (object of the preposition)

  As Woody Allen once said, "Eighty percent of life is **showing up**." (predicate noun)

634.3 Infinitives

An **infinitive** is usually introduced by *to*; the infinitive may be used as a noun, an adjective, or an adverb.

- **To succeed** is not easy. (noun)

  That is the most important thing **to remember**. (adjective)

  Students are wise **to work** hard. (adverb)

esl **Note:** It can be difficult to know whether a gerund or an infinitive should follow a verb. It's helpful to become familiar with lists of specific verbs that can be followed by one but not the other. (See **669.2–670.1**.)

634.4 Participles

A **present participle** ends in *ing* and functions as an adjective. A **past participle** ends in *ed* (or another past tense form) and also functions as an adjective.

- The students **reading** those study-skill handouts are definitely **interested**.
  The prospect of **aced** tests and assignments must be **appealing**.
  (These participles function as adjectives: *reading* students, *interested* students, *aced* tests and assignments, and *appealing* prospect. Notice, however, that *reading* has a direct object: *handouts*. Verbals may have direct objects.)

Using Verbals

Make sure that you use verbals correctly; look carefully at the examples below.

Verbal: **Diving** is a popular Olympic sport.
(*Diving* is a gerund used as a subject.)

Diving gracefully, the Olympian hoped to get high marks.
(*Diving* is a participle modifying *Olympian*.)

Verb: The next competitor was **diving** in the practice pool.
(Here, *diving* is a verb, not a verbal.)

Irregular Verbs

Irregular verbs can often be confusing. That's because the past tense and past participle of irregular verbs are formed by changing the word itself, not merely by adding *d* or *ed*. The following list contains the most troublesome irregular verbs.

Common Irregular Verbs and Their Principal Parts

Present Tense	Past Tense	Past Participle	Present Tense	Past Tense	Past Participle	Present Tense	Past Tense	Past Participle
am, be	was, were	been	fly	flew	flown	see	saw	seen
arise	arose	arisen	forget	forgot	forgotten, forgot	set	set	set
awake	awoke, awaked	awoken, awaked	freeze	froze	frozen	shake	shook	shaken
beat	beat	beaten	get	got	gotten	shine (light)	shone	shone
become	became	become	give	gave	given	shine (polish)	shined	shined
begin	began	begun	go	went	gone	show	showed	shown
bite	bit	bitten, bit	grow	grew	grown	shrink	shrank	shrunk
blow	blew	blown	hang (execute)	hanged	hanged	sing	sang	sung
break	broke	broken	hang (suspend)	hung	hung	sink	sank	sunk
bring	brought	brought	have	had	had	sit	sat	sat
build	built	built	hear	heard	heard	sleep	slept	slept
burn	burnt, burned	burnt, burned	hide	hid	hidden	speak	spoke	spoken
			hit	hit	hit	spend	spent	spent
burst	burst	burst	keep	kept	kept	spring	sprang	sprung
buy	bought	bought	know	knew	known	stand	stood	stood
catch	caught	caught	lay	laid	laid	steal	stole	stolen
choose	chose	chosen	lead	led	led	strike	struck	struck, stricken
come	came	come	leave	left	left	strive	strove	striven
cost	cost	cost	lend	lent	lent	swear	swore	sworn
cut	cut	cut	let	let	let	swim	swam	swum
dig	dug	dug	lie (deceive)	lied	lied	swing	swung	swung
dive	dived, dove	dived	lie (recline)	lay	lain	take	took	taken
do	did	done	make	made	made	teach	taught	taught
draw	drew	drawn	mean	meant	meant	tear	tore	torn
dream	dreamed, dreamt	dreamed, dreamt	meet	met	met	tell	told	told
			pay	paid	paid	think	thought	thought
drink	drank	drunk	prove	proved	proved, proven	throw	threw	thrown
drive	drove	driven				wake	woke, waked	woken, waked
eat	ate	eaten	put	put	put			
fall	fell	fallen	read	read	read			
feel	felt	felt	ride	rode	ridden	wear	wore	worn
fight	fought	fought	ring	rang	rung	weave	wove	woven
find	found	found	rise	rose	risen	wind	wound	wound
flee	fled	fled	run	ran	run	wring	wrung	wrung
						write	wrote	written

Adjective

636.1   An **adjective** describes or modifies a noun or pronoun. The articles *a*, *an*, and *the* are adjectives.

➤ Advertising is **a big** and **powerful** industry.
   (*A*, *big*, and *powerful* modify industry.)

Numbers are also adjectives.

➤ **Fifty-three** relatives came to my party.

636.2   *Note:* Many demonstrative, indefinite, and interrogative forms may be used as either adjectives or pronouns (*that, these, many, some, whose,* and so on). These words are adjectives if they come before a noun and modify it; they are pronouns if they stand alone.

➤ **Some** advertisements are less than truthful.
   (*Some* modifies *advertisements* and is an adjective.)
   Many cause us to chuckle at their outrageous claims.
   (*Many* stands alone; it is a pronoun and replaces the noun *advertisements*.)

Proper Adjectives

636.3

Proper adjectives are created from proper nouns and are capitalized.

➤ **English** has been influenced by advertising slogans. (proper noun)
   The **English** language is constantly changing. (proper adjective)

Predicate Adjectives

636.4

A **predicate adjective** follows a form of the *be* verb (or other linking verb) and describes the subject.

➤ At its best, advertising is **useful**; at its worst, **deceptive**.
   (*Useful* and *deceptive* modify the noun *advertising*.)

Forms of Adjectives

636.5

Adjectives have three forms: *positive, comparative,* and *superlative*.

The **positive form** is the adjective in its regular form. It describes a noun or a pronoun without comparing it to anyone or anything else.

➤ Joysport walking shoes are **strong** and **comfortable**.

The **comparative form** (*er, more,* or *less*) compares two things. (*More* and *less* are used generally with adjectives of two or more syllables.)

➤ Air soles make Mile Eaters **stronger** and **more comfortable** than Joysports.

The **superlative form** (*est, most,* or *least*) compares three or more things. (*Most* and *least* are used most often with adjectives of two or more syllables.)

➤ My old Canvas Wonders are the **strongest, most comfortable** shoes of all!

esl **Note:** Two or more adjectives before a noun should have a certain order when they do not modify the noun equally. (See **674.1**.)

Adverb

An **adverb** describes or modifies a verb, an adjective, another adverb, or a whole sentence. An adverb answers questions such as *how, when, where, why, how often,* or *how much.*

➤ The temperature fell **sharply**. (*Sharply* modifies the verb *fell.*)

The temperature was **quite** low. (*Quite* modifies the adjective *low.*)

The temperature dropped **very quickly**.
(*Very* modifies the adverb *quickly,* which modifies the verb *dropped.*)

Unfortunately, the temperature stayed cool.
(*Unfortunately* modifies the whole sentence.)

Types of Adverbs

Adverbs can be grouped in four ways: *time, place, manner,* and *degree.*

Time (These adverbs tell *when, how often,* and *how long.*)

➤ **today, yesterday   daily, weekly   briefly, eternally**

Place (These adverbs tell *where, to where,* and *from where.*)

➤ **here, there   nearby, beyond   backward, forward**

Manner (These adverbs often end in *ly* and tell *how* something is done.)

➤ **precisely   regularly   regally   smoothly   well**

Degree (These adverbs tell *how much* or *how little.*)

➤ **substantially   greatly   entirely   partly   too**

Forms of Adverbs

Adverbs have three forms: *positive, comparative,* and *superlative.*

The **positive form** is the adverb in its regular form. It describes a verb, an adjective, or another adverb without comparing it to anyone or anything else.

➤ With Joysport shoes, you'll walk **fast**. They support your feet **well**.

The **comparative form** (*er, more,* or *less*) compares two things. (*More* and *less* are used generally with adverbs of two or more syllables.)

➤ Wear Jockos instead of Joysports, and you'll walk **faster**. Jockos' special soles support your feet **better** than the Roksports do.

The **superlative form** (*est, most,* or *least*) compares three or more things. (*Most* and *least* are used most often with adverbs of two or more syllables.)

➤ Really, I walk **fastest** wearing my old Canvas Wonders. They seem to support my feet, my knees, and my pocketbook **best** of all.

Regular Adverbs			**Irregular Adverbs**		
positive	comparative	superlative	positive	comparative	superlative
fast	faster	fastest	well	better	best
effectively	more effectively	most effectively	badly	worse	worst

638.1

Preposition

A **preposition** is a word (or group of words) that shows the relationship between its object (a noun or pronoun following the preposition) and another word in the sentence.

- ▶ **Regarding** your reasons **for** going **to** college, do they all hinge **on** getting a good job **after** graduation?

    (In this sentence, *reasons, going, college, getting,* and *graduation* are objects of their preceding prepositions *regarding, for, to, on,* and *after.*)

638.2

Prepositional Phrases

A **prepositional phrase** includes the preposition, the object of the preposition, and the modifiers of the object. A prepositional phrase may function as an adverb or adjective.

- ▶ A broader knowledge **of the world** is one benefit **of higher education.**

    (The two phrases function as adjectives modifying the nouns *knowledge* and *benefit* respectively.)

    Exercising your brain may safeguard **against atrophy.** (The phrase functions as an adverb modifying the verb *safeguard.*)

638.3

Prepositions

aboard	back of	except for	near to	round
about	because of	excepting	notwithstanding	save
above	before	for	of	since
according to	behind	from	off	subsequent to
across	below	from among	on	through
across from	beneath	from between	on account of	throughout
after	beside	from under	on behalf of	till
against	besides	in	onto	to
along	between	in addition to	on top of	together with
alongside	beyond	in behalf of	opposite	toward
alongside of	but	in front of	out	under
along with	by	in place of	out of	underneath
amid	by means of	in regard to	outside	until
among	concerning	inside	outside of	unto
apart from	considering	inside of	over	up
around	despite	in spite of	over to	upon
as far as	down	instead of	owing to	up to
aside from	down from	into	past	with
at	during	like	prior to	within
away from	except	near	regarding	without

esl **Note:** Prepositions often pair up with a verb and become part of an idiom, a slang expression, or a two-word verb. (See pages **671** and **682-684.**)

Conjunction

639.1

A **conjunction** connects individual words or groups of words.

- When we came back to Paris, it was clear **and** cold **and** lovely.

—Ernest Hemingway

Coordinating Conjunctions

639.2

Coordinating conjunctions usually connect a word to a word, a phrase to a phrase, or a clause to a clause. The words, phrases, or clauses joined by a coordinating conjunction are equal in importance or are of the same type.

- Civilization is a race between education **and** catastrophe.

—H. G. Wells

Correlative Conjunctions

639.3

Correlative conjunctions are a type of coordinating conjunction used in pairs.

- There are two inadvisable ways to think: **either** believe everything **or** doubt everything.

Subordinating Conjunctions

639.4

Subordinating conjunctions connect two clauses that are not equally important. A subordinating conjunction connects a dependent clause to an independent clause.

- Experience is the worst teacher; it gives the test **before** it presents the lesson. (The clause *before it presents the lesson* is dependent. It connects to the independent clause *it gives the test.*)

639.5

Conjunctions

Coordinating: and, but, or, nor, for, so, yet

Correlative: either, or; neither, nor; not only, but (but also); both, and; whether, or

Subordinating: after, although, as, as if, as long as, because, before, even though, if, in order that, provided that, since, so that, than, that, though, unless, until, when, whenever, where, while

Note: Relative pronouns and conjunctive adverbs (580.2) can also connect clauses.

Interjection

639.6

An **interjection** communicates strong emotion or surprise (*oh, ouch, hey,* and so on). Punctuation (often a comma or an exclamation point) is used to set off an interjection.

- **Hey! Wait! Well,** so much for catching the bus.

A Closer Look
at the Parts of Speech

Noun

A **noun** is a word that names something: a person, a place, a thing, or an idea.

- **Toni Morrison/author** *Lone Star*/**film**
  UC-Davis/university **Renaissance/era**
  ***A Congress of Wonders*/book**

Pronoun

A **pronoun** is a word used in place of a noun.

I	my	that	themselves	which
it	ours	they	everybody	you

Verb

A **verb** is a word that expresses action, links words, or acts as an auxiliary verb to the main verb.

are	break	drag	fly	run	sit	was
bite	catch	eat	is	see	tear	were

Adjective

An **adjective** describes or modifies a noun or pronoun. (The articles *a, an,* and *the* are adjectives.)

- **The carbonated** drink went down easy on **that hot, dry** day. (*The* and *carbonated* modify *drink*; *that, hot,* and *dry* modify *day*.)

Adverb

An **adverb** describes or modifies a verb, an adjective, another adverb, or a whole sentence. An adverb generally answers questions such as *how, when, where, how often,* or *how much.*

greatly	precisely	regularly	there
here	today	partly	quickly
slowly	yesterday	nearly	loudly

Preposition

A **preposition** is a word (or group of words) that shows the relationship between its object (a noun or pronoun that follows the preposition) and another word in the sentence. Prepositions introduce prepositional phrases.

- **across for with out to of**

Conjunction

A **conjunction** connects individual words or groups of words.

- **and because but for or since so yet**

Interjection

An **interjection** is a word that communicates strong emotion or surprise. Punctuation (often a comma or an exclamation point) is used to set off an interjection from the rest of the sentence.

- **Stop! No! What,** am I invisible?

Sentence Issues

CONTENTS

Chapter 39
Constructing Sentences

A **sentence** is made up of one or more words that express a complete thought. Sentences are groups of words that make statements, ask questions, or express feelings.

- The Web delivers the universe in a box.

Using Subjects and Predicates

643.1

Sentences have two main parts: a **subject** and a **predicate**.

- Technology frustrates many people.

Note: In the sentence above, *technology* is the subject—the sentence talks about technology. *Frustrates many people* is the complete predicate—it says something about the subject. (A predicate can also show action.)

The Subject

643.2

The **subject** names the person or thing either doing the action in a sentence or being talked about. The subject is most often a noun or a pronoun.

- **Technology** is an integral part of almost every business.
  Manufacturers need technology to compete in the world market.
  They could not go far without it.

A phrase or a clause may also function as a subject.

- **To survive without technology** is difficult. (infinitive phrase)
  Downloading information from the Web is easy. (gerund phrase)
  That the information age would arrive was inevitable. (noun clause)

Note: To determine the subject of a sentence, ask yourself a question that begins with *who* or *what* and ends with the predicate.

In most sentences, the subject comes before the verb; however, in questions and some exclamations, that order is reversed. (See **652.1**.)

esl *Note:* Some languages permit the omission of a subject in a sentence; English does not. A subject must be included in every sentence. (The only exception is an "understood subject," which is discussed at **644.4**.)

Simple Subject

644.1

A **simple subject** is the subject without the words that modify it.

- Thirty years ago, reasonably well-trained **mechanics** could fix any car on the road.

Complete Subject

644.2

A **complete subject** is the simple subject and the words that modify it.

- Thirty years ago, **reasonably well-trained mechanics** could fix any car on the road.

Compound Subject

644.3

A **compound subject** is composed of two or more simple subjects joined by a conjunction and sharing the same predicate(s).

- Today, **mechanics** and **technicians** would need to master a half million manual pages to fix every car on the road.

  Dealerships and their service **departments** must sometimes explain that to the customers.

Understood Subject

644.4

Sometimes a subject is **understood**. This means it is missing in the sentence, but a reader clearly understands what the subject is. An understood subject is most likely in an imperative sentence. (See **649.3**.)

- **(You)** Park on this side of the street. (The subject *you* is understood.)

  Put the CD player in the trunk.

Delayed Subject

644.5

In sentences that begin with *There is, It is, There was,* or *It was,* the subject usually follows the verb.

- **There were 70,000 fans in the stadium**. (The subject is *fans; were* is the verb. *There* is an expletive, an empty word.)

  It was a **problem** for stadium security. (*Problem* is the subject.)

The subject is also delayed in questions.

- Where was the **event**? (*Event* is the subject.)

  Was **Dave Matthews** playing? (*Dave Matthews* is the subject.)

Note: In sentences that begin with *It is* or *It was* and describe the weather, distance, time, and some other conditions, the word *it* serves as the subject.

- **It** was raining.

  It is 90 miles from Chicago to Milwaukee.

  It is three o'clock.

The Predicate (Verb)

The **predicate**, which contains the verb, is the sentence part that either tells what the subject is doing or says something about the subject.

- Students **need technical skills as well as basic academic skills**.

Simple Predicate

A **simple predicate** is the verb without the words that describe or modify it.

- Today's workplace **requires** employees to have a range of skills.

Complete Predicate

A **complete predicate** is the verb and all the words that modify or explain it.

- Today's workplace **requires employees to have a range of skills**.

Compound Predicate

A **compound predicate** is composed of two or more verbs and all the words that modify or explain them.

- Engineers **analyze problems and calculate solutions**.

Direct Object

A **direct object** is the part of the predicate that receives the action of the verb. A direct object makes the meaning of the verb complete.

- Marcos visited several **campuses**.
  (The direct object *campuses* receives the action of the verb *visited* by answering the question "Marcos visited what?")

Note: A direct object may be compound.

- An admissions counselor explained the academic **programs** and the application **process**.

Indirect Object

An **indirect object** is the word(s) that tells *to whom/to what* or *for whom/for what* something is done. A sentence must have a direct object before it can have an indirect object.

- I showed our **children** my new school.
  Use these questions to find an indirect object:

What is the verb?	*showed*
Showed what?	school (direct object)
Showed *school* to whom?	children (indirect object)

- I wrote **them** a note.

Note: An indirect object may be compound.

- I gave the **instructor** and a few **classmates** my e-mail address.

Using Phrases

646.1

A **phrase** is a group of related words that functions as a single part of speech. A phrase lacks a subject, a predicate, or both. There are three phrases in the following sentence.

➤ Examples of technology can be found in ancient civilizations.

   of technology
   (prepositional phrase that functions as an adjective; no subject or predicate)
   can be found
   (verb phrase; no subject)
   in ancient civilizations
   (prepositional phrase that functions as an adverb; no subject or predicate)

Types of Phrases

There are several types of phrases: *verb*, *verbal*, *prepositional*, *appositive*, and *absolute*.

Verb Phrase

646.2

A **verb phrase** consists of a main verb, its helping verbs, and sometimes its modifiers.

➤ Students, worried about exams, **have camped at the library all week**.

Verbal Phrase

646.3

A **verbal phrase** is a phrase based on one of the three types of verbals: *gerund*, *infinitive*, or *participle*. (See **634.1–634.4**.)

A **gerund phrase** consists of a gerund and its modifiers. The whole phrase functions as a noun. (See **634.2**.)

➤ **Becoming a marine biologist** is Rashanda's dream.
   (The gerund phrase is used as the subject of the sentence.)
   She has acquainted herself with the various methods for **collecting sea-life samples**. (The gerund phrase is the object of the preposition *for*.)

An **infinitive phrase** consists of the introductory word *to*, the fundamental form of a verb, and its modifiers. The whole phrase functions as a noun, an adjective, or an adverb.

➤ **To dream** is the first step in any endeavor.
   (The infinitive phrase functions as a noun used as the subject.)
   Remember **to make a plan to realize your dream**.
   (The infinitive phrase *to make a plan* functions as a noun used as a direct object; *to realize your dream* functions as an adjective modifying *plan*.)
   Finally, apply all of your talents and skills **to achieve your goals**.
   (The infinitive phrase functions as an adverb modifying *apply*.)

A **participial phrase** consists of a past or present participle (a verb form ending in *ing* or *ed*) and its modifiers. The phrase functions as an adjective.

➤ **Doing poorly in biology**, Theo signed up for a tutor.
   (The participial phrase modifies the noun *Theo*.)
   Some students **frustrated by difficult course work** don't seek help.
   (The participial phrase modifies the noun *students*.)

Functions of Verbal Phrases				647.1
	Noun	**Adjective**	**Adverb**	
Gerund	■			
Infinitive	■	■	■	
Participial		■		

Prepositional Phrase

647.2

A **prepositional phrase** is a group of words beginning with a preposition and ending with a noun or a pronoun. Prepositional phrases are used mainly as adjectives and adverbs. See **638.3** for a list of prepositions.

➤ Denying the existence **of exam week** hasn't worked **for anyone** yet.
(The prepositional phrase *of exam week* is used as an adjective modifying the noun *existence*; *for anyone* is used as an adverb modifying the verb *has worked*.)

Test days still dawn and GPAs still plummet **for the unprepared student**.
(The prepositional phrase *for the unprepared student* is used as an adverb modifying the verbs *dawn* and *plummet*.)

esl Note: A prepositional phrase may contain adjectives, but not adverbs. Do not mistake the following adverbs for nouns and incorrectly use them with a preposition: *here, there, everywhere, inside, outside, uptown, downtown.*

Appositive Phrase

647.3

An **appositive phrase**, which follows a noun or a pronoun and renames it, consists of a noun and its modifiers. An appositive adds new information about the noun or pronoun it follows.

➤ The Olympic-size pool, **a prized addition to the physical education building,** gets plenty of use. (The appositive phrase renames *pool.*)

Absolute Phrase

647.4

An **absolute phrase** consists of a noun and a participle (plus the participle's object, if there is one, and any modifiers). Because the noun acts like a subject and is followed by a verbal, an absolute phrase resembles a clause.

➤ **Their enthusiasm sometimes waning,** the students who cannot swim are required to take lessons. (The noun *enthusiasm* is modified by the present participle *waning;* the entire phrase modifies *students.*)

Phrases can add valuable information to sentences, but some phrases add nothing but "fat" to your writing. For a list of phrases to avoid, see page **83**.

Using Clauses

A **clause** is a group of related words that has both a subject and a predicate.

Independent/Dependent Clauses

648.1

An **independent clause** presents a complete thought and can stand alone as a sentence; a **dependent clause** (also called a subordinate clause) does not present a complete thought and cannot stand alone as a sentence.

➤ Though airplanes are twentieth-century inventions (dependent clause), people have always dreamed of flying (independent clause).

Types of Clauses

There are three basic types of dependent, or subordinate, clauses: *adverb, adjective,* and *noun.*

Adverb Clause

648.2

An **adverb clause** is used like an adverb to modify a verb, an adjective, or an adverb. All adverb clauses begin with subordinating conjunctions. (See **639.4**.)

➤ **Because Orville won a coin toss,** he got to fly the power-driven air machine first. (The adverb clause modifies the verb *got.*)

Adjective Clause

648.3

An **adjective clause** is used like an adjective to modify a noun or a pronoun. Adjective clauses begin with relative pronouns (*which, that, who*). (See **627.3**.)

➤ The men **who invented the first airplane** were brothers, Orville and Wilbur Wright. (The adjective clause modifies the noun *men. Who* is the subject of the adjective clause.)

The first flight, **which took place December 17, 1903,** was made by Orville. (The adjective clause modifies the noun *flight. Which* is the subject of the adjective clause.)

Noun Clause

648.4

A **noun clause** is used in place of a noun. Noun clauses can appear as subjects, as direct or indirect objects, as predicate nominatives, or as objects of prepositions. They are introduced by subordinating words such as *what, that, when, why, how, whatever, who, whom, whoever,* and *whomever.*

➤ He wants to know **what made modern aviation possible**.
(The noun clause functions as a direct object.)

Whoever invents an airplane with vertical takeoff ability will be a hero.
(The noun clause functions as the subject.)

TEST IT! If you can replace a whole clause with the pronoun *something* or *someone*, it is a noun clause.

Using Sentence Variety

A sentence can be classified according to the kind of statement it makes and according to the way it is constructed.

Kinds of Sentences

Sentences can make five basic kinds of statements: *declarative, interrogative, imperative, exclamatory,* or *conditional.*

Declarative Sentence

649.1

Declarative sentences make statements. They tell us something about a person, a place, a thing, or an idea.

➤ **In 1955, Rosa Parks refused to follow segregation rules on a bus in Montgomery, Alabama.**

Interrogative Sentence

649.2

Interrogative sentences ask questions.

➤ **Do you think Ms. Parks knew she was making history?**
Would you have had the courage to do what she did?

Imperative Sentence

649.3

Imperative sentences give commands. They often contain an understood subject (you). (See **644.4**.)

➤ **Read Chapters 6 through 10 for tomorrow.**

esl **Note:** Imperative sentences with an understood subject are the only sentences in which it is acceptable to have no subjects stated.

Exclamatory Sentence

649.4

Exclamatory sentences communicate strong emotion or surprise.

➤ **I simply can't keep up with these long reading assignments!**
Oh my gosh, you scared me!

Conditional Sentence

649.5

Conditional sentences express two circumstances. One of the circumstances depends on the other circumstance. The words *if, when,* or *unless* are often used in conditional statements.

➤ **If** you practice a few study-reading techniques, college reading loads will be manageable.
When I manage my time, it seems I have more of it.
Don't ask me to help you, **unless** you are willing to do the reading first.

exercise

Structure of Sentences

A sentence may be *simple, compound, complex,* or *compound-complex,* depending on the relationship between the independent and dependent clauses in it.

Simple Sentence

650.1

A **simple sentence** contains one independent clause. The independent clause may have compound subjects and predicates, and it may also contain phrases.

- My **back aches**.
  (single subject: *back;* single predicate: *aches*)
  My **teeth** and my **eyes hurt**.
  (compound subject: *teeth* and *eyes;* single predicate: *hurt*)
  My **memory** and my **logic come** and **go**.
  (compound subject: *memory* and *logic;* compound predicate: *come* and *go*)
  I must be in need of a vacation.
  (single subject: *I;* single predicate: *must be;* phrases: *in need, of a vacation*)

Compound Sentence

650.2

A **compound sentence** consists of two independent clauses. The clauses must be joined by a semicolon, by a comma and a coordinating conjunction (*and, but, or, nor, so, for, yet*), or by a semicolon and a conjunctive adverb (*besides, however, instead, meanwhile, then, therefore*).

- I had eight hours of sleep**, so** why am I so exhausted?
  I take good care of myself**;** I get enough sleep.
  I still feel fatigued**; therefore,** I must need more exercise.

Complex Sentence

650.3

A **complex sentence** contains one independent clause (in bold) and one or more dependent clauses (underlined).

- <u>When I can,</u> **I get eight hours of sleep**. (dependent clause; independent clause)
  <u>When I get up on time, and if someone hasn't used up all the milk,</u>
  I eat breakfast. (two dependent clauses; independent clause)

Compound-Complex Sentence

650.4

A **compound-complex sentence** contains two or more independent clauses (in bold type) and one or more dependent clauses (underlined).

- <u>If I'm not in a hurry,</u> **I take leisurely walks, and I try to spot some wildlife**.
  (dependent clause; two independent clauses)
  I saw a hawk <u>when I was walking,</u> **and other smaller birds were chasing it**.
  (independent clause, dependent clause; independent clause)

audio

Chapter 40
Avoiding Sentence Errors

Subject-Verb Agreement

The subject and verb of any clause must agree in both *person* and *number*. *Person* indicates whether the subject of the verb is *first, second,* or *third person*. *Number* indicates whether the subject and verb are *singular* or *plural*.

	Singular	Plural
First Person	I think	we think
Second Person	you think	you think
Third Person	he/she/it thinks	they think

exercise

Agreement in Number

A verb must agree in number (singular or plural) with its subject.

- The **student was** rewarded for her hard work. (Both the subject *student* and the verb *was* are singular; they agree in number.)

Note: Do not be confused by phrases that come between the subject and the verb. Such phrases may begin with words like *in addition to, as well as,* or *together with.*

- The **instructor**, as well as the students, **is** expected to attend the orientation. (*Instructor*, not *students*, is the subject.)

Compound Subjects

Compound subjects connected with *and* usually require a plural verb.

- **Dedication and creativity are** trademarks of successful students.

Note: If a compound subject joined by *and* is thought of as a unit, use a singular verb.

- **Macaroni and cheese is** always available in the cafeteria.

Delayed Subjects

652.1

Delayed subjects occur when the verb comes *before* the subject in a sentence. In these inverted sentences, the true (delayed) subject must be made to agree with the verb.

- There **are** many nontraditional **students** on our campus.
  Here **is** the **syllabus** you need.
  (*Students* and *syllabus* are the true subjects of these sentences, not *there* and *here*.)

Note: Using an inverted sentence, on occasion, will lend variety to your writing style. Simply remember to make the delayed subjects agree with the verbs.

- However, included among the list's topmost items **was "revise research paper."** (Because the true subject here is singular—one item—the singular verb *was* is correct.)

Titles as Subjects

652.2

When the subject of a sentence is the title of a work of art, literature, or music, the verb should be singular. This is also true of a word (or phrase) being used as a word (or phrase).

- *Lyrical Ballads* **was** published in 1798 by two of England's greatest poets, Wordsworth and Coleridge. (Even though the title of the book, *Lyrical Ballads*, is plural in form, it is still a single title being used as the subject, correctly taking the singular verb *was*.)
  "Over-the-counter drugs" is a phrase that means nonprescription medications. (Even though the phrase is plural in form, it is still a single phrase being used as the subject, correctly taking the singular verb *is*.)

Singular Subjects with *Or* or *Nor*

652.3

Singular subjects joined by *or* or *nor* take a singular verb.

- Neither a **textbook** nor a **notebook is required** for this class.

Note: When the subject nearer a present-tense verb is the singular pronoun *I* or *you*, the correct singular verb does not end in *s*. (See the chart on page **651**.)

- Neither **Marcus** nor **I feel** (not *feels*) right about this.
  Either **Rosa** or **you have** (not *has*) to take notes for me.
  Either **you** or **Rosa has** to take notes for me.

Singular/Plural Subjects

652.4

When one of the subjects joined by *or* or *nor* is singular and one is plural, the verb must agree with the subject nearer the verb.

- Neither the **professor** nor her **students were** in the lab. (The plural subject *students* is nearer the verb; therefore, the plural verb *were* agrees with *students*.)
  Neither the **students** nor the **professor was** in the lab. (The singular subject *professor* is nearer the verb; therefore, the singular verb *is* is used to agree with *professor*.)

Collective Nouns 653.1

Generally, **collective nouns** (*faculty, pair, crew, assembly, congress, species, crowd, army, team, committee,* and so on) take a singular verb. However, if you want to emphasize differences among individuals in the group or are referring to the group as individuals, you can use a plural verb.

> My lab **team takes** its work very seriously. (*Team* refers to the group as a unit; it requires a singular verb, *takes.*)
>
> The **team assume** separate responsibilities for each study they undertake. (In this example, *team* refers to individuals within the group; it requires a plural verb, *assume.*)

Note: Collective nouns such as *police, poor, elderly,* and *young* use plural verbs.

> The **police direct** traffic here between 7:00 and 9:00 a.m.

Plural Noun with Singular Meaning 653.2

Some nouns that are plural in form but singular in meaning take a singular verb: *mumps, measles, news, mathematics, economics, robotics,* and so on.

> **Economics is** sometimes called "the dismal science."
>
> The economic **news is** not very good.

Note: The most common exceptions are *scissors, trousers, tidings,* and *pliers.*

> The **scissors are** missing again.
>
> **Are** these **trousers** prewashed?

Be Verbs (*am, is, are, was, were*) 653.3

When a sentence contains a form of the *be* verb—and a noun comes before and after that verb—the verb must agree with the subject, not the *complement* (the noun coming after the verb).

> The cause of his problem **was** poor study habits. (*Cause* requires a singular verb, even though the subject's complement, *habits,* is plural.)
>
> His poor study habits **were** the cause of his problem. (*Habits* requires a plural verb, even though the subject's complement, *cause,* is singular.)

Nouns Showing Measurement, Time, and Money 653.4

Mathematical phrases and phrases that name a period of time, a unit of measurement, or an amount of money take a singular verb.

> Three and three **is** six.
>
> Eight pages **is** a long paper on this topic.
>
> In my opinion, two dollars **is** a high price for a cup of coffee.

654.1 Relative Pronouns

When a **relative pronoun** (*who, which, that*) is used as the subject of a clause, the number of the verb is determined by that pronoun's antecedent. (The antecedent is the word to which the pronoun refers.)

➡ This is one of the **books that are** required for English class.
(The relative pronoun *that* requires the plural verb *are* because its antecedent is *books,* not the word *one.* To test this type of sentence for agreement, read the *of* phrase first: *Of the books that are . . .*)

Note: Generally, the antecedent is the nearest noun or pronoun and is often the object of a preposition. Sometimes, however, the antecedent is not the nearest noun or pronoun, especially in sentences containing the phrase "the only one of."

➡ Dr. Graciosa wondered why Claire was the only **one** of her students **who was** not attending lectures regularly. (In this case, the addition of the modifiers *the only* changes the sense of the sentence. The antecedent of *who* is *one,* not *students.* Only one student was not attending.)

654.2 Indefinite Pronoun with Singular Verb

Many indefinite pronouns (*someone, somebody, something; anyone, anybody, anything; no one, nobody, nothing; everyone, everybody, everything; each, either, neither, one, this*) require a singular verb.

➡ **Everybody is** welcome to attend the chancellor's reception.
No one was sent an invitation.

Note: Although it may seem to indicate more than one, *each* is a singular pronoun and requires a singular verb. Do not be confused by words or phrases that come between the indefinite pronoun and the verb.

➡ **Each** of the new students **is** (not *are*) encouraged to attend the reception.

654.3 Indefinite Pronoun with Plural Verb

Some indefinite pronouns (*both, few, many, most,* and *several*) are plural; they require a plural verb.

➡ **Few are** offered the opportunity to study abroad.
Most take advantage of opportunities closer to home.

654.4 Indefinite Pronoun with Singular or Plural Verb

Some indefinite pronouns (*all, any, most, none,* and *some*) may be either singular or plural, depending on the nouns they refer to.

➡ **Some** of the students **were** missing. (*Students,* the noun that *some* refers to, is plural; therefore, the pronoun *some* is considered plural, and the plural verb *were* is used to agree with it.)

Most of the lecture **was** over by the time we arrived. (Because *lecture* is singular, *most* is also singular, requiring the singular verb *was.*)

Pronoun-Antecedent Agreement

655.1

exercise

A pronoun must agree in number, person, and gender (sex) with its *antecedent*. The antecedent is the word to which the pronoun refers.

- **Yoshi** brought **his** laptop computer and e-book to school.
  (The pronoun *his* refers to the antecedent *Yoshi*. Both the pronoun and its antecedent are singular, third person, and masculine; therefore, the pronoun is said to agree with its antecedent.)

Singular Pronoun

655.2

Use a singular pronoun to refer to such antecedents as *each, either, neither, one, anyone, anybody, everyone, everybody, somebody, another, nobody,* and *a person.*

- **Each** of the maintenance vehicles has **their** doors locked at night. (Incorrect)
  Each of the maintenance vehicles has **its** doors locked at night.
  (Correct: Both *Each* and *its* are singular.)
  Somebody left **his or her** (not *their*) vehicle unlocked. (Correct)

Plural Pronoun

655.3

When a plural pronoun (*they, their*) is mistakenly used with a singular indefinite pronoun (such as *everyone* or *everybody*), you may correct the sentence by replacing *their* or *they* with optional pronouns (*his or her* or *he or she*), or you may make the antecedent plural.

- **Everyone** must learn to wait **their** turn. (Incorrect)
  Everyone must learn to wait **his or her** turn.
  (Correct: Optional pronouns *his or her* are used.)
  People must learn to wait **their** turn.
  (Correct: The singular antecedent, *Everyone*, is changed to the plural antecedent, *People*.)

Two or More Antecedents

655.4

When two or more antecedents are joined by *and*, they are considered plural.

- **Tomas** and **Jamal** are finishing **their** assignments.

When two or more singular antecedents are joined by *or* or *nor*, they are considered singular.

- Either **Connie** or **Shavonn** left **her** headset in the library.

Note: If one of the antecedents is masculine and one feminine, the pronouns should likewise be masculine and feminine.

- Is either **Ahmad** or **Phyllis** bringing **his or her** laptop computer?

Note: If one of the antecedents joined by *or* or *nor* is singular and one is plural, the pronoun is made to agree with the nearer antecedent.

- Neither **Ravi** nor **his friends** want to spend **their** time studying.
  Neither **his friends** nor **Ravi** wants to spend **his** time studying.

Shifts in Sentence Construction

A shift is an improper change in structure midway through a sentence. The following examples will help you identify and fix several different kinds of shifts.

Shift in Person

656.1

exercise

Shift in person is mixing first, second, or third person within a sentence.

Shift | **One** may get spring fever unless **you** live in California or Florida. (The sentence shifts from third person, *one*, to second person, *you*.)

Corrected | **You may get spring fever unless you live in California or Florida.** (Stays in second person)

Corrected | **People may get spring fever unless they live in California or Florida.** (*People*, a third person plural noun, requires a third person plural pronoun, *they*.)

Shift in Tense

656.2

exercise

Shift in tense is using more than one tense in a sentence when it is unnecessary.

Shift | Sheila **looked** at nine apartments in one weekend before she **had chosen** one. (Tense shifts from past to past perfect for no reason.)

Corrected | **Sheila looked at nine apartments in one weekend before she chose one.** (Tense stays in past tense.)

Shift in Voice

656.3

Shift in voice is mixing active with passive voice. Usually, a sentence beginning in active voice should remain so to the end.

Shift | As you look (active voice) for just the right place, many interesting apartments will probably be seen. (passive voice)

Corrected | **As you look** (active voice) **for just the right place, you will probably see** (active voice) **many interesting apartments.**

Unparallel Construction

656.4

exercise

Unparallel construction occurs when the kind of words or phrases being used shifts or changes in the middle of a sentence.

Shift | In my hometown, people pass the time shooting pool, pitching horseshoes, and at softball games. (Sentence shifts from *ing* words, *shooting* and *pitching*, to the phrase *at softball games*.)

Parallel | **In my hometown, people pass the time shooting pool, pitching horseshoes, and playing softball.** (Now all three activities are *ing* words—they are consistent, or parallel.)

Fragments, Comma Splices, and Run-Ons

Except in a few special situations, you should use complete sentences when you write. By definition, a complete sentence expresses a complete thought. However, a sentence may actually contain several ideas, not just one. The trick is getting those ideas to work together to form a clear, interesting sentence that expresses your exact meaning. Among the most common sentence errors that writers make are fragments, comma splices, and run-ons.

Fragment

657.1

A **fragment** is a group of words used as a sentence. It is not a sentence, however, because it lacks a subject, a verb, or some other essential part. That missing part results in an incomplete thought.

Fragment	Pete gunned the engine. Forgetting that the boat was hooked to the truck. (This is a sentence followed by a fragment. This error can be corrected by combining the fragment with the sentence.)
Corrected	**Pete gunned the engine, forgetting that the boat was hooked to the truck.**
Fragment	Even though my best friend had a little boy last year. (This clause does not convey a complete thought. We need to know what is happening despite the birth of the little boy.)
Corrected	**Even though my best friend had a little boy last year, I do not comprehend the full meaning of "motherhood."**

Comma Splice

657.2

A **comma splice** is a mistake made when two independent clauses are connected ("spliced") with only a comma. The comma is not enough: a period, semicolon, or conjunction is needed.

Splice	People say that being a stay-at-home mom or dad is an important job, their actions tell a different story.
Corrected	**People say that being a stay-at-home mom or dad is an important job, but their actions tell a different story.** (The coordinating conjunction *but*, added after the comma, corrects the splice.)
Corrected	**People say that being a stay-at-home mom or dad is an important job; their actions tell a different story.** (A semicolon—rather than just a comma—makes the sentence correct.)
Corrected	**People say that being a stay-at-home mom or dad is an important job. Their actions tell a different story.** (A period creates two sentences and corrects the splice.)

Run-Ons

exercise

A **run-on sentence** is actually two sentences joined without adequate punctuation or a connecting word.

Run-on	The Alamo holds a special place in American history it was the site of an important battle between the United States and Mexico.
Corrected	**The Alamo holds a special place in American history because it was the site of an important battle between the United States and Mexico.** (A subordinating conjunction is added to fix the run-on.)
Run-ons	Antonio de Santa Anna, the president of Mexico who once held a funeral for his amputated leg, is the same Santa Anna who stormed the Alamo he led his troops to victory over the Texan rebels defending that fort. Two famous American frontiersmen died they were James Bowie and Davy Crockett. Santa Anna enjoyed fame, power, and respect among his followers. He died in 1876 he was poor, blind, and ignored.
Corrected	**Antonio de Santa Anna, the president of Mexico who once held a funeral for his amputated leg, is the same Santa Anna who stormed the Alamo. He led his troops to victory over Texan rebels defending that fort. Two famous American frontiersmen were killed in the battle; they were James Bowie and Davy Crockett. Santa Anna enjoyed fame, power, and respect among his followers. When he died in 1876, he was poor, blind, and ignored.**

658.2   The writer corrected the run-on sentences in the paragraph above by adding punctuation. While doing so, the writer also made a few changes to improve the ideas. The writer makes further improvements in the paragraph below by combining two sets of short sentences into two stronger sentences.

Improved	**Antonio de Santa Anna, the president of Mexico who once held a funeral for his amputated leg, is the same Santa Anna who stormed the Alamo. He led his troops to victory over Texan rebels defending that fort. Two famous American frontiersmen, James Bowie and Davy Crockett, were killed in the battle. Santa Anna enjoyed fame, power, and respect among his followers; but when he died in 1876, he was poor, blind, and ignored.**

fyi

Once you make a correction, you may see an opportunity to add, cut, or improve something else. Correcting and editing sentences is frustrating at times, but with practice, it can become one of the more enjoyable parts of the writing process.

Misplaced and Dangling Modifiers

Writing is thinking. Before you can write clearly, you must think clearly. Nothing is more frustrating for the reader than writing that has to be reread just to understand its basic meaning. Look carefully at the common errors that follow. Then use this section as a checklist when you revise. Always avoid leaving misplaced or dangling modifiers in your finished work.

exercise

Misplaced Modifiers

659.1

video

Misplaced modifiers are descriptive words or phrases so separated from what they are describing that the reader is confused.

Misplaced	The neighbor's dog has nearly been barking nonstop for two hours. (*Nearly* been barking?)
Corrected	**The neighbor's dog has been barking nonstop for nearly two hours.** (Watch your placement of *only, just, nearly, barely,* and so on.)
Misplaced	The commercial advertised an assortment of combs for active people with unbreakable teeth. (*People* with unbreakable teeth?)
Corrected	**The commercial advertised an assortment of combs with unbreakable teeth for active people.** (*Combs* with unbreakable teeth)
Misplaced	The pool staff gave large beach towels to the students marked with chlorine-resistant ID numbers. (*Students* marked with chlorine-resistant ID numbers?)
Corrected	**The pool staff gave large beach towels marked with chlorine-resistant ID numbers to the students.** (*Towels* marked with chlorine-resistant ID numbers)

Dangling Modifiers

659.2

Dangling modifiers are descriptive words that modify a subject that isn't stated in the sentence. These often occur as phrases containing *ing* words.

Dangling	After standing in line all afternoon, the manager informed us that all the tickets had been sold. (It sounds as if the manager has been *standing in line all afternoon.*)
Corrected	**After we stood in line all afternoon, the manager informed us that all the tickets had been sold.**
Dangling	After living in the house for one month, the electrician recommended we update all the wiring. (It sounds as if the electrician has been *living in the house.*)
Corrected	**After living in the house for one month, we hired an electrician, who recommended we update all the wiring.**

exercise

Ambiguous Wording

Sloppy sentences confuse readers. No one should have to wonder, "What does this writer mean?" When you revise and edit, check for indefinite pronoun references, incomplete comparisons, and unclear wording.

660.1 Indefinite Pronoun References

An **indefinite reference** is a problem caused by careless use of pronouns. There must always be a word or phrase nearby that a pronoun clearly replaces.

Indefinite	When Tonya attempted to put her dictionary on the shelf, it fell to the floor. (The pronoun *it* could refer to either the dictionary or the shelf.)
Corrected	**When Tonya attempted to put her dictionary on the shelf, the shelf fell to the floor.**
Indefinite	Juanita reminded Kerri that she needed to photocopy her résumé before going to her interview. (Who *needed to photocopy her résumé,* Juanita or Kerri?)
Corrected	**Juanita reminded Kerri to photocopy her résumé before going to her interview.**

660.2 Incomplete Comparisons

Incomplete comparisons—leaving out words that show exactly what is being compared to what—can confuse readers.

Incomplete	After completing our lab experiment, we concluded that helium is lighter. (*Lighter* than what?)
Corrected	**After completing our lab experiment, we concluded that helium is lighter than oxygen.**

660.3 Unclear Wording

One type of ambiguous writing is wording that has two or more possible meanings due to an unclear reference to something elsewhere in the sentence. (See **660.1**.)

Unclear	I couldn't believe my sister bought a cat with all those allergy problems. (Who has the *allergy problems*—the cat or the sister?)
Corrected	**I couldn't believe my sister, who is very allergic, bought a cat.**
Unclear	Dao intended to wash the car when he finished his homework, but he never did. (It is unclear which he *never did*—wash the car or finish his homework.)
Corrected	**Dao intended to wash the car when he finished his homework, but he never did get around to washing the car.**

Nonstandard Language

Nonstandard language is language that does not conform to the standards set by schools, media, and public institutions. It is often acceptable in everyday conversation and in fictional writing, but seldom in formal speech or other forms of writing.

exercise

Colloquial Language

661.1

Colloquial language is wording used in informal conversation that is unacceptable in formal writing.

Colloquial	Hey, wait up! Cal wants to go with.
Standard	**Hey, wait! Cal wants to go with us.**

Double Preposition

661.2

The use of certain **double prepositions**—*off of, off to, from off*—is unacceptable.

Double Preposition	Pick up the dirty clothes from off the floor.
Standard	**Pick up the dirty clothes from the floor.**

Substitution

661.3

Avoid substituting *and* for *to*.

Substitution	Try and get to class on time.
Standard	**Try to get to class on time.**

Avoid substituting *of* for *have* when combining with *could, would, should,* or *might*.

Substitution	I should of studied for that exam.
Standard	**I should have studied for that exam.**

Double Negative

661.4

A **double negative** is a sentence that contains two negative words used to express a single negative idea. Double negatives are unacceptable in academic writing.

Double Negative	After paying for essentials, I haven't got no money left.
Standard	**I haven't got any money left. / I have no money left.**

Slang

661.5

Avoid the use of **slang** or any "in" words in formal writing.

Slang	The way the stadium roof opened was way cool.
Standard	**The way the stadium roof opened was remarkable.**

Avoiding Sentence Problems

QUICK GUIDE

Does every subject agree with its verb? (See pages 651–654.)

- In person and number?
- When a word or phrase comes between the subject and verb?
- When the subject is delayed?
- When the subject is a title?
- When a compound subject is connected with *or*?
- When the subject is a collective noun (*faculty, team,* or *crowd*)?
- When the subject is a relative pronoun (*who, which, that*)?
- When the subject is an indefinite pronoun (*everyone, anybody,* or *many*)?

Does every pronoun agree with its antecedent? (See page 655.)

- When the pronoun is a singular indefinite pronoun such as *each, either,* or *another*?
- When two antecedents are joined with *and*?
- When two antecedents are joined with *or*?

Did you unintentionally create inappropriate shifts? (See page 656.)

- In person?
- In tense?
- From active to passive voice?
- Other unparallel construction?

Are all your sentences complete? (See pages 657–658.)

- Have you used sentence fragments?
- Are some sentences "spliced" or run together?

Did you use any misplaced modifiers or ambiguous wording? (See pages 659– 660.)

- Have you used misplaced or dangling modifiers?
- Have you used incomplete comparisons or indefinite references?

Did you use any nonstandard language? (See page 661.)

- Have you used slang or colloquial language?
- Have you used double negatives or double prepositions?

Addressing Multilingual/ESL Issues

CONTENTS

41   Multilingual and ESL Guidelines

ADDITIONAL INFORMATION FOR MULTILINGUAL/ESL LEARNERS

Chapter 41
Multilingual and ESL Guidelines

English may be your second, third, or fifth language. As a multilingual learner, you bring to your writing the culture and knowledge of the languages you use. This broader perspective enables you to draw on many experiences and greater knowledge as you write and speak. Whether you are an international student or someone who has lived here a long time and is now learning more about English, this chapter provides you with important information about writing in English.

The Parts of Speech

Noun

Count Nouns

665.1

Count nouns refer to things that can be counted. They can have *a*, *an*, *the*, or *one* in front of them. One or more adjectives can come between the *a*, *an*, *the*, or *one* and the singular count noun.

> ➤ **an apple, one orange, a plump, a purple plum**

Count nouns can be singular, as in the examples above, or plural, as in the examples below.

> ➤ **plums, apples, oranges**

Note: When count nouns are plural, they can have the word *the*, a number, or a demonstrative adjective in front of them. (See **667.1** and **667.3**.)

> ➤ I used **the** plums to make a pie.
> He placed **five** apples on my desk.
> **These** oranges are so juicy!

The *number* of a noun refers to whether it names a single thing (book), in which case its number is *singular*, or whether it names more than one thing (books), in which case the number of the noun is *plural*.

Note: There are different ways in which the plural form of nouns is created. For more information, see pages **597–598**.

Noncount Nouns

666.1

Noncount nouns refer to things that cannot be counted. Do not use *a*, *an*, or *one* in front of them. They have no plural form, so they always take a singular verb. Some nouns that end in *s* are not plural; they are noncount nouns.

➤ **fruit, furniture, rain, thunder, advice, mathematics, news**

Abstract nouns name ideas or conditions rather than people, places, or objects. Many abstract nouns are noncount nouns.

➤ The students had **fun** at the party. Good **health** is a wonderful gift.

Collective nouns name a whole category or group and are often noncount nouns.

➤ **homework, furniture, money, faculty, committee, flock**

Note: The parts or components of a group or category named by a noncount noun are often count nouns. For example, *report* and *assignment* are count nouns that are parts of the collective, noncount noun *homework*.

Two-Way Nouns

666.2

Some nouns can be used as either count or noncount nouns, depending on what they refer to.

➤ I would like a **glass** of water. (count noun)
  Glass is used to make windows. (noncount noun)

Articles and Other Noun Markers
Specific Articles

666.3

Use articles and other noun markers or modifiers to give more information about nouns. The **specific** (or **definite**) **article** *the* is used to refer to a specific noun.

➤ I found **the** book I misplaced yesterday.

Indefinite Articles

666.4

exercise

Use the **indefinite article** *a* or *an* to refer to a nonspecific noun. Use *an* before singular nouns beginning with the vowels *a*, *e*, *i*, *o*, and *u*. Use *a* before nouns beginning with all other letters of the alphabet, the consonants. Exceptions do occur: *a* unit; *a* university.

➤ I always take **an** apple to work.
  It is good to have **a** book with you when you travel.

Indefinite pronouns can also mark nonspecific nouns—*all, any, each, either, every, few, many, more, most, neither, several, some* (for singular and plural count nouns); *all, any, more, most, much, some* (for noncount nouns).

➤ **Every** student is encouraged to register early.
  Most classes fill quickly.

Determining Whether to Use Articles

667.1

Listed below are a number of guidelines to help you determine whether to use an article and which one to use.

Use *a* or *an* with singular count nouns that do not refer to one specific item.
- **A zebra** has black and white stripes. **An apple** is good for you.

Do not use *a* or *an* with plural count nouns.
- **Zebras** have black and white stripes. **Apples** are good for you.

Do not use *a* or *an* with noncount nouns.
- **Homework** needs to be done promptly.

Use *the* with singular count nouns that refer to one specific item.
- **The apple** you gave me was delicious.

Use *the* with plural count nouns.
- **The zebras** at Brookfield Zoo were healthy.

Use *the* with noncount nouns.
- **The money** from my uncle is a gift.

Do not use *the* with most singular proper nouns.
- **Mother Theresa** loved the poor and downcast.

    Note: There are many exceptions: the Sahara Desert, the University of Minnesota, the Fourth of July

Use *the* with plural nouns.
- **the Joneses** (both Mr. and Mrs. Jones), **the Rocky Mountains, the United States**

Possessive Adjectives

667.2

Possessive nouns and pronouns are used to mark nouns.

possessive nouns: *Tanya's, father's, store's*
- The car is **Tanya's**, not her **father's**.

possessive pronouns: *my, your, his, her, its, our*
- **My** hat is purple.

Demonstrative Adjectives

667.3

Demonstrative pronouns can mark nouns.

demonstrative pronouns: *this, that, these, those* (for singular and plural count nouns); *this, that* (for noncount nouns)
- **Those** chairs are lovely. Where did you buy **that** furniture?

Quantifiers

668.1

Expressions of quantity and measure are often used with nouns. Below are some of these expressions and guidelines for using them.

The following expressions of quantity can be used with count nouns: *each, every, both, a couple of, a few, several, many, a number of.*

- We enjoyed **both** concerts we attended. **A couple of** songs performed were familiar to us.

Use a number to indicate a specific quantity of a continuum.

- I saw **fifteen** cardinals in the park.

To indicate a specific quantity of a noncount noun, use *a* + quantity (such as *bag, bottle, bowl, carton, glass,* or *piece*) + *of* + noun.

- I bought **a carton of milk, a head of lettuce, a piece of cheese**, and **a bag of flour** at the grocery store.

The following expressions can be used with noncount nouns: *a little, much, a great deal of.*

- We had **much** wind and **a little** rain as the storm passed through yesterday.

The following expressions of quantity can be used with both count and noncount nouns: *no/not any, some, a lot of, lots of, plenty of, most, all, this, that.*

- I would like **some** apples (*count noun*) and **some** rice (*noncount noun*), please.

Verb

exercise

As the central part of the predicate, a verb conveys much of a sentence's meaning. Using verb tenses and forms correctly ensures that your readers will understand your sentences as you intend them to. For a more thorough review of verbs, see pages **630–635**.

Progressive (Continuous) Tenses

668.2

Progressive or continuous tense verbs express action that is in progress (see page **632**).

To form the **present continuous** tense, use the helping verb *am, is,* or *are* with the *ing* form of the main verb.

- He **is washing** the car right now.
  Kent and Chen **are studying** for a test.

The **past continuous** tense, use the helping verb *was* or *were* with the *ing* form of the main verb.

- Yesterday he **was working** in the garden all day.
  Julia and Juan **were watching** a movie.

To form the **future continuous** tense, use *will* or a phrase that indicates the future, the helping verb *be*, and the *ing* form of the main verb.

- Next week he **will be painting** the house.
  He **plans to be painting** the house soon.

Note that some verbs are generally not used in the continuous tenses, such as the following groups of frequently used verbs:

- Verbs that express thoughts, attitudes, and desires: *know, understand, want, prefer*
- Verbs that describe appearances: *seem, resemble*
- Verbs that indicate possession: *belong, have, own, possess*
- Verbs that signify inclusion: *contain, hold*
  - ➤ Kala **knows** how to ride a motorcycle.
    NOT THIS: Kala **is knowing** how to ride a motorcycle.

Verb Complements

Verb complements are words used to complete the meaning of transitive verbs. A verb complement can be a direct object (sometimes with an indirect object), an object complement, or a subject complement in the case of a linking verb.

Verb complements include verb forms called verbals. There are three kinds of verbals: infinitives, gerunds, and participles (see page 634). There are no grammar rules describing which verbs accompany which complements, so take note of the following information.

Infinitives as Complements

Infinitives can follow many verbs, including these: *agree, appear, attempt, consent, decide, demand, deserve, endeavor, fail, hesitate, hope, intend, need, offer, plan, prepare, promise, refuse, seem, tend, volunteer, wish.* (See 634.3 for more on infinitives.)

➤ He **promised to bring** some samples.

The following verbs are among those that can be followed by a noun or pronoun plus the infinitive: *ask, beg, choose, expect, intend, need, prepare, promise, want.*

➤ I **expect you to be** there on time.

Note: Except in the passive voice, the following verbs must have a noun or pronoun before the infinitive: *advise, allow, appoint, authorize, cause, challenge, command, convince, encourage, forbid, force, hire, instruct, invite, order, permit, remind, require, select, teach, tell, tempt, trust.*

➤ I will **authorize Emily to use** my credit card.

Unmarked infinitives (no *to*) can follow these verbs: *make, have, let, help.*

➤ These glasses **help me see** the board.

Gerunds as Complements

Gerunds can follow these verbs: *admit, avoid, consider, deny, discuss, dislike, enjoy, finish, imagine, miss, postpone, quit, recall, recommend, regret.* (Also see 634.2.)

➤ I **recommended hiring** Ian for the job.

670.1

Infinitives or Gerunds as Complements

Either gerunds or infinitives can follow these verbs: *begin, continue, hate, like, love, prefer, remember, start, stop, try.*

➤ I **hate having** cold feet. **I hate to have** cold feet.

Note: Sometimes the meaning of a sentence will change depending on whether you use a gerund or an infinitive.

➤ I **stopped to smoke**. (I *stopped* weeding the garden *to smoke* a cigarette.)
  I **stopped smoking**. (I no longer smoke.)

670.2

Common Modal Auxiliary Verbs

Modal auxiliary verbs are a kind of auxiliary verb. (See **630.3**.) They help the main verb express meaning. Modals are sometimes grouped with other helping or auxiliary verbs.

Modal verbs must be followed by the base form of a verb without *to* (not by a gerund or an infinitive). Also, modal verbs do not change form; they are always used as they appear in the following chart.

Modal	Expresses	Sample Sentence
can	ability	I **can** program a VCR.
could	ability	I **could** baby-sit Tuesday.
	possibility	He **could** be sick.
might	possibility	I **might** be early.
may, might	possibility	I **may** sleep late Saturday.
	request	**May** I be excused?
must	strong need	I **must** study more.
have to	strong need	I **have to** (have got to) exercise.
ought to	feeling of duty	I **ought to** (should) help Dad.
should	advisabillity	She **should** retire.
	expectation	I **should** have caught that train.
shall	intent	**Shall** I stay longer?
will	intent	I **will** visit my grandma soon.
would	intent	I **would** live to regret my offer.
	repeated action	He **would** walk in the meadow.
would + you	polite request	**Would you** help me?
could + you	polite request	**Could you** type this letter?
will + you	polite request	**Will you** give me a ride?
can + you	polite request	**Can you** make supper tonight?

Common Two-Word Verbs

This chart lists some common verbs in which two words—a verb and a preposition—work together to express a specific action. A noun or pronoun is often inserted between the parts of the two-word verb when it is used in a sentence: break *it* down, call *it* off.

break down	to take apart or fall apart
call off	cancel
call up	make a phone call
clear out	leave a place quickly
cross out	draw a line through
do over	repeat
figure out	find a solution
fill in/out	complete a form or an application
fill up	fill a container or tank
* **find out**	discover
* **get in**	enter a vehicle or building
* **get out of**	leave a car, a house, or a situation
* **get over**	recover from a sickness or a problem
give back	return something
give in/up	surrender or quit
hand in	give homework to a teacher
hand out	give someone something
hang up	put down a phone receiver
leave out	omit or don't use
let in/out	allow someone or something to enter or go out
look up	find information
mix up	confuse
pay back	return money or a favor
pick out	choose
point out	call attention to
put away	return something to its proper place
put down	place something on a table, the floor, etc.
put off	delay doing something
shut off	turn off a machine or light
* **take part**	participate
talk over	discuss
think over	consider carefully
try on	put on clothing to see if it fits
turn down	lower the volume
turn up	raise the volume
write down	write on a piece of paper

* These two-word verbs should not have a noun or pronoun inserted between their parts.

Spelling Guidelines for Verb Forms

The same spelling rules that apply when adding a suffix to other words apply to verbs as well. Most verbs need a suffix to indicate tense or form. The third-person singular form of a verb, for example, usually ends in *s*, but it can also end in *es*. Formation of *ing* and *ed* forms of verbs and verbals needs careful attention, too. Consult the rules below to determine which spelling is correct for each verb. (For general spelling guidelines, see page **604**.)

 There may be exceptions to these rules when forming the past tense of irregular verbs because the verbs are formed by changing the word itself, not merely by adding *d* or *ed*. (See the chart of irregular verbs on page **635**.)

672.1 Past Tense: Adding *ed*

Add *ed* . . .

- When a verb ends with two consonants:
  - ➤ touch—**touched**, ask—**asked**, pass—**passed**
- When a verb ends with a consonant preceded by two vowels:
  - ➤ heal—**healed**, gain—**gained**
- When a verb ends in *y* preceded by a vowel:
  - ➤ annoy—**annoyed**, flay—**flayed**
- When a multisyllable verb's last syllable is not stressed (even when the last syllable ends with a consonant preceded by a vowel):
  - ➤ budget—**budgeted**, enter—**entered**, interpret—**interpreted**

Change *y* to *i* and add *ed* when a verb ends in a consonant followed by *y:*
- ➤ liquefy—**liquefied**, worry—**worried**

Double the final consonant and add *ed* . . .

- When a verb has one syllable and ends with a consonant preceded by a vowel:
  - ➤ wrap—**wrapped**, drop—**dropped**
- When a multisyllable verb's last syllable (ending in a consonant preceded by a vowel) is stressed:
  - ➤ admit—**admitted**, confer—**conferred**, abut—**abutted**

672.2 Past Tense: Adding *d*

Add *d* . . .

- When a verb ends with *e:*
  - ➤ chime—**chimed**, tape—**taped**
- When a verb ends with *ie:*
  - ➤ tie—**tied**, die—**died**, lie—**lied**

Present Tense: Adding *s* or *es*

Add es . . .

- When a verb ends in *ch, sh, s, x,* or *z*:
  - ➡ watch—**watches**, fix—**fixes**
- To *do* and *go*:
  - ➡ do—**does**, go—**goes**

Change y to *i* and add es when the verb ends in a consonant followed by *y*:
  - ➡ liquefy—**liquefies**, quantify—**quantifies**

Add s to most other verbs, including those already ending in *e* and those that end in a vowel followed by *y*:
  - ➡ write—**writes**, buy—**buys**

Present Tense: Adding *ing*

Drop the *e* and add *ing* when the verb ends in *e*:
  - ➡ drive—**driving**, rise—**rising**

Double the final consonant and add *ing* . . .

- When a verb has one syllable and ends with a consonant preceded by a vowel:
  - ➡ wrap—**wrapping**, sit—**sitting**
- When a multisyllable verb's last syllable (ending in a consonant preceded by a vowel) is stressed:
  - ➡ forget—**forgetting**, begin—**beginning,** abut—**abutting**

Change *ie* to *y* and add *ing* when a verb ends with *ie*:
  - ➡ tie—**tying**, die—**dying**, lie—**lying**

Add *ing* . . .

- When a verb ends with two consonants:
  - ➡ touch—**touching**, ask—**asking**, pass—**passing**
- When a verb ends with a consonant preceded by two vowels:
  - ➡ heal—**healing**, gain—**gaining**
- When a verb ends in *y*:
  - ➡ buy—**buying**, study—**studying**, cry—**crying**
- When a multisyllable verb's last syllable is not stressed (even when the last syllable ends with a consonant preceded by a vowel):
  - ➡ budget—**budgeting**, enter—**entering**, interpret—**interpreting**

Note: Never trust your spelling to even the best computer spell checker. Carefully proofread. Use a dictionary for questionable words your spell checker may miss.

exercise

674.1

Adjective

Placing Adjectives

You probably know that an adjective often comes before the noun it modifies. When several adjectives are used in a row to modify a single noun, it is important to arrange the adjectives in the well-established sequence used in English writing and speaking. The following list shows the usual order of adjectives when you use more than one.

First, place . . .
1. articles . . . . **a, an, the**
   demonstrative adjectives . . . . **that, those**
   possessives . . . . **my, her, Misha's**

Then, place words that . . .
2. indicate time. . . . . **first, next, final**
3. tell how many . . . . **one, few, some**
4. evaluate. . . . . **beautiful, dignified, graceful**
5. tell what size. . . . . **big, small, short, tall**
6. tell what shape . . . . **round, square**
7. describe a condition . . . . **messy, clean, dark**
8. tell what age . . . . **old, young, new, antique**
9. tell what color . . . . **blue, red, yellow**
10. tell what nationality . . . . **English, Chinese, Mexican**
11. tell what religion . . . . **Islam, Jewish, Protestant**
12. tell what material . . . . **satin, velvet, wooden**

Finally, place nouns . . .
13. used as adjectives . . . . **computer [monitor], spice [rack]**

> ➤ **my second try** (1 + 2 + noun)
> **gorgeous young white swans** (4 + 8 + 9 + noun)

Present and Past Participles as Adjectives

674.2

Both the **present participle**, which always ends in *ing*, and the **past participle** can be used as adjectives. Exercise care in choosing whether to use the present or the past participle. A participle can come either before a noun or after a linking verb.

A **present participle** used as an adjective should describe a person or thing that is causing a feeling or situation.

> ➤ His **annoying** comments made me angry.

A **past participle** should describe a person or thing that experiences a feeling or situation.

> ➤ He was **annoyed** because he had to wait so long.

Note: Within each of the following pairs, the present (*ing* form) and past participles (*ed* form) have different meanings.

➤ **annoying/annoyed**	**depressing/depressed**	**fascinating/fascinated**
boring/bored	**exciting/excited**	**surprising/surprised**
confusing/confused	**exhausting/exhausted**	

Nouns as Adjectives

Nouns sometimes function as adjectives by modifying another noun. When a noun is used as an adjective, it is always singular.

- Many European cities have **rose** gardens.
  Marta recently joined a **book** club.

TIP: Try to avoid using more than two nouns as adjectives for another noun. These "noun compounds" can get confusing. Prepositional phrases may get the meaning across better than long noun strings.

- Omar is a **crew** member in the **restaurant** kitchen during **second** shift.
  NOT THIS: Omar is a **second-shift restaurant kitchen crew** member.

Adverb

Placing Adverbs

exercise

Consider the following guidelines for placing adverbs correctly. See page **637** for more information about adverbs.

Place adverbs that tell how often (*frequently, seldom, never, always, sometimes*) after a helping verb and before the main verb. In a sentence without a helping verb, adverbs that tell *how often* are placed before an action verb but after a "be" verb.

- The salesclerk will **usually** help me.

Place adverbs that tell when (*yesterday, now, at five o'clock*) at the end of a sentence.

- Auntie El came home **yesterday**.

Adverbs that tell where (*upside-down, around, downstairs*) usually follow the verb they modify. Many prepositional phrases (*at the beach, under the stairs, below the water*) are used as adverbs that tell *where*.

- We waited **on the porch**.

Adverbs that tell how (*quickly, slowly, loudly*) can be placed either at the beginning, in the middle, or at the end of a sentence—but not between a verb and its direct object.

- **Softly** he called my name. He **softly** called my name. He called my name **softly**.

Place adverbs that modify adjectives directly before the adjective.

- That is a **most** unusual dress.

Adverbs that modify clauses are most often placed in front of the clause, but they can also go inside or at the end of the clause.

- **Fortunately**, we were not involved in the accident.
  We were not involved, **fortunately**, in the accident.
  We were not involved in the accident, **fortunately**.

Note: Adverbs that are used with verbs that have objects must *not* be placed between the verb and its object.

- Luis **usually** catches the most fish. **Usually**, Luis catches the most fish.
  NOT THIS: Luis catches **usually** the most fish.

exercise

Preposition

A **preposition** combines with a noun to form a prepositional phrase, which usually acts as an adverb or adjective. See pages **638** and **640** for a list of common prepositions and for more information about prepositions .

Using *in, on, at,* and *by*

676.1

In, on, at, and *by* are four common prepositions that refer to time and place. Here are some examples of how these prepositions are used in each case.

To show time

➤ **on** a specific day or date: *on* June 7, *on* Wednesday

in part of a day: *in* the afternoon

in a year or month: *in* 2003, *in* April

in a period of time: completed *in* an hour

by a specific time or date: *by* noon, *by* the fifth of May

at a specific time of day or night: *at* 3:30 this afternoon

To show place

➤ **at** a meeting place or location: *at* school, *at* the park

at the edge of something: standing *at* the bar

at the corner of something: turning *at* the intersection

at a target: throwing a dart *at* the target

on a surface: left *on* the floor

on an electronic medium: *on* the Internet, *on* television

in an enclosed space: *in* the box, *in* the room

in a geographic location: *in* New York City, *in* Germany

in a print medium: *in* a journal

by a landmark: *by* the fountain

TIP: Do not insert a preposition between a transitive verb and its direct object. Intransitive verbs, however, are often followed by a prepositional phrase (a phrase that begins with a preposition).

➤ I **cooked** hot dogs on the grill. (transitive verb)
I **ate** in the park. (intransitive verb)

Phrasal Prepositions

676.2

Some prepositional phrases begin with more than one preposition. These **phrasal prepositions** are commonly used in both written and spoken communication. A list of common phrasal prepositions follows:

➤ **according to**	**because of**	**in case of**	**on the side of**
across from	**by way of**	**in spite of**	**up to**
along with	**except for**	**instead of**	**with respect to**

Understanding Sentence Basics

Simple sentences in the English language follow the five basic patterns shown below. (See pages 643–650 for more information.)

Subject + Verb

```
┌─ S ─┐┌─V ─┐
```
Naomie winked.

Some verbs like *winked* are intransitive. Intransitive verbs *do not* need a direct object to express a complete thought. (See 630.2.)

Subject + Verb + Direct Object

```
┌─ S ─┐┌─ V ─┐┌─DO─┐
```
Harris grinds his teeth.

Some verbs like *grinds* are transitive. Transitive verbs *do* need a direct object to express a complete thought. (See 630.2.)

Subject + Verb + Indirect Object + Direct Object

```
┌─ S ─┐┌─ V ─┐┌─ IO ─┐┌─ DO ─┐
```
Elena offered her friend an anchovy.

The direct object names who or what receives the action; the indirect object names to whom or for whom the action was done.

Subject + Verb + Direct Object + Object Complement

```
┌─── S ───┐┌─V─┐ DO ┌─────── OC ───────┐
```
The chancellor named Ravi the outstanding student of 2002.

The object complement renames or describes the direct object.

Subject + Linking Verb + Predicate Noun (or Predicate Adjective)

```
┌─S─┐LV┌──── PN ────┐   ┌─S─┐LV┌── PA ──┐
```
Paula is a computer programmer.   Paula is very intelligent.

A linking verb connects the subject to the predicate noun or predicate adjective. The predicate noun renames the subject; the predicate adjective describes the subject.

Inverted Order

In the sentence patterns above, the subject comes before the verb. In a few types of sentences, such as those below, the subject comes *after* the verb.

```
LV┌─S─┐ ┌ PN ┐
```
Is Larisa a poet? (A question)

```
LV ┌── S ──┐
```
There was a meeting. (A sentence beginning with "there")

Sentence Problems

This section looks at potential trouble spots and sentence problems. For more information about English sentences, their parts, and how to construct them see pages 643 through 650 in the handbook. Pages 651 through 662 cover the types of problems and errors found in English writing. The guide to avoiding sentence problems found on page 662 is an excellent editing tool.

678.1 Double Negatives

When making a sentence negative, use *not* or another negative adverb (*never, rarely, hardly, seldom*, and so on), but not both. Using both results in a double negative (see 661.4).

678.2 Subject-Verb Agreement

Be sure the subject and verb in every clause agree in person and number.

- The **student was** rewarded for her hard work.
  The **students were** rewarded for their hard work.
  The **instructor**, as well as the students, **is** expected to attend the orientation.
  The **students**, as well as the instructor, **are** expected to attend the orientation.

678.3 Omitted Words

Do not omit subjects or the expletives *there* or *it*. In all English clauses and sentences (except imperatives, where the subject *you* is understood), there must be a subject.

- Your mother was very quiet; **she** seemed to be upset.
  NOT THIS: Your mother was very quiet; seemed to be upset.

  There is not much time left.
  NOT THIS: Not much time left.

  It is well known that fruits and grains are good for you.
  NOT THIS: Well known that fruits and grains are good for you.

678.4 Repeated Words

Do not repeat the subject of a clause or sentence.

- The doctor prescribed an antibiotic.
  NOT THIS: The doctor, **she** prescribed an antibiotic.

Do not repeat an object in an adjective clause.

- I forgot the flowers that I intended to give to my hosts.
  NOT THIS: I forgot the flowers that I intended to give **them** to my hosts.

Note: Sometimes, the beginning relative pronoun is omitted but understood.

- I forgot the flowers I intended to give to my hosts.
  (The relative pronoun *that* is omitted.)

Conditional Sentences

679.1

Conditional sentences express a situation requiring that a condition be met in order to be true. Selecting the correct verb tense for use in the two clauses of a conditional sentence can be problematic. Below you will find an explanation of the three types of conditional sentences and the verb tenses that are needed to form them.

1. **Factual conditionals:** The conditional clause begins with *if, when, whenever,* or a similar expression. Furthermore, the verbs in the conditional clause and the main clause should be in the same tense.
   - **Whenever** we **had** time, we **took** a break and **went** for a swim.

2. **Predictive conditionals** express future conditions and possible results. The conditional clause begins with *if* or *unless* and has a present tense verb. The main clause uses a modal (*will, can, should, may, might*) plus the base form of the verb.
   - **Unless** we **find** a better deal, we **will buy** this sound system.

3. **Hypothetical past conditionals** describe a situation that is unlikely to happen or that is contrary to fact. To describe situations in the past, the verb in the conditional clause is in the past perfect tense, and the verb in the main clause is formed from *would have, could have,* or *might have* plus the past participle.
   - **If** we **had started out** earlier, we **would have arrived** on time.

Note: If the hypothetical situation is a present or future one, the verb in the conditional clause is in the past tense, and the verb in the main clause is formed from *would, could,* or *might* plus the base form of the verb.
   - **If** we **bought** groceries once a week, we **would** not **have** to go to the store so often.

Quoted and Reported Speech

679.2

Quoted speech is the use of exact words from another source in your own writing; you must enclose these words in quotation marks. It is also possible to report nearly exact words without quotation marks. This is called **reported speech**, or indirect quotation. (See pages **586–587** for a review of the use of quotation marks.)
   - **Direct quotation:** Felicia said, "Don't worry about tomorrow."
   - **Indirect quotation:** Felicia said that you don't have to worry about tomorrow.

In the case of a question, when a direct quotation is changed to an indirect quotation, the question mark is not needed.
   - **Direct quotation:** Ahmad asked, "Which of you will give me a hand?"
   - **Indirect quotation:** Ahmad asked which of us would give him a hand.

Notice how pronouns are often changed in indirect quotations.
   - **Direct quotation:** My friends said, "**You**'re crazy."
   - **Indirect quotation:** My friends said that **I** was crazy.

Note: In academic writing, the use of another source's spoken or written words in one's own writing without proper acknowledgment is called *plagiarism.* Plagiarism is severely penalized in academic situations. (See pages **471–473**.)

Numbers, Word Parts, and Idioms
Numbers

As a multilingual/ESL learner, you may be accustomed to a way of writing numbers that is different than the way it is done in North America. Become familiar with the North American conventions for writing numbers. Pages **599** and **600** show you how numbers are written and punctuated in both word and numeral form.

680.1
Using Punctuation with Numerals

Note that the **period** is used to express percentages (5.5%, 75.9%) and the **comma** is used to organize large numbers into units (7,000; 23,100; 231,990,000). Commas are not used, however, in writing the year (2002).

680.2
Cardinal Numbers

Cardinal numbers are used when counting a number of parts or objects. Cardinal numbers can be used as nouns (she counted to **ten**), pronouns (I invited many guests, but only **three** came), or adjectives (there are **ten** boys here).

Write out in words the numbers one through one hundred. Numbers 101 and greater are often written as numerals. (See **599.1**.)

680.3
Ordinal Numbers

Ordinal numbers show place or succession in a series: the fourth row, the twenty-first century, the tenth time, and so on. Ordinal numbers are used to talk about the parts into which a whole can be divided, such as a fourth or a tenth, and as the denominator in fractions, such as one-fourth or three-fifths. Written fractions can also be used as nouns (I gave him **four-fifths**) or as adjectives (a **four-fifths** majority).

Note: See the list below for names and symbols of the first twenty-five ordinal numbers. Consult a college dictionary for a complete list of cardinal and ordinal numbers.

First	**1st**	**Tenth**	**10th**	**Nineteenth**	**19th**
Second	**2nd**	**Eleventh**	**11th**	**Twentieth**	**20th**
Third	**3rd**	**Twelfth**	**12th**	**Twenty-first**	**21st**
Fourth	**4th**	**Thirteenth**	**13th**	**Twenty-second**	**22nd**
Fifth	**5th**	**Fourteenth**	**14th**	**Twenty-third**	**23rd**
Sixth	**6th**	**Fifteenth**	**15th**	**Twenty-fourth**	**24th**
Seventh	**7th**	**Sixteenth**	**16th**	**Twenty-fifth**	**25th**
Eighth	**8th**	**Seventeenth**	**17th**		
Ninth	**9th**	**Eighteenth**	**18th**		

Prefixes, Suffixes, and Roots

Following is a list of many common word parts and their meanings. Learning them can help you determine the meaning of unfamiliar words as you come across them in your reading. For instance, if you know that "hemi" means "half," you can conclude that "hemisphere" means "half of a sphere."

Prefixes	Meaning	Suffixes	Meaning
a, an	not, without	able, ible	able, can do
anti, ant	against	age	act of, state of
co, con, com	together, with	al	relating to
di	two, twice	ate	cause, make
dis, dif	apart, away	en	made of
ex, e, ec, ef	out	ence, ency	action, quality
hemi, semi	half	esis, osis	action, process
il, ir, in, im	not	ice	condition, quality
inter	between	ile	relating to
intra	within	sion, tion	act of, state of
multi	many	ish	resembling
non	not	ment	act of, state of
ob, of, op, oc	toward, against	ology	study, theory
per	throughout	ous	full of, having
post	after	some	like, tending to
super, supr	above, more	tude	state of
trans, tra	across, beyond	ward	in the direction of
tri	three		
uni	one		

Roots	Meaning	Roots	Meaning
acu	sharp	ject	throw
am, amor	love, liking	log, ology	word, study, speech
anthrop	man	man	hand
aster, astr	star	micro	small
auto	self	mit, miss	send
biblio	book	nom	law, order
bio	life	onym	name
capit, capt	head	path, pathy	feeling, suffering
chron	time	rupt	break
cit	to call, start	scrib, script	write
cred	believe	spec, spect, spic	look
dem	people	tele	far
dict	say, speak	tempo	time
erg	work	tox	poison
fid, feder	faith, trust	vac	empty
fract, frag	break	ver, veri	true
graph, gram	write, written	zo	animal

Idioms

Web

Idioms are phrases that are used in a special way. An idiom can't be understood just by knowing the meaning of each word in the phrase. It must be learned as a whole. For example, the idiom *to bury the hatchet* means "to settle an argument," even though the individual words in the phrase mean something much different. These pages list some of the common idioms in American English.

a bad apple	● One troublemaker on a team may be called **a bad apple**. *(a bad influence)*
an axe to grind	● Mom has **an axe to grind** with the owners of the dog that dug up her flower garden. *(a problem to settle)*
as the crow flies	● She lives only two miles from here **as the crow flies**. *(in a straight line)*
beat around the bush	● Dad said, "Where were you? Don't **beat around the bush**." *(avoid getting to the point)*
benefit of the doubt	● Ms. Hy gave Henri the **benefit of the doubt** when he explained why he fell asleep in class. *(another chance)*
beyond the shadow of a doubt	● Salvatore won the 50-yard dash **beyond the shadow of a doubt**. *(for certain)*
blew my top	● When my money got stolen, I **blew my top**. *(showed great anger)*
bone to pick	● Nick had a **bone to pick** with Adrian when he learned they both liked the same girl. *(problem to settle)*
break the ice	● Shanta was the first to **break the ice** in the room full of new students. *(start a conversation)*
burn the midnight oil	● Carmen had to **burn the midnight oil** the day before the big test. *(work late into the night)*
chomping at the bit	● Dwayne was **chomping at the bit** when it was his turn to bat. *(eager, excited)*
cold shoulder	● Alicia always gives me the **cold shoulder** after our disagreements. *(ignores me)*
cry wolf	● If you **cry wolf** too often, no one will come when you really need help. *(say you are in trouble when you aren't)*
drop in the bucket	● My donation was a **drop in the bucket**. *(a small amount compared to what's needed)*
face the music	● José had to **face the music** when he got caught cheating on the test. *(deal with the punishment)*
flew off the handle	● Tramayne **flew off the handle** when he saw his little brother playing with matches. *(became very angry)*

floating on air	► Teresa was **floating on air** when she read the letter. *(feeling very happy)*
food for thought	► The coach gave us some **food for thought** when she said that winning isn't everything. *(something to think about)*
get down to business	► In five minutes you need to **get down to business** on this assignment. *(start working)*
get the upper hand	► The other team will **get the upper hand** if we don't play better in the second half. *(probably win)*
hit the ceiling	► Rosa **hit the ceiling** when she saw her sister painting the television. *(was very angry)*
hit the hay	► Patrice **hit the hay** early because she was tired. *(went to bed)*
in a nutshell	► **In a nutshell**, Coach Roby told us to play our best. *(to summarize)*
in the nick of time	► Zong grabbed his little brother's hand **in the nick of time** before he touched the hot pan. *(just in time)*
in the same boat	► My friend and I are **in the same boat** when it comes to doing Saturday chores. *(have the same problem)*
iron out	► Jamil and his brother were told to **iron out** their differences about cleaning their room. *(solve, work out)*
it stands to reason	► **It stands to reason** that if you keep lifting weights, you will get stronger. *(it makes sense)*
knuckle down	► Grandpa told me to **knuckle down** at school if I want to be a doctor. *(work hard)*
learn the ropes	► Being new in school, I knew it would take some time to **learn the ropes**. *(get to know how things are done)*
let's face it	► "**Let's face it**!" said Mr. Sills. "You're a better long distance runner than a sprinter." *(let's admit it)*
let the cat out of the bag	► Tia **let the cat out of the bag** and got her sister in trouble. *(told a secret)*
lose face	► If I strike out again, I will **lose face**. *(be embarrassed)*
nose to the grindstone	► If I keep my **nose to the grindstone**, I will finish my homework in one hour. *(working hard)*
on cloud nine	► Walking home from the party, I was **on cloud nine**. *(feeling very happy)*
on pins and needles	► I was **on pins and needles** as I waited to see the doctor. *(feeling nervous)*

over and above	➤ **Over and above** the assigned reading, I read two library books. *(in addition to)*
put his foot in his mouth	➤ Chivas **put his foot in his mouth** when he called his teacher by the wrong name. *(said something embarrassing)*
put your best foot forward	➤ Grandpa said that whenever you do something, you should **put your best foot forward**. *(do the best that you can do)*
rock the boat	➤ The coach said, "Don't **rock the boat** if you want to stay on this team." *(cause trouble)*
rude awakening	➤ I had a **rude awakening** when I saw the letter *F* at the top of my Spanish quiz. *(sudden, unpleasant surprise)*
save face	➤ Grant tried to **save face** when he said he was sorry for making fun of me in class. *(fix an embarrassing situation)*
see eye to eye	➤ My sister and I finally **see eye to eye** about who gets to use the phone first after school. *(are in agreement)*
sight unseen	➤ Grandma bought the television **sight unseen**. *(without seeing it first)*
take a dim view	➤ My brother will **take a dim view** if I don't help him at the store. *(disapprove)*
take it with a grain of salt	➤ If my sister tells you she has no homework, **take it with a grain of salt**. *(don't believe everything you're told)*
take the bull by the horns	➤ This team needs to **take the bull by the horns** to win the game. *(take control)*
through thick and thin	➤ Max and I will be friends **through thick and thin**. *(in good times and in bad times)*
time flies	➤ When you're having fun, **time flies**. *(time passes quickly)*
time to kill	➤ We had **time to kill** before the ballpark gates would open. *(extra time)*
to go overboard	➤ The teacher told us not **to go overboard** with fancy lettering on our posters. *(to do too much)*
under the weather	➤ I was feeling **under the weather**, so I didn't go to school. *(sick)*
word of mouth	➤ We found out who the new teacher was by **word of mouth**. *(talking to other people)*

Note: Like idioms, **collocations** are groups of words that often appear together. They may help you identify different senses of a word; for example, "old" means slightly different things in these collocations: *old* man, *old* friends. You will find sentence construction easier if you check for collocations.

Web

Credits

Index